PSYCHOPATHOLOGY AND PSYCHOTHERAPY

PSYCHOPATHOLOGY AND PSYCHOTHERAPY

From DSM-IV Diagnosis to Treatment
Second Edition

Edited by
Len Sperry, M.D., Ph.D.
Jon Carlson, Psy.D., Ed.D.

ACCELERATED DEVELOPMENT
A member of the Taylor & Francis Group

USA	Publishing Office	Accelerated Development
		A member of the Taylor & Francis Group
		325 Chestnut Street, Suite 800
		Philadelphia, PA 19106
		Tel: (215) 625-8900
		Fax: (215) 625-2940
	Distribution Center	Accelerated Development
		A member of the Taylor & Francis Group
		7625 Empire Drive
		Florence, KY 41042
		Tel: (800) 634-7064
		Fax: (800) 248-4724
UK		Taylor & Francis
		27 Church Road
		Hove
		E. Sussex BN3 2FA
		Tel: +44 (0) 1273 207411
		Fax: +44 (0) 1273 205612

PSYCHOPATHOLOGY AND PSYCHOTHERAPY: From DSM-IV Diagnosis to Treatment, Second Edition

3 4 5 6 7 8 9 0   BRBR   9 8 7 6

This book was set in Times Roman by Monotype Composition, Inc. The editor was Judith L. Aymond. Technical development by Cindy Long. Cover design by Michelle Fleitz. Printing and binding by Braun-Brumfield, Inc.

A CIP catalog record for this book is available from the British Library.
⊗ The paper in this publication meets the requirements of the ANSI Standard Z39.48-1984 (Permanence of Paper)

Library of Congress Cataloging-in-Publication Data

Sperry, Len.
    Psychopathology and psychotherapy: from DSM-IV diagnosis to treatment/Len Sperry, Jon Carlson.—2nd ed.
        p. cm.
    Includes bibliographical references and index.
    1. Psychology, Pathological.   2. Psychotherapy.   3. Psychiatry—Differential thera-peutics.   4. Adler, Alfred, 1870–1937.   5. Diagnostic and statistical manual of mental disorders.   I. Carlson, Jon.   II. Title.
    [DNLM: 1. Adler, Alfred, 1870–1937.   2. Mental Disorders—diagnosis.   3. Mental Disorders—therapy.   4. Mental Disorders—classification.   5. Psychopathology.
6. Psychotherapy—methods.   WM 140 S751p 1996]
RC454.S68   1996
616.89—dc20
DNLM/DLC
for Library of Congress   95-48202
                                                                                                        CIP

ISBN 1-56032-492-9

TABLE OF CONTENTS

Part I
INTRODUCTION

CHAPTER 1
PSYCHOPATHOLOGY AND THE DIAGNOSTIC AND
TREATMENT PROCESS   3
Len Sperry

Part II
PSYCHOSES AND MOOD DISORDERS

CHAPTER 5
DEPRESSIVE DISORDERS
Ronald J. Pancner and Carl W. Jylland

Part III
ANXIETY, SOMATOFORM, AND
DISSOCIATIVE DISORDERS

CHAPTER 6
ANXIETY DISORDERS I
Len Sperry

Part IV
ADJUSTMENT REACTIONS, PERSONALITY DISORDERS, ADDICTIONS, AND SEXUAL DYSFUNCTIONS

Part V
CHILDHOOD AND ADOLESCENT DISORDERS

LIST OF FIGURES

LIST OF TABLES

FOREWORD

Perhaps the highest order skill necessary for effective clinical work is the ability to develop a therapeutic conceptual framework for understanding each patient. This conceptual framework is much like an architect's model of a structure to be built. The model can be viewed as to how it would fit onto the proposed site, it can be manipulated to allow the architect to view the model from different perspectives, and it is open for modification, as needed. The therapeutic conceptualization must be simple, data-based, useful, theoretically coherent, and internally consistent. If we have an effective and accurate conceptualization, it will help us understand the patient's past behavior, make sense of the patient's present behavior, and predict the patient's future behavior.

The conceptual model necessary for effective therapy has several specific elements, including an understanding of normal and pathological states; a theoretical model to offer guidelines for understanding the patient; a protocol for assessment or data collection; a capacity to develop clinical hypotheses, to use the data to build a picture of the psychological disorder(s), to develop a strategic treatment plan, to build a working alliance and develop motivation to change, to implement the treatment strategy by using specific interventions, and to evaluate progress or change; and a relapse prevention strategy. Without a conceptual framework as a starting point, the therapist is limited to either random application of techniques with the hope and prayer that something will work (i.e., the throw everything at the problem and let's see what sticks school of therapy) or the application of techniques done in a rote fashion (i.e., the it worked before; let's do it that way again school of therapy). Too often the necessary parts of the therapeutic process noted above are not integrated into a coherent treatment model. Often the therapist's personal style dictates his or her adherence to a particular treatment model or, indeed, to no model at all.

There are several different types of therapist that I would identify. I label them the *Theoretician,* the *Rhetorician,* the *Politician,* the *Technician,* the *Magician,* and the *Clinician*. Each type has its own particular style and approach to clinical issues and problems.

The *Theoretician* sees all of the world within the perspective of his or her theory. There is no need to empirically validate his or her model, as it seems to be more of a religion. Any deviation from the "law" is seen as improper, inappropriate, or even blasphemous. The theoretician may write volumes based on a theory without ever believing that there is a need to collect the data to support the theory.

The second type of therapist is the *Rhetorician*. For this type of therapist, therapy is something to talk about. This therapist talks, writes, and teaches about therapy but does not do it. He or she even may have the incredible "chutzpah" to supervise students who are doing therapy. In this therapist's view, the doing of therapy is an elementary task that even may be seen as beneath him or her.

The third type of therapist is the *Technician*. The technician learns therapy via a cookbook approach. He or she masters specific interventions and performs them with facility. Using DSM-IV criteria, they offer a discussion of psychopathological states and then describe many treatment possibilities and strategies.

In this excellent revision of their earlier volume, they have kept the strengths intact, including the clear and concise connection between assessment, diagnosis, and treatment. They have updated all diagnoses in keeping with DSM-IV criteria and have expanded many sections.

This volume's richness requires several readings. It must be studied, rather than perused. It has value as a text for graduate courses in clinical psychology, counseling, social work, and psychiatry but also has great utility as an up-to-date treatment guide and reference for practicing professionals.

I am pleased to offer this introduction to the second edition, just as I was pleased and flattered to be able to introduce the first volume.

Arthur Freeman
Philadelphia, Pennsylvania

PREFACE

Most mental health clinicians and trainees complain that abnormal psychology and psychopathology texts are typically lifeless and boring. These books tend to be packed with too many facts, criteria, and lists of symptoms with too few case examples. More importantly, they have limited value and utility for day-to-day clinical practice. This is particularly true of texts that are based primarily on the American Psychiatric Association's *Diagnostic and Statistical Manual of Mental Disorders* (DSM-IV) with its seemingly endless and arbitrary lists of categories, labels, and criteria. Clinicians wonder, besides providing diagnostic labels and codes for insurance forms and agency and government records, what value do standardized diagnostic criteria have for treatment? many systems of psychotherapy have eschewed standardized diagnostic systems claiming that theory were irrelevant for treatment. Beutler's research bears out the observations of practicing clinicians and psychotherapy theorists. He reported that, except for specific diagnostic entities such as phobic disorders and sexual dysfunctions like premature ejaculation and primary orgasmic dysfunction, it is not possible to predict effective outcomes for therapeutic interventions based solely on diagnosis (Beutler & Crago, 1987).

Clinicians have suggested that DSM-IV could be more useful in planning treatment if it provided dynamic or systems formulations for each disorder. Is it unreasonable to expect that a psychopathology text provide both diagnostic criteria and dynamic or systemic formulations?

One of the main purposes of the revised edition of *Psychopathology and Psychotherapy* is to combine DSM-IV diagnostic criteria with dynamic/systemic formulations. Specifically, this book integrates the diagnostic feature of DSM-IV with the dynamic and systems-based theory of Individual Psychology. DSM-IV and Individual Psychology—the theory of personality and treatment developed by Alfred Adler—are surprisingly complementary. This text emphasizes this mutual complementarity and provides the reader a straightforward and easily comprehensible understanding of why a particular client or patient develops one disorder rather than another. Factors such as early childhood experiences, family dynamics, temperament, and other biological considerations as well as dysfunctional cognitions and beliefs are correlated with DSM-IV descriptions and diagnostic criteria.

A second purpose of the revision of *Psychopathology and Psychotherapy* is reflected in the subtitle: *From DSM-IV Diagnosis to Treatment*. Based on our clinical practice, teaching, and supervision, we find that understanding why and how an individual develops a particular disorder is extremely valuable and useful in developing treatment intervention and guiding the psychotherapeutic process. Accordingly, a discussion of treatment goals, strategies, and methods supplements follows the description and clinical formulation of each DSM-IV disorder discussed in this text.

This book is arranged in five sections, beginning with an overview of psychopathology and the diagnostic and treatment process. The more common clinical presentations of children and adults are described in the next four sections. Diagnostic, clinical, and treatment formulation for these disorders are provided along with a representative case example.

We believe that the Individual Psychology perspective is particularly valuable and timely as the trend toward integration of the various psychotherapeutic systems gains momentum. The contemporary view of Individual Psychology presented in this text integrates much information from psychodynamic, cognitive-behavioral, and systems schools as well as the neurosciences. Essentially, Individual Psychology is an integrative theory approach.

This book will be useful as both a text for undergraduate and graduate psychopathology courses in all mental health disciplines as well as for interns and residents in clinical and counseling psychology and psychiatry programs. It also should have clinical value and utility for experienced practitioners in the various mental health professions.

REFERENCE

Beutler, L., & Crago, M. (1987). Strategies and techniques of prescriptive psychotherapeutic intervention. In R. Hales & A. Frances (Eds.), *Psychiatry Update: Annual Review Vol. 6*. Washington, DC: American Psychiatric Press.

ACKNOWLEDGMENTS

We would like to acknowledge the outstanding work of the many contributors to this text, particularly Michael Maniacci, Harold Mosak, Bernard Shulman, Walter "Buzz" O'Connell, Donald Lombardi, Dorothy Peven, Jim Croake, Kathy Myers, Ronald Pancner, Mark Mays, and Judy Lewis. Dr. Heinz Ansbacher, the dean of Individual Psychology, provided invaluable comments and critiques of parts of the manuscript, as well as inestimable encouragement in the darker moments of this project's life course.

We also would like to acknowledge the gentle direction and support from publisher and colleague Dr. Joe Hollis. Finally, we acknowledge the word processing assistance of Candace Ward Howell, Dawn Stalbaum, and Kim James-Jones.

PART I
INTRODUCTION

OVERVIEW

In Chapter 1 an overview is provided of Alfred Adler's Individual Psychology and its relation to psychopathology. The three formulations—diagnostic, clinical, and treatment—are discussed to show the relationship.

Differences and similarities between the *Diagnostic and Statistical Manual of Mental Disorders, Fourth Edition* and Individual Psychology are identified and discussed. The DSM-IV system is based on a pathological model and a psychology of possession, whereas the Adlerian approach is based on a growth model and a psychology of use. The Adlerian approach emphases are (a) psychological reasons in explaining behavior and symptoms (Psychodynamic focus); (b) attitudes and beliefs about self and the world (cognitive focus); and (c) family constellation, social interactions, and psychological movement (systems focus).

This first chapter concludes with a case example to illustrate the progression from diagnosis to treatment.

Chapter 1

PSYCHOPATHOLOGY AND THE DIAGNOSTIC AND TREATMENT PROCESS

Len Sperry

Today more is known about the process of normal development and psychopathology than ever before. Similarly the hope is greater that treatment interventions can effectively reduce and even reverse psychopathological processes than in past decades. This chapter has three purposes: First, it describes Alfred Adler's basic view of normality and psychopathology along with some observations that extend and clarify it. Second, it compares the Individual Psychology or Adlerian view with the nosological or classification system of the *Diagnostic and Statistical Manual of Mental Disorders, Fourth Edition* (DSM-IV) (American Psychiatric Association, 1994). Third, it suggests how diagnostic considerations can be linked to treatment interventions. A case example will be used to highlight these considerations by suggesting how a famous historical case might be formulated by a contemporary clinician.

ALFRED ADLER'S VIEW

Alfred Adler (Ansbacher & Ansbacher, 1956) was the founder of the psychological theory and system called Individual Psychology. Adler chose the term *individual*—as its Latin derivation meant *indivisible*—referring to the essential unity of the person. Adler believed that the hallmark of the healthy, nonpathological person was the capacity to move through life meeting the various life tasks with courage and common sense. Adler called this hallmark **social interest.** In no way did Adler infer that such an individual was perfect or fully self-actualized. Actually, healthy persons can use private logic, experience some discouragement and a sense of inferiority for which they compensate in ways that are outside the reaches of social interest. The common perception is that imperfections and failures are part of the human condition. On the other hand, pathological persons believe that they must be perfect and then justify their thinking and actions as the only way to achieve perfection. For Adler, all personality dysfunction was the outcome of erroneous conceptions of how to achieve personal superiority. For the most part, he believed that these faulty conceptions were formed early in one's life (Ansbacher & Ansbacher, 1956).

A neurotic disposition, Adler's term for the predisposing conditions that can result in psychopathology, stems from childhood experiences characterized either by overprotection or neglect, or by a confusing admixture of both. From these experiences, the young child develops a set of psychological convictions—about self, the world, and life goal, which becomes the *lifestyle*—of his or her inability to develop mastery or cope with the tasks of life. This conviction is confounded and reinforced either by the child's perception of a hostile, punishing, or depriving environment at home or school or by one that is subtly demanding or frustrating. Rather than providing encouragement to engage in other efforts involving mastery and achievement, these experiences leave the youngster feeling discouraged and fearful. Rather than experiencing trusting and loving relationships, the young child grows to become distrustful and manipulative. To compensate for these exaggerated feelings of insecurity and anxiety, the child becomes self-centered and uncooperative.

So what is a pathological or dysfunctional lifestyle? The dysfunctional lifestyle is an inflexible lifestyle. Problem-solving is based upon a self-protective "private sense" rather than a more task-oriented and socially useful "common sense." Once this set of faulty psychological convictions has coalesced and self-protective patterns of coping are established, the individual has difficulty seeing or responding to life in any other way. The end result is that the dysfunctional individual cannot cope productively with the tasks of life or really enjoy the rewards of his or her labors, much less his relationships with others. In contrast, a set of psychological convictions and coping patterns that are shaped positively by the child's healthy experiences of mastery, creativity, and loving and pleasurable relationships will result in a flexible lifestyle.

Adler presented a unitary theory of psychopathology wherein the individual "arranges" symptoms uniquely to serve as excuses for not meeting the tasks of life or to safeguard self-esteem either by aggression or distancing from others. Adler discriminated dysfunctional behavior along the dimensions of social interest and degree of activity. For instance, neurotics respond to the life tasks with "yes—but." With the "yes" the individual acknowledges social responsibilities, and with the "but" symptoms are presented that excuse responsibility. Mosak (1984) described two types of "yes—but" responses: "yes—but I'm sick," the classic response of the psychoneurotic, and "yes—but I defy it," the acting-out response of the character neurosis or personality disorder. On the other hand, psychotics respond to life tasks with "no" and cut themselves off from the common world. As to activity level, Adler noted a lower degree in neurotic conditions such as depression and obsessive-compulsion and a higher degree in anxiety neurosis, schizophrenia, and alcoholism. The highest levels were in instances of manics and sociopaths (Ansbacher & Ansbacher, 1964).

DEVELOPMENTS IN THE ADLERIAN VIEW

Adler believed that three main components were common to all psychopathology: *discouragement, faulty conceptions,* and *lifestyle beliefs.* Furthermore, he posited that undeveloped social interest and personality dysfunction were basically the outcome of an erroneous way of living. This represents Adler's views of normality versus abnormality at the time of his death. It should be noted that at the outset of his career, Adler felt that psychopathology stemmed from various organ inferiorities. This was a rather biological and reductionistic position. Later, his view changed to a more intrapsychic view in which dysfunctional behavior was seen as a conflict between inferiority and superiority feelings. He described the "neurotic disposition" as the predisposing factor in the development of neurosis. The term "pampered lifestyle" eventually replaced this term. Still later Adler developed a more sociopsychological view in which psychopathology represented movement toward self-importance at the expense of the common good. In many respects, the last version of Adler's theory represented one of the first attempts at developing a holistic view of psychopathology (Adler, 1964). Although it encompassed features from the biological (organ inferiority and organ dialect) and the social realms, it was primarily a theory of emotional development and dysfunction that integrated all processes through the prism of the lifestyle.

> This is notably the case with the lungs, the heart, the stomach, the organs of excretion and the sexual organs. The disturbance of these functions expresses the direction which an individual is taking to

> attain his goal. I have called these disturbances the organ dialect,
> or organ jargon, since the organs are revealing in their own most
> expressive language the intention of the individual totality. (Adler,
> 1964, p. 156)

Neufield (1954) differentiated the early psychosomatic approaches from the biopsychosocial and integrative approaches like Individual Psychology. Most psychosomatic theories failed to appreciate fully the multifaceted dynamics and interdependence of *all* of the biological, the psychological, and the social dimensions of human existence. Failure to appreciate all of these multifaceted dimensions leads to the same narrow reductionism Neufield criticized in many early psychosomatic theories.

A tendency among those espousing an integrative theory has been to downplay some of these multifaceted dynamics, particularly the biochemical and neuropharmacological ones. This is particularly true in the treatment of depressive disorders. A growing awareness is that depression is not a single entity but rather a spectrum disorder. As such, depression currently is viewed by many as a group of discrete illnesses that span a biopsychosocial continuum in which symptom patterns appear to be more influenced by biochemical factors at one end of the continuum and more by psychological factors at the other end. To illustrate the biopsychosocial perspective, a helpful procedure is to speculate about how a depressive disorder develops. One speculation, based on recent research findings, is that people who experience a major depressive episode are in some ways genetically susceptible to depression—that is, their brain pathways and circuits dealing with emotions like pleasure are fragile and poorly buffered from external influences. If added to this are some early life traumas that undermine self-confidence and self-esteem, such as the loss or separation from a significant other such as a parent, then these individuals respond with safeguarding patterns. When individuals are subjected to a severe psychological stressor at a later point in life, they interpret this a threat that in some way echoes their early experience of loss or separation. When existing social support systems and personal coping strategies or safeguarding methods are not sufficient to neutralize this stressor, the already compromised brain biochemistry is overtaxed, resulting in the familiar biological symptoms of depression such as sleep and appetite disturbance, psychomotor retardation, reduced energy, inability to experience pleasure, and somatic symptoms such as constipation and headache. This reduced physiological functioning serves to reinforce further individuals' lifestyle beliefs about self, the world, and the future. Pancner (1985a) suggested a similar hypothesis. On the other hand, a dysthymic disorder, previously called neurotic depression, probably has more psychosocial loading than genetic and biological loading. The dysthymic disorder most often presents with fewer biological symptoms and more dysfunctional lifestyle beliefs and coping skills. Thus, it is not surprising that dysthymic disorders respond well primarily to psychosocial therapies, whereas major depressive disorders are more likely to respond to biochemical therapies such as antidepressant medications, often in conjunction with psychotherapy. Psychotherapy will be a necessary adjunctive treatment assuming that a pampered lifestyle or neurotic disposition interferes with functioning in life tasks. But, when little or no life task dysfunction exists, as is sometimes the situation, then psychotherapy is probably not warranted. Pancner (1985b) proposed a similar view.

FORMULATION: DIAGNOSTIC, CLINICAL, AND TREATMENT FORMULATIONS

A case formulation is a way of summarizing diverse information about a patient in a brief, coherent manner for the purpose of better understanding and treating of the individual. Basically, case formulations consist of three aspects: diagnostic formulations, clinical formulations, and treatment formulations. A *diagnostic formulation* is a descriptive statement about the nature and severity of the individual's psychiatric presentation. The diagnostic formulation aids the clinician in reaching three sets of diagnostic conclusions: (a) whether the patient's presentation is primarily psychotic, characterological, or neurotic; (b) whether the patient's presentation is primarily organic or psychogenic in etiology; and (c) whether the patient's presentation is so acute and severe that it requires immediate intervention. In short, diagnostic formulations are descriptive, phenomenological, and cross-sectional in nature. They answer the "What happened?" question. For all practical purposes the diagnostic formulation lends itself to being specified with DSM-IV criteria and nosology. A *clinical formulation,* on the other hand, is more explanatory and longitudinal in nature and attempts to offer a rationale for the development and maintenance of symptoms and dysfunctional life patterns. Just as various theories of human behavior exist, so do various types of clinical formulations exist: psychoanalytic, Adlerian, cognitive, behavioral, biological, family systems, and biopsychosocial. Clinical formulations answer the "Why did it happen?" question. A *treatment formulation* follows from a diagnostic and clinical formulation and serves as an explicit blueprint governing treatment interventions. Rather than answering the "What happened?" or the "Why did it happen?" question, the treatment formulation addresses the "What can be done about it, and how?" question. The most useful and comprehensive formulations are *integrative formulations* that encompass all three dimensions: diagnostic, clinical, and treatment. The format of the following chapters of this book will highlight integrative formulations. Diagnostic formulation material will emphasize DSM-IV criteria and codes. Clinical formulation material will review Adlerian interpretations and dynamics, whereas the treatment formulation material will suggest briefly treatment goals and methods. Because DSM-IV is so prominent in diagnostic formulation, the DSM-IV theory will be related to Adlerian psychology throughout this book.

INDIVIDUAL PSYCHOLOGY AND DSM-IV

Quite unlike other psychological systems, which are based on a pathology- or disease-model, Adlerian theory is based on a growth-model. It emphasizes the element of discouragement in the dysfunctional individual rather than focusing primarily on psychopathological symptoms (Mosak, 1984). Similarly, because it is a psychology of use rather than of possession, Adlerian theory does not emphasize the diagnostic classification of symptoms. Instead, Adlerians empha- size the meaning, purpose, and use of dysfunctional thinking, behavior, and symptoms. Because the Adlerian approach emphasizes the psychological reasons or mechanisms considered to be important in explaining behavior and symptoms, it has a *psychodynamic focus*. Because it also emphasizes attitudes and beliefs about self and the world, it has a *cognitive focus*. Finally, because it emphasizes family constellation, social interactions, and psychological movement it has a *systems focus*. In short, a clinical formulation for an Adlerian integrates psychody- namic, cognitive, and systems features. With this emphasis on the clinical formula- tion, we do not mean to imply that Adlerian clinicians do not specify a diagnostic formulation. Adlerians will assign a formal diagnosis if requested by an insurance carrier or by clinic policy. Because observations about the individual's movement and descriptions about the uniqueness of the individual are considered more useful than diagnostic categories, nosologies and personality typologies have utility in clinical practice among Adlerians. For didactic purposes, however, Adler did characterize four personality types: the ruling person, the getting person, the avoiding person, and the healthy, socially useful person. The first three types describe individuals who are discouraged and low in social interest and so would be considered dysfunctional. Mosak (1959, 1971, 1973, 1985) has briefly de- scribed several other personality types and has provided in-depth analyses of the getting and controlling types. Adler considered the obsessive-compulsive neurosis to be the prototype of all neuroses, whereas the hysterical neurosis was the prototype for Freud. Indecisiveness and doubt, depreciation of others, god-like strivings, and focus on minutiae were the safeguarding methods that Adler rou- tinely noted were used by his compulsive neurotic patients in seeking their goal of personal superiority. He noted that various neurotic and psychotic individuals might use different safeguarding methods, but their movement was nevertheless the same: avoidance or rejection of the life tasks. The standard diagnostic classification adopted by many clinicians and insurance carriers in the United States is the fourth edition of the *Diagnostic and Statistical Manual of Mental Disorders* (1994), usually referred to as DSM-IV. Unlike the Adlerian approach with its unitary theory of psychopathology, DSM-IV describes 18 distinct major classifications and diagnostic criteria for more than 200 mental disorders. Each disorder has a unique set of descriptive—rather than dynamic—diagnostic criteria. A DSM-IV diagnosis can be made when a match exists between the facts from a particular individual's history and clinical presentation and the diagnostic criteria for a particular mental disorder. In short, *the DSM-IV system is based on a pathological model and a psychology of possession, while the Adlerian approach is based on a growth model and a psychology of use.* Consequently, the Adlerian therapist might not be as concerned about making a DSM-IV type of descriptive diagnosis as he or she would be in understanding the individual's dynamics, that is, movement and lifestyle themes. But just as differences exist between the two approaches, some important similarities also exist.

Similar to the Adlerian emphasis on life-task functioning, DSM-IV views pathology as clinically significant behavioral or psychological syndromes or patterns associated with maladaptive functioning in one or more of three areas: social relations, occupation, and leisure. As the Adlerian approach strives toward an integrative-biopsychosocial understanding of the individual, DSM-IV allows for a multiaxial classification so that interrelated biopsychosocial or systems facets of a person's life may be considered. Five axes are used:

Axis I: Clinical Disorders (e.g., 309.0: Adjustment Disorder with Anxious Mood)

Axis II: Personality Disorder or Mental Retardation (e.g., 301.6: Dependent Personality Disorder)

Axis III: General Medical Conditions (e.g., 244.9: Hypothyroidism)

Axis IV: Psychosocial and Environmental Problems (e.g., death of spouse and change of job)

Axis V: Global Assessment of Functioning (e.g., GAF = 55 [current]; GAF = 70 [highest level past year]

In Adlerian terms, the Axis I diagnoses would be the presenting problems. These would be determined by examining, in part, what Dreikurs referred to as the "subjective condition" (Dreikurs, 1967). Axis II diagnoses provide a glimpse of the lifestyle. Given a certain set of beliefs, clients will present with a particular style. For Adlerians, Axis III would provide information about organ inferiorities, medical conditions, organ dialects, or other potential handicapping conditions that individuals might subjectively perceive as overburdening situations (Ansbacher & Ansbacher, 1956). Regarding Axis IV, Individual Psychology has long emphasized understanding people in their social field. Adler (Ansbacher & Ansbacher, 1956) referred to understanding the "exogenous factor" (p. 296). In fact, he listed 10 "typical occasions for the onset of a neurosis or psychosis," which are similar to those listed in the DSM-IV (Ansbacher & Ansbacher, 1956, pp. 296-297). In terms of Axis V, the corresponding component in Adlerian psychology for the GAF Scale would be an assessment of the life tasks. Whereas Axis I would examine the subjective condition, Axis V would be an assessment of what Dreikurs (1967) referred to as the "Objective Situation": Understanding Axis V has another benefit—assisting clinicians in minimizing resistance. Adler (Ansbacher & Ansbacher, 1956), Dreikurs (1967), and other Adlerians have defined a cardinal characteristic of resistance as being a misalignment of goals between the therapist and client. The GAF Scale offers two scores, the current level of functioning and the highest level of functioning, or baseline, in the past year. A discrepancy between the current level and the highest level in the past year is usually indicative of an acute condition with a good prognosis (Sperry & Maniacci, 1992).

Putting the above into a unified case formulation involves practice and supervision, but once learned, it can prove to be quite beneficial. Briefly summarized, it would be something like this: A client with this particular lifestyle (Axis II) has encountered a situation for which he or she is not adequately prepared (Axis IV). In order to safeguard, the client selects a particular group or cluster of symptoms to use to sidestep the demands and create distance (Axis I). The "chosen" symptoms may be due to an organ inferiority or an overburdening situation such as a handicap (Axis III). The adequacy for which the client meets the tasks of life can be assessed. Similarly, the degree of involvement he or she expects to return to also can be assessed to gain a quick barometer of the amount of social interest present as well as to help align treatment goals (Axis V). In such a formulation, the principles of Individual Psychology are not violated, and Adlerians can become integrated in contemporary clinical practice, thus allowing their ideas and conceptualizations to be heard in a common language of their peers. An investigation of the lifestyle using traditional methods would only add to the formulation.

Many integrative-oriented therapists, including Adlerians, would argue for the inclusion of a sixth axis: a biopsychosocial formulation. The mere listing of biopsychosocial information in the various axes, however, does not in and of itself constitute an integrative formulation. Practically speaking, can DSM-IV categories be interrelated with Adlerian theory? Mosak (1968), in what many consider to be a classic in the psychopathology literature, has helped a generation of clinicians to interrelate central themes or basic lifestyle convictions with

DSM diagnostic categories. These central themes are determined from clinical observation, psychological testing, and particularly through early recollections. Mosak listed the eight most common themes: getter; controller; driver; to be good, perfect, right, martyr; victim; "aginner"; feeling avoider; and excitement seeker. He also interrelated combinations of these themes with nineteen diagnostic categories. For example, the lifestyle of a person who traditionally would be traditionally diagnosed as a depressive neurotic would likely be a composite, in varying degrees, of the getter, the controller, and the person needing to be right (Mosak, 1979). For the antisocial personality, the themes would likely be those of the getter, the aginner, and the excitement seeker.

FROM DIAGNOSIS TO TREATMENT

How does a clinician know whether or not a client is receiving the most appropriate clinical care? The current consensus favors treatment that is matched or tailored to the client's needs and expectations. Tailored treatment is a logical extension of cooperation between clinician and client in Adlerian Theory. Tailored treatment is based on a comprehensive evaluation and integrative case formulation as well as on a negotiated, mutual agreement about treatment expectations and methods.

Briefly, a comprehensive clinical evaluation usually includes the presenting complaints and their history, mental status, social and developmental history, health status, previous treatment, and the client's explanation of the condition and expectations for treatment. These last two items represent the client's formulation. In addition, the Adlerian clinician would observe and elicit information on the life tasks and of lifestyle themes and convictions. The integrative case formulation suggests the origins and meaning of the client's concerns. Because it is an integrative statement, it accounts for biological and familial predispositions, the client's coping skills, faulty lifestyle convictions, as well as interpersonal, occupational, and social system factors. A five axes DSM-IV diagnosis, problem list, statement of the client's motivation and capacity for treatment, and prognosis round out the formulation.

The *negotiation process* begins with the clinician acknowledging the client's formulation and the similarities and differences from the clinician's formulation. The ensuing discussion allows the clinician to educate the client about his or her illness and clarify misconceptions about it and the treatment process. Discussion of the client's expectations for the treatment process and outcomes facilitates negotiating a mutually agreeable direction for treatment and a therapeutic relationship based on cooperation. Then, the specifics of treatment selection can be discussed.

CASE EXAMPLE: THE CASE OF MRS. A REVISITED

Perhaps the most famous of Adler's (1969) cases was that of Mrs. A. Following is a summary of the Case of Mrs. A as it might be reported by a clinician today along with diagnostic, clinical, and treatment formulations. The reader is reminded that Adler did not treat Mrs. A. She was an ongoing patient of Dr. Hilda Weber, a non-Adlerian at the time Adler was asked to comment on parts of Dr. Weber's written case study. Although he did not personally interview Mrs. A, Adler was able to deduce Mrs. A's lifestyle themes from a few pages of Dr. Weber's case report. These lifestyle themes are noted in the clinical formulation section.

Summary

This is a 31-year-old married housewife with two children who presents with a dysphoric mood, a cleaning compulsion, a knife phobia, and a fear of seriously harming her younger son.

History of Present Illness

The patient dates these progressively worsening symptoms of 18 months to a terrifying dream in which angels surrounded a coffin. But it appears the symptoms span the eight years of her marriage probably beginning with her immense disappointment that her first child was a boy rather than a girl. In time she became jealous of her husband's popularity and friends, had difficulty relating to her neighbors, and as their marital discord increased, threatened to kill herself and her son if things did not change. Her vanity was severely wounded when a second son was born about three years later. Soon thereafter, a drunken neighbor threatened to kill her with a knife. She soon moved out of their home and took her two children and moved in with her parents. During her absence, her husband had a 'nervous breakdown' and begged her to return to care for him. After she returned, her obsessive thoughts and compulsions incapacitated her to the point that she sought psychotherapy.

Past Psychiatric Treatment

Following her suicidal threats, her husband took her for an evaluation at which time she was diagnosed with a "nervous stomach," a functional or psychosomatic condition. Psychotherapy was neither recommended nor requested. This was approximately four years ago.

Family History

The patient denies any family history of psychiatric illness but notes alcoholism on her father's side of the family. Father was described as a construction worker who was impulsive, physically abusive, and a binge drinker. Mother was described as hardworking but nonassertive. Marital conflict was precipitated by her father's drinking and loud threats to "cut everyone's throat." The patient was the third of eight children, four girls followed by four boys. She described herself as a child as being cheerful, fun-loving and well-liked by everyone except her oldest brother, whom she described as selfish and inconsiderate. She described her older sister as selfish because she was silent and reserved, and as having herself been severely disciplined for small matters.

Social/Developmental History

She reports being in excellent health as a child, doing well in school and having many friends. She left high school before graduation—which was not uncommon among her female friends—and had a number of unskilled jobs before marrying. While she lived at home and worked, she did well. But when jobs necessitated, she lived away from home and developed numerous somatic symptoms including a severe skin condition and an enlarged thyroid gland. After her physician insisted that she return to live at home, her symptoms subsided. Thereafter she was able to return to work choosing male-oriented jobs. She explained she did not want to work around things like fine glassware or china because she dreaded breaking such items. One day her father threatened to kill her with a shovel because her return home had become a financial drain on the family. She ran from the house and hid at a nearby church, vowing she would never return to live at home again. At the age of 21 she broke off an engagement of three years to a rather passive and clinging male. Soon thereafter, she met her husband while he was recuperating from wounds sustained in the military. He was all she had dreamed of in a mate: tall, handsome, and a non-drinker. Like their marriage, their courtship was conflictive. He left her, and she pursued him when she learned that she was pregnant with their child. A "shotgun" wedding followed.

Diagnostic Formulation

A list of acute problems or symptoms exhibited by Mrs. A include a cleaning compulsion and obsession involving aggressive behavior and fear of knives, indication of an Obsessive Compulsive Disorder; dysphoric mood of sufficient duration to warrant the diagnosis of Dysthymia; and concerns about the safety of her children given her impulsive style leading to the V-code diagnosis of the Parent-Child Problems. Longer-term problems or issues include chronic marital problems (V code), and characterological issues of impulsivity, affective instability, and other symptoms characterized by the Axis II diagnoses.

Axis I: Obsessive Compulsive Disorder (300.30)
           Dysthymic Disorder (300.40)
           Partner Relational Problem (V61.20)
Axis II: Borderline Personality Disorders (301.83) with Histrionic, Narcissistic, Compulsive, and Dependent traits
Axis III: Somatic complaints, Thyroid goiter by history
Axis IV: Chronic marital-family issues; Homicidal ideation
Axis V: GAF = 46 (current); GAF = 58 (highest level past year)

Clinical Formulation

Based on Adler's analysis and Shulman's (1969) accompanying commentary on the case, the following lifestyle themes and convictions are noted. Mrs. A viewed life as hostile, unfair, and overcontrolling. She saw herself as a victim who expected to be humiliated, but she also believed she was entitled to be treated differently. Therefore, she demanded that others take care of her, and she utilized obsessions, compulsions, and threats of harming herself and her child to insure that her husband and family continued in their caretaking roles. Mrs. A. also utilized interpersonal relationships as a means of gaining dominance and resisting submission and tended to construe cooperation as conquest. Therefore, a clinician might anticipate that the development of cooperative therapeutic relationships would take some time and that the negotiation phase of therapy would be very important and could not be downplayed. Also, because Mrs. A showed relatively little insight and psychological mindedness, and was rather ambivalent, the initial phase of treatment would not focus primarily on insight and interpretation. In short, a clinician would endeavor to gain Mrs. A's cooperation from the very onset by attending to her expectations of treatment and by encouraging her involvement, while being aware of her ambivalent, controlling, and entitled lifestyle.

Plausible Treatment Formulation

The initial focus of treatment would be to elicit Mrs. A's expectations for treatment, for the therapist's role in treatment, and for her role in treatment. A mutually agreed upon treatment plan then would be negotiated. Presumably, the treatment plan would involve symptom reduction at first, followed by stabilization of marriage and family relations, and in the later stages, focus more on character-ological or Axis II issues. A short course of treatment with a trial of an antidepres-sant, anti–obsessive-compulsive medication (i.e., Prozac or Anafranil), and/or focused behavior therapy aimed at symptom reduction is indicated. In addition, whatever measures might be needed to insure that Mrs. A did not harm her children or herself such as consultation with a child protective services agency would be advised. Then, because of the chronic severity of her condition, psycho-social stressors, as well as her histrionic, narcissistic, and borderline personality features, a course of individual supportive therapy, with adjunctive sessions involving her husband and/or children, as well as a consideration of group therapy would be indicated. Half-hour sessions probably would be scheduled twice weekly until sufficient symptom reduction was achieved and a stable therapeutic relation-ship had developed.

In the second phase of treatment, sessions might be weekly and focus on longer-term problem issues such as parent–child relations, marital relations, and her characterological features and faulty lifestyle convictions about entitlement and overcontrol, as well as her need to somatize, and threats of acting out, masculine protest, and so on. Because of these characterological features, Mrs. A likely might prove to be a difficult patient; however, she would merit a fair to good prognosis, assuming she would continue in her commitment to treatment.

REFERENCES

Adler, A. (1964). *Problems of neurosis: A book of case histories.* New York: Harper and Row.

Adler, A. (1969). *The case of Mrs. A: The diagnosis of a life style* (2nd ed., with commentary by B. Shulman, M.D.). Chicago: Alfred Adler Institute Publishers.

American Psychiatric Association. (1994). *Diagnostic and statistical manual of mental disorders* (4th ed). Washington, DC: Author.

Ansbacher, H.L., & Ansbacher, R.R. (Eds.). (1956). *The Individual Psychology of Alfred Adler*. New York: Harper & Row.

Ansbacher, H.L., & Ansbacher, R.R. (Eds.). (1964). *Superiority and social interest*. Evanston, IL: Northwestern University Press.

Dreikurs, R. (1967). The psychological interview in medicine. In R. Dreikurs (Ed.), *Psychodynamics, psychotherapy and counseling* (pp. 75–102). Chicago: Alfred Adler Institute.

Mosak, H. (1959). The getting type, a parsimonious social interpretation of the oral character. *Journal of Individual Psychology, 15*(2), 193–198.

Mosak, H. (1968). The interrelatedness of the neuroses through central themes. *Journal of Individual Psychology, 24*(1), 67–70.

Mosak, H. (1971). Lifestyle. In A. Nikelly (Ed.), *Techniques for behavior changes: Applications of Adlerian theory*. Springfield, IL: Charles C. Thomas.

Mosak, H. (1973). The controller: A social interpretation of the anal character. In H.H. Mosak (Ed.), *Alfred Adler: His influence on psychology today* (pp. 43–52). Park Ridge, NJ: Noyes Press.

Mosak, H. (1979). Mosak's typology: An update. *Journal of Individual Psychology, 35*(2), 92–95.

Mosak, H. (1984). Adlerian psychology. In R. Corsini & B. Ozaki (Eds.), *Encyclopedia of psychology* (pp. 16–19). New York: Wiley-Interscience.

Mosak, H. (1985, May). *Mosak's typology: Behaviors, psychopathology, and psychotherapy.* Paper presented at North American Society of Adlerian Psychology, Atlanta, GA.

Neufield, I. (1954). Holistic medicine versus psychosomatic medicine. *American Journal of Individual Psychology, 10*(3,4), 140–168.

Pancer, R. (1985a). *Biochemical theory and Adlerian psychotherapy.* Audiotape. Montreal: International Association of Individual Psychology.

Pancner, R. (1985b). Impact of current depression research on Adlerian theory and practice. *Individual Psychology: The Adlerian Journal of Individual Psychology, 41*(3), 289–301.

Shulman, B. (1969). Forward. In F.G. Crookshank (Ed.), *The case of Mrs. A: The diagnosis of a life style* (2nd ed.). Chicago: Alfred Adler Institute.

Sperry, L., Gudeman, J., Blackwell, B., & Faulkner, L. (1992). *Psychiatric case formulations*. Washington, DC: American Psychiatric Press.

Sperry, L., & Maniacci, M. (1992). An integration of DSM-III-R diagnoses and Adlerian case formulations. *Individual Psychology, 48*(2), 175–181.

PART II
PSYCHOSES AND MOOD
DISORDERS

OVERVIEW

Adler (Ansbacher & Ansbacher, 1956) stated that "The loftiest goals are to be found in the most pathological cases, that is, in the psychoses" (p. 314). Although Freud developed a theory about psychotic disorders, he felt that, by and large, they were not amenable to psychoanalytic treatment. Adler disagreed, unequivocally stating that psychosis

> represents a greater distance from fellow man than any other expression except, perhaps, suicide. But . . . [it] is not incurable if the interest in others can be aroused. It is an art to cure such cases, and a very difficult art. We must win the patient back to cooperation; and we can do it only by patience and the kindliest and friendliest manner. (Ansbacher & Ansbacher, 1956, p. 316)

In the next four chapters, the authors examine four of the most difficult and theoretically controversial disorders in DSM-IV. Ever since the French philosopher Descartes made the distinction between mind and body, theoreticians have struggled with the problem of how to conceptualize "mental illness." For Adlerians, the distinction between mind and body is irrelevant; given the holistic hypothesis and teleological perspective of Individual Psychology, the issue is not what causes what, but for what purpose is this being used. Adlerians are generally receptive to the recent advances and discoveries in the biological sciences, believing that seeking a single, unitary cause to any condition is reductionistic (of note is Freud's opinion in this respect; he felt that symptoms were "overdetermined" and to search for any single cause was fruitless).

Dreikurs (1967) made a distinction that has proved quite useful. He noted the difference between psychosis, neurosis, and character disorders as the relationship of common sense to private logic. In the psychotic disorders (including the organic conditions), common sense is discarded. Private logic prevails, and individuals act as if their private logic were "fact" rather than "fiction." Regardless of the etiology, psychotic individuals operate upon premises that are not grounded in common sense. Whether a condition is primarily psychological or biological is not as relevant for Adlerians as is the individuals' stance about their conditions. People must learn to adapt to survive, and as Adler frequently noted, survival is greatly facilitated when it is done cooperatively, with the support and mutual assistance of others.

Sperry and Shulman present Chapter 2 entitled "Schizophrenia and Delusional Disorders." They review the DSM-IV diagnostic criteria and the classic Adlerian perspectives of each condition. Using up-to-date research, they present an insightful discussion of the work of Gazzaniga (1988), whose recent work on split-brain patients has offered some fascinating conceptualizations that appear to support a basic Adlerian construct: the lifestyle as organizer and interpreter of experience.

In Chapter 3, Maniacci discusses "Mental Disorders Due to a General Condition and Other Cognitive Disorders." After presenting an overview of the DSM-IV criteria, he discusses the differences among inferiorities, inferiority feelings, and inferiority complexes and presents a discussion of the three levels of compensation individuals make when adjusting to illness. He highlights the necessity of understanding patients' conditions not only from a biomedical perspective but also from an individual, family systems, and rehabilitation perspective.

Peven in Chapter 4 discusses "Individual Psychology and Bipolar Mood Disorder." She presents an extensive review of the history and various theoretical perspectives taken toward the condition throughout the years and discusses the Adlerian perspective cogently and insightfully. Peven offers eight cardinal features found in patients with Bipolar Mood Disorders and the subsequent implications for treatment.

The final chapter in Part II, Chapter 5, is written by Pancner and Jylland and is entitled "Depressive Disorders." After an extensive review of the DSM-

IV, biological, familial, and psychological factors of these varied conditions, he presents an integrated, comprehensive perspective of the conditions based upon the concept of depression as a spectrum disorder existing along a continuum.

REFERENCES

Ansbacher, H.L., & Ansbacher R.R. (Eds.). (1956). *The Individual Psychology of Alfred Adler.* New York: Harper and Row.

Dreikurs, R. (1967). *Psychodynamics, psychotherapy, and counseling.* Chicago: Alfred Adler Institute.

Gazzaniga, M.S. (1988). *Mind matters.* Boston: Houghton Mifflin.

Chapter 2

SCHIZOPHRENIA AND DELUSIONAL DISORDERS

Len Sperry
Bernard H. Shulman

Schizophrenia and Delusional Disorders occur frequently in patients with one or more mental health disorders. In this chapter is provided information on Schizophrenia and Delusional Disorders as to phases, types, and Adlerian perspectives on psychosis.

SCHIZOPHRENIA

Approximately one-fourth of all hospital beds and roughly one-half of the psychiatric beds in the United States are occupied by individuals who have been diagnosed with a schizophrenic disorder. Estimates are that the lifetime risk of developing this disorder is approximately one percent. Basically, schizophrenia is a syndrome consisting of a highly altered sense of inner and outer reality to which the individual responds in ways that impair his or her life. This altered sense of reality, which is the psychotic core of this disorder, shows itself in disturbances of speech, perception, thinking, emotion, and physical activity. The term literally means "splitting of the mind," which in popular parlance connotes a "split personality" or multiple personality. Rather, schizophrenia refers to the incongruity between different mental functions, that is, between thought content and feeling or between feeling and overt activity. For example, the schizophrenic may talk of sad or terrifying events while laughing or showing no affect whatsoever.

Schizophrenia is a syndrome that involves multiple disorders with varying causes, courses, and treatment outcomes. As a diagnostic label, schizophrenia includes a wide variety of clinical presentations. Symptoms can vary so greatly from one individual to another that to present a classic textbook picture of the disorder is difficult. For example, the diagnostic presentation could be that of a hypervigilant accountant who suspects that others are plotting against him or her, the housewife who believes she is controlled by her dead mother's voice, or the withdrawn and apathetic college student who broods incessantly about the reality of existence. Symptoms also can vary within the same individual over time so that the schizophrenic may be floridly psychotic and totally unable to function one week, and then be capable of adequate reality testing and reasonable performance in the work place the next week.

DSM-IV Diagnostic Features

The major features of schizophrenia can be specified in terms of a series of diagnostic criteria that include an age of onset, disorganization of prior level of functioning, and a tendency toward chronicity, as well as characteristic symptoms such as bizarre delusions, prominent hallucinations, incoherence or marked loosening of associations, catatonic behavior, flat or grossly inappropriate affect, and marked dysfunctioning in the tasks of life. Furthermore, certain other psychiatric conditions that may mimic the disorder must be ruled out. These include schizoaffective disorder, mood disorder with psychotic features, psychoactive substance abuse disorder, organic mental disorder, delusional disorder, or other psychiatric disorders such as brief reactive psychoses and induced psychotic disorder. The diagnostic criteria in *Diagnostic and Statistical Manual of Mental Disorders, Fourth Edition* (American Psychiatric Association, 1994, pp. 285–286), for schizophrenia are noted in Table 2.1.

The onset of schizophrenia is most likely to be noted in late adolescence or early adulthood. Except in rare instances, the diagnosis is not made unless the illness begins before age 45. Clinical experience has indicated that the diagnosis should be reserved for illnesses of at least six months duration. The diagnosis of Schizophreniform Disorder is reserved for individuals with symptoms of less than six months duration who otherwise meet the diagnostic criteria for schizophrenia. If the symptoms persist for more than six months the diagnosis is then corrected to that of Schizophrenic Disorder.

TABLE 2.1
Criteria and course of Schizophrenia

Diagnostic criteria for Schizophrenia

A. *Characteristic symptoms:* Two (or more of the following, each present for a significant portion of time during a 1-month period (or less if successfully treated):

   (1)   delusions
   (2)   hallucinations
   (3)   disorganized speech (e.g., frequent derailment or incoherence)
   (4)   grossly disorganized or catatonic behavior
   (5)   negative symptoms, i.e., affective flattening, alogia, or avolition

Note: Only one Criterion A symptom is required if delusions are bizarre or hallucinations consist of a voice keeping up a running commentary on the person's behavior or thoughts, or two or more voices conversing with each other.

B. *Social/occupational dysfunction:* For a significant portion of the time since the onset of the disturbance, one or more major areas of functioning such as work, interpersonal relations, or self-care are markedly below the level achieved prior to the onset (or when the onset is in childhood or adolescence, failure to achieve expected level of interpersonal, academic, or occupational achievement).

C. *Duration:* Continuous signs of the disturbance persist for at least 6 months. This 6-month period must include at least 1 month of symptoms (or less if successfully treated) that meet Criterion A (i.e., active-phase symptoms) and may include periods of prodromal or residual symptoms. During these prodromal or residual periods, the signs of the disturbance may be manifested by only negative symptoms or two or more symptoms listed in Criterion A present in an attenuated form (e.g., odd beliefs, unusual perceptual experiences).

D. *Schizoaffective and Mood Disorder exclusion:* Schizoaffective Disorder and Mood Disorder With Psychotic Features have been ruled out because either (1) no Major Depressive, Manic, or Mixed Episodes have occurred concurrently with the active-phase symptoms; or (2) if mood episodes have occurred during active-phase symptoms, their total duration has been brief relative to the duration of the active and residual periods.

TABLE 2.1 (Continued)
Criteria and course of Schizophrenia

Diagnostic criteria for Schizophrenia

E. *Substance/general condition exclusion:* The disturbance is not due to the direct physiological effects of a substance (e.g., a drug of abuse, a medication) or a general medical condition.

F. *Relationship to a Pervasive Developmental Disorder:* If there is a history of Autistic Disorder or another Pervasive Developmental Disorder, the additional diagnosis of Schizophrenia is made only if prominent delusions or hallucinations are also present for at least a month (or less if successfully treated).

Classification of longitudinal course (can be applied only after 1 year has elapsed since the initial onset of active-phase symptoms):
   Episodic With Interepisode Residual Symptoms (episodes are defined by the reemergence of prominent psychotic symptoms); *also specify if:* **With Prominent Negative Symptoms**
   Episodic With No Interepisode Residual Symptoms
   Continuous (prominent psychotic symptoms are present throughout the period of observation); *also specify if:* **With Prominent Negative Symptoms**
   Single Episode In Partial Remission; *also specify if:* **With Prominent Negative Symptoms**
   Single Episode In Full Remission
   Other or Unspecified Pattern

From *Diagnostic and Statistical Manual of Mental Disorders, Fourth Edition* (DSM-IV). Copyright © 1994 by American Psychiatric Association. Reprinted with permission.

Phases and Course of Schizophrenic Disorder

Generally speaking, this disorder first presents with prodromal symptoms, yet manifestations of the active phase sometimes occur without these. Usually, the prodromal phase begins with a noticeable deterioration of functioning prior to the active phase and involves the presence of specific symptoms. These symptoms include social isolation or withdrawal; marked impairment of role functioning; peculiar behavior; poor hygiene; blunted, flat, or inappropriate affect; unusual perception experiences; odd or bizarre ideation or "magical thinking"; and vague, circumstantial, or metaphorical speech. The diagnosis is not made unless two of these symptoms are present.

The active phase is recognized by the presence of certain characteristic symptoms combined with gross impairment in the tasks of life: work, love, and friendship. Symptoms characteristic of this phase include delusions, hallucinations, and marked disorganization of thought and verbal behavior. Typically, delusions are bizarre and include content of either religious, somatic, grandiose, nihilistic, or prosecutory nature. Typically, auditory hallucinations involve two conversing voices, or one voice providing a running commentary on the patient's behavior, or is repetitive but unrelated to a depressed or elated mood. Typically, thought disturbance is evidenced by incoherence, illogicality, loose associations, or poverty of content. Thought disturbance, however, is not a dependable criterion unless accompanied by a flat, blunted, or inappropriate affect; grossly disorganized behavior; or some type of delusions and/or hallucinations. Other symptoms may include a disturbance in a sense of self, autistic preoccupation, difficulty in making and carrying out decisions, confusion, obsessions or ritualistic behavior, ideas of reference, or dysphoric moods.

The residual phase gradually follows from the active phase. It is manifested by the same symptoms already described for the prodromal phase. Persistence of at least two of the prodromal symptoms are required by DSM-IV diagnostic criteria.

According to DSM-IV, the diagnostician should classify the longitudinal course of schizophrenic disturbance as episodic, continuous, single episode, or unspecified pattern.

A patient who has a documented diagnosis of schizophrenic disorder but recovers fully is usually considered to be *in remission*. If no recurrences intervene over a period of five years without medication, the diagnosis is then changed to that of "no mental disorder." Patients in remission frequently experience an acute exacerbation of their symptoms, possibly re-hospitalization. Clinicians talk about the "rule of thirds," which predicts that approximately one-third of all patients who meets the diagnosis for schizophrenia will recover fully after a single episode, and another one-third will experience periodic exacerbations of symptoms and periods of remission, while the remaining one-third will experience the ongoing chronic form of this disorder.

Subtypes of Schizophrenia

In DSM-IV are recognized five subtypes of schizophrenic disorder. In actual practice, clinicians have found these subtypes of limited value since schizophrenic presentations do not neatly fit into a single diagnostic category. The five subtypes are paranoid, disorganized, catatonic, residual, and undifferentiated. Table 2.2

TABLE 2.2
Criteria for subtypes of Schizophrenia

Diagnostic criteria for 295.30 Paranoid Type

A type of Schizophrenia in which the following criteria are met:

A. Preoccupation with one or more delusions or frequent auditory hallucinations.

B. None of the following is prominent: disorganized speech, disorganized or catatonic behavior, or flat or inappropriate affect.

Diagnostic criteria for 295.10 Disorganized Type

A type of Schizophrenia in which the following criteria are met:

A. All of the following are prominent
    (1)   disorganized speech
    (2)   disorganized behavior
    (3)   flat or inappropriate affect

B. The criteria are not met for Catatonic Type.

Diagnostic criteria for 295.20 Catatonic Type

A type of Schizophrenia in which the clinical picture is dominated by at least two of the following:

(1)   motoric immobility as evidence by catalepsy (including waxy flexibility) or stupor

(2)   excessive motor activity (that is apparently purposeless and not influenced by external stimuli)

(American Psychiatric Association, 1994, pp. 287–290) presents the diagnostic criteria for these subtypes.

DELUSIONAL DISORDERS

The essential feature of the delusional disorder is the presence of a persistent, nonbizarre delusion that is not due to any other mental disorder. Delusionally

TABLE 2.2 (Continued)
Criteria for subtypes of Schizophrenia

---

(3)   extreme negativism (an apparently motiveless resistance to all instructions or maintenance of a rigid posture against attempts to be moved) or mutism

(4)   peculiarities of voluntary movement as evidenced by posturing (voluntary assumption of inappropriate or bizarre postures), stereotyped movements, prominent mannerisms, or prominent grimacing

(5)   echolalia or echopraxia

Diagnostic criteria for 295.60 Residual Type

A type of Schizophrenia in which the following criteria are met:

A.   Absence of prominent delusions, hallucinations, disorganized speech, and grossly disorganized or catatonic behavior.

B.   There is continuing evidence of the disturbance, as indicated by the presence of negative symptoms or two or more symptoms listed in Criterion A for Schizophrenia, present in an attenuated form (e.g., odd beliefs, unusual perceptual experiences).

Diagnostic criteria for 295.90 Undifferentiated Type

A type of Schizophrenia in which symptoms that meet Criterion A are present, but the criteria are not met for the Paranoid, Disorganized, or Catatonic Type.

From *Diagnostic and Statistical Manual of Mental Disorders, Fourth Edition* (DSM-IV). Copyright © 1994 by American Psychiatric Association. Reprinted with permission.

disordered patients do not display the pervasive disturbances of mood and thought found in other psychotic disorders. Absent are flat or inappropriate affect, prominent hallucinations, or markedly bizarre delusions. They, however, do have one or more systematic and circumscribed delusions often of a persecutory nature but also involving infidelity, grandiosity, being deceived by spouses or lovers, somatic changes or erotomania. In Table 2.3 (American Psychiatric Association, 1994, p. 301) are presented the DSM-IV diagnostic criteria for this disorder.

The delusional disorder is relatively uncommon and the lifetime risk of this disorder is between 0.05 percent and 0.1 percent. For the most part, this is a mid-life disorder and usually not recognized until the individual's delusional

TABLE 2.3
Criteria and types of Delusional Disorder

Diagnostic criteria for 297.1 Delusional Disorder

A. Nonbizarre delusions (i.e., involving situations that occur in real life, such as being followed, poisoned, infected, loved at a distance, or deceived by spouse or lover, or having a disease) of at least 1 month's duration.

B. Criterion A for Schizophrenia has never been met. **Note:** Tactile and olfactory hallucinations may be present in Delusional Disorder if they are related the delusional theme.

C. Apart from the impact of the delusion(s) or its ramifications, functioning is not markedly impaired and behavior is not obviously odd or bizarre.

D. If mood episodes have occurred concurrently with delusions, their total duration has been brief relative to the duration of the delusional periods.

E. The disturbance is not due to the direct physiological effects of a substance (e.g., a drug of abuse, a medication) or a general medical condition.

Specify type (the following types are assigned based on the predominant delusional theme):

Erotomanic Type: delusions that another person, usually of higher status, is in love with the individual

Grandiose Type: delusions of inflated worth, power, knowledge, identity, or special relationship to a deity or famous person

Jealous Type: delusions that the individual's sexual partner is unfaithful

Persecutory Type: delusions that the person (or someone to whom the person is close) is being malevolently treated in some way

Somatic Type: delusions that the person has some physical defect or general medical condition

Mixed Type: delusions characteristic of more than one of the above types but no one theme predominates

Unspecified Type

From *Diagnostic and Statistical Manual of Mental Disorders, Fourth Edition* (DSM-IV). Copyright © 1994 by American Psychiatric Association. Reprinted with permission.

system is noted by friends or family. One reason why this disorder may appear to be relatively rare is that these individuals tend to be distrustful of others, particularly psychiatrists, and typically do not voluntarily seek treatment. Delusionally disordered individuals tend to be hypersensitive, argumentative, and litigious and may be referred for psychiatric evaluation because of ill-founded legal actions that they have initiated. Although these individuals may perform well occupationally and in areas outside the parameter of their delusions, they tend to be social isolates and have difficulty maintaining marriages and friendships.

The delusional disorder appears midway on a continuum between the paranoid personality disorder and schizophrenia, paranoid type. Delusions are common among the elderly and among the stimulant-drug abusers. Similarly, delusional or paranoid reactions are common in medical or surgical patients who experience delirium and in patients who are bed-ridden, hearing or sight impaired individuals as well among refugees and minority groups. Delusionally disordered individuals have family relationships that are characterized by turbulence, callousness, and coldness. The etiology for this disorder is unknown, and though genetic and biological factors have been postulated none have actually been identified.

Types of Delusional Disorders

DSM-IV recognizes seven types of delusional disorders based on the predominant delusional being noted. In Table 2.3, these types are specified.

The differential diagnosis for this disorder includes organic mental disorders, such as dementia and organic delusional syndromes, those due to amphetamines, or those due to a brain tumor. Other disorders that must be ruled out are schizophrenia, paranoid type, schizophreniform disorder, mood disorders with psychotic features, body dysmorphic disorder, and the paranoid personality disorder. According to DSM-IV, when an individual meets the criteria for a delusional disorder and has a preexisting paranoid personality disorder, the personality disorder should be listed on Axis II followed by the modifier *premorbid*.

ADLERIAN PERSPECTIVE ON PSYCHOSIS

The theory of functional psychosis presented in this section reflects the Adlerian perspective particularly as it has been articulated by Bernard Shulman

(1968, 1984) and supplemented with the research-based theory of Michael Gazzaniga (1988), the noted mind-body researcher.

Shulman's model of the psychotic process can be summarized as follows:

Vulnerability + Lifestyle Convictions + Decision

+ Self-training and Discouragement →

Psychotic Process and Symptoms

Briefly, vulnerability (i.e., positive family history for a major psychiatric disorder, some biological predisposition to psychosis, and/or faulty training) when combined with psychotic-like lifestyle convictions, personal decision, self-training and discouragement can result in a psychotic process. One becomes schizophrenic over a period of time in response to cumulative life stresses and a feeling of failure. The "choice" is neither conscious nor planned ahead of time. It is a series of small steps—a self-training in which one step makes taking the next step easier, so that in the end one somehow arrives at one's own illness without recalling the past by which one came.

Like other Adlerians, Shulman espouses a cognitive theory of personality development and psychopathology. Cognitive theory offers a description, an explanation of the internal cognitive structures of the individual. This explanation includes the individual's consistent style of perceiving. For example, schizophrenics extract and process information differently from other persons. They are 'over-inclusive'; that is, they include too many categories in their thoughts. They do not filter out extraneous information well. Furthermore, they do not abstract with precision and thus make errors in logic. They do not pay proper attention to differences in the semantic context of language, and thus they do not understand precisely what others are saying to them. Therefore, they invest what they hear with meaning prompted by the inner fantasies. In addition, cognitive theory describes the internal schemata apperception—the self-concepts of individuals, their world designs, and their plans for coping with the world. Kelly (1955) devised the term *personal constructs* for the idiosyncratic way people construe events. The word "construe" is apt, because it implies that events are actually *constructs* devised by individuals themselves. It is a personal conclusion about life and themselves that produces a seemingly appropriate action. These personal constructs are contained in the memory organization of individuals and influence how subsequent events are stored in their memory.

The personal constructs contain the world design and the plan of action in the schizophrenic, the *extravagant ideals* that Binswanger (1960) mentioned.

Self-concept, world design, and plan of action are all part of what Adler called the lifestyle (1926). Extravagant ideals grow from normal human motives that have gone awry. Finally, a cognitive theory describes the coping program devised by individuals. If we know the lifestyle of individuals, we will know their cognitive blueprint for behavior. Then, we shall be able to see how those who become psychotic have followed a step-by-step progression in their journey toward psychosis. We shall understand how they integrate the events of their lives into this journey in accord with their unconscious blueprint. Thus, knowing their master plan for perceiving stimuli, we shall be able to understand their subjective experiences—the phenomenology of their life. From knowing their phenomenology, we also may reason backwards and plot out their cognitive blueprint.

Arieti (1974, 1980) and Binswanger (1960) have offered useful insights for understanding the psychotic process from a cognitive perspective. Arieti (1980) begins his inquiry by noting the importance of a child's subjective perceptions:

> Certainly it is very important to study what kind of interpersonal world the patient met early in life. That is the first term on our list of inquiries, but only the first. It is also of crucial importance to determine how the child experienced this world, how he internalized and how such internalization affected the subsequent events of his life, which in turn acted as feedback mechanisms. (p. 242)

A more thorough cognitive-phenomenological theory of psychosis and schizophrenia is offered by Binswanger (1960). Starting from the premise the individuals construct their own *world design,* Binswanger asked, "Who is this man and how does this man interpret himself?" He went on to say that schizophrenics construct a world design in which they set up a set of rigid alternatives, a hard and fast either/or:

> These alternatives are totally inadequate to escape from an unescapable situation. . . . [h]e shuts himself off from the world of others and himself, and most especially . . . he shuts himself off from . . . a loving relatedness with others. (Binswanger, 1960, p. 160)

Binswanger was saying that those who will become psychotic have created an impossible situation for themselves. As part of their world design, they have constructed a distorted and misguided goal that is impossible to achieve. They do not give themselves permission to cease pursuit of this goal, and they believe they will be a total failure if they do not achieve it. This notion that schizophrenics have inordinate and inappropriate goals is similar to that of Adler (1926)—a concretized, rigid and dogmatic aspiration to be in some way superhuman and a greater interest in this personal goal than in fellowship or enjoyment of life.

What few studies on level of aspiration that have been done on schizophrenics and preschizophrenics confirm that, unlike controls, schizophrenics and preschizophrenics either maintain high levels of aspiration after repeated failure or raise those levels (Lu, 1962).

Vulnerability to Psychosis

Even in high-risk situations, most individuals do not experience the psychotic process. Specifically, why does one child in the family become psychotic while others do not? Vulnerability is an important consideration. The basic assumption here is that a person who has a vulnerability to a psychiatric illness has the propensity to develop or express symptoms of the disorder under certain stressful conditions. This, of course, is the basis of what is called the **stress-diathesis model**. Neuchterlein and Dawson (1984) and Liberman (1987) have described vulnerability-stress models of schizophrenia in which the course and outcome of the disorder are in dynamic flux, influenced by biological, psychological, and social-environmental variables. This vulnerability is manifested by genetic predisposition, neurotransmitter abnormalities, and other unknown neurological factors resulting in cognitive, autonomic, and attentional dysfunctions, as well as a host of premorbid psychosocial factors such as faulty early childhood training, high flown goals, and lifestyle convictions, to name some.

Neuchterlein and Dawson (1984) emphasize the information-process deficits that along with autonomic reactivity anomalies, social competence, and coping limitations (called enduring vulnerability characteristics) interact with environmental stimuli (social stressors and nonsupportive social networks) and transient intermediate states (processing capacity overload, autonomic hyperarousal, and deficient processing of social stimuli) to yield the psychotic symptoms of schizophrenia.

Some schizophrenics seem to start life with what Alfred Adler called an **organ inferiority**, a central nervous system organization that is unstable or somehow defective. Gazzaniga (1988) has developed a cognitive theory of psychopathology that addresses this issue of central nervous system dysfunction and incorporates research findings from both the neurosciences and cognitive theory. Gazzaniga proposes that individuals generate a series of internally consisted schemas or beliefs about themselves and life that allow daily living to be both predictable and meaningful. He labels these cognitive schemas the **brain's interpreter**, which appears similar to what Adlerians call lifestyle convictions. Gazzaniga's "brain interpreter" is reminiscent of Kurt Goldstein's (1939) compensatory tendency and Adler's theory of compensation. The interpreter does not always have correct data but must interpret this information anyway the brain can. Gazzaniga further postulated an urge to create order in the information being processed, which is an effort to compensate for central nervous system dysfunctioning, or "organ inferiority" as it was called by Adler. Gazzaniga believed that schizophrenia is a disease in which the brain's interpreter, typically the verbal, left hemisphere, attempts to create order out of what is most likely endogenous, or inner-generated, brain chaos. By brain chaos, he referred to spurious neural actions precipitated by faulty biochemical brain states, such as sharp rises or decreases in neurotransmitters that adversely affect the typically symbolic, image-generating right hemisphere. The interpreter makes decisions about what meaning to assign to chaotic events.

The psychotic process in general and schizophrenia in particular reveals how powerful the interpreter may be and how much it wants to succeed in generating reasonable ideas about unreasonable experiences and thoughts that arise out of dysfunctional brain states. As the right hemisphere continues to generate odd, unexplainable images and impressions, the left hemisphere desperately attempts to "interpret" and integrate these aberrations according to some consistent, logical, rule-governing system, which Adlerians would term the lifestyle.

Endogenous brain changes, particularly changes in the levels of neurotransmitters such as dopamine, create new circumstances to which the brain's interpreter must continually react. That reaction in turn produces perceptions that can become powerful guides for the mental outlook of the patient. An endogenous state that is quickly induced by a change of brain chemistry—such as with a mind-altering drug like LSD—can be fairly easily dismissed as an apparition after the brain's biochemistry returns to a more normal state. If the brain change lasts longer, however, then the interpretations generated by the altered state of mind become more embellished and the memories associated with them take on their own life and can become powerful influences on the personal history of the individual. Gazzaniga noted that "crazy thoughts" are manageable for the normal person because they occur as part of some unusual context, and thus are easily rejected. On the other hand, continually crazy thoughts, evoked by chronic brain dysfunction, become more difficult to reject. This occurs because of the accumulative effect of one "crazy memory" welcoming other "crazy ideas."

Gazzaniga speculated that schizophrenia is the fate of the human mind exposed to long-term distortions of reality. The brain's interpreter tries to bring order to the chaos brought about by biochemical or structural brain abnormalities.

As a result of processing erroneous data about self, social relationships, and life circumstances over long periods of time, the brain's interpreter constructs strange and psychotic theories about reality, which become the bizarre images generated by the right hemisphere.

Gazzaniga was not saying that chronic brain dysfunction such as schizophrenia is the result merely of the overproduction of the neurotransmitter dopamine. Rather, he believed that the dopamine abnormality impacts nerve circuits such that they misfire. In turn, the brain's interpreter creates a specific delusion or set of hallucinations that allow the patient to 'make sense' of this phenomenon.

Gazzaniga offered a useful phenomenological description of the overwhelming feelings of vulnerability of individuals entering a psychotic state. The nonpsychotic person's sense of worth is usually sustained by the positive feedback from social contacts, interactions, and personal relationships. While individuals may have doubts about the future in known and unknown situations, they can cope with such feelings, because life in the past with other people has worked out. But what happens if these individuals start to lose their perception of these automatic rewards? Assuming that accurate perceptions reflect brain circuitry that is functional, good feelings are automatically triggered when individuals have contact with a good friend. But what if seeing that friend did not trigger that response? Gazzaniga believed that this new, negative experience evolves into a state much like schizophrenia. With their personal reference system at loose ends, because they had trouble producing those automatic rewards, they feel suddenly uncertain and vulnerable. In this disorienting state, they begin to see the world through a haze of paranoia. Such a change in neurotransmitter activity in the limbic system, also called the reward-generating system, alters brain circuits so that pleasant associations and rewards are no longer produced. Thus, it is easy to imagine how bizarre thoughts fill this void. Without input of thoughts from the normal reward system, schizophrenics are in a chronic information vacuum. They search for information from their current environment, but because of their increasing social isolation, little is to be found. As consensual validation decreases, their interpreter creates an alternative reality, which accounts for hallucinations and delusions.

Intrusive thoughts may begin to flood this chronic informational vacuum. As schizophrenics cope with these unwanted intrusions into thought, thought itself becomes very disordered and interrupted. The first response can be wild embarrassment, and schizophrenics withdraw from social contact as much as possible. Rather than helping, however, social isolation further compounds the problem. At first, the brain's interpreter had to deal with imagined sounds and voices, but it now has to comprehend them without the steadying influence provided by contact with friends and family. The same can be said about delusions. At times, all persons experience some paranoid thinking. Episodes of overwhelming vulnerability that arise in the absence of a threatening stimulus is usually due to some transitory biochemical imbalance in neurocircuitry, which the brain's interpreter easily dismisses as unsubstantiated. When, however, the condition moves beyond the episodic to a chronic condition, the brain's interpreter can create prominent delusions in its attempt to "explain" its neurochemical dysfunction.

Besides brain dysfunction, other vulnerabilities to schizophrenia include a positive family history for a major psychiatric disorder predisposing an individual biologically and psychosocially for an expression of psychotic process, and a difficult childhood in which the individual has become systematically and persistently discouraged by the demands of life. *The childhood of schizophrenics is characterized by unsatisfactory human relationships*, not only with parents but also with siblings and peers. Such unsatisfactory childhood situations, containing deviant personal methods of relating, distorted and confusing methods of communication, marital problems, suppressive parental behavior, and other peculiar and unsatisfying interactions have been described by many theorists and researchers. Adlerians believe that these unsatisfactory situations are not what result in psychosis but rather the child's personal reaction to these childhood problems.

Shulman (1984) noted that the child must conspire with environmental pressures to bring about situations that lead to schizophrenia. He noted four common syndromes that predispose or increase the individual's vulnerability to schizophrenia. The four syndromes are (a) the special child syndrome, (b) the bossy child syndrome, (c) the inadequate childhood syndrome, and (d) the child who has to be something to satisfy others syndrome.

Schizophrenia seems to be a final common pathway to which different people can come. Perhaps these concepts do not yet explain who becomes schizophrenic. By looking at the internal schemata of the individual, researchers inevitably find evidence of the kind of world design described by Binswanger (1960) and the kind of lifestyle described by Kurt Adler (1958).

Shulman proposed that both a vulnerability to psychosis and an extreme stressor are necessary but insufficient conditions for the expression of psychosis. He argued that the sufficient condition is a decision. Therefore, he proposed that the child with a predisposition toward psychosis can choose to be or not to be schizophrenic. The question is basically one of choosing a course of life that is likely to lead to schizophrenia. In their study of families of schizophrenics, Hoover and Franz (1972) found that both normal and schizophrenic siblings selected their responses to parental demands and life situation stimuli by either letting themselves become involved in intense embroilment with the parent or refusing to do so. In each case, some kind of decision or choice is made. Thus, in addition to hereditary and environmental determinants, a *creative self* also is at work. Shulman (1984) stated that this creative self becomes a crucial factor in the etiology of schizophrenia because it leads to the notion that schizophrenia is a personal choice—unconscious perhaps, but a choice nevertheless. Like Gazzaniga, Shulman is convinced that schizophrenia is more likely to be the result of a plan rather than simply the result of a defect in brain functioning only.

Shulman's theory of schizophrenia and other psychotic disorders will be presented in the remaining sections of this chapter. This material has been adapted from Shulman (1968, 1984).

Lifestyle Convictions, Decisions, and Self-training for Psychosis

Psychotic individuals create their own meaning for their existence according to their underlying *convictions*. These same convictions are schizophrenogenic; that is, they predispose individuals to schizophrenia. Shulman assumes that a teleological factor must be present, namely, a set of *personal values*, which are largely self-determined and which "call forth" the psychosis.

Such personal values are developed during childhood in the context of the family. They include convictions about self and life drawn from childhood relationships, the raw material from which they must select data and fashion beliefs. These psychotogenic values or convictions grow out of faulty training in responding to life's demands and result in the syndromes of behavior described above. The convictions are described in the following hypothesis:

Hypothesis 1   *Individuals who will become schizophrenic are the recipients of faulty training, which leads to the following faulty beliefs.*
  a   The conviction that they have no place in the world because of their deficiencies and/or the hostilities of the environment.
  b   The conviction that they must achieve some special state or position, which frees them from all defects in order to have a satisfactory life. This special state or position is always an exaggerated goal, e.g., to be perfect, to be godlike, to be impregnable, to hurt and humiliate, to be utterly masculine, to have "perfect" interpersonal relationships, and so on. Only this longed for state can give them a place. Their goals are

therefore relatively inflexible, have an all-or-none quality, and demand absolute fulfillment. They see few or no alternatives.

c   The conviction that any defeat or anticipated defeat, no matter how minor, in the pursuit of this goal is a major threat to their desperate attempt to overcome their defects and will "spoil" their life. From this grows the idea that the schizophrenics are abnormally sensitive to slights or defeats, whereas normal individuals are able to withstand certain disappointments. Schizophrenics are thus seen as having "low frustration tolerance" and "weak egos." For Shulman, persons who are so "sensitive" to failure exaggerate the importance of succeeding in all endeavors. Life must not bring any defeat because that would topple the whole structure. In this sense, schizophrenics have all their eggs in one basket. Thus they make unreasonable demands on life.

d   The conviction that common sense, social participation, and acceptance of the rules of life according to which society operates interfere with their movement toward their chosen goal. Therefore, in order to better pursue the goals and/or avoid defeat in their pursuits, they make all other considerations of lesser value. Thus, good human relations, the customs of society, sex, health, even life itself have less value than the continuation of their pursuits. In short, schizophrenics train themselves to be different because being like others will not work for them.

Hypothesis 2   *The crisis occurs when they perceive their life situation does not allow achievement of the goal in accord with "common sense" in socially acceptable and useful way.*   Therefore, "common sense" and consensuality are discarded because they interfere with the pursuit of the goal. They decide to stop living in the consensual world. This is the *decision* that constitutes the "psychotic break." This is the point at which they discard the obligation to function like other human beings.

Hypothesis 3   *Having discarded common sense, they are free to develop their own private logic that permits them to create the fiction that they have reached or will reach their goal of superiority.* For example, a divinity student, convinced of his own sinfulness and failing in his schoolwork, spent three days and nights in prayer and fasting eventually resulting in a state of confusion in which he felt himself drawn to Jesus. When found by the school authorities, he claimed that he *was* Jesus, and he was subsequently hospitalized. Schizophrenics-in-process systematically and autistically build a fantasy life to suit themselves. They become independent of the rules that others feel obliged to obey. They can even publicly defecate or masturbate without shame.

Hypothesis 4   *Because the world and other people, by their very existence, tend to intrude on their privacy, they must take steps to protect their private world.* To this end they isolate themselves and take steps to nullify the efforts of others who attempt to communicate with them. They remove themselves by stupor or drive others away by threats and bizarre behavior. They decide that what others do is wrong, harmful, silly, or crazy, and otherwise blunt, impede, or hide from the efforts of others to reach them. They make themselves immune to logic and sentiment: two consensual ways of communicating by which one person can possibly influence another. All this is made easier by having discarded "common sense." If one wants to stop being part of this world and live in the world of one's own making, the efficient procedure is not to accept "common sense."

Once the schizophrenogenic convictions have been reached and the crisis situation has occurred, the decision to discontinue social participation leads to forms of behavior that prevent continued social integration. Such behavior may be universal or limited to certain specific life areas, because sometimes schizophrenics can accomplish their goals by discarding only some aspects of consensuality. They need not discard all of them or all of them all of the time.

By continued isolation from social participation, what begins as a device for avoiding personal defeat or catastrophe becomes itself a catastrophe. Schizophrenics may start by playing a game of pretense but often find themselves caught in their own devices. Scher (1962) said that schizophrenics begin to believe their own fanciful constructs; they have discarded the social system and now have only their schizophrenic system as a *modus vivendi*. Their only choice is to continue their attempts to strengthen their *fort sans foundation* to work harder at reifying their private sense until they succeed at reaching a state hospital or halfway house. There they are relatively free from the demands of life or until their transcension into schizophrenia permits them to escape the defeats they fear, after which the "acute psychosis" may remit and they resume limited social participation. Otherwise, only strong intercurrent events affect their system. Psychotropic drugs, electroshock therapy, or a skillful therapist may sidetrack them from the pursuit of this fiction; or, if they are soldiers and the military situation does not permit them to withdraw from social participation, they may be forced to make some kind of peace with the demands of life.

The "decision" to disregard consensuality is thus the *sine qua non* of the psychotic break. Boisen (1947) compared this to creative thinking, saying that observation of a person experiencing this psychotic process shows evidence of an "unsolved personal problem"; attempts at solution are made that proceed by stages similar to the development of insight and creative thinking. Boisen considered the psychosis as a chosen "solution" to the problem.

Shulman (1984) also noted that schizophrenics must be convinced that common sense is an obstacle, rather than an aid to their purpose. Since common sense is not only sufficient but also necessary for the achievement of those personal goals that are chosen by the majority of persons, it becomes logical to assume that psychotics aspire to achievements that are impossible, or at least highly unlikely, when they remain within the bounds of consensuality. Research has shown that schizophrenics have a higher level of aspiration than nonschizophrenics, and they tend to raise these levels after repeated failures rather than lowering them as normal persons do (Lu, 1962). Their goal may not only be very high and perfectionistic but also extremely inappropriate, such as wanting to be the Messiah, God, supersexed, nonhuman, wanting relationships only on their own terms, wanting to have no human relationships at all, or wanting to live in a completely different kind of world.

Schizophrenics also must decide that their private personal goals are imperatives that outweigh all other considerations and values. Nothing else has an appeal for them equal to this rigid goal. In their ambitions, all else is considered chaff for the wind. Only in dreams, in toxic states, in narcotic fantasies, in artificial psychoses, in experiments on sensory deprivation, or in times of severe exhaustion can those living by consensual rules arrange to discard common sense and operate according to a private sense that is completely personal and extrasocial. At other times, the *Weltanschauung* we accept constrains us to heed the commonly accepted forms of behavior and communication even though we may resent their limitations.

Because "private sense" cannot stand too much daylight without crumbling, schizophrenics must protect it from close scrutiny. To this end, they severely limit interpersonal communications, either by not speaking at all or deliberately misleading those attempting to speak with them. They may be willing to transact business with others when such transactions do not threaten their private logic, either because the area of transaction is innocuous or because a therapist or other person is willing to accept their rules of the game. This last situation is called "participating in the patient's psychosis."

Basically, schizophrenics remain well integrated in their *own way*. An outside observer may be impressed with the inappropriate quality of the psychotic solution and may think he or she sees a person whose "defenses have disintegrated." Actually psychotic individuals have discarded their previous consensual defenses because they were related to consensual modes of functioning and therefore no longer useful to them. This is why they do not use the usual "defense mechanisms" that require that they accept the rules of common sense. The decision to discard common sense still leaves psychotics with the continuing problem of reifying their private sense. In Gazzaniga's language, the brain's interpreter now has to make sense out of chaos. They must support, justify, and defend their point of view until it becomes an article of faith, as when paranoid individuals provoke others to abuse them so they can feel justified in being "victims." At this point, some of their behavior will be exploratory in nature—that is, they will determine empirically which varieties of behavior best serve their purpose of keeping distance. This is why *a far greater variety of behavior is seen in earlier stages of psychosis than in later stages.* Eventually, effective ways of creating distant are evolved, tested, sharpened and refined, and the behavior becomes no longer exploratory and relatively open, but rigid, stereotyped, and concrete.

What others have called "poor ego functioning," "poor drive control," and "emergence of primary processes" are the schizophrenic's careful inattention to those stimuli and perceptions (in attempt to filter them out) and the consequent availability of illogic, unreason, illusion, fantasy, and so on, used both as modes of perception and as modes of communication. This allows them to be and act "crazy" since the consensual rejection of "crazy" behavior is absent. For example, psychotics first fantasize that the world is askew; then they are justified in rejecting as unreal and false any evidence that the world exists. Now they are free from obligation to observe rules; they emancipate themselves from all powers other than their own and save their self-respect by either blaming the outside world or refusing to acknowledge its existence.

The "decision" seems often to occur at times of physical exhaustion or illness. The crisis situation with its attendant fear, indecision, restlessness, exhaustion, sleeplessness, and sleep deprivation provide an easier transition into a psychotic state. When physical resistance is lowered, the integrating functions of the central nervous system are diminished as the brain's interpreter 'tires,' and nonconsensual experiences are more likely to occur. Perhaps if they set out to become reactively psychotic, an easy procedure would be to work themselves into a state of frenzy, unclarity, exhaustion, and extreme subjectivity, just as warriors engage in a war dance to work themselves into frenzied readiness before a battle.

Differential Diagnosis and Dynamics of Schizophrenia

Some patients, however, meet the criteria for other psychoses but in some way do not completely fit these hypotheses for schizophrenia. While having had some childhood difficulties, they were neither schizotypal or paranoid personality types. Yet, they can relate interpersonally with families and peers but from time to time become psychotic under stress. Once the acute psychotic state clears, their underlying personality disorder, usually histrionic, passive-aggressive, or borderline, becomes evident.

The main difference between these cases and schizophrenia is that the psychosis in these cases is temporarily evident in the individual's life and not a way of existence. These individuals are not caught up in what Adler (1926) called the *high-flown goal*, and what Binswanger (1960) termed the *extravagant ideals*. Of the four sets of convictions mentioned earlier in this chapter, seemingly they suffer only from the fourth. This distinction fits the criteria in DSM-IV for Brief Psychotic Disorder (298.8) as distinguished from schizophrenia.

The psychosis in these cases may be more easily understood if we compared it to a partial retreat from reality in the face of a most unpleasant demand for life. It provides a temporary way out and starts to recede as soon as the life demand is no longer present. It can be compared to the behavior of a child losing a game: One child will lose graciously; another will hide its hurt; the third will depreciate the game; a fourth will accuse the others of cheating; a fifth will cheat to influence the outcome; the sixth will rationalize; and, a seventh will grit its teeth and determine to win next time. The eighth child, however, will deny, distort, disturb, and even destroy the game, refusing to let it come to its natural end. This is the mode of reaction of a patient who fits the criteria for "brief reactive psychosis."

Shulman (1984) differentiated the *paranoid* features of the schizophrenic from those seen in the *delusional disorder* and the *bipolar disorder*. In the delusional and bipolar disorders, Shulman noted that they develop some private logic while retaining some consensuality. Delusional patients can become very upset, but do not appear to have undergone an acute disoriented episode. They may have their own private explanation of "causes" and "evil forces at work" and have no intention to expose these explanations to rules of consensual logic. The bipolar disorder, on the other hand, often can look as bizarre as the schizophrenic so that the differentiations become difficult. The acute disoriented state in the manic phase of the bipolar disorder is similar to that of a schizophrenic.

Both states can show perceptual distortions and autistic thinking. *Manic states* may contain considerable paranoid features. Manics, however, do not wish to keep a distance between themselves and others. Although they change the rules of the "reality game," they continue to want social relationships. Their behavior is that of people who constantly seek close relationships. Even in the distrust phase of the bipolar disorder, their behavior is designed to keep others involved with them. This is the essential difference between the bipolar disorder and the schizophrenic. Between attacks, individuals with the bipolar disorder usually accept the human role as the rest of us do, whereas schizophrenics do not.

Psychotic Process and Symptoms

The symptoms of schizophrenia themselves also can be understood as a form of surrealistic creation and its consequences. Schizophrenics have manifold symptoms, not all of them limited to psychotic processes. They can worry, be fearful, become despondent, be self-conscious, suffer feelings of inadequacy, be cynical, be lonely, lose sleep and appetite, have obsessive thoughts, overindulge in alcohol, and be able to concentrate as does the so-called neurotic. On the other hand, some of their symptoms are specific manifestations of schizophrenia, particularly those involving their refusal to use consensuality.

With this in mind, Shulman (1984) has classified the symptoms of schizophrenia as specific markers along the continuum moving away from or toward consensuality. Symptoms are arranged in a developmental sequence rather than in a chronological order. As in any developmental sequence, stages may merge and overlap and should not be considered as sharply delimited from another. In addition, stages may be repeated since schizophrenics sometimes proceed through the same process over and over again. What is more, many schizophrenics will not pass through all these stages but will skip some of them in the course of their illness. Thus, one must not think that every patient follows this exact course of events. Note needs to be made that many psychotic disorders such as acute organic brain syndromes and delusional disorders will not fit into this scheme.

The sequence is described in terms of the symptoms evident to an observer and related to the schizophrenic's subjective experience at the time. Not all of the schizophrenic's symptoms are psychotic symptoms *per se*. Some can more rightly be called neurotic. The sequence of psychotic symptoms is as follows:

1. Symptoms with a purpose of permitting and facilitating the withdrawal from social integration. These include seclusiveness, secretiveness, apa-

thy, shallow affect, lack of interest in normal events, deep concentration, practicing autistic thinking, and even suicide.

2. Symptoms with a purpose of defeating the appeal of social living and the insistence of social demands. These include inappropriate affect, loose associations, private language, mutism, negativism, self-neglect, violence, disgusting behavior, and assaultiveness.

3. Symptoms with a purpose of reinforcing schizophrenic private logic in insuring the correctness of their position. These include hallucinations, delusions, provocation of others, impulsiveness, the need to prove self as no good, and playing the game of being "crazy."

4. Symptoms with a purpose of admitting the reestablishment of conditional social relationships sometimes so bizarre that we are constrained to consider them as indications of psychoses. These include some bizarre methods of behavior; however, obsessive-compulsive and hypochondriacal symptoms may be used for the same purpose. Perhaps these symptoms, bizarre as they may be, should be included among those we consider restitutive, because they are not intended to further separate the individual from society.

A *composite model* of psychotic disorders now can be presented that incorporates the stress-vulnerability research, Gazzaniga's neuroscience theory and Shulman's view:

$$\text{Stress } + \text{ Brain-Mind Vulnerability}$$
$$+ \text{ Coping/Self-training } + \text{ Decision} \rightarrow$$
$$\text{Psychotic Process}$$

Essentially, stressors such as losses, conflicts, lack of social support, etc. can precipitate a psychotic process and symptoms when brain-mind vulnerability—positive family psychiatric history or other biological predisposing factors as well as psychosis-prone lifestyle convictions/cognitive schema—interacts with deficits in coping skills, self-training and decisions based on discouragement.

TREATMENT OF SCHIZOPHRENIC DISORDER

Since the middle 1950s antipsychotic medications have been the treatment of choice for schizophrenics, particularly in the active phase. The introduction of antipsychotic medications has had a powerful influence on the management of schizophrenia. Some pharmacologists believe that the antipsychotic medication is the only proven mode of treatment and that psychotherapeutic interventions are of little use. On the other hand, advocates of psychotherapy for schizophrenia argue that medication alone is not sufficient and that the effectiveness of medication depends on the psychosocial context in which it is given. They also contend that medication only reduces psychotic symptoms but does not affect the patient's social or personality functioning. For all practical purposes, talking about a single "correct" treatment is not useful since schizophrenia is a syndrome consisting of a number of disorders. The range of treatments and combinations of treatments used reflect the variability inherent in this disorder. What is useful to some schizophrenic individuals may not be useful or even may be harmful to others. Most effective treatment regimens combine psychopharmacology and psychosocial therapies (Beitman and Klerman, 1986).

Shulman (1984) has described an Adlerian perspective on treatment. He noted that the decision to reverse the psychotic process requires that the individual be willing to consider alternatives to current behavior, to experiment with these alternatives, and to train oneself in new directions. The task is not a simple decision to "buck up and stop thinking that way," but a willingness to reorder one's perception in order to permit the growth of a new frame of reference in regard to life. Shulman noted that change must proceed through a kindling of hope, a reestablishment of consensual ways of behaving, and an experiencing of satisfaction in consensual living. The keynote of the therapist's behavior is, thus, encouragement. Patient, persistent encouragement is a necessity. "The approach is continued," stated Kurt Adler (1958), "until the patient becomes convinced that fruitful cooperation is possible, becomes more hopeful as to the achievement of some of his goals, learns to feel less of an isolate and more likely the human being" (p. 72).

What must patients learn in order to change? That they have mistaken high-flown goals; that they have misunderstood what it means to be human; that they can become successfully human with human practice; that life will be more satisfying when they join the human community; that they have been training themselves away from the common sense way of looking at life and practicing the use of an isolating private logic; and, that their psychotic symptoms are purposeful maneuvers more under their control than they have recognized.

Shulman (1984) noted that neither will the great majority of schizophrenic individuals have any systematic individual psychotherapy, nor will the relationship between the great majority of therapists and patients be extended over a long enough term to be effective. Even brief encounters, however, can have far-reaching effects. While therapists will carry out a systematic long-term psychotherapy with relatively few schizophrenic individuals, they will briefly and perhaps casually come in contact with many more patients. Any of these encounters, while making ward rounds, while doing intakes in the clinic, while examining patients, or while making emergency admissions, provide therapists opportunities to intervene therapeutically albeit briefly. Shulman noted that treatment such as group therapy, milieu therapy, family and recreational therapy, music therapy, psychodrama, social clubs, and even medication groups can be very useful treatment interventions. They are social processes and tools of communication with a purpose of encouraging and clarifying self-awareness and self-understanding, overcoming isolation, promoting the use of social skills, and correcting faulty perceptions.

TREATMENT OF THE DELUSIONAL DISORDERS

Generally speaking, treatment of the delusional disorders is extraordinarily difficult. The longer the symptoms have been present, the more refractory they are to simple treatments such as psychoeducation, psychotherapy, or medication. Some culturally-induced syndromes, however, may respond to relocation—i.e., returning to the patient's country of origin—even if they have taken months to come to clinical attention (Reid, 1989).

When the delusionally disordered individual agrees to psychotherapy, it may be the treatment of choice, but it should be initiated in such a way that the patient is likely to see some benefit from it and some support from the therapist. Emphasis should be on developing a trusting relationship with a neutral and accepting therapist. Ritzler (1981) indicated that systematic desensitization has been effective in reducing delusional behavior. Antipsychotic medication has been noted to be effective in some cases. Most patients, however, are reluctant to take neuroleptics either because of their suspiciousness of the treatment or because of their exquisite sensitivity to the side effects of medication. Antipsychotic medication has been shown to take the "edge" off delusions, making psychosocial treatment much more possible. Recent use of antidepressants also has been effective (Reid, 1989).

Bullard's (1960) short paper on Adlerian psychotherapy with paranoid patients is a classic. Bullard described an approach to engaging the suspicious and distrustful, delusional, or paranoid patients. Shulman (1984) noted that insofar as possible he tries to save the pride of the paranoid. He stated

> Our explanations and interpretations are egosyntonic; we treat him
> with courtesy and respect, while we do not let his delusions pay

off; we try to discuss with him his feelings about life, and those areas where he feels threatened by defeat, and try to help him to feel that he is a worthwhile person. It will take longer to convince that he is not surrounded by a hostile world, and that he does not always need to win to be superior or to be right. (Shulman, 1984, p. 156)

CASE EXAMPLE

A 41-year-old single white male had been hospitalized for psychotic reactions five times in the previous 15 years. He presented as a dependent personality disordered individual who lived with an older married sister and was supported by a Veterans Administration pension. Although unmarried, he had had girlfriends in the past and still maintains a sexual liaison with one of them. He had male friends and enjoyed drinking, playing cards, and going to ball games with them. His downfall always came at work. He was able to get a job whenever he felt well and always showed himself to be a good worker. Soon he would be given more responsibilities. He feared and resisted, but he was not able to speak up affectively to his bosses. He would react by becoming slipshod in his work and taking days off. Shortly thereafter, he would begin to feel agitated and worried about his job and his health. He would lose his appetite and become unable to sleep. For several sleepless nights, he would begin "having thoughts," which were obsessive ideas that he was getting sick or that he would lose his mind. Eventually he became exhausted and disoriented, would hear voices, imagine that he was dying, fear that he was being poisoned, and so on. He would be brought to the hospital by his sister or sometimes would present himself for admission. His stays in the hospital tended to last from six months to two years. After a few months he would begin to calm down, recover his composure, and slowly regain his confidence to leave the hospital and try working again. He had never been discharged from a job but voluntarily left when he felt too sick to work. His greatest fear was that he would again have a psychotic episode.

During the psychotic episodes, this male fulfilled all the criteria for the diagnosis of schizophrenic, undifferentiated type. During his periods of remission he was a dependent personality with reasonably superficial adjustment to others. True, he never felt able to undertake many responsibilities such as marriage or advancement at work. He had dropped out of school in the 11th grade because he felt it was too much for him. He was the baby of his family and had been overprotected by his mother until her death. His older sister now filled his mother's role. The pattern of his life is a common one; but why did he become psychotic in times of stress rather than developing an anxiety disorder that might have served his purpose just as well? The psychotic episodes function as ordinary anxiety disorders, as a device for avoiding a difficult situation, or for saving face in it. When faced with the responsibility that is perceived as overwhelming, this patient could defeat the demands of the life situation by "flipping his lid," by "throwing everything up for grabs." He, however, does retain a bridge by the nonpsychotic states in two ways: First he always remains able to find a job; and second, he willingly returns to the dependent hospital situation where he is relieved of responsibility and stress. The psychotic episodes are situational reactions for this dependent personality.

REFERENCES

Adler, A. (1926). *Uber den nervosen charakter*. Wiesbaden: J. F. Bergman.

Adler, K. (1958). Life style in schizophrenia. *Journal of Individual Psychology, 14*, 68–72.

American Psychiatric Association. (1994). *Diagnostic and statistical manual of mental disorders* (4th ed.). Washington, DC: Author.

Arieti, S. (1974). An overview of schizophrenia from a predominantly psychological approach. *American Journal of Psychiatry, 131*, 241–249.

Arieti, S. (1980). Psychotherapy of schizophrenia: New or revised procedures. *American Journal of Psychotherapy, 34*, 464–476.

Beitman, B., & Klerman, G. (Eds.). (1986). *Combining psychotherapy and drug therapy in clinical practice*. New York: S.P. Medical & Scientific Book.

Binswanger, L. (1960). Existential analysis, psychiatry, schizophrenia. *Journal of Existential Psychiatry, 1*, 157–165.

Boisen, A. (1947). Onset in acute schizophrenia. *Psychiatry, 10*, 159.

Bullard, D. (1960). Psychotherapy of paranoid patients. *Archives of General Psychiatry, 2*, 137–141.

Gazzaniga, M. (1988). *Mind matters: How mind and body interact to create our conscious lives*. Boston: Houghton-Mifflin.

Goldstein, K. (1939). *The organism: A holistic approach to biology derived from pathological data in man.* New York: American Book Co.

Hoover, G., & Franz, J. (1972). Siblings in the families of schizophrenia. *Archives of General Psychiatry, 26,* 334–342.

Kelly, G. (1955). *The psychology of personal constructs.* New York: Norton.

Liberman, R. (1987). *Psychiatric rehabilitation of chronic mental patients.* Washington, DC: American Psychiatric Press.

Lu, Y. (1962). Contradictory parental expectations in schizophrenia. *Archives of General Psychiatry, 6,* 219–234.

Neuchterlein, K., & Dawson, M. (1984). A heuristic vulnerability/stress model of schizophrenic episodes. *Schizophrenia Bulletin, 10*(2), 300–312.

Reid, W. (1989). *The treatment of psychiatric disorders: Revised for the DSM-III-R.* New York: Brunner/Mazel.

Ritzler, B. (1981). Paranoia—prognosis and treatment: A review. *Schizophrenia Bulletin, 7,* 710–728.

Scher, J. (1962). *Theories of the mind.* New York: Free Press of Glencoe.

Shulman, B. (1968). *Essays in schizophrenia.* Baltimore: Williams and Wilkins.

Shulman, B. (1984). *Essays in schizophrenia* (2nd ed.). Chicago: Alfred Adler Institute.

Chapter 3

MENTAL DISORDERS DUE TO A GENERAL MEDICAL CONDITION AND OTHER COGNITIVE DISORDERS

Michael P. Maniacci

Alfred Adler developed a theory and technique of counseling and psychotherapy that has, in time, gained in recognition and acceptance. Individual Psychology, the name he gave his system, postulates a theory of human nature and behavior that emphasizes the holistic, phenomenological, teleological, and interpersonal aspects of people. Adler, perhaps above all else, was a pragmatist. His theory grew out of his work as a clinician, practicing physician, and psychotherapist who placed treatment and prevention highest on his list of priorities. Sigmund Freud, Adler's senior colleague and the founder of psychoanalysis, was a scientist and had a much more theoretical, research-oriented perspective in mind when he developed his system. For Freud, psychoanalysis was the focus of his work; he was interested in developing and elaborating upon his theory and technique. Hence, his clinical work was limited by (and directed to) the type of patient who would fit his theoretical system, typically psychoneurotics and patients with certain conversion (psychosomatic) disorders. Patients with severe personality disorders, psychotics, and children and families, because they did not fit his system of treatment, were excluded. Adler, by contrast, was much more patient/clinical-oriented. He worked not only in individual outpatient psychotherapy, but also in large clinics, schools, and even prisons. In addition, Adler worked in hospitals and sanatoriums with varieties of patients. His emphasis was upon what worked, regardless of setting, mode, duration, or patient selection. If a family needed to be seen, he would develop a strategy for working with them. He did the same in his work with children, criminals (for whom he recommended group psychotherapy), and psychotics (Adler, in Ansbacher & Ansbacher, 1956).

The variety of patients with whom Individual Psychologists work is rather broad. Adler's system provides not only the theoretical conceptualizations necessary for such work, but, in many instances, the clinical guidelines and strategies. Patients with general medical conditions that lead to mental disorders are challenging; yet Adler and his followers have provided clinicians the requisite guidelines and theoretical framework upon which to base treatment. Not only is Adlerian theory applicable to understanding such conditions, but it is also well- suited for working with such individuals. Medical supervision and interventions are required in the treatment of all these conditions and syndromes, although the psychosocial aspects are gaining in recognition and importance, even in the medical field (Berg, Franzen, & Wedding, 1987; Miller, 1990; Rule, 1984; Strub & Black, 1993). As Gallatin (1982) pointed out,

> Perhaps the most significant point that emerged [from her research] had to do with the role of social factors . . . whether or not a patient feels "isolated." A person's attitude . . . can help to determine how well he or she recovers from a brain injury. Indeed, it is possible that these social and emotional factors may enter the picture from the start—that some people may be more susceptible to organic disorders because of their isolation and lack of support. . . . (p. 201)

It is against this ever increasing theoretical awareness that Adler's conceptualizations will be presented.

AN OVERVIEW OF THE ADLERIAN PERSPECTIVE

At the time Adler (1907) first presented his theory of organ inferiority, he was still a member of the Freudian inner circle, and his conceptualizations were quite mechanistic and deterministic. In effect, he was writing as a Freudian, not an Adlerian. His position evolved and changed radically since that early monograph. A discussion of the process is beyond the scope of this work; interested individuals are referred to Ansbacher and Ansbacher's commentaries in their seminal volume (Ansbacher & Ansbacher, 1956). For present purposes, Adler's views will be discussed in their final form.

Dreikurs (1948) pointed out that Adler's final formulation of organ inferiority involved three aspects: (a) a somatic level, (b) a sympathetic level, and (c) a psychic level. An inferior organ, that is, an organ that is deficient in structure or function (for reasons detailed below), typically requires compensatory efforts in at least one or more of the three areas. A person with a dysfunctional limb may compensate somatically by unconsciously developing the unaffected limbs to a greater degree than normal; on the sympathetic side, that same person may assume a certain way of moving that compensates for the deficiency; and on the psychical side, the person may either attempt to deal with the deficiency as best as he or she can, or place others into his or her service. In keeping with Adler's conceptualizations of striving from a perceived minus situation to a perceived plus situation, individuals compensate according to the degree of social interest and level of activity they have (Adler, in Ansbacher & Ansbacher, 1956).

For example, John has epilepsy. He has a low degree of social interest (a sense of community feeling, an interest in the interest of others) and a high degree of activity. His compensatory efforts most likely will develop on the useless side of life, through very assertive, aggressive means. He may use his epilepsy to bully others into his service and "blackmail" those in his social field into yielding to his demands by not taking his medication, by overstimulating himself at times he knows he should not, and by being hypersensitive to environmental cues that arouse his sympathetic nervous system too easily (Swonger & Constantine, 1983). How useful or useless John's compensation is for his organic inferiority is contingent upon how much social interest he has and how active he is. Adler conceptualized a fourfold personality description that utilized these two constructs (Adler, 1935).

Erickson and Doppelt (1987), Mosak and Maniacci (1989), and Sperry (1988) all recently have detailed and discussed the biopsychosocial aspects of Individual Psychology. In a holistic theory, the biological, psychological, and social dimensions of individuals all need to be examined to obtain a better grasp on the situation. When working with the mental disorders caused by general medical conditions, practitioners must examine and deal with all three areas to better treat the individual—the goal Adler placed foremost in his work. Stopping interventions either at the somatic or psychosocial level is not enough in most cases; it is providing less than optimum care to the patient and is in itself reductionistic. Somatic and psychological problems can and often do coexist. In fact, research is beginning to postulate an interconnectedness that Adler stressed as early as 1907 (Gallatin, 1982; Ornstein & Sobel, 1987). Whether or not the etiological significance of psychosocial factors in biological conditions is ever clarified, one thing is clear: A biopsychosocial perspective entails working with the entire person, not just parts or symptoms.

DSM-IV: MENTAL DISORDERS DUE TO A GENERAL MEDICAL CONDITION AND OTHER COGNITIVE DISORDERS

The fourth edition the *Diagnostic and Statistical Manual of Mental Disorders* (DSM-IV) (American Psychiatric Association, 1994) has reconceptualized the Organic Mental Disorders section of previous editions. The changes are more than cosmetic; in fact, they represent a major conceptual shift toward a more holistic, biopsychosocial perspective. As the authors themselves have stated, "organic mental disorder is no longer used in DSM-IV because it incorrectly implies that 'nonorganic' mental disorders do not have a biological basis" (American Psychiatric Association, 1994, p. 123). What once were categorized as discrete entities now are seen as occurring along a continuum in which the degree of biological loading varies from one end of the spectrum to another. Hence anxiety can be caused either by a predominantly biological factor (as in 293.89, Anxiety Disorder Due to a General Medical Condition) or a predominantly psychosocial factor (as in 309.24, Adjustment Disorder with Anxiety), with many of the other anxiety-related disorders falling relatively in -between (such as 300.01, Panic Disorder without Agoraphobia).

In DSM-IV, there are now three major sections that compose what used to be termed Organic Mental Disorders. The new sections are as follows:

Delirium, Dementia, and Amnestic and Other Cognitive Disorders,
Mental Disorders Due to a General Medical Condition, and
Substance-Related Disorders.

The first group, Delirium, Dementia, and Amnestic and Other Cognitive Disorders, have the following in common:

> The predominant disturbance is a clinically significant deficit in cognition or memory that represents a significant change from a previous level of functioning. For each disorder in this section, the etiology is either a general medical condition (although the specific general medical condition may not be identifiable) or a substance (i.e., a drug of abuse, medication, or toxin), or a combination of these factors. (American Psychiatric Association, 1994, p. 123)

The second group, Mental Disorders Due to a General Medical Condition, have in common: "the presence of mental symptoms that are judged to be the direct physiological consequence of a general medical condition" (p. 165).

A related, but beyond the scope of this chapter, section entails a description of the Substance-Related Disorders. Besides the issues of dependence, intoxication, withdrawal, and use, this section details the various medical complications that can produce aberrant behavior and dysfunction, such as

Alcohol-Induced Delirium,
Alcohol-Induced Sleep Disturbance,
Cocaine-Induced Mood Disorder, and
Inhalant-Induced Psychotic Disorder, With Delusions.

In other words, all sorts of cognitive and behavioral impairments can be produced from the ingestions of substances that produce symptoms descriptively similar to other disorders listed in the DSM-IV. There are over 130 different codes assigned to just this one section—the amount of damage these various substance can produce is quite extensive. A full discussion is, as mentioned above, well beyond the scope of this work, and interested readers are referred to the DSM-IV for a detailed discussion. Far more detail will be devoted to the first two sections.

DELIRIUM, DEMENTIA, AND AMNESTIC AND OTHER COGNITIVE DISORDERS

An examination of each of the four major disorders in this section will begin with a look at delirium. The criteria for this disorder have changed in the DSM-IV.

Delirium

Primarily a disorder of consciousness, or what the DSM defines as a "reduced clarity or awareness of the environment" (American Psychiatric Association, 1994, p. 129), Delirium causes patients to have a "reduced ability to focus, sustain, or shift attention" (American Psychiatric Association, 1994, p. 129). It typically is characterized by a rapid onset and is resolved quickly. It is seen most often in cases of high fevers and acute trauma to a localized area of the brain. Delirium tends to occur most frequently at either end of the age spectrum (i.e., the very young and those over 60) but can occur at any age. Damage to the right parietal lobe and inferomedial surface of the occipital lobe, as well as encephalopathy, renal disease, and certain metabolic disorders (e.g., hypoglycemia, ionic imbalances) ca precipitate it. The slower the onset (usually no more that hours or, at the most, days), the more likely the underlying pathology is systemic or metabolic as opposed to traumatic. The clinical picture tends to fluctuate over the course of a day, with the patient being worse during sleepless nights or in the dark (commonly referred to as "sundown syndrome"). The person may appear incoherent or rambling and display increased or decreased motor activity. Especially during acute periods, orientation to person, place, time, and situation is grossly impaired.

In DSM-IV, delirium can be diagnosed according to five subtypes:

Delirium Due to a General Medical Condition (diagnosticians would list the specific medical condition),
Substance Intoxication Delirium (diagnosticians would refer to the Substance-Related section),
Substance Withdrawal Delirium (once again, diagnosticians would refer to the Substance-Related section),
Delirium Due to Multiple Etiologies (for types that have more than one causal factor), and
Delirium NOS (Not Otherwise Specified) (for residual conditions that fail to meet any of the above subtypes).

Dementia

The essential features of Dementia are memory impairment and a more insidious onset. Prognosis may be static, progressive, or remitting, depending upon the particular case presentation. Memory impairment typically follows the following course: Short-term memory is lost first, followed by immediate and, finally, long-term memory (usually only in the most advanced cases). Subsequently, identity confusion, gross errors in judgment, and lack of impulse control take place. This is a condition found primarily in the elderly. Dementia is diagnosed only when there is loss of intellectual functioning sufficient enough to interfere severely with social or occupational life tasks.

In DSM-IV, dementia can be diagnosed with six specifiers:

With Early Onset,
With Late Onset,
With Delirium,
With Delusions,

With Depressed Mood, and
Uncomplicated.

In addition, clinicians are encouraged to note whether Behavioral Disturbance (i.e., wandering) is evident in any of the above situations. There are 13 subtypes of Dementia, such as Dementia of the Alzheimer's Type, Vascular Dementia, Dementia Due to HIV Disease, and Substance-Induced Persisting Dementia. Interested readers are referred to the DSM-IV for a more detailed discussion of these subtypes.

Amnestic Disorders

DSM-IV has clarified the criteria for these sets of disorders. Memory impairment is defined as impairment in the "ability to learn new information or the inability to recall previously learned information" (American Psychiatric Association, 1994, p. 160). In patients with these disorders, the memory disturbance causes impairment in functioning and does not occur only during a delirium or a dementia. In addition, long-term memory of events from the distant past sometimes can be remembered better than more recent events. Immediate memory, such as the ability to recall digits presented in sequence, is typically not impaired; such a dysfunction is more indicative of attentional disturbances (e.g., delirium). In order to fill in the memory loss, confabulation is often present (i.e., imaginary events are substituted for the forgotten information). The most common form of this disorder usually is associated with thiamine deficiency, but head trauma or certain forms of encephalitis can precipitate it as well.

In DSM-IV, amnestic disorders can be diagnosed according to three subtypes:

Amnestic Disorder Due to a General Medical Condition (diagnosticians would list the specific medical condition and specify if the impairment is transient or chronic),
Substance-Induced Persisting Amnestic Disorder (once again, referring to the Substance-Related section), and
Amnestic Disorder NOS.

Other Cognitive Disorders

In this category, the DSM-IV lists Cognitive Disorder NOS. In the proposed categories section located as an appendix, two specific subtypes that await further research are described:

Mild Neurocognitive Disorder (for impairment as evidenced by testing or quantified clinical assessment) and

Postconcussional Disorder (for impairment in memory or attention associated with head trauma).

In addition, the Cognitive Disorder NOS category can be used to diagnose other disorders of cognition that do not meet the exact criteria of any particular disorder.

MENTAL DISORDERS DUE TO A GENERAL MEDICAL CONDITION

Five of the Eight Conditions

In DSM-IV, the following conditions are listed:

Psychotic Disorder Due to a General Medical Condition (discussed in the Schizophrenia and Other Psychotic Disorders section of DSM-IV),

Mood Disorder Due to a General Medical Condition (discussed in the Mood Disorders section of DSM-IV),

Anxiety Disorder Due to a General Medical Condition (discussed in the Anxiety Disorders section of DSM-IV),

Sexual Dysfunction Due to a General Medical Condition (discussed in the Sexual Dysfunctions section of DSM-IV), and

Sleep Disorder to a General Medical Condition (discussed in the Sleep Disorder section of DSM-IV).

In previous editions of DSM, most of these conditions were discussed under the Organic Mental Disorders as separate entities. Under the current system, as discussed in the beginning of this chapter, they are discussed in the sections encompassing their traditionally more psychosocially loaded counterparts. For clinicians, the issue is first to diagnose the particular condition, such as a particular sleep disturbance, and determine on which end of the spectrum of biological to biopsychosocial to psychosocial it belongs. In other words, a patient has a sleep disturbance. Is it primarily related to his or her psychological stressors at this time or to some medical condition he or she has? Descriptively, the presentations may be identical, but with regard to etiology, the causes can be very different.

For example, psychotic symptoms such as hallucinations and delusions can be caused by many factors, including drug use, strokes, and cancers. Mood disorders can be caused by endocrine dysfunction, pancreatic cancer, or right hemisphere damage. Anxiety symptoms can be commonly produced by caffeinism, hyperthyroidism, or certain brain tumors. When diagnosing these disorders, clinicians need to be aware of what Taylor (1989) referred to as *alerting* and *presumptive clues*. He noted that by attending to each type of clue, clinicians can be more sensitive to "possible psychological masquerade" of a more biological loading to the above noted conditions (p. 586).

Alerting Clues	Presumptive Clues
No history of similar symptoms	Symptoms of brain syndrome (cognitive
No readily identifiable cause	disorders)
Age 55 or older	Head injury
Chronic physical disease	Change in headache pattern
Drug use	Visual disturbances
	Speech deficits
	Abnormal body movements
	Changes in consciousness

Alerting clues are those that should raise suspicion of a more biological loading, and they are addictive in that the more noted, the greater the chance of biological loading. Presumptive clues indicate a "strong probability" of a major biological loading (Taylor, 1989, p. 586).

Adlerians have their own criteria for differential diagnosis (Adler, in Ansbacher & Ansbacher, 1956; K. Adler, 1989; Mosak, 1977). Generally, whereas traditional diagnosis has been based upon exclusion, that is, ruling out what type of disorder cannot exist given the presenting symptoms, Adlerians employ another set of criteria: diagnosis by purpose.

For example, when assessing patients, Adlerians examine if the presenting symptoms serve a purpose for them. As Kurt Adler (1989) noted, three criteria are examined:

> (a) The symptom must be usable and necessary in the pursuit of the patient's goal. . . . (b) The use of this particular symptom must be traceable throughout his history from childhood on. (c) The symptom, which is thus part of his lifestyle, must be found to pervade all his attitudes, all his movements, his dreams, his memory, and all his feeling life and relations. (p. 63)

As Kurt Adler wrote, "If these criteria are not fulfilled, the chances are that his condition has some organic basis" (p. 63).

To assess criterion (a), Adlerians typically use *The Question*. Patients are asked, "What would be different in your life if you did not have this problem?" Should the answer be, "I'd be able to work/love/socialize, etc.," the symptom is probably more psychosocially loaded. If the answer is something like, "Well, then my head would hurt less/my concentration would be better, etc.," greater attention should be afforded to the biological loading. In cases in which the answer is "mixed," that is, has elements of both types of responses (e.g., "I'd be able to concentrate better, and my parents wouldn't nag me so much"), a mixture of biological *and* psychosocial factors is possibly at work. In other words, the patient probably has some organic pathology that is being used to move him or her toward some neurotic goal.

Criteria (b) and (c) are measured via a lifestyle assessment. Mosak (1977), building on the work of Adler (Ansbacher & Ansbacher, 1956), has delineated several lifestyle types with characteristic patterns of interacting, such as pleasers, controllers, getters, babies, and excitement seekers, to name but a few. By examining the early childhood situation of patients, including how they got along with siblings, peers, teachers, and parents, characteristic styles can be detected. Their early recollections are also examined to assess their current views of themselves, others, and the world. From such a process, the characteristic style can be determined.

As Kurt Adler (1989) detailed, the presenting symptoms should have some consistency throughout the patient's life. For instance, a pleaser, someone who typically is "sensitive to criticism," and feels "crushed" when rejected or disapproved of, characteristically does *not* engage in symptoms designed to push others away (Mosak, 1977, p. 184). If the symptoms do not seem to match the style, an organic basis should be considered.

In questionable cases, referral to a medical specialist always should be strongly considered. Further guidelines for screening for such conditions are presented below in the section discussing the role of private logic in psychotic disorders (see also Cummings, 1988).

Three of the Eight Conditions

In addition to the five categories previously listed in this section, DSM-IV has three other disorders that should be noted:

Catatonic Disorder Due to a General Medical Condition,
Personality Change Due to a General Medical Condition, and
Mental Disorder NOS Due to a General Medical Condition.

Catatonic Disorder. In this disorder, motoric immobility, mutism, echolalia, echopraxia, and excessive motor activity that is apparently purposeless are present. Unlike Schizophrenia, Catatonic Subtype, the loading is clearly biologically weighted. Neoplasms, cerebrovascular disease, heptic encephalopathy, and toxicity because of drug ingestion are typical causes of such conditions.

Personality Change. In DSM-III-R, this was called the Organic Personality Disorder. For a diagnosis of this condition, "a persistent personality disturbance that represents a change from the individual's previous characteristic personality pattern" must be evident (American Psychiatric Association, 1994, p. 173). Such changes are related to biological factors, including (but not limited to) head trauma, frontal lobe damage, temporal lobe epilepsy, multiple sclerosis, and Huntington's Chorea. There are eight subtypes:

Labile Type,
Disinhibited Type,
Aggressive Type,
Apathetic Type,
Paranoid Type,
Other Type,
Combined Type, and
Unspecified Type.

In all of these subtypes, the personality change is the result of a general medical condition.

Mental Disorder NOS. This is the residual category for mental disturbances that occur because of general medical conditions that may not be listed in the DSM.

What is the significance of the changes in the DSM-IV? On one level, it appears that the sections simply have been reorganized. On a more profound level, however, the changes represent a move toward a more holistic conceptualization. They put a much heavier burden on non-medically trained clinicians to be sensitive to the end of the continuum traditionally reserved for psychiatrists and neurologists. The ability to work collaboratively with the medical specialists is a requirement, and non-medically trained clinicians should be alert not only to overstepping their boundaries, but also to being unaware of such boundaries. Psychologists, counselors, social workers, and marriage and family therapists should be trained to identify alerting and presumptive clues, as well as to make appropriate referrals when needed.

DYNAMICS: AN ADLERIAN PERSPECTIVE

This is a difficult section to write because of the diverse nature of the above-mentioned disorders. Which particular disorder appears is primarily biologically determined, as is the course of the disorder. As Adler pointed out, however, how a patient reacts to a disability is dependent on whether his or her compensatory efforts are useful or useless. On level (a), the somatic level, and level (b), the sympathetic level, biological processes and medical interventions predominate; level (c), the psychic level, is contingent on the degree of social interest and level of activity the person has developed and mastered. As Shulman and Klapman (1968) pointed out, the agitation or confusion seen in delirium or the affective instability seen in the mood disorders due to a general medical condition secondary to temporal lobe epilepsy is beyond the individual's control; however, how he or she reacts to having it and how compliant he or she is to managing it usefully are matters of psychic compensation, and that is a matter of subjective perception and choice.

Nature of the Inferiority

Dreikurs (1948) made the useful distinction between inferiority, inferiority feelings, and inferiority complex. Briefly, an *inferiority* is objective; that is, it can be measured according to situationally determined standards and criteria. *Inferiority feelings* are subjective; that is, they may have nothing to do with actual inferiorities. *Inferiority complexes* are open declarations of bankruptcy, that is, behaviorally observable presentations of subjectively felt inferiorities. For instance, Sally may have cerebral palsy, an actual inferiority. She may feel inferior because of it and declare bankruptcy; she may refuse to participate in life and force others into her service. In contrast, Kate, with the same organic inferiority, may not feel inferior; she may choose to overcompensate on the useful side of life and become exceptionally helpful, courageous, and productive. The nature of the inferiority imposes certain limits upon what is possible but not on the attitude adopted.

Inferiorities can be genetic/inherited (Cystic Fibrosis, Huntington's Chorea), chromosomal (Down's Syndrome, Turner's Syndrome), situational/accidental (head trauma, metabolic or endocrine dysfunction, infarcts), or self-induced (substance abuse, damage from anoxia secondary to some suicide attempts, etc.). The location of the damage may have certain effects on behavior depending upon a number of complex, interrelated factors (such as central nervous system, left or right hemisphere, temporal or occipital lobes, cerebrovascular, etc.). The idiographic nature of Individual Psychology is perhaps nowhere more relevant than here. The numerous factors that make up the particular disorder must be taken into account.

Many Adlerians make a distinction between organ inferiority and handicap. An *organ inferiority* is traditionally referred to when an inherited inferiority is passed down from generation to generation. A *handicap* is any inferiority that is not inherited. For present purposes, such a distinction is not necessarily to articulate; whether compensatory efforts are useful or useless is the relevant issue.

Childhood Training

Adler (1932) classified three situations that he considered "intensified minus" situations, that is, situations that severely tax the social interest and cooperative spirit of individuals. The first of these situations was discussed previously— *organ inferiority*. Having an inferior organ or organ systems can lead to useless compensation on the part of the individual, who may become discouraged in efforts to fit into society in a prosocial way.

The second situation Adler (1932) said predisposed certain individuals to useless compensations was *pampering*. Pampering can be operationally defined as doing anything for children that they can do for themselves (Dreikurs & Soltz, 1964). For Adler, pampering established an expectant attitude in individuals of continued service throughout the life span. Such people begin to become dependent upon others for solutions to the challenges of life. As Adler cautioned, pampering is not only the result of the actions of parents and caregivers, but it is also "the creation of the child himself" (Adler, 1932, p. 89). It is "the exacting attitude of the child which induces pampering" (Adler, 1932, p. 89).

The third situation that Adler said predisposed individuals to useless compensatory activity was *neglect*. Children who are neglected, hated, or abused can understandably be deficient in developing their social interest. Also, Adler cautioned, "every pampered child will automatically find himself, later in life, in situations which will make him feel neglected" (Adler, 1932, p. 89). These forms of training in meeting life's challenges can lead individuals to adopt hesitant, dependent attitudes toward their disabilities.

Family Training

Family training encompasses a more systems-oriented perspective (Sherman & Dinkmeyer, 1987). As Barlow (1984) and Traver (1984) pointed out, families can sometimes encourage the useless compensatory efforts of disabled individuals. The "systemic lifestyles" of certain families, according to Barlow, can significantly affect the onset, adjustment, exacerbation, and maintenance of many physical conditions and disabilities (Barlow, 1964, p. 63). Family purposes, as well as individual purposes, need to be examined in the training of individuals who use their disabilities for neurotic purposes. Interested individuals are referred to the chapters by Barlow and Traver for detailed family systems descriptions in line with the principles of Individual Psychology.

Clinging to the Shock Effects

Adler (Ansbacher & Ansbacher, 1956) spoke of certain patients who tended to cling to the shock effects of some situations, which can be either biological or psychological. For example, on the psychological side, an individual may experience a disappointment from a "real," exogenous situation, such as the loss of a job; however, the person can cling to the effect and use it to further movement toward goals that are self-centered. The disappointment may be used as an excuse to extract special treatment or consideration from others. On the biological side, much the same can be seen with someone who uses a broken leg to dominate those in his or her social field. For example, a person with an anxiety disorder secondary to hyperthyroidism was quite adept at manipulating his family—his mother and older sister especially—into assuming all his major chores and tasks, much to the resentment of his siblings and father. Not only did his father subsequently become angry and resentful at his wife and her overly sensitive posture toward her "ill" son, but the already existing distance between certain family members also increased. This young man clung to his anxiety symptoms long after therapeutic blood levels were attained on his medication.

Private Logic

Adler (1928) discussed the difference between common sense and private sense, logic, or intelligence. *Common sense* is that which is shared by the general population: it is a sign of empathy, identification with others, and social interest. *Private intelligence,* or *logic,* is that which is not in line with common sense. The closer that private logic is to common sense, the more socially adaptive the individual is (Dreikurs, 1945). In the organic psychoses, private logic of the individual is exposed; that is, as in all psychoses (functional, ideopathic or organic), "as the perception of our common world vanishes or disintegrates, the inner world of the patient becomes dominant" (Dreikurs, 1945, p. 135). This dynamic plays a crucial role in understanding the lifestyle of the disabled individual (Rule, 1984). DSM-IV, with its multiaxial classification system, utilizes a similar concept with its inclusion of Axis II personality disorders. Someone with an obsessive-compulsive personality disorder may react to a disability in a radically different way than someone with a premorbid histrionic personality disorder. The particular presentation will depend upon the various factors discussed above.

Cummings (1988) provided a useful set of guidelines for distinguishing between organic and ideopathic (functional) psychoses. He listed seven characteristics that may be indicative of a clear-cut organic pathology:

Late onset—typically after the age of 45
Atypical features—that is, features that do not ordinarily occur in schizophrenia or manic psychoses
A coexistent deficit syndrome—such as delirium, dementia, or aphasia, for example
A normal premorbid personality
An absent history of psychiatric illness
An absent history of psychiatric mental illness in the family
A coexisting neuromedical illness

In addition, two additional signs of which clinicians should be aware when screening for organic psychosis are visual hallucinations and a tendency to make the unfamiliar familiar. In the first case, visual hallucinations are usually (but not exclusively) indicative of toxic processes in clients. In the second, individuals who claim to know strangers or treat people they have never met as if they were relatives ("That nurse, that's my sister Patty!") are compensating for severe perceptual or memory impairment. Both are telltale signs of organic pathology in a number of cases.

GENERAL TREATMENT STRATEGIES

As mentioned previously, medical interventions always are required in the organic conditions. In addition, treatment strategies are directed in four other areas: education, structure, and support, counseling, and family interventions. Each will be examined briefly.

Medical

In general, medical intervention typically is directed along two fronts, surgical and chemical. Surgery to relieve intercranial pressure from a tumor producing an Amnestic Disorder can be extremely beneficial. Medication with antipsychotic medication, such as haloperidol, can be very helpful in controlling some cases of Psychotic Delusional Disorder. The role of anticonvulsants in managing a number of organic conditions is being acknowledged (Martin, 1986).

Typically, medical assessments are structural assessments, that is, they involve examining the brain and its surrounding structures. CAT scans, PET scans, MRI scans, and the like primarily provide glimpses into the brain itself. Functional assessment, the role of determining what patients can and cannot do will be discussed later in this chapter.

Education

This is very crucial. Individual Psychology emphasizes the educational component of counseling and therapy. Patients and families can be given information and facts about the type of illness, its course, relapse rate, prognosis, and associated features. Increasing their awareness and ability to make informed choices can prove especially beneficial in virtually all cases.

Structure and Support

In most of the acute conditions, hospitalization is required. Someone in a full-blown delirium should be medically monitored and treated. The structure of the hospital and support of the professional staff is necessary. Similarly, rehabilitation centers and support groups can ease the burden and greatly facilitate recuperation.

Counseling

Rule (1984) has provided an excellent volume on this topic for use by Adlerians. In general, counseling interventions involve two dimensions: counseling for rehabilitation and counseling for adjustment.

Rehabilitation involves the distinction between impairment and disability. Two individuals with the same impairment will not necessarily be equally disabled. For example, the loss of a finger to a construction worker is less disabling than to a concert pianist. Again, the idiographic components of the particular case, lifestyle and family structure in particular, need to be examined.

Adjustment involves adaptation to the impairment. Lifestyle factors are crucial for an understanding of this phase (Rule, 1984). The ability of someone to adjust to the organic condition will influence the efficacy of the rehabilitative efforts.

Functional assessment involves an understanding of what given patients can and cannot do, depending upon the type and severity of the organic condition. Briefly, some of the main assessment instruments are the following.

The Mental Status Examination. Strub and Black (1993) provided an excellent discussion of the procedure. When used by an experienced clinician, it can be done in less than an hour and quite successfully serve as a screening device for organic pathology. Two other rapid screening devices used by clinicians are the *Hutt Adaptation to the Bender-Gestalt Test* (1985) and the *Quick Neurological Screening Test—Revised.*

Luria-Nebraska Neuropsychological Battery. This instrument provides a comprehensive overview of patients' functioning, and it can be useful in localizing the site of many injuries to the brain and central nervous system. Along with the *Halsted-Reitan,* it is one of the most frequently used neuropsychological assessment instruments.

Understanding of Personality. In addition to the neuropsychological assessment instruments mentioned, clinicians may be interested in gaining an understanding of the personality variables of their clients. As Rule (1984) aptly pointed out, a Lifestyle Assessment can prove invaluable. The *Rorschach* test, particularly using Exner's (1986) system, can be extremely helpful. Whereas the Lifestyle Assessment can provide a longitudinal view of personality functioning, the *Rorschach* test can provide a rich cross-sectional view of cognitive-perceptual, emotional, and interpersonal functioning in a relatively short time.

In general, as Gallatin (1982) and Ornstein and Sobel (1987) pointed out, the individual's adaptation to society can prove crucial in the recovery from serious organic pathology. Clients need to feel connected, useful, and a part of their network. Feelings of inferiority only serve to disrupt rehabilitation efforts and recovery.

Family Interventions

Barlow (1984) and Traver (1984) discussed the role of family dynamics in rehabilitation. Clinicians need to be sensitive and willing to work with concerned family members as partners in the process. In many cases, simply imparting knowledge to the family about the nature, course, and prognosis of the condition can do much to relieve fears and tensions. Explaining the limits of the patients' future functioning and possible, potential difficulties can prove beneficial as well. Many of the specific conditions listed in DSM-IV are of short duration, and recovery is rapid and without complication; however, some such as dementia or the Personality Changes Due to a General Medical Condition can have long-lasting and very disruptive effects upon the lives of patients and families alike. Counseling strategies need to be directed in these cases towards adjustment and compensatory efforts, and the family's role in the process can be crucial.

CLINICAL EXAMPLES

Two brief examples will highlight many of the aforementioned issues. The first involved a relatively acute condition needing immediate medical attention; the second case was of a more chronic, debilitating nature.

Case of Eddie

Eddie was a young, rebellious man who had been in therapy at a local community clinic for several months. He had an antisocial personality disorder with narcissistic features on Axis II with a long history of polydrug abuse on Axis I. He was in treatment under pressure from his family, who threatened to send him back to a halfway house should some improvement not be noticed in his overall behavior. He appeared at the treatment center agitated, somewhat confused, and extremely paranoid. The night before, he had been taken home by a friend who dropped him off at his front door and turned to leave. Eddie came running after the friend in a panic claiming there was a dead body in Eddie's front room. The police were called only to find that there was no body in the room. His friend had calmed Eddie down and told the police he would take Eddie to the treatment center first thing in the morning. When Eddie was examined, he was oriented times four (he knew who he was, where he was, what time it was, and why he was there) and had a relatively normal presentation except for the agitation and paranoia. He was claiming that others were after him and that the treatment staff (the psychiatric nurse, who was Eddie's primary therapist, and the author, who was called in to evaluate Eddie's current condition) were going to destroy his life and take away his family. After questioning Eddie and his friend, the possibility of an organic versus functional delusional disorder was raised. The rapid onset of the delusions, the agitation, and Eddie's overall physical condition (extremely rapid pulse, pupil dilation, sweating) lent credence to the possible organic nature of the condition, and laboratory tests were ordered. Eddie had ingested a large quantity of amphetamines. His diagnosis was as follows:

Axis I: 292.11 Amphetamine-Induced Psychotic Disorder with Delusion
Axis II: 301.70 Antisocial Personality Disorder with narcissistic features
Axis III: None
Axis IV: Psychosocial Stressors: parents' divorce threatening family stability
Axis V: GAF: 50 (current)

A Lifestyle Assessment was conducted when Eddie was released back to the treatment center for outpatient psychotherapy. In short, he is a "getter" (Adler, in Ansbacher & Ansbacher, 1956; Mosak, 1959). His early recollection summary stated that

> I am entitled to special treatment, enjoy creating excitement and being rebellious. There are two types of women—those who give to me and those who are unstable, hysterical, and no fun (they are the ones who expect me to be accountable for my actions). There are some things in this world that have to be accepted, but I don't like it.

Eddie and his therapist began work on these issues. His substance abuse was related to his style of life. Also of issue was his relationship to his female therapist, whom, as predicted from his Lifestyle Assessment, he viewed as "no fun" and out to hold him "accountable" for his actions. The content of his delusions—his private logic—reflected these themes as well: His life was in threat of being "destroyed" from his perspective, and his family might be taken away if he did not "clean up" his life.

Case of Jenny

The second case was very different in nature from Eddie's. Jenny was a woman in her 30s and had been living in a suburban community with her family (husband and two children). In the past several months, she had begun acting out, becoming intermittently violent and explosive over apparently inconsequential situations. She would settle down, feel terribly guilty, confused, and at a loss for her behavior. Despite numerous attempts to "control" herself, she was unsuccessful, and her marriage was in jeopardy. During consultation, it was discovered that she had a very brittle diabetic condition, which was exacerbated by the birth of her two children. When she was having trouble regulating her insulin, she occasionally would go into a seizure in violent, grand mal episodes, on one occasion dislocating her shoulder. Neuropsychological assessment was undertaken.

Intelligence testing found Jenny to be functioning in the low average range, below her college history and professional occupational status. Testing with the *Bender-Gestalt, Stoop Neuropsychological Screening Test, Trail Making Test* (parts A & B), and the *Quick Neurological Screening Test—Revised* found nonspecific, diffuse impairment. Memory assessment with the *Wechsler Memory Scale—Revised* found numerous impairments. In addition, her score on the *Beck Depression Inventory* found her to be moderately depressed and hopeless. She was referred for neurological assessment, and an MRI was performed, revealing frontal and temporal lobe lesions believed to be secondary to her severe seizures. Her diagnosis was as follows:

Axis I: 310.1 Personality Change Due to a History of Seizures secondary to unregulated diabetes, Combined Type (labile & Aggressive); 294.9 Cognitive Disorder NOS (Mild Neurocognitive Disorder); 300.4 Dysthymic Disorder, late onset
Axis II: Obsessive-Compulsive features
Axis III: History of diabetes, seizures
Axis IV: Medical problems, marital problems
Axis V: GAF: 55 (current)

Her primary care physician placed her in a hospital. An insulin pump was surgically implanted, anticonvulsant medication was instituted, and behavioral training was undertaken with the help of her husband. Jenny learned to manage herself well using a number of compensatory strategies, and the couple began their long, hard road back to reestablishing their marriage.

Discussion of Cases

In the first case, Eddie's lifestyle strongly influenced his eventual diagnostic presentation. His getting style and excitement-seeking tendencies led him to an amphetamine-induced psychosis. Further complications and management issues could be expected unless some change occurred in his lifestyle. Even during his acute condition, his delusions reflected his private logic.

In the second case, Jenny's medical condition affected portions of her brain that influenced her ability to regulate and control her behavior and impulses. No overt lifestyle issues were involved; in fact, she had a history of controlling tendencies in opposition to her symptoms. It is generally acknowledged that patients with damage to the frontal and temporal lobes display similar dysfunction.

Eddie's case was more an issue of psychotherapy and reorientation after the acute condition was successfully managed. For Jenny, the issue became one of rehabilitation and adjustment to her disorders. It was *not* a psychotherapeutic issue; it was more of a counseling situation (i.e., adaptation to the situation without changing the underlying lifestyle). In her case, family members needed to be counseled as to the extent and prognosis of her conditions as well as to the importance of Jenny being consistent on her diet and medications.

CONCLUSION

Adler developed a system of psychotherapy and a model of personality that emphasized the biopsychosocial aspects of individuals. For Adler, the patient was the focus of treatment and the crucial component upon which his theory was based. Adler developed techniques for dealing with numerous and varied disorders, ranging along a wide spectrum of clinical presentations. Within his theory, Adler offered guidelines for work to be directed to a whole array of conditions, including mental disorders that had more of a medical, biological loading.

In general, patients with Mental Disorders Due to General Medical Conditions and Other Cognitive Disorders can be taught to compensate for their conditions in socially useful ways. Through the help of family members and professionals (medical and nonmedical alike), patients with disorders can be helped. The important aspects of the case to be taken into consideration are the nature of the patients' organ inferiorities/dysfunctions, the direction of the compensatory efforts in either useful or useless ways, the type of support provided by the social network, and the particular lifestyle of the patient in question.

SUGGESTED READINGS

Berg, R., Franzen, M., & Wedding, D. (1987). *Screening for brain impairment: A manual for mental health practice*. New York: Springer Publishing.

This is an excellent overview of screening procedures and techniques. It is easily readable and covers areas such as neuropsychological history taking, screening for memory functions, verbal functions, and a perceptual and motor functions.

Martin, R. (1986). *Matters gray and white*. New York: Fawcett Crest.

This is an interesting discussion of many of the common neurological disorders clinicians encounter. The author follows a neurologist for one year and learns about the various clinical disorders and the brain and central nervous system functioning.

Miller, L. (1990). *Inner natures: Brain, self and personality*. New York: Ballantine Books.

The author, a neuropsychologist, discusses the neuropsychological under pinnings of personality, including some of the more frequently diagnosed DSM personality disorders. This book is quite helpful in learning to apply neuropsychological data to humans, rather than to parts of a person.

Ornstein, R., & Sobel, D. (1987). *The healing brain*. New York: Simon & Schuster.

This book clearly and convincingly discusses the interrelationship between biological functioning and our psychosocial relationships. In addition, the authors discuss the role of beliefs and expectations in managing health and illness.

Rule, W.R. (Ed.). (1984). *Lifestyle counseling for adjustment to disability*. Rockville, MD: Aspen Publications.

This is *the* textbook for applying Adlerian psychology to various issues of rehabilitation and counseling of the impaired. Rule has assembled many experienced clinicians (many of whom he trained) and asked them to write chapters on their particular areas of specialty.

Strub, R.L., & Black, F.W. (1993). *The mental status examination in neurology* (3rd ed.). Philadelphia: F.A. Davis.

One of the best books available on administering and interpreting the mental status examination. The authors, in a surprisingly concise fashion, discuss what various responses and findings mean in relation to brain and central nervous system functioning. A book of which every clinician should be aware.

Taylor, R.L. (1989). Screening for medical referral. In R.J. Corsini & D. Wedding (Eds.), *Current psychotherapies* (4th ed.) (pp. 585–588). Itasca, IL: F.E. Peacock.

This is a readable, brief overview based on his book from the early 1980s. Taylor discusses the difference between altertive and presumptive clues and provides useful guidelines for differential diagnosis.

REFERENCES

Adler, A. (1907). *Study of organ inferiority and its psychical compensation.* New York: Nervous and Mental Diseases.

Adler, A. (1928). Brief comments on reason, intelligence and feeble-mindedness. In H.L. Ansbacher & R.R. Ansbacher (Eds.), *Superiority and social interest* (pp. 39–49). New York: W.W. Norton.

Adler, A. (1932). The structure of neurosis. In H.L. Ansbacher & R.R. Ansbacher (Eds.), *Superiority and social interest* (pp. 83–95). New York W.W. Norton.

Adler, A. (1935). Typology of meeting life problems. In H.L. Ansbacher & R.R. Ansbacher (Eds.), *Superiority and social interest* (pp. 66–70). New York: W.W. Norton.

Adler, K. (1989). Techniques that shorten psychotherapy: Illustrated with five cases. *Individual Psychology, 45,* 62–74.

American Psychiatric Association. (1994). *Diagnostic and statistical manual of mental disorders* (4th ed.). Washington, DC: Author.

Ansbacher, H.L., & Ansbacher, R.R. (Eds.). (1956). *The Individual Psychology of Alfred Adler.* New York: Basic Books.

Barlow, M.S. (1984). Lifestyle and the family of the disabled. In W.R. Rule (Ed.), *Lifestyle counseling for adjustment to disability* (pp. 61–80). Rockville, MD: Aspen Publications.

Berg, R., Franzen, M., & Wedding, D. (1987). *Screening for brain impairment.* New York: Springer Publishing.

Cummings, J.L. (1988). Organic psychosis. *Psychosomatics, 29,* 16–26.

Dreikurs, R. (1945). Psychological differentiation of psychopathological disorders. In R. Dreikurs (Ed.), *Psychodynamics, psychotherapy and counseling* (pp. 5-24). Chicago: Alfred Adler Institute.

Dreikurs, R. (1948). The socio-psychological dynamics of physical disability. In R. Dreikurs (Ed.), *Psychodynamics, psychotherapy and counseling* (pp. 167–188). Chicago: Alfred Adler Institute.

Dreikurs, R., & Soltz, V. (1964). *Children: The challenge.* New York: Duell, Sloan & Pearce.

Erickson, R.C., & Doppelt, L.H. (1987). Rehabilitation of the chronic psychiatric patient. *Individual Psychology, 43,* 296–307.

Exner, J.E. (1986). *The Rorschach: A comprehensive system. Volume 1: Basic foundations* (2nd ed.). New York: John Wiley & Sons.

Gallatin, J. (1982). *Abnormal psychology.* New York: Macmillan.

Hutt, M.L. (1985). *The Hutt adaptation of the Bender-Gestalt test* (4th ed.). New York: Grune & Stratton.

Martin, R. (1986). *Matters gray and white.* New York: Fawcett Crest.

Miller, L. (1990). *Inner natures: Brain, self and personality.* New York: Ballantine Books.

Mosak, H.H. (1959). The getting type: A parsimonious social interpretation of the oral character. *Journal of Individual Psychology, 15,* 193–198.

Mosak, H.H. (1977). *On purpose.* Chicago: Alfred Adler Institute.

Mosak, H.H., & Maniacci, M.P. (1989). An approach to the understanding of "schizophrenese." *Individual Psychology, 45,* 465–472.

Ornstein, R., & Sobel, D. (1987). *The healing brain.* New York: Simon & Schuster.

Rule, W.R. (Ed.). (1984). *Lifestyle counseling for adjustment to disability.* Rockville, MD: Aspen Publications.

Sherman, R., & Dinkmeyer, D. (1987). *Systems of family therapy: An Adlerian integration*. New York: Brunner/Mazel.

Shulman, B.H., & Klapman, H.J. (1968). Organ inferiority and psychiatric disorders in childhood. In E. Harms (Ed.), *Pathogenesis of nervous and mental diseases in children* (pp. 49–62). New York: Libra.

Sperry, L. (1988). Biopsychosocial therapy: An integrative approach for tailoring treatment. *Individual Psychology, 44*, 225–235.

Strub, R.L., & Black, F.W. (1993). *The mental status examination in neurology* (3rd ed.). Philadelphia: F.A. Davis.

Swonger, A.K., & Constantine, L.L. (1983). *Drugs and therapy: A handbook of psychotropic drugs* (2nd ed.). Boston: Little, Brown and Company.

Taylor, R.L. (1989). Screening for medical referral. In R.J. Corsini & D. Wedding (Eds.), *Current psychotherapies* (4th ed.) (pp. 585–588). Itasca, IL: F.E. Peacock.

Traver, M.D. (1984). Using selected lifestyle information in understanding multigenerational patterns. In W.R. Rule (Ed.), *Lifestyle counseling for adjustment to disability* (pp. 81–103). Rockville, MD: Aspen Publications.

Chapter 4

INDIVIDUAL PSYCHOLOGY AND BIPOLAR MOOD DISORDER

Dorothy E. Peven

This chapter is adapted from "Individual Psychology and Bipolar Mood Disorder" by D. Peven and B. Shulman, *Individual Psychology,* 39, 2-16. Used by permission of the authors and the University of Texas Press.

Preface to the Second Edition

A review of the most current literature demonstrates once again that there are fashions in science as well as in symptoms. The great success of current biological treatments for mood disorders has resulted by promoting biological theories while ignoring psychological theories about the nature and etiology of mood disorders. As the quest for understanding of our psychological origins continues, reductionistic, deterministic answers become popular. Yet the pendulum swings and most likely we can expect psychoanalytic (even brain hemispheric?) concepts to reemerge in the next decade since there is, as yet, no unequivocal biochemical basis for mood disorders.

Current biologic/genetic theories of causation of affective disorders do not conflict, per se, with Adler's theories about depression and mania since he stated that the bipolar seems to have a constitutional tendency toward mood swings.

Bodily influences on affect and on motivation were part of his theory of organ inferiority. He also stressed that actions are motivated and that behavior has a goal—thinking and feeling are actions taken by the organism in pursuit of the "final goal." Mental life is conceptualized in circular terms since it would not be possible to understand one facet of the triad—thinking, feeling, or acting—without understanding that any one of these facets has an inexorable effect on the other two. Comprehension of human behavior does not lend itself to linear concepts, that is, thinking leading to feeling leading to acting as Beck and Ellis understand behavior (Beck, 1987; Ellis & Harper, 1970). Nor does the Individual Psychologist understand human behavior by observing *only* behavior as do the behaviorists, since, or course, in the circular mode, acting (behaving) in certain ways influences the environment, and the feed back from the environment influences feeling which influences thinking and so on. (This is actually similar to an understanding of human behavior from the viewpoint of Systems theory.)

Because Adler, as a holistic theorist, believed there could be no comprehension of personality without an understanding of the biological basis of behavior, current biological/genetic theories fit easily into an Adlerian conception of psychiatric disorders. But the most current *Diagnostic and Statistical Manual of Mental Disorders* (DSM-IV) of the American Psychiatric Association (1994) makes no attempt to integrate biological and psychological systems and cites etiology very carefully. Therefore, DSM-IV is to be understood as a descriptive system, "an attempt to place some order in the universe of human behavior" (Avram, Mack, Forman, Brown, & Frances, 1994, p. 515) and not to be understood as an *explanation* of behavior.

For example, there has been a change in the diagnostic categories for Bipolar Mood Disorder. Previously DSM-III-R (1987) listed Bipolar Disorder as the following: Bipolar Disorder, Mixed; Bipolar Disorder, Manic; and Bipolar Disorder, Depressed. DSM-IV distinguishes between Bipolar I Disorder with subcategories—Most Recent Episode Depressed, Manic, Mixed, or Hypomanic—and Bipolar II Disorder defined as Recurrent Major Depressive Episodes with Hypomanic Episodes. (Cyclothymic Disorder is the same in DSM-III-R and DSM-IV.)

Historically, it was 1962 before recurrent mood disorders were divided into monopolar and bipolar types, and by 1966 the monopolar was renamed unipolar. In 1975, bipolar disorders were subdivided into Type I, in which the manic phase is mild, and Type II, in which the manic phase is severe. DSM-III (1980) and DSM-III-R (1987) identified bipolar disorder by most current episode. DSM-IV asks the clinician to diagnose in very discrete units. Sedler (1983, translated by Sedler & Dessain) suggested

> . . . classification that bases the distinctions among mental disorders
> on an ensemble of characteristics, where each depends on the
> others, and on the clinical course, i.e., on the orderly development
> of the phenomena . . . [leading to] a set of principles that are more
> likely to yield a regular classification, a clear prognosis, and a
> rational course of treatment. (Sedler, 1983, p. 1129)

Individual Psychological understanding of affective disorders grows out of
a 1914 paper on *Melancholia and Paranoia* by Alfred Adler (Adler, 1968), just
as psychoanalytic understanding comes from Abraham (1957) and Freud's 1917
Mourning and Melancholia (Freud, 1960). Later elaborations by psychoanalysts
and Individual Psychologists have expanded the theories, but there has as yet
been no integration of psychodynamic theories with the vast amount of biological
research of the past few decades. Perhaps exploration of the next few decades
will help us understand, for as Avram et al. pointed out

> Like its predecessors, DSM-IV is [only] a descriptive system, and
> it too gradually will be replaced by an etiologic model—one, it is
> hoped, that is more scientifically valid than previous attempts at
> etiologic explanation. . . . (Avram et al., 1994, p. 522)

A search of the literature at a hospital library, the public library, and two
university libraries disclosed no empirical studies in the past two years that offer
a psychodynamic explanation of bipolar disorders. Personality theorists, on the
other hand, have discussed the psychodynamics of bipolar mood disorder but
have published few, if any, empirical studies. Neither Adler nor the psychoanalysts
have addressed themselves at any length to the psychodynamics of bipolar disorder nor has any theorist or geneticist yet distinguished between major depressive
disorder and the depression of the bipolar. In fact, bipolar depression is distin-
guishable from major depressive disorder only by history.

This author's purpose is to review some theoretical formulations and recent
research findings to attempt a synthesis toward an understanding of bipolar
disorder from the viewpoint of Individual Psychology. The discussion of the
psychodynamics of bipolar disorder follows a previous paper by this author and
Shulman (1983), and some ideas were originally presented in that paper.

DIAGNOSIS OF BIPOLAR DISORDER

The phenomenon of dysphoric and euphoric episodes following one another
was identified as a syndrome by poets and physicians as early as Homer and

Plutarch and was described by Aretaeus of Cappadocia in the first century A.D. Current understanding and classification of bipolar disorder derives from the ideas of Emil Kraepelin who had been influenced by J. Falret who, in 1946, said

> . . . there is a certain category of patient who continually exhibits a nearly regular succession of mania and melancholia. This seemed sufficiently important to us to serve as a basis for a specific mental disorder, which we call circular insanity. . . . (Sedler & Dessain, 1983)

In 1896 Kraepelin proposed the name ***manic depressive insanity*** for this group of disorders and wrote vivid and complete descriptions of the syndrome (Kraepelin, 1902). He added his own observation that a large proportion of manic-depressive patients came from "tainted" families (i.e., his patients had close relative who had experienced some form of affective [mood] disorder).

Bipolar disorders are distinguished from other affective disorders because of the circularity of the moods: depression follows mania which follows depression in a fashion that colors the whole psychic life even though there are euthymic periods when functioning is not disturbed. Mood Episodes do not have their own diagnostic codes and are not diagnosed separately but form the criteria for the Disorder diagnoses. The DSM-IV includes specifiers that describe either the most recent mood episode of the course of recurrent episodes. The disorders are as follows:

> Bipolar I Disorder—characterized by one or more Manic or Mixed Episodes, usually accompanied by Major Depressive Episodes,
> Bipolar II Disorder—characterized by one or more Major Depressive Episodes accompanied by at least one Hypomanic Episode, and
> Cyclothymic Disorder—characterized by at least two years of numerous periods of hypomanic symptoms that do not meet criteria for a Manic Episode and numerous periods of depressive symptoms that do not meet criteria for a Major Depressive Episode.

MAJOR MOOD DISORDER

The diagnosis of a major mood disorder is made only after a finding of the typical criteria defining episodes. The ability to distinguish between a disorder and an episode depends on whether or not the episode is severe enough to cause marked impairment in social or occupational functioning or to require hospitalization. Even though some hypomanic episodes evolve into full manic episodes, the diagnosis depends on the degree of impairment.

Manic Episode

Manic episodes are characterized by a period of an abnormally and persistently elevated and/or irritable mood lasting at least one week. In order to diagnose a manic episode, at least three of the following symptoms must be present (American Psychiatric Association, 1994, p. 332):

1. inflated self-esteem or grandiosity,

    > Three young men were hospitalized on the psychiatric unit (St. Joseph Hospital, Chicago) at the same time, all three of whom claimed to be Jesus Christ. The staff resolved any dissension by allowing each one to have a turn at being Jesus . . . John could be Christ on Monday, Michael on Tuesday, and Peter on Wednesday. (Within a week they had all changed identifications.)

2. decreased need for sleep,
3. press of speech,
4. flight of ideas,
5. distractibility,
6. psychomotor agitation, and
7. what can be the most disturbing aspect of this particular disorder, poor judgment demonstrated by the inability to understand the consequences of behavior in unrestrained buying sprees, promiscuous sexual behavior, and foolish business investments. Manics often put themselves in dangerous situations.

    > M, a young man in a manic state, planted himself in the middle of one of Chicago's busiest streets (the Outer Drive) and with his coat held as a cape played toreador with the oncoming traffic.

    > A, a young woman in a manic state, would sit on a park bench during pleasant weather and trip the male joggers going by in order to start a conversation. She then would invite them to her apartment for a sexual interlude. She later developed an STD.

Occasionally during the manic state, paranoid delusions or hallucinations occur. The uncritical self-esteem and marked grandiosity are often of a delusional nature. Some people either believe they are on a special mission from God or believe they are being persecuted by "strange" forces.

> A very frightened young man, S, had been in a manic state marked by extreme fear paranoia and had been hospitalized for several weeks. After discharge he told me that during the hospitalization he thought the staff were cannibals and whenever they came to his room to take care of him, he believed they were going to cut out pieces of his flesh and eat them.

> Another male bipolar, B, would drink to excess when he felt "high" and one day threw 20-dollar bills out of the second-floor window of his office to all his "peasants" on the street.

People who are suffering from a manic disorder have a decreased need for sleep and awaken full of energy. Usually there is a flight of ideas and a nearly continuous flow of accelerated speech with abrupt changes from topic to topic. Sometimes the speech is disorganized and incoherent, with a loosening of associations.

The most commonly associated feature is lability of mood with rapid shifts from laughter to anger to extreme irritability and depression. The depression may last moments, hours, or days, and not uncommonly the depressive and manic symptoms intermingle and either occur at the same time or alternate rapidly.

Some mania occurs secondary to other conditions like epilepsy, drugs, infections, and metabolic disturbances. It is always well to inquire about medications and, especially with younger patients, street drugs.

Depressive Episode

The Depressive Episode is characterized by a change of mood from a usual "normal" mood to a predominantly dysphoric mood, and/or by a loss of interest or pleasure in all, or almost all, of the patient's usual activities. At least four of the following eight symptoms have to be present for a least a two-week period (American Psychiatric Association, 1994, p. 327):

1. depressed mood all day every day, usually subjective;
2. little interest or pleasure in activities all day every day;
3. significant weight loss when not dieting or weight gain (e.g., a change of more than 5% of body weight in a month), or decrease or increase in appetite nearly every day;
4. sleep difficulty, either measurable insomnia or measurable hypersomnia;
5. psychomotor agitation or retardation;
6. decrease of energy, chronic fatigue;

> L, a 23-year-old woman who was recovering from a manic episode felt herself beginning to get depressed and felt anergic. She needed a job and found it very difficult to arouse herself for interviews. She sat heavily in her chair, facing me, and said plaintively, "Dorothy, why not let me go off the medicine (lithium) for three days and I'll bet you I'll have five job offers."

7. feelings of worthlessness, hopelessness, and helplessness;
8. diminished ability to think or concentrate; and
9. suicidal ideation, thoughts of dying.

> A, the woman mentioned earlier, had been through several manic and depressive cycles and had been hospitalized many times. During a depressed episode, A jumped in front of a train and nearly lost her left leg. She was subdued and cooperative during the long recovery and responded well to my efforts to raise her spirits. Afterwards, she did not want to discuss the episode but vowed never to try to suicide again. (And she hasn't.)

PHYSIOLOGICAL THEORY AND RESEARCH

Recent researchers have tried to prove Kraepelin's observations about "tainted" families, and many research findings seem to demonstrate a familial proclivity to bipolar disorders. The most recent research has focused on the application of recombinant DNA technology and the chromosomal linkage of markers to bipolar disorders. A recent study by Berrettini and his coworkers in Philadelphia found ". . . a gene that helps create a predisposition to manic depression . . . in a substantial minority of cases . . . [and] lies along a short stretch of chromosome 18" (Science News, 1994). But an active controversy exists over the reproducibility of the X-chromosome findings (Blehar, Weissman, Gershon, & Hirschfeld, 1988). In a study of 266 first-degree relatives of Bipolar I and Bipolar II probands, Simpson, Folstein, Meyers, McMahon, Brusco, & DePaulo (1993) found Bipolar II Disorder was the most common affective disorder in both family groups where 40% of the 47 first-degree relatives of the Bipolar II probands and 22% of the 219 first-degree relatives of the Bipolar I probands were diagnosed with Bipolar II Disorder. The conclusion is that Bipolar II Disorder is "genetically related to but less complex than Bipolar I Disorder" (Simpson et al., 1993).

DSM-IV (1994, p. 353) reports that first-degree biological relatives of individual with Bipolar I Disorder have elevated rates of Bipolar I Disorder (4% to 24%), Bipolar II Disorder (1% to 5%), and Major Depressive Disorder (4% to 24%). Twin and adoption studies provide strong evidence of a genetic influence for Bipolar I Disorder.

Remember the black and white movies of the 1930s and 1940s where marriage was abjured and a reason was refused? *Jane Eyre*? *King's Row*? The "reason" was the fear of inherited insanity. "You can't marry darling," said father to daughter or mother to son. "I've tried to keep this from you, but the truth is that your mother [father, grandmother, grandfather] died in an insane asylum."

Bipolars do tend to have close relatives suffering from affective disorders, and it is difficult not to believe that an inherited factor is at work. Winokur wrote that two ingredients "seem to be necessary" for Bipolar Mood Disorder to occur: (a) a propensity for significant mood change, and (b) a tendency for the mood change to vary in a bipolar fashion (Winokur, 1975). Kretschmer thought that a disproportionately large number of pyknic body-type individuals develop bipolar disorder (Kretschmer, 1936), whereas Sheldon suggested that a constitution of high mesomorphy coincided with a higher than average representation of cyclothymic disorders.

In the past there also has been considerable discussion that no distinction is made between the depressed state in bipolar disorder and the depressed state in a major depressive disorder. Winokur, Coryell, Endicott, and Akiskal (1993) pointed out that there are distinctions between manic-depressive illness and primary depressive disorder. They contended, based on their study, that patients with bipolar disorder differ from patients with unipolar depression by having family histories of mania with an earlier onset, and that they have more episodes over a lifetime. Data were collected from clinical interviews, and results demonstrated that bipolar patients had an earlier, more acute, onset; had more total episodes, had more familial mania, and were more likely to be male than unipolars.

The authors of the study concluded that there would be considerable usefulness to distinguishing between bipolar and unipolar patients in treatment and research studies (Winokur et al., 1993).

Blacker and associates agreed with Winokur's findings and said that epidemiologic studies show consistent differences between unipolar and bipolar disorder in sex ratio, age at onset, and affective episodes. They added, "Depressive episodes in bipolar disorder appear to be more severe, even psychotic, and to have so-called reverse neurovegetative signs" (Blacker & Tsuang, 1992, p. 1474).

In addition to hereditary factors, constitutional factors, and premorbid personality factors, other etiological theories have been advanced, for example, dysfunctions of (a) the endocrine system, (b) the diencephalic centers involved in affective expressions, and (c) the processes that in lower animals are involved in hibernation (consideration of the seasonal factor). Genetic and family studies, neurophysiological studies, and neurochemical studies have produced results suggesting that most likely a relationship exists among the various functional, anatomical, and neurochemical systems in the brain and that brain disturbances can lead to affective disorders.

Sleep neurophysiologic and neuroendocrine abnormalities have been investigated and support the hypothesis that mood disorders are limbic-diencephalic disturbances and "give credence to the notion that midbrain homeostatic mechanisms are disrupted" (Akiskal, 1989, p. 7).

One of the most interesting discussions in the literature concerns the relationship of creativity to mental illness, especially bipolar disorder.

> . . . bouts of black melancholy alternating with paroxysms of creative drive figure prominently in the life histories of many productively creative persons. [We] . . . examined rates of mental illness in 30 creative writers, 30 matched control subjects, and the first-degree relatives of both groups. . . . [It showed that] the writers had a substantially higher rate of bipolar affective disorder and there was also a higher rate of affective disorder and creativity in the writers' first-degree relatives. (Miller, as cited in Hoppe, 1988, p. 388)

Jamison (1994) and Goodwin and Jamison (1990) discussed George Gordon (Lord Byron, 1788-1824) who was subject to wild changes in mood, severe depression, hallucinations, financial extravagance, and extreme eccentricity (he kept a bear in his rooms). Jamison believed that "it is probably this psychological suffering which caused him to produce some of the most eloquent and moving poetry about the human condition" (Jamison, 1994, p. 480). It is suggested, however, that mania is valuable only if it is joined to ability, and while the notion of the "mad genius" is beguiling, obviously mania cannot serve an inspirational purpose unless it is accompanied by talent.

Finally, there were researchers in the 1980s attempting to analyze the relationship between psychopathology and neuropsychological abnormalities of the right and left hemispheres of the brain. Kyle reported

> In studies of affective disorders versus schizophrenia, the schizophrenic patients showed significantly more left temporal and left parietal lobe errors. Both schizophrenic and affective disorder subjects (a majority of whom were manic) had more errors relating to both hemispheres than did controls. In general, depressive patients show impairment of the right hemisphere and right frontal functions compared to schizophrenics and to normals. (Kyle, 1988, p. 370)

Apparently a relationship exists among the various functional, anatomical, and neurochemical systems, but we are just beginning to understand the relationships between these systems and psychopathology. Genetic and family studies all seem to point to some essential difference between the physiology of "normal" people and the bipolar disorder of others.

PSYCHODYNAMIC THEORIES: THE RELATIONSHIP OF PERSONALITY TO BIPOLAR DISORDER

The relationship of personality to affective disorders is described in the literature using several hypotheses such as (a) personality as an expression of affective illness, (b) personality as altered by affective illness, and (c) personality as predisposition to affective illness. It is this latter hypothesis with which this chapter is concerned.

Both the empiricists and the personality theorists suggest that the premorbid personality of the bipolar is cyclothymic; that is, marked alternations of lively and depressed moods are common before a psychotic episode. Kraepelin (1902); Kretschmer (1936); Turns (1978); Akiskal, Djenderedjian, Rosenthal, and Khani (1977); and Adler (Ansbacher & Ansbacher, 1956) believed that a certain type of person who has either a particular kind of temperament or a particular set of personality traits becomes ill with bipolar disorder. For example, Adler said, "alterations in manic-depressive insanity are manifested by individuals who showed slight phases of conduct of this pattern in their earlier life . . ." (Ansbacher & Ansbacher, 1956, p. 323). More recent theorists suggested

> While the nature of cyclothymia's relation to bipolar disorder re-
> mains unclear, the fact of a relationship seems well established.
> By definition, the phenomenology is closely linked . . . cyclothymia
> itself does cluster with bipolar disorder. . . . Clinicians frequently
> note that many patients with bipolar disorder have a history of
> antecedent cyclothymia, and Akiskal et al. (1977) confirmed this
> on a prospective basis in a group of outpatients with cyclothymia.
> (Blacker & Tsuang, 1992, p. 1478)

But Pope suggested that "everyone is vulnerable if you create overwhelming conditions" [and] "there have been patients whose symptoms had been considered to represent disordered personality traits or 'character disorders' and who became dramatically better while taking an anti-depressant drug" (Pope, 1994, p. 39). It is possible that, in the future, theorists and laboratory researchers alike will be forced to reconsider their findings.

Freud, like Adler and other personality theorists using naturalistic observations, generated hypotheses linking personality to affective disorders but, as mentioned above, made no distinction between depression in bipolar disorder and in other types of depression. In *Mourning and Melancholia*, Freud (1960) interpreted depression by comparing it with the normal mourning reaction that follows the death of a loved one.

> The mourning work consists of a slow, gradual dissolution of the
> emotional ties with the lost object, and the incorporation of its
> idealized picture into the subject. . . . [it] is as if the patient
> unconsciously lost an object for which he had ambivalent feelings
> of love and hatred. As a consequence of its incorporation, the
> shadow of the object has fallen upon the ego, hence the melancholic
> self-hatred and suicidal tendencies. (Ellenberger, 1970, p. 512)

What had been an external struggle between the patient and the love object becomes an internal battle.

For Abraham (1957), following Freud, depression represented the reaction of a feeling of narcissistic injury and loss, as the ego fears the punitive and disapproving superego. Abraham thought that manic patients without a clinical history of depression had experienced what he called a primal depression very early in childhood. Those children who never learn to tolerate early depression or who lose a depression deny "the reality of their developmental tragedy and become manic" (Silber, in Kaplan & Sadock, 1989, p. 890).

The psychoanalysts believe manic patients are trying to ward off depressed feelings; otherwise the superego would flood the ego and overwhelm it. Mania is the ego's insistence that the injury has been repaired and the superego conquered. Because ego has defeated the superego, the need to inhibit impulses no longer exists and manic has a triumphant feeling of omnipotence, and manics enjoy the release of their inhibitions. But superego fears persist in the mania. Thus, "the behavior found in the manic attack . . . is in itself a defense reaction. By taking the offensive [the manic] . . . keeps himself safe from the approach of the painful thought or feeling . . . a realization of some failure or degradation" (Dooley, 1921, in Goodwin & Jamison, 1990, p. 316). Mania is understood as an attempt to stave off and deny depression.

Later, Freud (1960) changed the sequence and hypothesized that, when the depression is finally resolved, the energy bound up in the depression is liberated and mania appears. No explanation is given for the fact that mania does not follow every episode of depression.

Rado (1956) explained both mania and melancholia by a double incorporation. He believed the lost loved object has been split into good and bad objects. The bad object, incorporated into the ego, is punished leading to melancholia. The good object remains for reconciliation. Mania is understood to be achieved through a denial of guilt.

The neo-Freudian Fromm-Reichmann, with associates, studied 12 patients with manic-depressive illness and made the following observations: Bipolar patients seem to come from families that are upward striving, and the parents' values lead to the development of ambitious, driven children who feel an obligation to achieve success in accordance with the high achievement standards of the family. Future patients become outwardly extroverted and set their life goals impossibly high, which makes them susceptible to any small setback. This orientation is not intrinsic to the child but comes from conforming to family values (Cohen, Baker, Cohen, & Fromm-Reichmann, 1954).

Sullivan believed the psychic pathogen is anxiety:

> The behavior of cyclothymic people may be looked upon as an obscure expression of movements away from the experience of anxiety . . . or an unhappy manic state being more tolerable than anxiety itself. The anxiety is apparently rarely felt as such, and it

is extraordinarily difficult to isolate the event which threatens to
expose the anxiety and in turn sets up the patterns known as manic
depressive. . . . (Sullivan, 1954, p. 201)

Cognitive theorists like Beck (1987) and Ellis and Harper (1970) have
noted that people with affective disorder use cognitive strategies that lead to the
disorders. These cognitive mistakes include (a) arbitrary inferency—they jump
to conclusions that are contrary to fact, (b) overgeneralization—something that
happened once was always that way, (c) selective inattention—choosing to view
the worst aspect of a situation while ignoring the positive aspects, and (d)
magnification—turning an insignificant event into a catastrophic one. These
mistakes are considered inaccurate judgments about people and events in life
and can, ultimately, lead to major affective disorders.

Even though Kohut did most of his writing during the last few decades, his
followers suggest that he did not adequately address the issue of biological
predisposition. Kohut had concluded that all psychopathology was best explained
by "developmental arrests which inevitably result from parental shortcomings
[of empathic failure]" (Baker & Baker, 1987, p. 2).

While later contributions to theory do not always follow the original formulations of Freud and Abraham, only fragmentary discussions are in the literature
suggesting psychodynamic hypothesis for manic-depressive illness.

ALFRED ADLER AND INDIVIDUAL PSYCHOLOGY

Adler and Organ Inferiority

Genetic and family studies, neurophysiological studies, and neurochemical
studies all seem to point to physiological factors in the etiology of bipolar disorder.
This hypothesis is consistent with Adlerian thinking, especially Adler's early
formulations about organ inferiority. Early in his theoretical thinking (about
1907), Adler proposed that some children are born with organs that are "developmentally retarded" and that ". . . an inherited [organ] inferiority corresponds to
an inherited disease" (Ansbacher & Ansbacher, 1956, p. 24).

Although Adler had not as yet completed his thinking about the role of the
"creative self" in the development of personality, he suggested that organ inferiority is not deterministic: Beethoven, who was deaf, wrote music; Renoir, who
was blind, painted; and so on.

> The fate of the inferior organs is extremely varied. Development
> and the external stimuli of life press toward overcoming the expres-
> sions of such inferiority. Thus we may find approximately the
> following outcomes . . . inability to survive, anomaly of form,
> anomaly of function, compensation within the organ, compensa-
> tions through a second organ, compensation through the psycholog-
> ical superstructure, and organic or psychological overcompensa-
> tion. . . . (Ansbacher & Ansbacher, 1956, p. 24)

Later, Adler gave primacy to the psychological processes:

> . . . organ inferiority becomes one of the important objective factors
> which provide certain probabilities for . . . development, such
> factors being ultimately subject to the individual's own interpreta-
> tion. Second, the inferior organ, as the point of least resistance,
> becomes the preferred means by which the psyche expresses itself
> through the body. (Ansbacher & Ansbacher, 1956, p. 222)

In conclusion, the findings of laboratory researchers lead to the suggestion
that bipolar disorder is an illness that occurs to those people who are predisposed
to it by virtue of a familial inherited organ inferiority; but, the lessons of Individual
Psychology suggest that the *appearance* of the illness in its morbid form is a
function of each individual personality. Thus, bipolar disorders can be precipitated
by life situation stresses or by personality-driven stresses that disrupt the "midbrain homeostatic mechanisms" (Akiskal, 1989). This leads to the evidence for
the etiologic role of psychodynamic personality susceptibility factors.

Adler and the Affective Disorders

Mania.   By 1920, Adler had developed his unitary theory of the neurosis
and, therefore, never did address himself at any length to the psychodynamics
of bipolar illness.

Adler believed that all humans are motivated to overcome a subjective
experience of inferiority by striving for a "fictional" goal of superiority. Those
who direct this striving toward *personal* supremacy over their fellow human
beings are, to the extent that their goal lacks social interest, more or less neurotic.

> . . . the essential tendency of the neurotic is the striving from the
> feeling of inferiority toward "above . . . [and] the combination
> of". . . these two moods . . . [leads to] a neurotic constant back
> and forth . . . the conduct of powerless exaltation, where at one
> time the trait of powerlessness, at another time the trait of exaltation,

becomes more prominent. This process is most clearly visible in manic depressive insanity. (Ansbacher & Ansbacher, 1956, p. 273)

Bipolar patients are those who display in the most extreme fashion the "hesitating," "back and forth" movement that Adler saw in all neurotic behavior. For Adler, all neurosis is an attempt to evade what is subjectively perceived as a challenge. Those who see challenges as situations to be dealt with will move forward directly into problem-solving behavior. Those who see challenges as threats to a precarious self-esteem will either falter or move away from the perceived "danger."

According to Adler, neurotics are distinguished from psychotics by their ability to retain their grasp on reality; that is, they understand a challenge exists that has to be faced and steps must be taken, but they do not like the idea. They feel frightened and behave in timid ways. Psychotics, on the other hand, try to deceive themselves as well as others by acting I *as if* the threatening situation is either not there at all and they deal with other issues like "voices," or they behave *as if* the problem already has been solved successfully.

Given these theoretical foundations, it is understandable why Adler saw mania as "a bluff to overrun others" (Ansbacher & Ansbacher, 1956, p. 323). Later, in *Life-Lies and Responsibility*, Adler (1968) elaborated further by stating that mania occurs in ambitious people who do not believe in themselves to the extent of imagining that they would be able to gain their goal of superiority by direct methods. Therefore, the mania is an "act" meant to deceive both the manic person and his or her fellow humans into believing the deed has been done already. But bipolars cannot continue their deception indefinitely; so even though they begin "every act enthusiastically . . . [they lose] interest soon after . . ." (Adler, 1968, p. 247), and the mania is "a sudden blaze which consumes its fuel. . . . [excitement] rapidly wanes into depression . . . [and] brilliant beginnings and sudden anticlimaxes are repeated at intervals through [the manic-depressives'] life histories" (Adler, 1964, p. 27).

Peven and Shulman summarized Adler's statements on bipolar disorder: (a) a premorbid cyclothymic personality exists, (b) moods swing back and forth between a feeling of omnipotence and exaltation (they feel able to meet any challenge) to a feeling of powerlessness and feeling overwhelmed by the slightest task, (c) bipolars lack faith in their own competence, and (d) mania can be seen as a maneuver to deceive themselves and others (Peven & Shulman, 1983, p. 5).

Depression.   Alfred Adler (1968), in "Melancholia and Paranoia," presented his ideas on the etiology, phenomenology, and interpersonal transactions of the depressed "melancholic" person. And Kurt Adler, in 1961, gave an eloquent review of the Individual Psychological position on depression.

For the Adlers, the depressed adult is one who has from early childhood on put other people into his or her service. A. Adler said, "The discouraged child who finds he can tyrannize best by tears will be a cry-baby; and a direct line of development leads from the cry-baby to the adult depressed patient" (A. Adler, 1968). Depressed persons force others to submit to them by acting "as if" they were weak, helpless babies. Their method of operation (which is called "the exploitation of others' good will") is developed early on and carried throughout life.

The self-image of "pampered" children is that of inadequacy. Pampered children are those who have everything done for them. Consequently, they never develop their problem-solving abilities, feel unable and inadequate, and prefer never to be put to a test. This leads to an exaggeration of the inability to meet life's challenges.

According to Alfred Adler, this low assessment of the self suggests that an opportunity for extraordinary success has somehow been missed. Depressives imply, in a disguised manner, how important and extraordinary they are when they take upon themselves ostentatiously the blame for world calamities.

The purpose of the depression is the achievement of a fictive superiority and irresponsibility. By putting a claim on the services of others, by blaming others to induce guilt, by frustrating all efforts to help them, by depreciating others, "the depressive is led to a concealed increase in the feeling of importance" (K. Adler, 1961, p. 58).

> This, then, is the relentless effort of the depressed [the goal of the depression]: to prevail with his will over others, to extort from them sacrifices, to frustrate all their efforts to help him, to blame them . . . overtly or secretly . . . for his plight, and to be free of all social obligations and cooperations, by certifying to his sickness. (K. Adler, 1961, p. 66)

The symptoms of depressives are seen as offensive weapons and have as their purpose to increase the "shock" to the environment.

As a holistic theorist, Adler believed the organs of the body are induced to cooperate with the purpose of the behavior. Thus, appetite, sleep, digestion, etc. adjust their functions in response to the depression. This is not to be considered an argument for causation: Adler was not a determinist. For decades the research has shown that all emotions (affects) are accompanied by chemical changes. Emotions, by definition, always include physiological processes. By influencing the chemical processes, however, some illnesses (cancer of the pancreas) as well as some drugs can produce symptoms of depression. It is believed these drugs produce the same chemical changes produced by a depression from psychogenic causes. The chemical findings in depression remind us that body and mind influence each other as interacting systems and that the source of trouble can be either system.

For the two Adlers, depression is an attitude toward life, an accommodation to life as perceived through the eyes of a spoiled child who exploits and depreciates others and will force his body knowingly or unknowingly to accommodate to this pathological way of life by producing distressing symptomatology. Under these circumstances, whether the depression is part of a unipolar or a bipolar illness makes no difference. Adler said:

> It is neither heredity nor environment which determines our rela-
> tionship to the [world]. Heredity only endows us with certain
> abilities. Environment only gives us certain impressions. . . . the
> interpretation we make of these experiences . . . are the bricks
> which we use in our own "creative" way in building up our attitude
> toward life. It is our individual way of using these bricks . . . which
> determines our relationship to the outside world. (Ansbacher &
> Ansbacher, 1956, p. 206)

THE WORK OF PEVEN AND SHULMAN

The material in this section is taken from a 1983 paper by Peven and Shulman. They studied 17 well-established cases of bipolar disorder from their private files in an attempt to establish an Individual Psychological viewpoint of bipolar disorder. They also reviewed the literature on bipolar disorder and found some personality factors that seemed to be universally accepted and had implications for psychodynamic theory. The outstanding factors discussed in historical litera-ture were (a) bipolars have strong affiliative tendencies, (b) bipolars have a high achievement motive, (c) bipolars seem to have little faith in themselves and their ability to solve life's problems in a straightforward fashion, and (d) bipolars' attitudes and energies shift from one extreme to another.

The group studied consisted of 11 men and 6 women, and an analysis of their personalities was obtained from *Lifestyle Analysis, Rorschach* tests, *16 PF* tests, and the *Lusher, MMPI,* and *WAIS.* Of the 17, 5 had a definite family history of affective disorder.

All the tests and anamneses were reviewed for common material, and the material then was factored. No statistical analysis was done, and no control group was used. The authors found the following 8 common personality factors in their 17 bipolar patients.

1. Affectivity in the Perceptual Style

Bipolar people seem to meet Jung's concept of people who use feeling rather than thinking, sensing, or intuiting as their superior function (1971); that is, they pay a great deal of attention to their feelings. They often will be found taking their emotional temperature: "I feel great," "I feel sad," and so on. The early recollection of R (a young man) is an example:

> Age 6: I was alone with my mother in our apartment. It was dark and dingy and smelled. I hated the smell. My mother was angry about something, and I was very unhappy. I felt terrible in that dark, smelly place.

2. Ambition to Achieve

All 17 patients studied either showed a high achievement motive or described themselves as coming from families in which a strong press was a strong press for achievement. This finding concurs with earlier studies mentioned in this chapter.

Adlerians see the achievement motive as competitive movement toward an ambitious goal of superiority. Whenever private goals are inordinate, insatiable, or improbable of attainment, they contribute to psychopathology. Although the goals of the patients in the study were not necessarily the "lofty goals" of psychosis (Adler, 1964), they were "inappropriate to the time, place, and method of pursuit. The patients preferred giant steps to ordinary ones, large bites to small ones" (Peven & Shulman, 1983, p. 8).

But sometimes the goal is "too high up" as in the young man whose *Rorschach* report reads: "His main goal in life is to become the most amazing person in the world."

3. Covert Rebellion against the Obligation to Achieve

Although achievement was a dominant goal for the bipolars studied, they seemed to harbor resentment toward it. Overt or covert opposition to the burden of achievement was always present.

The summary of the Family Constellation of one patient reads, "He accepted the family value that one had to achieve all the time, even when he didn't want to." The psychologist's interpretation of this patient's *Rorschach* states, "He views himself as being called upon to accomplish special feats, but he does not want to be pushed around by life; he wants unlimited freedom."

Even when bipolars are angry about the necessity, they cannot permit themselves to stop achieving.

> Perhaps one reason achievement becomes burdensome is the fact that true achievement is most often a gradual, step-by-step process over time—a time sequence bipolars can hardly tolerate since they are characterized by the trait of impatience. As mentioned above, when bipolars are manic they act as if the success were imminent. The achievement is considered either complete and the burden is lifted or, as in the depression, the burden has returned heavier than ever and paralyzed the bipolar. (Peven & Shulman, 1983, p. 8)

4. Birth Order

Firstborn and only children were overrepresented in the 17 patients. Thirteen of the 17 were either firstborn or only children. (All six women were firstborn or only children.) This factor has been found in other studies (Berman, 1933) and begs the question: If some kind of physiological causality does occur, why does it appear to morbidly affect firstborns more than others?

> The achievement orientation of firstborn children has been cited by several investigators (Altus, 1970; Fakouri, 1974). . . . Perhaps the reason firstborn and only children are overrepresented . . . is that these . . . children are also more likely to have a high desire for parental approval. Thus, firstborns may feel less free to reject the values and tasks their parents assign to them. They may feel rebellious, but are less able to disregard the parental injunction that achievement is important. (Peven & Shulman, 1983, p. 9)

5. Cognitive Styles

Two common cognitive styles were found in the patient group: sharpening (versus leveling) and a high internal locus of control (versus an external locus of control). Those people who tend to minimize differences between two similarly viewed figures are called *levelers.* Those who accentuate differences are called *sharpeners.* Holzman and Gardner (1960) found that sharpeners are more open to new experiences, are willing to expend great effort to get what they want, and show more emotional intensity (than levelers). Peven and Shulman (1983) believed bipolars are sharpeners because they always demonstrate emotional intensity.

Sharpening fits also with the bipolars' search for excitement and extroversion. One of B's early recollections demonstrates this trait.

> Age 5: I went to Florida with my parents to visit some friends. I was playing around the house and I heard the dog barking at something and I saw it was a rattlesnake. I just stood there terrified. The man came out with a shotgun and yelled "get away!" He shot the snake and picked it up on a pitchfork while it was still moving. He said, "They don't stop moving until sundown." It was a grand experience. I was exhilarated.

According to Rotter (1975), people with an internal locus of control see themselves as the responsible agents for the events of their lives and allocate excessive responsibility to themselves. In mania, bipolars attribute great power to themselves; in depression, they attribute exaggerated failures to themselves. This seems to fit Adler's idea that bipolars alternate between feelings of powerlessness and exaltation, and that they start projects enthusiastically and lose interest quickly.

6. The Value of Excitement

Zuckerman (1979) called the tendency to always seek out high levels of excitement the *sensation-seeking motive.* Adlerians would see this behavior as movement toward the goal of excitement.

> In clinical studies Zuckerman found this motive associated with hypomania, impulsiveness, and overactivity. . . . It follows that

people who use feeling in this way will seek out feeling experiences. But bipolars value excitement so much that they intensify these experiences until they provide the amount of emotional arousal with which they feel most comfortable. (Peven & Shulman, 1983, p. 10)

The early recollection about the rattlesnake is an example of the high priority given to excitement. Another example is the early recollection of M, the young man who played toreador in the street:

Age 7: My aunt, uncle, cousin, and all my family piled into the station wagon and went to Riverview (an amusement park). I had never seen Riverview, let alone at night when it was all lit up. It was very exciting to me. I said, "This is heaven!" Everybody laughed but I was very, very excited and enthralled.

7. Extremism

Adler believed that one of the mistakes neurotic people make is to see the world in terms of concrete opposites. Antithetical thinking does not allow for shades of gray; things are either black or white, good or evil, and these kinds of cognitions lead to maladaptive behavior. Kurt Adler believed this tendency to be present in the bipolars' emotions and behavior as well as their cognition: "[They] appear to take literally the 'all' in the 'all or nothing' proposition. . . . The effort usually fails, as does the gambler's when he puts all his money on one horse in a desperate attempt to recoup his losses" (K. Adler, 1961, p. 60).

One patient decided to be a coin collector. He through himself into the activity to the extent that he bought them in huge quantities, attended every exhibition, visited all the dealers, and filled a whole room in his house. Then he lost interest and stopped the activity altogether.

Bipolars are either-or people. They throw themselves into life or just as intensely shrink from it. Kurt Adler pointed out that the seemingly contradictory behavior has a singleness of purpose—the pursuit of personal superiority through impressive achievements. But, "they never really believe in themselves, [and] they negate reality at the use of a delusion . . . either by foreseeing that everything will be wonderful and that [they] can do anything . . . [or] that everything will be dismal and that [they] can do nothing . . ." (K. Adler, 1961, p. 60). This extremism is exemplified in the Family Constellation Summary of one of the young men previously mentioned; it is an example of early training in extremism.

An only child who grew up in a family with an authoritarian, distance-keeping father and a sweet, close, giving mother. The atmosphere was one of extremes and stressed the closeness to mother and the distance from father. He was both pampered and felt deprived; and while father required accomplishments, mother accepted him as he was.

Bipolars see themselves as first or last, Caesar or nobody.

Their behavior is like Don Quixote who managed to live in the world as a heroic knight even though the age of chivalry was past. He would either attack windmills forcefully or lie under a tree unmoving and claim to be enchanted. (Peven & Shulman, 1983, p. 12)

Another of the men previously mentioned described himself in extremes by saying, "I was very skinny until I was eight and then I became very fat." He talked about school in the same manner—"Sometimes I got an A, and sometimes I flunked."

Peven and Shulman (1983) saw the extremism of the bipolar as a response style. It is the way bipolars respond to the responsibilities of life and is another way to understand the cyclical nature of the illness.

8. Inept Feelings and the Desire to Impress

Both Adlers believed that bipolars do not really believe in their own competence. The goal of achievement is set too high, and since they are unable to reach their goals they feel inadequate and try to compensate. One way in which they compensate is to try to impress others with their greatness. The *Rorschach* of one man states this very clearly:

Mr. T uses a snow job to impress people when he cannot deliver the goods. He uses a verbal smoke screen from unconventional areas of knowledge to impress others while disguising his inability to understand and deal with what is really going on around him. By attracting attention to the esoteric, he can distract others from the fact that he produces very little by common sense standards and can bamboozle others into regarding him as a whiz. He creates for himself a substitute world of achievement and power, with grandiose future plans, which he may believe himself, but which are hardly convincing to someone who looks for the evidence . . . by selecting areas difficult to put to the test, he enjoys the liberty of taking the benefit of the doubt about power and achievement, and believing that he is superior to others.

He may make a good beginning, but fails in the follow through.

The world for Mr. T is both strange and frightening; he feels small and overpowered in it. He is at the bottom, and the only way he feels he can make it up is through power and prestige.

He is a discouraged person who sees others as either above or below him (in power, prestige, and achievement), and he is a long way from the top. He has given up trying to reach the top through conventional channels . . . and is reaching for magic. . . . He relieves the discouragement by entertaining grandiose plans and substituting fictitious prestige and achievements. (Testing done by Bede Smith, Ph.D.)

This *Rorschach* interpretation of a 28-year-old man reads like an analysis of bipolar disorder as understood from an Adlerian viewpoint. In the face of high achievement goals, bipolars feel inadequate, and they attempt to compensate for feelings of inferiority by impressing others with grandiose plans. The plans serve as substitutes for real achievement, for bipolars are concerned with the impression they make on others. They need people for their purposes and do not isolate or withdraw as schizophrenics do. They demonstrate little social interest, however, as their desire for approval is for the recognition of their own importance and not about concern for others. (Yet they are often warm, compassionate friends.) The early memory of S demonstrates the kind of relationships bipolars enjoy—impressing others:

Age 9: We had just moved to a new neighborhood and I was with this guy. I told him I was with a gang in my old neighborhood. I had on this great leather jacket and the wind came along and blew my jacket open. There were four little holes in the lining and I told the guy the holes were from shots from a gun. I was hoping he would believe me.

As mentioned above, many writers point to the affiliative tendencies of the bipolars. They say that bipolars, especially in the manic phase, seek out people. In contrast to the schizophrenic, who withdraws from others and seeks to *ex*clude, the manic wants company. They are people-persons. It is as if in order to carry out their plans for living, manics have to *in*clude others (Shulman, 1962; Cohen et al., 1954; Goodwin & Jamison, 1990).

SUMMARY

Peven and Shulman (1983) believed that bipolar disorder may very well be an organ inferiority, a constitutional predisposition to mood swings. Following Adler, however, they argued that the existence of an organ inferiority does not determine behavior. The "creative self," i.e., that which intervenes between the stimuli (heredity and environment) acting on people, and the response to those stimuli is what "determines" behavior. Thus, no matter the "cause" of the disorder, the behavior has psychological significance.

Birth order is not a personality trait, of course. But firstborns, more often than others, are known to be highly achievement oriented, and their overrepresentation in the studied cases is explained in this way. But the desire to achieve prominence, status, and prestige was evident in all cases studied. Bipolars are ambitious people who burden themselves with inappropriate goals of achievement. Their method of operation is an impatient lunge in the general direction of their goal, which often results in failure. The failure does not end the desire to impress; so when they are in the manic phase, they try to overwhelm others with their grandiose plans and fantasies. Because their method of operation does not allow for gradual, straightforward movement, they experience feelings of inferiority at their "failures" and withdraw as if in defeat.

Bipolars do not hold themselves in high regard. They suffer from low self-esteem and the belief that they are the responsible parties (common feelings in a firstborn). Therefore, instead of recognizing their goals and methods as inappropriate, they blame themselves for their failures.

One finding was the discovery that bipolars carry within themselves a deep feeling of rebellion against what they consider the "burden" of impressive achievement. Consider the following *Rorschach*:

> S views himself as called upon to accomplish special feats. He is supposed to be big, but does not feel that he is. The test indicates that he does not really test himself to see whether he has what it takes. Instead, S only goes through the motions while fooling himself into believing that he is making sincere efforts to achieve. His desire is not to be

pushed around by life and to have unlimited freedom. Since he sees life as a struggle (full of hassles), S's immediate goal is to be independent and free of constraints.

But bipolars are not free to throw off the burden because in their limited-range thinking, impulsive and antithetical, they see the world only in concrete opposites. If no grand overwhelming success exists, then only dismal failure occurs. They are people of extremes in what they think, feel, and do.

The relationship between mania and depression is considered.

Mania can be seen as a heightened attempt to achieve impressive feats; depression as the exhausted refusal to participate in life when it denies bipolars their achievement but leaves them still faced with the *burden* of achieving. . . . [We] do not believe that the purpose of mania is to stave off depression nor do we believe that it is the resulting freedom of energy following resolution of depression. For us, *mania . . . is an intensified protest against the "burdensome task."* . . . Mania can be a denial of fear (as Kurt Adler says) as well as a denial of sadness (as Freud says). One may attack a challenge when one feels inept or fears defeat, but one can also attack when one smells success. Given the constitutional predisposition and the characteristic ways of behaving, it is also quite possible that mania can result from being aroused by a success or by pleasant excitement and not knowing when to stop or moderate the arousal. Bipolars, in fact, court the arousal since that is the way they feel most comfortable. (Peven & Shulman, 1983, p. 14) (author's emphases)

CASE EXAMPLE

Case of Martha

The following case history demonstrates many of the psychodynamics explained in this chapter.

Martha was 30 years old when she was hospitalized for the first time under the care of our group private practice. She was brought to the hospital by her husband who recognized her behavior as manic and realized she needed psychiatric care.

The couple, who had a son four years old, had recently moved to the Chicago area because the husband, Paul, had just become the vice-president of a medium-sized corporation in Chicago. They lived in a suburb known for its upward mobility and transiency; as the men moved up the corporate and financial ladders, couples moved out of suburb A up to suburb B.

The women in suburb A were "corporate" minded and had formed social clubs and voluntary organizations designed to help their husbands' upward mobility. The year was 1971, and large socioeconomic sections of the U.S. had not taken up the banner of the 60s revolution.

Martha wanted to "belong," to be like the other women whom she saw as successful wives and mothers. She worked part-time as a teacher to help them "up" financially and joined as many of the women's groups as she could. Within a few months she was not sleeping nights, had no appetite, and felt "shaky and excited all the time." She lost control of her classroom and started calling the women in her groups at all hours trying to "make plans" for all the schemes she had concocted. Soon, the women were bewildered by Martha and began to question her judgment. She was beginning to get periods of crying spells mixed with her hyperactivity and excited state. Martha speaks:

> Paul was out of town on business and I got all involved in the overplanning of the women's groups. I called Bob [the corporate President] in the middle of the night. I realized something was wrong, and I thought I'd better get home to my parents [in Minnesota], so I put Richard [the son] in the car and drove two blocks. I knew right away I couldn't make it, so I went to my girlfriend's house and she saw I wasn't normal and she got me and Richard to sleep by telling me I had to lay down with Richard. I fell asleep immediately.... I hadn't slept in days. She called the office and the President called Paul who came right home and took me to the hospital.
>
> I felt terrible. Paul was trying so hard and I fell apart. I was in the hospital for six weeks and all I wanted was to get out of the hospital. I hadn't accepted it [her illness]. I was determined not to be like my mother.

Family Constellation.   Martha's mother had been diagnosed manic-depressive for many years, and apparently, mother never did get "regulated" on her medications. Although mother had not shown extreme signs of mania or depression in Martha's early years, by the time Martha was a teenager, mother was spending more and more time in the hospital until, by the time I met Martha, the family considered it a good year when mother spent only two or three months in the hospital.

Martha has a sister three years younger, Jeanette, whom she describes [as a child] as "Belligerent. She fought a lot with the other children and didn't want to go to school. She wet the bed and we didn't get along." Jeanette grew up to be an unhappy, unpleasant adult. Married three times, she is now divorced, has moved all over the country from job to job and is currently back in their home town living with her parents.

The family history of Martha and Jeanette also includes a maternal grandfather who committed suicide by hanging himself. Such a family history, (grandfather, mother, Jeanette) is characteristic of the primary relatives of those suffering from affective disorders. Although Jeanette may not present with classical bipolar signs, she does suffer the irritability and restlessness that is common to subaffective mood disorders (Akiskal, 1989).

While Martha was in the hospital in 1971 she was treated with phenothiazines and discharged after six weeks, already started on a downward turn toward depression. Within a few weeks she

> . . . got depressed because things weren't all well [perfect]
> and I took all my pills at once. Paul took me to the hospital
> where they pumped my stomach, and then I was back in
> your hospital for three weeks.

Martha recovered from that bout of depression and neither was seen nor did she need treatment for 10 years.

Then, in 1982, Paul noticed a change in Martha's behavior and brought her back into treatment. The records show she was "high" and was put on phenothiazines for a while, but it was not until 1984 that Martha was hospitalized again as "manic." She began psychotherapy with me at that time and also was seen by a psychiatrist for medication.

My major problem during Martha's therapy was to get her to accept the fact of her illness. She had grown up with two "difficult" women and was considered the "star" of her family, the "good girl" who did everything right. She had no room in her self-image for being "sick." A summary of her Family Constellation reads as follows:

The older of two girls who stayed in the number one position by being the kind of child the parents wanted: a "good girl scout." Sister was discouraged and found her place by being the angry baby. The children were expected to have a "smile on their face and a song in their hearts" because the family values were to have a nice disposition and conduct yourself properly and constructively. The good opinion of others was also important.

The family atmosphere was warm and affectionate, and the people were concerned about each other. Father guided the family as a benevolent authority because he knew what was "right" and had the final say over the kindly but "sick" mother.

Martha took the family values seriously and tried to do the right thing and to please others. She became "Miss Goody Two-Shoes."

Martha's Early Recollections.   Some of Martha's 1971 early recollections were as follows:

Age 4:   I was swinging in a swing from the cottonwood tree. Grandmother was swinging me . . . long, huge, soaring swings so that I could look out over everything. Grandmother was saying she would go to town and buy groceries and every time she pulled me back she would tell me another grocery she'd buy . . . bread . . . butter . . . milk. . . . Long, huge, majestic swings to swing out as far as I want to. Warm and all engulfing. A soaring feeling.

Age 6:   There was a big bonfire. Father had roasted wieners and marshmallows and all the neighborhood kids were there. We put together all the leaves and piled them high and there was the smell of the bonfire and all the kids jumping on the leaves. Happy and excited and romantic.

Age 8:   Father ran the town movie projector. A bunch of us went to father's movie house on Saturday night. The popcorn girl was making popcorn. We all held hands while one person touched the machine because it had a short in it so the shock from the machine went around everybody and through everybody. I was frightened. I was not enjoying the fun. I was frightened, but everybody else thought it was fun.

Age 8:   It was gym and everybody chose up teams for the softball team, and I was the very last person chosen. Sports was not my thing, but I was crushed. Nobody wanted me, neither team wanted me. It was important to be popular. I felt humiliated.

Summary of the Early Recollections.   "I want life to be beautiful, everybody to be happy and have a good time, and life to go smoothly. (Life should be like a picnic.) When life becomes unpleasant I suffer and I don't know what to do."

Discussion of Case.   Out of the summary of the Family Constellations and the summary of the Early Recollections were found three self-defeating apperceptions:

1. She doesn't even think in terms of being a decision-maker. She is interested only in meeting the requirements and following the directions.
2. She exaggerates the importance of being a "good girl." In fact, this is all she has, and it is the only way she has of solving problems.
3. When being a good girl does not work, she feels completely at a loss and suffers.

In 1971, in the new situation, Martha tried hard to "shine." She wanted so much to do the right thing, to please everybody, to be accepted, that she created a "crisis situation." She stopped sleeping, increased her activity, and developed a manic state. When she believed she had failed completely, she became depressed and attempted suicide.

During the years from 1971 to 1984 when we started psychotherapy together, Martha had given up teaching and had learned not to overtax herself. She and Paul made the difficult decision not to have any more children because they were concerned about Martha's mental health. She was working in an office in a nonmanagement position and was happy there: "I don't have to take any work home."

During the course of a session one day, I casually asked after Paul, and Martha told me he had "non-Hodgkins lymphoma," that it was "under control," and she did her best never to think about it: "It's very background, and I don't pay any attention to it," and she didn't have to for over four years. (More about this later.)

In March, 1985, my notes read: "She wonders why she cycles. We agree that too much stimuli for her sets her off, and she says, "Any time I'm in a group situation and I have to find my place in the group, it's a difficult situation for me.'"' This is reminiscent of one of her early recollections where she wasn't chosen. By then, she understood this constitutes stress for her. In June of 1985 her son graduated from high school, both her family and Paul's came in and stayed with her, the toilet broke down, her car stopped running, and she "got high." Paul called and she was put on phenothiazines again for several weeks.

Paul began to notice "differences" in her and was concerned that she was "going crazy" again. But Martha and I dug deeply and discovered she was literally changing her lifestyle: She no longer believed she had to please everybody. She did not believe that she had to say "yes" to anything asked of her, and always be a "good girl." She started to do more of what she pleased, and Paul found it disconcerting although it was not a threat to the marriage. An early recollection from that time shows her admitting "nasty" feelings:

> *Age 7:* My sister had done something, and I said to my grandmother, "I hate her." My grandmother said, "No you don't, you love her, she's your sister." I knew my grandmother was wrong and that I really did hate her.

In September, 1985, Martha came in looking dull and bleary and complained of feeling anergic. She said, "I'm a little down right now, but it's not a problem." Yet my notes read, "I think she's more than a little depressed and (maybe) going to get worse." By October she was reporting early morning awakening, loss of appetite, low energy, social withdrawal, and inability to concentrate. At this point, we wrestled each other to the ground.

Martha always had resisted taking lithium, the medicine of choice for bipolar disorder. (The latest research is directed toward the use of anticonvulsant medication for the treatment of bipolar disorder [pope, 1994].) She was still "very hung up on the embarrassment and shame of her "mental illness'." I begged and entreated her to treat herself as if she had any other illness, like diabetes, for example, where she would have to be on insulin. I said she had to finally accept the fact that she cycled *like mother* and had to take medicine *like mother* whether she liked it or wanted it or not.

Martha struggled and evaded; I pleaded, cajoled, and threatened. She started to cry and finally agreed to start lithium and other medicines as prescribed by a physician. By December, 1985, she was "neither up nor down," and she has continued in this mode for many years. Her lithium level stayed between 0.76 and 0.95 (therapeutic level is between 0.75 and 1.50), and she managed to go through some unpleasant situations without cycling too high or too low.

Suddenly, in the fall of 1986, Paul's lymphoma took a bad turn. Martha reported it to me but said she "preferred not to think about it." Yet all during 1986 and 1987 Paul kept getting worse and failed to respond for any length of time to more and more drastic treatment. Martha came to see me more often and, in an interesting development, she became even more open and honest. She stopped denying her fears about Paul's illness and told me of her real doubts and worries. She confessed she had never liked her mother, only her father, and really hated being on medicine because it made her think of her mother. She couldn't understand why she was without medicine or treatment of any kind for 10 years and then began to cycle again.

Paul kept getting worse until by February of 1988 Martha and I were discussing what she would do if Paul died. Paul did die in October of 1988, and my notes throughout 1988 and 1989 consistently read, "She is doing very well." She managed the death, the funeral arrangements, the burial, and the grieving with extreme grace under pressure and watched herself carefully for any untoward signs of depression or mania.

By 1990 Martha had not cycled for five years, although she did have a grief reaction after Paul died. Her mother, however, had been hospitalized for several months every year. Martha had made a good adjustment to her single, widowed life. Paul had left her well provided for, she had friends, and her son finished graduate school.

In 1990, Martha was almost 50 years old. She talked about wanting to be free of all constraints and burdens and said she was enjoying the freedom from responsibility she was experiencing and had no desire to accommodate herself to others. Martha had developed a belief in herself and was no longer frightened of being like mother. At that time she watched herself closely, got plenty of rest, and was living a somewhat quiet, relaxed life. She had hired a financial advisor and was pleased with her financial situation. And then . . .

Paul had been dead for several years when Martha decided she would try her hand at singles groups. She went to a Parents Without Partners meeting, and the first night there she met Frank, a divorced man, who instantly was attracted to her. He courted her assiduously; she went out with him and told me she thought his manners were "coarse." But Frank was persistent, and Martha was flattered and excited. Within a relatively short period of time they were planning marriage.

I felt ambivalent. I was happy for Martha because she felt loved and wanted and curious because Frank's behavior as she described it sounded "strange."

Why did Frank's children not speak to him? Why was he not working? Why didn't he have any money? And why did Richard "hate" Frank? Like most bipolars, Martha had trouble being analytical, and she was enjoying her feelings. Although I asked to meet Frank, he did not want to come to the office.

Martha and Frank were married, and within a few months, there was trouble. While he was courting her, Frank was kind, considerate, thoughtful, and flattering. Shortly after the wedding, Martha began telling me that Frank would go into rages late at night and scream at her for hours. It seems Frank had a violent temper and was secretly drinking. He frequently complained about Richard, and Richard did likewise about Frank. Martha never had been treated like that before and did not know what to make of such behavior. Within six months, Martha was hospitalized "high" but left the hospital within one week. Then she lost her job.

Martha had told Frank about her disorder, but he did not understand and did not change his behavior. Drinking and fighting continued. Finally, Martha threatened Frank with divorce, and he agreed to marriage counseling on the condition that they go to a mental health center near their home. (I had moved my office, and now we are more than an hour's drive apart.) Martha agreed and since that time we have kept in touch by telephone.

The last time we talked, Martha reported that she had a new job as a secretary in a large institution. She had been hospitalized three times in the last two years and was now on heavy medication. Richard had his first job since graduate school, Martha's mother had not been hospitalized in a year, and Frank's behavior had "improved." She was glad to hear from me and said that she was "happy" and that she and Frank were "doing fine."

In the first edition of this book (Peven, 1992), I reported the early recollections that I collected from Martha in 1990. They were as follows:

Age 3:   There was a big, huge tree with a long swing attached, and my grandmother pushed me and told me she was going to take me to places like Japan and Ireland, and China [different from the food of the first time] and all those places that the swing could take me. I knew she loved me. It was fun and there were no rules; you're on your own.

I can go wherever I want and do whatever I want. There are no rules. I'm getting help from someone who loves me so I can do what I want.

Age 7:   My dad had built cupboards in the bathroom and had put in the towels and linens. My sister and I got in there and we hid there and scrambled up and down. We climbed and crawled around the cabinet. I had a great sense of freedom.

Age 7:   It was the middle of winter and we lived up on a hill. They closed the streets and there was no traffic. Lots of kids, and my father, and we took sled rides. We went clear to the top and all the way to the bottom even to the railway tracks. It was fun.

At that time, I suggested that these new recollections showed that Martha felt her burden relieved, that she no longer had to please in order to fit in, and that she had stopped trying to accommodate herself to others. Then I wrote the following:

> I don't believe Martha has completely conquered her bipolar illness: Her early recollection about the swing compels me to see symbolic significance in the glorious, soaring feelings she enjoys as she hovers over the world. . . . I am concerned that if she ever loosens up her control of herself, she might climb into mania again. (Peven, 1992, p. 117)

Unfortunately, I was right.

Under continual stress, Martha was unable to accommodate herself. As long as she lived a relatively quiet, subdued life and continued maintenance medication, her moods did not cycle. The stress of continually troubled marriage, under pressures that would not cease and over which she had no control, the circuits overloaded, and it is not surprising that the built-in cycling system was activated. Martha is a gentle, quiet woman by nature, and I believe that she was genuinely startled to be living with a man who kept the emotional intensity so high. Perhaps it is not so surprising.

Earlier in this chapter I discussed how much bipolars value excitement, and Martha may well find this relationship exciting. Fighting is one method some people use to maintain intimacy. It certainly keeps many people involved with each other, and, if nothing else, it keeps up the emotional arousal, a condition comfortable for bipolars. Martha's first husband, Paul, was a quiet, educated, unemotional, rational man, whereas her second husband, Frank, is loud, much more sexually intense, uneducated, somewhat coarse, and expresses himself in rather vulgar terms; Martha went from one extreme to another. Lastly, I think Martha is a mischief maker and secretly is enjoying herself. (See the last Early Recollections.)

Perhaps I overemphasize the importance of the swing recollection. Yet, 4 of the 17 people Shulman and I studied had swing recollections, and it is tempting to believe that the back and forth, up and down, soaring, swinging feeling exhibited in a swing memory is symbolic of the mood swings of the bipolar. In the literature, Kohut mentioned a swing dream from a bipolar patient:

> The patient is on a swing, swinging forward and backward, higher and higher—yet there is never a serious danger of the patient's flying off. . . . [the] narcissistic transference protected the patient against a potentially dangerous overstimulation of the ego (a hypomanic state) . . . an overstimulation that had become a threat as a result of the mobilization of archaic exhibitionistic libido during analysis. (Kohut, 1971, p. 110)

Apparently, we both agree that swinging back and forth is a feeling that is common to bipolars. But, as an Individual Psychologist, I would understand this dream as a warning that the patient is going to start cycling and caution is advised.

Summary.   Martha's case illustrates the interplay between a physiological disorder and personality factors. A firstborn girl born into a family with first-degree relative suffering from mood disorders, Martha took as her goal to be the "goodest" girl in the world. This inhibited her problem-solving ability since she was only able to see the world in terms of doing the "right thing" and impressing others with her goodness or, failing that, disaster—the extremism at work. During stressful life situations (the original move into suburb A and the current marriage), she tries harder and becomes emotionally aroused (the inherited factor). The cycling starts.

Martha's case also demonstrates the beneficial use of psychotherapy in mood disturbances. During psychotherapy, Martha learned to regard her bipolar disorder as an illness and to treat herself accordingly. She did stop seeing the world in concrete opposites and became able to qualify and make gradations. As much as she loved Paul (and she did), she did not turn his death into a disaster.

Martha decided she was lonely, however, and tired of living alone and taking care of herself. When a man pursued her, she saw a way out. Disregarding common sense in a typical impulsive bipolar fashion, Martha moved into a marriage in spite of her misgivings and the caution of her therapist. When Frank came out of the closet as an alcoholic with a rather violent temper, Martha, true to her lifestyle, could only try harder to be "gooder" and started cycling (swinging) again. She has stopped individual psychotherapy and accommodated herself to the marriage at the cost of continual cycling.

Finally, I would like to take under consideration the survival value of bipolar disorder. Is the bipolar disorder a pathological deviation of a normal adaptive mechanism? Does mania (or hypomania) have survival value?

> Every social organization needs enthusiastic, energetic members who help to motivate others. Enthusiasm in behavior, facial expression, and tone of voice can arouse and motivate. Perhaps we should give thanks to our ancestor of the ice age who looked around one chilly day and enthusiastically said to his fellows, "I know a great place down south. Why don't we pack up and move down there and get out of this cold?" (Peven & Shulman, 1983, p. 15)

REFERENCES

Abraham, K. (1957). *Selected papers of Karl Abraham*. New York: Basic Books.

Adler, A. (1964). *Problems of neurosis*. New York: Harper & Row

Adler, A. (1968). *The practice and theory of Individual Psychology*. Towota, NJ: Littlefield, Adams.

Adler, K. (1961). Depression in the light of Individual Psychology. *Journal of Individual Psychology, 17*, 56–67.

Akiskal, H. (1989). New insights into the nature and heterogeneity of mood disorders. *Journal of Clinical Psychiatry, 50*, 5.

Akiskal, H., Djenderedjian, A., Rosenthal, R., & Khani, M. (1977). Cyclothymic disorder: Validating criteria for inclusion in the bipolar affective group. *American Journal of Psychiatry, 134*, 1227–1233.

Altus, W.D. (1970). Marriage and order of birth. *Proceedings of the Annual Convention of the American Psychological Association, 5*, 361–362.

American Psychiatric Association. (1980). *Diagnostic and statistical manual of mental disorders* (3rd ed.). Washington, DC: Author.

American Psychiatric Association. (1987). *Diagnostic and statistical manual of mental disorders* (3rd ed., rev.). Washington, DC: Author.

American Psychiatric Association. (1994). *Diagnostic and statistical manual of mental disorders* (4th ed.). Washington, DC: Author.

Ansbacher, H.L., & Ansbacher, R.R. (Eds.). (1956). *The Individual Psychology of Alfred Adler*. New York: Basic Books.

Avram, A., Mack, A., Forman, L., Brown, R., & Frances, A. (1994). A brief history of psychiatric classification from the ancients to DSM-IV. In S. Romm & R. Friedman (Eds.), *The psychiatric clinics of North America: History of Psychiatry, 17*(3). Philadelphia: W.B. Saunders.

Baker, H., & Baker, M. (1987). Heinz Kohut's self-psychology: An overview. *The American Journal of Psychiatry, 144*, 1.

Beck, A. (1987). Cognitive models of depression. *Journal of Cognitive Psychotherapy: An International Quarterly, 1*, 1.

Berman, H. (1933). Order of birth in manic-depressive reactions. *Psychiatric Quarterly, 7*, 430–435.

Blacker, D., & Tsuang, M. (1992). Contested boundaries of bipolar disorder and the limits of categorical diagnosis in psychiatry. *American Journal of Psychiatry, 149*, 1473–1483.

Blehar, M., Weissman, M., Gershon, E., & Hirschfeld, R. (1988). Family and genetic studies of affective disorders. *Archives of General Psychiatry, 45*, 289–292.

Cohen, M., Baker, G., Cohen, R., & Fromm-Reichmann, F. (1954). An intensive study of twelve cases of manic-depressive psychoses. *Psychiatry, 17*, 103–137.

Ellenberger, H. (1970). *The discovery of the unconscious*. New York: Basic Books.

Fakouri, M.E. (1974). Relationship of birth order, dogmatism, and achievement motivation. *Journal of Individual Psychology, 30*, 216–220.

Freud, S. (1960). Mourning and melancholia. In *Collected papers, Vol. 4* (pp. 152–170). New York: Basic Books.

Goodwin, F.K., & Jamison, K.R. (1990). *Manic-depressive illness*. New York: Oxford Press.

Holzman, P., & Gardner, R. (1960). Leveling and sharpening and memory organization. *Journal of Abnormal and Social Psychology, 61*, 176–180.

Jamison, K. (1994). George Gordon, Lord Byron, 1788–1824 (Images in psychiatry). *American Journal of Psychiatry, 151*, 480.

Kaplan, H., & Sadock, B. (1981). *Modern synopsis: A comprehensive textbook of psychiatry* (3rd ed.). Baltimore: Williams & Wilkins.

Kohut, H. (1971). *The analysis of the self*. Madison, CT: International Universities Press.

Kraepelin, E. (1902). Dementia praecox and manic-depressive disease. In T. Millon (Ed.), *Theories of personality and psychopathology* (3rd ed.). New York: Holt, Rinehart & Winston.

Kretschmer, E. (1936). *Physique and temperament*. London: Routledge and Kegan Paul.

Kyle, N. (1988). Emotions and hemispheric specialization. In K. Hoppe (Ed.), *The psychiatric clinics of North America: Hemispheric specialization, 11*(3). Philadelphia: W. B. Saunders.

Miller, L. (1988). Ego autonomy, creativity, and cognitive style. In K. Hoppe (Ed.), *The psychiatric clinics of North America: Hemispheric specialization, 11*(3). Philadelphia: W. B. Saunders.

Peven, D., & Shulman, B. (1983). The psychodynamics of bipolar affective disorder: Some empirical findings and their implications for cognitive theory. *Individual Psychology, 39*, 2–16.

Pope, H. (1994). An algorithmic approach to mania and depression in bipolar disorder. *Currents in affective illness, XIII*, 5.

Rado, S. (1956). *Psychoanalysis of behavior: Collected papers*. New York: Grune & Stratton.

Rotter, J. (1975). Some problems and misconceptions related to the construct of internal versus external control of reinforcement. *Journal of Consulting and Clinical Psychology, 43*, 56–57.

Science News. (1994, July 1). Gene clues to manic depression emerge. *Science News, 146*, 13.

Sedler, M. (1993). Falret's discovery: The origin of the concept of bipolar affective illness. Translation by M. Sedler & E. Dessain. *American Journal of Psychiatry, 140*(9), 1127–1133.

Shulman, B. (1962). The meaning of people to the schizophrenic and the manic-depressive. *Journal of Individual Psychology, 18*, 151–156.

Simpson, S. Folstein, S., Meyers, D. McMahon, F., Brusco, D. & DePaulo, R. (1993). Bipolar II: The most common bipolar phenotype? *American Journal of Psychiatry, 150*(3), 901.

Sullivan, H. (1954). In H. Perry & M. Gawel (Eds.), *The psychiatric interview* (taken from two lecture series given in 1944–45 and 1945–46) (pp. 94–112). New York: W. W. Norton.

Turns, D. (1978). The epidemiology of major affective disorders. *American Journal of Psychotherapy, 35*, 5–19.

Winokur, G. (1975). Heredity in the affective disorders. In E. Anthony & T. Benedek (Eds.), *Depression and human existence* (pp. 7–20). Boston: Little, Brown.

Winokur, G., Coryell, W., Endicott, J., & Akiskal, H. (1993). Further distinctions between manic-depressive illness (bipolar disorder) and primary depressive disorder (unipolar depression). *American Journal of Psychiatry, 150*, 1176.

Zuckerman, M. (1979). *Sensation seeking: Beyond the optimum level of arousal.* Hillsdale, NJ: Lawrence Erlbaum.

Chapter 5

DEPRESSIVE DISORDERS

Ronald J. Pancner
Carl W. Jylland

When depression is discussed among mental health professionals, profound disagreements often emerge. Some profess that the use of somatic therapy (medication or electroconvulsive therapy) is unnecessary (if not deleterious) to outcome. They reason that depression emerges from limited coping techniques to meet life's challenges and one's perception about life and themselves. Those trained in medical settings (and thus more likely to work with inpatient populations) tend to treat those depressions that profoundly interfere with functioning. They will assert that medications and electroconvulsive therapy are highly effective and should be utilized.

The polarity of these attitudes stems from various factors such as being trained by teachers who were heavily biased toward one approach or the other and later reinforced by selective perceptions of the therapist's experiences in practice. Another factor is the practice setting. Those who primarily have an outpatient practice will usually see milder varieties of depression than the hospital-based practitioner. Since Adlerian psychology is a holistic psychology, the challenge to Adlerian practitioners is to keep all factors in perspective and to recognize that perception affects biochemistry and biochemistry affects perception in formulating an effective treatment approach and understanding of the patient.

Much of the psychiatric literature is devoted to research trying to help determine which depressions are most likely to respond to medications, identifying subgroups that will likely respond to specific classes of medications or psychotherapy, and discovering the biochemical changes occurring in depression. The vast majority of psychiatrists, however, recognize the environmental and perceptual factors in the etiology, and the importance of psychotherapy in successful treatment of depressions.

In any discussion of depression, several factors need to be kept in mind. The first is that depression is a universal affect. In other words, all human beings feel sad or depressed at times. The "feeling" of depression is not an illness. Only when the feeling of depression interferes with functioning does the condition qualify for a diagnosis or become a disorder. Adler recognized this concept by citing that psychopathology exists when people avoid the life tasks—work, social and sex. Avoidance is justified by these individuals either claiming, "Yes, but I'm sick," if neurotic techniques are utilized or saying, "No" and utilizing their own private logic (perceptions without conceptual validation) to excuse themselves when the disorder is psychotic.

A second factor in any discussion of depression is that psychological, psychiatric, and Adlerian literature is often confusing. Older articles usually do not cite where the studied depressive patient group fits in the continuum of symptoms and functional incapacity. In other words, when depression is discussed, it often is not specified whether or not the symptoms fulfill the criteria of melancholia, major depression, dysthymia disorder or cyclothymic disorder, adjustment disorder with depressed mood, etc.

A third factor is that diagnostic criteria have changed markedly in this century and even in the last 10 years. The changes followed research that was conducted in the Untied States and United Kingdom regarding diagnostic concepts. In North America, schizophrenia and character disorder diagnoses were found to be unnecessarily broad (Cooper, Kendall, & Gurland, 1972). Extensive studies of diagnostic liability and validity ultimately resulted in the development of DSM-III. This led to supporting diagnostic decisions by (1) inclusion and exclusion criteria; (2) familial genetic history; (3) considerations of age of onset, premorbid course, and prospective follow-up; and (4) treatment response. This practice is continued in DSM-III-R and DSM-IV. In addition, laboratory tests that provide confirmatory evidence for affective diagnoses are being used increasingly in clinical practice (Akiskal, 1989; Carroll, Feinberg, Greden, Tarika, Albala, Haskett, James, Kronfol, Lohr, Steiner, de Vigne, & Young, 1981).

The difficulty in the diagnosis and treatment of depression is that fundamental symptoms in the spectrum of depression remain very similar. From clinical observation and history alone, those conditions that are likely to respond to medications are often nearly impossible to differentiate. In the DSM-IV are at least 14 mood disorders that include depressive symptoms: normal sadness, normal bereavement, Adjustment Disorder with Depressed Mood, Dysthymic Disorder, Cyclothymic Disorder, Major Depressive Disorder, Depressive Disorder NOS (not otherwise specified), Bipolar I Disorder, Bipolar II Disorder, Bipolar Disorder NOS, as well as Mood Disorder to a General Medical Condition, Substance Induced Mood Disorder, and Organic Affective Syndrome. In addition, there are modifiers as to severity and whether psychotic, melancholic, atypical, or catatonic features are present. There are also course specifiers as to whether there is a seasonal pattern or a postpartum onset to the symptoms. The reason for accurate diagnosis is to minimize patient risk, treatment selection, prognostication, and communication. As an example, now that we have a specific agent for treating bipolar disorder, no longer do these patients need to be exposed to antipsychotics with the risk of tardive dyskinesia. Many psychotic patients who formerly were diagnosed as schizophrenic are now found to fulfill the criteria of psychotic major depression. Many patients who previously were believed to be hypochondriacs, or were diagnosed as having character disorders, are being found to have varieties of depressive illness and treated accordingly. The result has been the broadening of the boundaries of affective disorder (Akiskal & Lemmi, 1983).

STATISTICS: THE EXTENT OF THE PROBLEM

Depression is by far the most common psychiatric disorder in this country and is a major public health problem. Weissman, Klerman, Prusoff, Sholomskas, and Padian (1981) reported studying a community in Connecticut that at any one point in time, three percent of the population met the criteria of major depression with an approximate lifetime risk of up to 20%. Bipolar disorder was much less common, with only one percent lifetime risk. In any six-month period, four percent of all women and two percent of all men could be diagnosed as having major depression. In addition, an equal proportion could be diagnosed as having dysthymia. The highest prevalence for both sexes tended to be in the young and middle adult years with a drop-off in frequency after age 65 (Myers, Weissman, & Tischler, 1984; Weissman & Boyd, 1982). However, this may be due to underrecognition; various studies more recently have reported prevalence rates from 25% to 50% of some depressive symptoms.

No clear relationship exists between the syndrome of major depression and social class or race. The prevalence of bipolar disorder is less, 0.6 to 0.9 percent, with the male to female ratio as 1:1.2.

Several risk factors for major depression have been reported. The two most powerful risk factors for major depression are being female and having a family history of depressive illness (Hirschfeld & Cross, 1982). Studies of stressful life events have found that depressed patients tend to have an excess of negative events, particularly losses, in the six months prior to the onset of depression. Such events increase the relative risk of depression by a factor of 6.5 (Paykel, 1978). Loss of a parent because of death or separation during childhood, long considered a predisposing factor to a major depression, has not been substantiated by empirical research. However, major depression occurs most often in persons who have no close interpersonal relationships and are divorced or separated. Studies of recovered persons with major depression have often shown a dependent, emotionally unstable, and introverted personality (Hirschfeld, Klerman, & Clayton, 1983).

Mortality is high with an estimated 15% suicide risk for recurrent depressions (Robins & Guze, 1970). Moreover, studies indicate a high rate of cardiovascular disease in depressives. Depressives often utilize the health care system heavily, seeking relief for their often vague somatic distress such as stomachaches and headaches. The majority of depressives, however, are not treated. Only 33% are seen by physicians and mental health professionals, and only 6% are treated by psychiatrists. This is unfortunate, since many studies have shown that effective treatment is available.

Depression is one of the most common mental disorders, affecting an estimated 10 to 12% of the population in this country. This figure does not include the normal bereavement and adjustment disorders with depressed mood (Regier, Narrow, Rae, Manderscheid, Locke, & Goodwin, 1993).

MAJOR DEPRESSION

Diagnosis—DSM-IV

Depression can be understood best as a spectrum condition. The symptoms of depression can be a normal human condition designated in DSM-IV as normal bereavement (for example, when a loss occurs of a love object, such as the death or separation from a loved one, or loss of status or position). At the other end of the spectrum is major depression, where the person has marked impairment of functioning and may exhibit psychotic symptoms, such as delusions and hallucination, and marked physiological manifestations, such as psychomotor slowing or agitation and constipation. Accurate diagnosis is often difficult because the distinction among groups is often slight.

The category of major depression in all probability does not delineate one illness but rather a symptom cluster as a manifestation of a group of illnesses. Probably several etiologies are involved in major depression. In DSM-IV, the criteria for major depressive episode include the presence of either (1) depressed mood, which can express itself in irritability in children and/or adolescents, or (2) markedly diminished interest or pleasure in almost all activities. One of these symptoms must have been present for at least two weeks and represent a change from previous function.

Additional symptoms need to be present for the same two-week period— (3) significant weight loss or weight gain, (4) insomnia or hypersomnia, and (5) psychomotor agitation or retardation. The symptom needs to be observed by others and not be merely a subjective feeling. Also, (6) a fatigue or loss of energy; (7) feelings of worthlessness or excessive or inappropriate guilt may occur, which need to be beyond merely self-reproach or guilt for being ill and may reach delusional proportions; (8) a diminished ability to think or concentrate and indecisiveness; or (9) recurrent thoughts of death, including recurrent suicidal ideation with or without a specific plan or a suicide attempt. The preceding symptoms need to be present most of the day nearly every day. A total of five of the above factors need to be present for the diagnosis of major depressive episode. In addition, the symptoms cause significant distress in occupational, social, or other important areas of functioning.

Exclusion criteria are first, that an organic factor cannot be established that would account for the initiation and maintenance of the disturbance including a general medical condition or the physiological effects of a substance (drug abuse or medication) and second, that the disturbance is not a normal reaction to the death of a loved one (uncomplicated bereavement). A morbid preoccupation with worthlessness, suicidal ideation, impairment of function, or psychomotor retardation over two months, however, would suggest bereavement complicated by a major depression. At no time during the disturbance would delusions or hallucinations have been present for as long as two weeks in the absence of prominent affective symptoms.

Lastly, these symptoms are not superimposed on either schizophrenia, schizophreniform disorder, delusional disorder, or psychotic disorder not otherwise specified.

Major depression is a category that encompasses several conditions previously diagnosed separately such as involutional depression, psychotic depression,

unipolar affective disease, and some more severe forms of psychoneurotic depressive reaction. Major depression can further be subclassified into mild, moderate, severe without psychotic features, severe with psychotic features, with catatonic features, with melancholic features, with atypical features, with postpartum
onset, and with seasonal pattern. The term "double depression" is also found in
the literature but not in DSM-IV. It refers to those patients who have an underlying
chronic depression with a superimposed major depressive episode. The prognosis
for this group is relatively unfavorable, with remission of both chronic and acute
symptoms being only one-half as likely as from major depression alone. Thirty-
nine percent of double depressives recovered after two years, compared with
79% for depression alone. The relapse rate also is twice as frequent among those
with double depression who do recover (Keller, Lavori, & Endicott, 1983).

Subtypes of Major Depressive Disorders

The DSM-III-R was modified from the DSM-III by adding seasonality and
reformulating endogenous depression into a subheading of melancholia. This
was done to eliminate etiologic implications. The DSM-IV also required that the
diagnostician delineate between summer and winter seasonal pattern.

The diagnostic criteria for the melancholic type of major depressive episode
include either (a) loss of interest or pleasure in almost all activity; (b) lack of
reactivity to usual pleasurable stimuli; and at least three of the following: (a)
does not feel better even temporarily; (b) the depression has diurnal variation,
namely, the depressive feels worse in the morning; (c) has early morning waking
at least two hours before the usual time of wakening; (d) psychomotor retardation
or agitation is observable and not based solely on subjective complaints; (e)
significant anorexia or weight loss occurs which equals more than five percent
of body weight in a month; (f) excessive or inappropriate guilt.

Obviously many of these symptoms are found in non-melancholic depressions as well. Those symptoms most characteristic of melancholia are the lack
of reactivity and the psychomotor changes.

Haslam and Beck (1994) have analyzed five subtypes of Major Depression.
These included endogenous form, autonomous form, sociotropic form, a hopelessness form and a self-critical form. The authors analyzed 531 personality
profiles of outpatient clients with a primary diagnosis of Major Depression. They
attempted to determine whether the clinical features of the proposed subtypes
co-varied. Significant evidence for discreetness was found only for the endogenous form subtype.

This is further complicated by the high rates of co-morbidity between major depression and dysthymia. Co-occurrence has been found in studies of outpatients, inpatients, and community samples. A high rate of co-morbidity has also been found across the life span from children to adulthood (Klein & Salisbury-Kelly, 1993).

Psychotic Features

The diagnostic criteria for psychotic features requires delusions and/or hallucinations. These features need to be further categorized into either mood congruent or incongruent. Mood congruent psychotic depression requires delusions and/or hallucinations with mood congruent content. The themes of the delusions would be personal inadequacy, deserved punishment, guilt, and/or nihilism. To receive a diagnosis of psychotic depression with mood incongruent features, the delusions and hallucinations must be inconsistent with a depressed mood. Examples are thought broadcasting, thought projection, delusions of persecution (not related to depressive themes and delusions of control).

Those patients who are psychotic have recovery rates essentially the same as non-psychotic, depressed patients. However, they tend to recover more slowly and have lower short-term (six-month) recovery rates (Coryell, Lavori, & Endicott, 1984).

Seasonal Pattern Specifier

The seasonal nature of moods has long been known to man, and references to that phenomenon can be found in ancient writings. Modern-day evidence demonstrates that attacks of mania are more frequent in the summer, while hospitalizations for depression are relatively more common in the late spring. Only in recent years has this syndrome been investigated systematically (Rosenthal, Sack, & Gillin, 1984). The winter-type seasonal pattern appears to be more common and increases with higher latitudes. Women comprise the majority of individuals experiencing seasonal pattern comprising 60 to 90% and younger persons appear to be at higher risk for winter-depressive episodes. Winter seasonal pattern depression usually begins in October and November and has an atypical depressive symptom such as hyper-somnia, carbohydrate craving, lack of energy, and weight gain, along with typical features of hopelessness, suicidal thoughts, decreased libido, and social withdrawal. Usually considerable functioning impairment is associated.

The onset appears to occur in the second and third decades of life and the patients appear to be predominately women with the symptoms of Bipolar II illness (depression with hypomanic episodes). Depressions usually begin in October or November and have atypical depressive symptoms such as hypersomnia, carbohydrate craving, lack of energy, and weight gain, along with typical features.

Successful treatment of this syndrome includes exposure to high intensity (2,500 lux) light for two hours in the morning immediately upon arising or 10,000 lux for 30 minutes. Improvement often occurs within one week (Lewy, 1987; Rosenthal, 1993).

Atypical Features

Identifying a type of depression with atypical features is the result of research that indicated patients with symptoms referred to as hysteroid dysphoria or reverse vegetative symptoms had an improved therapeutic response with monoamine oxidase inhibitors compared to tricyclic antidepressants. The symptoms must include a mood reactivity (i.e., the mood brightens in response to actual or potential positive events), and two of the following features must be present most of the time for at least two weeks: 1) significant weight gain or increase in appetite; 2) hypersomnia—sleeping more than usual; 3) leaden paralysis defined as a heavy feeling in the arms or legs as if they were lead; 4) a long-standing pattern of sensitivity to interpersonal rejection, not limited to episodes of mood disturbance, which results in significant social or occupational impairment. If melancholic or catatonic features exist, then the criteria for atypical features are not met, (Quitkin, McGrath, & Stewart, 1989; Workman & Short, 1993).

Catatonic Feature Specifier

Having the catatonic feature specifier to mood disorders brings into focus that catatonic states are not only found in schizophrenia but also found with major depression, bipolar disorder, and medical conditions. Thus, catatonic symptoms do not imply a specific diagnosis. In all probability, the presence of these features in mood disorders will have prognostic and treatment significance in the future.

Catatonic features criteria include a clinical picture dominated by at least two of the following: (a) motoric immobilities such as catalepsy (waxy flexibility) or stupor; (b) excessive motor activity that seems purposeless and not influenced by external stimuli; (c) mutism or extreme negativism showing a resistance to all instructions and maintaining a rigid posture against all attempts to be moved; (d) stereotyped movements or peculiarities of voluntary movement as evidenced by posturing in which the person assumes inappropriate or bizarre postures voluntarily; and (e) echolalia (the apparent senseless repetition of a word or phrase just spoken by another) or echopraxia (a repetitive imitation of a movement of another).

This condition can lead to danger to self or others either in stupor or in excitement. The consequences include malnutrition, exhaustion, or self-inflicted injury.

Postpartum Onset Specifier

If a mood disturbance occurs within four weeks after giving birth, the use of postpartum onset specifier should be used. The mothers so afflicted usually have thoughts of harming themselves or the infant. They complain of fatigue, insomnia, restlessness, and have episodes of tearfulness and emotional lability. Later suspiciousness, confusion, obsessive concerns about the baby's health, incoherence and irrational statements occur. In about 50% of the cases, delusions are present—usually that the baby is dead or defective or the birth is denied. Other delusions are the mother claiming to be virginal, unmarried, persecuted, or influenced in some fashion. Hallucinations occur in about 25% of the cases, usually voices telling the mother to kill the baby.

DYSTHYMIC DISORDERS OR DEPRESSIVE MOODS

Dysthymic disorders are not synonymous with the traditional definitions of neurotic depression. Many of the previous neurotic depressions would now be classified starting with DSM-III-R as major depression. There is controversy about the placement of dysthymic disorder with mood disorders because of implied similarities in cause—genetic predisposition, treatment, and prognosis (Klein & Salisberry-Kelly, 1993). Some psychodynamic psychiatrists and psychologists disagree and believe that the disorder is a result of incompletely resolved issues in the psychodynamic development and faulty perception of self and others.

Dysthymic disorder is fairly common, affecting three to five percent of persons but is very high in a clinic setting where it affects between one-third to one-half of all clinic patients. In young adolescents, one study reports a five percent prevalence in girls and eight percent in boys. It is more common in young unmarried persons and those with low income.

Dysthymic disorder is characterized as a chronic condition with nonepisodic symptoms as contrasted to major depression, which is characterized by discreet episodes of symptoms. The symptoms are similar to that of major depression but are generally not as severe in intensity. The age of onset varies from young adolescence to late life and frequently coexists with other psychiatric disorders such as alcohol and drug abuse, anxiety disorders (especially panic disorder), borderline personalities, and major depressive episodes (Markowitz, 1993).

The DSM-IV criteria for dysthymic disorder includes depressed mood (which can express itself as irritable mood in children and adolescents) for most of the day, more days than not, as indicated either by subjective account or the observation of others, for at least two years (one year for children and adolescents). During this period individuals are not without the symptoms of depression or irritable mood for more than two months at a time. While depressed, at least two of the following must be present: (a) poor appetite or overeating, (b) insomnia or hypersomnia, (c) low energy or fatigue, (d) low self-esteem, (e) poor concentration or difficulty making decisions, and (f) feelings of hopelessness. Also, the symptoms must have caused significant distress or impairment in social occupation or other important areas of functioning.

Exclusions criteria are (a) no evidence of an unequivocal major depressive episode during the first two years of the disturbance (one year for children and adolescents)—if that occurred then major depression disorder in partial remission or chronic major depression may better describe the condition; (b) never a manic episode, mixed or hypomanic episode; (c) the lack of symptoms being superimposed on a chronic psychotic disorder such as schizophrenia or delusional disorder; and (d) establishing that the physiological effect of a medication or drug of abuse or a general medical condition initiate and maintain the disturbance. One should note that a previous major depressive episode may have occurred prior to the diagnosis of dysthymic disorder if a full remission had been present for two months before development of the dysthymic disorder. In addition, if a patient fulfills the criteria for dysthymic disorder, a superimposed episode of major depression may occur and in that case both diagnoses are given. This is the double depression previously mentioned.

It has been difficult either to determine the severity of dysthymia or to attempt to predict the client's response to treatment. This is partially due to the fact that most of the instruments utilized to measure severity were originally developed for measuring major depression. The symptoms measured, for example in the HAM-D (*Hamilton Rating Scale for Depression*), are heavily weighted toward vegetative symptoms of depression. The *Beck Depression Inventory* (BDI) was developed to measure acute or episodic depression as opposed to chronic depression. Recently, the 20-item *Cornell Dysthymia Rating Scale* (CDRS) was developed to assist in measuring the degree of severity of dysthymic disorders (Mason, Kocsis, Leon, Thompson, Frances, Morgan, & Parides, 1993).

Unusual Affective Presentations

Depression also can exhibit itself in various "unusual" affective presentations (Akiskal & Lemmi, 1983). These include grief that progresses to melancholia, and melancholia with anxious presentations in which the primary presentations are panic, fear of death, breathlessness, profuse sweating, and nightmares. Also included are somatic presentations in which the person primarily complains of vague somatic complaints such as headache, abdominal discomfort, weakness, and dizzy spells without associated medical findings. Characterological presentations of recurrent affective disorder include repeated romantic or marital failure, substance abuse, job instability, and dilettantism. Pseudo-demented presentation of retarded depression may be diagnosed in some elderly subjects who present with confusion, disorientation, and memory difficulties. They may actually suffer from irreversible affective disorder that responds to antidepressants or electroconvulsive therapy. In presentation of affective psychosis (schizophreniform), some severe depressions show classical schizophrenic symptoms.

Many depressives show obsessive-compulsive symptoms, and some resort to alcohol or other mind-altering drugs for relief. This compounds and complicates the clinical picture and patients' problems. From the complexity of symptomatology and the overlapping with other psychiatric conditions, one can easily understand why considerable research is being done to try to find trait markers and state markers for various depressive syndromes so that the most effective and least risky medication can be utilized.

Differential Diagnosis

The diagnosis of depression is an extremely complicated process. Not only can depression be superimposed on other psychiatric illnesses such as panic disorder or schizophrenia but it also is found frequently with substance abuse, particularly in the withdrawal from alcohol and cocaine. Moreover, depression accompanies many physical illnesses such as endocrine disorders, including those of the pituitary, adrenals, and thyroid; vitamin and mineral deficiencies and excesses; infections, such as hepatitis and tuberculosis; neurological disorders, such as multiple sclerosis; collagen disorders, such as systemic lupus erythematosus; cardiovascular disease, such as myocardial infarction or cerebral ischemia; and also some malignancies.

Further complicating this picture is the presence of several classifications of medications that frequently produce depressive reactions. These include the hormones estrogen and progesterone; the antihypertensives, such as reserpine, propranolol (Inderal), clonidine, and methyldopa; the corticosteroids, such as cortisone; anti-cancer medications, such as Vincristine and Vinblastine; anti-tuberculins, such as cycloserine; and the anti-Parkinsonian medications, such as Levodopa, Carbidopa, and Amantadine.

In addition, except for a history of mania or hypomania, the depressive symptoms of major depression and dysthymia are indistinguishable from those of the bipolar disorders. Obtaining a family history may be helpful to make this differentiation because of genetic predisposition.

Accurate diagnosis is important in ascertaining which treatment is most likely to be effective. The medication armamentarium has multiplied dramatically. The utilization of proper medication when indicated can dramatically shorten the length of suffering and perhaps prevent the dire complication of suicide (Debattista & Schatzberg, 1994; Hirschfeld & Goodwin, 1988). Moreover, psychotherapy has been highly effective in several types of depression (Sotsky, Glass, Shea, Pilkonis, Collins, Elkin, Watkins, Imber, Leber, Moyer, & Oliveri, 1991).

Genetic Studies

Mounting evidence has been that some forms of depression have a genetic factor. Affective disorders that have been the most closely studied genetically, and the most impressive, are those studies of bipolar (manic depressive) illness. A large twin study was accomplished by Bertelson, Harvald, and Hauge (1977) that showed that monozygotic (75%) twin pairs are significantly more likely to be concordant for bipolar illness than dizygotic (17%) twin pairs. Recently a specific gene location of bipolar disorder was found on the short arm of chromosome 11 in a large Amish pedigree (Egeland, Gerhard, & Pauls, 1987); however, with extension of the pedigree and the development of the disorder in additional family members, the statistical association ceased to apply. The conclusion reached from these data by many researchers is that a genetic factor is responsible for bipolar illness and that bipolar disorder is a specific illness, in contrast to major depression, which is a group of disorders.

Research data also include a high concordance rate in unipolar depression: 43% for monozygotic twins and 19% for dizygotic twins. These data, however, are not considered conclusive evidence of the presence of a genetic factor (Bertelson et al., 1977). More recent studies have shown consistently that identical twins are far more concordant for major affective disorder (65 to 75%) than are fraternal twins (14 to 19%). This strongly supports the genetic contribution to vulnerability. Additional evidence from adoption and family pedigree studies confirm these findings; however, the etiology of affective illness is still unknown (Pancner, 1985).

BIOCHEMICAL THEORIES

Biogenic Amine Hypothesis

The biogenic amine hypothesis arose from observations of the effect of various pharmacological substances on patients. Theoretically, depression is linked with disorders in the functioning of two major amine neurotransmitter systems: norepinephrine and serotonin. This theory developed from observations that reserpine caused a depressive syndrome in 10 to 15% of patients and that the medication depleted brain monoamine stores. Also, iproniazid, a medication used to treat tubercular patients, elevated their mood. It is a monamine oxidase inhibitor and thus increases brain monamine concentration. In addition, tricyclic antidepressants (Tofranil, Pamelor, Norpramine, etc.) block the re-uptake of amine neurotransmitters into the presynaptic neurons, and Lithium Carbonate, which is effective in bipolar affective disorders, facilitates monamine re-uptake. The serotonin specific re-uptake inhibitors (Prozac, Zoloft, Paxil) inhibit the re-uptake of serotonin in the synapse. All the above add further evidence of the role of biogenic amines in depression.

Studies have been made on the relationship of serotonin, norepinephrine, and dopamine levels in cerebral spinal fluid (CSF) and in human behavior. A study performed by Traskman, Asberg, Bertilsson, and Sjostrang (1981) on patients who were treated in a hospital emergency room after a suicide attempt found that those who had low serotonin levels in their spinal fluid had a 20% mortality rate by suicide within a year. Depression was more closely related to low levels of the dopamine metabolite, homo-vanillic acid (HVA). Although psychoanalytic theories have suggested an integral association between aggression and depressed states (Freud, 1953), an important point to remember is that not all suicide victims suffer from depression.

Those persons in the psychiatric unit of a naval hospital with diagnosed personality disorders had a robust inverse correlation between aggression, suicide, and levels of a serotonin metabolite, 5-HIAA. In other words, those persons who were admitted because of aggressive behavior and suicide attempts had low serotonin levels, again suggesting a link between aggression and central serotonin mechanisms (Brown, Ebert, & Goyer, 1982).

Low levels of CSF 5-HIAA have been reported in other psychiatric conditions such as alcoholism (Ballenger, Goodwin, & Major, 1979) and obsessive-compulsive disorder (Thoren, Ansberg, & Bertilsson, 1980). These findings may indicate that low levels of the serotonin metabolite are associated with increased vulnerability to a spectrum of psychiatric disturbances and to suicidal behavior and not associated with any specific illness. Depending upon genetic predisposition and/or environmental circumstances, aggressive impulses can lead to psychopathic behavior, excessive drinking, murder, or violent suicide (Georgotos, 1983). This seems to be validated by the SSRI's effectiveness in the treatment of major depression and obsessive-compulsive disorder. There is also preliminary evidence of their effectiveness in bulimia a nervosa, panic disorder, dysthymic disorder, and borderline personality disorder as well.

The recent patient popularity and clinical success of SSRIs should not be confused with across-the-board pharmacological efficacy. While many patients do in fact respond positively to SSRIs, 20% to 30% of the patient population fail to exhibit a substantial response (Nierenberg, 1994). Eleven studies of re-uptake-blocker antidepressants have found that the occurrence of depression relapse is higher in patients who discontinue their medication than in patients who are on a maintenance regime (Littrell, 1994). Relapse becomes a substantial problem for clinicians and clients. Over 50% of patients treated for depression will experience relapse within three months of discontinuing medical treatment. More than 80% will experience recurrence of depression three years following the discontinuation of a maintenance level regime of antidepressants (Fava & Kaji, 1994).

This selective efficacy of the SSRIs and the limitations presented by an apparent need for a maintenance regime of medications points out the complications inherent in treating such a heterogeneous group of disorders. One current attempt to bring order to the treatment of a disorder with distinct pathophysiologies and treatment responses is the development of an algorithm for the treatment of depression (Debattista & Schatzberg, 1994). The algorithm focuses on three subtypes of major depression: melancholia, atypical depression, and psychotic depression. The algorithm also contains a decision tree for recurrent depressive episodes and addresses seasonal depression. The advantage of such an approach is that it provides clear guidelines and criteria to assist in the planning of treatment—this includes clear indicators of when ECT is warranted.

BIOLOGIC TESTS

Whenever a depressed patient is seen, the question is raised, "Is this a biologically-based condition accompanied by a chemical abnormality, or is this a method of coping with a life challenge or loss?" Currently, no lab tests or X-ray imagery that conclusively determine depressive diagnoses are available; nonetheless, several tests have recently been applied to this question.

The most studied and currently utilized test is the *Dexamethasone Suppression Test* (DST). DST abnormalities imply the existence of an imbalance in the hypothalamic-pituitary-adrenal axis (H-P-A). The neurotransmitters implicated in depression, norepinephrine, and serotonin have an effect on hypothalamic hormones. Dexamethasone is a potent glucocorticoid that suppresses ACTH and cortisol production for up to 24 hours. Failure of a single dose to suppress cortisol secretion indicates over-activity of the H-P-A axis. The DST is not a trait marker; it is abnormal only when the person is depressed. An abnormal finding is considered 95% valid in diagnosing a major depression; however, the test only detects 50% of those persons diagnosed as a major depression based on symptom criteria.

Other studies (Targum, 1983) have pointed out that eight percent of nondepressed patients and seven percent of persons diagnosed schizophrenic also have positive *Dexamethasone Suppression Tests*. Similarly, recent studies by the collaborative depression program at the National Institute of Mental Health indicate that the *Dexamethasone Suppression Test* for depression has not been found to have diagnostic specificity. Eight of 77 controls were nonsuppressors, with eight of 16 manic patients, 10 of 37 bipolar patients, and 20 of 74 unipolar depressions demonstrating nonsuppression. Thus the hope that the test would be of diagnostic usefulness was not realized.

A helpful feature of the test is that a person's improvement is reflected in the normalization of the abnormal DST. Those patients who appear to improve clinically, but whose DST is still abnormal, are at high risk of relapse if treatment is discontinued, and their prognosis is poor. This aspect is still clinically useful.

Some medications and disease states interfere with the results of the DST, among which are alcoholism during and after withdrawal, hemodialysis, diabetes mellitus, anorexia nervosa, anticonvulsant medication, and high doses of the benzodiazepines (Valium and related medications). For the majority of the population, however, it remains a useful tool to confirm a biochemical disorder and to decrease guilt and self-blame in the depressive person.

Thyrotropin Releasing Hormone Test

More recently, a correlation between depression and thyroid function has been found. The usual tests that most physicians utilize to test for thyroid dysfunction are within the normal range in depression. *Thyrotropin releasing hormone* (TRH), which is an hypothalamic tripeptide, regulate the release of *thyroid stimulating hormone* (TSH) from the anterior pituitary. Normally, giving TRH to a person will stimulate production of large amounts of TSH; however, in patients with major depression, this response is blunted.

Thirty percent of depressed patients are positive to both the DST and TRH tests; 34% are abnormal on the TRH test alone, and 20% are abnormal only on the DST. The two tests together confirmed 84% of the major unipolar depressive patients with a diagnostic confidence greater than 95% (Gold, Pottash, Extein, & Sweeney, 1981). Only a few false positive results are obtained, excluding alcoholics in withdrawal and hyperthyroidism (Loosen, Prange, Wilson, Lara, & Pettus, 1977).

Although the neurochemical mechanisms for these and other widely-reported neuroendocrine abnormalities in major depression await explanation and do not prove causality, the diagnostic tests described are useful today. Sachar, Asnis, and Halbreich (1980) stated that an abnormal DST can assist in diagnosis, provide information about genetics, and predict treatment response to medication or electroconvulsive therapy. Furthermore, these same tests repeated after treatment can help document response to treatment and help in determining whether the underlying disease is in remission or in an active state, which would leave the patient extremely vulnerable to relapse if medication were stopped.

Serum Antidepressant Levels

In the last few years, serum levels of the antidepressants have been available to clinicians. Studies have found that only 15 to 20% of the depressed patients referred to psychiatrists have had the proper medication prescribed in adequate doses. A Columbia University study treated depressives with dosages usually considered adequate: 200 mg for females; 250 mg for males. The study found 40% of patients were below what was considered therapeutic levels. Moreover, in the elderly, small quantities of medication can produce high serum levels and often toxic symptoms that resemble depression and psychosis. Other studies have shown that 60 to 70% of patients respond to tricyclic medications after two weeks or more, but another 15 to 16% improve if the serum level is adjusted (Pancner, 1985).

Polysomnography

Abnormalities of polygraphically-monitored sleep have been reported consistently in major depression, specifically, the short latency in time from the beginning of sleep to the onset of rapid eye movement (REM); the increased frequency of rapid eye movement during REM sleep (increased REM density); reduced slow wave sleep; a shift in the temporal distribution of REM sleep so that more of it occurs in the early part of the night (shorter REM latency and longer first REM periods); and reduction of sleep, which includes longer latency intermittently awakening at night, early a.m. wakening, and therefore decreased sleep efficiency (Hirschfeld & Goodwin, 1988). Most of these abnormalities, however, lack diagnostic specificity.

Interestingly, well-established studies have shown that total sleep deprivation (Pflug & Tolle, 1971) or deprivation of sleep in the second half of the night (Schilgen & Tolle, 1980) is able to induce remissions in depressed unipolar and bipolar patients temporarily. In fact, shifting the timing of sleep also appears to influence mood. Bipolar and unipolar patients who went to sleep five or six hours earlier than usual are at times relieved of depressive symptoms (Sack, Nurnburger, & Rosenthal, 1985). Such a remission can be sustained for one to two weeks.

Brain Imaging

Findings from computed tomography (CT), magnetic residence imaging (MRI), positron emission tomography (PET), and single photon emission computerized tomography (SPECT) studies of patients with depression suggest that the disorder is associated with dysfunction in specific brain regions. CT and MRI studies have found structural subtle reductions in size in the hippocampus, basal ganglia and frontal and temporal lobes; however, these differences are detectable only on group data and are not visible on individual scans for diagnostic purposes.

These changes have been speculated to be due to high levels of endogenous cortisol (George, Kettler & Post, 1993).

It has long been noted that functional deficits do not correspond to abnormalities in structure—in other words, brain structure may be largely normal but for some reason may not function properly. The development of PET and SPECT technology opened the realm of studying brain functioning. PET reflects glucose metabolism in the brain while SPECT demonstrates blood flow—both indicative of activity. Studies with PET have demonstrated hypometabolism in the frontal lobe in depression regardless of whether the depression is primary or secondary—primary referring to idiopathic clinical depression in distinction from secondary depression, which is a consequence of another illness such as epilepsy or multiple sclerosis affecting the brain.

It has been shown that the severity of depression is often related to the degree of frontal hypometabolism. Preliminary studies show that hypometabolism normalizes after treatment in tandem with the patient's improved mood. Studies have consistently implicated the left prefrontal and frontal cortices, portions of the anterior temporal lobes, the amygdala, and the cingulate gyrus bilaterally. SPECT studies in depressed patients basically confirmed the PET findings with decreases in regional cerebral blood flow bilaterally in the frontal and temporal lobes cingulate gyri and left caudate nucleus. A recent study utilizing SPECT demonstrated that the left frontal lobe normalized with symptomatic improvement of depressive symptoms and that it normalized regardless of whether the patient was treated with drugs or with cognitive therapy. Thus, a compelling convergence of information from psychiatric and neurological investigations indicates that depression is mediated by a restrictive set of brain structures (Cummings, 1993; George et al., 1993).

CHILDHOOD FORERUNNERS OF DEPRESSION

Alfred Adler studied the interpersonal aspect of depressive symptoms. He viewed psychological symptoms as a way of coping with social demands. The development of a depressive style as a method of coping with life's challenges theoretically begins in early childhood when children try to master their environment. The process of learning occurs when children try various methods of obtaining their desires. When a method is found to be successful, children will utilize the method repeatedly. Moreover, Adler believed that after these behaviors are found to be useful, they may then be utilized in later life to reach goals (Ansbacher & Ansbacher, 1956, p. 288).

In 1914, Adler wrote

> The discouraged child finds that he can tyrannize best by tears will be a crybaby; the direct line of development leads from the crybaby to the adult depressed patient. Tears and complaints—the means which I have called "water power"—can be extremely useful weapons for disturbing cooperation and reducing others to a condition of "slavery." (Ansbacher & Ansbacher, 1956, p. 288)

In another article, Adler stated

> Melancholia develops in individuals whose method of living has from early childhood been dependent upon the achievement and support of others. Such individuals will always try to lean on others and will not scorn the use of exaggerated hints at their own inadequacy to force the support, adjustment, and submissiveness of others. . . . Their self-esteem from childhood on is clearly low as can be concluded from their unceasing attempts to achieve greatest importance. (Ansbacher & Ansbacher, 1956, p. 319)

Adler theorized that several types of children are in danger of developing neuroses, psychoses, and personality disorders. The commonality was that they tended to concentrate too much on themselves and too little on other people; their development of social interest (*Gemeinschaftsgefühl*) was limited. He outlined three reasons for why a child might become so self-focused. First, the child might have organ inferiorities, such as being lame or stuttering. These problems, he theorized, would require so much of the child's attention to master that little time was left to develop positive relationships with other people except to depend on them.

Second, some children develop a pampered style of life. This state does not necessarily require actual pampering of children, but rather that children interpret life to mean that they should get everything without any effort on their part, that everyone should be supportive, and that children should be catered to by everyone. To such persons, their often unconscious goal in life is to take from others, to be in a superior position in order to better exploit others. The attitude may be modeled after a parent or taught by concepts such as "You better get it while you can." It may have been learned from people who always gave material gifts, attention, or accolades to the depressive. Because of receiving throughout life, some people expect such treatment as adults and feel entitled (Mosak, 1985).

The third category of children in danger of developing such difficulties later in life are those who were neglected or even hated. These are children who never have experienced a loving, friendly relationship, nor ever had a loving, friendly relationship modeled for them. They usually have the misconception that getting from others or manipulating others into giving to them represents the main goal in life. Children who are more active will tend to enter more easily into delinquency, crime, and those behavior disorders that utilize threatening and coercive methods. The more passive children tend to use alcohol or other substances or develop symptoms of psychoses or neuroses (K. Adler, 1978).

When confronted with rejection, neglect, or refusal of their wishes, children who become depressed adults are more likely to crawl under the bed and daydream of finding their real parents (the stepchild fantasy), a passive way of criticizing and depreciating their parents. Some children, however, also develop a method of hurting themselves in order to hurt the opponents. Children have many ways of hurting themselves in order to strike out against a parent and thus gain revenge or establish dominance. A refusal to eat is one such method that is usually successful in centering attention on the child while the parents become irritated and upset. Another method might be lying on a cold stone floor refusing to get up, thinking, "It will serve her right if I get pneumonia. Then she'll be sorry for not letting me have my way." The extent of this pattern of hurting self in order to affect others can be viewed as a forerunner to the utilization of suicidal threats, ideation, gestures, and attempts in later life (K. Adler, 1980).

Adler did not believe that any event in childhood was causal of any particular symptom or psychological illness. Rather, when people develop a "neurosis," they bring up from memory events long past to give explanation to their current position (Ansbacher & Ansbacher, 1956, p. 289).

PSYCHODYNAMICS

Adler believed neurosis was not a disease in the sense of a medical illness but a "mistaken way of living." The patient is not viewed as a victim of symptoms; rather, the symptoms are viewed as purposeful and chosen for some unconscious goal. The symptoms of depression are chosen because of lifestyle predisposition, specifically, the convictions formed from our interpretation of life experiences as we develop. The depressive unconsciously decides to meet life challenges with depressive symptoms.

Mosak (1985) stated that depressives can be grouped into two categories. The first group focuses on feelings of guilt. These people attribute all their ills to what they either have done in the past or should have done but didn't. They feel that they are failures and create a litany of how their acts have resulted in negative consequences. They depreciate themselves, verbalizing guilt for their shortcomings or what they consider evil actions in their past. They seem to hold themselves responsible for unfortunate happenings within the family, within the neighborhood, and, as their thinking becomes psychotic, for disasters in the nation and the world.

The second group attributes their feelings to something external that happened to them, some past misfortune. They create a litany about how life defeats them, is unjust, and how they never have been given a "fair shake." They have a feeling of hopelessness and helplessness about their situation.

Adler stated

> Neurosis and psychosis have the ultimate purpose (unconscious) of safeguarding people from a clash with life tasks—that is with reality—and of sparing them the danger of having the dark secret of their inferiority (or inadequacy) revealed to themselves and to others. (K. Adler, 1978, p. 14)

Whenever they are confronted with a problem for which they have not been sufficiently prepared, their mind, their feelings, and much of their body will strain to find a way to deal with this unexpected difficulty that would threaten to expose their inadequacy to deal with the situation. Therefore, they will apply those methods of safeguarding self-image and self-esteem that they found effective as children. They usually will adhere to these techniques tenaciously, even when to all observers they are inappropriately and ineffectively dealing with the problem. Adler termed the methods *safeguarding devices.* Twelve years later, Freud introduced the term *defense mechanisms* for this phenomenon (K. Adler, 1978, p. 14).

Depression is a special safeguarding device with specific characteristics. The individual, however, seldom demonstrates all the psychodynamic manifestations of depression, since all individuals are creative and develop other defenses such as phobias, compulsions, or withdrawal, depending upon their previous learning and experience (K. Adler, 1961).

A description of the interrelatedness and various purposes of symptoms was explored by Mosak and Shulman (1967) and Mosak (1968).

The depressive tries to be better than others in some way in an attempt to overcome inferiority feelings and gain superiority (defined as moving from a perceived minus to a felt plus). This often is demonstrated by a lack of "social interest" or caring about other people and lack of cooperation. It also is manifested in intense competition in what has been described as vertical striving, focusing on who is better and who is a winner or a loser, rather than extending oneself to fellow human beings as an equal and a contributor.

This attitude of superiority, which is just under the surface of depressives, can be seen more clearly in the depressives who become psychotic. For example, they often claim to be the *worst* sinner or the personification of the devil. They strive to be number one in a negative direction. This phenomenon has been described as downward ambition.

Mosak (1985) postulated that depressive symptomatology is chosen because of problems in the self-ideal and themes in the lifestyle. Depressives have the mistaken convictions that in order to have a place, to belong, to be significant, they should get, they should be good, and they should control or be in control. These convictions exist in various proportions in many people, but with depressives, the problem is compounded because the "shoulds" become the imperative—"I must always." And if they do not or others do not provide, they then feel worthless and without significance.

The first theme, "having to get," becomes a demand that the world should give to them. If the world does not, then something is wrong and the world is blamed. As the person becomes angry, life then is accused of being unfair and inconsistent. Moreover, the demand includes that life should provide what is wanted on schedule; thus, the depressive is impatient.

These people also want "good things," not "bad things." Because of this factor, anger is not expressed, because if depressives expressed anger, others or life may not like them and may retaliate, and then they may not get what they want. Further, these persons are trained or have trained themselves to do only in order to get. Since they rely on others to provide for them, they are poor problem solvers; thus, when life provides difficulties, they often become discouraged, resigned, and give up. They have learned that if they create a good appearance, smile, and are enticing, the world will rescue them This maneuver also is know as "learned helplessness" (Seligman & Maier, 1967).

The second theme, "I should always be good," is linked to perfectionism and can be seen as an "aspiration for sainthood." These people are often in a dilemma about doing what is good because people define "good" differently: Should they do what they think is good or what others think is good? Often they are in conflict about "Which is the higher good?" or "Which is the lesser of two evils?" the result is vacillation and doubt. Therefore, they seek guidelines and standards and often are attracted to the study of philosophy and to churches that emphasize dogma. Since goodness is an imperative demand, being good 99% of the time is not sufficient. They strive for absolute perfection. Thus, any transgressions perpetrated in the past are constantly in their thoughts.

Individuals so engrossed with being good and perfect often find that people tend to stay away from them because they do not permit others to live their own lives. They moralize and tell others how to live better lives. "It is difficult living with a saint." They compensate by trying to convert others to their point of view in an attempt to have companionship.

The third central theme is wanting to control others or not wanting life to control them. Again, the key element is the imperative "always." In this particular theme, the person appears to aspire "to be God." Since the task is impossible as no one can be in control of everything all the time, the demand is frustrating. They begin to view the world as unfair and unjust and as an adversary (a place where one must be careful; otherwise, without vigilance, adversity can "sneak up on you"). Thus, these people are always on guard. They fear any sort of physical disability, even of a short duration like the flu, because they lose control. The also fear loss of control of their minds. They often state that they are afraid they are "going crazy" or "losing their minds." They also often verbalize fear of death and dying. This is based on the inability to control death; death will control them. Death is the realm of the unknown; thus, it is impossible to control.

Since these themes coexist in various proportions, they often interact and cause conflict within individuals. The "chocolate bar conflict" illustrates the interaction between the themes, "I should be good" and "I should always get." In this scenario, those who believe they need always to be good have a chocolate bar. They decide they would like some chocolate, but they are with a friend. In order to be "nice and good," they should share. So, they break the bar in half only to note quickly that the bar is not broken exactly in half. As a getter, they tell themselves they have to take the bigger piece; but to be good, they should take the smaller piece. If they are good, however, they will reason that they were "suckers" not to get the most. Thus, they put themselves into a "double bind" in which either choice will result in distress.

The next scenario is a conflict between "I should be good" and "I should control." This is known as the "cookie jar conflict." The persons in this instance want cookies that are in a jar. As they grasp as many of the cookies as they can, they discover the narrow opening stops them as they try to extract their hands. Thus, they perceive a loss of control. To drop some cookies places them in the dilemma of not getting as much as they want. Either way, they find themselves in another "double bind."

The last scenario involves the themes of having to be in control and "I have to be good." This Mosak (1985) called the "stoplight conflict." In this instance, people driving through a bad neighborhood at night stop at a stoplight. A possible assailant comes and starts smashing the window in order to gain access to the inside of the car. The companion asks why they don't drive away and they point to the red light. If they obey the law and be good, they are not in control of the situation; however, if they gain control and drive away, the will be rule-violating and therefore not be good. The again are in a "double bind" because of the imperative "always" they impose upon themselves.

These themes also are a contributing factor to the choice of depressive symptomatology. People who are nice and good do not give themselves permission to express anger to register a protest. When life does not permit the depressives to be in control, they will not allow themselves to express anger either because they are afraid of losing control or they fear the consequences of their expression of anger. "If I lose my temper, someone may get hurt." The theme of getting will inhibit the expression of anger because of the fear that if anger is expressed, they may not like what they get or retaliation may occur, thus resulting in the holding back of further receiving.

Not only do the depressives not allow themselves to demonstrate anger, they deny anger and avoid acknowledging the emotion. When asked about anger, they often will respond, "No, I am depressed." When asked further, they may reply that they are annoyed, or they sometimes resent certain actions or they feel hurt. They refuse to use the word "angry." One reason for this avoidance is that if they acknowledge anger, then they might have to do something about the situation or the person provoking the anger. If *they* are hurt, however, then all they need to do is deal with themselves rather than with the external problem. Thus, they develop a "sideshow" of depressive symptoms to "cloud the issue." Their ruminations about how they have to change themselves because they are failures and bad persons give them an excuse not to deal directly with the life task that is presenting a challenge. This is in contrast with the well-known concept of depression's aggression turned inward. Depression is better described as "a silent temper tantrum" or protest about the way life is proceeding (Mosak, 1985).

Desperation, Exploitation, and Guilt

Adler believed that neurotics are like people who believe they are drowning. Their focus is entirely on saving themselves. In such a situation, they cannot appreciate the beautiful scenery around them. When others come to help them and try to save them, they frantically will try to clutch at them, jeopardizing everybody's lives. If they could cooperate with those who want to be of help, they could be saved. Similarly, neurotics are like people who constantly feel in danger of drowning and of succumbing to the dangers of life. The depreciate those who are trying to help them by proving them either incapable or not willing to try hard enough to help them (K. Adler, 1978).

The depressives' method of attaining superiority is not detected easily from their self-debasing statements. But the goal can be ascertained from examining the effect these verbalizations have on those who care about them. Those who care worry about the depressives constantly; they reassure the depressives of their devotion and love. Because of the depressives' inability to function, those who care become forced into the depressive persons' service at great personal sacrifice. The new outcome is that the depressives are placed at the center of attention, their importance to others is reinforced, and they are relieved of obligations and given license to do whatever they want. "Only in fairly tales can a prince or princess command such a privileged position" (K. Adler, 1961, pp. 56-67).

Since they are unaware of the hidden purpose of gaining superiority, yet are aware of how much others are doing for them, they express guilt feelings about exploiting others and being such a burden. Such guilt feelings are viewed as a prestige enhancer in which the depressives elevate themselves to a position of judge of their own behavior. In so doing, they profess even higher moral "goodness" than their behavior demonstrates. Guilt feelings have been described as an expression of "good intentions which one does not have" (Dreikurs, 1950, pp. 12-21).

In many case, the feelings are verbalized when the person does not want to end the morally-violating behavior but still wants to appear good. An example would be married persons verbalizing depression and guilt because they have been having an affair for the past two or three years. Solutions are sought such as deciding with one of the partners is to be discarded by the persons who profess love for both, and depressives utilize guilt feelings as proof of their high moral character in spite of their rule-violating behavior. "Adler explained their purpose and function as a device for appearing to oneself and others as noble and socially minded while persistent in exploitive actions" (K. Adler, 1961, p. 57). Alfred Adler wrote, "In depression, the patient contents himself with merely expressing the sense of guilt while he would never think of exercising active contrition in the form of improved behavior" (Ansbacher & Ansbacher, 1956, p. 307).

Depreciation

When depressives are relatively free of symptoms, ambition compels them to pursue achievements where little risk for failure exists and where little effort is required. Whenever failure looms, however, they tend to shrink from the task and claim that, as usual, they are failures. They repeat to themselves and to all others who are willing to listen a litany of pessimism. The repetition of pessimistic self-defeating ideation, of course, leads them to fulfill their own prophecy as they further undermine their self-confidence. Indirectly, however, the failure often is blamed on relatives or friends who somehow did not fulfill their obligations, the method by which they were reared, some "biochemical imbalance," and/or heredity (A. Adler, 1979, p. 249). They depreciate those trying to help by not responding, proving them incapable or not trying hard enough to help. They are usually unaware of how their thinking and actions are actually contributory or generating the depression. Pessimistically, they anticipate dire outcomes from which they cannot be saved or helped by anyone or by themselves.

Depressives tend to catastrophize. They become preoccupied with the thought of how miserable they will become if the undesired occurs. Alfred Adler stated

> That dynamic can best be observed in depressed or melancholic individuals who live as if the misfortune has already happened. (Ansbacher & Ansbacher, 1956, p. 283)
> The categorical imperative of melancholia is "act, think, feel in such a way as if the horrible fate that you have conjured up had already befallen you and was inevitable." (Ansbacher & Ansbacher, 1956, p. 321; A. Adler, 1979, p. 250)

Proving Illness and Maintenance of Symptoms

The suffering of depressed persons is genuine although usually exaggerated. The depressives want relief and sincerely want to give up their symptoms; however, since symptoms were generated as a protection against a loss of prestige and self-esteem, depressives are prevented from relinquishing symptoms because they fear the consequences. As Alfred Adler stated, it is "The danger of death through loss of prestige" (Ansbacher & Ansbacher, 1956, p. 266).

In their attempts to certify their illness, persons' continuous ruminations over misfortune, hopelessness, helplessness, and inadequacy affect their whole body. The depressives begin to neglect themselves and their outward appearance, sleep becomes disordered, they do not care about eating and may actually lose weight, and even bodily functions, such as bowel movements, are disturbed. An interesting point to note is that Adler remarked, "We want to stress especially that toxins are released by the endocrine glands through the effect of rage and grief by way of the vegetative nervous system" (K. Adler, 1961, p. 59). The result of all these obvious signs of deterioration and physical complications is definite proof to all that a truly serious condition exists that needs care and assistance from others, and that they must be relieved from all obligations to occupation, social relations, and marriage (K. Adler, 1961).

In addition, a depressive has to maintain his or her symptoms. For this purpose, several mechanisms are utilized. One is not to take responsibility for the symptom, to believe that the symptoms spontaneously recur and remit and that nothing can be done to change the pattern. The second mechanism is to fight against the symptoms and, by fighting against them, actually reinforce the symptoms. The third is to feel sorry for oneself constantly for having the symptoms and to search endlessly for the cause or worry about the dire consequences if the symptoms continue.

Sometimes recognition of the success of their suffering is evidenced by the occasional slight secret smile observed on the faces of depressives when they count the extent others have tried to help because of their depression or how frustrated others are about the situation. Kurt Adler (1961, p. 61) cited a Viennese playwright, Mestroy, as recognizing this phenomenon years ago through a character who states, "If I could not annoy people with my melancholia I wouldn't enjoy it at all."

If persons actually did enjoy suffering the symptoms, it would mean that they had lost contact with the ties of social interest and of "the logical reason that binds us all," and thus they have become psychotic. Some depressives do develop delusions and hallucinations. This theoretically occurs when inferiority feelings are so great, and the overambitious idealized goals are so lofty that distortion of reality is the only possible protection (K. Adler, 1961).

Suicide

A common symptom that occurs with depressives is that of suicidal ideation, intent, or attempts. The childhood forerunners of such symptoms have been discussed previously as methods of revenge and protest. Similar motives can be suspected in adults. Sometimes suicidal persons even will admit that they fantasized family and friends crying and feeling guilty for what they had done to or not done for the person. This also reveals the aggressive, hostile, unconscious motivation of the act against significant others.

The attempt to commit suicide may seem a contradiction to the theme of "being good"; however, depressed individuals use various techniques to justify such an action. They may just give up and decide that the possibility of being good all the time is impossible; therefore, they might as well give up and no longer be good and decide to end their lives. Others, however, rationalize suicide as being an altruistic act. They state that their friends and family will be better off without them, that the family will collect insurance and be able to clear up many debts accrued because of the way the depressive persons have failed.

Suicide can have other interpersonal dynamics. As an example, some people have a difficult time admitting they need help because of fear of loss of prestige or sometimes because of a self-concept or family concept that to seek help means weakness. In these situations, the suicide attempt may be a cry for help. It forces people to recognize the desperation of depressive persons and places these persons in a position where they can be "forced" legally to receive treatment. In many suicide attempts, patients finally arrange the opportunity to discuss dissatisfactions with their lives or their marriages when previous attempts to do so were unsuccessful.

Threats of suicide also have been used as a form of coercion and "blackmail." Perhaps the most common example would be the lover who is using coercive tactics to continue a relationship: "If you leave me, my life is not worth living; I'll kill myself." Threats of suicide have been effective in preventing parents from insisting that a child in the mid-twenties or older become employed or leave home. Similarly, suicide attempts can be used as an escape from a potentially disgraceful situation. As an example, a college student facing final examinations with insufficient preparation and high personal goals for achievement may make a suicide attempt in order to be hospitalized and thus have an excuse not to take the final examinations.

Even in the escape motivation, an element of revenge due to perceived unfairness is often visible with the refrain, as stated by Kurt Adler (1961, p. 60), "See what you have driven me to do; now you will suffer for the rest of your life for it. Missing me you will realize what a rare and sensitive person I was." Perhaps the statement needs to be made again that these interpersonal dynamics are usually unconscious; the person is usually unaware of the hidden motivations for such an action.

INTEGRATION OF SOMATIC AND PSYCHOLOGICAL THERAPIES

Although Adler believed firmly that the medical model was not valid for neuroses (and to some extent psychoses) and believed them to be "mistaken ways of living," he nevertheless acknowledged that physicians were the ones who were best trained for the supervision, if not for the actual treatment, of neuroses and psychoses because of their understandings of the diseases associated with depressive symptoms, the somatic concomitants of mental disorders, and the differential diagnosis that was necessary to ascertain where an organic, physical factor was present (K. Adler, 1980). However, he also wrote that some mental disorders, specifically psychosis, epilepsy, melancholia, and schizophrenia, might have an organic etiology: although "here, too, a part is played by the exogenous situation" (Ansbacher & Ansbacher, 1979, p. 230).

Since many somatic treatments can offer significant relief of suffering within two to eight weeks, an essential first step in any therapy process is to conduct an active differential diagnosis to ascertain whether the depressive's symptoms are partially or completely correctable by medications or electroconvulsive therapy.

Since Individual Psychology is a holistic, not a reductionistic psychology, many have taught that diagnosis can interfere with understanding the dynamics of a patient and the therapeutic process. With the dissemination of recent depression research to the public and the demands of third-party payers, this position is increasingly untenable. The reductionistic process of accurate diagnosis is imperative in establishing whether or not the person is likely to respond to a somatic therapy and what treatment approach is most likely to benefit the patient.

The proof of any theory, whether it be psychodynamic, genetic, or biochemical, is its usefulness. One benefit of somatic theories is that they alleviate guilt feelings that prevent improvement. The blockage that guilt produces often is removed with the discovery of a physical cause of depression, such as a probable genetic basis or abnormal cortisol levels. Patients are then free to learn how to manage their illness and use all the treatment modalities that are available. Often they are then more open to learning psychological techniques that will lessen the probability of relapse and enable them to lead more productive lives.

Trying to treat a psychotic depression or even a nonpsychotic melancholic depression with psychotherapy alone is somewhat similar to trying to use psychotherapy with an intoxicated alcoholic or an alcoholic going through withdrawal.

A certain amount of supportive dialogue is essential to explain what is being done and to establish a positive relationship; however, often an impairment of concentration and memory and a preoccupation with current physical symptoms occur to such an extent that to establish meaningful insight is difficult. Once acute withdrawal is completed and less organic disruption of cognitive functioning is present, the patient is not only more open to learn but also better able to learn. A parallel can be made to the depressive. during melancholic stupor or when psychotically depressed, to develop psychological insight is difficult. Once the major symptoms are cleared with medication or ECT and a determination is made as to whether or not psychological symptoms persist, the more insight-oriented therapies can be very helpful. The previously described psychodynamics fit some depressed patients. What remains to be ascertained is to which diagnostic categories they are applicable. We can speculate that they are more apt to fit the characterological depressives, although some dysthymics and major depressives also can demonstrate these psychodynamics. Moreover, these traits can be seen in some nondepressive persons.

Kurt Adler (1983) stated that in evaluating the biochemical findings we must ask, what is really proved? Can these biochemical changes such as low serotonin levels in people who have made suicide attempts be brought about by attitudes, ways of looking at life, as well as some biochemical deficiency? Every time a person sees, hears, feels, tastes, or thinks, the biochemistry of the body is changed, and the endocrine output is changed. As an example, if something is said to bring a blush to a person's face, the blush is a reaction to what was heard and how it was interpreted. The person's thinking affects this feeling and produces an endocrine biochemical change that results in the dilation of blood vessels in the face. Blushing requires an endocrine reaction to be transmitted. With medication, often

> the patient feels amelioration of the symptoms that accompany depression. The patient feels encouraged and psychotherapy will often be more accepted by the patient. When I give some of my patients antidepressant drugs, and I do with some, not many, patients, I usually tell them that this drug will ameliorate their physical symptoms and they may find that they can life without depression. But, we have to work very hard together to find for what purpose they always create depression, how they develop the idea that this was the best way to achieve significance. Because only they can make the depression. (K. Adler, 1983, p. 298)

A recent multi-center study comparing two psychotherapies with an antidepressant (Imiprimine) and a placebo demonstrated that for less severely depressed patients (*Hamilton Rating Scale for Depression* total score less than 20), all the therapies, including the placebo with case management, produced significant improvement. Moreover, they did not differ significantly from each other. For the subgroup of patients who were more severely depressed and functionally impaired, however, Imipramine was much more effective than the placebo, and the two psychotherapies fell between those treatments in effectiveness. Several surprises came from these findings, namely that the placebo in clinical management was unexpectedly effective in the mildly depressed patients. Apparently encouragement, attention, and empathy may be more therapeutic than previously thought. One limitation of the study was that the patients all were relatively well-educated outpatients who were nonpsychotic (Elkin, Shea, Watkins, Imber, Stotsky, Collins, Glass, Pilkonis, Leber, Docherty, Fiester, & Parloff, 1989).

The same authors further studied predicted outcome across various treatments including interpersonal psychotherapy, cognitive behavior therapy, imipramine with clinical management, or placebo with clinical management. They identified significant patient predictors of differential treatment outcome. If there was low social dysfunction, it predicted a superior response to interpersonal psychother-apy. If there was low cognitive dysfunction, this predicted a superior response to cognitive behavior therapy and to imipramine. If there was high work dysfunc-tion, this predicted a superior response to imipramine alone. If high depression severity and impairment of function were present, this predicted a superior re-sponse to imipramine and to interpersonal psychotherapy. Their conclusions were that the study demonstrated the relevance of patient characteristics including social, cognitive, and work function for the prediction of the outcome of major depressive disorder, and indirect evidence was provided for treatment specificity by identifying characteristics responsive to different modalities, which may be of value in the selection of patients for alternative treatments (Sotsky et al., 1991).

These results corroborate many of the points made earlier, that depression is a complex group of disorders for which a variety of effective interventions exist. Since criteria on effective treatment for specific subgroups have not yet been established, factors such as patient's goals, time, financial limitations, sensi-tivity to side effects, and severity of symptoms will have to be considered in deciding which intervention to utilize.

ADLERIAN PSYCHOTHERAPY OF DEPRESSION

Change can transpire in many ways. To discuss comprehensively the proce-dure of Adlerian psychotherapy is beyond the scope of this chapter. The reader is referred to Dreikurs' (1967) and Mosak's (1984) discussions of the process; however, some specific applications of techniques will be outlined.

Generally, the Adlerian therapist is a teacher, and the teacher shares what he or she knows about the illness. Thus, if the symptoms include a melancholic or psychotic aspect, the biochemical and genetic theories of the illness are explained as well as references to readings designed for the layperson. When psychological issues are identified, the steps of self-understanding through the gathering of lifestyle data and the purpose of psychotherapy are discussed with the patient.

At the beginning of treatment, both Alfred and Kurt Adler advocated avoiding conflicts or battle with patients. Depressive patients are already irritable, angry, and ready for battle. The recommendation is that the therapist establish with patients the fact that the therapist is completely powerless without patients' cooperation. To people who have developed patterns of depending upon others for assistance and expect the "doctor" to save them miraculously from their symptoms, this approach often comes as a shock. The second tactic is to make clear to patients that nothing is demanded or expected from them. Adler said, "Never do anything you don't like" (Ansbacher & Ansbacher, 1956, p. 346). This tactic has several effects. First, it relieves depressives of pressures of having to perform. The depressive is given a status to do as he or she wants, free from social pressure and restraint. The therapist thus removes himself or herself as an adversary. This tactic can be enhanced further by initially advising relatives that the patients are too ill to fulfill their usual roles and responsibilities and that they will need several weeks to recover.

The process of psychotherapy is compared, on occasion, with Dorothy's quest in *The Wizard of Oz* (Pancner & Pancner, 1988). Parables and fables are utilized to illustrate various crucial dynamics found in the patient's behavior or thinking (Pancner, 1978). For example, to illustrate how we maintain symptoms by fighting against them, we use the fable of the king who gave one-half of his kingdom for the power to turn lead into gold; however, he was informed after making the agreement that the ability would only be present if he would not think about the word "crocodile." And, of course, with that requirement, he would dwell on how not to think about crocodile and thus constantly think about crocodiles.

The antidote to this dilemma is the technique of "antisuggestion" as described by Ervin Wexberg, later named *paradoxical intention* by Victor Frankl (1960). In this technique, instead of fighting the symptoms, the person is encouraged to act out the symptoms and try to create them even more often. Adler utilized paradox in treatment, calling it "prescribing the symptoms." He utilized this technique when patients indicated they wanted to stay in bed all day. Adler agreed that this was what patients needed to do. When patients complained of being in bed all day, they would be reminded of the rule of not doing anything they disliked doing; thus, they were free to get up from bed if they so wished.

To deal with the areas of distrust of others and competitiveness, Adler (Ansbacher & Ansbacher, 1956, p. 47) utilized the statement, "You can be cured in 14 days if you will follow my prescription to try to think every day, 'How I can please someone.' " This can be further magnified by actually assigning the task of doing something to be helpful to another on a daily basis. Adler stated the following:

> All my efforts are devoted to increasing social interest of a patient. I know that the real reason for his malady is lack of cooperation, and I want him to see it too. As soon as he can connect himself with his fellow men on an equal and cooperative footing, he is cured. (Ansbacher & Ansbacher, 1956, p. 347)

Another useful modality for attaining this goal is the therapeutic group, particularly with other depressives with whom identification can easily occur. This imparts a felling of belonging, of not being alone, of not being unique, and eventually of more courage and of increased self-esteem.

Another therapy was systemized by Dreikurs (1967) as consisting of four essential overlapping stages in the therapeutic process. First, establish a rapport between the therapist and client. In this relationship, mutual trust, cooperation, and respect need to develop. An agreement as to goals and objectives for the relationship is essential. In the second stage, the patient's current behavior is examined in relationship to their perceptions that have been developed. Specifically, the current life situation is examined in light of the lifestyle assessment (Mosak, 1958; Mosak & Gushurst, 1972). The possible purpose of the current symptoms is identified. The emphasis in this process is on investigating, uncovering, and seeking to perceive life from the patient's point of view.

In the third stage, the therapist extracts from these personality characteristics an underlying behavior pattern and explains the dynamics to the patient. They learn about their self-concept or self-ideal, their view of their environment, what people are like, what life is like, what their ethical convictions are, how they believe they should act and others should act, and their method of operation for attaining their goals. In addition, they are mad aware of their mistaken apperception, those convictions that somehow interfere with their optimal functioning.

In therapy, patients' distorted perceptions and pessimistic predictions must be pointed out and patients convinced that these perceptions are produced for a purpose, the purpose being to avoid assuming responsibility because of the crippling perceptions about themselves and the world that were formed in child-hood. With more optimistic anticipation, they can recognize the strengths within their personalities. They then will enjoy entering into cooperative relationships with others, removing the need to attempt to dominate others since people no longer will seem so hostile and threatening.

In the last stage, clients are encouraged to implement these insights into changing their behavior. The hope is that patients will learn to recognize patterns of the past and how they tend to recur persistently. They first learn to catch themselves on the verge of repeating the pattern; then patients are asked to make a decision whether or not to do things differently. If they try a new method and it is successful, then with support they are urged to continue the new method until it becomes comfortable. With successful practice of the new methods, their perceptions on life are influenced and changed (Nikelly, 1971).

Throughout treatment, the therapist needs to demonstrate to patients that they are held in high esteem and that they should recognize that some of their actions and perceptions are based on childhood perceptions. Their misperceptions can be corrected through education and their effort. As they develop their human potential, they will discover how this experience is gratifying and expanding.

Mosak (1985) advocated the use of the "pushbutton technique" to demon-strate to patients that they do not have to remain unhappy. In this exercise, patients are asked to recall some positive and pleasant event, then to picture the experience in their minds and enjoy the feelings that came from the situation. Next, they are asked to do the same with an episode that was unpleasant. When they have opportunity to picture, project, and feel those emotions, they are again assigned to pick a positive incident and repeat the process. Mosak then asked patients if they noticed anything during the exercise. They usually respond that they felt happy and enthusiastic during the first and third exercises. This technique is utilized to illustrate to them that when they think about disasters and unpleasant experiences, they are going to feel bad. It further demonstrates that what one thinks has a large effect on how one feels, leading to the conclusion that patients create their own feelings and also maintain them. Once that is discovered, they often no longer feel as helpless or as hopeless (Mosak, 1985).

PREVENTION OF SUICIDE

Perhaps the most critical psychological treatment situation is the emergency brought forth by suicidal ideation or attempt. Kurt Adler (1980, p. 173) advocated treating suicidal, depressed patients with vigorous open confrontation to uncover the hidden rage, hostility, and revenge. This is necessary because the patients try to hid their inner motives by noble motives such as to relieve others of the burden of having to care for them. when the therapist exposes the rage, hostility, and revenge motives against those whom they profess to love, patients have difficulty maintaining the illusion that their pretended high and noble motives will be believed. Thus, patients' hope that suicide will make them appear noble and well-meaning disappears. Moreover, when faced with the anger and revenge interpretation, suicide becomes ego-dystonic, and the act of suicide will not be consistent with the idealized self-image.

Kurt Adler (1980) recommended telling patients that the revenge motive of suicide is well-known, that people hide suicides, do not talk about them, and try to forget them as quickly as possible. Many religions do not permit suicides to be buried with the faithful because the deviousness of the act is such common knowledge. Adler pointed out that, contrary to some glorified notions and stories to indicate that suicide is a heroic act that requires courage, escape from one's problems shows a lack of courage. Suicide is doing exactly that—running from one's problems.

To counter the rationale that, "This is my life and my decision as to whether or not I want to live or die," Adler would tell clients that they fool themselves, but they cannot fool him as to why they consider suicide. They actively are thinking of someone else whom they want to punish, make feel guilty, and make suffer. He then further would add that the suffering of the significant other is not a certainty, that they may be relieved finally to be rid of the burden of the relationship. Adler would try to put a doubt in their minds that the suicide will fulfill their goal of making their significant other suffer. In the attempt at making suicide ego-alien, Adler would emphasize that they will not look noble, but by committing suicide, they will look hateful, mean, and stupid.

For those who profess a love so strong that they cannot live without their chosen other, Kurt Adler again would counter strongly, telling them

> not to make such phony pretenses; everyone can see that they want
> their mates to feel guilt and want to punish them for leaving. The
> main drive is not love, but hatred and lust for revenge. Since when
> is blackmailing a person proof of undying love? (K. Adler, 1980,
> p. 174)

To those depressives who are suicidal, professing that they want to free their relatives to whom they are a burden, Kurt Adler again would confront sharply, stating that their purpose is only to show relatives how noble-minded the de-pressives are while the relatives are low-minded. The depressives' inner motive is for relatives to suffer guilt for the rest of their lives, which is an unloving act, a tactic that again makes suicide ego-alien.

Kurt Adler (1980) believed that although these tactics may seem unfair and even cruel, this is justified in such an emergency. Strong, quick action has to be taken to smash the illusion under which a suicidal depressive operates, making it virtually impossible for them to attempt suicide. He stressed the importance, however, of first having convinced clients that while they are valued by the therapist, their actions or manipulations are not (K. Adler, 1961). Clients are advised that their actions are understandable, that they stem from attitudes and techniques learned in early childhood, and that they have utilized these tactics without realizing the tactics' self-defeating aspects (K. Adler, 1980). It also can be pointed out that other ways exist to express dissatisfaction and anger to others that have a much greater chance of succeeding and bringing about significant change and that they have the capability to learn these new techniques and ways of coping with life's challenges.

CONCLUSION

An important point is to conceptualize major depressive illness holistically, to view the process as a function of many factors. The genetic, biochemical, and organic factors probably are activated by the level of stress in most cases. The level of stress is determined by individuals' perception of life events. Stress can be reduced by certain positive factors such as individuals' extent of competence or capacity to cope, their self-esteem, and their support system. Mental illness from all indications is not attributable to simple "cause and effect" but is the product of an interplay of many factors.

Bernard H. Shulman (1983) has point out that it would be a mistake to diagnose on the basis of the biochemical tests alone and to make etiological inferences about any biochemical tests. A test is a measurement at a certain point in time of what is happening in a certain process. Tests are useful for suggesting that depression should be considered and that the client may respond to certain types of antidepressant medication. Whereas the organic theorist will tend to view abnormal tests as causal, the psychodynamic theorist will tend to perceive them only as a correlation or possibly as a consequence of psychological events inside the person rather that a cause.

Adlerian theory is a psychodynamic theory but also recognizes the existence of constitutional factors.

> It gives us direction for research, for re-examining the old Adlerian ideas of "organ inferiority" or the constitutional diathesis. Are people who suffer from depression more inclined to do so because they are born with a tendency in that direction, or are they more likely to become depressed because they have been exposed to certain life experiences, have come to certain conclusions about them, and on the basis of their creative selves have devised a method of response and attitude toward life which we would call a tendency to become depressed when life becomes difficult? It is difficult to determine how much is learning, how much is the creative self, how much is in the constitutional diathesis.
>
> The challenge of these discoveries is to bring together what we are learning about the body and what we believe psychodynamically and fit them together. After all, Adlerian theory says that the body and mind work together and if Adlerian theory cannot make the mind and body work together we will have to invent a new theory. (Shulman, in Pancner, 1985, p. 299)

Acknowledgment

We are deeply grateful to Kurt Adler and Harold Mosak, whose lectures and presentations provided most of the concepts for the psychodynamics of this chapter. We also are indebted to Robert Doyal and Ann Wheeler for their editorial assistance.

REFERENCES

Adler, A. (1979). Melancholia and paranoia (1914). In *Practice and theory of Individual Psychology* (pp. 246–262). Patterson, NJ: Littlefield Adams.

Adler, K. (1961). Depression in the light of Individual Psychology. *Journal of Individual Psychology, 17*, 56–67.

Adler, K. (1978, March). *The contribution of Individual Psychology to the mental health professions.* Lecture delivered at Kean College of New Jersey.

Adler, K. (1980). Depression and suicide as they relate to intimacy and communication. *Modern Psychoanalysis, 5*(2), 167–176.

Adler, K. (1983, May). Discussion at symposium presented at the North American Society of Adlerian Psychology, Boulder, CO.

Akiskal, H.S. (1989). New insights into the nature of heterogeneity of mood disorders. *Journal of Clinical Psychiatry, 50*(Supplement), 6–10.

Akiskal, H.S., & Lemmi, H. (1983, March). Clinical, neuroendocrine, and sleep EEG diagnosis of "unusual" affective presentations: A practical review. *In Psychiatric Clinics of North America, 6*(1), 69–83.

American Psychiatric Association. (1994). *Diagnostic and statistical manual of mental disorders* (4th ed.). Washington, DC: Author

Ansbacher, H.L., & Ansbacher, R.R. (Eds.). (1956). *The Individual Psychology of Alfred Adler* (pp. 239–349). New York: Harper & Row.

Ansbacher, H.L., & Ansbacher, R.R. (Eds.). (1979). *Superiority and social interest* (3rd ed.). New York: W.W. Norton.

Ballenger, J.C., Goodwin, F.K., & Major, L.F. (1979). Alcohol and central serotonin metabolism in man. *Archives of General Psychiatry, 36*, 224–227.

Bertelson, A., Harvald, B., & Hauge, M. (1977). A Danish twin study of manic-depressive disorders. *British Journal of Psychiatry, 130*, 330–351.

Brown, G.L., Ebert, M.H., & Goyer, P.F. (1982). Aggression, suicide, and serotonin: Relationships to CSF amine metabolites. *American Journal of Psychiatry, 139*, 6.

Carroll, B.J., Feinberg, M., Greden, J.F., Tarika, J., Albala, A.A., Haskett, R.F., James, N.M., Kronfol, Z. Lohr, N., Steiner, M., deVigne, J.P., & Young, E. (1981). A specific laboratory test for the diagnosis of melancholia: Standardization, validation, and clinical utility. *Archives of General Psychiatry, 38*, 15–22.

Cooper, J.E., Kendall, R.E., & Gurland, B.J. (1972). *Psychiatric diagnosis in New York and London: A comparative study of mental hospital admissions.* (Institute of Psychiatry, Maudsley Monograph No. 20). London: Oxford University Press.

Coryell, W., Lavori, P., & Endicott, J. (1984). Outcome in schizophrenia, affective, psychotic and non-psychotic depression course during a 6- to 24-month follow-up. *Archives of General Psychiatry, 41*, 787–791.

Cummings, J.L. (1993). The neuroanatomy of depression. *Journal of Clinical Psychiatry, 54*(11) (Supplement), 14–20.

Debattista, C., & Schatzberg, A.F. (1994). An algorithm for the treatment of major depression and its sub-types. *Psychiatric Annals, 24*(7), 341–347.

Dreikurs, R. (1950). Guilt feelings as an excuse. *Individual Psychology Bulletin, 8*, 12–21.

Dreikurs, R. (1967). *Psychodynamics, psychotherapy and counseling. Collected Papers.* Chicago: Alfred Adler Institute.

Egeland, J.A., Gerhard, D.S., & Pauls, D.L. (1987). Bipolar disorders linked to DNA markers on chromosome II. *Nature, 325*, 783–787.

Elkin, I., Shea, M.T., Watkins, J.T., Imber, S.D., Stotsky, S.M., Collins, J.F., Glass, D.R., Pilkonis, P.A., Leber, W.R., Docherty, J.P., Fiester, S.J., & Parloff, M.B. (1989). National Institute of Mental Health treatment of depression collaborative research program. *Archives of General Psychiatry, 46*, 971–982.

Fava, M., & Kaji, J. (1994). Continuation and maintenance treatments of major depressive disorders. *Psychiatric Annals, 24*(6), 281–290.

Frankl, V. (1960). Paradoxical intention: A logotherapeutic technique. *American Journal of Psychotherapy, 14*, 520–535.

Freud, S. (1953). Mourning and melancholia. In *Complete psychological works* (standard ed., 14). London: Hogarth Press.

George, M.S., Kettler, T.A., & Post, R.M. (1993). SPECT and PET imaging in Mood Disorders. *Journal of Clinical Psychiatry, 54*(11)(Supplement), 6–13.

Georgotos, A. (1983). Monoamine metabolites in CSF and suicidal behavior. *Intelligence Reports in Psychiatric Disorders, 2*(15).

Gold, M.S., Pottash, L.C., Extein, I., & Sweeney, D.R. (1981). Diagnosis of depression in the 1980s. *Journal of the American Medical Association, 245*, 1562–1564.

Haslam, N., & Beck, A.T. (1994). Sub-typing major depression: a taxometric analysis. *Journal of Abnormal Psychology, 103*(4), 686–692.

Hirschfeld, R.M.A., & Cross, C.K. (1982). Epidemiology of affective disorders: Psychosocial risk factors. *Archives of General Psychiatry, 39*, 35–46.

Hirschfeld, R.M.A., & Goodwin, F.K. (1988). Mood disorders. In J.A. Talbott, R.E. Hales, & S.C. Yudofsky (Eds.), *Textbook of psychiatry* (pp. 403–441). Washington, DC: American Psychiatric Press.

Hirschfeld, R.M.A., Klerman, G.L., & Clayton, P.J. (1983). Personality and depression: Empirical findings. *Archives of General Psychiatry, 40*, 993–998.

Keller, M.B., Lavori, P.W., & Endicott, J. (1983). "Double depression:" Two-year follow-up. *American Journal of Psychiatry, 140*, 689–695.

Klein, D.N., & Salisbury-Kelly, H. (1993). Diagnosis and classification of dysthymia. *Psychiatric Annals, 23*(11), 609–616.

Lewy, A.J. (1987). Treating chronobiological sleep and mood disorders with bright light. *Psychiatric Annals, 17*, 664–669.

Littrell, J. (1994). Relationship between time since reuptake-blocker antidepressant discontinuation and relapse. *Experimental and Clinical Psychopharmacology, 2*(1), 82–94.

Loosen, P.T., Prange, A.J., Jr., Wilson, I.C., Lara, P.P., & Pettus, C. (1977). Thyroid stimulating hormone response after thyrotropin releasing hormone in depressed schizophrenic and normal women. *Psychoneuroendocrinology, 2*, 137–148.

Markowitz, J.C. (1993). Comorbidity of Dysthymia. *Psychiatric Annals, 23*(11), 617–624.

Mason, B.J., Kocsis, J.H., Leon, A.C., Thompson, S., Frances, A.J., Morgan, R.O., & Parides, M.K. (1993). Measurement of severity and treatment response in dysthymia. *Psychiatric Annals, 23*(11), 625–631.

Mosak, H.H. (1958). Early recollections as a projective technique. *Journal of Projective Techniques, 22*(3), 302–311.

Mosak, H.H. (1968). The interrelatedness of the neurosis through central themes. *Journal of Individual Psychology, 24*, 67–70.

Mosak, H.H. (1984). Adlerian psychotherapy. In R. Corsini and Contributors

(Eds.), *Current psychotherapies* (3rd ed.) (pp. 56–107). Itasca, IL: F.E. Peacock Publishers.

Mosak, H.H. (1985). *The assumptive universe of the depressive*. Paper presented at the meeting of the North American Society of Adlerian Psychology, Atlanta, GA.

Mosak, H.H., & Gushurst, R.H. (1972). Some therapeutic uses of psychologic testing. *American Journal of Psychotherapy, 26*(4), 539–546.

Mosak. H.H., & Shulman, B.H. (1967. Various purposes of symptoms. *Journal of Individual Psychology, 23*, 79–87.

Myers, J.K., Weissman, M.M., & Tischler, G.L. (1984). Six-month prevalence of psychiatric disorders in three communities. *Archives of General Psychiatry, 41*, 959–967.

Nierenberg, A. (1994). Treatment-resistant depression in the age of serotonin. *Psychiatric Annals, 24*(5), 217–219.

Nikelly, A.G. (Ed.). (1971). *Techniques for behavior change: Applications for Adlerian theory*. Springfield, IL: Charles C. Thomas.

Pancner, K.L. (1978). The use of parables and fables in Adlerian psychotherapy. *The Individual Psychologist, 15*, 19–29.

Pancner, K.L., & Pancner, R.J. (1988). The quest, gurus, and the yellow brick road. *Individual Psychology, 44*, 158–166.

Pancner, R.J. (1985). Impact of current depression research on Adlerian theory and practice. *Individual Psychology, 41*, 289–301.

Paykel, E.S. (1978). Contribution of life events to causation of psychometric illness. *Psychol Med, 8*, 245–253.

Pflug, B., & Tolle, R. (1971). Disturbance of the 24-hour rhythm in endogenous depression and the treatment of endogenous depression by sleep deprivation. *International Pharmacopsychiatry, 6*, 187–196.

Quitkin, F.M., McGrath, A.J., & Stewart, J.W. (1989). Phenelzine and Imipramine in mood reactive depression: further delineation of the syndrome of Atypical depression. *Archives of General Psychiatry, 46*, 787–793.

Regier, D.A., Narrow, W.E., Rae, D.S., Manderscheid, R.W., Locke, B.Z., & Goodwin, F.K. (1993). The de Facto US mental and addictive disorders service system. *Archives of General Psychiatry, 50*(2), 85–94.

Robins, E., & Guze, S.B. (1970). Suicide and primary affective disorder. *American Journal of Psychiatry, 126*, 107–111.

Rosenthal, N.E., Sack, D.A., & Gillin, J.C. (1984). Seasonal affective disorder: A description of the syndrome and preliminary findings with light therapy. *Archives of General Psychiatry, 41*, 72–80.

Rosenthal, N.E. (1993). Diagnosis and treatment of seasonal affective disorder. *Journal of American Medical Association, 270*, 2717–2720.

Sachar, E.J., Asnis, G., & Halbreich, U. (1980). Recent studies in the neuroendocrinology of major depressive disorders. *Psychiatric Clinics of North America, 3*, 313–326.

Sack, D.A., Nurnburger, J., & Rosenthal, N.E. (1985). The potentiation of antidepressant medications by phase-advance of the sleep-wake cycle. *American Journal of Psychiatry, 142*, 606–608.

Schilgen, B., & Tolle, R. (1980). Partial sleep deprivation as therapy for depression. *Archives of General Psychiatry, 37*, 267–271.

Seligman, M., & Maier, S. (1967). Failure to escape traumatic shock. *Journal of Experimental Psychology, 74*, 1–9.

Shulman, B.H. (1983, May). Discussion at meeting of the North American Society of Adlerian Psychology, Boulder, CO.

Sotsky, S.M., Glass, D.R., Shea, M.T., Pilkonis, P.A., Collins, J.F., Elkin I., Watkins, J.T., Imber, S.D., Leber, W.R., Moyer, J., & Oliveri, M.E. (1991). Patient predictors of response to psychotherapy and pharmacotherapy: Findings in the NIMH treatment of depression collaborative research program. *American Journal of Psychiatry, 148*(8), 997–1008.

Targum, S.D. (1983). Neuroendocrine challenge studies in clinical psychiatry. *Psychiatric Annals, 13*, 385–395.

Thoren, P., Ansberg, M., & Bertilsson, L. (1980). Clomipramine treatment of obsessive-compulsive disorder: II. Biochemical aspects. *Archives of General Psychiatry, 37,* 1289–1294.

Traskman, L., Asberg, M., Bertilsson, L., & Sjostrang, L. (1981). Monoamine metabolites in CSF and suicidal behavior. *Archives of General Psychiatry, 38,* 631–636.

Weissman, M.M., & Boyd, J.H. (1982). The epidemiology of affective disorders, rates and risk factors. In L. Grinspoon (Ed.), *American Psychiatric Association Annual Review, 2,* 406–428. Washington, DC: American Psychiatric Press.

Weissman, M., Klerman, G.L., Prusoff, B.A., Sholomskas, D., & Padian, N. (1981). Depressed outpatients. *Archives of General Psychiatry, 38,* 51–55.

Workman, E.A., & Short, D.D. (1993). Atypical antidepressants versus imipramine in the treatment of major depression: A meta-analysis. *Journal of Clinical Psychiatry, 54*(5).

PART III
ANXIETY,
SOMATOFORM,
AND
DISSOCIATIVE
DISORDERS

OVERVIEW

Prior to the publication of DSM-III in 1980, a distinction was made between psychotic and neurotic disorders. The first section of this book dealt with what used to be called the psychoses. This section deals with what used to make up the neuroses. Whereas Adler (Ansbacher & Ansbacher, 1956) considered psychosis to be a "No!" in response to the challenges of life, he believed

> Neurosis is always behavior which can be expressed in two words, the words "Yes—but." This is the best and easiest definition because it distinguishes a neurosis from all other types of failure and the neurotic from the normal person. (p. 302)

Adlerians believe that, when faced with challenges, normal—that is, socially interested people—will respond with a "Yes—I can" attitude. These people will focus not upon themselves and their own prestige (i.e., inferiorities) but upon the task at hand. They are task-oriented rather than prestige-oriented. Psychotics will respond with a "No!" attitude, refusing to even acknowledge the request or demand. Neurotics will acknowledge the demand (the "Yes" part of the response), but they will hesitate and attempt to excuse themselves (the "but" portion of the response): "Yes, I know what to do, but I can't, because of . . . fears . . . pains . . . etc."

Dreikurs (1967), in differentiating neurotic from psychotic disorders psycho-dynamically, noted that whereas psychotics discarded common sense in favor of their private logic, neurotics had a firmly developed common sense that they hoped to disqualify. Neurotics followed their private logic, but they maintained enough of the common sense to at least act as if they were outwardly compliant. Unlike the psychotics, neurotics at least acknowledged the challenge.

In Chapter 6, "Anxiety Disorders I," Sperry begins this section with a discussion of the Panic, Obsessive-Compulsive, and Agoraphobic Disorders. He discusses the biopsychosocial components of each condition, along with latest research into treatment strategies.

In Chapter 7, "Anxiety Disorders II," O'Connell and Hooker discuss Posttraumatic Stress Disorder, Generalized Anxiety Disorder, and Social Phobia. This chapter presents O'Connell's unique interpretation of Individual Psychology and his many years of experience working with very troubled individuals from a multiplicity of life experiences, ranging from such common occurrences as worry about attending social gatherings to the horrors and devastation in being in a combat zone, fighting for survival.

Mays, in Chapter 8, elaborates upon the "Somatoform Disorders and Psychological Factors Affecting Physical conditions." He introduces the Adlerian concept of organ jargon and analyzes from the vantage point of the holistic hypothesis in order to understand and intervene in conditions that, by definition, "speak through the body."

In Chapter 9, the final chapter in this section, the rather infrequently discussed topic of "Dissociative Disorders" is discussed. Sperry, in a truly integrative fashion, reviews the works of not only Adler but also Janet, Freud, and Prince in order to illuminate what traditionally have been some of the most elusive of all conditions to conceptualize and treat.

REFERENCES

Ansbacher, H.L., & Ansbacher, R.R. (Eds.). (1956). *The Individual Psychology of Alfred Adler*. New York: Basic Books.

Dreikurs, R. (1967). *Psychodynamics, psychotherapy, and counseling*. Chicago: Alfred Adler Institute.

Chapter 6

ANXIETY DISORDERS I

Len Sperry

The anxiety disorders are perhaps the most common clinical condition diagnosed and treated by mental health professionals. The designation Anxiety Disorders in DSM-IV refer to eleven discrete clinical entities: Panic Disorder with Agoraphobia, Panic Disorder without Agoraphobia, Agoraphobia without a history of Panic Disorder, Specific Phobia, Social Phobia, Obsessive-Compulsive Disorder, Posttraumatic Stress Disorder, Acute Stress Disorder, Generalized Anxiety Disorder, Anxiety Disorder Due to a General Medical Condition, and Anxiety Disorders Not Otherwise Specified (NOS). Previously these disorders were classified in DSM-I and DSM-II as neuroses or neurotic disorders.

The terms fear and anxiety have been variously defined, but in this chapter we will utilize the definitions of Beck and Emery (1985). They distinguished anxiety from fear by defining fear as a cognitive assessment of a threatening stimuli, whereas anxiety is an emotional reaction to that assessment. As anxiety is experienced, a number of physiological reactions, particularly symptoms associated with the autonomic nervous system, may occur simultaneously. When we speak of the anxiety disorders, we can differentiate the variety of manifestations of anxiety. For instance, overwhelming anxiety is either the predominant disturbance as it is manifested in Panic Disorders without Agoraphobia and Generalized Anxiety Disorders or anxiety experienced as a person attempts to master symptoms, as when confronting a dreaded object or situation in phobic disorder. When the anxiety is manifested when resisting an obsession or a compulsion, however, then an Obsessive-Compulsive Disorder is diagnosed.

A few generalizations need to be made about the anxiety disorders. With a possible exception of Social Phobia, these disorders develop most frequently in young women and generally have a poor prognosis and a chronic unremitting course when appropriate treatment is not provided. These disorders occur relatively frequently. The most comprehensive epidemiological study of mental illness in the United States, the *Epidemiologic Catchment Area* (ECA) study reported high lifetime problems rates between 10% and 25% (Robins, Helzer, & Weissman, 1984). Even though the prevalence rate is quite high, only a small percentage of individuals with these disorders is ever treated by a professional therapist. In this chapter will be described three anxiety disorders: Panic Disorder without Agoraphobia, Obsessive-Compulsive Disorder, and Agoraphobia without history of Panic Disorder. In the next chapter, other anxiety disorders will be described. The plan for this chapter is to present each disorder descriptively or phenomenologically, including DSM-IV criteria, a clinical formulation in terms of Adlerian theory, and a brief section on treatment goals and methods. Also, a case study is provided that exemplifies each disorder.

PANIC DISORDER WITHOUT AGORAPHOBIA

Panic attacks are the cardinal feature for panic disorders. The panic or anxiety attack has dramatic, acute symptoms lasting minutes to hours and is usually self-limited. Symptoms are perceived by the individual as medical in nature and are characterized by strong autonomic nervous system discharges: heart pounding, chest pains, trembling, choking, sweating, and dizziness. Individuals also may experience feeling disorganized, confused, and a sense of impending doom. The panic disorder is primarily recurrent and episodic rather than chronic in nature. The panic attacks are clearly separate incidents, but the anxiety experienced is not a response to a phobic stimuli or to any event that is very dangerous in reality. The terror experiences are not unlike "free-floating anxiety," described as an experienced anxiety with the inability to specify any source or reason. It is probably for this reason that Freud combined two forms of anxiety, panic attacks and chronic anxiety, under the rubic of the anxiety neurosis. This convention was followed in both DSM-I and DSM-II; however, researchers found that the tricyclic antidepressant imipramine produced remission of panic symptoms in anxiety individuals without altering the severity of their generalized anxiety (Klein, 1980). This finding suggested the panic attacks might distinguish a Panic Disorder from a Generalized Anxiety Disorder. Subsequently DSM-III, DSM-III-R, and DSM-IV adopted this distinction by specifying separate diagnoses for Panic Disorder and Generalized Anxiety Disorder.

TABLE 6.1
Diagnostic criteria for 300.01 Panic Disorder Without Agoraphobia

A. Both (1) and (2):
   (1) recurrent unexpected Panic Attacks
   A discrete period of intense fear or discomfort, in which four (or more) of the following symptoms developed abruptly and reached a peak within 10 minutes:
   　(1) palpitations, pounding heart, or accelerated heart rate
   　(2) sweating
   　(3) trembling or shaking
   　(4) sensations of shortness of breath or smothering
   　(5) feeling of choking
   　(6) chest pain or discomfort
   　(7) nausea or abdominal distress
   　(8) feeling dizzy, unsteady, lightheaded, or faint
   　(9) derealization (feelings of unreality) or depersonalization (being detached from oneself)
   　(10) fear of losing control or going crazy
   　(11) fear of dying
   　(12) paresthesias (numbness or tingling sensations)
   　(13) chills or hot flushes
   (2) at least one of the attacks has been followed by 1 month (or more) of one (or more) of the following:
   　(a) persistent concern about having additional attacks
   　(b) worry about the implications of the attack or its consequences (e.g., losing control, having a hearth attack, "going crazy")
   　(c) a significant change in behavior related to the attacks
B. Absence of Agoraphobia
C. The Panic Attacks are not due to the direct physiological effects of a substance (e.g., a drug of abuse, a medication) or a general medical condition (e.g., hyperthyroidism).
D. The Panic Attacks are not better accounted for by another mental disorder, such as Social Phobia (e.g., occurring on exposure to feared social situations), Specific Phobia (e.g., on exposure to a specific phobic situation), Obsessive-Compulsive Disorder (e.g., on exposure to dirt in someone with an obsession about contamination), Posttraumatic Stress Disorder (e.g., in response to stimuli associated with a severe stressor), or Separation Anxiety Disorder (e.g., in response to being away from home or close relatives).

From *Diagnostic and Statistical Manual of Mental Disorders, Fourth Edition* (DSM-IV). Copyright © 1994 by American Psychiatric Association. Reprinted with permission.

The DSM-IV offers specific criteria for Panic without Agoraphobia (300.01), which are noted in Table 6.1 (American Psychiatric Association, 1994, p. 395 & 402). Some individuals attempt to cope with these panic attacks with an anticipatory fear of helplessness and by becoming increasingly reluctant to leave the comfort and familiarity of their homes. If this fear increases, the diagnosis will likely change to panic disorder with agoraphobia. With the panic disorder, it is important to rule out physical disorders that mimic panic attacks such as hypoglycemia and hyperthyroidism or withdrawal symptoms from alcohol or other drugs, or mitral valve prolapse, which cause approximately 40% of all panic episodes.

Course of the Disorder

Typically, panic disorder begins with a spontaneous panic attack, that is, an anxiety attack with no environmental precipitant. Most frequently, this panic attack occurs in the third decade of life and within six months of a stressful life event such as a marital separation or death of a parent. Generally, when individuals experience this first panic attack they misinterpret its significance, frequently believing that they are either dying of a heart attack or going crazy. Psychosocial factors can significantly affect the course of the panic disorder. As mentioned earlier, adverse life events are associated with the onset of the disorder and probably with the course of the panic symptoms. Individuals with panic disorders tend to display poor problem-solving ability. Coexisting personality disorders or traits such as the dependent, avoidant, or histrionic personality disorders are present in approximately 50% of panic patients. The presence of an Axis II personality disorder tends to worsen treatment prognosis. Hypersensitivity to bodily sensations and cognitive distortions tends to exacerbate symptoms and tends to increase the risk of complications. Under very stressful circumstances, usually following an illness or a loss of sleep, an individual often will experience an anxiety attack. In the normal individual, no progression in terms of frequency or severity will occur to meet the DSM-IV criteria. In the biologically and psychologically predisposed individual, however, panic episodes tend to continue with sufficient severity and frequency to meet DSM-IV criteria within two months or so of the first panic attack. In the first year after the onset of panic symptoms, most patients will develop anticipatory anxiety and agoraphobia (Breier, Charney, & Heninger, 1986). About 20% of individuals with panic also have histories of alcoholism. Panic-disordered individuals with panic also have histories of alcoholism. Panic-disordered individuals often use alcohol as a self-treatment for their panic attacks.

The lifetime prevalence of panic disorders is in the range of 0.4% and 2.5% according to the ECA (Robins et al., 1984). Panic symptoms were shown to be two to three times more frequent in women, mainly because men use alcohol to self-treat their panic and subsequently are given a diagnosis of alcoholism rather than panic disorder. In both men and women, panic is most prevalent in the second through fourth decades and decreases in frequency thereafter.

PANIC DISORDER WITHOUT A HISTORY OF AGORAPHOBIA

Literally, agoraphobia means a fear of the marketplace or of being in open spaces. Clinically, agoraphobia is a fear of being trapped in such places as crowded theaters, traffic jams, bridges, and elevators. Typically, agoraphobia develops in individuals already experiencing panic attacks. A useful procedure is to think of agoraphobia as a learned fear response to panic attacks. Following the onset of agoraphobia, individuals generally begin avoiding the setting of anxiety attacks. This avoidance generalizes as a disorder and becomes more severe, thus resulting in the individual becoming housebound.

Agoraphobics develop a strong sense of helplessness and anticipate that panic will set in at any time, leaving them without any means of control. Their ultimate fear is that they will be trapped, left alone, and overwhelmed with panic attack. The increasing incidence of agoraphobia may reflect increasing interpersonal alienation, increasing competitiveness, as well as rising divorce rate, breakdown of the family unit, and high levels of social and geographic mobility. These changes in demands increase the likelihood that the individual will experience being alone in the face of change and stress. These stresses and changes are often first noted in adolescence, though they may have been preceded by attacks of separation anxiety and occurrences of school phobia in childhood. Social and vocational role changes can make the individual particularly vulnerable to agoraphobia. Thus, women in a traditional housewife role who are experiencing menopause at the same time their children are leaving home are likely to be vulnerable to agoraphobia. Housebound agoraphobics are noted for their manipulative behaviors toward significant others. These individuals may, with time, become bothersome to those around them, and subsequently depression will complicate their agoraphobia. Needless to say, the agoraphobic who utilizes alcohol or other drugs to diminish his or her anxieties has a high propensity toward substance addiction. The lifetime prevalence of this disorder is approximately five percent. The DSM-IV criteria for Agoraphobia Without History of Panic Disorder (300.22) are noted in Table 6.2 (American Psychiatric Association, 1994, pp. 404–405).

The DSM-IV also lists criteria for Panic Disorder With Agoraphobia. The Criteria are noted in Table 6.3 (American Psychiatric Association, 1994, pp. 402–403).

Developmental Antecedents

Although Panic Disorder and Agoraphobia with panic episodes usually begin in early adulthood, they can be preceded by childhood anxiety or psychological

TABLE 6.2
Diagnostic criteria for 300.22 Agoraphobia Without History of Panic Disorder

A. The presence of Agoraphobia related to fear of developing panic-like symptoms (e.g., dizziness or diarrhea).

Anxiety about being in places or situations from which escape might be difficult (or embarrassing) or in which help may not be available in the event of having an unexpected or situationally predisposed Panic Attack or panic-like symptoms. Agoraphobic fears typically involve characteristic clusters of situations that include being outside the home alone; being in a crowd or standing in a line; being on a bridge; and traveling in a bus, train, or automobile.

Note: Consider the diagnosis of Specific Phobia if the avoidance is limited to one or only a few specific situations, or Social Phobia if the avoidance is limited to social situations.

The situations are avoided (e.g., travel is restricted) or else are endured with marked distress or with anxiety about having a Panic Attack or panic-like symptoms, or require the presence of a companion.

The anxiety or phobic avoidance is not better accounted for by another mental disorder, such as Social Phobia (e.g., avoidance limited to social situations because of fear of embarrassment), Specific Phobia (e.g., avoidance limited to a single situation like elevators), Obsessive-Compulsive Disorder (e.g., avoidance of dirt in someone with an obsession about contamination), Posttraumatic Stress Disorder (e.g., avoidance of stimuli associated with a severe stressor), or Separation Anxiety Disorder (e.g., avoidance of leaving home or relatives.)

B. Criteria have never been met for Panic Disorder
C. The disturbance is not due to the direct physiological effects of a substance (e.g., a drug of abuse, a medication) or a general medical condition.
D. If an associated general medical condition is present, the fear described in Criterion A is clearly in excess of that usually associated with the condition.

From *Diagnostic and Statistical Manual of Mental Disorders, Fourth Edition* (DSM-IV). Copyright © 1994 by American Psychiatric Association. Reprinted with permission.

trauma. Individuals with Panic Disorder report more childhood fears, recall being more anxious as children, and have more disturbed childhood environments than individuals with Generalized Anxiety Disorder. Females with agoraphobia and panic attacks are increasingly likely to have experienced childhood separation anxiety. Several studies have confirmed this history of separation anxiety (Aronson & Logue, 1987). The development of phobias in individuals with Panic Disorders also is associated with the history of childhood depression, Obsessive-Compulsive Disorder, and Overanxious Disorder. Individuals with such a history

TABLE 6.3
Diagnostic criteria for 300.21 Panic Disorder With Agoraphobia

A. Both (1) and (2):
  (1) recurrent unexpected Panic Attacks
  (2) at least one of the attacks has been followed by 1 month (or more) of one (or more) of the following:
    (a) persistent concern about having additional attacks
    (b) worry about the implications of the attack or its consequences (e.g., losing control, having a heart attack, "going crazy")
    (c) a significant change in behavior related to the attacks
B. The presence of Agoraphobia
C. The Panic Attacks are not due to the direct physiological effects of a substance (e.g., a drug of abuse, a medication) or a general medical condition (e.g., hyperthyroidism).
D. The Panic Attacks are not better accounted for by another mental disorder, such as Social Phobia (e.g., occurring on exposure to feared social situations), Specific Phobia (e.g., on exposure to a specific phobic situation), Obsessive-Compulsive Disorder (e.g., on exposure to dirt in someone with an obsession about contamination), Posttraumatic Stress Disorder (e.g., in response to stimuli associated with a severe stressor), or Separation Anxiety Disorder (e.g., in response to being away from home or close relatives).

From *Diagnostic and Statistical Manual of Mental Disorders, Fourth Edition* (DSM-IV). Copyright © 1994 by American Psychiatric Association. Reprinted with permission.

of separation anxiety do show an earlier onset of panic attacks. Since separation anxiety is not a significant feature of individuals with Panic Disorder without Agoraphobia, a history of childhood separation experiences or a formal diagnosis of Separation Anxiety Disorder appears to be a marker for Agoraphobia.

The history of childhood fearfulness in anxiety disorders in agoraphobics may represent an earlier manifestation of the same disorder or a predisposing factor increasing their vulnerability to panic and other phobias. This increasing vulnerability to agoraphobia suggests a temperamental difference. The agoraphobic individual was most likely an overanxious and clinging child who experienced parental withdrawal, which contributed to the development of this disorder.

OBSESSIVE-COMPULSIVE DISORDER

Obsessive-Compulsive Disorder is distinguished by its two cardinal features, obsessions and compulsions. Obsessions are persistent, unwanted ideas or impulses that cannot be overcome easily by logic or reason. Compulsions are persistent, repetitive, and intrusive urges to perform an action that is contrary to one's wishes and standards. Compulsions may be performed in response to an obsession or without a clear percipient. Obsessions may be distinguished from delusions by the retention of reality testing that permits the sufferer to recognize the intrusive thought as irrational, excessive, or uncharacteristic. For example: "I know I just washed my hands, but I keep thinking that they're dirty." Obsessions also may be distinguished from depressive ruminations, which characteristically are "owned" by the person. For example: "I'm worthless because I lost my job." Compulsions rarely are confused with symptoms of other diagnoses. The most common obsessions are fears of contamination such as by dirt, toxins, or germs. Other common obsessions involve aggression or violence, or doubts about self, religion, or duties. The most common compulsions include checking behaviors, hand-washing, and repetitive actions. The Obsessive-Compulsive Disorder does not include compulsions to perform behaviors that are in themselves pleasurable such as alcohol use or overeating. Even though the users of alcohol or food may not be able to control these behavior patterns, these patterns are not ego-alien. In fact, these behaviors are inherently pleasurable and, thus, would not be considered compulsions.

Individuals diagnosed with Obsessive-Compulsive Disorder give a history of subclinical ritualistic behaviors dating back to early childhood. Avoiding stepping on cracks in the sidewalk, touching a lucky chair or book when walking into a room, or rubbing objects or a particular part of their bodies in a repetitive almost mechanical way are examples of these subclinical rituals. The usual onset for the Obsessive-Compulsive Disorder is late adolescence or early adulthood. By the age of 25 years, the majority of individuals who will be diagnosed with this disorder already will have expressed clinical symptoms.

Obsessive-Compulsive Disorder syndrome occurs proportionately more often in middle- and upper-class individuals. In a culture that highly values achievement, individuals with compulsive patterns are often quite efficient and productive and are likely to have been rewarded for their compulsiveness. Obsessive-Compulsive individuals tend to be brighter than individuals with other anxiety disorders. This is probably because obsessions are basically intellectual coping strategies to reduce anxieties.

Obsessive-Compulsive Disorder was considered relatively uncommon; however, the recent ECA study found the lifetime prevalence of Obsessive-Compulsive Disorder to be two to three percent, which was approximately 20 times more than had previously been thought (Robins et al., 1984). Males and females appear to be approximately equally affected with Obsessive-Compulsive Disorder, although the childhood form of this disorder appears to develop more frequently in males. A high incidence of major depression occurs in individuals with Obsessive-

Compulsive Disorder. Typically, depressive symptoms appear after the Obsessive-Compulsive disorder already has produced functional impairment. Also, Obsessive-Compulsive Disorder may exist concurrently with panic disorder as well as Tourette's syndrome. The belief was that Obsessive-Compulsive Disorder and Obsessive-Compulsive Personality Disorder were either one in the same, or that individuals who exhibited the Axis I Obsessive-Compulsive Disorder would exhibit an Axis II Obsessive-Compulsive Personality Disorder. This belief was fostered, in large part, by Freud's case of "The Rat Man." The Rat Man displayed an Obsessive-Compulsive Personality Disorder as well as the obsessions and rituals characteristic of the Obsessive-Compulsive Disorder. The ego-alien quality discriminates the Obsessive-Compulsive Disorder from the personality disorder. If the personality-disordered individual does engage in occasional rituals, these compulsions are ego-satanic; that is, they are not viewed as conflictual. Based on research data (Jenike, Baer, & Minichiello, 1986; Rappoport, 1989) Obsessive-Compulsive Personality Disorder is noted in less that 40% of individuals with the Obsessive-Compulsive Disorder. DSM-IV criteria for Obsessive-Compulsive Disorder are noted in Table 6.4 (American Psychiatric Association, 1994, pp. 422–423).

AN ADLERIAN INTERPRETATION OF PANIC DISORDER, AGORAPHOBIA, AND OBSESSIVE-COMPULSIVE DISORDER

Adler (1964) taught that anxiety is utilized to create distance between the individual and life tasks so as to safeguard self-esteem when the individual feels defeat. Adler considered the neurotic individual as an ambitious person who had lost his or her courage and so lived in constant dread of his or her weaknesses being discovered by others. Adler would say that the neurotic has a "hesitating attitude" or a "yes-but" response to life. The anxious individual postpones decisions and tries to keep a safe distance from others and difficult tasks.

> Agoraphobia, anxiety neurosis, and all the forms of phobia may originate at this point (the individual's unwillingness to admit his defeat), but, whichever may be, it fulfills its purpose of blocking the way to further activity. Thus, what was desired is obtained—namely, the ordeal is evaded without disclosing, even to its owner, the hated feeling of inferiority. All other symptoms, such as compulsions, ideas, fits, fatigue, sleeplessness, functional disturbances such as neurotic heart, headaches, migraines, and so on, develop out of the severe tension of this very difficult concealment. (Adler, 1964, p. 11)

TABLE 6.4
Diagnostic criteria for 300.3 Obsessive-Compulsive Disorder

A. Either obsessions or compulsions:
   Obsessions as defined by (1), (2), (3), and (4):
   (1) recurrent and persistent thoughts, impulses, or images that are experienced, at some time during the disturbance, as intrusive and inappropriate and that cause marked anxiety or distress
   (2) the thoughts, impulses, or images are not simply excessive worries about real-life problems
   (3) the person attempts to ignore or suppress such thoughts, impulses, or images, or to neutralize them with some other thought or action
   (4) the person recognizes that the obsessional thoughts, impulses, or images are a product of his or her own mind (not imposed from without as in thought insertion)
   Compulsions as defined by (1) and (2):
   (1) repetitive behaviors (e.g., hand washing, ordering, checking) or mental acts (e.g., praying, counting, repeating words silently) that the person feels driven to perform in response to an obsession, or according to rules that must be applied rigidly
   (2) the behaviors or mental acts are aimed at preventing or reducing distress or preventing some dreaded event or situation; however, these behaviors or mental acts either are not connected in a realistic way with what they are designed to neutralize or prevent or are clearly excessive

B. At some point during the course of the disorder, the person has recognized that the obsessions or compulsions are excessive or unreasonable. **Note:** This does not apply to children.

C. The obsessions or compulsions cause marked distress, are time consuming (take more that 1 hour a day), or significantly interfere with the person's normal routine, occupational (or academic) functioning, or usual social activities or relationships.

D. If another Axis I disorder is present, the content of the obsessions or compulsions is not restricted to it (e.g., preoccupation with food in the presence of an Eating Disorder; hair pulling in the presence of Trichotillomania; concern with appearance in the presence of Body Dysmorphic Disorder; preoccupation with drugs in the presence of a Substance Use Disorder; preoccupation with having a serious illness in the presence of Hypochondriasis; preoccupation with sexual urges or fantasies in the presence of a Paraphilia; or guilty ruminations in the presence of Major Depressive Disorder).

E. The disturbance is not due to the direct physiological effects of a substance (e.g., a drug of abuse, a medication) or a general medical condition.

Specify if:
   With Poor Insight: if, for most of the time during the current episode, the person does not recognize that the obsessions and compulsions are excessive or unreasonable

These neurotic patterns are laid down in early childhood. Because pampered children are ill-prepared to perform the tasks of life, they find their courage taxed when another child is born, school life begins, or a major change takes place in their environment, such as a move to another neighborhood or the death of a parent. The first anxious symptoms often take the form of organ dysfunction, such as abdominal pains, respiratory symptoms, anuresis, or temper tantrums. Their purpose is to compel the parents to give in to their children and relieve them of certain responsibilities. Dreikurs noted that these symptoms are among the first weapons children use to get their way (Dreikurs, 1950).

Like Freud, Adler did not distinguish the Panic Disorder from Agoraphobia or from the other anxiety disorders. On the other hand, Adler (1964) described the Obsessive-Compulsive Disorder in considerable detail. In fact, he considered the Compulsive Neurosis as the prototype of all mental disorders.

Adler delineated at least eight features of the Compulsive Neurosis. First, there is a striving for personal superiority that is diverted into easy channels. This striving for personal superiority is encouraged in the child by excessive parental pampering. The onset of the Compulsive Neurosis occurs in the face of actual situations where the dread of a blow to vanity through failure leads to the "hesitating attitude." The compulsive symptoms then provide a means of relief. And once fixed upon, they provide the individual with an excuse for failing. The construction of the compulsive neurosis as seen by Adler is identical with that of the lifestyle. Adler was careful to point out that the compulsion did not reside in the compulsive actions themselves but originated in the demands of social living that represented a menace to the individual's prestige and courage. The lifestyle of the compulsive neurotic adopted only those forms of symptom expression that suited its purpose while rejecting other forms of expression. And finally, the ever-present guilt feelings experienced by the compulsive neurotic were efforts to kill time in order to gain time. This then is a summary description of the dynamics of the Obsessive-Compulsive Disorder formulated by Adler and his followers. Parenthetically, Leon Salzman's formulation in the book *The Obsessive Personality* (1968) is consistent with Adler's formulation.

TREATMENT CONSIDERATIONS

Treatment of Panic and Agoraphobia

Biological and psychosocial factors have a significant effect on the time of onset, course, treatment, and response of Panic and Agoraphobic Disorders. For this reason, these factors need to be considered in the treatment of Panic Disorder and Agoraphobia. Therefore, assessment of an individual with Panic Disorder should include careful attention to Axis II features, major coping strategies used, lifestyle convictions, and the cognitive interpretation of the significance of panic symptoms, history of childhood disorders, and recent or impending life changes. Many individuals, especially those with Axis II personality disorder diagnoses, poor coping skills, or significant cognitive distortions, will require psychotherapy in addition to medication for panic and agoraphobic symptoms. Antidepressant and/or anxiolytic medications such as Xanax and Tranzene have been shown to quickly abate and prevent panic attacks. Psychotherapy will be most helpful if it is targeted specifically for the person's current deficits and includes cognitive restructuring techniques and psychoeducation about effective problem solving. Common issues in the therapy of panic and agoraphobia include dependency, autonomy, and defensive overcontrol.

In the course of treatment, individuals can learn to identify, anticipate, and deal with some of their adverse life changes that have exacerbated their illness in the past. Encouragement and education are important in helping individuals with their first panic attacks, especially if they are concerned about life-threatening illnesses or "going crazy." These concerns, as well as a history of childhood anxiety, indicate a need for encouragement from the therapist to help these individuals confront feared situations and avoid the development of agoraphobia. Treatment of individuals with established agoraphobia must include careful attention to significant interpersonal relationships.

Treatment of the Obsessive-Compulsive Disorder

Surprisingly, treatment of the Obsessive-Compulsive Disorder is moderately successful, with approximately 70% to 80% of individuals reporting resolution of their symptoms. Medication has been found to be particularly useful in this disorder. Drugs like Prozac and Anafranil and other drugs with serotonergic properties like Desyrel are most likely to reduce symptoms. Behavior therapy also has been found particularly helpful. For ritualizers, the most effective combination of behavioral interventions are *exposure therapy* and *response prevention*. In exposure therapy, the individual is exposed to the fearful situation, whereas in response prevention the compulsive response is blocked or prevented from occurring. For individuals who experience obsessions only, two behavioral methods are recommended. They are *imaginal exposure* and *thought stopping*. In imaginal exposure, the individual is helped to mentally experience the dreaded situation and become systematically desensitized, and in time the fear is extinguished. In thought stopping, the therapist, and then later the individual, interrupts obsessional thoughts by either seeing the word "stop" mentally on a large T.V. screen or billboard, or whispering or shouting out the word "stop" at the moment the obsessional thought comes to consciousness. Since this disorder is not solely a biological dysfunction, not surprisingly, a combination of medications and psychotherapy results in significant improvement. Therapeutic issues, particularly lifestyle convictions about control and feeling avoidance, are the focus of insight-oriented therapy. Readers are referred to Salzman's book on *Treatment of the Obsessive Personality* (1980) or his more recent article for a review of the psychotherapy of obsessions and compulsions (Salzman, 1985).

CASE EXAMPLES

Case of Mr. Z

Mr. Z is a 41-year-old claims adjuster who was referred by his family doctor for psychological evaluation. He related a six-month history of recurrent bouts of extreme fear of sudden onset, accompanied by sweating, shortness of breath, palpitations, chest pain, dizziness, numbness in his fingers and toes, and the fear that he was going to die. His family physician had given him a complete medical workup and could not find an organic cause for these symptoms. Mr. Z and his wife had been married for eight years and have no children. He had served with distinction in the military before his marriage. Afterwards, he began working at a large insurance company during the day while going to college at night to complete a bachelor's and master's degree in business administration. He was quite successful and well-liked at his place of employment. He and his wife generally got along quite well and had an active social life. Because of the attacks, which occurred unexpectedly and in a variety of situations several times a week, Mr. Z started to avoid driving his car and going into shops and office buildings, fearing he might have an anxiety attack. He convinced his wife to accompany him on all errands; and during the last four weeks, he had felt comfortable only at home with his wife. Finally, he could not face the prospect of leaving home to go to his office and applied for a medical leave of absence. While at home, he experienced only occasional "twinges" of chest pain and slight numbness in his fingers, but no full-blown anxiety attacks. When asked about circumstances surrounding the onset of his attacks, Mr. Z noted that he and his wife had discussed buying a home and moving from their apartment. He admitted that the responsibilities of owning a home intimidated him and related the significance of the move to similar concerns his parents had that had prevented them from ever buying a house.

This case exemplifies the DSM-IV diagnosis of Panic Disorder with Agoraphobia (300.21). Mr. Z's recurrent, unexpected anxiety attacks in the absence of an organic cause indicate Panic Disorder. Agoraphobia developed as Mr. Z increasingly constricted his normal activities because of a fear of being in situations from which escape would be difficult or embarrassing, or where help might not be available in the event of a panic attack. For Mr. Z, the significant life-change event was the anticipation of home ownership. Similar concerns to those of his parents, Mr. Z's "hesitating attitude" about assuming the added financial and day-to-day responsibilities for owning a home resulted in his panic and agoraphobic symptoms. These symptoms effectively safeguarded Mr. Z from having to move into a home he owns. Ironically, the symptoms, particularly the agoraphobia, "force" Mr. Z to remain in his apartment.

Case of Mrs. A

For an example of the Obsessive-Compulsive Disorder, we return again to the case of Mrs. A that was described in some detail in Chapter One of this text. The reader will recall that Mrs. A was a housewife with two children who presented with a dysphoric mood, a cleaning compulsion, a night phobia, and a fear of seriously harming her younger son. She also experienced significant marital and other family problems. Her obsessions and compulsions progressively worsened in the 18 months following a terrifying dream in which angels surround a coffin. About this time she had problems with her neighbors and difficulty with her husband to such an extent that she moved out of her home, took her children, and returned to live with her parents. During this time her husband experienced a "nervous breakdown" and begged for her to return to care for him. After returning, her obsessive thoughts and compulsive behaviors incapacitated her to such an extent that she sought psychotherapy. Her faulty lifestyle convictions include the following: Mrs. A viewed life as hostile, unfair, and overcontrolling. She saw herself as a victim who expected to be humiliated but also believed she was entitled to be treated differently. Therefore, she demanded that others take care of her. Furthermore, she utilized obsessions, compulsions, and threats of harming herself and her children to ensure that her husband and family continued in their caretaking roles. In short, Mrs. A utilized interpersonal relationships as a means of gaining dominance and resisting submission. For her, cooperation was construed as conquest and defeat rather than mutual helpfulness and social interest.

SUMMARY

This chapter focused on three anxiety disorders: Panic Disorder Without Agoraphobia, Obsessive-Compulsive Disorder Without Agoraphobia, and Agoraphobia Without a History of Panic Disorder. Each disorder was described with DSM-IV criteria, an Individual Psychology formulation, treatment goals and interventions, and a case example. The following chapter focuses on additional DSM-IV anxiety disorders.

REFERENCES

Adler, A. (1964). *Problems of neurosis*. New York: Harper Torchbooks.

American Psychiatric Association. (1994). *Diagnostic and statistical manual of mental disorders* (4th ed.). Washington, DC: Author.

Aronson, T., & Logue, H. (1987). On the longitudinal course of panic disorder: Developmental history and predictors of phobic complications. *Comprehensive Psychiatry, 28*, 344–355.

Beck, A.T., & Emery, G. (1985). *Anxiety disorders and phobias*. New York: Basic Books.

Breier, A., Charney, D.S., & Heninger, G.R. (1986). Agoraphobia with panic attacks. *Archives of General Psychiatry, 43*, 1029–1038.

Dreikurs, R. (1950). *Fundamentals of Adlerian psychology*. New York: Greenburg Publishers.

Jenike, M.A., Baer, M., & Minichiello, W.E. (1986). *Obsessive-compulsive disorders: Theory and management*. Littleton, MA: PSG Publishing.

Klein, D. (1980). Anxiety reconceptualized. *Comprehensive Psychiatry, 21*, 411–427.

Rappoport, J.L. (Ed.). (1989). *Obsessive-compulsive disorder in children and adolescents*. Washington, DC: American Psychiatric Press.

Robins, L.M., Helzer, J.E., & Weissman, M.M. (1984). Lifetime prevalence of specific psychiatric disorders in three sites. *Archives of General Psychiatry, 41*, 949–958.

Salzman, L. (1968). *Obsessive personality: Origins, dynamics, and therapy*. New York: Science House.

Salzman, L. (1980). *Treatment of the obsessive personality*. New York: Jason Aronson.

Salzman, L. (1985). Psychotherapeutic management of obsessive-compulsive patients. *American Journal of Psychiatry, 39*, 323–330.

Chapter 7

ANXIETY DISORDERS II

Walter E. O'Connell
Elizabeth Hooker

The honest psychologist cannot shut his eyes to social conditions which prevent the child from becoming a part of the community and from feeling at home in the world, and which allow him to grow up as though he lived in enemy country. Thus the psychologist must work against nationalism when it is so poorly understood that it harms mankind as a whole; against wars of conquest, revenge, and prestige; against unemployment which plunges people into hopelessness; and against all other obstacles which interfere with the spreading of social interest in the family, the school, and society at large. (Adler, in Ansbacher & Ansbacher, 1956, p. 454)

This chapter will cover the Adlerian diagnosis, understanding, and treatment of three DSM-IV categories of the anxiety disorders (American Psychiatric Association, 1994). These are Posttraumatic Stress Disorder (PTSD), Generalized Anxiety Disorder (GAD), and Social Phobias (SP). Diagnosis, understanding, and treatment of these problem patterns of inner and outer movement will follow the insightful conceptualizations of Alfred Adler. His wisdom is summarized succinctly in the above quotation originally published in 1933.

Psychological truth, according to the Adlerian view, is expressed by those inner and outer movements that maximize experiences of *self-esteem* (SE), *social interest* (SI), and *sense of humor* (SH). Anxiety, on the other hand, is the cause and effect of the negative certainty that the future is out of control. Powerful negative forces, it is feared, will overwhelm the spurious solid, permanent separateness of the psyche. These negative inner and outer threats must be resisted and/or denied to maintain this tremulous ego trance state (O'Connell & Gomez, 1990). Of course, the anxiety-ridden person does not express these self-defeating assumptions and purposes with any psychic distance and subsequent humor. Popular certainties of solid, permanent, and separateness must be threatened by such negative misconceptions for tension to be reframed into a habitual set of objectless fears.

A precursor to distress is the normal shock of an unexpected overwhelming stimulation that subsequently cannot be shared without "awfulizing." This shock reaction follows from the abrupt realization that one is mortal and not able to predict perfect control over persons and events. This perception of mortality and limited control over persons and events stimulates psychic and physical reactions. When such out-of-control states are resisted and catastrophized, they are called "anxiety." Strong persons, those who generate SE, SI, and a buoyant SH, recover their psychic balance quickly; that is, such actualized and individuated persons resist the temptations to identify with guilt and other subsequent negative judgments of the discouraging ego identity. The hallmarks of ego identity movements (see Figures 7.1 and 7.2) is perceptions of separation and boundaries, feelings of deprivation, anxiety and guilt. Stimulating and believing such negative perceptions will guarantee anxiety, and, of course, no anxiety is possible without this central belief that one is weak and isolated and, therefore, "out of control."

POSTTRAUMATIC STRESS DISORDER (PTSD)

Persons with the diagnosis of PTSD have been faced with experiences that have shattered their sense of personal identity (worth and belonging). The physical or psychic disabling or death, actual or implied, of oneself and/or one's significant others can seriously disrupt perceptions of significance and continuity. The absurd and excessive, meaningless violence of our times (in multiple contexts) threatens the existence of ideals, connectedness, and purposes of living. Traumatic termination, linked to sudden, shocking outer events, is the essence of the PTSD phenomenology.

The presence of PTSD is reflected by persistent reexperiencing of the traumatic event. Habitual attempts are made to avoid stimuli connected with the negativized and resisted happening. Increased arousal also reflects the presence of the PTSD syndrome. Excessive reexperience, arousal, and avoidance must be inferred from at least one, two, and three actions, respectively. Persistent *reexperiencing* is inferred from the presence of at least one of the following four

GUILT FEELINGS: Negative judgments of persons and events, mainly unconscious—"Worthless, now and forever, because of what was done or not done":

1. Focus on guilt feelings does not stimulate positive changes in behavior.

2. Guilt feelings diminish self-esteem (SE), social interest (SI), and the sense of humor (SH).

3. Guilt feelings have gluttonous and grandiose purposes:

   a. Gluttonous guilt feelings grab all the blame by ignoring the influence of other persons and events.

   b. Grandiose guilt feelings are negative certainties about the future (selective perceptions, provoked reactions).

4. Guilt feelings can be projected (dumped on others). And so we have prejudices and wars.

5. "Guilt Gluttons" unconsciously seek *and* fear punishment at the same time.

6. Guilt feelings can be used to gain minimal power (ego esteem through social influence) while neglecting strength (SE, SI, SH). These are the useless social goals of attention, special service, excitement, being boss, getting even, and displaying dis-ability (Dreikurs, 1972).

7. Once weakened by guilt-addiction, the Guilt Glutton becomes the dumping ground for the projected guilt of others. Not the magnetic attraction of the Guilt Dumper and Guilt Glutton, which makes for Gruesome Twosomes in marriages.

8. Guilt feelings grow out of the horrible confusion of judgment of worth of persons and events with judgments of worth and actions. All persons are *more than* their actions.

Figure 7.1. The constrictive power of guilt feelings.

The learned ego delusions that worth and belonging depend upon taking seriously (or otherwise attempting to make virtuous) the following vices, with their hidden commands:

1. Awfulizing Attitudes—"It not only happened, it was awful, terrible, catastrophe."
2. Boundary Building—"I must fragment, with impenetrable walls, certain thoughts, acts, and persons."
3. Control—"I must be the boss of thoughts, events, and persons."
4. Active Competition—"If I am not number one, in competitive combat, I am nothing."
5. Dependent Competition—"I need the perfect person or belief" to give a (pampering) fix for worthlessness and isolation.
6. Passive Competition—"I will do my secret avoid-dance and remove myself by depreciating any learning situation in which I am not the perfect master."
7. Double Denial—Two negative certainties, one at the beginning and the other much later, in the neurotic struggle with anxiety, initial denial of the ego defenses, followed later by denial of the necessity for self-training.
8. Distancing—"Stay out of my territory, or I'll waste you."
9. Futile Force—"Only a cowardly wimp would be too scared to use force to teach any lessons."
10. Self-guilt—The core and kingpin of the ego identity movements. "I am worthless, now and forever, for what I did and did not do." All facts of ego identity illustrate ego-diminishments. Subsequent social movements to restore worth and belonging conditionally make for dependency.
11. Projected Guilt—This distrusting stance is an interpersonal reaction to basic guilt and depression. Substitute specific others for the "I" in the Self-guilt formula above. Self-guilt destroys passionate $\overline{SE}$. Paranoia destroys compassionate $\overline{SI}$.
12. Invidious Comparisons—Comparisons designed to stimulate the learning of excellence is fine. "Invidious" means judgment of persons and event negatively, and so guarantees misery making.
13. Perfectionism—The dualism of antithetical thinking. "I am perfect or else I am nothing." Perfectionism devalues persons.
14. Resistance—"Stop essential change at all costs" is the ego's motto: clinging, grasping, and hanging on to clinging, grasping, and hanging on.
15. Time Addiction—Keep the past alive with guilt, and vice versa. Anticipate future catastrophic failures of worth and belonging for anxiety's sake. Watch the images, words, and sensations. BASH for self-cure of ego-induced dis-eases and pre-tensions.

Figure 7.2.   The pull of ego gravity.

movements: harrowing recollections, dreams, symbolizations, or expectations of the reliving of the traumatic event. At least two activities assumed to show the presence of increased *arousal* need to be reported: sleep disturbances, anger, excessive vigilance, overreactions to symbolic connections, and the inability to concentrate. The criteria for *hyperavoidance* are at least three of the following actions: resistances to thoughts or feelings or memories of the traumatic event, feelings of detachment or loss of interest, restriction of interest range, or the sense of an impending finish to one's future.

GENERALIZED ANXIETY DISORDER (GAD)

Persons diagnosed as suffering from GAD have persistent, excessive, irrational, ruminating, agonizing, and obsessing thoughts about two or more life situations for at least six months ("bothered more days than not").

For a GAD diagnosis, the candidate must report at least one-third of the following 18 symptoms when experiencing "anxiety." The four *motor tension* movements are trembling, muscular complaints, restlessness, and fatigue. *Autonomic hyperactivity* is marked by nine bodily complaints. These are feelings of being smothered, palpitations, sweating, dry mouth, vertigo, abdominal distress, flushes or chills, excessive urination, and "lump-in-throat." *Hypervigilance* has five characteristics: "keyed up," exaggerated startle response, blank mind, irritability, and sleep disturbances. From that wide range of emotional reactions, at least six are required for the GAD diagnosis.

Generalized anxiety is a manifestation of the individual's inability to cope. The primary source of the fear is often not conceptualized, and the individual is consistently in a state of high anxiety. Almost every person and event can be a serious threat to well-being, worth, and belonging, depending on the extent of the lowering and narrowing of SE, SI, and SH. Even when the fear has generalized to a broad range of people, places, and/or things, the source of the fear or anxiety is not perceived as being related to misery-making ego demands.

SOCIAL PHOBIA (SP) (Social Anxiety Disorder)

The person with the diagnosis of SP experiences chronic, intense anxiety in social situations. Social phobics irrationally believe that they are being critically judged by others. Consequently, they "know" that they will perform acts of commission or omission by which their tenuous worth and belonging will be severely threatened.

When exposed to the negative social stimuli, the person reacts with the feared symptoms of anxiety. Such displays or signs of loss of control are especially repugnant to social phobics. They usually endure phobic situations without any self-disclosure of anticipatory anxiety. Social phobics believe their suffering is excessive, irrational, and often crippling to vocational goals.

Social phobias are another way the individual conserves energy and obtains psychic distance from the problem by externalizing the object of the fear. The ego identity is defended by focusing on a specific target rather than generalized fear. ("It is only this specific situation in which I am not acceptable.") Externalizing the fear can be seen as a creative, laudable coping mechanism (like all learned movements), for which the client deserves congratulations; however, if symptoms are framed as "necessary safeguard skills," those symptoms would cease to be hated and would disappear. Symptoms owe their painful existence to ego resistance and negativization of happenings.

Social phobias can serve the purpose of giving structure to the individual's fear and at least a limited sense of power and control. A sense of power and control is an essential element in avoiding, alleviating, or forestalling the learned helplessness of depression. With a sense of control, even if judged as delusional, the person is able to remove himself or herself from the position of being helpless and thus hopeless. Any level of control, even pseudo-control, allows the person to keep hope alive, the remote but possible chance of being happy. One temporary value of social phobias is that the certainty of total worthlessness and inherent isolation is not generalized indiscriminately. People practicing and clinging to social phobias are considerably more tragicomic than most of us. Their awkward "avoid-dances," seen as so unnecessary to the disinterested observer, is the stuff of comedy. Their monumental misery-making triggers acute sadness in those aware of their inner struggles. Social phobias do not make sense: panic and "avoid-dances" are sad and mad, in the absence of life-threatening situations.

The phobic sufferer lacks self-esteem and social interest. It is the psyche that invites and fights the death threat. What we call psychopathology or mental "dis-ease" is a perceived threat to ego-esteem (or the ability to get strokes from other folks). Ego-esteem feels like self-esteem, but the risks involved in addiction to it are tremendous. Just as Arab oil "feels" like Texas oil, so ego-esteem feels like self-esteem. There is, however, the ever-present danger of being cut off for not performing up to the ego demands of the *other*. Ego-esteem is, as we all know, a pleasant experience. It is esteem or worth that gives the impetus to move about, carry on, and take risks. But to rely on ego entirely for the energy of esteem is a grievous error.

Another important point to be made is that ego-esteem is tied to a certain role. For example, if I have adequate ego-esteem as a doctor, I may show plenty of confidence and feel significant in the doctor's office. Unfortunately I may feel guilty and grossly inferior as a father. To avoid these feelings in the father's role, I may try to compensate by repeating behaviors I trust to "work"—those behaviors I am comfortable with and know well. Therefore, as a father, I will "act" the same way I do as a "good doctor." For obvious reasons, I will be without much success. Self-esteem, on the other hand, is self-generated from within. In this state the images, words, and bodily tensions of guilt and anxiety are noted and let go. Meditative practices and conscious efforts to give oneself strokes for effort, uniqueness, and simply "food-for-being" lead to the experience of unconditional expansive worth (SE). Practice in interpersonal encouragement stimulates cooperation-as-equals (active social interest). Self-training in cooperation-as-equals makes for anxiety-free persons, in any role in life. The twin keystones are the experience of worth (SE) and belonging (SI) while helping others to develop this capacity fully (O'Connell, 1984b).

In Adlerian terms, often mistaken social goals are involved in the maintenance of the mislabeling and avoidance stance toward anxiety, for example, attention, power, revenge, and the display of inadequacy (Dreikurs, 1972). Yet, social phobias are a result of the individual's discouragement and mistaken belief that he or she is somehow imperfect and unable to live up to self- or other-imposed standards. For example, the most common social phobia, the fear of speaking in public, usually has an identifiable premorbid incident in which the messages of "not good enough" were given and/or "heard" by the person plagued by this social phobia. The ego-imposed guilt ("worthless-now-and-forever") is persistently experienced, but by an uncomplete projection: The originator of the judgement is "the other" in social phobias. We believe that in more "skilled" projections, the self-guilt affect disappears. In such a paranoia, "the other" is forever unworthy; hence, the popularity of prejudices.

Although it may seem contradictory, a person with this phobia may not be phobic of all forms of public speaking. In fact, he or she could be paralyzed with fear of extemporaneous speaking, but be perfectly comfortable in a play, speaking memorized lines. Another possibility is for the individual to be phobic of addressing or making a presentation to peers or those vital to his or her welfare, but perfectly at ease when he or she is "the authority" or when addressing a nonthreatening audience. Once again, the specific area of phobic involvement often can be traced to an earlier incident in which the individual's ego-esteem was damaged, but the *present* state of worth and belonging is far more crucial for change.

PTSD, GAD, SP: SIMILARITIES AND DIFFERENCES

The Adlerian approach to anxiety (the copeless appraisal of future catastrophic failure) is immensely promising. The precipitating external conditions that stimulate the internal appraisal and coping incapacities may be varied. External stimuli may be symbolically widespread GAD. They may be more limited to competitive social environments that can be avoided (SP) at the cost of even more ego punitiveness. (The fear of negative evaluation is the best long-term predictor of the behavior of the social phobic, for example.) In other instances, the anxiety might arise from the perceptions of helplessness or hopelessness after one's identity has been shattered by an overwhelming experience with death. In all cases, the disordered person needs to develop an orderly way to create esteem, belonging, and a playful switch to alternative perceptions. Trower and Gilbert (1989) detail this necessary movement from the atonic (competitive) to a hedonic (cooperation, equality, and mutual support) sense of relatedness.

In essence, what they are saying is that the therapist needs to model and reinforce the "hedonic" style of life and ". . . give people a (sometimes prolonged) exposure to a hedonic relationship in which the therapist always respects . . . never attacks, puts down or ridicules the client" (Trower & Gilbert, 1989, p. 32). We believe that the state-of-art diagnosis and treatment of anxiety disorders has roots in the Adlerian philosophy of healing, no matter what the label used.

The Adlerian psychotherapist knows that psychotherapy, and the progression of other maturity as well, moves faster and surer when the motivation of therapist, patient, and the patient's social surroundings is toward the experience and understanding of self-identity. This self-identity is more intensely curative the more SE, SI, and SH energize inner and outer movements. Foremost with our thinking is the ability of therapist (healer, teacher, leader) to be an encourager (O'Connell & Gomez, 1990). The encourager takes literally the old cliché of "loving the sinner and hating the sin," both simultaneously and wholeheartedly. Institutions do not foster this kind of enchantment and enthusiasm. Institutions create images but forego the actual healing. Institutions move as if impelled by a giant ego identity (see Figure 7.2).

The anxiety-ridden patient's tongue sings a litany of change, but the feet move in tune with ego-identity demands. Anxiety patients are suffering from starvation of SE, SI, and SH but do not know it. They are focused upon disruptions of external supports (ego "props" or "fixes") that they cannot control. Anxiety patients learn to identify bodily sensations with the negative certainty that some events that they cannot control will render them helpless and hopeless. In this ego-induced state, the "victim" does not think of his or her part in the wellness of others (SI). What would happen if we had culturally-approved anxiety contests in which the anxiety client became a pop artist? If the client received adulation for symptoms, the guilt (worthlessness) and isolation would be difficult to create. Moreover, without resisting and negativizing the tensions, reexperiences, avoidances, arousals, and numbing, they would be more difficult to produce. When we imagine these overstatements, we imagine the laughable. We might then have patients having anxiety over not having anxiety (O'Connell, 1987)!

Adler believed that the therapist who could not teach happiness was a charlatan. We also see the SE, SI, and SH of the therapist—the qualities never taught in medical and graduate schools—to be the most crucial elements of the healing equation. Like Adler, we perceive the diagnosis of the patient to be less crucial by far than the encouragement of the healer. In our diagnoses, we find the symbols and metaphors of discouragement in overwhelming force. The inner and outer ways in which the client loses the struggle for security and satisfaction are noted in our diagnoses. The breadth and depth (intensity, certainty) of discouragement are seen along with the client's discouraging ways of fighting discouragement. At the same time, we can gauge in our diagnoses the extent of the client's knowledge of the struggle and the discouraging ways that this knowledge does not lead to SE, SI, and SH.

We always give students two aphorisms to contemplate initially. When they begin to understand them, they begin to be real healers. These are, "Never diagnose unless you treat," and "Don't even treat anyone here; just understand them." After all, a diagnosis is just a diagnosis. But with Adlerians, a diagnosis also can be a true treatment for discouragement.

To us, the DSM-IV categories reflect the various erosions of esteem, belonging, and inflexibility of ego-mindset. The inner and outer unsuccessful compensatory movements for weaknesses are likewise part of the diagnostic function. In brief, we could say that the categories show similarity of movements that *create* and *maintain* dis-courage. The therapist must use compassion, knowledge, and adroitness to have the strength to keep encouraging strength.

What are the differences suggested among diagnoses? The psychic pain of SP is in the lust for certain others to confirm clients' worth and belonging. The tragicomic twist is that clients are the ones who unwittingly decide between the movements of "strokes" and the movements of "slights" from others. Initially, clients never believe that when they banish ego identity and become socially responsible, they will find the energy to fuel encouragement within themselves.

GAD does have the order of ego-fighting-ego and ego-winning by misery-making. The client fights symptoms (rejects, denies, awfulizes, negativizes, resists them) but eventually uses them for useless power (to get attention, to be the boss, to get revenge, to be let alone). Motor tension, autonomic hyperactivity, apprehensive expectation, and hyperalertness taken seriously generate more of the same. The flight from crises and challenges into labeling negatively (as a passive victim: "Anxiety makes me miserable.") is the start of the tragicomic journey into the land of chemical addiction. Anxiety, like most psychic symptoms, is a big tar baby. The more it is fought as a hated enemy, the more it sticks and grows (O'Connell, 1984b, 1988).

Would PTSD be prevalent in a society that welcomed and honored awareness and sharing of death (O'Connell, 1981b)? Would suicide be such an epidemic if death lost its sting and thereby its useless power? In PTSD we see the loss of control over life suddenly erupting into a consciousness where that issue of death is never allowed easy entry. If we had no guilt (neither self-blame nor its sequel, other-blame), we would not have PTSD, with regression into psychoses or character disorders. The abrupt loss of control (with death as its extreme) wreaks havoc with the lifestyle that is unprepared to live fully (SE, SI, SH focus) and die fully (without guilt). Once feelings of unworth, isolation, and super-seriousness become foremost, so do the defenses against the multimeanings and occasions of anxiety. Healers of *combat-related PTSD* wish that the angry, defensive veteran could continue as a warrior, but a warrior of peace (Blackburn, O'Connell, & Richman, 1984; Egendorf, 1985; Lifton, 1985). The same type of emotional logic would be involved in wishing that each anxiety victim would develop an anxiety dictum: Anxiety can be a blessed message showing our defective (inner and outer) movements. After accepting this *blessing*, there is a lifetime of *being aware, sharing, honoring*, and *humoring*. This *BASH*-dance is the prologue to the creation of a full and happy life in a discouragenic, but not necessarily discouraging, world (O'Connell, 1981a, 1984b, 1988).

CASE EXAMPLE: SOCIAL PHOBIA CASE LIFESTYLE

Jimmy's Joke: Smiling in Phobic Relationships with Phobias

Jimmy has been a chronic dis-ease carrier. His symptomatic social phobias have contributed to narrow circumscribed lives for his wife, Jane, and daughter,

Mary. Jane has had chronic colitis throughout most of their 40-year marriage. Surgery and increasing use of tranquilizers have narrowed the ambience of her quiet desperation. The 30-year-old daughter has been under psychiatric care for a score of years for "hatred toward men."

Jimmy only felt good ego-esteem when his favorite football team (the Dallas Cowboys) won. He videotaped victories and went into depression when they lost. Jimmy and the wife, Jane, attended a weekly group for six months 12 years ago with the Adlerian therapist. They were satisfied that Jimmy learned to be happy (when he was praised by the boss and the Cowboys actually won). Jane believed the marriage was saved when her anger toward her symptoms, toward Jimmy, and toward the daughter, Mary, disappeared. However, encouragement (how to solve life's tasks with SE, SI, SH) was never reached. Jimmy returned to the therapist (now 150 miles away from Jimmy's home) when he could not tolerate retirement (no strokes from bosses) and the Cowboys' losing season.

Jimmy's early recollections all could be summed up as "Poor Little Jimmy" and a dethroned older brother whose only connection with his younger sibling was the shared family value of "Everything's horrible and will only get worse." Jimmy's father deserted the family in infancy; his mother never remarried. Jimmy, in effect, has been her henpecked husband, even at a distance. Jimmy believed he had never succeeded at anything. He had even faked getting himself fired at his saleswork and failed that too. He never stopped competing (and losing in his mind) with every other salesman. He made invidious comparisons with every quality constantly. Then he would avoid giving presentations before groups at all costs (faking sicknesses, deaths, etc.); yet he occasionally would make a presentation for which he never credited himself.

The therapeutic relationship became positive from the first session, because the therapist readily predicted how Jimmy would make himself miserable and gave him credit for the effort and success at failure. Jimmy now had a new father figure, the therapist, who stroked him for effort. He was confirmed as being wonderful, even at the creation of the numbing control that Jimmy put on all feelings in an effort to avoid "catastrophes" (failures that the excessive effort successfully brought about). Jimmy wanted rituals and strokes from bosses. He got them, in line with Adler's implied dictum of encouraging the display of a symptom, provided it is performed (paradoxically) with SI (O'Connell, 1975). In this way, behavior that is not negativized and resisted and is done for practice of human expansion (SE, SI, SH) is no longer symptomatic of disorders.

Jimmy now has a ritualistic time for work-play. He plays Adlerian tapes of theory, relaxation, and letting-go meditations (O'Connell, 1984a, 1988). He had a tape made for him by the therapist of his favorite sounds, images, thoughts, and bodily sensations. He also has a personalized tape bringing awareness of avoided words, images, and feelings, with practice at letting them go (without negative judgements). In therapy, Jimmy laughs at the therapist's *Reductio Ad Absurda*. These remarks are relevantly overstated irreverences such as: "How many centimeters must the boss' mouth turn upward?" and "How many seconds before *you* will allow yourself to feel loved?"

According to our way of thinking, transforming anxiety into positive challenges follows identification with the encouraging therapist who is able to perceive and reinforce a nimbus of light in even the most discouraged, anxiety ridden, anxiety-avoider (O'Connell & Gomez, 1990).

TREATMENT FOR ANXIETY DISORDERS

Creative Cooperation-as-equals for Treatment of Anxiety Disorders

We perceive ourselves, others, and the world according to the goals of our lifestyle premises (Adler, 1964; Adler, in Ansbacher & Ansbacher 1956). In short, believing is seeing. Our common nonsense renders certain psychiatric diagnoses easier to relate to than others. Most people have had direct or indirect experiences coping with an irrational avoiding of harmless persons or in temporarily being overwhelmed with torrents of anxiety, SP, and GAD. There are far fewer people, however, with the creativity of imagination to empathize with youth who have faced months or even years of death-threatening experiences under the domination of senseless authorities and contradictory goals (Veninga & Wilmer, 1985; Wilmer, 1989). Further traumata to the lifestyle (ego-identity ideals) came with the killing of women and children who at unpredictable times were friends or enemies.

Consider, for example, statements often made by some Vietnam war veterans who in summary form report experiences such as the following. These youth fought in an unpopular war in an inhospitable climate, where drugs were easy to obtain as self-medication for the effects of guilt and isolation. A mechanical dehumanized technique was used to avoid psychiatric casualties caused by losing friends in combat. These boys were flown in alone to battle and given a personal date of expected departure. Within hours of firefights, they arrived suddenly at home, again alone. Leadership of the kind needed by these Vietnam soldiers or even older role models were rare. The murdering of officers ("Fraggings") was far worse than in any other American army. Covert operations were often dishonest, stupid, and just plain evil. When the youth found comrades in their shared repeated battles and withdrawals over the same bit of land, the composite of this camaraderie was interracial at a time when the home front was afire with interracial riots. The boy soldiers were too often targets of hostility, attacked and spat upon as baby-killers and dope-fiends. And, of course, no parades were given to the losers. The boy soldiers, wielders of the most tremendous power of destruction the world has ever known, had been beaten by skinny, small persons in "pajamas," often armed with homemade and foraged weaponry.

The Adlerian orientation, with its emphasis on the guiding fictions of life-styles and embedded in ironclad logic of communal living, relates empathically to the inner needs of such youth for esteem and belonging or encouragement (Blackburn et al., 1984). References to worthlessness, isolation, and purpose-lessness as precursors for disturbed and disturbing lifestyles are recorded through-out Adlerian literature. Lifton (1985) noted comparable pathological processes of disintegration, disconnectedness, and stasis (purposelessness). His finding also concurred with studies of PTSD from other disciplines (Baritz, 1985; Egendorf, 1985; Manchester, 1979; Veninga & Wilmer 1985). Combat-related PTSD is simply, yet destructively, an intense magnification of the shocking confrontation with psychic and physical death. From the Adlerian perspective, the death that terrorizes is the feared death of inner guiding fictions: goals, conscious or uncon-scious, presumed to generate esteem and belonging (O'Connell, 1981a, 1981b, 1984b, 1988).

Delayed and chronic PTSD presents problems for professionals who are not of Adlerian frame of reference. Adlerians see the "delay" of the disorder more in terms of thresholds of attention that fail to note the initial losses of worth, belonging, and humor. The PTSD victim (and victimizer) intensifies his or her safeguarding tendencies with movements patently doomed to fail (antithetical thought, deprecation, overcompensation, power strivings, isolation). Accelerated disturbed and disturbing actions ensue. As the communal ideal of cooperation-as-equals disappears, both individual and social tension increase drastically.

The failure to relate losses (or fear of losses) in shared ways with others, perceived as equal and similar, keeps restorative grief out of awareness. Violence is a popular cultural choice to cover this grief-denial. Once again, Adlerian theory and practice provides the frame of understanding and treatment. Diagnosis here is identifying the breadth and intensity of movements constricting the experiences of unconditional worth (SE) and universal belonging (SI). Treatment is aimed at promoting such awareness without more negative attitudes or constrictions. Treatment moves from initial learning *how* to cooperate as equals (with all participants) to learning how to let go of one's own negative certainties by helping others to do so. Professionals soon learn that Adlerians do not view monadic catharsis ("release of bottled up emotions") as a treatment goal. Emotions are seen as energies devoted to goal-fulfillment and are therefore socially purposive. No units of one are in the Adlerian open system of creative community existence. One is not automatically victimized by the past, present, or future. All determinisms are "soft," decided by goals of one's guiding fictions rather than external factors alone. What other therapists might see as healthy catharsis, the Adlerian would see as an example of social responsibility, admitting hidden goals without negativity.

Adlerians excel at uniting the poles of "living concepts" (O'Connell & Gomez, 1990). From his early writings, Adler (1964; Ansbacher & Ansbacher, 1956) did not isolate the social conditions of tailors from their subsequent diseases or the neuroses of children from the movements of teachers and classroom peers. In fact, this Adlerian method is neither boundary-ridden subjectivity nor objectivity but "phenomenological operationalism" (Ansbacher, 1965), an interaction of subjective guiding fictions and goals with overt behavior. The patient who represses *awareness* of hostility does show hostile *behavior* (e.g., depreciation of self and others). According to the Adlerian emphasis on both polar opposites, living concepts, social units, and ends of any stick are not without polar opposites. An overemphasis on one role ("no hostility") may be in the service of the disowned polar opposite (subtle violence).

Such Adlerian dialectics pioneered paradoxical and strategic therapies (Mozdzierz, Marchitelli, & Lisiecki, 1976; O'Connell & Gomez, 1990). In Adler's dialectics, one-sided behavior often reflected the deflected energy of a disowned pole of a living concept. "Too much" or "too little" movement (awareness) of the polar opposites of living concepts destroys the experience balance. A balanced encouraging lifestyle has a "both/and" orientation, not an "either/or" dichotomy, for example, angry depreciatory tendencies of the chronic severe PTSD victim-victimizer. Violence can hide the soft, sad impotence of loss of person and symbols that gave life positive meaning. The pole where we feel the most vulnerability (of worth and belonging) is the pole where the defenses are stacked. An Adlerian would understand the need to share the grieving process. Such a helper would see the symptom as a painful blessing, showing us where our "weaknesses" are and how they are hidden and become blocks to community. Honoring happenings without blame and humoring blame away is part of the healing process. In healing, there is a distancing from *identification* with constricting symptoms to an identification with universal community. ("I am more than my negative fears. I am always in community," *sub specie aeternitatis*.)

Allopathic Quietment for Anxiety Disorders

One of the discouraging fallacies of allopathic psychiatry is the implied ease of optimal development. In the allopathic framework, good living follows automatically upon freedom from the symptoms of mental disease; however, in Adlerian terms, good living and freedom from mental disease are anchored in the processes of courage and encouragement. Adler (Ansbacher & Ansbacher, 1956) made a distinction between courage and social interest. Courage is *active* social interest. Courage is a distinct step beyond the more passive acceptance of others "as if" they are equals, sharing in the human need to experience unconditional worth (SE) and purposive belonging (SI). Courage is *active* risk-taking (SI) (O'Connell, 1975). Courage reflects the strength of the individual (SE, SI) as well as knowledge of and skill with the encouragement process. To Adler (1964; Ansbacher & Ansbacher, 1956), the mother's task was to stimulate the appearance of the search for similarities and extend it broadly to others. That role is a similar goal for the Adlerian therapist with the courage to give feedback and self-disclosure (O'Connell, 1984a).

We see the physician identified with allopathic-model premises to be the shadow-opposite of the Adlerian healer. The latter is a rare occurrence in institutional settings (O'Connell, 1983). Allopathic psychiatrists often have not expanded their narrow training of search-and-destroy of symptoms into concerns about the processes of spirit and soul as did Jung, Adler, and Milton Erickson (O'Connell & Gomez, 1990). If the goal is immediate reduction of symptoms, no emphasis is upon cooperation-as-equals between peers. The serious allopaths deal only with the abstract logic world of so-called "solid" facts (Weil, 1983). Like the madman, this hard determinist acknowledges no doubt. On the other hand, the Adlerian healer can play, guessing without the lack of certitude, in a world of changing perceptions, possibilities, and attitudes. Allopathic understanding and treatment can be dehumanized to following geometric models of "fitting" chemical receptors with "blocking" locks. Then, the human needs of spirit (SE) and soul (SI) are victims of reductionistic regression. The growth possibility of reframing negative emotions as complementary challenges that develop character (when resistance and negativity cease) is not acknowledged in the standard allopathic model of quick quietment (Weil, 1983).

In our estimation, the orthodox allopathic model in psychiatric institutions is hostile to treatments whose metaphors are more congruent with psychospiritual pilgrimages, developing athletic prowess, or skill games than with reductionistic and isolated physical focus. Adlerians would be on the side of treatment for chronic and severe PTSD rather than simple allopathic quietment of symptoms by chemical constraints. Adlerian therapy for anxiety disorders of all types would be more similar to homeopathic medicine (Weil, 1983). That is, the inner state of the sufferer would be strengthened (SE, SI, SH) using individualized, "diluted injections" of the events labeled "traumatic." Putting the patient back into a psychodramatic simulation of the stressors (O'Connell, 1975), now encouraged with Adlerian knowledge and trusting democratic relationships, is a fine example of Adlerian treatment (O'Connell, 1987).

Psychiatrists doing research for the Pentagon are still enamored with the goal of inventing a "Brave Pill" to overcome the physical fatigue and fear of dying and killing connected with absurd round-the-clock violence (Gabriel, 1987). Such institutional ego-thinking does not take into consideration the human needs for integrity, connectedness, and inspiring goals, which are affected by the encouraging or discouraging, caring or careless, actions of others. Institutional thinking ignores the power (social influence) of psychic weakness that is seen in the belief of the necessity of guilt. It is the diminuting actions and useless reactions of living with the unlimited technology of absurd death that promotes wartime PTSD (Lifton, 1985). Perceiving the absurdity of ego identity in the context of a shattered self-identity equals severe PTSD. Most humans would go to their deaths without PTSD if that death would guarantee the continued existence of idealized goals and persons. The trauma of PTSD is the result of experiencing the death of worth, belonging, and humor. Similarly, PTSD follows the death of integrity, connectedness, and movement, an equivalent process translated by Lifton (1985) as "Death Anxiety." One can be ego-sustaining in the face of pervasive death and dying as long as the dead are no more than external objects. But such unfortunate and shocking sadness can be opportunity for expansive growth when *BASH*ed (seen as *b*lessings with *s*hared *a*wareness, while *h*onored and *h*umored). If what are dying are inner values (SE, SI, SH), however, there is no immediate possibility of positive transformation of lifestyle (Blackburn et al., 1984).

Individual psychologists who perceive mental illness as stemming from deficiencies of SE, SI, and SH as did Alfred Adler (Ansbacher & Ansbacher, 1956; Adler, 1964), are concerned with the *uses* of diagnoses. The diagnosed are not perceived by Adlerians as passive victims or malicious monsters. The diagnostic process, in Adlerian terms, needs to highlight the inner and outer movements of *how* innate worth (SE) and belonging (SI) are *not* realized and experienced. Diagnostic concepts are our guiding fictions to understand *how* the client constricts perceptions and experiences of well-being. It is up to the Adlerian therapist to create mutual trust, relate to, interpret discouraging movements, and offer corrective experiences of cooperation-as-equals. The discouraging diagnosis and quietment of wartime PTSD in institutions is proof positive that diagnoses are allied to guiding fictions, used either to discourage or to encourage. Diagnoses are not palpable essences, reliable and valid for all persons, for all social conditions diagnoses.

Our observations of hundreds of combat-era patients and scores of diagnosticians and healers lead us to believe that the manner in which a hospitalized psychiatric patient is diagnosed and treated for PTSD depends as equally on the lifestyle of the mental health professional as on that of the patient. PTSD is a relatively new diagnosis. When given the choice, some diagnosticians will resist acknowledging that diagnosis. Moreover, the diagnostic change that accompanied inclusion of PTSD in DSM-III deemphasized the longstanding contention that predisposition was essential for the presence of psychiatric casualties. PTSD could be a delayed reaction, another change in the traditional time frame of immediate reaction and past predispositions. There is, however, a hidden ambivalence about the limits of life-threatening (and psychic identity) stress upon the lifestyle. By arbitrary definition of many practitioners, one can contract an *anxiety* disorder from life-threatening stress but not a *psychotic* disorder. So while contemporary stress is given more importance as an independent factor in anxiety reactions of PTSD by most therapists, often an arbitrary ceiling is placed on its allowed severity. PTSD is "only" an anxiety disorder. If your identity is extremely shattered, if life (or psychic) threat is severe enough to precipitate a psychotic reaction, then PTSD often is ruled out of the diagnostic picture.

(Note: PTSD was a relatively new diagnosis when the DSM-III was first published and, in the DSM-IV, combat-related PTSD receives almost no attention. On the other hand, it was because of the initial interest in finding an "explanation" for the symptomatology related to Vietnam combat veteran behavior that the diagnosis was identified and used. Today, PTSD delayed is recognized as a viable diagnosis or "real condition" and often is used where childhood trauma such as sexual, physical, and/or extreme emotional abuse, abandonment, or neglect has occurred.)

An alarming example of what happens to a chronic and severe combat-related PTSD (all of whom are now middle-aged "youths") follows. We believe that the orthodox diagnosis of PTSD requires a knowledge of the interaction between individual preconditions and the perception of threat of the stressors. In a recent case of ours, a local district attorney sought to establish a morbid precondition by finding relatives who confessed to engaging in incestuous homosexual activities with the defendant when he was young. She also said the defendant could not be diagnosed as being "under stress" since he was not now in combat. (She saw "stress" in terms of counting, weighing, and measuring current firepower. Destruction to the lifestyle from two combat tours and eight years in prison did not count as "stress" now.)

The district attorney did not investigate the psychiatric hospitalization and documented dissociative states experienced by this individual while he was in Vietnam. She stated her reasons for ignoring these highly relevant facts as being "irrelevant" because they did not "explain" current violence toward women whose behavior contributed to the defendant's self-perceived helplessness. The defendant himself muddied the waters with his emphasis on causative "flash-backs" rather than on his decompensated lifestyle. His defense lawyer would not accept the validity of flashbacks because the defendant was not reexperiencing the externals of combat. It appears that the defendant used the slang of his youth in Nam, but no one understood the meaning. Therefore, no one empathized with the one who was capable of crimes of violence toward females. Using these irrational arguments, punishment of imprisonment rather than treatment for PTSD was initiated. When O'Connell could not offer long-term treatment under locked ward conditions, the defendant's fate was sealed.

HOW ANXIETY DISORDERS CAN BECOME CHRONIC CHARACTER DISORDERS

Si Me Disturbes, Te Occidero (which when translated means, "If you hassle me, I'll waste you"). When a group of PTSD Nam vets were moving as if they would trust the intentions of the therapist, had at least an intellectual understanding of ego and self-identity, and were learning to work-play their way to self-awareness, the above "humorous" quotation was written on the blackboard in the ward by the therapist. It was a dignified Latin rendition of a common threat by chronic and severe PTSD combat veterans. In essence, this Latin inscription is a succinct statement of how to change a neurosis into a character disorder. The same theme was often incorporated into the belief systems of gullible boys as early as basic training. Particularly during the Vietnam era, the drill instructors' goal seems to have been to transform scared kids into disciplined killers with admonitions such as "Whenever you get scared, kill!" Given the isolation, confusion, anxiety, and art of weaponry of the Vietnam conflict, the killing was prodigious indeed, and the fragmenting and negativizing of the ego identity (called "delayed") under conscious and unconscious guilt was harrowing.

The Adlerian practitioner can readily understand the self-destructive course and discouraging outcome of prolonged intense negativity and isolation. One

criticism of both DSM-III-R and DSM-IV is that PTSD remains under the classification of anxiety. For everyone except chronic saints, the lack of encouraging
models leads to progressive dehabilitation of unconditional worth (SE) and SI.
Even the narrower and conditional ego-esteem and dependent interests fade away
in threatening, discouraging atmospheres.

Given only a community of violent discouragement, the constricted PTSD
can resemble more of a character disorder (little or no social interest and too
much ego-esteem). If treatment participants have the hidden goals of ego-esteem
without SI and the therapist is unaware of how to counter with encouraging
movements (quality of SE, SI, SH), no therapy is likely. The most to hope for
is narrow SI, confined to an in-group, with hostility against the rest of the
universe. True social interest means cooperation-as-equals, *sub specie aeternitatis*
(O'Connell, 1984b). Researchers now know that some of the best therapy with
PTSD Nam vets was through using World War II veterans, in empathic sharing
relationships (O'Connell, 1975, 1987). Beyond creating helpfulness in identifying
and moving beyond constrictions, the World War II veteran demonstrated in his
misery that time and external assets would not likely cure the chronic and severe
PTSD lifestyle (ego identity).

We have noted a crucial difference between those veterans whose PTSD
remained on an anxiety level (resisting, negativizing) and those who dumped
this diminuting guilt on others. For the latter, youth who went on to develop
character disorder-type behavior, moving against others, in one form or another,
became an addiction. "Justified" hostility toward those now regarded as worthless
and less-than-human became acts calculated to show masculine "overcoming"
of fears. "Love thy neighbor" became "Hassle me and I'll waste you" in a world
peopled with competitive dissimilarities.

Figure 7.3 presents our views on the emergence of two types of PTSD. They
often become pronounced following the existential crises of prolonged exposure
to the unlimited and absurd violence of modern combat. Type A, the more
neurotic variety, is emphasized in both DSM-III-R and DSM-IV. Type B reflects
the unacknowledged choice to continue killing (actually or psychic-symbolically).
This striving for power (ego-esteem) through degrees of violence contributes to
the development of psychopathic, borderline character types. Veterans in this
more disturbing category are less amenable to treatment. In fact their ego-justified
and wide range of hostility ("joking" verbal to provoking physical) makes them
a chronic dis-ease carrier. Type B's extroverted disturbing style stimulates burnout
epidemics in any program that does not contain encouragement training for staff
(O'Connell, 1983).

	Type A—"Neurotic"	Type B—"Psychopathic"
1. Basic attitude	Introverted.	Extroverted.
2. Hostility toward authority	Narrow range of directed verbal hostility: "I should have 'fragged' that ignorant bastard who led the squad into that ambush."	Wide range of directed verbal hostility: "You bastards can never know what we went through."
3. Guilt	Lacerating. Numbing of all affects: "I am worthless, now and forever, because of what I did/did not do."	Projected on others: "You are no good, now and forever, because of what you did/did not do."
4. Sleep disturbances	Chronic, severe, witnessed by others.	Quality of controlled purposiveness: In service of ego image (top macho). Usually not seen by others.
5. Combat memories	Repressed. Traumatic rearousal may accompany sharing.	Excellent memory for details. Dotes on atrocity nuances.
6. Symptomatology	Disturbed, depressive.	Disturbing, paranoid.
7. Reactions to symptoms	Expresses need to eradicate symptoms.	Uses symptoms to create and maintain actively competitive image.
8. Safeguarding tendencies	Avoid-dance.	Power ploys.
9. Ego-esteem	Low esteem. Lifton's (1985) stasis (little movement).	High ego esteem, brittle sense of worth. manipulates environment for worth and belonging.
10. Social interest	Present, but restricted to narrow range of people and situations.	Very little and temporary if any at all.
11. Prognosis toward SE, SI, SH	Good, with friendly, firm encouragement.	Poor because close personal relationships are rejected and disdained.

Figure 7.3.   Main reactions to shock of unlimited absurd violence of modern combat.

Addendum to Figure 7.3

These observations of drastic (but necessary, at the time) reactions to inner and outer extreme violence were made on hundreds of PTSD patients in our (VA) drug and PTSD treatment programs. Veterans, upon entering the PTSD ward, were given the opportunity to design their treatment programs, which varied from medications only to combinations of medication, individual and group therapies, psychodrama, art therapy, and a PTSD "rap" group. The veteran was offered all these treatment possibilities. In true Adlerian fashion, the patients' diagnosis (and prognosis) depended on the extent to which they would fight or invite encouragement. The type B reaction to violent and absurd killing was, as a rule, in an intense and habitual avoid-dance. With the B type PTSD, the possibilities of positive change and renewed relationships with others (who did not obsess and ruminate on the impossibility of change) were resisted and negativized. Type B dedication is toward maintaining and enhancing negative certainties of "Once a trauma, always a trauma" and "Hassle us, and we'll waste you."

The Axis I diagnosis for most program patients included PTSD; however, the type B patterns often had (or a least deserved) the Axis II code of personality disorders. Such disorders, "characteristic of the individual's current and long-term functioning" were seen more in the habitual rejection of training in worth, belonging, and humor (Natural High Theory and Practice). Guesses about possible disorders based on patients' reports of early childhood and combat experience were not as predictive of outcome as were the patients' movements of foot and tongue when presented with an opportunity to fight for encouragement.

Both patient types A and B, in our opinion, overestimate the importance of externals of combat and underestimate the importance of friendly, firm affection in creating prognoses for their own futures. We believe, on the other hand, that *psychic* deaths (numbing and lacerating of esteem and belonging) lead directly to the deep discouragement of the worthless, isolated, super-serious candidate for violence and other useless addictions.

Figure 7.3.   continued.

CASE EXAMPLES: TWO PTSD CASE LIFESTYLES

Saving Sammy

Sammy S. was an actively competitive ex-Marine. His ego identity (of which he was unaware) was to be praised as the best in every task he undertook. His desired image was that of ultra-masculine, always in command, taking "no crap" from anyone, especially males with whom he competed. He was a well conditioned boxer and dancer and excelled in martial arts. He was hospitalized for seizures (as well as for PTSD) and heavily medicated on standard medications for epilepsy. Sammy was discouraged about this condition. He was certain that he would have his physical defects all his life and was told that he was totally and permanently disabled by more than one allopathic physician. Moreover, the useless power he had acquired through his sick role of ten years was tremendous. He was compensated "100%—permanent and total"—because his first seizures appeared in combat conditions. Along with Social Security payments, Sammy received over $1,500.00 monthly plus room and board during hospitalization. Sammy had the useless luxury of being able to talk of his potential without ever risking the loss of ego-esteem by undertaking training. That training at government expense was automatically ruled out by Sammy's receipt of a "total and permanent" rating. Even if the disability was lessened, the fact of reported seizures remained, although none had ever been seen during his frequent hospitalizations.

Sammy was seeing himself as a passive victim of an insufferable fate that reluctantly and paradoxically rewarded him for taking on the sick role so readily. He was considered a "good patient"; therefore, doctors and nurses could easily see themselves as good professionals. Sammy was being schooled in trained incapacity in the vital areas of social responsibility (love, cooperation-as-equals, work). He loved to complain about his chronic social rejection as a Vietnam vet and obsessed about having his compensation tragically reduced some day. One of the dangers of forming groups exclusively for Vietnam veterans is that once out of total isolation, the group's social interest will not advance beyond the "us against them" competitive stance.

Veterans like Sammy were pampered but rejected as persons capable of being trained to fulfill lifestyle tasks of social, vocational, and loving commitments. They were trained in quietment and discouragement. In quietment, no acceptance is made of the primacy of expanding one's identity (SE), which is made strong through learning the technology of spirit and soul (SI) growth. Treatment of the human identity requires empathic therapists who will model and reinforce the striving for loving worth (SE) and universal belonging (SI).

Treatment for combat PTSD in *Natural High Therapy* has used psychoactive drugs at times but only as facilitators for learning encouragement in the face of deeply intense discouragement.

Sammy moved into and through the grief that signals letting go of useless power, but he did so only through the loving care of equals who accepted, without ridicule, his diminuting, depreciatory tendencies. At the same time, participants in Adlerian psychodrama (O'Connell, 1975) urged Sammy to reexperience the content that he hid under the cloak of isolating violence. The key incident was the killing of a Vietnamese boy whom he loved. Sammy was certain that the boy was moving toward him with a concealed grenade. Such incidents were becoming commonplace with his unit at that time. In actuality, the child was hiding a gift carving he had made for Sammy. With the help of a fellow PTSD patient who played the "wasted" boy, Sammy, with hesitant back and forth movements, reenacted the scene while shaking and sobbing violently. He wanted to retreat to the nursing station to take his standing (PRN) order for dilantin. He admitted that he wanted to avoid an emotional "female" out-of-control experience. However, staff dialogued with Sammy to show the courage to express "weakness" and shake without guilt. Sammy did it enveloped in a circle of staff who hummed his favorite tune ("The Rose"). This incident in itself was not "curative" catharsis, but was a giant step to shared SI and the courage to admit imperfections without guilt. The incident was then available for giving Sammy strokes for effort, free from negative judgments. Today, Sammy is a teacher of meditation and a college student. He has long been discharged from the hospital and is now married to a fellow student of recreational therapy.

The Timeless Trials of Tim

The diagnostic ambivalence of the case of Tim certainly contributed something to his habitual look of confusion. His working diagnosis on the VA hospital ward was PTSD, delayed, severe. But the VA rating board, which decides if a psychiatric condition is worthy of financial compensation, considered him to have the disease of schizophrenia, paranoid type, without service connection.

Tim's bearing was always military. He dressed and moved as if always on inspection. Tim's upright frame moved at a brisk pace, as though he had an important secret mission. During all of his frequent hospitalizations, Tim was never known to miss a ward or therapy group meeting. He was also never known to speak spontaneously except during Natural High Walkabouts (Blackburn, O'Connell, & Richman, 1984), in which he voluntarily, briskly, and rapidly expressed his angry frustrations about the diagnostic confusions.

The staff of the psychiatric section believed Tim deserved compensation and treatment for delayed and severe PTSD. Since no one knew for certain the reasons for his claim rejection, rumors abounded. A social worker held that some rating boards wanted to know and evaluate the intensity of enemy action in places where patients served. The ward psychiatrist noted that Tim's diagnosis was made in 1976, before the diagnosis of PTSD became officially recognized in 1980. And, once a patient is diagnosed, changing it is difficult, especially if subsequent psychiatrists "Didn't believe that PTSD was a real disease." O'Connell, the ward psychologist, lamented that many psychiatrists had no idea of the connections between guilt (both lacerating and numbing), the ego identity, and paranoid reactions. An Adlerian would be far more likely to see that self-guilt ruins feelings of worth (SE), belonging (SI), and joy (SH).

Such grandiose overcompensations cannot succeed in the ironclad law of communal living as equals (Salzman, 1968). To O'Connell, Tim was certainly paranoid, but more numbed in SI than ego inflated with grandiosity. Tim even may have had predispositions toward paranoid reactions, but would not likely have had "irrational" discouragement (low SE, narrow SI, super-seriousness) without lacerating and numbing guilt: "I am no good now and forever because of what I did not do." Without a doubt, Egendorf (1985) and Lifton (1985) would agree with O'Connell's contentions that Tim's "paranoid" death fears and fear of punishment were dynamically related to his continuing guilt. This inner weakness resulted from deflation of esteem and belonging, and disappearance of humor. Tim identified more and more with negative images, words, and bodily sensations of discouragement (O'Connell, 1975, 1988).

Tim's case is not uncommon in the diagnosing and treating of combat-related PTSD. Tim did not fire a gun at the enemy, nor was he fired upon. He took on too much responsibility for perfection and control in a futile effort to prove his worth and belonging. Even as he drove his fire-fighting and rescue trucks at his air base, Tim dreamed of burning pilots and awoke in fear and panic for years. Tim's sense of patriotic pride and duty, his ignorance of psychic matters, and his lack of introspection kept him from reporting to a psychiatrist in Vietnam, if he could have found one. Like many of the Vietnam veterans, Tim had the flashbacks, arousals, numbing, reexperiences, and avoidances after traumatic events (outside the range of usual human experience). Symptoms were "delayed," however, in the sense that they were not recorded in official documents until Tim believed that help was available and reported to that location.

Tim still wallows in self-guilt because he believes that officials regard him as "unworthy of PTSD." He projects his worthlessness outwardly, and now evil "others" are responsible for his weaknesses. That delusional set is not systemic and specific; Tim expects and fears punishment. Because of his unworthiness and the presence of evildoers, Tim stays in the past with images, words, and sensations that are not shared, honored, and humored. This weakness and self-loathing of guilt set Tim up for anticipatory anxiety of the future. Tim feels so weak, inept, and inadequate that he knows he will be victimized in the future by things out of his control. The success of other Vietnam veterans in securing the payments for compensation and rehabilitation only accentuates his unsuccessful competition and guilt. His invidious comparisons with fellow vets create more paranoid distrust.

While Tim repeats his predictable tragicomic scenarios from day to day, his future gets bleaker. Instrumental PTSD programs in institutions were always rare but now are exceedingly rare. One reason is that PTSD veterans upset authorities with their intense and direct "hostile" demands toward them. Another is that with all of their overt reexperiencing, arousing, avoiding, and numbing, these veterans are not apt candidates for traditional institutional quietment. A third reason is that successful PTSD treatment requires helper-experts who stimulate, allow, and share the natural lows of grief (O'Connell, 1981a, 1987) that are so necessary for the letting go of hostility (O'Connell, 1983, 1984a, 1984b). Cultural and economic pressures and ego needs to reframe problems of living into easy medicalized solutions have also contributed to the early demise of authentic and effective PTSD treatment programs in institutions (O'Connell, 1983).

And so, Tim marches on, losing his few empathic encouragers as nonallopathic PTSD treatment fades away. Soon he will be engulfed by chronic schizophrenics, lost on an orthodox quietment ward. He will be distinguished from the others only by his brisk upright parade step, as if on a confusing mission of tragicomic proportions.

FLASHBACK: CAUSE OR EFFECT?

An Adlerian psychotherapist would not regard "flashbacks" as an explanatory concept necessary to understand human behavior. Popular media and a number of ill-advised veterans have misused the descriptive metaphor of flashbacks as "the cause" of untoward actions. In psychotherapy, the chronic PTSD client learns to "let go" of the negativity and resistance toward being aware of and sharing the actual or feared loss. He or she begins to lose the "John Wayne: numbed but violent" defensiveness as the necessary grief work proceeds. At the same time, work-play continues on concentrating (contemplating) previously unacknowledged strength (SE) and belonging (SI). ("I'm learning now that I've always been more than my old need to show super-toughness, which eventually cracked"; "I never knew that we are all so weak. Maybe real strength is in sharing our mutual human defects"; "I now know that he who laughs—without anger—lasts.")

Another quality that changes (often automatically) with the unfolding of the natural low of grief and the construction of strength is the reframing of "flashbacks." It becomes obvious to those who work closely with chronic and severe PTSD clients, like the Nam vets, that there is misuse for power (SI) of flashbacks and violence. The threat of violence frightens others and gets the user the attention, special service, power over others, revenge, and/or avoidance of social responsibility that he or she misperceives as necessary (Dreikurs, 1972). The threat of violence protects the weak, brittle macho overcompensation, which continues to generate increasingly disturbed or disturbing behaviors (e.g., violence toward authority). In therapy, flashbacks are reframed as similes, ways of hiding the avoidance of responsibility ("I didn't want to attack that woman. The flashbacks made me do it"). Similes add the "like" (symbolic) dimension to a metaphoric statement: "It seems, at times, *like* the flashbacks make me do things." In successful lifestyle changes, the patient becomes aware (while sharing, honoring, and humoring) of a previously hidden, denied, and disguised sequence. That perception is the unwanted perceived helplessness (seen as negative and resisted) triggering the out-of-control panic. Then the images, words, and bodily sensations hit. The client has lacked the psychic distance and *becomes* the feared weakness, equivalent to psychic death (Lifton, 1985). Helplessness and loss of control—which have been repressed, negativized, resisted—now are that person. The chronic and severe PTSD patient who learns to evolve beyond quietment of symptoms into an encouraging lifestyle ceases to resort to violence and flashbacks to protect ego-esteem and ego interests. In the cure of all psychic disorders, the direction is the same: increase of unconditional worth, belonging, and joy. This task becomes more difficult with increase of disintegration, disconnection, and stasis (lack of psychic movement), the more chronic and severe the death anxiety.

GROUP TECHNOLOGY FOR NATURAL HIGH THERAPY FOR ANXIETY DISORDERS
(Order-for-Disorder)

> ... childlike foolishness is the calling of mature men. Just this way, Rank prescribed the cure for neurosis: as the "need for legitimate foolishness." The problem of the union of religion, psychiatry and social science is contained in this one formula. (Becker, 1973, p. 202).

A *strong* ego in effect disappears. That is, the identification with the lacks and desires of the weak ego "wants" (see Figure 7.1) is at least temporarily defused. Distance from ego demands means that one no longer judges persons and events negatively, on a contingency basis for allowing the experience of values of worth and belonging. All striving for external proof of esteem and belonging (the basis of ego-identity standards) is then seen as absolutely crazy-making! When the person is strong enough (SE, SI, SH) to break out of all forms of ego addictions (enslavement to externals for the "feel-goods"), he or she is in touch with the natural birthright of self-identity: unlimited worth and belonging, the universal free gift. Self-identity is never contingent upon what others do, say, think, or feel. In fact, once a person is afflicted with that "spell," the enthusiasm, inspiration, and enchantment of encouraging living pops like a bubble. Now one can see the purpose of metaphoric images of fairy tales (spells, "rationally" incomprehensible connections), games (teamwork, conditioning, arbitrary rules), and psychospiritual pilgrimages (searches beyond the ego addictions).

Following this way of imaging, the orthodox allopathic medical model can be seen with its "evil" pole. When transposed beyond medical emergencies and physical illnesses, the allopathic model can be the losing game, or a blatant sin for optimal psychic and spirit-soul development (Weil, 1983). To avoid this discouraging medicalized existence, one must be self-trained for skills in the sport of unconditional worth (SE), universal belonging (SI), and psychic dialectics (SH). The allopathic model in psychiatry, which emphasizes reductionism and hard determinism, has no place for the type of courageous play that is needed.

ACUTE STRESS DISORDER

This is new in the DSM-IV. It has much the same symptom criteria as PTSD, including flashbacks. The difference is in time and duration. With this diagnosis, the disturbance lasts for a minimum of two days and a maximum of four weeks and must occur within four weeks of the trauma.

NONCOMBAT PTSD: SIMILARITIES AND DIFFERENCES

The individual experiencing and exhibiting the symptomatology of PTSD resulting from events that are not combat-related likewise has suffered from overwhelming, absurd violence over which he or she had no control. Combat- and noncombat-related PTSD manifest many of the same symptoms. These include *hypervigilance, exaggerated startle reaction, somatization,* and the *exclusive use of specific coping mechanisms*—ones that once were successful but that now contribute to the maintenance of the problem (Hooker, 1985).

A common pattern in both etiologies of PTSD is perceived or actual lack of power and inability to control the situation; little or no sense of belonging, resulting in low SI; lack of, or inability to access past successes, resulting in low SE; and scarcity of potential resources that the individual could marshal in order to cope with, or make sense of, the situation. The level or intensity of each of these impacts the way the individual will internalize and respond to the initial, and any subsequent, trauma. For example, individuals who have been victimized, yet experience or internalize the traumatic event as less severe than those whose experience results in PTSD symptomatology, are theorized to have some mitigating factor. Perhaps the individual was able to exert control in a situation resulting in higher SE. Perhaps supportive, protective siblings banded together, resulting in feelings of belonging and higher SI. These same factors contribute to the recovery prognosis.

In the noncombat PTSD patient or client, the principal differences are in the *flashbacks, selective repression,* and *use of dissociation* as survival tools while the trauma is occurring and afterward when the memories begin to surface. These differences are noted as follows:

Flashbacks

Less frequently one of the earlier manifestations of the disorder. Because the use of denial and/or repression of the memory are preferred defense mechanisms with noncombat PTSD, considerable energy is required to break through that block. Initially, when a flashback does occur, it is often in the form of a nightmare in which the face of the perpetrator is distorted, demonic, blank, or dark and blurred. Such dreams, especially initially, tend to be symbolic rather than realistic portrayals of the event. Flashbacks are frequently fragments at first, with the person remaining consciously in the here-and-now, rather than reliving the trauma.

With PTSD of both types, when the individual totally returns to the trauma and loses contact with the present time, a danger is that of the individual remaining locked in the memory, unable to return to the present. When this happens, the event is diagnosed as a psychotic break. Temporary flashbacks have also resulted in this diagnosis, particularly in individuals where exposure of the trauma would jeopardize someone more influential.

Memory Loss

The individual reports periods of time unexplainably lost. These periods may be days, months, or as extensive as a number of years. Although these time periods are no longer part of the person's *conscious* memory, the individual continues to relive and to have his or her decisions influenced by the experience at the unconscious level.

Regression During a Flashback

In cases where the trauma being reexperienced occurred when the individual was young, during the flashback or reliving of the memory the individual appears to "become" that age. With especially severe and/or chronic trauma, care needs to be taken to keep the bridge between past and present open for "safety" and to prevent a "psychotic" break in which the individual could become developmentally "stuck" or fixed at that age. Many PTSD patients have a great fear of "going crazy," due in part to previous occurrences of such flashbacks, and having no other label or frame of references with which to "make sense" of the flashback experience.

One coping or survival mechanism often selected while PTSD-inducing trauma is occurring is to mentally dissociate. This psychological distancing leaves the memory of the trauma unavailable to the *conscious* mind; however, the trauma continues to be reality for the unconscious. Another complication is that trauma, particularly chronic, creates a block or impasse beyond which the individual cannot proceed with subsequent developmental tasks (Erikson, 1963). The outcome is a person whose emotional, moral, or intellectual development appears arrested, often in more than one area. (Hooker, 1985, discussed the effects of trauma on the person's ability to access intellectual resources due to the mental drain of obsessively reliving the experience or reviewing the tape, so to speak, which in turn affects his or her ability to focus on the here-and-now.) This inability to access and/or focus means that the individual who experiences trauma resulting in PTSD symptomatology often will have both the complication of memory loss and of being psychologically frozen at the age or stage when the debilitating trauma occurred. When this is the case, expect an increasing disparity between the person's chronological age and the behaviors he or she is exhibiting. Some people with high natural intelligence are very creative in hiding this;

however, if even a hint or glimpse of behavior does not correspond with the "rest of the picture," the possibility of early trauma should be explored.

Once the decision is made that remembering the event could jeopardize the individual's survival, the flashback or repression cycle is put in place. This means the individual then will be unable to access consciously or verbalize memories or feelings concerning the event. Repression of the memory will continue until the individual, often with the help of an encouraging therapist, is able to somehow perceive the ego strength as sufficient to risk remembering some portion of the event without total destruction. The exception to this is, of course, the flashback. One criterion of PTSD is that the traumatic memory(s) is(are) powerful enough to force through the wall of repression and reach the consciousness, that is, the flashback. A major problem here is that the flashback occurs *spontaneously* before the ego strength has improved sufficiently for the necessary psychological distance to be obtained and for the guilt and shame surrounding the original trauma to be assigned appropriately.

Another problem with the flashback is that the same emotions and intensity are experienced. (When dissociation was the coping mechanism used to survive, the individual may be consciously experiencing these emotions for the first time.) For example, during a flashback, the physical pain of a violent act will be felt. The individual may go into shock, scream, faint, become hysterical—anything that would have been appropriate at the time but may or may not have been options for the individual when the event occurred.

During therapy, if the trauma occurred at an early age, during therapy the client's attempts to verbalize or express the feelings connected with the event often result in moans, guttural visceral cries, or an inability to produce any sound even while the entire body is positioned to scream. That is, the body is tense, the head is back, the chin is up, the mouth is open, the face is contorted in a grimace, but the person is still unable to produce any sound. This silent scream is most prevalent either in the individual initially traumatized under the age of six and not allowed to make a sound even when in great pain or in the person who was told not to let anyone know.

Individuals suffering from noncombat-related PTSD report periods of mental confusion, emotional numbness, frequent dissociation, or taking a mental "trip," with the accompanying inability either to focus on present events or to remain in the here and now. These symptoms intensify when the person is under stress. This includes therapy when the individual is working to recall the traumatic event or memory. Typically, a client who mentally *checks out* will have the most difficulty staying in the present time when a mental connection is made between what is being said and the trauma. This connection may be made with information that seems totally unrelated to an outsider and often to the person with PTSD.

Several factors are at work to produce this effect. First, because PTSD-invoking trauma is intense, extensive generalization can take place quickly, and the connections made during the generalization will remain in effect until the power of the trauma is somehow diminished or negated. Second, due to the intensity of the emotions at the time, and the high levels of energy involved in repressing the memory, a great deal of power is brought to bear anytime the wall of repression or denial is threatened. Although what is being said, in reality, may have no connection with the event, the fear of discovery will be so strong that the most effective coping mechanism will be utilized and at an extremely high level. One patient would go to sleep during lectures about the possibility of changing or in a small group when the subject of incest or any form of abuse was being discussed or disclosed. Discovering the memory is particularly frightening with sexual abuse and/or incest, especially when the child has been told not to tell and/or has been threatened with terrible consequences if he or she does tell. Typical threats are the child's death and/or the harm or death of a loved one.

Treatment Techniques

In therapy, a clue that the memory is beginning to surface is when the client reports either having had a disquieting dream or recalling a recurring nightmare he or she had as a child. Asking the client what the dream meant to him or her and allowing the *client* to do the **interpreting** is the most effective tool. This includes the times when the therapist is completely sure of the meaning and the client "doesn't have a clue." It is important for the client to do the discovering work so he or she can take the credit. The client may report unexplained nervousness or perhaps "a feeling of sadness I just can't seem to shake. I don't know where it comes from or what it is about. It is just that most of the time, I feel so sad." When this happens, the therapist should normalize it, that is, frame it as a normal, natural part of the process, as a signal that a memory is getting ready to surface. The client also is assured that this is the proper time for the reason for the sadness, for example, to come up. The therapist should assure the client that, whatever the memory is, he or she will have the resources to deal with it; otherwise, the memory and the feelings associated with the memory would not be moving to the conscious level. With the mature adult or inner-child work, the therapist should remind the client that the child no longer has to protect the adult (conscious mind) from what happened, that the adult is strong and powerful. The adult has the ability and is willing to protect the child now; that is the adult's job.

If an impasse has been reached, with the client unable to bring the memory to consciousness, one tool is to ask the client to draw or write what happened with his or her nondominant hand. The nondominant hand seems to have access to the visual memories. Drawing and writing also circumvent the "don't tell" injunction.

Inner-child work involves utilizing a specific tool to access the memory. The inner child is framed as the part of the person that experienced the event(s). With some clients, it is necessary to separate the concept of multiple personalities from having a part of the personality that remembers exactly what happened. One way it can be framed is that everything that ever happened is stored in our memory banks, and using the concept of the inner child allows quicker access to that particular time. The unconscious or subconscious is identified as that part holding the memory. The conscious mind is then seen as the rational, objective part, the part that can be logical in all thinking and processing—the mature adult. Epstein (1994) discussed reuniting the cognitive with the dynamic unconscious and the value of this type work. The uniting of both areas and functions of the brain, the accessing of the previously hidden material or memory through the inner-child or adult concept is part of the value of inner-child work. Again, it is about taking away shame and guilt, offering protection and a way for the individual to feel powerful, with less disruption of his or her current reality. As the therapy progresses, a reintegration of the adult and child is accomplished (Hooker, 1991).

Beginning the memory retrieval work is a terribly frightening time for the individual who has been abused to the point where these symptoms or coping strategies are used and leaving therapy becomes an inviting alternative. Leaving is often judged the safest course of action. Although the client may or may not verbalize this fear, as memories begin to surface, one can expect the client to threaten to or actually leave therapy. This is a time when bonding or level of trust will be critical. It is important to offer safety and encouragement, to be completely nonjudgmental, and to convey these attributes to the client sufficiently so that he or she will trust the therapist to provide these at all times and in all circumstances. Safety, encouragement, and nonjudgmentalness are scarce commodities for PTSD survivors. This is one reason the Adlerian approach is so effective in working with PTSD. Again, when using the concept of the adult-child, it is important that instructions be given that the above are qualities of the mature adult and that the therapist is merely modeling "adult" behavior.

At times, the client may report having a flashback much like a snapshot that appears briefly, often incomplete seemingly nonsensical. These fragments may take the form of a sound, a partial view of a room, an article of clothing, a weapon, a color, something the person was looking at or focusing on while the trauma occurred, or a symbolic image.

It is helpful for the therapist to *frame* these as "trial runs" or "tests" that the unconscious is using to see if the individual is now strong enough to remember the event and survive. The Adlerian practitioner should also encourage the client with statements such as, "You are safe. You can trust that regardless of what you remember, you will be able to deal with it. If not, it would not have come up at this time." If the initial memories do not prove too frightening and are accepted, owned, and honored, another fragment will be supplied. If not, the repression and denial mechanisms will be reinstated. These pieces of the jigsaw may be given in various patterns, for example, one fragment one day, with the next one in two weeks, the next day, or an hour later. Again, what surfaces and the timing are determined by the way in which the person accepts and deals with each one. Denial is commonly the first defense. When denial is being used, the client will say things such as, "I'm making this all up. It never did happen. It was just a bad dream," or "I wanted to be loved by and be special to my Dad, and that's why I had the dream. It was just a fantasy. I feel awful for telling you those things. None of them were true. I lied; Daddy would never do anything to hurt me. He loves me."

The Adlerian practitioner also congratulates the client for any mental confusion, numbness, and inability to remain in the present. This is done by telling the client the truth: "These coping mechanisms allowed you to survive." The individual used these as a way to protect himself or herself from a reality that was too severe, too punishing, too traumatic to have been tolerated otherwise. The fact that he or she still uses these familiar devises as protective mechanisms also can be a source of encouragement. One can remind the person that he or she is continuing to use the techniques that "worked," which is very wise. The therapist then helps the client see that, although these mechanisms worked very well and served a useful purpose initially, it is no longer necessary to protect himself or herself in this way. Helping the client learn new ways to protect himself or herself and deal more effectively with situations that are or have been anxiety producing, is the logical next step.

One useful technique is to have the client congratulate the *inner child* (the part of the psyche that experienced and endured the trauma), to thank the inner child for his or her continuing help, and then to assure the child that he or she no longer needs to protect the *adult self* from the truth, that the adult self is now strong enough to protect them both. In this process, the child self is not discounted and thus discouraged. Rather, the inner child is encouraged through praise and is thanked for all his or her hard and diligent work. Even the most negative client, one who is unable to accept praise or thanks at the adult, conscious level, is often able to thank the inner child, thereby indirectly raising his or her SE as well as feelings of worthiness and belonging (SI).

Another basic difference between the combat veteran and the person with noncombat PTSD is the former's inability to establish and maintain psychological distance. The combat veteran is subjected to intense, continual, real, and/or anticipatory anxiety; in combat, no relief occurs from this. The proximity, the intensity, and the lack of control all contribute to the inability of the individual with combat-related PTSD to establish and maintain appropriate, necessary, healthy, survival-essential, psychological distance.

On the other hand, the noncombat sufferer of PTSD who has been able to maintain his or her sanity has found a way to obtain this distance. Being able to establish this distance is critical. The individual's way of getting this distance may seem dysfunctional or even "crazy," yet the therapist needs to recognize that establishing distance is an essential survival technique for the trauma survivor. Basically, we have encountered four ways this distance is established: (a) *denial* of the perpetrator's identity or the full extent of the trauma, (b) *repression,* (c) *dissociation,* and (d) *self-blame.* For example, a victim of sexual abuse such as incest with multiple perpetrators may recall and/or admit that sibling incest occurred but deny that a parent was involved as well. The victim of the abuse may remember that "something bad" happened but remember monsters, grotesque faces, demons as being present and/or responsible for what happened (again, having memory of the event at one level, while maintaining denial of the actual perpetrator's identity).

Repression as a safeguarding tendency frequently occurs with abuse victims with PTSD. When repression is being used as a coping or defense mechanism, amnesia of the event may be total. At the conscious level, the individual is unaware the traumatic event occurred. This type of client may report reacting or behaving in strange ways for no apparent reason. The person will be genuinely puzzled by his or her actions, which are residual effects of the traumatic event that has been repressed.

Dissociation in one form or another, especially when reinforced later by repression, is the most common and most effective method of dealing with noncombat trauma resulting in PTSD. Dissociation may take one of several forms. One, an *out-of-body experience* where the person views the scene as an observer rather than as a participant. Two, *imploding*, which is going *inside*, resulting in a complete shutdown of all sensations and thoughts. This is a state in which the person actually neither feels or experiences the physical pain involved nor hears, on the conscious level, the verbal abuse. Three, the individual may create a pseudo-self to take the place of the real self (during the experience). For example, one victim of incest assumed a different identity by "becoming" one of her dolls during the actual sexual intercourse with her father. The girl had a large collection of dolls, each of which had a different name. The ritual was that when her father entered the room, she would say, "Hello, my name is Melanie." Her father would then refer to his daughter as "Melanie" during the act. The next day, the child would bury the "bad" doll who died the night before. What a wonderful way to establish the psychological distance needed to survive. Regardless of the coping mechanism used, it is important to focus on the creativity, wisdom, and functionality of the solution. The Adlerian therapist always congratulates and thus encourages the client.

Lastly, the individual may mentally **check out,** to absent himself or herself from the scene completely. Although on the surface this may seem safer and more effective, in some ways, checking out is more dangerous. The reason being that here, the dissociation is so complete that it becomes more appealing, even addictively alluring to the individual using it. The greatest danger of the use of this dissociative technique of mental numbing or blanking out of all reality is that it is so effective that it is difficult to convince the client that it is no longer necessary to use this defense mechanism. Plus, the client often is not aware of doing it. The other reason this form of dissociation is so dangerous is that its use results in behavior and a mental state frighteningly close to a psychotic break. Individuals who have consistently used this escape or coping mechanism as children often report having lost years of time. As adults, these same people report having difficulty concentrating and staying in the here-and-now in any situation, but especially when any type stressor is present.

CASE EXAMPLES

Case of Bill

When any form of dissociation is used, the individual will report lost time or disjointed, partial, fragmented memories. For example, one patient whom we will call "Bill" reported feeling as if he were in a piece of a room. He said there was a pair of shoes in the room and nothing else; then everything disappeared and the "bad" thoughts (thoughts of becoming violent) started. When queried about the feelings, Bill became emotional and screamed: "I didn't feel anything! I never feel anything. There was nothing there. There never is anything there. It is all in my head. Nothing is real." He was very uncomfortable during the entire time he was recounting what he called "this fragment" but did have the courage to continue.

At one point during the session, Bill looked directly at the therapist and said, "I have thoughts like wanting to stick my fist through your face and knock the back of your head off." The therapist calmly assured Bill that such feelings of rage and powerlessness were a natural result of the childhood abuse he suffered. The therapist then said to Bill, "I want you to look at me for a minute and listen." As soon as eye contact was established, the therapist immediately said, "You are not crazy. You are not going to go crazy. You are safe. It is safe to remember what happened and feel your feelings. You are strong enough to hear the truth and deal with the past. You have strength to work through anything that surfaces." It is helpful to encourage clients with this type of strategy. Do not expect the highly or chronically traumatized client to be able to maintain eye contact for more than one or two seconds at first. The important thing is breaking through the protective wall, even for a moment.

Another important part of working with the PTSD-delayed client is to prewarn him or her not to worry if the memories are not complete or clear immediately. Reassure the client that, as the scared part feels safer, more memories will surface; that some of what happened may never be remembered, and that is fine; and that it is not necessary to remember everything in order to be free of the past. Ask the client when he or she gets scared to say, "I am safe. I will never be given any memory that is more than I can deal with. I will never be confronted with anything that will make me lose control and go crazy. I have the power and strength to deal with anything from the past." When using the inner-child approach, the therapist has the mature adult assure the child self that the adult will protect the child, will believe what is said, will be nonjudgmental, and will do all the necessary work of healing.

Perceived inability to control or predict either the level or the timing of the violence of future events remain key elements in the prognosis of individuals with PTSD. Were the individual able to predict or control the level of violence in future similar events, he or she would be able to avoid the continuing feelings of powerlessness and worthlessness (low SE) that are integral parts of the belief system of a person experiencing the residual effects of trauma or PTSD.

Changing the person's internal belief system regarding the ability to control future events; addressing and correctly assigning responsibility for the original trauma; and absolving the victim of trauma-connected shame and guilt (which often are assumed as ways of gaining some feeling of control, that is, being able to change, stop, avoid, or lessen past and future trauma) all are essential. Changing the belief system and dealing with the past help end the necessity of recreating or reliving the event. When an individual keeps reexperiencing similar traumatic events, not always with the same perpetrator or victimizer, it may be an attempt by the unconscious to "correct the error" and change the script. Mentally replaying the videotapes of the event is often an attempt to find this perfect answer. The reason for seeking the "right way" is to regain the power lost during the trauma; to be able to protect one's self; to abolish the constant fear connected with being revictimized and the need for hypervigilance; and to stop the cycle of fear and pain, the continuous mental (and frequently physical) reenactment of the trauma, looking for clues. Adler's dynamic of "clinging to the shock effects" may be a manifestation of this; an attempt to make sense of insanity; or to this time "get it right," in order to erase the "fatal flaw," and thus deserve to belong (SI) and finally to feel better about one's self (SE).

Case of Female Incest Victim

Phobias often can be tied to a traumatic event. In one case, a female incest victim came into therapy complaining of nervousness and an intense though "foolish" fear of bugs. In the course of therapy, it was discovered that her perpetrator was her grandfather, with whom she was living, and the sex act always took place in a root cellar where there were a number of bugs. As a survival tool, she associated the pain and the terror with the bugs. It was easier (safer) to fear and hate bugs; they were not responsible for her well-being or survival; her grandfather was. Her grandfather also gave her love and affection, praise and ego-based feelings of self-worth. It is only natural that it had to be the bugs that were "bad," not Papa. Papa loved her. This dichotomy, this survival-level conflict between needs and reality, must be addressed in therapy. Fortunately, Adlerian therapists have the ideal tools.

Feelings of emptiness, worthlessness, overwhelming isolation, and poorly defined, undefined, or generalized irrational fear (anxiety and/or phobic responses) also are frequently reported feelings when the client is asked to recall what it was like to grow up in his or her family.

Assuming the blame, guilt, or self-blame affords the individual a pseudo, though inaccurate, feeling of power and/or the ability to control the situation and, thus, to prevent future similar traumatic events from occurring. By assuming responsibility or blame for causing the event, the individual feels, in part, in control and obtains a feeling of having some power—real or not—over the situation and his or her life. Any amount, any level, of power is a crucial factor in preventing the debilitation of helplessness and the despair of hopelessness in the individual.

GLOBAL APPROACH TO TREATMENT

Two of the most crucial factors in Adlerian treatment of PTSD are the practitioner's ability to help the client reconnect with his or her intrinsic value or worth (SE) and sense of belonging to the wider community (SI). Increasing the client's SI (which includes a sense of worthiness to belong to the community and, therefore, basic worth as a person who is a capable, important, and necessary member of society) also is related to the psycho-spiritual healing phase completing the integration of all levels—body, mind, and spirit. Healing at any of these levels is important and necessary, but, in and of itself, insufficient to accomplish reestablishment of wholeness and ultimate reconnectedness of the integrated and thus "healthy" individual with the community (at the universal level). Integration, a sense of worth and belonging across all levels of the psyche is implicit in the definition of adjustment and/or mental "health" in the Adlerian sense. This *global approach* of total reintegration may seem grandiose; however, to these writers, it remains both the ultimate and minimal criteria for true healing.

Adlerians believe that the client's level of discouragement or displayed damage to SE predetermines or predisposes the individual's expressed symptomatology as well as which therapeutic approach(es) might be most helpful. These authors agree. For example, the person who has been discouraged since childhood with resulting low SE and little SI would have a great deal of difficulty tackling, much less chance of accomplishing, a task or challenge designed to help teach a client whose SE and SI have sustained only recent damage or trauma. With the former, basic trust issues (Erikson, 1963) need to be addressed, and rudimentary teaching of techniques, such as stroking for strength and use of affirmations, is required. Clients with longstanding histories of rejection (or perceived rejection) by others have learned not to trust, and trust is the basic building block of self-esteem (SE), followed by SI. With the chronically discouraged client, joy, a sense of humor (SH), and feelings of connectedness and worthiness to be or feel connected are notably absent. It has been our experience that joy—a sense of humor (SH)—and a zest for living and life are the first casualties in the PTSD victim's lifestyle, belief system, and drama. O'Connell (1981a) addressed this need to restore SH and SI in his work on psycho-spiritual healing.

SEPARATING DISCOURAGING EVENTS FROM BASIC WORTH

Most noncombat and many combat PTSD victims have a great deal of difficulty separating the discouraging event(s) from their basic worth (SE). It is not unusual to hear clients with a PTSD diagnosis assuming the guilt and/or blame for the event. For example, the client will say, "If I hadn't been there," or "dressed that way," or "looked at him like that . . . said what I did, it would never have happened." "I knew better. I knew what would happen. It's all my fault." These messages are not always created without help from others. Many incest and/or rape victims and battered women and children are told, "It's your fault. You provoked him(her)" or "You should have stopped it. You knew better," or "If that was going on, why did you go back? You knew what would happen. It's your own fault it kept going on. You wanted it to go on or else you wouldn't have kept going back," or "You let it happen" or "Why didn't you tell me?", which corroborates the myth that if the victim had told, then magically some help would have been forthcoming or that the parent or protector would have been there for the victim, giving aid, assistance, protection, and love. Again, the underlying message is that what happened is the victim's fault and responsibility—the same type of message the victim has been giving himself or herself all along. Victims mentally abuse or beat themselves up, using discouraging messages such as assuming the blame (Hooker, 1985).

One client assumed the blame for a violent rape. Her reasoning? "I knew better than to pick up my car alone after office hours." Unfortunately, this client's belief that she had been solely to blame for the rape was reinforced by several hours of interrogation by police officers while she sat in ripped, blood-stained clothes, unable even to shower because she had not yet been "permitted" to go to the county hospital for a medical examination to see if indeed a rape had occurred. This sense of being to blame, somehow responsible, was compounded by the victim's husband's and mother's tirades. Her husband accused the victim of lying about the rape—using it to cover up an extramarital affair. Her mother insisted that the daughter put herself in the position of "asking for it" by picking up her car after working hours (and that she had probably had on a dress that was too tight or in some way provocative). Mother went on to say that under no circumstances was the daughter ever to tell her father because "the shame would kill him." This client carried the shame of her "guilty secret" and therefore her intrinsic lack of worth for over 20 years before ever sharing it. The facts about the rape came out in therapy after the client began to trust and as a result was able to begin releasing the discouraging, negative aspects of the past and then start building and accepting her true worth.

SUMMARY

The level of self-acceptance (SE) affects one's ability to tolerate change, to recognize the power to initiate and make needed changes. The individual who can accept personal responsibility for all his or her actions and decisions, particularly positive ones (because victims seem to instinctively assume responsibility for everything negative), is well on his or her way to mental health and integration. As teachers, Adlerian practitioners should know that accepting responsibility, seeing challenges instead of obstacles, the ability to laugh at oneself, knowing that "I belong," and this is the way it should be are all goals of treatment and/or therapy. To move the client to this point of acceptance, or as close to it as possible, is our mission. Some Adlerians are crusaders. We often are considered the "outsiders"—the ones who are out of step—but we know the truth. Adlerian therapy makes a difference with Generalized Anxiety Disorder, Social Phobias, and Posttraumatic Stress Disorder because we encourage, teach, and model change and bring about integration, hope, and acceptance of our human imperfections. We see our flaws and challenges as a chance to humor ourselves as we "laugh-dance" through the reality we have created in our lives.

Natural High Haiku

Discouragement grasps

separation, fear, and guilt.

Humor lets them go.

O'Connell

REFERENCES

Adler, A. (1964). *Problems of neurosis*. New York: Harper Torchbooks. (originally published 1929)

American Psychiatric Association. (1987). *Diagnostic and statistical manual of mental disorders* (3rd ed., revised). Washington, DC: Author.

Ansbacher, H. (1965). The structure of Individual Psychology. In B. Wolman (Ed.), *Scientific psychology* (pp. 340–364). New York: Basic Books.

Ansbacher, H.L., & Ansbacher, R.R. (Eds.). (1956). *The Individual Psychology of Alfred Adler*. New York: Basic Books.

Baritz, L. (1985). *Backfire: A history of how American culture led us into Vietnam and made us fight the way we did*. New York: William Morrow.

Becker, E. (1973). *Denial of death*. New York: Free Press.

Blackburn, A., O'Connell, W., & Richman, B. (1984). Post-traumatic stress disorder, the Vietnam veteran, and Adlerian Natural High Therapy. *Individual Psychology: The Journal of Adlerian Theory, Research, and Practice, 40*, 307–332.

Dreikurs, R. (1972). Technology of conflict resolution. *Journal of Individual Psychology, 28*, 203–206.

Egendorf, A. (1985). *Healing from the war: Trauma and transformation after Vietnam*. Boston: Houghton Mifflin.

Epstein, S. (1994). Integration of the cognitive and psychodynamic unconscious. *American Psychologist, 9*(8), 709–724.

Erikson, E. (1963). *Childhood and society*. New York: Norton.

Gabriel, R. (1987). *No more heroes: Madness and psychiatry in war*. New York: Farrar, Straus and Giroux.

Hooker, B. (1985). *Rx for victims: A clinician's guide to recognizing and treating victim behavior*. Dallas, TX: Thompson Publishing.

Hooker, E. (1991). *Facilitating personal change*. Dissertation Abstracts.

Lifton, R. (1985). *Home from the war*. New York: Basic Books.

Manchester, W. (1979). *Goodbye, darkness*. Boston: Little, Brown.

Mozdzierz, C., Marchitelli, F., & Lisiecki, J. (1976). The paradox in psychotherapy. *Journal of Individual Psychology, 32*, 169–184.

O'Connell, W. (1975). *Action therapy and Adlerian theory: Selected papers by Walter O'Connell*. Chicago: Alfred Adler Institute.

O'Connell, W. (1981a). Natural high therapy. In R. Corsini (Ed.), *Handbook of innovative psychotherapies* (pp. 554-568). New York: Wiley.

O'Connell, W. (1981b). Spirits in thanatology. *Death Education, 4*, 397–409.

O'Connell, W. (1983). The impossible dream: Institutionalized actualization of self-esteem and belonging. In R. Steffenhagen (Ed.), *Hypnotic techniques for increasing self-esteem* (pp. 163–180). New York: Irvington.

O'Connell, W. (1984a). Letting go and hanging on: Confessions of a Zen Adlerian. *Individual Psychology: The Journal of Adlerian Theory, Research, and Practice, 40*, 71–82.

O'Connell, W. (1984b). Cutting edges: PTSD. *V.A. Chief Psychologist, 7*(2).

O'Connell, W. (1987). Natural high theory and practice: The humorist's game of games. In W. Fry & W. Salameh (Eds.), *Handbook of humor and psychotherapy: Advances in the clinical use of humor* (pp. 55–79). Sarasota, FL: Professional Resource Exchange.

O'Connell, W. (1988). Natural high theory and practice: A psychospiritual integration. *Journal of Integrative and Eclectic Psychotherapy, 7*(4), 81–94.

O'Connell, W., & Gomez, E. (1990). Dialectics, trances, and the wisdom of encouragement. *Individual Psychology: The Journal of Adlerian Theory, Research, and Practice, 46*, 431–442.

Salzman, L. (1968). *The obsessive personality*. New York: Science House.

Trower, P., & Gilbert, P. (1989). New theoretical conceptions of social anxiety and social phobias. *Clinical Psychology Review, 9*, 19–35.

Veninga, J., & Wilmer, H. (1985). *Vietnam in remission*. College Station, TX: Texas A&M University Press.

Weil, A. (1983). *Health and healing*. Boston: Houghton Mifflin.

Wilmer, H. (1989). *Evil and the American shadow: Lessons from Vietnam*. Dallas, TX: Isthmus Institute, February 4.

Chapter 8

SOMATOFORM DISORDERS AND PSYCHOLOGICAL FACTORS AFFECTING PHYSICAL CONDITIONS

Mark Mays

Somatoform disorders are those psychological conditions in which the focus is upon physical functioning, the soma. In these conditions, patients perceive themselves as physically ill, describe health symptoms, or describe worries about health, but they are without actual organic pathology. The diagnosis of Psychological Factors Affecting Physical Conditions refers to those conditions in which actual organic pathology is present, yet psychological factors are seen to trigger, intensify, or maintain the physical distress. In all of these conditions the focus is on the body. In all of these conditions, patients define themselves as physically ill. In all of these conditions, their physician disagrees partially or entirely with them.

HYPOCHONDRIASIS

Hypochondriacal patients are concerned about their health. Often they have had some experience that has made them unsure about the security of good health, or life itself. To them, the world is full of worries. The satisfactions and enjoyments that come with good health may be gone forever. The ultimate loss is just a heart beat, or lack thereof, away. Life to them seems somewhat gray and often unenjoyable, but worth holding on to. It is difficult for them to know how completely to rely upon their physicians, since their doctors' concerns are not as great, their worries not as intense, their personal investment not so high. Perhaps they have overlooked something? Perhaps some condition exists that they know about but are not disclosing? Support often seems lacking, both from doctors and nurses as well as friends and family who do not seem to understand how serious all of this is and how tragic the consequences might be.

The physical body and the world of physical enjoyments are to them more a source of frustration rather than satisfaction. The world of thought or caring matters more. Movement and energy are diminished in an attempt to control one's safety, all of which require abilities that they fear they may not possess.

In a more objective sense, the hypochondriacal patient starts off with the assumption that ill health is a likelihood and interprets ambiguous sensory events as indicating serious physical pathology. Much like an Alice in Wonderland, in which there is a "sentence first, trial later," the hypochondriacal patient assumes physical disease or ill health, sometimes catastrophic, and gathers data to support this assumption.

The DSM-IV diagnostic criteria for (300.7) Hypochondriasis are as follows (American Psychiatric Association, 1994, p. 465):

A.   Preoccupation with fears of having, or the idea that one has, a serious disease based on the person's misinterpretation of bodily symptoms.

B.   The preoccupation persists despite appropriate medical evaluation and reassurance.

C.   The belief in Criterion A is not of delusional intensity (as in Delusional Disorder, Somatic Type) and is not restricted to a circumscribed concern about appearance (as in Body Dysmorphic Disorder).

D.   The preoccupation causes clinically significant distress or impairment in social, occupational, or other important areas of functioning.

E.   The duration of the disturbance is at least 6 months.

F.   The preoccupation is not better accounted for by Generalized Anxiety Disorder, Obsessive-Compulsive Disorder, Panic Disorder, a Major Depressive Episode, Separation Anxiety, or another Somatoform Disorder.

Specify if:
With Poor Insight: if, for most of the time during the current episode, the person does not recognize that the concern about having a serious illness is excessive or unreasonable

SOMATIZATION DISORDER

Patients with a Somatization Disorder are those who are long suffering, act helpless, and feel physically out of control. To them, the world is truly a frightening place. They fear they may not be up to dealing with some of the challenges of life all by themselves. Security for them resides outside themselves, and only a helpful "other" such as a doctor or medicines can hold any hope for reducing the distress and suffering. Even these only help a little. People often do not seem to understand how much more is necessary.

The world is full of things that they might wish to do, but feel unable to do because physical symptoms preclude full participation in life. If all of these symptoms did not exist, my, but the world would be full and rich. As of now, they feel they need to settle for second best and to only hope that help in the form of a caretaker is down the road. Since for them power resides outside of one's self, an essential way of life for them is to please and avoid the disapproval of others who may hold the keys to some improvement or hope for betterment in the future. They feel dragons are out there, far bigger than any one person, and they must find the knight to rescue them. They believe one must avoid pain of any kind.

Indeed, those with a Somatization Disorder, by definition, have numerous physical symptoms. These may include conversion like phenomena, in which physical symptoms cannot be explained by organic, or physical, dysfunction, nor by those mechanisms that affect the body, such as medicines or alcohol. The Somatization Disorder patient usually complains of pain and is clear to present himself or herself as long suffering. Things are generally "all in a mess" physically without a singular focus for physical concern or symptomatology. These patients feel sick. Regardless of what their physicians say, and they usually have numerous physicians, they believe they have the proof of illness through their subjective distress. Unlike the hypochondriacal patient, who is concerned about possible medical illness, the somatization disorder patient actually has numerous symptoms. These persist over time, and, given their physical manifestation, the patient is convinced of their physical cause. Unlike the hypochondriacal patient who has reached a "sentence" of illness before the actual "trial," the person with the somatization disorder has vast and prolific evidence they offer to prove their point.

The DSM-IV diagnostic criteria for (300.81) Somatization Disorder are as follows (American Psychiatric Association, 1994, pp. 449-450):

A.   A history of many physical complaints beginning before age 30 years that occur over a period of several years and result in treatment being sought or significant impairment in social, occupational, or other important areas of functioning.

B.   Each of the following criteria must have been met, with individual symptoms occurring at any time during the course of the disturbance:

    (1)   *four pain symptoms*: a history of pain related to at least four different sites or functions (e.g., head, abdomen, back, joints, extremities, chest, rectum, during menstruation, during sexual intercourse, or during urination)

    (2)   *two gastrointestinal symptoms*: a history of at least two gastrointestinal symptoms other than pain (e.g., nausea, bloating, vomiting other than during pregnancy, diarrhea, or intolerance of several different foods)

    (3)   *one sexual symptom*: a history of at least one sexual or reproductive symptom other than pain (e.g., sexual indifference, erectile or ejaculatory dysfunction, irregular menses, excessive menstrual bleeding, vomiting throughout pregnancy)

    (4)   *one pseudoneurological symptom*: a history of at least one symptom or deficit suggesting a neurological condition not limited to pain (conversion symptoms such as impaired coordination or balance, paralysis or localized weakness, difficulty swallowing or lump in throat, aphonia, urinary retention, hallucinations, loss of touch or pain sensation, double vision, blindness, deafness, seizures; dissociative symptoms such as amnesia; or loss of consciousness other than fainting)

C.   Either (1) or (2):

    (1)   after appropriate investigation, each of the symptoms in Criterion B cannot be fully explained by a known general medical condition or the direct effects of a substance (e.g., a drug of abuse, a medication)

(2)   when there is a related general medical condition, the physical complaints or resulting social or occupational impairment are in excess of what would be expected from the history, physical examination, or laboratory findings

D.   The symptoms are not intentionally feigned or produced (as in Factitious Disorder or Malingering).

CONVERSION DISORDER

The person with the Conversion Disorder experiences a loss or alteration in physical functioning suggesting a physical disorder, but psychological factors cause this. Such symptoms as paralysis, loss of sensory functioning in one or more areas, or the like, initially appear to have a physical cause, but adequate medical evaluation excludes a physical basis.

The phenomenology of the Conversion Disorder patient is generally that of resigned acceptance. Their world is one in which there are losses, sometimes irretrievable losses. One can only deal with this by the quiet acceptance of situations beyond one's control. Since life seems full of loss, they feel that all that one can do now is to attempt to minimize further loss. Feeling disabled and impaired, helpless to change things beyond one's control, they try to look on the bright side and try to make the best of things. Fortunately, others are often helpful and seem to understand the sad blow that fate has dealt them. Others "understand" that they can do nothing to change things, except to try to make it a life a bit more endurable. If medical illness is a prison, then they attempt to be a trustee.

From a more objective viewpoint, conversion disorder patients seem to have accommodated all too well to their current difficulties. They seem to have little insight or understanding regarding the possible psychological rewards for their distress. Often these environmental supports or rewards are quite notable, but the patient treats all of this with an almost automatic emotional response of generally bland indifference. They appear to be only a rider in the car, with physical symptoms clearly driving. Their symptomatology is consistent over time, and they clearly are not malingering or consciously attempting to deceive others. Their own experience is that of having no control over aspects of their physical functioning.

The DSM-IV diagnostic criteria for (300.11) Conversion Disorder are as follows (American Psychiatric Association, 1994, p. 457):

A.   One or more symptoms or deficits affecting voluntary motor or sensory function that suggest a neurological or other general medical condition.

B.   Psychological factors are judged to be associated with the symptom or deficit because the initiation or exacerbation of the symptom or deficit is preceded by conflicts or other stressors.

C.   The symptom or deficit is not intentionally produced or feigned (as in Factitious Disorder or Malingering).

D.   The symptom or deficit cannot, after appropriate investigation, be fully explained by a general medical condition, or by the direct effects of a substance, or as a culturally sanctioned behavior or experience.

E.   The symptom or deficit causes clinically significant distress or impairment in social, occupational, or other important areas of functioning or warrants medical evaluation.

F.   The symptom or deficit is not limited to pain or sexual dysfunction, does not occur exclusively during the course of Somatization Disorder, and is not better accounted for by another mental disorder.

Specify type of symptom or deficit:
With Motor Symptom or Deficit
With Sensory Symptom or Deficit
With Seizures or Convulsions
With Mixed Presentation

PSYCHOLOGICAL FACTORS AFFECTING PHYSICAL CONDITION

Psychological Factors Affecting Physical Condition is the diagnosis given when actual organic pathology is present, but psychological stressors, causes, or stimuli serve to start or exacerbate the physical process. Such problems as ulcers, migraine headaches, arthritis, allergic reactions, dermatological conditions, and many other such conditions may have a psychosocial aspect. In fact, some very interesting research suggests that many health issues may have more of a psychosocial aspect than has been previously thought. Research studies suggest, for example, that psychosocial factors may affect the rate of cancer growth, may correlate with the onset of certain forms of cancer, may affect the resiliency of the immune system, or may affect physical functioning in a variety of other ways. While intriguing, these considerations are beyond the specific diagnostic criteria of Psychological Factors Affecting Physical Condition. Here a psychologically meaningful stimuli must be related in time to the initiation or intensification of a specific physical disorder. Although such correlations between psychosocial factors and more general health maintenance in fact may exist, this is a more general question regarding holistic theories of physical well being and beyond the more particular diagnostic questions raised by this DSM-IV category.

Patients who have this diagnosis experience physical distress. They know that they are ill and can point to X-rays, laboratory studies, and other such objective data for confirmation. They are sick and come with portfolios and credentials. From their point of view, physical pain and physical deterioration are realities, often frightening realities. Resources must be marshaled to avoid further loss, stress, and even risk of loss. They often feel powerless to control what occurs with their bodies and feel a sense of helplessness and powerlessness over other aspects of life as well. Life to them is stimulating but sometimes in painful ways. The focus on life is on outer stimuli, rather than on inner stimuli, because satisfaction for them is generally found externally. Unfortunately, it is difficult for them to predict or plan in a world that seems unpredictable and occasionally chaotic, one they believe is best controlled by attempts to deal with problems in a rational and orderly way, without the intrusion of disruptive emotion. Things already feel out of control enough they believe, so it is best not to further this with impulsive or expressive actions, or to cause further distress by focusing on unpleasant aspects of life.

From a more objective viewpoint, these patients clearly have illness, participate in continuing care for their illness, but are often only getting treated rather than getting better. Medical treatment focuses on the more visible threads of the tapestry of the illness syndrome, often neglecting the "binding weave" of psychological and physical factors into the holistic tapestry of human functioning. The range of conditions and the slightly differing dynamics behind these displays of psychologically influenced medical conditions makes it difficult to determine any specific syndrome or psychological mechanism. Furthermore, psychological assessment is sometimes complicated by the context of health care delivery. These patients may have changed somewhat as a result of kinds of treatment that they have received, either defining themselves as more passive participants in their own health process or becoming exceptionally frustrated with the lack of notable exchange that has occurred through their medical interventions. These contextual factors may complicate the patient's presentation and should be considered in understanding them.

The DSM-IV diagnostic criteria for (316) . . . [Specified Psychological Factor] Affecting . . . [Indicate the General Medical Condition] are as follows (American Psychiatric Association, 1994, p. 678):

A.   A general medical condition (coded on Axis III) is present.

B.   Psychological factors adversely affect the general medical condition in one of the following ways:

    (1)   the factors have influenced the course of the general medical condition as shown by a close temporal association between the psychological factors and the development or exacerbation of, or delayed recovery from, the general medical condition

    (2)   the factors interfere with the treatment of the general medical condition

    (3)   the factors constitute additional health risks for the individual

    (4)   stress-related physiological responses precipitate or exacerbate symptoms of the general medical condition

Choose name based on the nature of the psychological factors (if more than one factor is present, indicate the most prominent):

Mental Disorder Affecting . . . *[Indicate the General Medical Condition]* (e.g., an Axis I disorder such as Major Depressive Disorder delaying recovery from a myocardial infarction)

Psychological Symptoms Affecting . . . *[Indicate the General Medical Condition]* (e.g., depressive symptoms delaying recovery from surgery; anxiety exacerbating asthma)

Personality Traits or Coping Style Affecting . . . *[Indicate the General Medical Condition]* (e.g., pathological denial of the need for surgery in a patient with cancer; hostile, pressured behavior contributing to cardiovascular disease)

Maladaptive Health Behaviors Affecting . . . *[Indicate the General Medical Condition]* (e.g., overeating; lack of exercise; unsafe sex)

Stress-Related Physiological Response Affecting . . . *[Indicate the General Medical Condition]* (e.g., stress-related exacerbations of ulcer, hypertension, arrhythmia, or tension headache)

Other or Unspecified Psychological Factors Affecting . . . *[Indicate the General Medical Condition]* (e.g., interpersonal, cultural, or religious factors)

Of note is that the revision to DSM-IV from DSM-III-R allows for consideration of health-related behavior patterns that are maladaptive. This would include those behavior patterns that might cause health problems, such as unsafe sex or obesity as well as those behavior patterns that can interfere with effective medical treatment.

PAIN DISORDER

A revision in the DSM-IV is the addition of the diagnosis of a Pain Disorder. Very similar to the diagnosis of Psychological Factors Affecting Physical Condition, this diagnosis requires a specific complaint of physical pain with a psychological component. Pain must be sufficient to impair one's functioning and cause significant distress. Pain is usually the focus of medical attention. The patient's complaints of localized pain may or may not have a medical basis. This diagnosis can be given when only psychological factors are seen as causing a pain syndrome as well as when psychological factors interact with a general medical condition to produce pain not fully explainable from either an organic or a physical basis.

The psychodynamics of the person receiving the diagnosis of a pain disorder are quite similar to those receiving the diagnosis of Psychological Factors Affecting Physical Condition. There is generally some functional benefit, meaning that the pain tends to serve some function for the patient. It should be stressed that these physically involved psychological conditions are different from malingering, in which a patient has control over pain symptoms, manufacturing either the experience of pain or the report of pain. The patient with a Pain Disorder, and those with other somatoform disorders, is telling the truth. The person with a Pain Disorder really does hurt. The physician looks at the pain complaint, however, and concludes that one must also consider psychological factors in looking at the duration, intensity, or impairment caused by the patient's distress. Psychological factors may trigger pain, may make it worse, or may cause it altogether. Most frequently with such patients an examination of the social reinforcements of being in distress are quite relevant. (Also see Figure 8.1.)

The criteria for a pain disorder in DSM-IV are as follows (American Psychiatric Association, 1994, pp. 461-462):

A. Pain in one or more anatomical sites is the predominant focus of the clinical presentation and is of sufficient severity to warrant clinical attention.

B. The pain causes clinically significant distress or impairment in social, occupational, or other important areas of functioning.

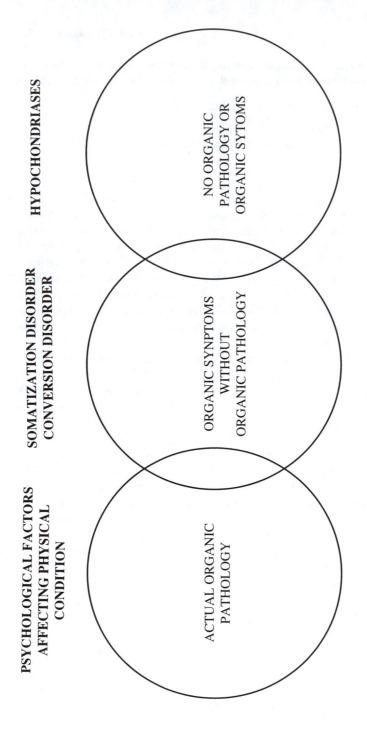

Figure 8.1. Psychological/physical continuum.

C. Psychological factors are judged to have an important role in the onset, severity, exacerbation, or maintenance of the pain.

D. The symptom or deficit is not intentionally produced or feigned (as in Factitious Disorder or Malingering).

E. The pain is not better accounted for by a Mood, Anxiety, or Psychotic Disorder and does not meet criteria for Dyspareunia.

Code as follows:

307.80 Pain Disorder Associated With Psychological Factors: psychological factors are judged to have the major role in the onset, severity, exacerbation, or maintenance of the pain. (If a general medical condition is present, it does not have a major role in the onset, severity, exacerbation, or maintenance of the pain.) This type of Pain Disorder is not diagnosed if criteria are also met for Somatization Disorder.

Specify if:
Acute: duration of less than 6 months
Chronic: duration of 6 months or longer

307.89 Pain Disorder Associated With Both Psychological Factors and a General Medical Condition: both psychological factors and a general medical condition are judged to have important roles in the onset, severity, exacerbation, or maintenance of the pain. The associated general medical condition or anatomical site of the pain (see below) is coded on Axis III.

Specify if:
Acute: duration of less than 6 months
Chronic: duration of 6 months or longer

Note: The following is not considered to be a mental disorder and is included here to facilitate differential diagnosis.

Pain Disorder Associated With a General Medical Condition: a general medical condition has a major role in the onset, severity, exacerbation, or maintenance of the pain. (If psychological factors are present, they are not judged to have a major role in the onset, severity, exacerbation, or maintenance of the pain.) The diagnostic code for the pain is selected based on the associated general medical condition if one has been established (see Appendix G) or on the anatomical location of the pain if the underlying general medical condition is not yet clearly established—for example, low back (724.2), sciatic (724.3), pelvic (625.9), headache (784.0), facial (784.0), chest (786.50), joint (719.4), bone (733.90), abdominal (789.0), breast (611.71), renal (788.0), ear (388.70), eye (379.91), throat (784.1), tooth (525.9), and urinary (788.0).

ADLERIAN APPROACH

A variety of ways exist to conceptualize these psychological conditions. The DSM-IV, with which we are primarily concerned here, divides them into the previously noted classifications as well as a few others not discussed. The ICDA, an international system of nomenclature, has defined them somewhat differently, referring to two categories: physical conditions with tissue injury, and physical conditions without such tissue injury. Previous diagnostic categories in the prior diagnostic manual referred to "psychophysiological reactions." Prior to that, "psychosomatic disorders" were the appropriate diagnosis.

The history of changes in diagnostic criteria and conceptualization shows how psychiatric medicine has attempted to deal with a dichotomy between mind and body. Today's DSM-IV implies this dichotomy of mind and body, with the criteria of psychological stimuli "triggering" organic pathology, and the distinction between psychological and physical events. Although Adlerian theory is quite helpful in understanding psychosomatic disorders, regardless of how labeled, a theoretical assumption in the current diagnostic conceptualization implies a subtle incompatibility with Adlerian theory. This can sometimes complicate communication with those of a dissimilar theoretical framework. One similarity among all of these conditions is the patient's presentation of physical symptoms or concerns having a psychological aspect. From an Adlerian viewpoint, in which all behavior is social, this would mean that a social-communicative value, a meaning, exists to all such conditions. In effect, the Adlerian definition of "psychological" suggests that the social context within which an individual lives and moves interacts with their own personal goals and lifestyle. With these conditions, this results in a reaction or disruption of psychological "movement" reflected in a physiological symptom or condition. This is one of the strengths of Adlerian theory. Adlerian theory is a holistic and phenomenological social psychology allowing exploration and understanding of an individual from a variety of perspectives. It allows consideration of the host of different levels of systems in which psychological movement occurs. These range from the cultural to the social to the familial to the psychological (see Figure 8.2).

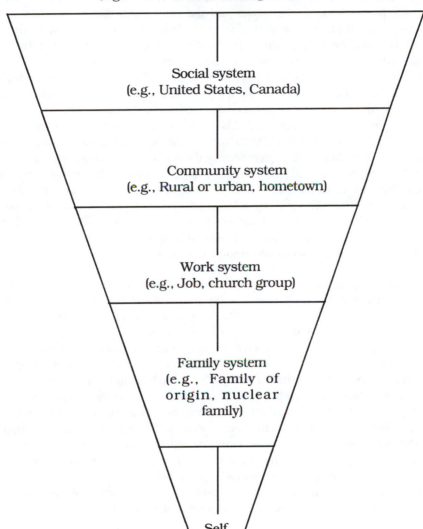

Cultural system
(e.g., Judeo-Christian, Anglo-American)

Social system
(e.g., United States, Canada)

Community system
(e.g., Rural or urban, hometown)

Work system
(e.g., Job, church group)

Family system
(e.g., Family of origin, nuclear family)

Self

Figure 8.2. Different levels of systems in which psychological movement occurs.

Adlerian psychology allows for an understanding of human movement that accounts for or takes into consideration not only the person but also the social fields in which he or she moves and the contributing holistic interaction of subsystems that form a psychological entity. In other words, Adlerian theory can "make sense" of an individual's personal and social situation more easily than can other theories because it takes into account the person's social context. Psychoanalytic attempts to interpret or infer generalized psychodynamics behind varying conditions have not been supported in the research literature. Psychoanalytic formulations employ a metaphor of human functioning that is biological rather than social psychological. These theories attempt to look at animalistic urges in conflict with external social forces. The focus remains intrapsychic rather than one that takes into complete account the ecology in which an individual lives and functions. The social psychological "payoff," or benefit, for psychosomatic conditions in other theories is seen as secondary, as is clear in the concept of "secondary gain." The primary gain, or psychological benefit, is a resolution of an unconscious conflict, according to traditional psychoanalytic theory. Unfortunately for the psychoanalyst, these theoretical positions have often been found wanting, both in analytical and empirical studies.

Adlerian theory looks at individuals in their social situation. Adlerians look at the meaning that a symptom has for an individual, the anticipated reactions of others, the social psychological "role" that an individual maintains by being medically ill, and a lifestyle in which such exaggerated goals as claiming, getting, avoiding, or revenge can play a role in contributing to a patient's symptoms. We explore the context to see in which ways an individual's lifestyle might be served by symptoms. Adlerian therapy is also helpful in terms of exploring the psychological meaning of being medically ill within our culture. Depending upon one's background and social circumstances, the role of the medical patient may have some profound implications and rewards. Some good things can happen when a person is sick. Friends and family pay attention. The rigors and demands of work and contributory activity can be avoided in a face-saving manner. Sometimes special favors are given, and social expectations shift when one is sickly. As most people view situations, one is expected not to have any "say so" over their medical condition and thus the consequences of being ill.

SOCIAL ROLE GAINED BY MENTAL ILLNESS

Anthropologists have explored the social role of the medically ill in differing cultures and during different eras. For example, a rather intense symptomatological response was once commonly expected as a response to "the change in life."

Swooning, fainting, and being incapacitated were all fairly normative, expected, and, given the general understanding of the syndrome, condoned. In the latter part of the twentieth century in America, perhaps following the rise of the feminist movement and an increase of women in the workplace, such expectations have changed. A woman who swoons and faints in response to "the change of life" would be viewed askance by males and females alike. A social role for what is accepted and expected of the medical patient is an anthropological variable. It shifts over time, it varies among subcultures, and it certainly plays a role in a person's symptoms.

Psychological theories differ regarding how to incorporate the understandings of the other social sciences. For example, an individual might develop a psychological paralysis of the vocal cords immediately preceding an audition for the opera. The psychoanalyst might see this as a reflection of rage directed towards a harsh and introjected father figure who has compelled excessive devotion to the precision of musical and operatic training, with a secondary psychological payoff of solicitousness from friends. One with a more physiological bent might see this as a laryngeal spasm secondary to heightened arousal, with psychological distress secondary to this, such distress reflecting itself in the most vulnerable organ system, coincidentally that of the voice. A behaviorist might see subvocalization and intense muscular tension secondary to performance distress as contributing to a buildup of lactic acid and resultant muscular discontrol.

An Adlerian, on the other hand, would explore a person's lifestyle and the social context, exploring what occurred as a result of the physical symptom without a physical cause. The Adlerian would look at the anticipated effect as well as the actual one and the meaning of this to the individual. Here an Adlerian would wonder if this reflects discouragement and might hypothesize that such an individual was discouraged and developed a "face-saving" way to avoid social evaluation, an evaluation that his or her discouragement and pessimism might make him or her wish to avoid. The development of a physical symptom, something consensually seen in our culture as beyond an individual's volitional or voluntary control, takes the person "off the hook." The individual, therefore, can say "I would have if I could have." Self-definition remains intact, and the person can see himself or herself, and, likely mistakenly, believe that others see them as still possessing such skill that, were it not for fate, certainly would reflect itself with an opening at the Met.

Although this is one hypothesis that such a symptom picture might reflect, the Adlerian therapist looking at a patient's unique and individual approach to situations might find a variety of different dynamics. It might not be quite so simple as avoidance of a psychologically threatening situation. It might well be, for example, that if the individual was a woman and was raised in a subculture in which, for example, the "good Mormon girl" deferred to her husband's directives, relinquished leadership to the husband, and would not wish to "overshadow" her spouse as such success might cause. The lifestyle of such an individual might be that of one who had an exaggerated need to do what was right, or an individual who had martyristic tendencies, gaining superiority through "righteous suffering."

This might also be, for example, an individual who wished to use physical symptoms to put others in one's service, reflecting a lifestyle of dominance more than avoidance. In one case, the situation might be analogous to the discouraged child who wishes to be left alone. In another case, it might be more akin to the individual who gets greater attention from family for frailties ("a bird in the hand") than she or he anticipates might occur following an audition in which fears are present that they might not have the skills to triumph over others ("two in the bush").

In making a diagnosis, the Adlerian would look at individuals' lifestyles and how these interact with the social context and consequences to produce a creative solution to personal problems. Psychological symptoms always are an individual's creative attempt to resolve a conflict between one's lifestyle and the social demands for cooperative living. The solution is sometimes a mistaken and socially useless one, yet a creative one nonetheless. In fact, the Adlerian practitioner can often shift the social psychological meaning of a symptom by reframing the symptom's meaning. For example, frequent nocturnal headaches might serve the purpose of distancing a wife from sexual contact with her spouse. A notable change might occur in symptom presentation if a credible and authoritative resource, such as a family doctor, announced to both her and her husband that her headaches were the result of muscle tightness, suggesting the need for emotional release, and that nothing would be better for this than sexual climax. This might cause the headaches to lead to the consequence of sexual activity rather than distancing one from it. The symptom might well change and another "solution" sought.

BRIDGE BETWEEN SOCIAL AND INDIVIDUAL

This bridge between the social psychological and the individual is fairly unique to Adlerian thought. This allows for the integration of the contributions of both the systems theorist and the personality theorist. Understanding goal-directed behavior in a social context is an understanding that Adlerians possess, yet a conceptual omission in many other theories of psychotherapy.

But what does all of this mean in real life? One result is that patients are referred to us who define themselves as merely medically ill. This often means that they are moving towards a personal goal of seeing themselves as ill and wishing to be seen by others as physically ill. If this is their goal, then one could expect that attempting to move them away from their goal would result in some notable lack of cooperative activity. The Adlerian therapist would either need to initially "make friends" with the private logic of a patient or challenge or change the patient's mistaken goals. Telling an individual who wishes to be seen as physically ill that "there is nothing wrong with you. It's all in your head" would often result in the individual seeking another, "more understanding" psychologist or therapist. A patient who is told that "your stomach problems are psychological in nature" might likely find this counter to his or her own personal experience, and certainly at great disharmony with his or her private goals of being seen as medically ill. A physician so diagnosing would likely be disbelieved, disregarded, or dismissed. Such patients are, however, quite comfortable with the diagnosis of "functional bowel syndrome," a label that implies the same condition, but still hints at physiology rather than personal motivation as being the cause or culprit in the patient's difficulties. A medical diagnosis such as this might be quite compatible with an individual's mistaken goals, for example, of being taken care of, suffering, avoiding, or getting from others as a result of their distress. A "psychological" diagnosis might not move one towards those goals. This makes treatment of such patients an art, demanding tact, timing, trust, and rapport.

So how does it all come about? Within Adlerian psychology, no specific antecedent leads directly and causally to these conditions. This is the beauty and elegance of Individual Psychology, an ideographic study of personality. Individuals' creativity is reflected in their choice of symptom, with the commonality being a lack of social interest and exaggerated or mistaken personal goals displayed in a conflict between their lifestyle and current circumstances.

Some historical antecedent predecessors are more common than others, however. Often the individuals who display physical disorders with a psychological component have aspects of their personality that are quite dependent. They wish to get from others or to be taken care of. These are more often youngest children. Overprotection on the part of parents may leave one with a discouraged perception of self as frail and unable to deal with life's hardships. Family constellations in which another sibling died often result in an overconcern and attentiveness to health on the part of family members. Early recollections of death, disease, injury, or medical treatment often are reflective of such a family focus. Chronic medical disabilities on the part of anybody in the family, elderly grandparents living at home, physically dangerous parental vocations, and the like, all might result in a family more attentive to health than the average.

Early recollections may show situations in which misfortune allowed an avoidance of stressful situations or described ways in which suffering, physical or situational, put others in one's service. These early recollections are quite compatible with the diagnoses of Somatoform Disorders or Psychological Factors Affecting Physical Condition. Early recollections that focus on kinesthetic processes, such as enjoying swinging, moving, tumbling, and the like, suggest a preference for kinesthetic representational systems, often associated with more reliance on physical forms of communication as often occurs in these diagnostic groups.

Individuals who have a heightened need for control often find the ultimate circumstance in which they lack control, that of death and life itself, as posing a particular stress for them. Hypochondriacal patients often have such an exaggerated need for control. Either those who seek stimulation excessively or those who are "getters" in their early recollections (Adler, 1957) often may be those who are vulnerable to prescription medicine dependence and somatoform dysfunction. Those who have experienced sexual abuse also may be more at risk for chronic pain syndromes or somatoform disorders. Deductions based on clinical experience suggest that this may play more of a role in the symptoms of female chronic pain patients than was previously thought. This would certainly suggest that early recollections in which physical aspects of life, or physical attractiveness, resulted in any unfortunate outcomes could certainly be consonant with a symbolic expression of distrust of physical forms of relating to the world. Those in occupations emphasizing physical activity, such as athletes, physical therapists, physical education teachers, dancers, and the like, may reflect a very positive way of relating to the world physically. Disruptions and discouragement for those in such vocational arenas may result in physical symptomatology, a more socially useless way of responding to life but still dealing with kinesthetic communicative systems.

TREATMENT

In treating such patients, an essential procedure is to examine the individual's psychological dynamics yet pursue assessment on both a medical and a psychological dimension. A diagnosis among the somatoform disorders implies the absence of physical pathology or other biologically based effects upon physical functioning. as can be found in drug misuse, alcohol abuse, or environmental influences. Some researchers have suggested that many patients thought to have a somatoform disorder are, in fact, misdiagnosed; they are medically ill patients. Such conditions as early presentation multiple sclerosis, endocrine disorders, certain neurologic conditions, environmental toxins, and a host of other situations may appear similar to these psychological conditions. This makes essential not only to gain a thorough medical understanding of the patient but also to have a lifestyle or psychological assessment that seems to "make sense" of the patient's symptoms. Both adequate medical and psychological findings should be present for these diagnoses to occur.

Physical symptoms also can occur as an individual attempts to express indirectly and metaphorically certain unacknowledged private goals. Attentiveness to such indirect communication is helpful, because this may reflect a patient's misguided effort to solve a personal problem. For example, individuals whose lifestyles limit them in being emotionally expressive, assertive, or confrontive with problematic people might develop functional neck pain that metaphorically reflects frustration and discomfort with their personal situation. Likely such a person would know immediately the answer to the question, "Who is the pain in your neck?" Some patients with functional bowel symptoms or ulcerative colitis with a psychogenic aspect often wish to rid themselves of something, their lifestyle inhibiting them from expressing this directly. Treatment that focuses on understanding, clarifying, and resolving lifestyle restrictions on full cooperative expressiveness aid in the resolution of such physical symptoms.

Individuals also may have as a private and unacknowledged goal to be like another person who has similar symptoms. Identification can occur upon occasion in somatic disorder, and an exploration of others who have been significant to a patient with similar syndromes may provide insight.

Dreikurs (1954) has recommended the use of The Question technique. He asked patients how their life would be different if one could wave a magic wand and take away all of these symptoms, exploring what they could do then that they cannot do now. He believed that this provided some indication of the psychological gains or benefits that accrue from the symptom. This technique is frequently helpful. Some believe that the absence of such anticipated life or behavioral changes with such an imagined miraculous cure tends to suggest a physical cause, with notable imagined changes suggesting a psychosocial component to the patient's problems. Another helpful procedure is to ask individuals with physical symptoms what it says about them to have such symptoms, how others understand and respond to them and their symptoms, if they have known anyone who has such symptoms, and if they can describe their symptoms metaphorically, asking what their symptoms are like or similar to. These are expansive questions that can help explore alternative ways in which an individual's lifestyle and personal movement can result in physical symptoms.

Treatment strategies focus on helping the patient understand and gain greater control over physical functioning while gradually building up other aspects of social embeddedness and social interest so that physical symptomatology erodes and fades away as it becomes unnecessary. Encouragement, greater understanding of mistaken goals in life, an increased feeling of social interest, and a less self-absorbed approach to life all tend to be good antidotes to these physical conditions.

CASE EXAMPLES

Case of Ethel

Ethel is 59 years old and a widow on her second marriage. Her first husband left her rather well-off financially, and she and her second husband now spend their time in their apartment, interacting marginally with a few long-standing friends. Ethel is the youngest of four children, having three older brothers. She described herself as "daddy's little girl." Her family was visible and highly regarded, if not wealthy. She grew up in the family as the "young princess," a person much taken care of by her older siblings.

Always concerned with fashion, she prided herself on looking good. She opened up a small boutique, financed in large part by her first husband, a physician quite older than she. Following her husband's death, the boutique began to fail and soon closed. She ultimately married a disabled laborer who frequented the coffee shop next to her store. Mildly depressed, she was referred to a psychiatrist for treatment and eventually became sexually involved with him during the course of treatment. When this relationship ended, she sought further care from a counselor who was supportive and saw her three times a week for several years until his retirement. Following his retirement, she developed episodes in which she had left-sided paralysis. Her husband, alarmed, referred her for neurological evaluation, but extensive studies were normal. Hospitalization showed muscle tone to continue, and irregularities of her presenting problems were noted that did not coincide with known medical processes. Her symptoms would vary over time, becoming acutely worse when her husband would have to spend time with his volunteer veterans association. This ultimately necessitated his abandoning his other activities to spend time with her. Ethel was diagnosed as having a Conversion Disorder.

Case of Ingrid

Ingrid is a 42-year-old obese female referred by her internist for a psychological evaluation. Her internist notes numerous medical problems, including bizarre sensory experiences, gastrointestinal difficulties and pain and symptom complaints that cover virtually every organ system. He is concerned about her prescription medicine dependence and notes that extensive medical exploration has not revealed a physiological basis to account for her symptoms. She is a long-term patient of the clinic, seen previously by the internist's former partner. He reports a history of having been adopted and raised in a foster home. She was removed at an early age by Child Protective Services workers as a result of neglect and abuse on the part of her alcoholic custodians. She has little information regarding her biological parents but reports them also to have been alcoholics. Her early recollections start at age seven and include memories of rocks thrown at her by an older boy and having had her gloves and coat stolen by a schoolmate. She has been unable to maintain consistent employment as a result of her health status and is supported by her husband—a sergeant in the Air Force who is frequently on remote assignment in his role as a safety instructor. She arrived at the clinic with a big handbag filled with all her medicines. assuming she would be asked about her health history She prepared for the social aspect of the interview by wearing thick blue eye shadow and heavy makeup. She is diagnosed as having a Somatization Disorder.

Case of Robert

Robert is a salesman for a tobacco company and has a large regional sales route. With recent health concerns, the tobacco industry has become increasingly competitive with quotas from the home office increasingly difficult to meet. Demoralized by the difficulties he experiences and concerned about the rather notable debts he has accumulated to support his indulgent lifestyle, Robert has taken on an additional sales territory. This causes him to be absent from home and family even more frequently. He notices that he has migraine headaches that seem to precede his monthly sales meetings and also correlate with his contacts with large accounts. These sometimes prohibit his making trips, but, more generally, he continues with his activities but believes his performance has diminished as a result of his physical distress. He is diagnosed as having Psychological Factors which Affect his Physical Condition.

Case of Henry

Henry is a 29-year-old only living son of a family with three children. One of his brothers died at infancy; the other was an alcoholic killed in an automobile accident. Henry has profound concerns about his health, concerns so pronounced as to make it difficult for him to concentrate on his academic activities. He has missed numerous classes for medical appointments and is delayed in his program as a result of not being able to complete required classes because of this. The oldest of his parents' three children, Henry wishes to be a success in his future career field of accounting, believing that likely he will need to support his potentially infirm parents as they age. He finds that his health concerns distract him from tending to his school activities, inhibit his dating, and are an almost constant source of worry. He takes his blood pressure daily, has complete physical exams at least twice a year, and is diagnosed as having Hypochondriasis.

Case of Karen

Karen is a laboratory technician at a local hospital, having previously worked professionally in the ballet. Her family constellation shows a family of three children, with Karen the middle sibling, and generally positive recollections and descriptions of her siblings and parents. Her early recollections show energy and physical movement and the involvement of others. She is referred for an evaluation of numerous physical complaints, including dizziness, problems with balance, and lapses of concentration and memory. Her family physician could not find a medical cause and referred her for psychological evaluation. An exploration of her lifestyle showed a high degree of social interest and involvement and no suggestion of psychopathology. Her referral back to her physician resulted in an ultimate diagnosis of exposure in the workplace to toxic levels of formaldehyde, which resulted in her symptoms. She received no psychiatric diagnosis.

BIBLIOGRAPHY

Adler, A. (1927). *The practice and theory of Individual Psychology.* New York: Greenberg.

Dreikurs, R. (1935). A case of functional disturbance of the digestive system. *International Journal of Individual Psychology, 1,* 57–62.

Dreikurs, R. (1936). The problem of neurasthenia. *International Journal of Individual Psychology, 2,* 14–34.

Dreikurs, R. (1948). The socio-psychological dynamics of physical disability. *Journal of Social Issues, 4,* 39–54.

Dreikurs, R. (1967). *Psychodynamics, psychotherapy and counseling: Collected papers.* Chicago: Alfred Adler Institute.

Manaster, G.J., & Corsini, R.J. (1982). *Individual Psychology.* Itasca: F.E. Peacock.

Mosak, H. (1977). *The psychological attitude in rehabilitation.* Chicago: Alfred Adler Institute.

Rule, W.R. (1984). *Lifestyle counseling for adjustment to disability.* Rockville: Aspen Publications.

Shulman, B.H. (1973). *Contributions to Individual Psychology.* Chicago: Alfred Adler Institute.

Shulman, B.H., & Mosak, H. (1967). Various purposes of symptoms. *Journal of Individual Psychology, 23*, 79–87.

REFERENCES

Adler. A. (1957). *Understanding human nature.* (W.B. Wolfe, Trans.). Greenwich, CT: Premier Books. (originally published 1918)

Adler. A. (1964). *Social interest.* New York: Capricorn Books.

American Psychiatric Association. (1994). *Diagnostic and statistical manual of mental disorders* (4th ed.). Washington, DC: Author.

Dreikurs, R. (1954). The psychological interview in medicine. *American Journal of Individual Psychology, 10*, 99-122.

Chapter 9

DISSOCIATIVE DISORDERS

Len Sperry

Dissociative Disorders represent a class of disorders considered so rare that some texts omit or limit their discussion. The reader should note that in older texts, as well as in DSM-I and DSM-II, these disorders were often termed Hysterical Neurosis-Dissociative type. Hysteria seems to have been highly prevalent among the leisure class of the late nineteenth century. Ellenberger (1970) believed this was due to cultural factors such as affectation and theatricality as well as puritanical ethos that fostered repression as a mechanism of defense or a neurotic safeguard. The virtual disappearance of hysteria or dissociative disorders amid the change to a more compulsive and work ethic driven culture in the early and middle part of the twentieth century may have accounted for the virtual disappearance of this disorder. Through the 1960s, the "me" and "now" generation, and a shift to a more narcissistic ethos, however, the apparent reappearance of this class of disorders suggests that they be included in this text.

Dissociation is a phenomenon commonly defined as a temporary alteration in the normally integrative functions of consciousness, identity, or memory. Dissociation involves a splitting off of thoughts, feelings, or behaviors that are ordinarily closely connected. Thus, thoughts can be dissociated from behaviors or from feelings. Dissociative phenomena are not necessarily associated with psychopathology. These phenomena may occur spontaneously, can be sought after, or can be induced for therapeutic purposes. It is believed that the ability to experience such is related to the same phenomenon underlying hypnotizability.

Hypnosis requires concentrated focal alteration with a relative reduction in awareness of stimuli (Spiegel & Spiegel, 1978).

Dissociation is a continuous rather than a singular or discrete phenomenon. Beahr (1982) referred to the "dissociative continuum" ranging from milder, more common forms of dissociation to pathological dissociative states included in the DSM-IV category of Dissociative Disorders. Commonplace dissociative events include daydreaming and absorption in reverie such that one can drive past one's freeway exit or not hear one's name being called by a class instructor. For the three-year-old child, having an imaginary playmate would be considered normal, as would a college student learning and practicing one of the many forms of meditation. Our culture tacitly supports and reinforces some degree of dissociation. In the process of becoming socialized, an American child is taught to take on a variety of roles that exist simultaneously but are expressed sequentially, depending on the demands of the situation. Among adults, the "part self" nature of the psyche has been accepted easily by the lay public and is a favorite theme in literature and the arts. We tacitly understand that we are not homogeneous, "single-minded" organisms, that conflict, diversity, and disparity within the self-structure are central features of being human.

The dissociative states are pathological forms in which complex behavior takes place outside the awareness of one's predominate consciousness and include trances, blackouts, amnesia, fugue, depersonalization disorder, and multiple personality disorder designated as dissociative identity disorder in DSM-IV. Although the etiologies of dissociative states usually are thought to be functional or psychological, they can have an organic etiology. Yaeger (1989) noted that blackouts—periods of amnesia—can be caused by alcohol or other substance intoxication as well as by head trauma. Yaeger also noted that dissociative states, including dissociative identity disorder, have been noted in individuals with temporal lobe epilepsy or partial complex seizures.

A BRIEF HISTORY OF THE CONCEPT OF DISSOCIATION

The phenomenon of dissociation has enthralled as well as puzzled philosophers, clinicians, and the lay public since the beginning of recorded history. For instance, the early Greeks employed dissociation in their "sleep therapy." Medical interest in dissociative disorders was reported beginning in the late nineteenth century with systematic studies of hysteria and hypnosis. Janet (Vander Kolk &

Vander Hart, 1989) is credited with introducing the term "dissociation." He hypothesized a model of idea complexes existing outside of consciousness as the cause of hysterical symptoms as well as the basis for hypnotic and posthypnotic phenomena. Janet used the term dissociation to describe a split in consciousness. He also believed that dissociation was the result of neuropsychological weakness (Vander Kolk & Vander Hart, 1989).

Freud and Breuer in their *Studies on Hysteria* (1955) claimed that thoughts kept out of conscious awareness to ward off painful affects could cause hysterical symptoms. Freud used the term repression rather than dissociation as a label for this phenomenon of thoughts kept out of consciousness. Unlike Janet, Freud's dissociation referred to both the observation of the split in consciousness and the mechanism of defense, that is, repression. Furthermore, Freud preferred a psychological rather than an organic explanation for dissociation. Finally, Freud's patients tended to be diagnosed as patients suffering from hysteria without a clear organic cause.

Prince (1906) also developed a theory of dissociation similar to Janet's in which different conscious states could exist in a person without awareness since his or her attention was not focused on them. He described co-consciousness as an explanation for phenomenon seen in both hysterical symptoms and multiple personality. Like Janet, Prince primarily studied patients with amnesia, fugue, gomnabulism, and multiple personality.

Freud and Prince had considerable impact on subsequent researchers and theorists on hysteria and multiple personality, and so it is not surprising that dissociative symptoms tend to be attributed to the existence of a split in consciousness and not to organic etiologies. Furthermore, even though Freud reported his observations on a more limited and distinct population—hysterical neurotics— than did Prince, the fact that both postulated "dissociation" as the underlying mechanism led many investigators to "lump" observations on the phenomena of amnesia, fugue, multiple personality, and hysteria together. This unwarranted assumption and consequent lumping of clinical presentations has led to diagnostic confusion. One result of this was that DSM-III, DSM-III-R, and DSM-IV approached diagnosis on the basis of similarities of signs and symptoms or known organic etiologies rather than on postulated psychological mechanisms. This change in focus has meant that some cases described in the literature as psychogenic fugue actually would meet criteria for psychogenic amnesia in DSM-III and DSM-III-R or dissociative amnesia in DSM-IV. Whereas the main character in Hannah Green's *I Never Promised You a Rose Garden* was diagnosed and was treated by her psychiatrist as a schizophrenic, today she would be classified as a dissociative identity disorder. For these, and perhaps other, reasons, there is considerable skepticism in the mental health profession about dissociation and the dissociative disorders. In the past 15 years, there has been a resurgence of interest in the multiple personality disorder. A small but vocal group believes that the diagnosis of dissociative identity disorder was overlooked, leaving untold numbers of patients undiagnosed or not treated adequately if they received a different diagnosis. This group has championed the diagnosis and developed its own organization, journal, and numerous workshops. A much larger group of mental health professionals believe that dissociative identity disorder is very rare, if it exists at all. A recent issue of the *Journal of Nervous and Mental Disorders* (1988, vol. 176, 9) was devoted to this "split" in the profession. This larger group is convinced that any increase in the number of reported cases of dissociative identity disorder represents a resurgence of interest in mental health professionals who in turn have influenced suggestible patients that they have this disorder. Furthermore, they contend that hypnosis is an introgenic treatment in that it probably induces the disorder.

DIAGNOSTIC FEATURES AND DSM-IV CRITERIA

With some background of the convoluted history of the phenomenon, dissociation, and its diagnosis, we now turn to descriptive features and diagnostic criteria of the five disorders listed in DSM-IV. These five are (a) dissociative amnesia, (b) dissociative fugue, (c) depersonalization disorder, (d) dissociative identity disorder, and (e) dissociative disorder NOS. A growing number of researchers and clinicians believe that Posttraumatic Stress Disorder, (PTSD) particularly the chronic form, is also a dissociative disorder, even though DSM-III, DSM-III-R, and DSM-IV assigned it to the Anxiety Disorders category. There was speculation that PTSD would be relocated to the Dissociative Disorders category in DSM-IV, but it was not.

DISSOCIATIVE AMNESIA

Dissociative amnesia, previously called psychogenic amnesia, is described as the sudden, but temporary, loss of ability to recall important personal information. This loss of memory can involve information about a specific topic or memories of the immediate or distant past. This memory loss is too extensive to be explained by ordinary forgetfulness, and it cannot be due to an organic etiology such as amnesia following a head injury, alcohol-induced blackouts, or

TABLE 9.1
Diagnostic criteria for 300.12 Dissociative Amnesia

A. The predominant disturbance is one or more episodes of inability to recall important personal information, usually of a traumatic or stressful nature, that is too extensive to be explained by ordinary forgetfulness.
B. The disturbance does not occur exclusively during the course of Dissociative Identity Disorder, Dissociative Fugue, Posttraumatic Stress Disorder, Acute Stress Disorder, or Somatization Disorder and is not due to the direct physiological effects of a substance (e.g., a drug of abuse, a medication) or a neurological or other general medical condition (e.g., Amnestic Disorder Due to Head Trauma).
C. The symptoms cause clinically significant distress or impairment in social, occupational, or other important areas of functioning.

From *Diagnostic and Statistical Manual of Mental Disorders, Fourth Edition* (DSM-IV). Copyright © 1994 by American Psychiatric Association. Reprinted with permission.

amnesia associated with a seizure disorder or induced by electroconvulsive therapy (ECT). Unlike the common portrayal of amnesia in T.V. shows and movies, dissociative amnesia very rarely involves a total loss of recall.

Epidemiologically, this disorder is diagnosed most commonly in female adolescents and young adults. It also is seen in young males under combat conditions, and it rarely is observed in the elderly. The frequency of the disorder is small, and at this time the rate of prevalence is unknown.

The etiology of dissociative amnesia involves dissociation usually secondary to severe psychosocial trauma or intrapsychic conflict. Unexpected loss is the most common catalyst for this disorder.

A hallmark of dissociative amnesia is that both the onset and termination of amnesia are rapid, and complete recovery of amnesias secondary to organic etiologies tends to be gradual and rarely is complete. The DSM-IV diagnostic criteria for this disorder are specified in Table 9.1 (American Psychiatric Association, 1994, p. 481).

The differential diagnosis of Dissociative Amnesia includes organic mental disorder, psychoactive substance-induced persisting amnestic disorder, substance intoxication, amnestic disorder due to a general medical condition or brain injury, dissociative identity disorder, malingering, and factitious disorder.

Appropriate assessment of amnesia requires a complete psychosocial evaluation including psychosocial stressors, history of drug use, trauma, tasks of life and lifestyle convictions. Referral for a medical evaluation must be considered to rule out physical trauma, neurological disease, and metabolic or drug-induced causes as primary or contributing factors.

Case Study—Mr. M

Mr. M was 21 years of age when he was found wandering along a busy freeway by a highway patrol officer. He did not appear to know who he was and could not account for his whereabouts prior to being picked up. He neither acknowledged the driver's license and credit cards in his wallet as his own nor recognized members of his family when they arrived at the highway patrol office where he was being held. He appeared confused and perplexed about these circumstances. Mr. M's family reported that he returned home early from a date with his steady girlfriend of three years, complaining of a headache and had gone to bed early. He awakened the next morning, appeared rather withdrawn, and said little to anyone. He left home and was found later that day about nine miles from home. Gradually, over a period of days, he recovered his awareness of his identity and his life prior to the onset of amnesia. Upon investigation it was learned that, on the day prior to leaving home, his best friend observed Mr. M's girlfriend with another man. When Mr. M confronted her, she told him she wanted to be free to date other men. A discussion of the amnestic period with a consulting psychologist prompted Mr. M's own spontaneous recollection. After a brief attempt to deny the loss of his girlfriend, he became dysphoric and briefly suicidal. Thereafter, he was able to grieve her loss and profited from short-term psychotherapy.

DISSOCIATIVE FUGUE

Dissociative Fugue, formerly called psychogenic fugue, is a specific form of amnesia in which the individual is unable to recall the essentials of his or her previous personality. The key features of this disorder are sudden, unplanned travel away from home or workplace, and the assumption of a new identity, with the inability to recall one's previous identity.

The course of this disorder is variable; however, in the majority of cases the fugue lasts for hours or days, though in rare cases it may continue for months. Recovery tends to be rapid and recurrences are rare. After recovery there is generally no recollection of what occurred during the fugue.

TABLE 9.2
Diagnostic criteria for 300.13 Dissociative Fugue

A. The predominant disturbance is sudden, unexpected travel away from home or one's customary place of work, with inability to recall one's past.
B. Confusion about personal identity or assumption of a new identity (partial or complete).
C. The disturbance does not occur exclusively during the course of Dissociative Identity Disorder and is not due to the direct physiological effects of a substance (e.g., a drug of abuse, a medication) or a general medical condition (e.g., temporal lobe epilepsy).
D. The symptoms cause clinically significant distress or impairment in social, occupational, or other important areas of functioning.

From *Diagnostic and Statistical Manual of Mental Disorders, Fourth Edition* (DSM-IV). Copyright © 1994 by American Psychiatric Association. Reprinted with permission.

Epidemiologically, this disorder is considered very rare. Its incidence and prevalence are unknown. The age of onset is variable, and it does not appear to be more common in women then in men. The etiology of this disorder is similar to dissociative amnesia. It often occurs as a reaction to a severe psychosocial stressor, such as the unexpected loss of a job, breakup of a marriage, or other serious disappointment. A history of heavy alcohol and substance use when combined with the above named psychosocial stressors can greatly facilitate the expression of this disorder. In addition, conflicts over money, sex, and aggressive behavior frequently coexist with this disorder. DSM-IV criteria are noted in Table 9.2 (American Psychiatric Association, 1994, p. 484).

The differential diagnosis of Dissociative Fugue includes temporal lobe epilepsy or complex partial seizure, dissociative amnesia, malingering, dissociative identity disorder, and schizophrenia.

A comprehensive assessment of fugue states requires a full psychosocial evaluation with emphasis on psychosocial stressors, history of drug and alcohol use, trauma, interpersonal difficulties, life tasks, and lifestyle convictions. Referral for a medical evaluation must be considered to rule out physical trauma, neurological disease, and metabolic and alcohol or drug-induced causes as primary or contributing factors.

Case Example—Dr. B

The family or Dr. B filed a missing persons report with the Chicago police two days after Dr. B's mysterious disappearance. Two weeks later, a Mr. S was found sleeping on a park bench in San Diego. When questioned by the San Diego police, he appeared confused as to where he was and what he was doing because nothing around his appeared familiar. He had no memory for Mr. S but insisted he was a physician, Dr. B, from Chicago. In running a description check, the San Diego police learned that he fit the description of the missing Dr. B. Mrs. B was contacted and immediately flew to San Diego and confirmed the man's identity. She explained that for six months prior to his disappearance, her husband had been very worried over a pending medical malpractice suit and had been considered troubled by two physicians leaving his group practice.

Previously an easy-going, affable person, he recently had become moody, irritable, and critical of his family. The last straw seemed to have been a phone call from his only child, a daughter whom he believed would go to medical school and join him in his practice upon completion of training. She had called to say she was dropping out of her freshman year of college to enter a commune. This call seems to have precipitated Dr. B's fugue.

DEPERSONALIZATION DISORDER

Depersonalization Disorder is unlike the other DSM-IV Dissociative Disorders in that consciousness is never actually segmented nor is significant memory loss a factor; in fact, bears little semblance to any DSM-IV category. Probably it was assigned to the Dissociative Disorders because it includes the feature of dissociation and "fits" even less well with other major DSM-IV categories.

Depersonalization usually is described as an alteration in the individual's perception of self. In this altered perception, individuals perceive and experience being estranged from their selves, feeling as though they were a separate observer of the self. Meditators and users of hallucinogens have reported "out of body" experiences, which is a form of depersonalization. It is estimated that 30% to 70% of young adults have had some experience of dissociation, suggesting that it is a very common phenomenon. In fact, some systems of meditation insist that the ability to regularly achieve a dissociative state in meditation is a marker of progress toward enlightenment. Since depersonalization is experienced by many individuals who are not bothered by it, the criteria for a diagnosable disorder then depends on its frequency or on the extent of distress brought about by the experience. A corollary phenomenon, called derealization, refers to alterations in one's perception of one's environment or object; it is as if the environment/object were alien or unreal. Derealization frequently accompanies depersonalization. Depersonalization is a symptom that is present in a number of psychiatric syndromes, particularly panic disorder, partial complex seizures, and schizo-phrenia.

Epidemiologically, the incidence and prevalence of Depersonalization Disor-der is unknown. Some studies have suggested that it is more common in females than males, but other studies have shown no gender differences. Since this disorder emphasizes the experiences of a changing identity, it should not be surprising that it occurs most often during adolescence, whereas onset after the age of 40 is very rare.

The etiology of Depersonalization Disorder is uncertain. A number of investi-gators, following Janet, have postulated a biological basis. Others have suggested that depersonalization follows the attempt to repudiate a self-image associated with unacceptable drives or alterations of ego boundaries, whereas others point to interpersonal influences. In addition to purely biological and psychological explanations, Putnam, Guroff, & Silberman (1986) believed that data on severe social stressors and life-threatening circumstances demonstrate that disassociation has a social basis. Perhaps a biopsychosocial explanation better explains and predicts this disorder as well as suggests treatment directives.

The course of the disorder is generally chronic and marked by remissions and exacerbations. The degree of impairment is minimal but can be exacerbated by anxiety or the fear of becoming insane. In that sense, it is similar to the conditioned anxiety response that many argue is the cause of the flashbacks occurring with certain drug experiences. Not surprisingly, abuse of alcohol or other substances facilitates the development and expression of this disorder. Other predisposing factors can be hypnotic induction, fatigue, and severe stress such as an accident, natural disaster, or combat experience. DSM-IV criteria are noted in Table 9.3 (American Psychiatric Association, 1994, p. 490).

The differential diagnosis of Depersonalization Disorder includes another dissociative disorder, schizophrenia, panic disorder, social or specific phobia, acute intoxication or withdrawal, posttraumatic or acute stress disorders, and temporal lobe epilepsy.

Case Example—Mr. P

Mr. P was a 21-year-old college student when he sought evaluation at the university student health service reporting he was losing his mind. Having begun to doubt his own reality, he felt he was living in a dream in which he saw himself from without, feeling connected to neither his thoughts nor his body. Through

TABLE 9.3
Diagnostic criteria for 300.6 Depersonalization Disorder

A. Persistent or recurrent experiences of feeling detached from, and as if one is an outside observer of, one's mental processes or body (e.g., feeling like one is in a dream).
B. During the depersonalization experience, reality testing remains intact.
C. The depersonalization causes clinically significant distress or impairment in social occupational, or other important areas of functioning.
D. The depersonalization experience does not occur exclusively during the course of another mental disorder, such as Schizophrenia, Panic Disorder, Acute Stress Disorder, or another Dissociative Disorder, and is not due to the direct physiological effects of a substance (e.g., a drug of abuse, a medication) or a general medical condition (e.g., temporal lobe epilepsy).

From *Diagnostic and Statistical Manual of Mental Disorders, Fourth Edition* (DSM-IV). Copyright © 1994 by American Psychiatric Association. Reprinted with permission.

his own eyes, he perceived his body parts as distorted in that his hands and feet seemed extraordinarily large. In addition, he thought people might be robots. He also had begun to ruminate about the recent onset of dizzy spells, thinking he might have a brain tumor. During the psychiatric evaluation, he was observed to be somewhat confused, moderately dysphoric, and given to obsessional brooding. He admitted spending so much time thinking about his circumstances that he had lost contact with all feelings except for a pervasive discontent about his predicament. In a follow-up session, he was preoccupied with the perception that his feet had grown too large for his shoes. He fretted about breaking up with his girlfriend, as he also had begun to perceive her in a distorted manner. A thorough medical and neurological evaluation ruled out an organic etiology. Various trials of medication were without significant effect. Yet over the course of two years of weekly psychotherapy, his symptoms gradually diminished. Although his obsessive-compulsive style remained, he now experienced himself and external reality more accurately.

DISSOCIATIVE IDENTITY DISORDER

Dissociative Identity Disorder, formerly called Multiple Personality Disorder, is characterized by the presence of two or more distinct identities or "alter egos" within the same individual. Each alter ego is dominant at a particular time. It should not be surprising that, because there can be a large number of alters in these individuals, it can be difficult to detect and diagnose especially early in the course of the disorder. Putnam et al. (1986) noted that the average duration of psychological treatment prior to the proper diagnosis of dissociative identity disorder is over six years. Because of the waxing and waning character of this disorder and the innumerable permutations of symptoms, the patient may present differently on different occasions. Thus, it should not be surprising that these patients usually have a history of being given several diagnoses. Kluft (1985) noted that this variable clinical picture is characteristic of 80% of patients with this disorder.

Individuals with dissociative identity disorder usually enter psychotherapy for any number of concerns from anxiety to sleep disorders. In the course of treatment, these individuals may complain of new concerns like the sudden onset of dizziness, difficulty finding their parked car, inordinate indecision about which clothes to wear, or denial of actions that were observed clearly by others. Upon further investigation, a different personality emerges or is discovered in the course of treatment. In some cases, alter egos continue to be produced. This may result either from the indirect suggestion of the clinician or through formal means like hypnotic induction or amobarbital interview.

Auditory hallucinations and some features of thought disorder commonly are noted in this disorder as are sudden mood swings. In fact, depression is the most commonly identified symptom of dissociative identity disorder. The more severely dysfunctional MPDs engage in para-suicidal behavior—including self-mutilation. Horevitz and Braun (1984) found that 70% of simple dissociative identity disorder cases met the DSM-III criteria for Borderline Personality Disorder. Finally, amnesia is considered a pathogenomonic sign of dissociative identity disorder.

Epidemiologically, this disorder is more common in females accounting for 70% to 90% of all cases. Though the actual prevalence rate is unknown, recent research studies suggest that this disorder is not as rare as once was believed.

Etiologically, a predisposing factor appears to be a history of repeated childhood abuse or trauma to which the child responded by dissociating; 97% have been found to have a repeated and severe history of physical and/or sexual abuse as children (Putnam et al., 1986). For these patients, dissociation becomes the predominant or only adaptive coping style.

The onset is usually in early childhood, and the course tends to be more chronic than any of the other dissociative disorders. The individual develops as many alter egos as are necessary to cope. Kluft (1985) noted that the alter egos have names that reflect their functions. Most common are the Protector, the Whore, the Little Girl (Child), and the Angry One. In their review of hundreds

TABLE 9.4
Diagnostic criteria for 300.14 Dissociative Identity Disorder

A. The presence of two or more distinct identities or personality states (each with its own relatively enduring pattern of perceiving, relating to, and thinking about the environment and self).
B. At least two of these identities or personality states recurrently take control of the person's behavior.
C. Inability to recall important personal information that is too extensive to be explained by ordinary forgetfulness.
D. The disturbance is not due to the direct physiological effects of a substance (e.g., blackouts or chaotic behavior during Alcohol Intoxication) or a general medical condition (e.g., complex partial seizures). **Note:** In children, the symptoms are not attributable to imaginary playmates or other fantasy play.

From *Diagnostic and Statistical Manual of Mental Disorders, Fourth Edition* (DSM-IV). Copyright © 1994 by American Psychiatric Association. Reprinted with permission.

of confirmed diagnoses of this disorder, Putnam et al. (1986) found an average number of 10 alters with a median of 7 and a mode of under 5.

Most dissociative identity disordered patients are diagnosed between the ages of late adolescence and early middle age. As they enter their late 50s, the majority begin to spend an increasing amount of time in one resilient personality with a wide range of functions. Some personalities even may integrate spontaneously. The ultimate goal of therapy becomes to reintegrate the personality. Fortunately, recent developments in therapy tailored to dissociative identity disorder suggest that individuals with this disorder may be quite responsive to therapy. DSM-IV criteria for this disorder are noted in Table 9.4 (American Psychiatric Association, 1994, p. 487).

Case Example—Ms. Y

Ms. Y is a 23-year-old undergraduate female who was admitted to the acute care psychiatric teaching unit at a university hospital with bandaged wrists that had required several stitches to close the self-inflicted horizontal lacerations. She reported that the day prior to admission she had found herself "waking up" in a liquor store checkout line with two bottles of scotch. This surprised and puzzled her because she never drank. She explained that she had lost track of time after leaving class that morning and could not account for her whereabouts between then and being in the liquor store later that afternoon. With some hesitation, she also admitted she had been experiencing nightmares for the past three nights. These involved watching her dead father lying in a casket while she held a knife in her hands. In addition, it was elicited that her father had died one year prior to her current admission.

Ms. Y admitted that she previously had been hospitalized once before for a "panic attack" and that she currently was in therapy with a counselor at student health services. Academically, she was a junior, although this was her fifth year in college. She gave a history of being physically abused repeatedly as a child by both her parents and of being molested by an older male cousin who lived next door.

During the initial psychiatric evaluation, she responded that she experienced episodes of depersonalization and derealization. When asked about her memory and the amnestic experience of the previous day, she noted that she often could not find where she had parked her car and that she sometimes would not recognize people who said they knew her. She volunteered that she always had been a daydreamer and was easily able to enter trance-like states. Upon hypnotic induction, two "personalities" presented themselves.

DISSOCIATIVE DISORDER NOT OTHERWISE SPECIFIED (NOS)

This catchall category is intended for those disordered presentations in which dissociation is the predominant feature but does not meet criteria for one of the four aforementioned Dissociative Disorders. Some examples include derealization unaccompanied by depersonalization, fugues in which the presence of a second identity cannot be documented, dissociated states following brainwashing in prison camps, duress associated with hostage situations, or indoctrination into cults. Dissociative trance disorders such as *ataque* or spirit/demon possession is another example. *Ganser syndrome*, which involves responding with "approximate answers" to questions and is associated with amnesia, conversion symptoms, or disorientation, is another disorder that merits the diagnosis of Dissociative Disorder NOS.

ADLERIAN VIEW OF DISSOCIATION

Alfred Adler wrote relatively little about dissociation, and, to the best of this author's knowledge, nothing about the dissociative disorder. What accounts for this? Of course, we do not know, but we can speculate. First of all, it should be noted that prior to DSM-III, the Dissociative Disorders usually were known as Hysterical Neuroses—Dissociative type to distinguish them from the Conversion type of the Hysterical Neuroses. In that regard, Ellenberger (1970) noted that Freud tended to limit his practice to the treatment of higher functioning, upper middle-class patients who for the most part presented with Hysterical Neuroses of both types. Adler, on the other hand, reportedly treated a wider variety of patients, many of lower-functioning working-class individuals with obsessive compulsive and characterological features. Thus, it might be that Adler had little or no therapeutic contact with dissociative disordered patients.

Yet Adler did at least once allude to the term "dissociation" as synonymous with "the apparent double-life of the neurotic" (Adler, 1968, p. 21). Adler was fond of discussing daydreams, which are a form of dissociation (Ansbacher & Ansbacher, 1956, 1964). His basic view of daydreams, and presumably of other dissociative phenomenon, was consistent with his overall theory of psychopathology: "The findings of Individual Psychology point to the fact that all behavior of a human being fits into a unit and is an expression of the individual's style of life" (Ansbacher & Ansbacher, 1956, p. 358). In discussing the retrogressive movement of the neurosis, Adler did mention psychogenic amnesia as one such manifestation (Adler, 1968).

Finally, Adler's aversion to hypnosis should be noted (Adler, 1968, pp. 161–162). Since hypnosis has and continues to be a basic diagnostic and treatment method of dissociative disorders, it would be even more unlikely that Adler or his protegees and later followers would focus much of their theoretical, clinical, and research efforts on the dissociative disorders. A review of the published Adlerian literature seems to support this observation.

There are some indications that this trend might be changing. As more and more dissociative disordered individuals present for treatment, more and more clinicians, including Adlerians, are "gearing up" to meet this therapeutic challenge. A recent rediscovery of the pioneering efforts of Pierre Janet holds considerable promise for those clinicians who were unconvinced or uncomfortable with the prevailing theories based on Freud's formulation (Vander Kolk & Vander Hart, 1989). Not only does Janet's formulation of dissociation provide a broad integrative framework for understanding and unifying elements for other theories, but it is quite compatible with Adlerian thinking (Shulman, 1990).

Essentially, Janet prepared a broad theory of perceptive and cognitive processes and memory that is now being validated by research in the neurosciences. Janet hypothesized that consciousness consisted of a unified memory of all psychological facets related to a particular experience and that memory was an act of creation rather than a passive and static recording of events. He speculated that memories were synthesized into a perceptual system that provided a matrix for categorizing and integrating subsequent data into what we today would call cognitive schemas. Janet believed that dissociations were sentiments of incompleteness or idea complexes that were split off or existed outside of consciousness. He believed that therapy is a process of bringing these split-off ideas into consciousness and that his process would be curative. For Adler, therapy was likewise a process of bringing these mistaken and missing ideas into consciousness. Of course, the "missing" element is social interest (Shulman, 1990).

TREATMENT OF THE DISSOCIATIVE DISORDERS

The goal of treatment for both dissociative amnesia and dissociative fugue is to recover lost memories and identity and to integrate the traumatic antecedent event(s) into the patient's consciousness. Regardless of the clinician's theoretical orientation, the general treatment strategy is to elicit the history in a supportive manner and listen empathetically. A supportive environment may be sufficient for spontaneous resolution to occur and may be all that is needed in some case. More active measures to recover missing memories are hypnosis, free association, suggestion, amobarbital interviews, and abreactive techniques. These methods often are utilized in conjunction with ongoing psychotherapy.

The literature on the treatment of Depersonalization Disorder is scant and inconclusive. Because the Dissociative Disorder is as much an identity development disorder as it is a dissociative phenomenon, the goal of treatment is a fuller integration of the personality and, correlatively, a more accurate perception of self and external reality. Treatment approaches that hold promise include hypnosis—especially for those of high hypnotizability—imagery techniques, and cognitive-behavioral approaches. Although the core pathology of the Dissociative Disorders is not influenced by medication, medication can be used to treat specific nondissociative symptoms that interfere with psychotherapy. These target symptoms include posttraumatic stress symptoms of anxiety, panic, phobia and sleep disturbance; mood symptoms like dysphoria; and crisis situations in order to restore order and regain control (Putnam, 1989). Thus, selective use of anxiolytics, antidepressants, sedative/hypnotics, or neuroleptics may be indicated as adjunct to psychotherapy.

The treatment of dissociative identity disorder tends to be long, demanding, and painful. The initial goal is to establish a trusting relationship, and the intermediate goal is to optimize the patient's function and potential. The ultimate goal, of course, would be the achievement of total integration of the alter egos into one personality; however, a reasonable degree of conflict-free collaboration among the personalities may be the only realistic goal for some patients.

Generally speaking, medications have been ineffective for the disorder, although they have been of some use with targets such as symptomatic depression, insomnia, and panic symptoms. Treatment success has been reported with hypnotherapy, psychoanalytical psychotherapy, group therapy with and without videotaping, and sodium amobarbital. Braun (1986) has described a series of thirteen steps that are sequential, but overlap and continue throughout treatment, which have been found useful regardless of the treatment orientation.

BIBLIOGRAPHY

Putnam, F. (1985). Dissociation as a response to extreme trauma. In R. Kluft (Ed.), *Childhood antecedents of multiple personality*. Washington, DC: American Psychiatric Press.

Wilbur, C., & Kluft, R. (1989). Multiple personality disorders. *In treatment of psychiatric disorders: A task force report of the American Psychiatric Association* (Vol. 3). Washington DC: American Psychiatric Press.

REFERENCES

Adler, A. (1968). The practice and theory of Individual Psychology (P. Radin, Trans.). Totawa, NJ: Littlefield, Adams and Co. (Original work published 1925)

American Psychiatric Association. (1986). *Diagnostic and statistical manual of mental disorders* (3rd., rev.). Washington, DC: Author.

American Psychiatric Association. (1994). *Diagnostic and statistical manual of mental disorders* (4th ed.). Washington DC: Author.

Ansbacher, H.L., & Ansbacher, R.R. (Eds.). (1956). *The Individual Psychology of Alfred Adler*. New York: Basic Books.

Ansbacher, H.L., & Ansbacher, R.R. (Eds.). (1964). *Superiority and social interest: A collection of later writings*. Evanston, IL: Northwestern University Press.

Beahr, J. (1982). *Unity and multiplicity: Consciousness of self in hypnosis, psychiatric disorder and mental health.* New York: Brunner/Mazel.

Braun, B. (1986). Issues in the psychotherapy of multiple personality disorder. In B. Braun, (Ed.), *Treatment of multiple personality disorder.* Washington, DC: American Psychiatric Press.

Ellenberger, H. (1970). *The discovery of the unconscious.* New York: Basic Books.

Freud, S., & Breuer, J. (1955). Studies on hysteria. In J. Strachey (Ed.), *The pre-standard edition of the complete psychological works of Sigmond Freud.* London: Hogarth Press.

Horevitz, R., & Braun, B. (1984). Are multiple personalities borderline? *Psychiatric Clinics of North America, 7,* 69–88.

Kluft, R. (1985). The natural history of multiple personality disorder: A study of thirty-three cases. In R. Kluft (Ed.), *Childhood antecedents of multiple personality.* Washington, DC: American Psychiatric Press.

Prince, M. (1906). *The dissociation of personality.* New York: Longmans, Green.

Putnam, F. (1989). *Diagnosis and treatment of multiple personality disorder.* New York: Guilford.

Putnam, F., Guroff, J., & Silberman, E. (1986). The clinical phenomenology of multiple personality disorder: Review of 100 recent cases. *Journal of Clinical Psychiatry, 47,* 285–293.

Spiegel, H., & Spiegel, D. (1978). *Trance and treatment.* New York: Basic Books.

Shulman, B. (1990). Personal communication.

Vander Kolk, B., & Vander Hart, O. (1989). Pierre Janet and the breakdown of adaptation in psychological trauma. *American Journal of Psychiatry, 146,* 1530–1540.

Yaeger, J. (1989). Manifestations of psychiatric disorders. In H. Kaplan & B. Sadockleds (Eds.), *Comprehensive textbook of psychiatry* (5th ed.). Baltimore: Williams and Wilkins.

PART IV
ADJUSTMENT REACTIONS, PERSONALITY DISORDERS, ADDICTIONS, AND SEXUAL DYSFUNCTIONS

OVERVIEW

Adler (Ansbacher & Ansbacher, 1956) noted that all lifestyles are adequate until life or other people present a challenge for which the individual is unprepared. At those times the lifestyle is tested, and the amount of social interest that is present is displayed. This section deals with a variety of conditions listed in DSM-IV that can be summarized according to one overriding dynamic: The lifestyles of individuals with these conditions generally have been sufficient to meet the tasks of life until an event or series of events occurs that severely taxes individuals, and their dysfunctional patterns come to the attention of others (be it law enforcement personnel, employers, or spouses).

The first chapter in this section (Chapter 10), by Carlson, focuses on the "Adjustment Disorders and V Codes." Carlson explores various types of conditions and responses individuals make to life's stresses and the effects those responses have upon self, family, and others.

Sperry and Mosak in Chapter 11 explore the "Personality Disorders" in general, and Sperry and Ansbacher in Chapter 12 explore the "Narcissistic Personality Disorder." Dreikurs (1967) noted that psychodynamically, psychotics discard common sense; neurotics acknowledge it but look for excuses in order not to follow it. what he referred to as character disorders might now be known as personality disorders. He noted that individuals with character disorders never fully developed common sense. for them, their private logic was fused intimately with a distorted common sense, so that the distinction between the two was difficult to make. When confronted with a challenge, these people responded with a "Yes—But I'll do it my way" approach. In other words, they felt that their way of solving the challenges of life was the way to solve it. Sperry presents an in-depth, biopsychosocial exploration of the DSM-IV personality disorders, along with an integrative analysis of the Narcissistic Personality Disorder based upon the works of Adler and Kohut.

Lewis and Carlson in Chapter 13 explore "Substance Abuse Treatment and Individual Psychology." They make the useful distinction between use, abuse, and dependence, and discuss the Adlerian perspective, which they note has quite a bit to offer current treatment intervention strategies, particularly with regard to some fundamental Adlerian concepts such as the social context of behavior, an awareness of lifestyle, and the purposefulness of symptoms.

"Antisocial Personality Disorder and Addictions" is the subsequent chapter, Chapter 14, by Lombardi. It explores the Antisocial Personality Disorder in greater depth, and relates fundamental attitudes of such individuals to addictions such as alcoholism, drugs, gambling, and food.

In the last chapter (Chapter 15) in this section, Peven deals with "Sexual Disorders from the Viewpoint of Individual Psychology." Adler (Ansbacher & Ansbacher, 1978) long ago noted the interrelatedness of sexuality to personality and felt that an individual's sex life could be one of the key barometers to the individual's amount of social interest. After a thorough review of DSM-IV criteria, Peven describes the relationship of the various disorders to lifesyle convictions and attitudes, noting not only Adler's early emphasis upon the social inequality of the sexes but also the current status of women and men in their interpersonal and sexual relationships.

REFERENCES

Ansbacher, H.L., & Ansbacher, R.R. (Eds.). *The Individual Psychology of Alfred Adler*. New York: Basic Books.

Ansbacher, H.L., & Ansbacher, R.R. (Eds.). (1978). *Co-operation between the sexes: Writings on women, love and marriage, sexuality and its disorders.* New York: Doubleday.

Dreikurs, R. (1967). *Psychodynamics, psychotherapy, and counseling.* Chicago: Alfred Adler Institute.

Chapter 10

ADJUSTMENT DISORDERS AND V CODES

Jon Carlson

Controversy continues as to whether or not adjustment disorders and V codes should be contained within the diagnostic description. Many clinicians believe the symptoms associated with adjustment disorders and V codes will take care of themselves with time and therefore do not need treatment. Critics indicate that adjustment disorders are, by definition, time-limited and to treat them wastes the clients' time, money, and effort. Additionally, intervention interferes with the natural recovery process, leaving the clients believing they are not able to take care of their own problems.

Adjustment disorders and V codes are very common and are a large part of clinical practice. Psychologists enjoy working with these conditions as they often are treated successfully and seem to respond well to traditional therapeutic intervention strategies designed for higher functioning individuals. Due to the high functioning nature of the clients, they not only resolve their disrupting and distressing situation, but many also are able to become even healthier and stronger as a result of this problem. Successful treatment builds self-confidence and skill development, making therapy a growth-promoting situation for most clients.

Both adjustment disorders and V codes are at the *least* severe end of Axis I problems. An important point to note, however, is that people with these diagnostic categories have problems that are more severe than normal problems in living.

DESCRIPTION

Adjustment disorders are more severe and less common than V code conditions. According to the DSM-IV (American Psychiatric Association, 1994), the essential feature of this disorder is a maladaptive reaction to an identifiable psychosocial stressor or stressors that occurs within three months of the onset of the stressor(s). Stressors may be single events, such as death, divorce, or birth, or continuous circumstances, such as marital discord, financial problems, or chronic illness. All, however, are within the normal realm of experience and would not meet the criteria for posttraumatic stress disorder. According to Maxmen (1986), the most common stressors for adults are marital difficulties, divorce or separation, and relocation, whereas for adolescents they are school-related problems, parental conflict, and substance abuse. In the DSM-IV are specified six types of adjustment disorders.

309.24 Adjustment disorder with anxious mood.   This subtype should be used when the predominant manifestations are symptoms such as depressed mood, tearfulness, or feelings of hopelessness.
309.24 With Anxiety.   This subtype should be used when the predominant manifestations are symptoms such as nervousness, worry, or jitteriness or, in children, fears of separation from major attachment figures.
309.29 With Mixed Anxiety and Depressed Mood.   This subtype should be used when the predominant manifestation is a combination of depression and anxiety.
309.3 With Disturbance of Conduct.   This subtype should be used when the predominant manifestation is a disturbance in conduct in which there is violation of the rights of others or of major age-appropriate societal norms and rules (e.g., truancy, vandalism, reckless driving, fighting, defaulting on legal responsibilities).
309.4 With Mixed Disturbance of Emotions and Conduct.   This subtype should be used when the predominant manifestations are both emotional symptoms (e.g., depression, anxiety) and a disturbance of conduct (see above subtype).
309.9 Unspecified.   This subtype should be used for maladaptive reactions (e.g., physical complaints, social withdrawal, or work or academic inhibition) to psychosocial stressors that are not classifiable as one of the specific subtypes of Adjustment Disorder. (American Psychiatric Association, 1994, pp. 623–624)

These six different types of adjustment disorders are classified according to their predominant symptoms. The diagnostic criteria for adjustment disorders of all types are as follows (American Psychiatric Association, 1994, p. 626):

A. The development of emotional or behavioral symptoms in response to an identifiable stressor(s) occurring within three months of the onset of the stressor(s).

B. These symptoms or behaviors are clinically significant as evidenced by either of the following:

(1) marked distress that is in excess or what would be expected from exposure to the stressor

(2) significant impairment in social or occupational (academic) functioning

C. The stress-related disturbance does not meet the criteria for another specific Axis I disorder and is not merely an exacerbation of a preexisting Axis I or Axis II disorder.

D. The symptoms do not represent Bereavement.

E. Once the stressor (or its consequences) has terminated, the symptoms do not persist for more than an additional six months.

Kaplan and Sadock (1985) reported that adjustment disorders are experienced by 10% to 15% of the population. Maxmen (1986) indicated that these disorders are even more prevalent and typically more severe in adolescents with as many as one-third experiencing adjustment disorders; however, because many people with adjustment disorders do not seek treatment, the number may be considerably higher than the above estimates.

FORMULATION

Nearly everyone has experienced an adjustment disorder or a V code condition or both. These disorders are often triggered by the normal life transitions that we all face. The transitions may be positive, such as the birth of a child or graduation from school, or negative, such as the loss of a job or the death of a loved one. These problems also may reflect and be related to the normal problems of living such as job dissatisfaction, marriage problems, and the care of an elderly or aging parent. To go through life without experiencing this type of problem seems almost impossible. People with effective coping mechanisms and ways of effectively handling stress, however, are less troubled by these life transitions.

Adjustment disorders will therefore occur in all types of people. They are likely, however, to be more prevalent in people who have limited resources and support sections, undeveloped coping mechanisms, or little experience in dealing effectively with previous stressful events and multiple stressors. Adlerians would view adjustment problems as resulting from faulty beliefs or lifestyle convictions. Likely individuals, due to early family learnings, have developed inferiority feelings and unrealistic goals and need assistance and education in learning healthier, more adaptive responses to the demands of life. Many need to learn the courage to be imperfect and to live in an imperfect world. Most clients with adjustment disorders have had a high level of previous functioning and are usually capable of handling the stressors themselves, but they have somehow lost self-esteem and need to be encouraged to increase their levels of confidence.

INTERVENTION STRATEGIES

Psychologists need to express confidence in clients with adjustment disorders and often by providing support and direction can help clients solve these problems themselves. An optimistic attitude will strengthen clients' self-esteem and encourage them to face the stressors in their lives.

As previously indicated, adjustment disorders often improve spontaneously without treatment; however, therapy can facilitate recovery. It can hasten improvement, provide coping skills and adaptive mechanisms to avert future problems, and minimize poor choices and self-destructive behaviors (Maxmen, 1986).

Many experts believe that the goals of therapy should be two-fold: (a) to help the client return to baseline level and (b) to capitalize on the emotional turmoil and to change longstanding maladaptive patterns to stress and to develop more useful and satisfying ones. The therapy then would be more likely to be called a flexible crisis intervention approach. This approach focuses both on relieving the acute symptoms and helping the clients learn more adaptive coping strategies. Therapy will use encouragement and support the clients' strengths and minimize or play down past problems unless a pattern is identified. Education and information are often a large part of treatment. This allows clients to look realistically at their situations, realize they are not alone, and become aware of resources that might be useful and helpful to them.

Often therapeutic interventions need to be tailored depending on the predominant symptoms. For example, if the client presents with depressive symptoms, cognitive techniques are often useful, whereas those with anxiety probably will benefit best from stress reduction procedures, and those who have academic or career problems often respond best to a more behavioral approach (Brown & Brown, 1990).

Due to the diversity of presenting problems, a variety of interventions are appropriate. Many therapists have found environmental change useful. Moving to a safer neighborhood, applying for a new job, or receiving further education are often useful. Bibliotherapy, or the use of books and reading material, seems to be an important part of treatment. Adlerian parenting materials (Dinkmeyer & McKay, 1989), marriage materials (Dinkmeyer & Carlson, 1984), career development materials (Bolles, 1989), etc. are often important tools. Many psychologists use inventories such as the Kern (1986) *Lifestyle Scale* and the *Millon Clinical Multiaxial Inventory* (Millon, 1984) to help clients understand why they are having difficulties with particular situations and on what resources they might draw and what options they have.

Therapy needs to be supportive, active, flexible, and goal-directed working within a time-limited context (Sperry, 1989). The brief therapy model seems particularly well-suited to problems of acute onset experienced by clients who have had good prior adjustment and who can relate well to others and engage in a therapeutic relationship. Often such patients are very highly motivated toward treatment. Some researchers have found group therapy to be a useful adjunct to treatment as well as family interventions. Such interventions provide a support system and can be used to teach and reinforce coping mechanisms, to improve self-esteem, and to provide alternative solutions to problems. Many people have found groups composed of clients going through similar life circumstances such as divorce, separation, and death of a loved one to be particularly helpful. Although group therapy does not provide the crisis intervention necessary to resolve the urgency of such a problem, it does provide a good support base and often is used in conjunction with individual approaches.

Medication seldom is used with adjustment disorders. In rare cases, however, time-limited prescriptions are provided for anxiety or sleep problems.

Adjustment disorders have a tendency to recur (Donovan, Bennett, & McElroy, 1981). Therefore, therapists need to be particularly vigilant with regard to treatment compliance and relapse. A useful procedure is to schedule follow-up appointments for 18 months following intervention in order to prevent future recurrence of this situation.

SPECIFIC SUGGESTIONS FOR ADJUSTMENT DISORDERS

Anxiety

In addition to the previous principles, the client needs to be reassured that the symptoms are transient and that the psychologist and client together can alleviate them. Unobtrusive support, crisis intervention techniques, relaxation, meditation, self-hypnosis, and/or biofeedback may be used by therapists experienced in any of these techniques. Temporary anti-anxiety medications such as a benzodiazepine may be considered. The emphasis needs to be on clients' ability to weather the stress as well as encouragement for their ability to strengthen coping mechanisms.

Depressed Mood

Clients with depressive symptoms are often more uncomfortable than those with any other adjustment disorder. They actually may appear disabled and have undergone considerable behavioral change such as sleep disturbance and lack of energy. Some even present with suicidal ideation. Most likely, these clients will not need medication. If medication is warranted, adjustment disorder is likely to be the wrong diagnosis. These clients will benefit from the support and reassurance of the therapist that the experience is short-term. Simple and often practical suggestions for problems of sleeplessness and energy show good results. Clients should be questioned about any suicidal thoughts, and these should be pursued seriously. Most likely, however, these thoughts are more anxiety-producing than real. Nevertheless, the therapist needs to discuss this topic thoroughly and take whatever precautions seem warranted.

Disturbance of Conduct

The therapist, the client, and often the client's family need to understand the difference between this diagnosis and a more chronic antisocial personality disorder. The therapist needs to recognize that the treatment for these problems is often preventive of future antisocial symptoms. The therapist needs to make sure that a harsh approach is not taken with these clients in spite of the problems that they may have caused others. Acceptance and attempts to have clients understand their symptoms as just characteristics of having a difficult time adjusting, rather than some deep-seated problem, is very important. This allows clients to see treatment as something logical and accomplishable. Another important point is to stress that the client needs to take responsibility and consequences for his or her own actions. The therapist's acceptance of the client and reassurance of the person's fragile condition do not really imply acceptance of the behavior but rather of the person.

Mixed Disturbance of Emotions and Conduct

This category should be treated using a combination of the principles already mentioned.

With Mixed Anxiety and Depressed Mood

The principles outlined earlier in this chapter also cover this disorder.

Unspecified

Physical Complaints.   The previous treatment principles will apply to this disorder. The therapist needs to acknowledge the presence of physical complaints along with the dysphoria they generate without elevating these problems to Axis III disorders. Once the therapist is confident, i.e., via medical examination, that no organic problem is present, this type of intervention should be limited. Psychologists working with this type of client often find the procedures mentioned in the somatoform/somatization disorders chapter very helpful. Therapy needs to focus on emotional issues and feelings rather than on the physical complaints. This can help the client attend to the real issues, clarify stressors, and improve coping skills and
emotional adaptation.

Social Withdrawal.   The therapist needs to be aware that withdrawal lends itself to isolation from sources of growth and support and that this disorder might evolve into a chronic avoidance or depression pattern. This client should receive encouragement and prescriptions to have considerable contact with other people. Therapists also find contacting the client's family to provide additional reassurance helpful.

Work or Academic Inhibition.   General principles previously mentioned or indicated work with this disorder. Assistance often is needed because an adjustment disorder with work or academic inhibition will endanger or postpone one's career or academic progress. Therapists usually find brief, supportive, goal-directed counseling such as that found in many student health centers or employee assistance programs useful. These programs should include encouragement to discuss current difficulties with the teacher or employer in person. This may clarify any misperceptions about the way the person is being treated and help him or her separate real-world situations from the distressing fantasies. If this problem continues and does not respond to these interventions, then likely the diagnosis needs to be changed.

V CODES

V codes is the name given for conditions that are not attributable to a mental disorder and are the focus of attention or treatment. These conditions are on a continuum *less* severe than those encountered in an adjustment disorder. These conditions are not mental disorders and have not resulted from mental disorders. These clients may or may not have coexisting and unrelated mental disorders, but the diagnosis of a V code implies that the focus of treatment will be on this condition rather than on any presenting mental disorder. In the DSM-IV are listed the following V code conditions:

V61.9 Relational Problem Related to a Mental Disorder or General Medical
    Condition
V61.20 Parent-Child Relational Problem
V61.1 Partner Relational Problem
V61.8 Sibling Relational Problem
V62.81 Relational Problem Not Otherwise Specified
V61.21 Physical Abuse of Child
V61.21 Sexual Abuse of Child
V61.21 Neglect of Child
V61.1 Physical Abuse of Adult
V61.1 Sexual Abuse of Adult
V15.81 Noncompliance With Treatment
V65.2 Malingering
V71.01 Adult Antisocial Behavior
V71.02 Child or Adolescent Antisocial Behavior
V62.89 Borderline Intellectual Functioning
V62.82 Bereavement
V62.3 Academic Problem
V62.2 Occupational Problem

V62.89 Religious or Spiritual Problem
V62.4 Acculturation Problem
V62.89 Phase of Life Problem

As one can see from the above list, these are problems of living that are experienced by most people. Usually these disorders go untreated, and people somehow manage to deal with them with varying degrees of success. The conditions are seldom troubling for long periods of time, and they do not cause extreme and persistent emotional pain. Typically clients with a V code diagnosis have good reality contact, and their reactions are consistent with the stressors or life experiences that they are experiencing. These clients, however, are experiencing considerable unhappiness and dissatisfaction with their lives and therefore often benefit greatly from therapy.

V codes often are diagnosed in fairly healthy clients with good ego strength and self-esteem. Traditionally these are what have been called YAVIS (Young Attractive Verbal Intelligent Social) clients.

INTERVENTIONS

Therapists intervene in a very similar fashion to the treatment for adjustment disorders. Clients respond best to therapists who are supportive and flexible but also challenge the clients to grow and develop. Therapists need to encourage clients to take responsibility for their own treatment, and, although nondirective strategies work very well, at times therapists need to prescribe resources and information as needed. Therapists usually have no difficulty maintaining a positive, optimistic attitude and anticipating short-term involvement.

Adlerians seem to be especially helpful treating clients with V code problems through encouragement and helping clients understand the universal nature of their problems. Clients tend not to feel abnormal and to feel empowered to make the changes necessary to cope successfully with their problems.

Support groups and self-help groups are often available for most V problems. Often these support groups are all a client will need.

Prognosis for V codes, as well as adjustment reactions, is very good, although the wide variety of conditions and clients who fit these diagnoses makes one cautious in terms of generalizing. Likely clients who have high levels of self-efficacy (Bandura, 1987) will have the highest prognosis of success. Clients with self-efficacy have high self-concepts and have had previous success at lifestyle changes.

CASE EXAMPLE

Case of Jim

Jim is a 30-year-old businessman who was referred by his family doctor because Jim wanted to talk to someone about his unhappy marriage. During the eight years of courtship and four years of marriage, there have been repeated problems that have usually been initiated by his overall dissatisfaction. Although he and his partner share many interests and have had an acceptable sexual relationship, he feels that his wife is too self-centered and cold. He is upset that she has no real concern about him, his work, or his interests. He is extremely upset with her and does not want to raise a family with her. His dissatisfaction periodically builds up to a point that leads to verbal fights, temporary separations, and then apologies. This leaves Jim feeling lonely, and he then comes crawling back to her. Jim appears to be in therapy looking for support to help him make a permanent break from his partner. Although he is currently in acute distress due to his marital situation, no evidence is noted of any of these difficulties in other aspects of his life. During the course of the intake interview, Jim often held back tears, had a voice that cracked, and reported having difficulty sleeping.

Diagnosis

Axis I:	V61.1 Partner Relational Problem
Axis II:	None
Axis III:	None
Axis IV:	Problems with primary support group—marital discord
Axis V:	Current GAF: 80; Highest GAF Past 12 Months: 80

In the client's interview, he revealed that he and his wife just had had a very serious fight, and today he felt pretty convinced that the marriage is over. The therapist's hypothesis was that the client's resolution probably will not continue. Discussion ensued in which he described that both his parents and his wife's parents had stormy relationships that were characterized by a family life with considerable ups and downs. Although both he and his wife do not like the current way of living, neither seems to know how to make it effectively different. Although he indicated that he was doubtful as to the prognosis of marriage therapy, he was more than willing to invite his wife to come in for conjoint sessions. Conjoint marital therapy was followed using the strategies developed by Sperry and Carlson (1991). The treatment was supplemented utilizing bibliotherapy with the TIME program materials (Dinkmeyer & Carlson, 1984). The couple was seen weekly for ten weeks, and then the sessions switched to monthly meetings. Both report increased satisfaction in the marriage and decreased conflict. Providing treatment to this type of client is rewarding because the progress is so readily observable.

SUMMARY OF TREATMENT RECOMMENDATIONS

Seligman (1990) has developed a procedure entitled "DO A CLIENT MAP" that effectively summarizes the recommendations for adjustment disorders and V code conditions.

> Diagnoses. Adjustment disorders and V codes for conditions not attributable to mental disorder.
> Objectives. Relieve symptoms, improve coping, restore at least prior level of functioning.
> Assessments. Generally none, although measures of transient anxiety, depression, and stress might be helpful.
> Clinician. Flexible yet structured. Present-oriented. Optimistic.
> Location. Outpatient.
> Interventions. Crisis intervention. Brief psychodynamically oriented psychotherapy, stress management. Other short-term active approaches.
> Emphasis. Encouragement of client responsibility. Moderately supportive. Probing only when relevant to current concerns with focus determined by specific precipitant and response.
> Nature. Individual therapy and/or peer support group. Possibly some family sessions.
> Timing. Brief duration, rapid pace.
> Medication. Rarely needed.
> Adjunct services. Inventories to clarify goals and direction. Education and information very important. Possibly environmental manipulation.
> Prognosis. Excellent, especially when no underlying mental disorder is present. (pp. 73–74)

REFERENCES

American Psychiatric Association. (1994). *Diagnostic and statistical manual of mental disorders* (4th ed.). Washington, DC: Author.

Bandura, A. (1987, May). *Self-efficacy*. University of California-Berkeley Wellness Letter, 1–2.

Bolles, R.N. (1989). *The 1989 what color is your parachute?* Berkeley, CA: Ten Speed Press.

Brown, D., & Brown, L. (1990). *Career choice and development*. San Francisco, CA: Jossey-Bass.

Dinkmeyer, D., & Carlson, J. (1984). *Time for a better marriage*. Circle Pines, MN: American Guidance Service.

Dinkmeyer, D., & McKay, G.D. (1989). *Systematic training for effective parenting*. Circle Pines, MN: American Guidance Service.

Donovan, J.M., Bennett, M.J., & McElroy, C.M. (1981). The crisis group: Its rationale, format, and outcome. In S.H. Budman (Ed.), *Forms of brief therapy* (pp. 283–303). New York: Guilford Press.

Kaplan, H.I., & Sadock, B.J. (1985). *Modern synopsis of comprehensive textbook of psychiatry*. Baltimore, MD: Williams and Wilkins.

Kern, R. (1986). *Lifestyle scale*. Coral Springs, FL: CMTI Press.

Maxmen, J.S. (1986). *Essential psychopathology*. New York: W. W. Norton.

Millon, T. (1984). *Millon clinical multiaxial inventory*. Minneapolis, MN: National Computer System.

Seligman, L. (1990). *Selecting effective treatments*. San Francisco: Jossey Bass.

Sperry, L. (Ed.). (1989). Special issue: Varieties of brief therapy. *Individual Psychology, 45*(1/2).

Sperry, L., & Carlson, J. (1991). *Marital therapy: Integrating theory and technique*. Denver, CO: Love Publishing Company.

Chapter **11**

PERSONALITY DISORDERS

Len Sperry
Harold H. Mosak

Personality can be defined as enduring patterns of thinking, feeling, and behaving and relating to the environment and oneself in a consistent manner and in various social contexts. When specific traits such as orderliness, rigidity, thriftiness, and emotional construction cluster together they can be referred to as a *personality style*. For instance, the four traits noted above would be labelled the obsessive-compulsive personality style. When these personality styles become inflexible and maladaptive so as to cause significant impairment in occupational or social functioning, or result in great subjective distress, the criteria in DSM-IV would cause them to be labelled as *personality disorders* and assign them Axis II codes. In the example above, the classification would be Obsessive-Compulsive Personality Disorder, 301.40. Whereas everyone exhibits a personality style, not everyone manifests a personality disorder or disorders. Personality disorders indicate the existence of a longstanding, maladaptive pattern of attitudes and behaviors of the way one relates to, perceives, and thinks about the environment and oneself that is of sufficient severity to cause either significant impairment in adaptive functioning or subjective distress. The manifestations of personality disorders are usually recognizable by adolescence and continue throughout most of life. According to DSM-IV, the pattern must be present by early adulthood (American Psychiatric Association, 1994).

The purpose of this chapter is to overview the 10 personality disorders described in DSM-IV and related information about their diagnostic, clinical, and treatment formulations. Before beginning this undertaking, we will clarify the place of personality disorders within the five axes system of DSM-IV and a few other classification systems. Unlike other chapters that describe one or two disorders, this chapter provides an overview of ten disorders. This overview is necessarily brief. A fuller description of these disorders and their treatment is available in Sperry's *Handbook of the Diagnosis and Treatment of DSM-IV Personality Disorders* (1995).

Why distinguish between Axis I and Axis II? Axis II personality disorders are conditions that are chronic and longstanding patterns of dysfunctional behavior. On the other hand, Axis I disorders tend to be acute, symptomatic, or episodic. Personality disorders are conditions that represent a more basic and chronic dysfunction than the superimposed Axis I symptom or syndrome. Another way of thinking about personality disorders is as the psychological vulnerability for an Axis I syndrome. In addition, Axis II disorders are much more resistant to change than a symptom or syndrome. Finally, personality disorders are ego-syntonic, which means that individuals are relatively comfortable with their behavior and usually are unwilling to enter treatment or to change once in treatment. This contrasts with Axis I disorders, which are ego-dystonic and more distressing. Here treatment is usually sought by the client in order to relieve distress. Table 11.1 (American Psychiatric Association, 1994, p. 633) lists the general diagnostic criteria for a personality disorder according to DSM-IV.

According to DSM-IV, personality disorder(s) are listed on Axis II. If no personality disorder is present, the clinician is encouraged to indicate the presence of prominent maladaptive personality features that do not meet the threshold for personality disorder. In addition, habitual use of maladaptive defense mechanisms can likewise be noted.

Earlier in this book, the analogy of pneumonia was presented to clarify multi-axial diagnoses. In terms of DSM-IV, Axis I and III represented all the individual symptoms of pneumonia whether they be physical, mental, or emotional. The bacteria eliciting pneumonia symptoms were represented by Axis IV—stressors—and Axis II represented the person's biological vulnerability or compromise of immune functioning. You will recall that treatment for pneumonia—Axis I—was quite aggressive if the patient was older, sickly, and immunosuppressed (had a disease like AIDS). Treatment was less aggressive or shorter term if the patient was an otherwise healthy, young college student. The first instance would be analogous to a severe personality disorder, whereas the second a personality style. In terms of psychological treatment, knowledge of the Axis II disorder or style can be prognostic regarding symptom expression as well as motivation for and compliance with treatment. For instance, the individual

TABLE 11.1
General diagnostic criteria for a Personality Disorder

A.   An enduring pattern of inner experience and behavior that deviates markedly from the expectations of the individual's culture. This pattern is manifested in two (or more) of the following areas:

  (1)   cognition (i.e., ways of perceiving and interpreting self, other people, and events)
  (2)   affectivity (i.e., the range, intensity, lability, and appropriateness of emotional response)
  (3)   interpersonal functioning
  (4)   impulse control

B.   The enduring pattern is inflexible and pervasive across a broad range of personal and social situations.
C.   The enduring pattern leads to clinically significant distress or impairment in social, occupational, or other important areas of functioning.
D.   The pattern is stable and of long duration and its onset can be traced back at least to adolescence or early adulthood.
E.   The enduring pattern is not better accounted for as a manifestation or consequence of another mental disorder.
F.   The enduring pattern is not due to the direct physiological effects of a substance (e.g., a drug of abuse, a medication) or a general medical condition (e.g., head trauma).

presenting with an Axis I adjustment disorder with depressed mood and an Axis II dependent personality style is likely to manifest a stable and mild course of symptoms and might be quite motivated and compliant with treatment. On the other hand, the same Axis I presentation with an Axis II passive-aggressive personality disorder would likely present with a more fluctuating and severe course of symptoms, and the individual would likely be uncooperative with treatment.

Adler did not discuss the personality disorders per se but did advance a two-dimensional theory of personality structure that was the basis for other Adlerians to develop personality typologies consistent with DSM-IV categories. Adler (1935) described two variables or dimensions: Social interest or usefulness (cooperative to uncooperative) and activity (active to inactive). These resulted in a four-fold personality typology: The ruling type (high active, low social interest); the avoiding type (low active, low social interest); the getting type (low active and high social interest); and socially useful, ideal type (high active, high social interest). Mosak (1968, 1979) expanded Adler's four-fold typology to eight types, which he correlated with DSM-II diagnostic codes. Mosak (1988) described the psychodynamics of personality disorders listed in DSM-III-R.

CLASSIFICATION OF PERSONALITY DISORDERS

In DSM-IV are listed ten distinct personality disorders that are grouped into three clusters. The clusters are Cluster A—odd or eccentric personality disorders (Paranoid, Schizoid, and Schizotypal); Cluster B—dramatic, emotional, or erratic personality disorders (Antisocial, Borderline, Histrionic, and Narcissistic); and Cluster C—anxious and fearful personality disorders (Avoidant, Dependent, and Obsessive-Compulsive). This classification of DSM-IV clusters is intuitive rather than being based on empirical data.

Finally, note that DSM-IV criteria include the designation and coding "Personality Disorder NOS" for listing disorders of personality functioning that are not classifiable as a specific personality disorder because the full criteria for one or more disorders cannot be met. When the features of one or more disorders are present, however, this diagnostic designation is to be used. In an appendix of DSM-IV, two other personality disorders are noted. They are depressive personality disorder and passive-aggressive personality disorder. Because the DSM-IV Task Force determined there was insufficient information to warrant inclusion of these two as Axis-II disorders, they were were given the status of proposed diagnoses in Appendix B. (It should be noted that passive-aggressive personality disorder had been classified as a full-fledged personality disorder in DSM-III-R. The diagnosis of either of these two disorders must be made with the "Personality Disorder NOS" classification and code.

CLINICAL PRESENTATION AND DEVELOPMENTAL ETIOLOGICAL FACTORS IN PERSONALITY DISORDERS

We began this chapter by defining personality as enduring patterns of thinking, feeling, and behaving or interacting. In the eleven personality disorders to be described, each disorder will be described in terms of its pattern of clinical presentation and its underlying predisposition or its etiological and developmental features.

The clinical presentation will be described by the observable pattern of the disorder in terms of its behavioral and interpersonal style, its thinking or cognitive styles, and its feeling or emotional style. This section also includes specific DSM-III-R diagnostic criteria for each disorder.

The section on developmental and etiological features describes how the personality style and disorder developed and are maintained. A biopsychosocial framework will form the basis of this section. A biopsychosocial formulation is an integrative effort to combine biological, psychological, and social data to explain and predict behavior. Biological factors can include predispositions associated with temperament, heredity, and central nervous system functioning. Temperament can be thought of as the biologically determined subset of personality. Each individual enters the world with a distinctive pattern of response, dispositions, and sensitivities. Thomas and Chess (1977, 1984) have described infant and child temperament patterns, while Burks and Rubenstein (1979) have described the application of these temperament types in adults, particularly adults in psychotherapy.

Psychological factors that influence personality development can be described in cognitive, dynamic, or behavioral terms. We will utilize the cognitive and dynamic approach of Individual Psychology to explain psychological development. Specially, lifestyle convictions referring to the individual's view of self, world, and life goals will be described (Mosak, 1954). In addition, levels of social learning and skill training will be noted.

Social factors will be described in terms of parenting style, parental injunction, as well as sibling, peer, and family relationship. In addition, those factors within the individual and the individual system and environment that reinforce and reconfirm this pattern and clinical presentation will be described.

DEPENDENT PERSONALITY DISORDER

DSM-IV Criteria

The Dependent Personality Disorder is characterized by a pervasive pattern of dependent and submissive behaviors. Those of this disorder are excessively passive, insecure, and isolated individuals who become abnormally dependent on one or more persons. While initially acceptable, this dependent behavior can become controlling, appear hostile, and even blend into a passive-aggressive pattern. This disorder is more common in females (2:1, females to males). In

TABLE 11.2

Diagnostic criteria for 301.50 Histrionic Personality Disorder

A pervasive pattern of excessive emotionality and attention seeking, beginning by early adulthood and present in a variety of contexts, as indicated by five (or more) of the following:

(1) is uncomfortable in situations in which he or she is not the center of attention

(2) interaction with others is often characterized by inappropriate sexually seductive or provocative behavior

(3) displays rapidly shifting and shallow expression of emotions

(4) consistently uses physical appearance to draw attention to self

(5) has a style of speech that is excessively impressionistic and lacking in detail

(6) shows self-dramatization, theatricality, and exaggerated expression of emotion

(7) is suggestible, i.e., easily influenced by others and circumstances

(8) considers relationships to be more intimate that they actually are

From *Diagnostic and Statistical Manual of Mental Disorders, Fourth Edition* (DSM-IV). Copyright © 1994 by American Psychiatric Association. Reprinted with permission.

females the dependent style often takes the form of submissiveness, whereas in males the dependent style is more likely to be autocratic, such as when the husband and boss depends on his wife and secretary to perform essential tasks that he himself cannot accomplish. In either case, this disorder is likely to lead to anxiety and depression when the dependent relationship is threatened.

As in the case of all personality disorders, this pattern begins by early adulthood and can be noted across a variety of situations and circumstances. The DSM-IV diagnostic criteria for this disorder are listed in Table 11.2 (American Psychiatric Association, 1994, pp. 657-658).

Clinical Presentation

The clinical presentation of the Dependent Personality Disorder can be described in terms of behavioral and interpersonal style, thinking style, and feeling style.

Their behavioral and interpersonal styles are characterized by docility, passivity, and nonassertiveness. In interpersonal relations, they tend to be pleasing, self-sacrificing, clinging, and constantly requiring the assurance of others. Their compliance and reliance on others lead to a subtle demand that others assume responsibility for major areas of their lives.

The thinking or cognitive style of dependent personalities is characterized by suggestibility. They easily adopt a Pollyannish attitude toward life. Furthermore, they tend to minimize difficulties and, because of their naivete, are easily persuadable and easily taken advantage of. In short, this style of thinking is uncritical and unperceptive.

Their feeling or affective style is characterized by insecurity and anxiousness. Because they lack self-confidence, they experience considerable discomfort at being alone. They tend to be preoccupied with the fear of abandonment and disapproval of others. Their mood tends to be one of anxiety or fearfulness as well as having a somber or sad quality.

Developmental and Etiological Features

In this section is described a biopsychosocial formulation of the development of the dependent personality. Biologically, these individuals are characterized by a low energy level. Their temperament is described as melancholic. As infants and young children they were characterized as fearful, sad, or withdrawn. In terms of body types they tend to have more endomorphic builds (Millon, 1981).

Psychologically, Dependent Personality Disorders can be understood and appreciated in terms of their view of themselves, their worldview, and their life goal. The self-view of these individuals tends to be a variant of the theme: "I'm nice, but inadequate (or fragile)." Their view of self is self-effacing, inept, and self-doubting. Their view of the world is some variant of the theme: "Others are here to take care of me, because I can't do it for myself." Their life goal is characterized by some variant of the theme: "Therefore, cling and rely on others at all cost."

The social features of this personality disorder can be described in terms of parental, familial, and environmental factors. The dependent personality is most likely to be raised in a family in which parental overprotection is prominent. It is as if the parental injunction to the child is "I can't trust you to do anything right (or well)." The dependent personality is likely to have been pampered and overprotected as a child. Contact with siblings and peers may engender feelings of unattractiveness, awkwardness, or competitive inadequacy, especially during the preadolescent and adolescent years. These can have a devastating impact on the individual and further confirm the individual's sense of self-deprecation and doubt. The Dependent Personality Disorder becomes self-perpetuating through a process that involves a sense of self-doubt, an avoidance of competitive activity, and the availability of self-reliant individuals who are willing to take care of and make decisions for the dependent person in exchange for the self-sacrificing and docile friendship of the dependent personality. A summary of characteristics of Dependent Personality Disorder is provided in Figure 11.1.

Treatment Considerations

The differential diagnoses for the Axis II personality disorder include the Histrionic Personality Disorder and the Avoidant Personality Disorder. Common Axis I diagnoses that are associated with the Dependent Personality Disorder include the Anxiety Disorders, particularly Simple and Social Phobias, and Panic Disorders with or without Agoraphobia. Other common DSM-IV disorders include Hypochondriasis, Conversion Disorders and Somatization Disorders. The experience of loss of a supportive person or relationship can lead to a number of affective disorders including Dysthymia and Major Depressive episodes. Finally, because Dependent Personality Disorders can have lifelong training in assuming the "sick role," they are especially prone to the Factitious Disorders.

In general, the long-range goal of psychotherapy with a dependent personality is to increase the individual's sense of independence and ability to function interdependently. At other times, the therapist may need to settle for a more modest goal, that is, helping the individual become a "healthier" dependent personality. Treatment strategies typically include challenging the individual's convictions or dysfunctional beliefs about personal inadequacy, and learning ways in which to increase assertiveness. A variety of methods can be used to increase self-reliance. Among these are providing the dependent person directives and opportunities for making decisions, being alone, and taking responsibility for his or her own well-being.

Case Example: Ms. A

Ms. A is a 34-year-old single, white female with a two-year history of partially treated panic attacks and major depression. Her panic symptoms began approximately three years previously and consisted of symptoms of hyperventilation, palpitations, lightheadedness, and a feeling of dread while she was working around her apartment. Because she believed she was having a heart attack, she

1.	Behavioral Appearance:	Docile Passive Nonassertive Lack of self-confidence
2.	Interpersonal Behavior:	Pleasing, Self-sacrificing Clinging, compliant Expect others to take responsibility for them
3.	Cognitive Style:	Suggestible: Pollyannish about interpersonal relations Overprotective (the "too good parent")
4.	Feeling Style:	Pleasant, but anxious, timid, or sad when stressed
5.	Parental Injunction/ Environmental Factors:	"You can't do it by yourself."
6.	Biological/Temperament:	Low energy level; fearful, sad, or withdrawn during infancy; melancholic
7.	Self-view:	"I'm nice, but inadequate or fragile." Self-doubting
8.	Worldview:	"Others are here to take care of me." (Because I can't do it myself)
9.	Self & System Perpetuant:	Avoidance of competitive activities Self-deprecation

Figure 11.1. Characteristics of Dependent Personality Disorder.

called for an ambulance and was taken to the emergency room of a local hospital. A heart attack was ruled out, and she was referred to her personal physician to be treated for anxiety symptoms. Over the course of the next several months, she was treated with Valium and the physician insisted she get psychotherapy. She did not, however, follow up with the recommendation for psychotherapy until 19 months after her first symptoms continued and, because of anticipatory anxiety of further panic attacks, she became increasingly homebound and agoraphobic. Over this period of time, she became more moody, irritable, fatigued, and tearful, and she had difficulty with initial insomnia as well as early morning awakening.

She is the younger of two siblings. Her brother was described as a successful attorney. Her parents were both alive, and since the panic attacks had begun, Ms. A moved back into her parents' home. She described both her parents as caring, concerned, and "my best friends." Ms. A had graduated from college and went on to complete a master's degree in education. Subsequently, she worked for four years as an elementary school teacher before her first symptoms occurred. Since then she had taken an indefinite leave of absence from her job. Ms. A reported being sickly as a young child and being taken by mother from doctor to doctor for various minor ailments. Even though she was a good student at school and had some friends, she preferred to come home after school and help mother around the house with the house cleaning and chores.

The following early recollections were reported: At age six she remembers her first day of going to school by herself. "I was proud. My mother said I could walk to school by myself. But when I turned the corner, I saw her out of the corner of my eye, following me." Ms. A recalls looking over her shoulder and seeing her mother behind a tree and feeling flustered and anger, and at the same time relieved that her mother was there. She remembers thinking, "Why can't she let me do this by myself?"

She remembers at age four getting her first puppy. "It was a mixed collie and a shepherd. Little Fluffy couldn't make it down the driveway on its own. When I tried to take him for a walk his legs just collapsed and he began to pant. So Fluffy became dependent on everyone. I had to pick him up and I said, 'He's too tired to do it by himself.' " She recalls bending down and picking up her dog and thinking "He's too tired" and feeling love for her puppy, and love and appreciation from him.

At age five, she recalls her mother asking her to go to the corner store to get some stamps. "She gave me instructions on how to cross the street, get change from the cashier, and put the money in the stamp machine. But when I went over to the stamp machine, I couldn't reach the coin slot because it was too high off the ground." Ms. A recalls standing in front of the machine and trying to get it to work, but not being able to reach the coin slot, and feeling puzzled and nervous, wondering if someone would see her and try to help her.

Ms. A's presenting symptoms, her early childhood and family history, and her early recollections are all suggestive of the clinical presentation and dynamics of the Dependent Personality Disorder. Not only was Ms. A overly dependent on her parents, she also became quite dependent on the Valium that she was prescribed for panic symptoms. The case of Ms. A is prototypic of many individuals who present with panic, agoraphobia, and depressive features; that is, the Dependent Personality Disorder is the most common Axis II presentation in individuals presenting with panic and agoraphobic symptoms.

HISTRIONIC PERSONALITY DISORDER

DSM-IV Description and Criteria

Histrionic personalities may initially seem charming, likable, energetic, and seductive, but as time passes they are likely to be seen as emotionally unstable, immature, and egocentric. This personality style and disorder predominate in females and presents with a caricature of femininity in dress and manner. DSM-IV diagnostic criteria are listed in Table 11.3 (American Psychiatric Association, 1994, pp. 668–669).

Clinical Presentation

The clinical presentation of the Histrionic Personality Disorder can be characterized with the following behavioral and interpersonal style, thinking style, and feeling style.

The behavioral style is characterized as charming, dramatic, and expressive, while also being demanding, self-indulgent, and inconsiderate. Persistent attention-seeking, mood lability, capriciousness, and superficiality further characterize their behavior. Interpersonally, these individuals tend to be exhibitionistic and flirtatious in their manner, with attention- seeking and manipulativeness being prominent.

TABLE 11.3
Diagnostic criteria for 301.6 Dependent Personality Disorder

A pervasive and excessive need to be taken care of that leads to submissive and clinging behavior and fears of separation, beginning by early adulthood and present in a variety of contexts, as indicated by five (or more) of the following:

(1)   has difficulty making everyday decisions without an excessive amount of advice and reassurance from others

(2)   needs others to assume responsibility for most major areas of his or her life

(3)   has difficulty expressing disagreement with others because of fear of loss of support or approval. **Note:** Do not include realistic fears of retribution.

(4)   has difficulty initiating projects or doing things on his or her own (because of a lack of self-confidence in judgment or abilities rather than a lack of motivation or energy)

(5)   goes to excessive lengths to obtain nurturance and support from others, to the point of volunteering to do things that are unpleasant

(6)   feels uncomfortable or helpless when alone because of exaggerated fears of being unable to care for himself or herself

(7)   urgently seeks another relationship as a source of care and support when a close relationship ends

(8)   is unrealistically preoccupied with fears of being left to take care of himself or herself

From *Diagnostic and Statistical Manual of Mental Disorders, Fourth Edition* (DSM-IV). Copyright © 1994 by American Psychiatric Association. Reprinted with permission.

The thinking or cognitive style of this personality can be characterized as impulsive and thematic rather than as analytical, precise and field-independent. In short, their tendency is to be non-analytic, vague, and field-dependent. They are easily suggestible and rely heavily on hunches and intuition. They avoid awareness of their own hidden dependency and other self-knowledge and tend to be "other-directed" with respect to the need for approval from others. Therefore, they can easily dissociate their "real" or inner self from their "public" or outer self. Their emotional or affective style is characterized by exaggerated emotional displays and excitability including irrational outbursts and temper tantrums. Although they are constantly seeking reassurance that they are loved, they respond with only superficial warmth and charm and are generally emotionally shallow. Finally, they are exceedingly rejection-sensitive.

Development and Etiological Features

The following biopsychosocial formulation may be helpful in understanding how the Histrionic Personality Disorder develops. Biologically and temperamentally, the Histrionic Personality Disorder appears to be quite different from the Dependent Personality Disorder. Unlike the dependent personality, histrionic personality is characterized by a high energy level and emotional and autonomic reactivity. Millon and Everly (1985) noted that histrionic adults tended to display a high degree of emotional lability and responsiveness in their infancy and early childhood. Their temperament then can be characterized as hyperresponsive and externally-oriented for gratification. Psychologically, Histrionic Personality Disorder has the characteristic view of self, worldview, and life goal. The self view of the histrionic will be some variant of the theme: "I am sensitive and everyone should admire and approve of me." The worldview will be some variant of: "Life makes me nervous so I am entitled to special care and consideration." Life goal is some variant of the theme: "Therefore, play to the audience, and have fun, fun, fun."

In addition to biological and psychological factors, social factors such as parenting style and injunction, and family and environmental factors influence the development of the histrionic personality. The parental injunction for the histrionic personality involves reciprocity: "I'll give you attention, if you do X." A parenting style that involves minimal or inconsistent discipline helps insure and reinforce the histrionic pattern. The histrionic child is likely to grow up with at least one manipulative or histrionic parent who reinforces the child's histrionic and attention-seeking behavior. Finally, the following sequence of self and system perpetuants are likely to be seen in the Histrionic Personality Disorder: denial of one's real or inner self; a preoccupation with externals; the need for excitement and attention seeking, which leads to a superficial charm and interpersonal presence; and the need for external approval. This, in turn, further reinforces the dissociation and denial of the real or inner self from the public self, and the cycle continues. Characteristics of Histrionic Personality Disorder are provided in Figure 11.2.

Treatment Considerations

The differential diagnosis of the Histrionic Personality Disorder includes the Narcissistic Personality Disorder and the Dependent Personality Disorder. In addition, in Axis II is combined the Histrionic-Borderline Disorder, which is a decompensated version of the Histrionic Personality Disorder. Also according

1.	Behavioral Appearance:	Charming/excitement-seeking Labile, capricious, superficial
2.	Interpersonal Behavior:	Attention-getting/manipulative Exhibitionistic/flirtatious
3.	Cognitive Style:	Impulsive, thematic, field-dependent Avoid awareness of their hidden dependencies
4.	Feeling Style:	Exaggerated emotional display
5.	Parental Injunction/ Environmental Factors:	"I'll give you attention when you do what I want." Manipulative/histrionic parental role models: minimal or inconsistent disciplining
6.	Biological/Temperament:	Hyperresponsive infantile pattern externally-oriented for gratification
7.	Self-view:	"I need to be noticed"; externally- oriented for gratification
8.	Worldview:	"Life makes me so nervous, so I'm entitled to special care and consideration."
9.	Self & System Perpetuant:	Preoccupation with external/repression Denial of shadow and inner life Reinforcement of need for approval

Figure 11.2.   Characteristics of Histrionic Personality Disorder.

to Millon (1981) is the Histrionic-Antisocial Personality Disorder. Associated DSM-IV Axis I diagnoses are in order of occurrence: Dysthymia; Acute Anxiety Syndromes such as Simple and Social Phobias; and the Somatoform Disorders, particularly Conversion Reactions and Hypochondriasis. Other disorders are the Obsessive-Compulsive Disorder and the Dissociative Disorders, particularly

Fugue States. Finally, Major Depression and Bipolar Disorders are common in the decompensated Histrionic Personality Disorder.

The treatment of the Histrionic Personality Disorder may present a considerable challenge to the clinician. For the purposes of this discussion, we will limit ourselves to some general considerations about treatment goals, limits, and medications. General treatment goals include helping the individual integrate gentleness with strength, moderating emotional expression, and encouraging warmth, genuineness, and empathy. Because the histrionic personality can present as dramatic, impulsive, seductive, and manipulative with potential for suicidal gestures, the clinician needs to discuss the matter of limits early in the course of therapy regarding professional boundaries and personal responsibilities. Some histrionic personalities, particularly those that bear some resemblance to "hysteroid dysphoria," respond to certain antidepressant agents particularly Parnate and Nardil (Liebowitz & Klein, 1979). Otherwise, unless a concurrent acute psychotic or major depressive episode is present, psychotherapy is the principal mode of treatment.

Case Example: Ms. J

Ms. J is a 19-year-old female undergraduate student who requested psychological counseling at the University Health Services for "boyfriend problems." Actually, she had taken a nonlethal overdose of minor tranquilizers the day before coming to the Health Services. She said she took the overdose in an attempt to kill herself because "life wasn't worth living" after her boyfriend had left the afternoon before. She was an attractive, well-dressed woman adorned with makeup and nail polish, which contrasted sharply with the very casual fashion of most coeds on campus. During the initial interview, she was warm and charming, maintained good eye contract, yet was mildly seductive. At two points in the interview she was emotionally labile, shifting from smiling elation to tearful sadness. Her boyfriend had accompanied her to the evaluation session and asked to talk to the therapist. He stated the reason he had left the patient was because she made demands on him that he could not meet, and that he "hadn't been able to satisfy her emotionally or sexually." Also, he noted that he could not afford to "take her out every night and party."

NARCISSISTIC PERSONALITY DISORDER

Although often symptom-free and well functioning, the Narcissistic Personality Disorder is chronically unsatisfied due to a constant need for admiration and

TABLE 11.4
Diagnostic criteria for 301.81 Narcissistic Personality Disorder

A pervasive pattern of grandiosity (in fantasy or behavior), need for admiration, and lack of empathy, beginning by early adulthood and present in a variety of contexts, as indicated by five (or more) of the following:

(1) has a grandiose sense of self-importance (e.g., exaggerates achievements and talents, expects to be recognized as superior without commensurate achievements)

(2) is preoccupied with fantasies of unlimited success, power, brilliance, beauty, or ideal love

(3) believes that he or she is "special" and unique and can only be understood by, or should associate with, other special or high-status people (or institutions)

(4) requires excessive admiration

(5) has a sense of entitlement, i.e., unreasonable expectations of especially favorable treatment or automatic compliance with his or her expectations

(6) is interpersonally exploitative, i.e., takes advantage of others to achieve his or her own ends

(7) lacks empathy: is unwilling to recognize or identify with the feelings and needs of others

(8) is often envious of others or believes that others are envious of him or her

(9) shows arrogant, haughty behaviors or attitudes

From *Diagnostic and Statistical Manual of Mental Disorders, Fourth Edition* (DSM-IV). Copyright © 1994 by American Psychiatric Association. Reprinted with permission.

habitually unrealistic self-expectations. The narcissist is impulsive and anxious, has ideas of grandiosity and "specialness," becomes quickly dissatisfied with others, and maintains superficial, exploitative interpersonal relationships. Under stress and when needs are not met, the narcissist may become depressed, develop somatic symptoms, have brief psychotic episodes, or display extreme rage.

DSM-IV Description and Criteria

The DSM-IV criteria for the Narcissistic Personality Disorder are noted in Table 11.4 (American Psychiatric Association, 1994, p. 661).

Clinical Presentation

The narcissistic personality is characterized by the following behavioral and interpersonal style, cognitive style, and affective style.

Behaviorally, narcissistic individuals are seen as conceited, boastful, and snobbish. They appear self-assured and self-centered, and they tend to dominate conversation, seek admiration, and act in a pompous and exhibitionistic fashion. They are also impatient, arrogant, and thin-skinned or hypersensitive. Interpersonally, they are exploitive and use others to indulge themselves and their desires. Their behavior is socially facile, pleasant, and endearing; however, they are unable to respond with true empathy to others. When stressed, they can be disdainful, exploitive, and generally irresponsible in their behavior.

Their thinking style is one of cognitive expansiveness and exaggeration. They tend to focus on images and themes rather than on facts and issues. In fact, they take liberties with the facts, distort them, and even engage in prevarication and self-deception to preserve their own illusions about themselves and the projects in which they are involved. Their cognitive style is also marked by inflexibility. In addition they have an exaggerated sense of self-importance and establish unrealistic goals of power, wealth, and ability. They justify all of this with their sense of entitlement and exaggerated sense of their own self-importance.

Their feeling or affective style is characterized by an aura of self-confidence and nonchalance that is present in most situations except when their narcissistic confidence is shaken. Then they are likely to respond with rage at criticism. Their feelings toward others shift and vacillate between overidealization and devaluation. Finally, their inability to show empathy is reflected in their superficial relationships with minimal emotional ties or commitments.

Developmental and Etiological Features

The following biopsychosocial formulation may be helpful in understanding how the Narcissistic Personality Disorder is likely to have developed.

Biologically narcissistic personalities tend to have hyperresponsive temperaments (Millon, 1981). As young children, they were viewed by others as being special in terms of looks, talents, or "promise." Often as young children they had early and exceptional speech development. In addition, they were likely keenly aware of interpersonal cues.

Psychologically, the narcissists' view of themselves, others, the world and life's purpose can be articulated in terms of the following themes: "I'm special and unique, and I am entitled to extraordinary rights and privileges whether I have earned them or not." Their worldview is a variant of the theme: "Life is a banquet table to be sampled at will. People owe me admiration and privilege." Their goal is, "Therefore, I'll expect and demand this specialness." Common defense mechanisms utilized by the narcissistic personality involve rationalization and projective identification.

Socially, predictable parental patterns and environmental factors can be noted for the narcissistic personality. Parental indulgence and overevaluation characterize the narcissistic personality. The parental injunction was likely: "Grow up and be wonderful—for me." Often they were only children, and, in addition, may have sustained early losses in childhood. From an early age they learned exploitive and manipulative behavior from their parents. This narcissistic pattern is confirmed, reinforced, and perpetuated by certain individual and systems factors. The illusion of specialness, disdain for others' views, and a sense of entitlement lead to an underdeveloped sense of social interest and responsibility. This, in turn, leads to increased self-absorption and confirmation of narcissistic beliefs. The characteristics of Narcissistic Personality Disorder are provided in Figure 11.3.

Treatment Considerations

Included in the differential diagnosis of the Narcissistic Personality Disorder are these other Axis II personality disorders: Histrionic Personality Disorder, Antisocial Personality Disorder, and Paranoid Personality Disorder. The most common Axis I syndromes associated with the Narcissistic Personality Disorder are Acute Anxiety Reactions, Dysthymia, Hypochondriasis, and Delusional Disorders.

In terms of treatment goals, a decision needs to be made as to whether the treatment is short-term and crisis-oriented or long-term and focused on personality restructuring. Crisis-oriented psychotherapy usually focuses on alleviation of the symptoms such as anxiety, depression, or somatic symptoms associated with the narcissistic injury or wound. This injury occurs when others fail to respond to the narcissist's sense of entitlement and specialness. Empathic mirroring or reflection and soothing are the treatments of choice (Kohut, 1971). The goals of

1. Behavioral Appearance: Conceited, boastful, snobbish
Self-assured, self-centered, pompous
Impatient, arrogant, thin-skinned

2. Interpersonal Behavior: Disdainful, exploitative, irresponsible
Socially facile but without empathy
Use others to indulge themselves

3. Cognitive Style: Cognitive expansiveness and exaggeration;
Focus on images and themes; Take
liberties with facts; Persistent and inflexible
Defense: projective identification

4. Feeling Style: Self-confidence—narcissistic rage

5. Parental Injunction/
Environmental Factors: "Grow up and be wonderful, for me."

6. Biological/Temperament: Special looks, talents, or "promise"; Early
and exceptional language development

7. Self-view: "I'm special and unique, and I'm entitled
to extraordinary rights and privileges
whether I've earned them or not."

8. Worldview: "Life is a banquet table to be sampled at
will. People owe me admiration and
privilege. Therefore, I'll expect and
demand this specialness."

9. Self & System
Perpetuant: Illusion of specialness + disdain for
others' views + entitlement—
underdeveloped social interest and
responsibility—increased self-absorption
and reinforcement of narcissistic beliefs

Figure 11.3. Characteristics of Narcissistic Personality Disorder.

longer term therapy involve the restructuring of personality. These goals include increasing empathy, decreasing rage and cognitive distortions, and increasing the individual's ability to mourn losses. Treatment methods and strategies include empathic mirroring (Kohut, 1971), anger management, cognitive restructuring, and empathy training as well as interpretation. When marital issues are involved, couples therapy has been shown to be a useful treatment modality (Feldman, 1982). Medication management is directed only at treatable Axis I conditions (Reid, 1989). Clinicians have noted that the majority of narcissistic personalities who present for treatment are interested only in having the narcissistic wound soothed; then they leave treatment.

Case Example: Mr. E

Mr. E is a 32-year-old male who presented for therapy after his wife of six years threatened to leave him, and because his employer was pressuring him to resign his position as a sales executive for a condominium project. Apparently, Mrs. E had told her husband that he loved himself "a hundred times more than you love me." Mr. E dismissed this by saying he needed to buy $600 suits because his job demanded that he look his best at all times and that he was "tall, dark, handsome and sexy, all any woman could want in a man." Mr. E denied that he used scare tactics, exaggerated claims, or other pressure-selling techniques with customers. "Sure, I'm a bit aggressive, but you don't get into the 'Millionaire's Club' by being a wimp." He added that his employer would "go belly up without me," and that he was too important to be dismissed for such petty reasons.

ANTISOCIAL PERSONALITY DISORDER

DSM-IV Description and Criteria

Antisocial behavior tends to begin in childhood or early adolescence and is characterized by aggressiveness, fighting, hyperactivity, poor peer relationships, irresponsibility, lying, theft, truancy, poor school performance, runaway behavior, and inappropriate sexual activity as well as drug and alcohol abuse. As adults, assaultiveness, self-defeating impulsivity, hedonism, promiscuity, unreliability, and continued drug and alcohol abuse may be present. Criminality may be involved. These individuals fail at work, change jobs frequently, tend to receive dishonorable discharges from the military, are abusing parents and neglectful spouses, have difficulty maintaining intimate relationships, and may be convicted and spend time in prison. Antisocial Personality Disordered persons are frequently

TABLE 11.5
Diagnostic criteria for 301.82 Avoidant Personality Disorder

A pervasive pattern of social inhibition, feelings of inadequacy, and hypersensitivity to negative evaluation, beginning by early adulthood and present in a variety of contexts, as indicated by four (or more) of the following:

(1) avoids occupational activities that involve significant interpersonal contact, because of fears of criticism, disapproval, or rejection

(2) is unwilling to get involved with people unless certain of being liked

(3) shows restraint within intimate relationships because of the fear of being shamed or ridiculed

(4) is preoccupied with being criticized or rejected in social situations

(5) is inhibited in new interpersonal situations because of feelings of inadequacy

(6) views self as socially inept, personally unappealing, or inferior to others

(7) is unusually reluctant to take personal risks or engage in any new activities because they may prove embarrassing

From *Diagnostic and Statistical Manual of Mental Disorders, Fourth Edition* (DSM-IV). Copyright © 1994 by American Psychiatric Association. Reprinted with permission.

anxious and depressed and show both conversion symptoms and factitious symptoms. Antisocial behavior often peaks in the late adolescence and early twenties and lessens in the late thirties. This is primarily a diagnosis of males with a prevalence rate being approximately 6:1, males to females.

DSM-IV criteria for this disorder are noted in Table 11.5 (American Psychiatric Association, 1994, pp. 664–665).

Clinical Presentation

The Antisocial Personality Disorder is recognizable by the following behavior and interpersonal style, cognitive style, and emotional style.

As previously noted with the DSM-IV criteria, the behavioral style of antisocial personalities is characterized by irresponsible parenting, poor job performance, repeated substance abuse, persistent lying, delinquency, truancy, and violations of others' rights. Antisocial Personality Disordered individuals are also noted for their impulsive anger, hostility, and cunning. They are forceful individuals who regularly engage in risk-seeking and thrill-seeking behavior. Their interpersonal style is characterized as antagonistic and belligerent. They tend to be highly competitive and distrustful of others and thus poor losers. Their relationships may at times appear to be "slick" as well as calculating. The flavor of this DSM-III-R diagnosis still retains much of the "criminal" diagnostic category. Yet these criteria also can characterize the behavior of successful businessmen, politicians, and other professionals who could be described as ambitious, hard-driving, and successful.

The cognitive style of the antisocial personality is described as impulsive and cognitively inflexible as well as externally-oriented. Because they are contemptuous of authority, rules, and social expectations, they easily rationalize their own behavior.

Their feelings or emotional style is characterized with shallow, superficial relationships that involve no lasting emotional ties or commitments. They avoid "softer" emotions such as warmth and intimacy because they regard these as signs of weakness. Guilt is seldom if ever experienced. They are unable to tolerate boredom, depression, or frustration and subsequently are sensation-seekers. They are callous toward the pain and suffering of others and show little guilt or shame over their own deviant actions.

Developmental and Etiological Features

The following biopsychosocial formulation may be helpful in understanding how the antisocial personality is likely to have developed.

Biologically, antisocial personalities manifested "difficult child" temperaments (Thomas & Chess, 1977). As such their patterns were unpredictable, tended to withdraw from situations, showed high intensity, and had a fairly low, discontented mood. This ill-tempered infantile pattern has been described by Millon (1981) as resulting in part, from a low threshold for limbic stimulation and a decrease in inhibitory centers of the central nervous system. Their body types tend to be endomorphic and mesomorphic (Millon, 1981).

Psychologically, the antisocials' view of themselves, others, the world, and life's purpose can be articulated in terms of the following themes. They tend to view themselves with some variant of the theme: "I am cunning and entitled to get whatever I want." In other words, they see themselves as strong, competitive, energetic, and tough. Their view of life and the world is variant of the theme:

"Life is devious and hostile, and rules keep me from fulfilling my needs." Not surprisingly their life's goal has a variant of the theme: "Therefore, I'll bend or break these rules because my needs come first, and I'll defend against efforts to be controlled or degraded by others." Acting out and rationalization are common defense mechanisms used by the antisocial personality.

Socially, predictable parenting styles and environmental factors can be noted for the Antisocial Personality Disorder. Typically, either the parenting style is characterized by hostility and deficient parental modeling, or the parents might have provided such good modeling that the child could not or refused to live up to high parental standards. The parental injunction is that, "The end justifies the means." Thus, vindictive behavior is modeled and reinforced. The family structure tends to be disorganized and disengaged. The antisocial pattern is confirmed, reinforced, and perpetuated by the following individual and systems factors: The need to be powerful and the fear of being abused and humiliated leads to a denial of "softer" emotions plus uncooperativeness. This, along with the tendency to provoke others, leads to further reinforcement of antisocial beliefs and behaviors. These characteristics of the Antisocial Personality Disorder are provided in Figure 11.4.

Treatment Considerations

The differential diagnosis for Antisocial Personality Disorder includes other Axis II personality disorders such as the Narcissistic Personality Disorder and the Paranoid Personality Disorder. The most common Axis I syndromes associated with the Antisocial Personality Disorder are Substance Abuse and Dependence, Acute Anxiety States, Delusional Disorders, and Factitious Disorders.

In terms of treatment goals, these individuals are usually not interested in presenting for treatment or are resistant to treatment if they are forced by the courts, employers, or other agencies. Individual therapy, in and of itself, has proved to be remarkably ineffective with these individuals; however, special residential treatment programs have shown some promise (Reid, 1989). If the antisocial personality is able to engage in psychotherapy, a clear sign of progress is noted with the appearance of depressive features.

Case Example: Mr. Z

Mr. Z is a 24-year-old Hispanic male who presented late in the evening to the emergency room at a community hospital complaining of a headache. His

1. Behavioral Appearance: Impulsively angry, hostile, cunning; Forceful, risk-taking, thrill-seeking; Temper, verbally or physically abusive; Avoid "softer" emotions such as warmth and intimacy = weakness

2. Interpersonal Behavior: Antagonistic to belligerent; "Slick" but calculating; Highly competitive and poor losers; Distrustful of others

3. Cognitive Style: Impulsive, inflexible, and externally-oriented; Hard-nosed, realistic, and devious
Defense: Acting out

4. Feeling Style: Glib, shallow, superficiality

5. Parental Injunction/ Environmental Factors: "The end justifies the means;"
Parental hostility—learned vindictive behavior + deficient authority figure
Disorganized family and/or subculture system

6. Biological/Temperament: Ill-tempered infantile pattern
Low threshold for limbic stimulation and inefficient inhibitory centers + mesomorphic-endomorphic body types (Subclass) Adult ADD-Residual

7. Self-view: "I'm cunning and I'm entitled to get what I want." View themselves as strong, competitive, self-reliant, energetic, tough

8. Worldview: "Life is devious and hostile and rules keep me from fulfilling my needs. Therefore, I'll bend or break them because my needs come first and I'll defend any efforts to be controlled or degraded."

9. Self & System Perpetuant: Need to be powerful + fear of being abused/ humiliated—denial of tender feelings and unwillingness to cooperate + tendency to provoke others—reinforcement of antisocial style

Figure 11.4.   Characteristics of Antisocial Personality Disorder.

description of the pain was vague and contradictory. At one point he said the pain had been present for three days, while at another point it was "many years." He indicated that the pain led to violent behavior and described how, during a headache episode, he had brutally assaulted a medic while he was in the Air Force. He gave a long history of arrests for assault, burglary, and drug dealing. Neurological and mental status examinations were with normal limits except for some mild agitation. He insisted that only Darvon—a narcotic—would relieve his headache pain. The patient resisted a plan for further diagnostic tests or a follow-up clinic appointment, saying unless he was treated immediately "something really bad could happen."

SCHIZOID PERSONALITY DISORDER

DSM-IV Description and Criteria

Individuals with Schizoid Personality Disorders are seclusive individuals who have little desire or capacity for interpersonal relationships and derive little pleasure from them; yet, they can perform well if left alone. For instance, they make excellent night watchmen and security guards. They have little emotional range, daydream excessively, and appear to be humorless and aloof. Research evidence does not confirm the belief that the schizoid personality has an increased risk of developing a schizophrenic pattern (Grinspoon, 1982).

DSM-IV criteria for the Schizoid Personality Disorder are noted in Table 11.6 (American Psychiatric Association, 1994, p. 641).

Clinical Presentation

The Schizoid Personality Disorder is characterized by the following behavior and interpersonal styles, thinking or cognitive styles, and emotional or affective styles.

The behavioral pattern of schizoids can be described as lethargic, inattentive, and occasionally eccentric. They exhibit slow and monotonal speech and are generally nonspontaneous in both their behavior and speech. Interpersonally, they appear to be content to remain socially aloof and alone. These individuals prefer to engage in solitary pursuits, are reserved and seclusive, and rarely respond to others' feelings and actions. They tend to fade into the social backdrop and

TABLE 11.6
Diagnostic criteria for 301.20 Schizoid Personality Disorder

A. A pervasive pattern of detachment from social relationships and a restricted range of expression of emotions in interpersonal settings, beginning by early adulthood and present in a variety of contexts, as indicated by four (or more) of the following:

(1) neither desires nor enjoys close relationships, including being part of a family

(2) almost always chooses solitary activities

(3) has little, if any, interest in having sexual experiences with another person

(4) takes pleasure in few, if any, activities

(5) lacks close friends or confidants other than first-degree relatives

(6) appears indifferent to the praise and criticism of others

(7) shows emotional coldness, detachment, or flattened affectivity

B. Does not occur exclusively during the course of Schizophrenia, a Mood Disorder With Psychotic Features, another Psychotic Disorders, or a Pervasive Developmental Disorder and is not due to the direct physiological effects of a general medical condition.

Note: If criteria are met prior to the onset of Schizophrenia, add "Premorbid," e.g., "Schizoid Personality Disorder (Premorbid)."

From *Diagnostic and Statistical Manual of Mental Disorders, Fourth Edition* (DSM-IV). Copyright © 1994 by American Psychiatric Association. Reprinted with permission.

appear to others as "cold fish." They do not involve themselves in group or team activity. In short, they appear inept and awkward in social situations.

Their thinking style can be characterized as cognitively distracted; that is, their thinking and communication can easily become derailed through internal or external distraction. This is noted in clinical interviews when these patients have difficulty organizing their thoughts, are vague, or wander into irrelevance such as the shoes certain people prefer (Millon, 1981). They appear to have little ability for introspection and no ability to articulate important aspects of interpersonal relationships. Their goals are vague and appear to be indecisive.

Their emotional style is characterized as being humorless, cold, aloof, and unemotional. They appear to be indifferent to praise and criticism, and they lack spontaneity. Not surprisingly, their rapport and ability to empathize with others are poor. In short, they have a constricted range of affective response.

Developmental and Etiological Features

The following biopsychosocial formulation may be helpful in understanding how the schizoid personality develops.

Biologically, the schizoid personality was likely to have had a passive and anhedonic infantile pattern and temperament. Millon (1981) suggested that this pattern results, in part, from increased dopaminergic postsynaptic limbic and frontal lobe receptor activity. Constitutionally, the schizoid is likely to be characterized by an ectomorphic body type (Sheldon, Dupertius, & McDermott, 1954).

Psychologically, schizoids view themselves, others, the world, and life's purpose in terms of the following themes. They view themselves by some variant of the theme: "I'm a misfit from life, so I don't need anybody. I am indifferent to everything." For schizoid personalities, the world and others are viewed by some variant of the theme: "Life is a difficult place and relating to people can be harmful." As such, they are likely to conclude, "Therefore, trust nothing and keep a distance from others and you won't get hurt." Alexandra Adler (1956) further describes these lifestyle dynamics. The most common defense mechanism utilized by them is intellectualization.

Socially, predictable patterns of parenting and environmental factors can be noted for schizoids. Parenting style is usually characterized by indifference and impoverishment. It is as if the parental injunction was: "You're a misfit," or, "Who are you, what do you want?" Their family pattern is characterized by fragmented communications and rigid, unemotional responsiveness. Because of these conditions, schizoids are grossly under-socialized and develop few if any interpersonal relating and coping skills. This schizoid pattern is confirmed, reinforced, and perpetuated by the following individual and systems factors: Believing themselves to be misfits, they shun social activity. This plus social insensitivity leads to reinforcement of social isolation and further confirmation of the schizoid style. In Figure 11.5 are listed characteristics of Schizoid Personality Disorder.

Treatment Considerations

Included in the differential diagnosis of the Schizoid Personality Disorder are the following Axis II personality disorders: the Avoidant Personality Disorder, Schizotypal Personality Disorder, and the Dependent Personality Disorder. The most common Axis I syndromes likely to be associated with the Schizoid Personality Disorder are Depersonalization Disorder, the Bipolar and Unipolar Disor-

1.	Behavioral Appearance:	Speech: slow and monotonous Lethargic, inattentive, nonspontaneous
2.	Interpersonal Behavior:	Minimal "human" interests and friends; "Cold fish" fades into social background; Rarely responds to feelings or actions of others, isolate; Content to remain aloof
3.	Cognitive Style:	Cognitively distracted (thoughts and communications are easily derailed and tangential or loose absent minded); Minimally introspective Defense: Intellectualization
4.	Feeling Style:	Aloof, indifferent
5.	Parental Injunction/ Environmental Factors:	"Who are you, what do you want?" Rigid, emotionally unresponsive family or origin; Fragmented family communications; Undersocialized in interpersonal skills
6.	Biological/ Temperament:	Passive and anhedonia infantile pattern; Excessive dopaminergic post-synaptic limbic and frontal lobe receptors; Ectomorphic build
7.	Self-view:	"I'm a misfit from life, so I don't need anybody." "I'm indifferent to everything."
8.	Worldview:	"Life is a difficult place and can be harmful. Therefore, trust nothing and keep distance from others and you won't get hurt."
9.	Self & System Perpetuant:	Infrequent social activity + social insensitivity—reinforcement of social isolation

Figure 11.5. Characteristics of Schizoid Personality Disorder.

ders, Obsessive-Compulsive Disorder, Hypochondriasis, Schizophreniform, and Disorganized and Catatonic Schizophrenias.

Schizoid personalities rarely volunteer for treatment unless decompensation is present; however, they may accept treatment if someone, like a family member, demands it. Treatment goals are focused on symptom alleviation rather than on restructuring of personality. Treatment strategy involves a crisis and supportive approach as well as providing a consistent and supportive therapeutic interaction. Medications, particularly the neuroleptics, do not appear to be useful with schizoid personality unless some psychotic decompensation has been noted (Reid, 1989).

Case Example: Mr. S

Mr. S is a 19-year-old freshman who met with the director of the introductory psychology course program to arrange an individual assignment in lieu of participation in the small group research project course requirement. Mr. S told the course director that because of a daily two hour commute each way, he "wouldn't be available for the research project", and that he "wasn't really interested in psychology and was only taking the course because it was required." Upon further inquiry, Mr. S disclosed that he preferred to commute and live at home with his mother, even though he had the financial resources to live on campus. He admitted he had no close friend or social contacts and preferred being a "loner." He had graduated from high school with a "B" average but did not date or participate in extracurricular activities, except the electronics club. He was a computer science major, and "hacking" was his only hobby. Mr. S's affect was somewhat flattened and he appeared to have no sense of humor and failed to respond to attempts by the course director to make contact through humor. There was no indication of a thought or perceptual disorder. The course director arranged for an individual project for the student.

AVOIDANT PERSONALITY DISORDER

DSM-IV Description and Criteria

Avoidant personalities are seemingly shy, lonely, hypersensitive individuals with low self-esteem. Although they are desperate for interpersonal involvement, they avoid personal contact with others because of their heightened fear of social disapproval and rejection sensitivity. In this regard, they are quite different than the schizoid personality who has little if any interest in personal contact.

TABLE 11.7
Diagnostic criteria for 301.7 Antisocial Personality Disorder

A. There is a pervasive pattern of disregard for and violation of the rights of others occurring since age 15 years, as indicated by three (or more) of the following:

> (1) failure to conform to social norms with respect to lawful behaviors as indicated by repeatedly performing acts that are grounds for arrest

> (2) deceitfulness, as indicated by repeated lying, use of aliases, or conning others for personal profit or pleasure

> (3) impulsivity or failure to plan ahead

> (4) irritability and aggressiveness, as indicated by repeated physical fights or assaults

> (5) reckless disregard for safety of self or others

> (6) consistent irresponsibility, as indicated by repeated failure to sustain consistent work behavior or honor financial obligations

> (7) lack of remorse, as indicated by being indifferent to or rationalizing having hurt, mistreated, or stolen from another

B. The individual is at least 18 years.
C. There is evidence of Conduct Disorder with onset before age 15 years.
D. The occurrence of antisocial behavior is not exclusively during the course of Schizophrenia or a Manic Episode.

From *Diagnostic and Statistical Manual of Mental Disorders, Fourth Edition* (DSM-IV). Copyright © 1994 by American Psychiatric Association. Reprinted with permission.

DSM-IV criteria for Avoidant Personality Disorder are noted in Table 11.7 (American Psychiatric Association, 1994, pp. 649–650).

Clinical Presentation

The avoidant personality disorder is characterized by the following behavioral and interpersonal styles, thinking or cognitive styles, and emotional or affective styles.

The behavioral style of avoidant personalities is characterized by social withdrawal, shyness, distrustfulness, and aloofness. Their behavior and speech is both controlled and inactive, and they appear apprehensive and awkward. Interpersonally, they are rejection-sensitive. Even though they desire acceptance by others, they keep distance from others and require unconditional approval before being willing to "open up." They gradually "test" others to determine who can be trusted to like them. They tend to see the world as some variant of the theme: "Life is unfair—people reject and criticize me—but, I still want someone to like me." As such, they are likely to conclude: "Therefore, be vigilant, demand reassurance, and if all else fails, fantasize and daydream about the way life could be." The most common defense mechanism of the avoidant personality is that of fantasy.

Socially, predictable patterns of parenting and environmental factors can be noted for the avoidant personality disorder. The avoidant personality is likely to have experienced parental rejection and/or ridicule. Later, siblings and peers will likely continue this pattern of rejection and ridicule. The parental injunction is likely to have been, "We don't accept you, and probably no one else will either." They may have had parents with high standards and worried that they may not have or would not meet these standards and therefore would not be accepted.

This avoidant pattern is confirmed, reinforced, and perpetuated by the following individual and systems factors: a sense of personal inadequacy and a fear of rejection leads to hypervigilance, which leads to restricted social experiences. These experiences, plus catastrophic thinking, lead to increased hypervigilance and hypersensitivity; leading to self-pity, anxiety, and depression; which leads to further confirmation of avoidant beliefs and styles. These characteristics of the Avoidant Personality Disorder are summarized in Figure 11.6.

Treatment Considerations

Included in a differential diagnosis of the Avoidant Personality Disorder are other Axis II personality disorders: Schizoid Personality Disorder, Schizotypal Personality Disorder, Borderline Personality Disorder and Dependent Personality Disorder. The most common Axis I syndromes associated with the Avoidant Personality Disorder are Generalized Anxiety Disorder, Dysthymia, Major Depressive episode, Hypochondriasis, Conversion Disorder, Dissociative Disorder, and Schizophrenia. It has been said that next to the Borderline Personality Disorder, the Avoidant Personality Disorder is the most liable and likely to decompensate (Reid, 1989).

In terms of treatment goals and strategies, there is little reported research on treating the avoidant personality; however, the goal of therapy should be to increase the individual's self-esteem and confidence in relationship to others and to desensitize the individual to the criticism of others. Desensitization techniques

1. Behavioral Appearance:

    Shy, mistrustful, aloof, apprehensive, socially awkward; Controlled, underactive behavior; Feelings of emptiness and depersonalization

2. Interpersonal Behavior:

    Guardedly "test" others
    Rejection sensitive as self-protectant;
    Desire acceptance but maintain distance;
    Have interpersonal skills, but fear using them

3. Cognitive Style:

    Perpetual vigilance; Thoughts easily distracted by their hypersensitivity

4. Feeling Style:

    Shy and apprehensive

5. Parental Injunction/ Environmental Factors:

    "We don't accept you, and probably nobody else will either." Parental rejection and/or ridicule; Later, peer group alienation

6. Biological/ Temperament:

    Hyperirritable infantile pattern
    Low arousal threshold for autonomic nervous system

7. Self-view:

    "I'm inadequate and frightened of rejection." Chronically tense, fatigued, self-conscious; Devalue their achievement, self-critical

8. Worldview:

    "Life is unfair, people reject and criticize me, but I want someone to like me. Therefore, be vigilant, demand reassurance, and, if all else fails, fantasize and daydream."

9. Self & Perpetuant:

    Fear of social rejection and humiliation— hypervigilance—restricted social experiences + catastrophizing—increased hypervigilance and hypersensitivity— increased self-pity

Figure 11.6.   Characteristics of Avoidant Personality Disorder.

appear to be much more useful and expedient in this regard. Assertiveness training and shyness training are reportedly very effective with the avoidant personality pattern (Turkat & Maisto, 1985). As with older personality disorders, medication is only useful for diagnosable Axis I conditions associated with the avoidant pattern.

Case Example: Ms. W

Ms. W is a 24-year-old female student who contacted the College Counseling Service for help with "difficulty concentrating." She indicated that the problem started when Ms. W's roommate of two years precipitously moved out to live with her boyfriend. Ms. W described herself as being "blown away and hurt" by this. She noted that she had no other close friends and described herself as being shy and having had only one date since high school. Since then she had foiled attempts by men to date her because of being rejected when she was a freshman by a guy who had dated her for a month and never contacted her again. On examination, she had poor eye contact with the admissions counselor and appeared very shy and self-conscious.

OBSESSIVE-COMPULSIVE PERSONALITY DISORDER

DSM-IV Description and Criteria

Obsessive-Compulsive Personality Disordered individuals are described as inhibited, stubborn, perfectionistic, judgmental, overconscientious, rigid, and chronically anxious. Characteristically, they are people who avoid intimacy and experience little pleasure from life. They may be successful but at the same time are indecisive and demanding. Often they are perceived as cold and reserved. Unlike the Axis I Obsessive-Compulsive Disorder, ritualistic compulsions and obsessions do not characterize this personality disorder.

DSM-IV criteria for the Obsessive-Compulsive Personality Disorder are noted in Table 11.8 (American Psychiatric Association, 1994, pp. 672–673).

Clinical Presentation

The Obsessive-Compulsive Personality Disorder can be recognized by the following behavior and interpersonal styles, cognitive style, and emotional style.

TABLE 11.8
Diagnostic criteria for 301.4 Obsessive-Compulsive Personality Disorder

A pervasive pattern of preoccupation with orderliness, perfectionism, and mental and interpersonal control, at the expense of flexibility, openness, and efficiency, beginning by early adulthood and present in a variety of contexts, as indicated by four (or more) of the following:

(1) is preoccupied with details, rules, lists, order, organization, or schedules to the extent that the major point of the activity is lost

(2) shows perfectionism that interferes with task completion (e.g., is unable to complete a project because his or her own overly strict standards are not met)

(3) is excessively devoted to work and productivity to the exclusion of leisure activities and friendships (not accounted for by obvious economic necessity)

(4) is overconscientious, scrupulous, and inflexible about matters of morality, ethics, or values (not accounted for by cultural or religious identification)

(5) is unable to discard worn-out or worthless objects even when they have no sentimental value

(6) is reluctant to delegate tasks or to work with others unless they submit to exactly his or her way of doing things

(7) adopts a miserly spending style toward both self and others; money is viewed as something to be hoarded for future catastrophes

(8) shows rigidity and stubbornness

From *Diagnostic and Statistical Manual of Mental Disorders, Fourth Edition* (DSM-IV). Copyright © 1994 by American Psychiatric Association. Reprinted with permission.

Behaviorally, this disorder is characterized by perfectionism. Individuals with this disorder are likely to be workaholics. In addition to dependability, they tend to be stubborn and possessive. They, like passive-aggressive disordered individuals, can be indecisive and procrastinating. Interpersonally, these individuals are exquisitely conscious of social rank and status and modify their behavior accordingly; that is, they tend to be deferential and obsequious to superiors, and haughty and autocratic to subordinates and peers. They can be doggedly insistent that others do things their way without an appreciation or awareness of how others react to this insistence. At their best they are polite and loyal to the organizations and ideals they espouse.

Their thinking style can be characterized as constricted and rule-based. They have difficulty establishing priorities and perspective. They are "detail" people and often lose sight of the larger project. In other words, they "can't see the forest for the trees." Their indecisiveness and doubts make decision making difficult. Their mental inflexibility is matched by their nonsuggestible and unimaginative style, suggesting they have a restricted fantasy life. Like passive-aggressive individuals, the obsessive-compulsives have conflicts between assertiveness and defiance, and pleasing and obedience.

Their emotional style is characterized as grim and cheerless. They have difficulty with the expression of intimate feelings such as warmth and tenderness. They tend to avoid the "softer" feelings, although they may express anger, frustration, and irritability quite freely. This grim, feeling-avoidant demeanor shows itself in stilted, stiff relationship behaviors.

Developmental and Etiological Features

The following biopsychosocial formulation may be helpful in understanding how the Obsessive-Compulsive Personality Disorder is likely to have developed.

Biologically, these individuals were likely to have exhibited an anhedonic temperament as an infant (Millon, 1981). Firstborn children have a greater propensity for developing a compulsive style than other siblings (Toman, 1961).

Psychologically, these individuals view themselves, others, the world, and life's purpose in terms of the following themes. They tend to view themselves with some variant of the theme: "I'm responsible if something goes wrong, so I have to be reliable, competent, and righteous." Their worldview is some variant of the theme: "Life is unpredictable and expects too much." As such, they are likely to conclude, "Therefore, be in control, right, and proper at all times."

Socially, predictable patterns of parenting and environmental conditioning are noted for this personality. The parenting style they experienced could be characterized as both consistent and overcontrolled. As children they were trained to be overly responsible for their actions and to feel guilty and worthless if they were not obedient, achievement-oriented, or "good." The parental injunction to which they were most likely exposed was "You must do and be better to be worthwhile."

This obsessive-compulsive pattern is confirmed, reinforced, and perpetuated by the following individual and systems factors: Exceedingly high expectations plus harshly rigid behavior and beliefs, along with a tendency to be self-critical, lead to rigid, rule-based behavior, and avoidance of social, professional, and moral unacceptability. This in turn further reconfirms the harshly rigid behaviors and beliefs of this personality. In Figure 11.7 are listed characteristics of Obsessive-Compulsive Personality Disorder.

Treatment Considerations

Included in the differential diagnosis of the Obsessive-Compulsive Personality Disorder are two other Axis II personality disorders: the Dependent Personality Disorder and the Passive-Aggressive Personality Disorder. The most common Axis I syndromes associated with the Obsessive-Compulsive Personality Disorder are the Obsessive-Compulsive Disorder, Simple Phobias, Generalized Anxiety Disorder, and Dysthymia. Other Axis I syndromes are Hypochondriasis, Somatization Disorder, and Psychological Factors Affecting Physical Conditions. Occasionally, a Brief Reactive Psychosis may be noted in the decompensated obsessive-compulsive.

The Obsessive-Compulsive Personality Disorder (OCD) has a long tradition of treatment dating back to Freud's case of the "Rat Man" and Adler's "Case of Mrs. A." Note that OCD is an Axis I disorder while the Obsessive-Compulsive Personality Disorder is an Axis II disorder. Since the "Rat Man" exhibited both Axis I and II disorders, many who have read Freud's account of this case and its treatment have incorrectly assumed that both disorders are the same and are treated the same. They are not the same disorder, but in about one-third of cases, both disorders have been shown to be present (Jenike, Baer, & Minichiello, 1986). When both disorders are present together, treatment has been shown to be much more challenging than if only OCD is present.

The goals of treatment include increased cognitive constriction and increased feeling expression so that a more reasonable balance can be obtained between thoughts and feelings. Treatment strategies for the Obsessive-Compulsive Personality Disorder usually involve long-term insight-oriented therapy. Unlike the Obsessive-Compulsive Disorder, where antidepressants plus behavior therapy can result in amelioration of obsessions and compulsions in a relatively short period of time, the Obsessive-Compulsive Personality Disorder does not lend itself to short-term treatment outcomes. Salzman (1968) and Turkat and Maisto (1985), however, offered dynamic and cognitive behavior intervention that has proved effective. Medication is usually not needed with this disorder if the restitution of the accompanying Axis I condition is attained.

1.	Behavioral Appearance:	Workaholic, dependable Stubborn, possessive Procrastination, indecisive Perfectionistic
2.	Interpersonal Behavior:	Feeling avoidance Autocratic to peers/subordinates Obsequious to superiors Polite, loyal
3.	Cognitive Style:	Constricted, rule-based, unimaginative; Conflict assertive (defiance) vs. pleasing (obedience)
4.	Feeling Style:	Grim, cheerless
5.	Parental Injunction/ Environmental Factors:	"You must do/be better to be worthwhile." Consistent parental overcontrol. Training in being overresponsible/guilty
6.	Biological/Temperament:	Anhedonia temperament First born
7.	Self-view:	"I'm responsible if some-thing goes wrong." See selves as reliable, competent, righteous
8.	Worldview:	"Life is unpredictable and expects much. Therefore, be in control, right and proper."
9	Self & System Perpetuant:	Very high expectations + harshly rigid behavior and beliefs + tendency to be self-critical—rigid rule-based behavior and avoidance of social, professional unacceptability—passive-aggressive behaviors

Figure 11.7. Characteristics of Obsessive-Compulsive Personality Disorder.

Case Example: Mr. Q

Mr. Q is a 37-year-old male business executive who wanted to begin a course of psychotherapy because his "whole world was closing in." He gave a history of longstanding feelings of dissatisfaction with his marriage, which had worsened in the past two years. He described his wife's increasing demands for time and affection from him, which he believed was a weakness she had. His professional life also had become conflicted when his partner of ten years wanted to expand their accounting firm to another city. Mr. Q believed this proposal was fraught with dangers and had come to the point of selling out his share of the business to his partner. He knew he had to make some decisions about his marriage and his business but found himself unable to do so. He hoped therapy would help with these decisions. He presented as neatly dressed in a conservative three-piece gray suit. His posture was rigid and he spoke in a formal and controlled tone with constricted affect. His thinking was characterized by preoccupation with details and was somewhat circumstantial.

The reader is referred to the Case of Mrs. A, one of Adler's (1969) most famous, for a detailed description and formulation of the Obsessive-Compulsive Disorder. It so happened that Mrs. A manifested a moderately severe borderline personality disorder.

PARANOID PERSONALITY DISORDER

DSM-IV Description and Criteria

Paranoid personalities are aloof, emotionally cold individuals who display unjustified suspiciousness, hypersensitivity, jealously, and a fear of intimacy. In addition, they can be grandiose, rigid, contentious, and litigious. Because of their hypersensitivity to criticism and tendency to project blame on others, they tend to lead isolated lives and are often disliked by others. Millon (1981) conceived of the Paranoid Personality Disorder as a pathological syndromal continuation of the Narcissistic Personality Disorder, the Antisocial Personality Disorder, or the Obsessive-Compulsive Personality Disorder. As a result, the clinical presentation of the paranoid personality takes on characteristics of these three respective precursors.

DSM-IV criteria for the Paranoid Personality Disorder are noted in Table 11.9 (American Psychiatric Association, 1994, pp. 637–638).

TABLE 11.9
Diagnostic criteria for 301.0 Paranoid Personality Disorder

A. A pervasive distrust and suspiciousness of others such that their motive are interpreted as malevolent, beginning by early adulthood and present in a variety of contexts, as indicated by four (or more) of the following:

(1) suspects, without sufficient basis, that others are exploiting, harming, or deceiving him or her

(2) is preoccupied with unjustified doubts about the loyalty or trustworthiness of friends or associates

(3) is reluctant to confide in others because of unwarranted fear that the information will be used maliciously against him or her

(4) reads hidden demeaning or threatening meanings into benign remarks or events

(5) persistently bears grudges, i.e., is unforgiving of insults, injuries, or slights

(6) perceives attacks on his or her character or reputation that are not apparent to others and is quick to react angrily or to counterattack

(7) has recurrent suspicions, without justification, regarding fidelity of spouse or sexual partner

B. Does not occur exclusively during the course of Schizophrenia, a Mood Disorder With Psychotic Features, or another Psychotic Disorder and is not due to the direct physiological effects of a general medical condition.

Note: If criteria are met prior to the onset of Schizophrenia, add "Premorbid," e.g., "Paranoid Personality Disorder (Premorbid)."

From *Diagnostic and Statistical Manual of Mental Disorders, Fourth Edition* (DSM-IV). Copyright © 1994 by American Psychiatric Association. Reprinted with permission.

Clinical Presentation

The Paranoid Personality Disorder is characterized by the following behavior interpersonal styles, cognitive style, and emotional style.

Behaviorally, paranoid individuals are resistive of external influences. They tend to be chronically tense because they are constantly mobilized against perceived threats from their environment. Their behavior also is marked by guardedness, defensiveness, argumentativeness, and litigiousness. Interpersonally, the tend to be distrustful, secretive, and isolative. They are intimacy-avoiders by nature and repudiate nurturant overtures by others.

Their cognitive style is characterized by mistrusting preconceptions. They carefully scrutinize every situation encountered and scan the environment for "clues" or "evidence" to confirm their preconceptions rather than objectively focus on data. Thus, although their perception may be accurate, their judgment often is not. The paranoid personalities' prejudices mold the perceived data to fit their preconceptions. Thus, they tend to disregard evidence that does not fit their preconceptions. When under stress their thinking can take on a conspiratorial or even delusional flavor. Their hypervigilance and need to seek evidence to confirm their beliefs lead them to have a rather authoritarian and mistrustful outlook on life.

The affective style of the paranoid personalities is characterized as cold, aloof, unemotional, and humorless. In addition, they lack deep sense of affection, warmth, and sentimentality. Because of their hypersensitivity to real or imagined slights and their subsequent anger at what they believe to be deceptions and betrayals, they tend to have few, if any, friends. The two emotions they experience and express with some depth are anger and intense jealousies.

Developmental and Etiological Factors

The following biopsychosocial formulations may be helpful in understanding how the paranoid personality disorder is likely to have developed.

Biologically, a low threshold for limbic system stimulation and deficiencies in inhibitory centers seem to influence the behavior of the paranoid personality. The underlying temperament can best be understood in terms of the subtypes of the paranoid disorder. Each of three subtypes are briefly described in terms of their underlying temperament and correlative parental and environmental factors. In the narcissistic type, a hyperresponsive temperament and precociousness, parental overevaluation and indulgence as well as the individual's sense of grandiosity and self behavior probably result in deficits in social interest and limited interpersonal skills. The antisocial type of the paranoid personality is likely to possess a hyperresponsive temperament. This plus harsh parental treatment probably contributes to the impulsive, hedonistic, and aggressive style of this type. In the compulsive type, the underlying temperament may have been anhedonic. This, as well as parental rigidity and overcontrol, largely accounts for the development of this type. Finally, a less common variant is the paranoid passive-aggressive type. As infants, these individuals usually demonstrated the "difficult child" temperament, and later temperament characterized by affective irritability. This plus parental inconsistency probably accounts in large part for the development of this type (Millon, 1981).

Psychologically, paranoid individuals view themselves, others, the world, and life's purpose in terms of the following themes. They tend to view themselves by some variant of the theme: "I'm special and different. I'm alone and no one likes me because I'm better than others." Life and the world are viewed by some variant of the theme: "Life is unfair, unpredictable and demanding. It can and will sneak up and harm you when you are least expecting it." As such, they are likely to conclude, "Therefore, be wary, counterattack, trust no one, and excuse yourself from failure by blaming others." The most common defensive mechanism associated with the paranoid disorder is projection.

Socially, predictable patterns of parenting and environmental factors can be noted for the Paranoid Personality Disorder. For all the subtypes the parental injunction appears to be "You're different. Don't make mistakes." Paranoid personality disordered individuals tend to have perfectionistic parents who expose these children to specialness training. This plus the parental style that has been articulated for the subtypes of the disorder and parental criticism leads to an attitude of social isolation and hypervigilant behavior. To make sense of the apparent contradiction between being special and being ridiculed, the children creatively conclude that the reason they are special and that no one likes them is because they are better than other people. This explanation serves the purpose of reducing their anxiety and allowing them to develop some sense of self and belonging.

This paranoid pattern is confirmed, reinforced, and perpetuated by the following individual and systems factors: A sense of specialness, rigidity, attributing malevolence to others, blaming others, and misinterpreting motives of others leads to social alienation and isolation, which further confirms the individual's persecutory stance. Figure 11.8 are lists these characteristics of the Paranoid Personality Disorder.

Treatment Considerations

Included in the differential diagnosis of the Paranoid Personality Disorder are the following Axis II personality disorders: Antisocial Personality Disorder, Narcissistic Personality Disorder, Obsessive-Compulsive Personality Disorder, and Passive-Aggressive Personality Disorder. The most common Axis I syndromes associated with the Paranoid Personality Disorder are Generalized Anxiety Disorder, Panic Disorder, and Delusional Disorder. If a Bipolar Disorder is present, an irritable manic presentation is likely. Decompensation into Schizophrenic reaction is likely. The Paranoid and Catatonic subtypes of Schizophrenia are most commonly noted.

1. Behavioral Appearance:	Guarded and defensive hypervigilant; Resistive of external influence; Chronically tense because constantly mobilized against perceived threats; Restricted affect, jealous
2. Interpersonal Behavior:	Distrustful, secretive, isolate, blaming; Provocative, counterattack, hypersensitive
3. Cognitive Style:	Mistrusting, preconceptions—tendency to disregard evidence to the contrary; May become conspiratorial or delusional under stress
4. Feeling Style:	Aloof, humorless, easily provoked
5. Parental Injunction/ Environment:	"You're different. Don't make mistakes." Perfectionistic parent(s) + specialness training + parental/peer criticalness—isolation + vigilant attitude
6. Biological/Temperament:	Low threshold for limbic system stimulation and deficient inhibitory centers Narcissistic type: hyperresponsive temperament + parental overevaluation and indulgence— deficits in cooperation and interpersonal skills + grandiosity/selfishness, aggressiveness style Compulsive type: anhedonic temperament + parental rigidity and control Passive-Aggressive type: affective irritability + parental inconsistency
7. Self-view:	"I'm so special and different. I'm alone and no one likes me because I'm better than others."
8. Worldview:	"Life is unfair, unpredictable, and demanding. It will sneak up and harm you. Therefore, be wary, counteract, trust no one, and excuse yourself from failure by blaming others."
9. Self & System Perpetuant:	Rigidity and interpersonal suspicion + blaming and attributing malevolent motives to others— social alienation and isolation—confirmation of persecutory stance

Figure 11.8.   Characteristics of Paranoid Personality Disorder.

Until recently, the prognosis for treatment of the Paranoid Personality Disorder was considered guarded. Today more optimism prevails in achieving these goals of treatment: increasing the benignness of perception and interpretation of reality, and increasing trusting behavior. The social skills training intervention described by Turkat (1985) focuses on changing the internal processes of attention, processing, response emission, and feedback from a pathological to a nonpathological mode of perceiving and thinking. In essence, individuals are taught how to reduce their perceptual scanning and attending to inappropriate cues to attending to more appropriate cues; and rather than using idiosyncratic logic and misinterpretation to process their cues, they learn to use more common logic and a more benign interpretation of cues. In so doing they are able to respond in a more socially graceful fashion and are more likely to interpret feedback, including criticism, as constructive. This social skills intervention approach can be combined with insight-oriented therapy to achieve positive therapeutic outcomes. Medication, particularly lower dose neuroleptics, has been shown useful for decreasing anxiety secondary to loss of control (Reid, 1989).

Case Example: Mr. Z

Mr. Z is a 59-year-old male referred for psychiatric evaluation by his attorney to rule out a treatable psychiatric disorder. Mr. Z had entered into five lawsuits in the past two and one-half years. His attorney believed that each suit was of questionable validity. Mr. Z was described as an unemotional, highly controlled male who was now suing a local men's clothing store "for conspiring to deprive me of my consumer rights." He contends that the store manager had consistently issued bad credit reports on him. The consulting psychiatrist elicited other examples of similar concerns. Mr. Z had long distrusted his neighbors across the street and regularly monitors their activity since one of his garbage cans disappeared two years ago. Mr. Z took an early retirement from his accounting job one year ago because he could not get along with his supervisor, whom he believed was faulting him about his accounts and paperwork. Mr. Z contends he was faultless. On examination, Mr. Z's mental status is unremarkable except for constriction of affect and for a certain hesitation and guardedness in his response to questions.

BORDERLINE PERSONALITY DISORDER

DSM-IV Description and Criteria

Individuals with borderline personalities present with a complex clinical picture including diverse combinations of anger, anxiety, intense and labile affect,

and brief disturbances of consciousness such as depersonalization and dissociation. In addition, their presentation includes chronic loneliness, a sense of emptiness, boredom, volatile interpersonal relations, identity confusion, and impulsive
behavior that can include self-injury or self-mutilation. Stress can even precipitate
a transient psychosis. The borderline personality is a heterogeneous diagnosis
that may be related to schizophrenia or the mood disorders. This personality
disorder remains controversial and first appeared in DSM-III. Some conceptualize
this disorder as a level of personality organization rather than as a specific
personality disorder (American Psychiatric Association, 1987).

DSM-IV criteria for the Borderline Personality Disorder are noted in Table
11.10 (American Psychiatric Association, 1994, p. 645).

Clinical Presentation

The borderline personality is characterized by the following behavior and
interpersonal styles, cognitive style, and emotional style.

Behaviorally, borderlines are characterized by physically self-damaging acts
such as suicide gestures, self-mutilation, or the provocation of fights. Their social
and occupational accomplishments are often less than their intelligence and ability
warrant. Of all the personality disorders, they are more likely to have irregularities
of circadian rhythms, especially of the sleep-wake cycle. Thus, chronic insomnia
is a common complaint.

Interpersonally, borderlines are characterized by their paradoxical instability;
that is, they fluctuate quickly between idealizing and clinging to another individual
to devaluing and opposing that individual. They are exquisitely rejection-sensitive
and experience abandonment depression following the slightest of stressors.
Millon (1981) considered separation anxiety as a primary motivator of this personality disorder. Interpersonal relationships develop rather quickly and intensely, yet
their social adaptiveness is rather superficial. They are extraordinarily intolerant of
being alone and they go to great lengths to seek out the company of others
whether in indiscriminate sexual affairs, late night phone calls to relatives and
recent acquaintances, or late-night visits to hospital emergency rooms with a
host of vague medical and/or psychiatric complaints.

Their cognitive style is described as inflexible and impulsive (Millon, 1981).
Inflexibility of their style is characterized by rigid abstractions that easily lead
to grandiose, idealized perceptions of others, not as real people, but as personifica-
tions of "all good" or "all bad" individuals. They reason by analogy from past

TABLE 11.10
Diagnostic criteria for 301.22 Schizotypal Personality Disorder

A. A pervasive pattern of social and interpersonal deficits marked by acute discomfort with, and reduced capacity for, close relationships as well as by cognitive or perceptual distortions and eccentricities of behavior, beginning by early adulthood and present in a variety of contexts, as indicated by five (or more) of the following:

(1) ideas of reference (excluding delusions of reference)

(2) odd believes or magical thinking that influences behavior and is inconsistent with subcultural norms (e.g., superstitiousness, belief in clairvoyance, telepathy, or "sixth sense"; in children and adolescents, bizarre fantasies or preoccupations)

(3) unusual perceptual experiences, including bodily illusions

(4) odd thinking and speech (e.g., vague, circumstantial, metaphorical, overelaborate, or stereotyped)

(5) suspiciousness or paranoid ideation

(6) inappropriate or constricted affect

(7) behavior or appearance that is odd, eccentric, or peculiar

(8) lack of close friends or confidants other than first-degree relatives

(9) excessive social anxiety that docs not diminish with familiarity and tends to be associated with paranoid fears rather than negative judgments about self

B. Does not occur exclusively during the course of Schizophrenia, a Mood Disorder With Psychotic Features, another Psychotic Disorder, or a Pervasive Developmental Disorder

Note: If criteria are met prior to the onset of Schizophrenia, add "Premorbid" e.g., "Schizotypal Personality Disorder (Premorbid)."

From *Diagnostic and Statistical Manual of Mental Disorders, Fourth Edition* (DSM-IV). Copyright © 1994 by American Psychiatric Association. Reprinted with permission.

experience and thus have difficulty reasoning logically and learning from past experiences and relationships. Because they have an external locus of control, the borderlines usually blame others when things go wrong. By accepting responsibility for their own incompetence, borderlines believe they would feel even more powerless to change circumstances. Accordingly, their emotions fluctuate between hope and despair because they believe that external circumstances are well beyond their control (Shulman, 1982). Their cognitive style is also marked by impulsivity, and just as they vacillate between idealization and devaluation of others, their thoughts shift from one extreme to another: "I like people, no I don't like them"; "Having goals is good, no it's not"; "I need to get my life together, no I can't, it's hopeless." This inflexibility and impulsivity complicate the process of identity formation. Their uncertainty about self-image, gender identity, goals, values, and career choice reflects this impulsive and flexible stance. Gerald Adler (1985) suggested that borderlines have an underdeveloped evocative memory, such that they have difficulty recalling images and feeling states that could structure and soothe them in times of turmoil. Their inflexibility and impulsivity are further noted in their tendency toward "splitting." Splitting is the inability to synthesize contradictory qualities, such that the individual views others as all good or all bad and utilizes "projective identification," that is, attributing his or her own negative or dangerous feelings to others. Their cognitive style is further characterized by an inability to tolerate frustration. Finally, micropsychotic episodes can be noted when these individuals are under a great deal of stress. These are ill-defined, strange thought processes especially noted in response to unstructured rather than structured situations and may take the form of derealization, depersonalization, intense rage reactions, unusual reactions to drugs, and intense brief paranoid episodes. Because of difficulty in focusing attention and subsequent loss of relevant data, borderlines also have a diminished capacity to process information.

The emotional style of individuals with this disorder is characterized by marked mood shifts from a normal or euthymic mood to a dysphoric mood. In addition, inappropriate and intense anger and rage may easily be triggered. On the other extreme are feelings of emptiness, a deep "void," or boredom.

Developmental and Etiological Features

The following biopsychosocial formulation may be helpful in understanding how the borderline personality pattern is likely to have developed.

Biologically, borderlines can be understood in terms of the three main subtypes: (a) borderline-dependent, (b) borderline-histrionic, and (c) borderline passive-aggressive. The temperamental style of the borderline-dependent type is that of the passive infantile pattern (Millon, 1981). Millon hypothesized that low autonomic nervous system reactivity plus an overprotective parenting style facilitates restrictive interpersonal skills and a clinging relational style. On the other hand, the histrionic subtype was more likely to have a hyperresponsive infantile pattern. Thus, because of high autonomic nervous system reactivity and increased parental stimulation and expectations for performance, the borderline-histrionic pattern was likely to result. Finally, the temperamental style of the passive-aggressive borderline was likely to have been the "difficult child" type noted by

Thomas and Chess (1977). This pattern plus parental inconsistency marks the affective irritability of the borderline passive-aggressive personality.

Psychologically, borderlines tend to view themselves, others, the world, and life's purpose in terms of the following themes. They view themselves by some variant of the theme: "I don't know who I am or where I'm going." In short, their identity problems involve gender, career, loyalties, and values whereas their self-esteem fluctuates with each thought or feeling about their self-identity. Borderlines tend to view their world with some variant of the theme: "People are great, no they are not"; "Having goals is good, no it's not"; or "If life doesn't go my way, I can't tolerate it." As such they are likely to conclude "Therefore keep all options open. Don't commit to anything. Reverse roles and vacillate thinking and feelings when under attack." The most common defense mechanisms utilized by the Borderline Personality Disordered individuals are regression, splitting, and projective identification.

Socially, predictable patterns of parenting and environmental factors can be noted for the Borderline Personality Disorder. Parenting style differs depending on the subtype. For example, in the dependent subtype, overprotectiveness characterizes parenting whereas, in the histrionic subtype, a demanding parenting style is more evident, and an inconsistent parenting style is more noted in the passive-aggressive subtype. But because the borderline personality is a syndromal elaboration and deterioration of the less severe Dependent, Histrionic, or Passive-Aggressive Personality Disorders, the family of origin in the borderline subtypes of these disorders is likely to be much more dysfunctional, increasing the likelihood the child will have learned various self-defeating coping strategies. The parental injunction is likely to have been, "If you grow up and leave me, bad things will happen to me (parent)."

This borderline pattern is confirmed, reinforced, and perpetuated by the following individual and systems factors: Diffuse identity, impulsive vacillation, and self-defeating coping strategies lead to aggressive acting out, which leads to more chaos, which leads to the experience of depersonalization, increased dysphoria, and/or self-mutilation to achieve some relief. This leads to further reconfirmation of their beliefs about self and the world as well as reinforcement of the behavioral and interpersonal patterns. Characteristics of this disorder are summarized in Figure 11.9.

Treatment Considerations

Included in the differential diagnosis of the Borderline Personality Disorder are these other Axis II personality disorders: Passive-Aggressive Personality

1.	Behavioral Appearance:	"Hemophiliacs" of emotion; Resentful, impulsiveness, acting out; Helpless, dysphoric, empty "void"; Irregular circadian rhythms (sleep-wake, etc.)
2.	Interpersonal Behavior:	Paradoxical (idealizing and clinging vs. devaluing and oppositional); Rejection sensitivity (abandonment depression); Separation anxiety as prime motivator; Role reversal
3.	Cognitive Style:	Inflexible, rigid abstracting, grandiosity and idealization, splitting; Reason by analogy, don't learn from experience; External locus of control, blaming; Poorly developed evocative memory
4.	Feeling Style:	Extreme liability of mood and affect
5.	Parental Injunction/ Environment:	"If you grow up, bad things will happen to me (parent)." Overprotective or demanding or inconsistent patenting
6.	Biological/ Temperament:	Dependent type: passive infantile pattern—low autonomic nervous system reactivity + parental overprotectiveness—restrictive interpersonal skills and pleasing, clinging style parental stimulation and demand for child to "perform." Passive Aggressive type: "difficult" infantile pattern—affective irritability + parental inconsistency
7.	Self-view:	"I don't know who I am or where I'm going." Identity problems involving gender, career, loyalties, and values. Self-esteem fluctuates with current emotion.
8.	Worldview:	"People are great, no they're not. Having goals is good, no it's not. If life doesn't go my way, I can't tolerate it. Therefore, keep all options open. Don't commit to anything. Reverse roles when under attack."
9.	Self & System Perpetuant:	Self-defeating coping strategies, particularly reversal" (i.e., from submissiveness to aggressiveness)—more chaos—depersonalization, brief psychotic episodes, increased dysphoria and/or self-mutilation to achieve relief—reconfirmation

Figure 11.9. Characteristics of Borderline Personality Disorder.

Disorder, Histrionic Personality Disorder, Dependent Personality Disorder, and the Schizotypal Personality Disorder. The most common Axis I syndromes associated with the personality disorder are Generalized Anxiety Disorder, Panic Disorder, and Dysthymia. In addition, other syndromes may be Brief Reactive Psychoses, Schizoaffective Disorder, Hypochondriasis, or the Dissociative Disorders, especially Psychogenic Fugue.

The Borderline Personality Disorder is becoming one of the most common Axis II presentations seen in both the public sector and in private practice. It can be among the most difficult and frustrating conditions to treat. Clinical experience suggests that it is important to assess the individual for overall level of functioning and for subtype. The higher functioning borderline-dependent personality has a higher probability for collaborating in psychotherapeutic treatment than the lower functioning borderline passive-aggressive personality. Higher functioning borderlines possibly may be engaged in insight-oriented psychotherapy without undue regression and acting out. Masterson (1976) suggested that rather than using traditional interpretation methods with borderlines, the therapist should utilize confrontational statements in which borderlines are asked to look at their behavior and its consequences.

With lower functioning patients, treatment goals may be much less limited. Here, the focus of treatment would be on increasing day-to-day stable functioning. Treatment strategies and methods are varied for the treatment of borderline subtypes. Strategies range from long-term psychotherapy, lasting two or more years, to rather short-term formats in which sessions are scheduled biweekly or even monthly, except when crises arise. Task-oriented group therapy has been shown to be a useful adjunct as well as a primary treatment in and of itself (Linehan, 1987). The rationale for group therapy with the borderline is that the intense interpersonal relationship that forms between the therapist and the patient and serves as the nidus for so much acting out is effectively reduced in a group format. Whether seen individually or in a group format, the therapist does well to clearly articulate treatment limits and objectives. For the lower functioning borderlines and the histrionic and passive-aggressive subtypes, a particularly useful procedure is to employ a written treatment contract. Medications are often used with borderline patients and are particularly aimed at target symptoms such as insomnia, depression, or anxiety disorders. Low dose neuroleptics are often utilized as well.

Case Example: Mr. T

Mr. T is a 29-year-old unemployed male who was referred to the hospital emergency room by his therapist at a community mental health center after two days of sustained suicidal gestures. He appeared to function adequately until his senior year in high school, when he became preoccupied with Transcendental Meditation. He had considerable difficulty concentrating during his first semester of college and seemed to focus most of his energies on finding a spiritual guru. At times, massive anxiety and feelings of emptiness swept over him, which he found would vanish suddenly if he lightly cut his wrist enough to draw blood. He had been in treatment with his current therapist for 18 months and became increasingly hostile and demanding as a patient, whereas earlier he had been quite captivated with his therapist's empathy and intuitive sense. Lately, his life seemed to center on these twice-weekly therapy sessions. Mr. T's most recent suicidal thoughts followed the therapist's disclosure that he was moving out of the area.

SCHIZOTYPAL PERSONALITY DISORDER

DSM-IV Description and Criteria

In addition to having features similar to that of the Schizoid Personality Disorder, the schizotypal disorder is characterized by eccentric behavior and peculiar thought content. Schizotypals describe strange intrapsychic experiences, think in odd and unusual ways, and are difficult to engage. Yet none of these features reach psychotic proportions. It has been suggested that the schizotypal personality is one of the schizophrenic spectrum disorders because schizophrenia occurs with increased frequency in family members of the schizotypal.

DSM-IV criteria for the Schizotypal Personality Disorder are noted in Table 11.11 (American Psychiatric Association, 1994, p. 654).

Clinical Presentation

The Schizotypal Personality Disorder is typically recognized by the following behavioral and interpersonal styles, cognitive styles, and emotional styles.

Behaviorally, schizotypals are noted for their eccentric, erratic, and bizarre mode of functioning. Their speech is markedly peculiar without being incoherent. Occupationally, they are inadequate, either quitting or being fired from jobs after short periods of time. Typically, they become drifters, moving from job to job and from town to town. They tend to avoid enduring responsibilities and in the process lose touch with a sense of social propriety.

TABLE 11.11
Diagnostic criteria for 301.83 Borderline Personality Disorder

---

A pervasive pattern of instability of interpersonal relationships, self-image, and affects, and marked impulsivity beginning by early adulthood and present in a variety of contexts, as indicate by five (or more) of the following:

(1) frantic efforts to avoid real or imagined abandonment. **Note:** Do not include suicidal or self-mutilating behavior covered in Criterion 5.

(2) a pattern of unstable and intense interpersonal relationships characterized by alternating between extremes of idealization and devaluation

(3) identity disturbance: markedly and persistently unstable self-image or sense of self

(4) impulsivity in at least two areas that are potentially self-damaging (e.g., spending, sex, substance abuse, reckless driving, binge eating). **Note:** Do not include suicidal or self-mutilating behavior covered in Criterion 5.

(5) recurrent suicidal behavior, gestures, or threats, or self-mutilating behavior

(6) affective instability due to a marked reactivity of mood (e.g., intense episodic dysphoria, irritability, or anxiety usually lasting a few hours and only rarely more than a few days)

(7) chronic feeling of emptiness

(8) inappropriate, intense anger or difficulty controlling anger (e.g., frequent displays of tempter, constant anger, recurrent physical fights)

(9) transient, stress-related paranoid ideation or severe dissociative symptoms

---

From *Diagnostic and Statistical Manual of Mental Disorders, Fourth Edition* (DSM-IV). Copyright © 1994 by American Psychiatric Association. Reprinted with permission.

Interpersonally, they are loners with few if any friends. Their solitary pursuits and social isolation may be the result of intense social anxiety that may be expressed with apprehensiveness. If married, their style of superficial and peripheral relating often leads to separation and divorce in a short period of time.

The cognitive style of schizotypals is described as scattered and ruminative and is characterized by cognitive slippage. Presentations of superstitiousness, telepathy, and bizarre fantasies are characteristic. They may describe vague ideas of reference and recurrent illusions of depersonalizing, derealizing experiences without the experience of delusions of reference, or auditory or visual hallucinations.

Their affective style is described as cold, aloof, and unemotional with constricted affect. They can be humorless and difficult individuals to engage in conversation probably because of their general suspicious and mistrustful nature. In addition, they are hypersensitive to real or imagined slights.

Developmental and Etiological Features

The following biopsychosocial formulation may be helpful in understanding how the Schizotypal Personality Disorder is likely to have developed.

This personality disorder was described by Millon (1981) as a syndromal extension or deterioration of the Schizoid or the Avoidant Personality Disorders. As such, a useful procedure is to describe the biological and temperamental features of both of these subtypes. The schizoid subtype of a schizotypal personality is characterized with a passive infantile pattern, probably resulting from low autonomic nervous system reactivity and parental indifference that led to impoverished infantile stimulation. On the other hand, the avoidant subtype is characterized by the fearful infantile temperamental pattern (Millon, 1981). This probably resulted from the child's high autonomic nervous system reactivity combined with parental criticalness and depreciation that was further reinforced by sibling and peer depreciation. Both subtypes of the schizotypal personality have been noted to have impaired eye tracking motions, which is a characteristic shared with schizophrenic individuals.

Psychologically, the schizotypals view themselves, others, the world, and life's purpose in terms of the following themes. They tend to view themselves by some variant of the theme: "I'm on a different wave length than others." They commonly experience being selfless, that is, they experience feeling empathy, estranged, and disconnected or dissociated from the rest of life. Their worldview is some variant of the theme: "Life is strange and unusual, and others have special magical intentions." As such, they are likely to conclude, "Therefore, observe caution while being curious about these special magical intentions of others." The most common defense mechanism utilized by them is undoing, the effort to neutralize "evil" deeds and thoughts by their eccentric, peculiar beliefs and actions.

Socially, predictable patterns of parenting and environmental factors can be noted for the Schizotypal Personality Disorder. The parenting patterns noted previously of the cold indifference of the schizoid subtype or the deprecating and derogatory parenting style and family environment of the avoidant subtype are noted. In both cases, the level of functioning in the family of origin then would be noted in the Schizoid Personality Disorder or the Avoidant Personality Disorder. Fragmented parental communications are a feature common to both subtypes of the Schizotypal Personality Disorder. The parental injunction is likely to have been "You're a strange bird." Figure 11.10 summarizes these characteristics of Schizotypal Personality Disorder.

Treatment Considerations

Included in the differential diagnosis of the Schizotypal Personality Disorder are three other Axis II personality disorders: Schizoid Personality Disorder, Avoidant Personality Disorder, and the Borderline Personality Disorder. The most common Axis I syndromes associated with Schizotypal Personality Disorder are the Schizophrenias, particularly the Disorganized, Catatonic and Residual types. Other disorders noted are the Anxiety Disorders, the Somatoform Disorders, and the Dissociative Disorders.

The Schizotypal Personality Disorder finds it very difficult to engage and remain in psychotherapeutic relationship. Rather than attempting personality restructuring, the realistic treatment goal for the schizotypal personality is to increase the individual's ability to function more consistently even though on the periphery of society. Some reports have been of utilizing long-term insight and dynamically-oriented therapies with the schizotypal. Those that have been successful report incorporating some psychoeducational or social skills training along with supportive psychotherapeutic methods. Reid (1989) noted that if these patients can remain in long-term treatment, they may be able to increase their ability to function more consistently and with less disease. Reid reported that homogeneous groups can occasionally be a useful adjunct to individual treatment. In terms of medication, low-dose neuroleptics have been found to be useful for the schizotypal personality even in the absence of psychotic features. Yet it should be noted that medication compliance is particularly a problem with the Schizotypal Personality Disorder.

Case Example: Ms. B

Ms. B is a 46-year-old single female who was referred to a community mental health clinic by her mother because Ms. B had no interests, friends, or outside activities and was considered by neighbors to be an "odd duck." Ms. B's father had recently retired, and because of a limited pension, the parents were having difficulty in making ends meet since Ms. B had been living with them for the past eight years after she had been laid off from an assembly line job

1.	Behavioral Appearance:	Eccentric, erratic, bizarre Speech: markedly peculiar but not incoherent Occupational: dropouts, drift from job to job
2.	Interpersonal Behavior:	Socially isolative, peripheral relationships; Intense social anxiety—apprehension or apathy Marriage: superficial relating—separation, divorce
3.	Cognitive Style:	"Cognitive slippage," scattered, ruminative; Magical thinking, superstitiousness Defense: undoing (neutralize "evil" deeds, thoughts)
4.	Feeling Style:	Hypersensitive, hostile, and aloof
5.	Parental Injunction/ Environmental Factors:	"You're a strange bird." Cold or derogatory family environment; Fragmented parental communications
6.	Biological/Temperament:	Schizoid types: passive infantile pattern— low autonomic reactivity RA's activity + impoverished infantile stimulation/parental indifference Avoidance type: fearful infantile pattern— hypersensitive RA's activity (+) parental/ peer deprecation; Impaired smooth (eye tracking) pursuit
7.	Self-view:	"I'm on a different wavelength from others." Experience of being "self-less," empty, estranged, depersonalization, dissociation
8.	Worldview:	"Life is strange and unusual and others have special magic intentions. Therefore, observe caution while being curious."
9.	Self & System Perpetuant:	Dependency training—social isolation—self-insulation which further reinforces social isolation and differentness

Figure 11.10.   Characteristics of Schizotypal Personality Disorder.

she had held for about 10 years. The patient readily admitted she preferred to be alone but denied that this was a problem for her. She believed that her mother was concerned about her because of what might happen to the patient after her parents' deaths. Ms. B was an only child who had graduated from high school with average grades but had never been involved in extracurricular activities while in school. She had never dated and mentioned she had a female friend whom she had not talked with in four years. Since moving back with her parents, she stayed in her room preoccupied with books about astrology and charting her astrological forecast. On examination, she was an alert, somewhat uncooperative female appearing older than her stated age, with moderately disheveled hair and clothing. Her speech was monotonal and deliberate. She achieved poor eye contact with the examiner. Her thinking was vague and tangential, and she expressed a belief that her fate lay in "the stars." She denied specific delusions or perceptual abnormalities. Ms. B's affect was constricted except for one episode of anger when she thought the therapist was being critical.

SUMMARY

Unlike the rest of the disorders surveyed in this book, the personality disorders are listed on Axis II of the Multiaxial system of DSM-IV. By definition, Axis II reflects personality structure rather than more acute symptomatology that would be assessed by Axis I criteria. The ten personality disorders of DSM-IV were described in terms of nine biopsychosocial variables: behavioral appearance, interpersonal behavior, cognitive style, feeling style, parental injunction, environmental factors, biological/temperament, self-view, worldview, and self and system perpetuants. The Adlerian formulation for each disorder, specific treatment goals and methods, along with a case example were provided for all ten disorders.

REFERENCES

Adler, A. (1935). The fundamental views of Individual Psychology. *International Journal of Individual Psychology, 1*(1), 5–8.

Adler, A. (1956). Problems in psychotherapy. *American Journal of Individual Psychology, 12*, 12–24.

Adler, A. (1969). *The case of Mrs A: The diagnosis of a life style* (2nd ed., with commentary by B. Shulman). Chicago: Alfred Adler Institute.

Adler, G. (1985). *Borderline psychopathology and its treatment*. New York: Jason Aronson.

American Psychiatric Association. (1987). *Diagnostic and statistical manual of mental disorders* (3rd ed., revised). Washington, DC: Author.

American Psychiatric Association. (1994). *Diagnostic and statistical manual of mental disorders* (4th ed.). Washington, DC: Author.

Burks, J., & Rubenstein, M. (1979). *Temperament styles in adult interaction: Applications to psychotherapy*. New York: Brunner/Mazel.

Feldman, L. (1982). Dysfunctional marital conflict: An integrative interpersonal-intrapsychic model. *Journal of Marital and Family Therapy, 8*, 417–428.

Grinspoon, L. (Ed.). (1982). The schizophrenic disorders. In *Psychiatric Update, Vol. 1*, 82–255. Washington, DC: American Psychiatric Press.

Jenike, M., Baer, L., & Minichiello, M. (1986). *Obsessive-compulsive disorder*. Littleton, MA: PSG.

Kohut, H. (1971). *The analysis of the self*. New York: International Universities Press.

Liebowitz, M., & Klein, D. (1979). Hysteroid dysphoria. *Psychiatric Clinics of North America, 2*, 555–575.

Linehan, M. (1987). Dialectical behavior therapy: A cognitive behavioral approach to parasuicide. *Journal of Personality Disorders, 1*(4), 328–333.

Masterson, J. (1976). *Psychotherapy of the borderline adult: A developmental approach*. New York: Brunner/Mazel.

Millon, T. (1981). *Disorders of personality: DSM-III Axis II*. New York: John Wiley and Sons.

Millon, T., & Everly G. (1985). *Personality and its disorders: A biosocial learning approach*. New York: John Wiley and Sons.

Mosak, H. (1954). The psychological attitude in rehabilitation. *American Archives of Rehabilitation Therapy, 2*, 9–10.

Mosak, H. (1968). The interrelatedness of the neurosis through central themes. *Journal of Individual Psychology, 24*(1), 67–70.

Mosak, H. (1979). Mosak's typology: An update. *Journal of Individual Psychology 35*(2), 92–95.

Mosak, H. (1988). Personality disorders. In *Course syllabus outline: Psychodynamics of psychopathology I and II*. Chicago: Alfred Adler Institute.

Reid, W. (1989). *The treatment of psychiatric disorders: Revised for the DSM-III-R*. New York: Brunner/Mazel.

Salzman, L. (1968). *The obsessive personality: Origins, dynamics and therapy*. New York: Science House.

Sheldon, W., Dupertius, C., & McDermott, E. (1954). *Atlas of men: A guide for somatotyping the adult male at all ages*. New York: Harper & Row.

Shulman, B. (1982). An Adlerian interpretation of the borderline personality. *Modern Psychoanalysis, 7*(2), 137–153.

Sperry, L. (1995). *Handbook of the diagnosis and treatment of the DSM-IV personality disorders*. New York: Brunner/Mazel.

Thomas, A., & Chess, S. (1977). *Temperament and development*. New York: Brunner/Mazel.

Thomas, A., & Chess, S. (1984). *Origins and evolution of behavior disorders*. New York: Brunner/Mazel.

Toman, W. (1961). *Family constellation: Theory and practice of a psychological game*. New York: Springer.

Turkat, I., & Maisto, S. (1985). Personality disorders: Application of the experimental method to the formulation and modification of personality disorders. In D.H. Barlow (Ed.), *Clinical handbook of psychological disorders* (pp. 502–570). New York: Guilford.

Chapter 12

THE CONCEPT OF NARCISSISM AND THE NARCISSISTIC PERSONALITY DISORDER

Len Sperry
Heinz L. Ansbacher

According to Greek mythology, Narcissus fell in love with his reflection as he gazed into a reflecting pond. Unable to tear himself away from his reflection, he died of languor. Although the story usually is told in this way, it omits the following larger context that is most significant from the Adlerian viewpoint as will be seen later. Echo, a beautiful nymph, loved Narcissus but failed to win him. All the other nymphs who loved him also were shunned by him. One nymph prayed that Narcissus might some time feel himself what it was to love and to be rejected. It is in response to this prayer that he was made to fall in love with his own image reflected in a pond, which led to his demise (Bulfinch, 1989).

The term narcissism apparently was introduced toward the end of the nineteenth century simultaneously by Paul Nacke and by Havelock Ellis. Freud first used the term in 1910. In 1925, Waelder (1960) detailed the "narcissistic personality." The "narcissistic personality disorder" received formal recognition as a clinical entity with its inclusion into DSM-III in 1980. Today, the concept of narcissism has been fully assimilated into common parlance aided by the mass media, advertising, and best sellers like *The Culture of Narcissism* (Lasch, 1978) and *The Self-seekers* (Restak, 1982). The "me generation" and Yuppies further popularized and reified narcissistic aphorisms such as "having it all," "have it your way," and "greed is good." Among mental health professionals, the concept of narcissism and discussion of treatment of the narcissistic personality have gained high visibility as witnessed by the spate of books, articles, and workshops on Self-Psychology and Narcissistic Disorders.

The designation of Self-Psychology and Narcissistic Disorders has become almost synonymous with the late psychoanalyst Heinz Kohut. Although Alfred Adler never used the term "narcissistic personality," his description of the neurotic personality is strikingly similar to that of a consensus of many contemporary writers (Ansbacher, 1985). Adler's psychology, which he proposed some 70 years ago, is strikingly similar to Kohut's self-psychology.

This chapter reviews the concept of narcissism and the Adlerian formulation of narcissism and narcissistic personality. Other formulations of this disorder and DSM-IV criteria also are reviewed. A case study concludes this discussion of the narcissistic personality.

CONCEPT OF NARCISSISM AND KOHUT'S SELF-PSYCHOLOGY

Narcissism can be described as an investment or concentration of energy or interest in the self. For Freud, narcissism refers to the withdrawal of libido and an investment in the self. In Kohut's thinking, narcissism implies the development of self-esteem through a relationship with a self-object. For Kohut, narcissism is normal and healthy. Furthermore, he believed narcissism has its own line of development separate from Freud's structural line of id, ego, and superego development (Kohut, 1971). Kohut believed that narcissism can be fixated at certain points, and, thus, has its own form of pathology requiring its own form of treatment (1977).

Kohut's Self-Psychology emphasized the structure and constituents of the self as well as the subjective conscious and unconscious experience of selfhood. He described the constituents of the self in terms of two poles: one from which emanates the basic strivings for power and recognition, and the other which maintains the guiding ideal. It is the arc of tension between the two poles that activates the individual's basic talents and skills. This view of self is remarkably similar to Adler's formulation detailed later in this chapter.

The core of Kohut's theory involves the experiential relationship between the self and the empathic "self-object." Self-object is Kohut's term for the child's partially fused view of self and others. It is the child's internal perception of persons in his environment who serve functions that, if development proceeds normally, later will be performed by the individual's own psychic structure. Kohut believed that a normal child grows up in an empathic-responsive environment peopled by others who are in tune with his or her psychological needs and wishes. As a result, the child experiences a merger with the all-powerful self-object. When the self-object is calm and collected, the child's needs, anxieties, and rage are calmed, such that he or she begins to experience the rudiments of a stable, cohesive self. Over the course of time, the child will experience disappointment and frustration or "empathic failure." To the extent that his or her "failure" does not exceed the child's capacity to manage it, maturation continues. But if the empathic failure occurs too early or too violently, the stability of the self is compromised, leading to loss of self-esteem and diminished capacity to function in the world. Kohut postulated that the self disorders, particularly the borderline and narcissistic personality disorders, result from early empathic failure on the part of the parents, particularly the mother. Repeated empathic failures result in a lack of cohesion in the child's sense of self. In adult life, the sequelae of these failures are typically rage, depression, substance abuse, splitting, projective identification, thrill-seeking, and sexual perversion. Kohut and his self-psychology colleagues agreed that treatment of narcissistic disorders is based on resolution of developmental deficits that interfere with the adult's capacity to deal with the frustrations of everyday life.

Kohut stressed the importance of the mother's mirroring and empathy out of which the infant and young child internalize a stable and cohesive sense of self. In Adler's self-psychology, the empathic/unempathic mother was not emphasized as much as the child's adaptiveness to his of her family environment.

Adler emphasized the child's initial adaptations to the significant persons in his or her environment, usually the parents. Adler focused on affective values in the parental response to the young child and the child's perception of the parent's response. When the child felt secure and loved, Adler believed the child felt worthwhile and a sense of belonging. When the child's feeling toward the parents reflected insecurity, the child experienced a sense of inferiority and would resort to neurotic safeguards to ward off inferiority feelings. This was Adler's formulation of the neurotic personality in general rather than of the narcissistic personality in particular.

Both Adler's and Kohut's formulations of self are radical departures from Freud's drive-reduction psychology. There are close similarities between Adler's and Kohut's formulations of self. Unfortunately, recognition of these similarities has not been forthcoming. In a somewhat obscure 1972 paper, Kohut does acknowledge some debt to Adler, and that was in regard to the concept of "organ inferiority" (Stepansky, 1983). Eagle (1984) criticized Kohut for failing to acknowledge the influences of predecessors. For instance, Eagle noted the striking parallels between Kohut and Carl Rogers on empathy but, like so many other commentators, failed to mention Kohut's parallels with Adler.

NARCISSISM AND INDIVIDUAL PSYCHOLOGY

Freud's paper "On Narcissism: An Introduction" (Freud, 1914/1949) published in 1914 was important as it marked the beginning of his ego psychology. Adler had challenged the basis of Freud's libidinal theory and notions of infant sexuality in his paper on "masculine protest" published in 1911 (Adler, 1911/1980). Freud's paper was his attempt to offer an alternative to Adler's masculine protest and to Jung's nonsexual libido.

For Adler, the masculine protest was the basic neurotic motive rather than the libidinal drive that Freud had promulgated. Freud criticized Adler's formulation saying that the masculine protest was "nothing other than fear of castration." Later, Freud faulted Adler for offering only an ego psychology and for basing masculine protest "on a social valuation." Instead, Freud proposed the concept of narcissism in which libido was directed toward the self as the basis of neurosis. This revised formulation marked the beginning of Freudian ego psychology.

Adler's concept of masculine protest is poorly understood by many. Even authoritative reference works have limited or misguided definitions. Typically, masculine protest is described as a compensatory process by which women overcome their feelings of inferiority by striving to gain the power of men (Walrond-Skinner, 1986). Adler indicated that masculine protest was tied to self-esteem. In 1912 he wrote, "The neurotic purpose is the enhancement of self-esteem, the simplest formula of which can be recognized in the exaggerated masculine protest. This formula, "I wish to be a real man," is the guiding fiction in every neurosis" (Adler, 1912/1917, pp. viii-ix). Masculine protest was a starting point in Adler's goal-oriented value psychology in which the self was central.

The term "masculine protest" in this broad sense was soon replaced by such terms as will to power, striving for an exaggerated personality ideal, superiority, conquest, security, perfection, completion, success as subjectively defined, or overcoming. All these are value terms denoting a movement from minus to plus toward enhancement of self-esteem or its preservation, an impetus that never ceases. They imply an actively striving individual, self, or ego rather than one dominated by some other "primary process." "Striving upward from below . . . represents the fundamental fact of our life. . . . Complementary to this, "The supreme law" of life is that "the sense of worth of the self shall not be allowed to be diminished" (Adler, in Ansbacher & Ansbacher, 1956, p. 358).

Freud made primary narcissism the basis of self-esteem and so gave the concept a positive connotation whereas previously it had been regarded negatively. In psychoanalytic circles, various forms of narcissism have been described: "normal," "primary," "secondary," "healthy," and "pathological." These different meanings of narcissism have been criticized by a number of psychoanalysts including Pulver (1970) and Dyrud (1983) as being of confusing and questionable meaning.

Adler's critique of psychoanalytic interpretations of narcissism predated the criticism of Balint and others. Adler maintained that the crucial feature in narcissism is not self-love; rather it is the exclusion of others. "In the conception of narcissism the most important part has been overlooked: the continuous exclusion of others, the narrowing of the sphere of action. This . . . signifies a lack of social interest." This lack in turn is to be attributed to a lack of self-confidence, "a feeling of weakness which originated from a feeling of inferiority. . . . This feeling seeks compensation through seemingly making the situation easier" (Adler, 1931/1979, p. 208).

The original Narcissus myth as described at the beginning if this chapter is quite in accord with Adler's understanding of the exclusion of others as the crucial part of narcissism, the myth presenting the fatal self-love of Narcissus as punishment for his exclusion of others.

Adler believed that the decisive basic difference between his psychology and that of Freud was that Freud starts with the assumption that by nature man only wants to satisfy his drives—the pleasure principle—and must, therefore, from the viewpoint of culture be regarded as completely "bad." By contrast, Adler held that "the indestructible destiny of the human species is social interest. In Individual Psychology this is the truth; in psychoanalysis it is a trick. Individual Psychology maintains that . . . the human being is inclined toward social interest, toward the good" (Adler, 1931/1979, p. 211).

NARCISSISTIC PERSONALITY DISORDER

The Narcissistic Personality Disorder (NPD) has been described variously by different authors. For Wolf (1988) and other followers of Kohut, the NPD is viewed as one of several "self disorders" in which there has been a significant failure of the self to achieve cohesion. Psychosis and Borderline States are self disorders in which serious damage to the self is either permanent or protracted, whereas the Narcissistic Behavior Disorders and NPD are less serious.

Wolf described the NPD as a self disorder in which damage to the self is temporary and restorable through appropriate psychoanalytic treatment and where the symptoms express the tensions associated with damage to the self or the tensions of autoplastic attempts to restore self-object functioning. He indicated that hypochondriasis, depression, and hypersensitivity are examples of autoplastic attempts to restore functioning.

Kernberg (1975, 1984) offered another psychoanalytic perspective on the NPD that is quite different from Wolf's or Kohut's. Kernberg believed that narcissism is not a separate line of development, as Kohut claimed, but an elaboration of psychosexual development and drive theory. Kernberg drew upon Freud and the object relations and development theories of Klein, Jacobson, Fairbairn, and Mahler to provide a systematic view of narcissism and the NPD. Kernberg concluded that narcissism is essentially pathological and includes the NPD within the wider category of the borderline personality disorder and conditions.

From a biopsychosocial perspective and based on psychometric data, Millon and Everly (1985) described persons with a narcissistic personality as passive-independent individuals who "possess an inflated sense of confidence and self-worth" (p. 73). Narcissistic personalities believe that they need merely be themselves to be secure and content. Their self-esteem is based on a blind assumption of superiority. Their behavior often is motivated by a desire to achieve the things they feel they deserve because of their "superiority." Millon and Everly (1985) described the NPD much less dysfunctionally than does DSM-IV. Millon also noted that the descriptions of the NPD in Kohut (1977) and Kernberg (1984) are different than DSM-IV. Finally, Millon and Everly (1985) noted that both Kernberg and Kohut described the NPD as a composite of both DSM-III-R Narcissistic and Passive Aggressive Personality Disorders.

From a psychiatric perspective, Ludwig (1986) described the NPD in terms of cognitive, behavioral, and emotional styles or features. The cognitive style of the NPD reflects an exaggerated sense of self-importance as well as unrealistic goals of power, wealth, and ability. It also reflects a sense of entitlement and self-deception or prevarication to preserve self-illusions. The behavioral style of the NPD suggests an individual who strives to be the center of attention, dominates conversations, and seeks admiration. Furthermore, this individual can be interpersonally exploitive, supercilious, and lacking humility. The emotional style of the NPD is characterized by a lack of empathy with others, ragefulness following

TABLE 12.1
Diagnostic criteria for 301.81 Narcissistic Personality Disorder

A pervasive pattern of grandiosity (in fantasy or behavior), need for admiration, and lack of empathy, beginning by early adulthood and present in a variety of contexts, as indicated by five (or more) of the following:

(1) has a grandiose sense of self-importance (e.g., exaggerates achievements and talents, expects to be recognized as superior without commensurate achievements)

(2) is preoccupied with fantasies of unlimited success, power, brilliance, beauty, or ideal love

(3) believes that he or she is "special" and unique and can only be understood by, or should associate with, other special or high-status people (or institutions)

(4) requires excessive admiration

(5) has a sense of entitlement, i.e., unreasonable expectations of especially favorable treatment or automatic compliance with his or her expectations

(6) is interpersonally exploitative, i.e., takes advantage of others to achieve his or her own ends

(7) lacks empathy is unwilling to recognize or identify with the feelings and needs of others

(8) is often envious of others or believes that others are envious of him or her

(9) shows arrogant, haughty behaviors or attitudes

From *Diagnostic and Statistical Manual of Mental Disorders, Fourth Edition* (DSM-IV). Copyright © 1994 by American Psychiatric Association. Reprinted with permission.

criticism, as well as feelings toward others that shift from overidealization to devaluation. Furthermore, affection will be largely directed toward the self, while projecting an aura of nonchalance, except when the individual's narcissistic confidence is shaken.

These criteria are quite similar to those of DSM-IV (American Psychiatric Association, 1994) where the NPD is described as a pervasive pattern of grandiosity in either behavior or fantasy as well as a lack of empathy and a hypersensitivity to others' criticism. DSM-IV also specifies that this disorder is present from early adulthood and is manifested in all aspects or contexts of the individual's life. Table 12.1 (American Psychiatric Association, 1994, p. 661) provides the DSM-IV criteria for this disorder.

Akhtar and Thompson (1982) offered an expanded view of the NPD that is a composite of DSM-III criteria, the object relations and self-psychology views of Kernberg and Kohut, and social and existential perspectives. They described the NPD as consisting of overt and covert deficits in six areas of functioning: (a) self-concept; (b) interpersonal relationships; (c) social adaptation; (d) ethics, standards, and ideals; (e) love and sexuality; and (f) cognitive style.

Shea (1988) noted that DSM-III-R criteria for NPD houses two rather distinctive types: the stable and unstable NPD. He described individuals with stable NPD as usually the product of a spoiled upbringing in which sharing was uncommon. As both children and adults, they find it difficult to view others as having needs, because they believe the world revolves around themselves. Their view of others may shift rapidly from idealizing others to devaluing them depending on how others meet or fail to meet their needs. According to Shea, stable narcissists are able to lead reasonably happy lives, especially if they are talented. Typically, they are difficult people to get along with. When they do not receive the adulation and subservience to which they believe they are entitled, they may pout, stomp about, or become depressed.

In contrast, unstable narcissists tend to inhabit a more hostile world. Because their sense of self is less developed and less cohesive, life is viewed as a constant threat. They experience themselves as worthless and constantly need to project a grandiose style. Few people are trusted, and bitterness becomes a way of life. They are wounded easily, and when this occurs they immediately react with narcissistic rage, projective identification, and cognitive distortions. Tantrums and rages are second nature to them. It is nearly impossible to please them, and they are prone to severe depressive episodes, substance abuse, and sexual perversion if their needs are not met. In addition, they may be prone to micropsychotic episodes. These unstable NPDs often are not successful in life since their self-absorbed behavior prevents advancement and their labile moods and anger make consistent work efforts difficult. At other times, they can demonstrate appropriate impulse control on the job or in public. This characterization of unstable NPD seems close to Wolf's description of the severe self disorders: the Psychotic and Borderline States. Shea's stable NPD more closely resembles Wolf's Narcissistic Personality and Behavior Disorders.

Finally, Bach (1985) described the NPD in terms of two types: Type I and II. Type I patients are well described by DSM-IV criteria. However, Type II patients present primarily with feelings of inferiority as well as insecurity, boredom, hypersensitivity, uncertainty, and chronic idealizations followed by disillusionment.

INDIVIDUAL PSYCHOLOGY FORMULATION OF THE NARCISSISTIC PERSONALITY

Alfred Adler described the neurotic personality as stemming from childhood experiences characterized by either overprotection or neglect, or a confusing admixture of both. From these experiences, the young child develops a set of psychological opinions about self, the world, and life goals. These opinions are reinforced and confirmed by the child's family and outer environment. These opinions help or hinder the person's ability to cope and master the tasks of life. Again, Adler did not describe the NPD per say. Yet as Ansbacher (1985) found, the prevailing view of NPD is reasonably consistent with Adler's general description of the neurotic personality. Ansbacher (1985) matched Akhtar and Thompson's (1982) description of deficits of functioning with Adler's description of the neurotic personality. Ansbacher notes that Adler's characterizations of overestimation of self, hypersensitivity, superiority complex, burning ambition, depreciation tendency, idealization, predestination complex, envy, prestige, pampered lifestyle, and lack of social interest are akin to DSM-III and other descriptions of the NPD.

The lifestyle opinions, or to use Shulman's term "convictions," can be expressed in terms of I am _____ (self-view); life is _____ (worldview); therefore _____ (life goal) (Shulman, 1973). For the NPD, the self-view is likely to be some variant of the theme: "I'm special and unique, and I'm entitled to extraordinary rights and privileges whether I've earned them or not." The worldview is likely to be a variant of the theme: "Life is a banquet table to be sampled at will. People owe me admiration and privilege." The life goal or pattern will be some variant of the theme: "Therefore, I'm entitled to have things my way, and I'll expect and demand this specialness. When I don't get what I demand, others will bear the brunt of my rage" (Sperry, 1990, p. 196).

TREATMENT CONSIDERATIONS

The goals of treatment of the NPD depend in large part on the expectations and needs of the patient. The treatment goal for reactive or superficial symptoms such as a reactive depression, marital discord, or acute anxiety symptoms typically are addressed with symptom-reduction methods. Treatment methods that salve and support the narcissistic injury are all that most NPDs want and expect. Often after symptoms have decreased, the narcissistic individual will leave or be unwilling to continue in longer-term psychotherapy. When longer-term therapy is indicated and desired by the patient, treatment goals will vary depending on the therapist's theoretical orientation. For psychoanalytically-oriented clinicians who emphasize the patient's narcissistic vulnerability and reaction to empathic failures, restructuring therapy is proposed. The goals of restructuring therapies are increased empathy for others and toward the self; decreased regression in the face of rebuff, failure, or separation; a capacity for flexible detachment and distancing oneself; the ability to feel gratified when working alone; the ability to give without personal gain; and the capacity to truly mourn an important loss (Nurnberg, 1984).

The Individual Psychology perspective tends to focus longer-term treatment of the NPD on the goals of increasing social interest specifically by reversing lifestyle convictions about entitlement, self-absorption, and specialness, and by developing alternatives to angry, rageful, and demanding behaviors. The Individual Psychologist might combine dynamic interpretations with cognitive restructuring and behavioral interventions. Among the behavioral interventions that have been shown effective with narcissistically-focused patients are empathy training, cognitive awareness training, and anger management (Feldman, 1982).

CASE EXAMPLE

Marilyn Monroe

Occasionally, the lives of public figures lend themselves well as case examples. Such is the life of Marilyn Monroe. She died of an overdose of sleeping pills at age 36. Ansbacher (1974) previously has demonstrated the application of Adlerian theory to understanding both the dynamics of Marilyn's life and untimely demise, the following being a brief summary of this analysis.

Marilyn was born to a lower-class mother in Los Angeles. Her mother previously had divorced and had two other children from that marriage, but these children were not in her custody. For much of her early years, Marilyn was raised in what appears to have been relatively stable foster homes. Yet her natural mother visited her weekly, and her maternal grandmother likewise visited Marilyn until the grandmother was committed to a mental institution. Later Marilyn's mother also was committed. In addition to this family history of unspecified psychiatric illness, an uncle reportedly committed suicide, further predisposing Marilyn to personality dysfunctioning.

As a child, Marilyn described herself as a tomboy who was quite good at athletics but uninterested and unskilled in feminine ways. Her earliest ambition was to be an actress, and her favorite pastime was movie matinees in which she would imagine herself on the big screen.

She became an actress after being discovered by an army photographer while she was working as a supervisor in a munitions factory during WWII. She became an overnight sensation, making 23 films before being dismissed by her studio for unjustified absences during filming. At the height of her career, she received 5,000 fan letters a week. Two months after her dismissal, and two years after her divorce from playwright Arthur Miller, her third husband, she took her life on August 5, 1962. She never had children, although she had two miscarriages. When under stress, she reportedly became sick to her stomach. Over the course of her career and up until the time of her death, she saw several psychoanalysts, with little apparent therapeutic success.

Colleagues described her as warm, likeable, good-humored, witty, and generous. Yet they also noted that she was self-absorbed much of the time, as well as having a bad temper, shown in rages and private furies.

Some of Marilyn's early recollections (ERs) have been reported in various biographical sketches. We will describe and analyze two of them as suggestive of her narcissistic personality.

> ER 1. She related the following childhood dream: "When I was maybe 6 or 7, I dreamed I was standing up in church without any clothes on, and all the people there were lying at my feet on the floor, and I walked naked, with a sense of freedom, being careful not to step on anyone."

Here we learn how her dream reflected her preoccupation with fantasies of unlimited success and beauty. She stands up like a goddess and everyone is lying at her feet in adoration, suggesting a grandiose self. Marilyn regarded herself as outside of this world. In the world she was just "poor little me" who should be protected and admired. But outside this world she could, at least her body could, be immortal (Ansbacher, 1974). Twenty-five years after her death, books of photo-essays of Marilyn continue to be published successfully as older generations worship and reminisce, and a new generation becomes enamored of her beguiling charm.

> ER 2. From the time she was 11 she remembered: "The whole world which was always closed to me suddenly opened up. Even the girls paid attention to me because they thought, "She is to be dealt with.' I had this long walk— 2 1/2 miles to school, 2 1/2 miles back—it was sheer pleasure. Every fellow honked his horn. . . . The world became friendly. All the newspaper boys when they delivered the paper would come around to where I lived. I used to hang

> from a limb of a tree, and I had a sort of a sweatshirt on. . . .
> Here they'd come with their bicycles and I'd get these free
> papers and the family liked that and they'd all pull their
> bicycles up around the tree and I'd be hanging. I was a little
> too shy to come down. I did get down to the curb . . . mostly
> listening. . . . I used to laugh so loud and so gay. . . . It was
> just this sudden freedom, because I would ask the boys,
> "Can I ride your bike now?' and they'd say, "Sure.' Then
> I'd go zooming, laughing in the wind, riding down the block,
> and they'd all stand around and wait till I came back, but I
> loved the wind; it caressed me."

Marilyn had become the center of constant attention and admiration. Further-more, her sense of entitlement is obvious: Girls must "deal with her," and every guy must honk his horn. This recollection also reflects her desire to be pampered. She receives newspapers and bicycle rides free. And without giving anything in return, she takes off on her own. That others would wait expectantly for her to return further suggests her pampered, special, and entitled status. There is no indication of Marilyn's ability to be empathetic. Rather than responding to her admirers, she "loved the wind; it caressed me."

Neither of these ERs, nor the other six reported by Ansbacher (1974), indicated that Marilyn believed life's goals could be obtained through cooperation and social interests. In the two ERs noted above, she is either above others (ER 1 and ER 2) or getting something for nothing (ER 2). With such underdeveloped social interest and elevated sense of narcissism, it is expected that Marilyn would have approached life situations from a self-centered viewpoint rather than one of mutuality.

In summary, Marilyn Monroe was an active person with extraordinary ambi-tion and little thought of others. Although she spent considerable time in foster care, there is no indication that she was abandoned by her mother or grandmother. In fact, she probably was a rather pampered child. She was rewarded by our society out of all proportion through her overnight stardom. Even after her death, her mystique appears actually to have increased. A view of biographical material and reported early recollections clearly suggests that she meets the DSM-IV criteria for Narcissistic Personality Disorder as well as the dynamic "criteria" for this disorder. Specifically, her view of herself, of the world, and of goals is similar to the views of other individuals who would be considered narcissistic personalities. In addition, biographical material on Marilyn suggests some Border-line and Dependent personality features or traits.

SUMMARY

The narcissistic personality has become one of the most prominent personality types today in the Western world. Psychoanalytic formulations of the narcissistic personality have evolved over the past several decades to parallel closely Adler's original description of the neurotic personality. Although not specifically using the term narcissistic personality, Adler's description of the neurotic personality and a recent Adlerian formulation are quite consistent with DSM-IV and other descriptions of the NPD.

BIBLIOGRAPHY

Sperry, L., & Carlson, J. (1993). *Psychopathology and psychotherapy: From diagnosis to treatment.* Muncie, IN: Accelerated Development.

Stepansky, P. (1983). *In Freud's shadow: Adler in context.* Hillsdale, NJ: The Analytic Press.

REFERENCES

Adler, A. (1911/1980). Masculine protest and a critique of Freud. In H.L. Ansbacher & R.R. Ansbacher (Trans. and Eds.), *Cooperation between the sexes.* New York: Jason Aronson.

Adler, A. (1912/1917). *The neurotic constitution: Outlines of a comparative individualistic psychology and psychotherapy.* (B. Glueck & J.E. Lind, Trans.). New York: Moffat, Yard.

Adler, A. (1931/1979). The difference between Individual Psychology and psychoanalysis. In H.L. Ansbacher & R.R. Ansbacher (Eds.), *Superiority and social interest.* New York: W.W. Norton.

Akhtar, S., & Thompson, T.A. (1982). Overview: Narcissistic personality disorder. *American Journal of Psychiatry, 139,* 12–20.

American Psychiatric Association. (1980). *Diagnostic and statistical manual of mental disorders* (3rd ed.). Washington, DC: Author.

American Psychiatric Association. (1987). *Diagnostic and statistical manual of mental disorders* (3rd ed., rev.). Washington, DC: Author.

American Psychiatric Association. (1994). *Diagnostic and statistical manual of mental disorders* (4th ed.). Washington, DC: Author.

Ansbacher, H.L. (1974). Goal-oriented Individual Psychology. In A. Burton (Ed.), *Operational theories of personality* (pp. 99–142). New York: Brunner/Mazel.

Ansbacher, H.L. (1985). The significance of Alfred Adler for the concept of narcissism. *American Journal of Psychiatry, 142*(2), 203–207.

Ansbacher, H.L., & Ansbacher, R.R. (Eds.). (1956). *The Individual Psychology of Alfred Adler*. New York: Harper & Row.

Bach, S. (1985). *Narcissistic states and the therapeutic process*. North Vale, NJ: Jason Aronson.

Bulfinch, T. (1989). *The age of fable or beauties of mythology* (rev. ed.). Philadelphia: David McKay.

Dyrud, J. (1983). Narcissism and nemesis. *Psychiatry, 46*, 106–112.

Eagle, M. (1984). *Recent developments in psychoanalysis: A critical evaluation*. New York: McGraw-Hill.

Feldman, L. (1982). Dysfunctional marital conflict: An integrative interpersonal-intrapsychic model. *Journal of Marital and Family Therapy, 8*, 417–428.

Freud, S. (1914/1949). On narcissism: Introduction. In *Complete psychological works, standard edition, volume 14*. London: Hogarth Press.

Kernberg, O. (1975). *Borderline conditions and pathological narcissism*. New York: Jason Aronson.

Kernberg, O. (1984). *Severe personality disorders: Psychotherapeutic strategies*. New Haven: Yale University Press.

Kohut, H. (1971). *The analysis of the self*. New York: International Universities Press.

Kohut, H. (1977). *The restoration of the self.* New York: International Universities Press.

Lasch, C. (1978). *The culture of narcissism.* New York: Norton.

Ludwig, A. (1986). *Principles of clinical psychiatry* (2nd ed.). New York: Free Press.

Million, T., & Everly, G.S. (1985). *Personality and its disorders.* New York: John Wiley & Sons.

Nurnberg, H. (1984). Survey of psychotherapeutic approaches to Narcissistic Personality Disorders. *Hillside Journal of Clinical Psychiatry, 6*(2), 204–220.

Pulver, S. (1970). Narcissism: The term and the concept. *Journal of American Psychoanalytic Association, 18,* 319–341.

Restak, R. (1982). *The self-seekers.* New York: Doubleday.

Shea, S.C. (1988). *Psychiatric interviewing.* Philadelphia: W.B. Saunders.

Shulman, B. (1973). Confrontation techniques in Adlerian Psychotherapy. In B. Shulman (Ed.), *Contributions to Individual Psychology* (pp. 196–206). Chicago: Alfred Adler Institute.

Sperry, L. (1990). Personality disorders: Biopsychosocial description and dynamics. *Individual Psychology, 46,* 193–202.

Stepansky, P. (1983). Perspectives on dissent: Adler, Kohut, and the idea of psychoanalytic research tradition. *The Annual of Psychoanalysis, XI.* New York: International Universities Press.

Waedler, R. (1960). *Basic theory of psychoanalysis.* New York: International Universities Press.

Walrond-Skinner, S. (1986). *A dictionary of psychotherapy.* London: Routledge & Kegan Paul.

Wolf, E. (1988). *Treating the self: Elements of clinical self psychology.* New York: Guilford Press.

Chapter **13**

SUBSTANCE ABUSE TREATMENT AND INDIVIDUAL PSYCHOLOGY

Judith Lewis
Jon Carlson

The use of psychoactive substances is so prevalent in our society that its negative effects have become impossible to overlook.

> Thirty-two million Americans smoke marijuana at least once a year; twenty million smoke it at least once a month. Annual cocaine users number over twelve million. Several million others take hallucinogens, stimulants, sedatives, and tranquilizers without medical supervision. And of course these figures are dwarfed by the number of people who use legal drugs, including alcoholic beverages (125 million) and tobacco cigarettes (70 million). (Polich, Ellickson, Reuter, & Kahan, 1984, p. v)

At least in the case of alcohol, an ample body of research indicates that there is a relationship between the general level of consumption among members of a population and the number of substance-related problems that can be expected to occur (Grant, 1986). Thus, the fact that substance use is widespread means that therapists are very likely to be confronted by drug- or alcohol-related problems with great frequency. Therapists need to understand, however, that there is a vast difference between substance *use* and substance *abuse* or *dependence*. The DSM-IV (American Psychiatric Association, 1994) guidelines make clear

353

that substance use is considered a disorder only when the individual demonstrates an inability to control his or her use despite the appearance of cognitive, behavioral, and physiologic symptoms. Mere use of a substance that modifies mood or behavior is not considered a substance abuse problem unless the user's functioning clearly is affected.

SUBSTANCE-RELATED DISORDERS: THE DSM-IV

The DSM-IV classifies the pathological use of substances in terms of two categories: Substance Dependence and Substance Abuse. Regardless of the specific substance used by individual clients, they are diagnosed as ***dependent*** only if at least three of the following seven symptoms have occurred at any time in the same 12–month period (American Psychiatric Association, 1994, p.181):

(1) tolerance, as defined by either of the following:
  (a) a need for markedly increased amounts of the substance to achieve intoxication or desired effect
  (b) markedly diminished effect with continued use of the same amount of the substance
(2) withdrawal, as manifested by either of the following:
  (a) the characteristic withdrawal syndrome for the substance (refer to Criteria A and B of the criteria sets for Withdrawal from the specific substances)
  (b) the same (or a closely related) substance is taken to relieve or avoid withdrawal symptoms
(3) the substance is often taken in larger amounts or over a longer period than the person intended
(4) there is a persistent desire or one or more unsuccessful efforts to cut down or control substance use
(5) a great deal of time spent in activities necessary to get the substance (e.g., visiting multiple doctors or driving long distances), use the substance (e.g., chain-smoking), or recover from its effects
(6) important social, occupational, or recreational activities given up or reduced because of substance use
(7) the substance use is continued despite knowledge of having a persistent or recurrent social, psychological, or physical problem that is likely to have been caused or exacerbated by the substance (e.g., current cocaine use despite recognition of cocaine-induced depression, or continued drinking despite recognition that an ulcer was made worse by alcohol consumption)

If the criteria for substance dependence are met, the disorder is categorized as *with physiological dependence* if symptoms include evidence of tolerance or withdrawal or *without physiological dependence* if there is no evidence of tolerance or withdrawal. Additionally, the course specifiers are included in the diagnosis. *Early partial remission* is used when the full criteria for dependence have not been met but one or more criteria for dependence have been met for at least 1 month, but less than 12 months. *Early full remission* is used when no criteria for dependence have been met for at least 1 month but less than 12 months. *Sustained partial remission* if the full criteria for dependence have not been met for a period of 12 months or longer; however, one or more criteria for dependence have been met. *Sustained full remission* is used if none of the criteria for dependence has been met at any time during a period of 12 months or longer. Finally the following specifiers apply if the individual is on agonist therapy or in a controlled environment: *On agonist* therapy is used if the individual is on a prescribed agonist medication and no criteria for dependence have been met for that class of medication for at least the past month (except tolerance to, or withdrawal from, the agonist), and *in a controlled environment* is used if the individual is in an environment where access to alcohol and controlled substances is restricted, and no criteria for dependence have been met for at least the past month (American Psychiatric Association, 1994, p. 180).

Substance Abuse is a diagnosis reserved for individuals who have never met the criteria for dependence for this class of substance but whose "maladaptive pattern of substance use lead[s] to clinically significant impairment or distress, as manifested by one (or more) of the following, occurring within a 12–month period" (American Psychiatric Association, 1994, pp. 182–183):

(1) recurrent substance use resulting in a failure to fulfill major role obligations at work, school, or home (e.g., repeated absences or poor work performance related to substance use; substance-related absences, suspensions, or expulsions from school; neglect of children or household)

(2) recurrent substance use in situations in which it is physically hazardous (e.g., driving an automobile or operating a machine when impaired by substance use)

(3) recurrent substance-related legal problems (e.g., arrests for substance-related disorderly conduct)

(4) continued substance use despite having persistent or recurrent social or interpersonal problems caused or exacerbated by the effects of the substance (e.g., arguments with spouse about consequences of intoxication, physical fights)

In the DSM-IV, nine classes of substances are associated with both abuse and dependence: alcohol; amphetamine or amphetamine-like; cannabis; cocaine;

hallucinogens; inhalants; opioids; phencyclidine or phencyclidine-like; and seda-tives, hypnotics, or anxiolytics. A tenth substance—nicotine—has a dependence diagnosis but not an abuse diagnosis. Each class of substances has its own code number.

303.90 Alcohol Dependence

305.00 Alcohol Abuse

Alcohol dependence and abuse are very common in the United States, with approximately 13% of the adult population having had one of these disorders at some time in their lives (American Psychiatric Association, 1994, p. 202). The behavior of people with either diagnosis may be characterized by a pattern of regular daily intake, of heavy drinking limited to weekends, or of periods of sobriety interspersed with binges. The diagnosis depends on the role of alcohol in the individual's life, the presence of symptoms of tolerance or withdrawal, and the degree of impairment in social and occupational functioning.

304.40 Amphetamine (or Amphetamine-Like) Dependence

305.70 Amphetamine (or Amphetamine-Like) Abuse

Substances in this category are nervous system stimulants generating patterns of dependence or abuse including either chronic, daily use or episodic use tending to be followed by unpleasant "crashes." Many amphetamine users also abuse alcohol or sedatives in an attempt to alleviate their symptoms. Psychological and behavioral changes include depression, irritability, anhedonia, anergia, and social isolation.

304.30 Cannabis Dependence

305.20 Cannabis Abuse

The DSM-IV suggests that Cannabis Dependence usually is characterized by daily, or almost daily, use of the substance (marijuana, hashish, or purified THC), whereas Cannabis Abuse involves episodic use with evidence of maladaptive behavior. Impairment tends to be less severe than is the case with alcohol, cocaine, and heroin; however cannabis often is used in combination with other substances. Cannabis Dependence may be characterized by such symptoms as lethargy, anhedonia, and attentional and memory problems.

304.20 Cocaine Dependence

305.60 Cocaine Abuse

The mode of administration is an important factor in Cocaine Dependence or Abuse. Smoking and intravenous administration tend to be associated with rapid progression to abuse or dependence, whereas intranasal administration tends to engender problems much more gradually. Over time, the individual tends to show a marked increase in tolerance so that vastly increased doses are needed to create the desired euphoria. Use may be chronic or episodic, with episodic binges being followed by very unpleasant crashes.

304.50 Hallucinogen Dependence

305.30 Hallucinogen Abuse

Hallucinogen Abuse is much more common than Hallucinogen Dependence. Use is generally episodic rather than chronic, with users taking "time out" to experiment with the substances and generally being successful in obtaining remission without treatment.

304.60 Inhalant Dependence

305.90 Inhalant Abuse

Individuals diagnosed as inhalant-dependent or abusing become intoxicated by inhaling volatile substances that are available commercially. The disorder frequently is found in children and adolescents and often is associated with other life problems and with abuse of other substances.

305.10 Nicotine Dependence

The DSM-IV does not include a classification of Nicotine Abuse because maladaptive use of nicotine is virtually always associated with dependence. Among Nicotine Dependent individuals, attempts to stop use are frequent and the relapse rate very high. Although there is little social or occupational impairment, there are, of course, serious physical complications associated with smoking.

304.00 Opioid Dependence

305.50 Opioid Abuse

This group of psychoactive drugs includes natural opioids, such as heroin and morphine, and synthetics that produce similar effects. Although some individuals may develop Opioid Dependence or Abuse based on use of prescription drugs, the more frequent pattern involves use of illegal opioids. In the United States, this problem may be exacerbated by long-term involvement in a drug-using subculture associated with violence and illegal activity.

304.50 Phencyclidine (or Phencyclidine-Like) Dependence

305.90 Phencyclidine (or Phencyclidine-Like) Abuse

The most common of this group of substances, PCP, has a euphoric effect and usually is used in episodic binges. Abuse or Dependence develops very quickly, but the presence of physical withdrawal symptoms or tolerance has not been proven.

304.10 Sedative, Hypnotic, or Anxiolytic Dependence

305.40 Sedative, Hypnotic, or Anxiolytic Abuse

Drugs in this group may be taken as treatment for anxiety or insomnia. Some individuals develop Abuse or Dependence patterns after increasing the frequency or dose of prescribed drugs. Others may use substances illegally in an attempt either to obtain euphoria or to balance the stimulant effects of cocaine or amphetamine. Heavy daily use and vastly increased tolerance are common.

304.80 Polysubstance Dependence

This diagnosis is reserved for individuals who have used at least three categories of psychoactive substances but with no single substance predominating. Furthermore, the Dependence criteria are met for substances as a group but not for any specific substance.

304.90 Other (or Unknown) Substance Dependence

305.90 Other (or Unknown) Substance Abuse

The Other (or Unknown) substance-related category is for classifying disorders associated with substances not listed above. Example of these substances include anabolic steroids, nitrite inhalants, nitrous oxide, catnip, betel nut, kava, and over-the-counter and prescription medications not otherwise covered by the categories above. In addition, this category may be used when the specific substance is unknown.

DIAGNOSIS OF THE DISORDER

Recognition of a client's pattern of substance use as pathological depends on the presence of a complex interaction of individual behaviors and social context. Diagnosis of the disorder thus requires an understanding of the individual's life situation; an awareness of the social, legal, and occupational difficulties associated with the substance use; and an assessment of the centrality of the drug to the individual's life goals. (Related nervous system effects of substance use are categorized as Substance-induced Organic Mental Disorders. For instance, Alcohol Intoxication, Alcohol Withdrawal Delirium, Alcohol Hallucinosis, and Dementia Associated with Alcoholism all are categorized as Alcohol-induced Organic Mental Disorders and described in a separate section.)

CONTRIBUTIONS OF ADLERIAN THOUGHT

The DSM-IV description of the range of symptoms that can be associated with substance dependence or abuse makes it clear that the diagnostic and treatment processes are complex. Traditionally, many substance abuse treatment providers have oversimplified their assessments, especially when dealing with alcohol dependence. Their erroneous belief that alcoholism is a unitary disease affecting all individuals in the same way frequently has led treatment providers to assume that, once a diagnosis has been made, a standardized course of treatment could be prescribed.

> The unitary concept assumes that there is a distinct class of persons who have the specific disease of alcoholism, who are substantively different from problem drinkers, heavy drinkers, prodromal alcoholics, and prealcoholics. . . . Most scientific authorities in the field of alcoholism now concur that the construct of alcoholism is most accurately construed as a multivariate syndrome. That is, there are multiple patterns of dysfunctional alcohol use that occur in multiple types of personalities, with multiple combinations of adverse consequences, with multiple prognoses, that may require different types of treatment interventions. (Pattison & Kaufman, 1982, p. 13)

Understanding the special needs and goals of a highly varied client population is equally important in the treatment of other drug problems. As Brill (1981) pointed out

> It is now generally accepted that nonmedical drug users comprise a great diversity of individuals who are drug dependent in different ways and degrees, use drugs to meet different needs, have different socio-economic backgrounds, are of both sexes, and represent a wide range of ages, races, and ethnic groups. No single treatment response will work for all: we need to match a particular approach to each individual. (pp. 5–6)

Effective treatment of substance use disorders can be provided only if therapists address these complexities, comprehending the social factors in substance abuse and using a holistic approach to understanding the individual client. Adlerian conceptualizations such as the social context of behavior, holism, encouragement, and teleology can provide a sorely needed alternative to "generic, global, diffuse, and nonspecific treatment of such singularly different dimensions of change as drinking behavior, psychological function, social interaction, physical function, and vocational competency" (Pattison, 1982, p. 225).

Social Context

Adlerians know that people cannot be understood in isolation from the social environment of which they are a part.

> Adler viewed man as embedded in the community of his fellowman, which furnishes both the resources and the problems of his life. . . . He knew that a person can overcome his fear of life only if he has a stable relationship to his human environment and that a person's all-powerful feeling of inferiority can be assuaged only when the voice of the community has begun to resound within him. (Rattner, 1983, p. 24)

One of the reasons that substance use disorders are difficult to treat is that, for many addicts, the "voice of the community" has long since been silenced. In fact, the community of fellow substance abusers may provide for them the only feeling of belonging that they know. Adolescent initiation into drug use has been termed a "group phenomenon" (Polich et al., 1984), as has maintenance of substance-abusing lifestyles among adults. Stephens (1985) described a "street addict subculture" with an accompanying role that may be highly valued by heroin-dependent individuals.

> The role is highly prominent (almost to the exclusion of all other roles), has a very great level of social support from other junkies, provides both intrinsic and extrinsic social and psychological rewards and can be enacted successfully in most social situations. (Stephens, 1985, p. 437)

Individuals who have become drug dependent spend more and more time with other addicts and learn to avoid non-substance-using friends and relatives.

Substance-abusing individuals frequently lack "the feeling of being a part of a larger social whole, the feeling of being socially embedded, the willingness to contribute in the communal life for the common weal" (Mosak, 1989, p. 66). Whether this lack of social interest is part of the etiology of the substance abuse problem or simply the result of years of drug use, the individual's recovery depends on his or her ability to rekindle the sparks of social reciprocity. Without *Gemeinschaftsgefuhl*, long-term sobriety becomes a difficult proposition at best. Among the most important factors affecting recovery from drug and alcohol problems are family and marital resources, positive work environments, and community support networks (Moos, Cronkite, & Finney, 1982). Encouraging the client to re-enter the social environment and find a place in it must be one of the therapist's first priorities.

Holism

Adlerian conceptualizations reject the reductionistic division of the individual into parts in favor of a holistic orientation that sees the person as a unity (Mosak, 1989). Similarly, the most realistic approaches to substance abuse recognize that "social, cultural, biological, and psychological factors interact reciprocally in both the etiology and the resolution of substance-related problems" (Lewis, Dana, & Blevins, 1988, p. 17). In addressing adolescent drug use, for instance

> Efforts toward prevention and rehabilitation aimed at changing adolescent alcohol and drug use may not be maximally effective if they are limited in focus to the use behavior itself or to an isolated domain of the adolescent's life. Instead, interventions should focus simultaneously on multiple domains. The multidimensional approach is also advisable because alcohol and drug use is intertwined with many issues and problems confronting adolescents, often to the extent that focusing solely on establishing the "cause and effect" relationship between substance abuse and life problems obscures the path to a successful intervention. (Pandina & Schuele, 1983, p. 971)

Some treatment providers mistakenly believe that they can address substance abuse problems in a vacuum, focusing solely on the drug issue and ignoring the interwoven concerns that make up the individual's life. In fact

> The client's substance abuse must also be considered in the context of other life problems, although not necessarily in terms of causality. Substance abuse tends to be associated with a variety of social, psychological, family, and financial problems. The counselor does not need to determine whether these problems are a cause of or a result of substance abuse. Each of a client's major concerns should be addressed as part of the counseling process under the assumption that a favorable outcome involves rehabilitation across several life domains." (Lewis et al., 1988, p. 11)

As Mejta (1988) has pointed out, "We need to think of a person who happens to have a drug problem, not a drug problem that happens to be expressed in this person."

Encouragement

The field of substance abuse treatment has a long history of controversy over the degree of responsibility that clients should assume for their problems and for the solution to those problems. The disease concept has helped clients understand that they should avoid self-blame for what were essentially involuntary behaviors (Fingarette, 1983). Unfortunately, the recognition that individuals' behavior was not under their own control may have brought with it an assumption of powerlessness.

> It is ironic that the major strength of the disease model, absolving the addict of personal responsibility for the problem behavior, may also be one of its major shortcomings. If alcoholics come to view their drinking as the result of a disease or physiological addiction, they may be more likely to assume the passive role of victim whenever they engage in drinking behavior if they see it as a symptom of their disease. . . . Relapse is the turning point where the disease model is likely to backfire. If an alcoholic has accepted the belief that it is impossible to control his or her drinking . . . then even a single slip may precipitate a total, uncontrolled relapse. Since drinking under these circumstances is equated with the occurrence of a symptom signifying the reemergence of the disease, one is likely to feel as powerless to control this behavior as one would with any other disease symptom. (Marlatt & Gordon, 1985, pp. 7–8)

Treatment would be enhanced in its effectiveness if therapists replaced the negative messages frequently given to clients ("You are unable to control your behavior") with positive, encouraging messages ("Through self-understanding, you can learn and change"). Through the encouragement process, treatment can begin to focus on enhancing the client's feeling that personal mastery is possible and desirable.

> In essence any psychological treatment is an attempt to increase the patient's self-confidence and to encourage him directly or indirectly. The Adlerian approach is characterized by its deliberate efforts to encourage the patient. Even exposure of the fraud which underlies the contradiction between what the patient "wants" to do and what he "can" do, between his apparent intentions and incapacity to give them effect, ultimately helps to encourage him. He sees that his failures have not been due to any weakness of character or equipment, but that he has been mistaken as to the nature of his intentions. (Dreikurs, 1953, p. 88)

Teleology

Adlerian psychology replaces the reductionism of oversimplified cause-and-effect relationships with a teleological orientation that sees behavior as a function of its goal.

> Alfred Adler stresses the fact that all living things move, and that
> every movement must have a goal. So, according to Adler, all
> living things seek a goal. With regard to man in particular, Alfred
> Adler declares that it is impossible for us to understand his behavior
> and actions unless we know their goal. (Dreikurs, 1953, p. 11)

In the substance abuse field, decades of searching for "the cause" of substance use disorders has been fruitless. A combination of many physiological, psychological, and social factors may contribute to the development of substance abuse problems. The ultimate resolution of these problems, however, depends on the client's understanding of the purpose that the psychoactive substance has performed in his or her life. Until the individual finds other ways to meet his or her life goals and makes appropriate lifestyle changes, maintenance of behavior changes may prove illusory.

> Addicts improve when their relationships to work, family, and
> other aspects of their environment approve. Addicts have come to
> count on the regular rewards they get from their addictive involve-
> ment. They can give up these rewards when they believe they will
> find superior gratifications from other activities in the regular fibre
> of their lives. (Peele, 1985, p. 154)

GENERAL TREATMENT STRATEGY

Whether the issue at hand is substance dependence or any other dysfunction, the therapist's first priority needs to be the establishment of a helping relationship. Some substance abuse treatment providers overlook the importance of this factor, moving quickly into direct confrontation and attempting to force each client into an acceptance of the therapist's point of view on the existence or seriousness of the problem. A more appropriate strategy is to establish a relationship based on the notion that the therapist can help the individual to reorient his or her thinking but that the decision to change or not to change is the client's. Miller's (1983) motivational interviewing approach, for instance, treats the substance dependent client as a responsible adult, based on a belief in "the individual's inherent wisdom and ability to choose the healthful path given sufficient support" (p. 490). *The substance abuse treatment provider walks a thin line, providing very active support and encouragement but refusing to take responsibility for the client's behavior.*

With the formation of a trusting relationship, the process of change can begin. Cooley (1983) suggested that formal lifestyle work should not begin too early in the client's recovery. In the early months of recovery, the client's attention needs to focus on the attainment of abstinence in the present. Once behavioral changes have become established, the client can begin to understand the nature of the faulty conclusions that have affected his or her lifestyle and use this knowledge to prevent relapse. This approach complements Washton's (1989) conceptualization of the stages in substance abuse treatment. In Stage 1 (stabilization and crisis intervention), clients are helped to resolve immediate crisis situations, to break off contacts with the drug world, to stop all drug and alcohol use, and to establish a connection to the treatment program. Stage 2 (early abstinence) involves learning about addiction, establishing support systems, and achieving stable abstinence. In Stage 3 (relapse prevention), clients learn about relapse and its prevention, start to identify and handle negative feelings, learn how to deal with problems, and make some beginnings in the direction of permanent lifestyle changes. Stage 4 (advanced recovery) involves deeper, more lasting changes in attitude, lifestyle, and behavior. At this stage, which is open-ended, the client is ready to examine the convictions upon which his or her lifestyle has been based, to recognize the faulty goals that have influenced his or her behaviors, and to deepen his or her involvement in the social milieu. Through this difficult but crucial process, the possibilities of long-term recovery can be enhanced.

Case of Harold "Hal" Willis

Diagnosis

Axis I: 303.90 Alcohol Dependence
            291.80 Uncomplicated Alcohol Withdrawal
Axis II: 301.81 Narcissistic Personality Disorder (R/O)
Axis III: Early liver disease; early heart disease
Axis IV: Psychosocial stressors: loss of job, estrangement from son; marital discord
            Severity: 3 (Moderate). Loss of job an acute event; family stressors enduring circumstances
Axis V: Current GAF: 55; Highest GAF past year: 70

Hal Willis is an engineer whose alcohol dependence was not recognized until he was in his mid-40s. Harold, who was the oldest of three children, always has suspected that his father, who died when Hal was quite young, was an alcoholic. Hal himself had only one serious alcohol-related episode in his youth, during a particularly stressful period in college.

After graduation from the university, Hal did not drink for well over 20 years. He married his college sweetheart immediately after graduation, and they led a quiet life, with Harold concentrating on his career and achieving considerable success. They remained together until after their son left for college. At that point, Harold became acutely aware of something missing in his marriage and asked for a divorce.

Hal continued to feel guilty about leaving his wife, whom he knew was dependent on him, and depressed that his son severed his relationship with Hal. When Hal later married Mildred, 15 years his junior, he vowed that he would make this marriage work.

Mildred, too, was counting on the success of this marriage, but it was because she felt that Harold—sober, responsible, and mature—would be able to rescue her from her own alcohol problems. Instead, Hal found himself stymied in his attempts to stop or control his wife's drinking and began to join her. He started going on binges almost immediately after his social drinking began. He and Mildred checked into hotels for binges of up to a week in duration, with Harold calling his office to say he was ill. The episodes occurred more and more frequently; after the last few episodes, the only way he was able to return to work at all was to spend several days being detoxified in an inpatient setting. During the last year of his drinking, he lost his job. He was able to find another position, but despite his competence, this job too was in jeopardy. During Hal's last stay at a detoxification facility, he was told by a physician that he was beginning to show early signs of heart disease and liver malfunction. At this point, Harold made a decision to try to change.

As important as this decision was, it was just a first step. When he returned home, he recognized that his own recovery was jeopardized by Mildred's contin-ued drinking. When she began to drink, he immediately drove her to the treatment center, telling her he would stay with her only when she was sober. After another solitary episode on Mildred's part, she, too, began the process of recovery.

At this point, Hal and Mildred were ready to assess their lives together. Both began attending Alcoholics Anonymous meetings several times a week, allowing them to participate in a positive social milieu for the first time. Mildred began working, which enabled her to become less dependent on her husband, and Hal, too, worked to reestablish himself in his profession. Hal began to reach out to his son and to his family of origin in an attempt to bridge his isolation. A therapist helped Hal and Mildred reexamine their relationship and develop a family life based on shared responsibility. In the long run, Harold was able to bring about permanent changes only when he recognized the importance of changing his lifestyle from one of striving to overcome inferiority and maintain power over others to one in which he was able to concentrate on the real tasks he needed to address.

RECOMMENDED READINGS

American Psychiatric Association. (1994). *DSM-IV sourcebook, vol. 1*. Washington, DC: Author.

Chapters 1–13 provide a comprehensive review of the literature upon which this section of DSM-IV was based.

Kaufman, E., & Kaufman, P. (Eds.). (1979). *Family therapy of drug and alcohol abuse*. New York: Gardner Press.

A classic collection of papers related to substance abuse and family systems.

Lewis, J.A., Dana, R.Q., & Blevins, G.A. (1988). *Substance abuse counseling: An individualized approach*. Pacific Grove, CA: Brooks/Cole.

An introduction to substance abuse counseling based on the recognition that substance abusers and their families are members of a heterogeneous population and must be treated from an individualized perspective. Describes the methods best supported by current research.

Marlatt, G.A., & Gordon, J.R. (1985). *Relapse prevention: Maintenance strategies in the treatment of addictive behaviors*. New York: Guilford Press.

Applications of Marlatt's well-established relapse prevention model to several substance-abuse-related issues.

Miller, W.E., & Heather, N. (1986). *Treating addictive behaviors: Processes of change*. New York: Plenum Press.

A collection of readings based on a comprehensive model of change; discusses approaches to addictive behaviors at the stages of contemplation, action, and maintenance.

Miller, W.E. (1985). *Alcoholism: Theory, research, and treatment*. Lexington, MA: Ginn Press.

An overview of empirically-validated approaches to alcoholism treatment. Includes reprints and original papers by Miller and others.

REFERENCES

American Psychiatric Association. (1994). *Diagnostic and statistical manual of mental disorders* (4th ed.). Washington, DC: Author.

Brill, L. (1981). *The clinical treatment of substance abusers.* New York: Free Press.

Cooley, H. (1983). Alcoholism and drug dependency: Some mistakes we can avoid. *Individual Psychology, 39*(2), 144–155.

Dreikurs, R.R. (1953). *Fundamentals of Adlerian psychology.* Chicago, IL: Alfred Adler Institute.

Fingarette, H. (1983). Philosophical and legal aspects of the disease concept of alcoholism. In R.G. Smart, F.B. Glaser, Y. Israel, H. Kalant, R.E. Popham, & W. Schmidt (Eds.), *Research advances in alcohol and drug problems* (pp. 1–35). New York: Plenum.

Grant, M. (1986). From contemplation to action: The role of the World Health Organization. In W.R. Miller & N. Heather (Eds.), *Treating addictive behaviors: Processes of change* (pp. 51–57). New York: Plenum Press.

Lewis, J.A., Dana, R.Q., & Blevins, G.A. (1988). *Substance abuse counseling: An individualized approach.* Pacific Grove, CA: Brooks/Cole.

Marlatt, G.A., & Gordon, J.R. (1985). *Relapse prevention: Maintenance strategies in the treatment of addictive behaviors.* New York: Guilford Press.

Mejta, C. (Speaker). (1988). Treatment. In *Substance abuse: Current concepts.* Videocassette series. University Park, IL: Governors State University.

Miller, W.R. (1983). Motivational interviewing with problem drinkers. In W.R. Miller (Ed.), *Alcoholism: Theory, research, and treatment* (pp. 484–503). Lexington, MA: Ginn Press.

Moos, R.H., Cronkite, R.C., & Finney, J.W. (1982). A conceptual framework for alcoholism treatment evaluation. In E.M. Pattison & E. Kaufman (Eds.), *Encyclopedic handbook of alcoholism* (pp. 1120–1139). New York: Gardner Press.

Mosak, H.H. (1989). Adlerian psychotherapy. In R.J. Corsini & D. Wedding (Eds.), *Current psychotherapies* (4th ed.) (pp. 65–118). Itasca, IL: F. E. Peacock.

Pandina, R.J., & Schuele, J.A. (1983). Psychosocial correlates of alcohol and drug use of adolescent students and adolescents in treatment. *Journal of Studies on Alcohol, 44*, 950–973.

Pattison, E.M. (1982). Decision strategies in the path of alcoholism treatment. In W.M. Hay & P.E. Nathan (Eds.), *Clinical case studies in the behavioral treatment of alcoholism* (pp. 251–274). New York: Plenum.

Pattison, E.M., & Kaufman, E. (1982). The alcoholism syndrome: Definitions and models. In E.M. Pattison & E. Kaufman (Eds.), *Encyclopedic handbook of alcoholism* (pp. 3–30). New York: Gardner Press.

Peele, S. (1985). *The meaning of addiction*. Lexington, MA: Lexington Books.

Polich, J.M., Ellickson, P.L., Reuter, P., & Kahan, J.P. (1984). *Strategies for controlling adolescent drug use*. Santa Monica, CA: Rand Corp.

Rattner, J. (1983). *Alfred Adler*. New York: Frederick Ungar.

Stephens, R.C. (1985). The sociocultural view of heroin abuse: Toward a role-theoretic model. *Journal of Drug Issues, 15*, 433–446.

Washton, A.M. (1989). *Cocaine addiction: Treatment, recovery, and relapse prevention*. New York: W. W. Norton.

Chapter 14

ANTISOCIAL PERSONALITY DISORDER AND ADDICTIONS

Donald N. Lombardi

The purpose of this chapter is to present the essence of Personality Disorders, Antisocial (Psychopathic) Personality, and the Addictive Disorders from the points of view of (a) DSM-IV (American Psychiatric Association, 1994) and (b) Individual Psychology. Evolving from this double-barreled presentation will come an awareness of the relationship between DSM-IV and Individual Psychology in regard to these disorders.

ACCORDING TO DSM

Personality Disorders were earlier known as Character Disorders (Zax & Cowen, 1976). Implicit in this conceptualization was the idea that the individual suffered a weakness of the will. Pinel named it *manie sans delire,* and later in 1935, a British psychiatrist, J. C. Pritchard, introduced the term "moral insanity" (McCord & McCord, 1964). It was not until the appearance of DSM-I in 1952 that Personality Disorders were recognized. DSM-I (1952) distinguished three different types of personality disturbances: personality pattern disturbances, personality trait disturbances, and sociopathic personality disturbances.

In DSM-II, which appeared in 1968, ten Personality Disorders are listed but one category was rarely used (Asthenic Personality), and two others (Cyclothymic

Personality and Explosive Personality) were later not classified among the Personality Disorders (DSM-III, 1980). In DSM-III (1980), Personality Disorders, coded on Axis II, were comprised of personality traits that are inflexible and maladaptive, causing either significant impairment in social or occupational functioning or subjective distress. The diagnosis of a Personality Disorder is made only when the characteristic features are typical of the individual's long-term functioning and are not limited to discrete episodes of illness. Twelve different Personality Disorders are grouped into three clusters. In DSM-III is stated that diagnosis of more than one Personality Disorder should be made if the individual meets the criteria for more than one (DSM-III, 1980).

According to the *Diagnostic and Statistical Manual of Mental Disorders* (DSM-IV) of the American Psychiatric Association (1987), the following organization of Personality Disorders exist:

Cluster A—Paranoid, Schizoid, Schizotypal Personality Disorders
Cluster B—Antisocial, Borderline, Histrionic, Narcissistic Personality Disorders
Cluster C—Avoidant, Dependent, Obsessive Compulsive, Passive Aggressive Personality Disorders

Two additional Personality Disorders (Self-defeating and Sadistic) are listed under the heading "Proposed Diagnostic Categories Needing Further Study" in Appendix B of the Manual (DSM-IV). Frequently, associated features are with Personality Disorders. Disturbances of mood, frequently involving depression or anxiety, are common and even may be the person's chief complaint (American Psychiatric Association, 1987).

Passive-Aggressive Personality Disorder has been left out of the most recent *Diagnostic and Statistical Manual of Mental Disorders* (DSM-IV) (American Psychiatric Association, 1994). This is a somewhat controversial diagnosis because a person is considered to be both passive and aggressive at the same time. Passive-Aggressive Personality Disorder also is referred to as Negativistic Personality Disorder. It is included in the Personality Disorder Not Otherwise Specified category in DSM-IV (1994).

Depressive Personality Disorder is included in Appendix B as a new classification in need of further study. Self-defeating and Sadistic Personality Disorders, which were so listed in DSM-III-R (1987), now are excluded from DSM-IV (1994).

ANTISOCIAL (PSYCHOPATHIC) PERSONALITY

The Personality Disorder that is probably best researched and understood is Antisocial Personality Disorder. In DSM-IV (1994) are listed a number of diagnostic criteria that must be met for this disorder. They include evidence of a Conduct Disorder with onset before age 15 and a pattern of irresponsible and antisocial behavior since the age of 15.

One of the more popular abnormal psychology textbooks, *Abnormal Psychology and Modern Life* (eighth edition) (Carson, Butcher, & Coleman, 1988), lists the following characteristics as typical of Antisocial Personality Disorders:

1. Inadequate conscience development and lack of anxiety and guilt;
2. Irresponsible and impulsive behavior, low frustration tolerance;
3. Ability to put up "a good front" to impress and exploit others, projecting blame onto others for their own socially disapproved behavior;
4. Rejection of authority and inability to profit from experience; and
5. Inability to maintain good interpersonal relationships.

Etiological explanations range from biological factors through disturbed family relationships to sociocultural considerations. A variety of therapeutic approaches have been utilized but none found to be too successful. The general topic of Personality Disorders, including Antisocial Personality, is confusing and an enigma from the point of view of etiology, dynamics, and treatment.

ADDICTIVE DISORDERS

Addictions are not found in the DSM-IV index. Alcohol and drug dependence and abuse are found in the chapter on Substance-Related Disorders. Pathological Gambling is under the heading, Impulsive Control Disorders Not Elsewhere Classified. Obesity is not in the section on Eating Disorders. Instead it is reserved for Psychological Factors Affecting Physical Condition (American Psychiatric Association, 1994).

The *Abnormal Psychology and Modern Life* textbook (Carson, Butcher, & Coleman, 1988) has a chapter on Substance Use and Other Addictive Disorders. Included in this chapter are alcohol abuse and dependence, drug abuse and dependence, extreme obesity, and pathological gambling. In another widely used text, *Abnormal Psychology* (Rosenhan & Seligman, 1984), drug and alcohol problems are treated in one chapter and obesity in another chapter under childhood disorders. No mention is made of pathological or compulsive gambling in either the index or the table of contents.

The classification and organization of mental disorders, especially Personality and Addictive Disorders, are a very confusing state of affairs. This is true historically and currently. Personality Disorders are often a factor in other disorders such as alcohol and drug problems, pathological gambling, and sexual deviations (Carson, Butcher, & Coleman, 1988). For example, Gilbert and Lombardi (1967) found a high incidence of psychopathic traits among heroin addicts.

FROM THE POINT OF VIEW
OF INDIVIDUAL PSYCHOLOGY

Before examining the syndromes from an Adlerian viewpoint, a number of basic concepts will be presented and explained. These concepts are critical in understanding and appreciating Alfred Adler's Individual Psychology. It is so-called because the emphasis is on the uniqueness of each person. The striving is in a social context in a goal-directed manner. Individual Psychology is an idiographic science (Ansbacher & Ansbacher, 1956).

Teleology

Teleology is concerned with the aim, purpose, or goal of human behavior. The prefix "tele" in derivation literally means distant, far, or end. A telephone is an instrument used to talk over a distance; a telescope can be used to view a distant or far object. In other words, in trying to understand behavior from a teleological point of view, the concern is with goals for which one is striving. The emphasis is not on the past antecedents of behavior. The traditional and Freudian approaches in psychology are to look to the past for the explanation of behavior occurring in the present. However, *teleology looks to the present and the future, not from where one is coming but to where one is going.* Ask why the rat in a Skinner box presses the bar and the respondent usually answers that the rat will get food. The answer is not in terms of past learning, although the past certainly is where the original learning took place. The point is that behavior is strategy and has an intention or purpose. Behavior is designed to accomplish a goal.

In a very real sense, behavior may be said to have less to do with cause and more to do with purpose. This can be seen when examining the concept of habit.

A habit usually is defined as an acquired response that is easily elicited and relatively invariable. It is a fixed behavior that occurs easily and automatically because it has been repeated frequently and requires decreased attention. Although a habit was learned in the past, it continues to serve a purpose in the present. A habit would cease to exist if it served no purpose (Beecher & Beecher, 1966).

Psychology of Use

A psychology of use can be contrasted with a psychology of possession (Ansbacher & Ansbacher, 1956). A psychology of possession states that you are what you are because of what you possess. This may be genetic endowment or environmental or social influence. A psychology of use means that you are what you are because of the use you make of what you possess, whether it be physical, genetic, or social. Two people may have the same height, handicap, or environment but make use of and live with it differently. Adler once expressed "Do not forget the most important fact that not heredity and not environment are determining factors. Both are giving only the frame and the influence which are answered by the individual in regard to his styled creative power" (Ansbacher & Ansbacher, 1956, p. xxiv). The raw material provided the individual is molded and shaped in his or her own way. It is not what one has but generally the use one makes of what one has that makes all the difference.

The relationship between a psychology of use and psychotherapy and psychopharmacology is beyond the scope of this chapter but is an issue that must be addressed. It was a topic of focus at the 36th Annual Convention of the North American Society of Adlerian Psychology, NASAP "88 (Mays, Sperry, Pancner, & Shulman, 1988). Regarding the matter of the relationship between DSM-III-R and Individual Psychology, Sperry (1989a, 1989b) has examined the two systems. He contrasted DSM-III-R based on the disease model and a psychology of possession with the Adlerian approach based on the growth model and a psychology of use. But Sperry also saw similarities and points of convergence between these two systems. Earlier, Mosak (1968) interrelated eight lifestyle themes with nineteen DSM-I diagnostic categories for the neuroses.

Unitary Concept of Motivation

From an Adlerian point of view, one basic dynamic force is behind all human activity—a striving from a felt minus situation towards a plus situation, from a feeling of inferiority towards superiority, perfection, and totality (Ansbacher &

Ansbacher, 1956). In his or her own way, the individual is trying to overcome a subjectively felt sense of weakness and looking for a feeling of worth and a place in the sun. In his or her unique way, each person is trying to belong and find personal significance (Lombardi, 1975). People are trying to overcome the difficulties of their lives and put themselves in a position of advantage so they feel a sense of security. But we must be aware that people in their overcoming felt weakness and searching for significance can do it in either the right (well-adjusted) or wrong (mistaken) way; however, one's interpretations and style of living are unique. Everyone is the same in wanting to feel significant but different in the ways of achieving that goal.

Lifestyle

This is one of Adler's major contributions. It is a series of opinions and conclusions that are come upon early in one's life, probably about the age of six. The three major components of lifestyle are (a) view of self, (b) view of others and the world, and (c) way of fitting oneself into life as one finds it. Once the lifestyle is formed, the inclination is to see and do things from that vantage point. Each person's lifestyle is patterned, organized, and consistent. This gives the individual a distinctive character and flavor. This is much like the modus operandi characteristic of an artist or criminal whose style of painting or criminal activity is easily detected and recognized.

To say that one's lifestyle is unique is a most important statement with many implications. To be unique means that you are one of a kind, unlike anybody else. When you were born, the mold was broken. There never has been, nor will there be, anyone just like you living with your exact genetics in your unique circumstances in this place and time. Even if you have an identical twin, you and your twin are not exactly alike. For example, one twin is born before the other, and twins do not always have identical fingerprints. People who live in the same family do not have the same familial environment. This is because one is not in one's own environment. For example, Mary and John are brother and sister in the same family. Mary has a younger brother (John), but John does not have a younger brother (himself). Instead he has an older sister. Thus, Mary and John's environments are quite different from each other.

As was brought out above, people may have erroneous ideas and faulty notions and conclusions that become the support and basis for mistaken lifestyles. This happens all too often resulting in a great variety of problems and disorders. One cannot understand a person on the basis of generalities but must always look at the individual case. A nomothetic approach in science must be supplemented with an idiographic approach (Allport, 1960). A concern has to be with a science of the individual person and an appreciation of not only commonalities but also individual differences.

Early Childhood Training and Family Dynamics

The family for the young child is the world in miniature. It provides the child with a basic training for life. Each member of the family constellation has distinctive traits and characteristics. The important relationships within the family are between parents, parent-child relationships, and sibling relations.

Another of Adler's major contributions is his calling attention to the importance of family dynamics and ordinal or birth position upon personality and lifestyle development (Adler, 1958). Much has been written and researched on this topic in the Adlerian literature (Dreikurs & Soltz, 1987; Leman, 1985; Watkins, 1986). Many probability statements can be made about a given birth-order position. For example, the oldest child is likely to be the most responsible, reliable, and dependable, and somewhat of a perfectionist. Again, however, caution must be taken regarding any general statement that applies to everyone, in this case, all oldest children. More importantly, attention must be paid to the unique circumstances of a particular person.

The important point here is that growing out of the family experience, the child develops values, beliefs, opinions, and conclusions about ever so many things. This includes a self-concept, and views of authority, the opposite sex, others, and the world. Out of the experience of living in a particular place (which includes one's family, neighborhood, culture) with a particular body (which includes heredity and physical makeup), one reaches certain conclusions, and the nucleus of lifestyle is formed. This summary set of conclusions grows out of one's experience and is affected by heredity, environment, family constellation, relationships, and birth-order dynamics. These opinions, conclusions, and cherished values are the foundation of lifestyle and serve as a basis for living lives. But so many ideas, opinions, and conclusions are mistaken certaintudes that make living lives intelligently difficult to say the least.

Unitary Concept of Psychopathology

A dynamic similarity exists to all incidences of clinical psychopathology regardless of the classification and names used to describe them. People in these incidences of clinical psychopathology can best be understood by an idiographic assessment, not a classification system. All the various psychopathologies (syndromes, abnormal behavior patterns) are efforts to find personal significance, but these individuals go about it in the "wrong way" with mistaken lifestyles. As Adler would put it, they live on the useless side of life (Ansbacher & Ansbacher, 1956). A person's symptoms or syndrome are less important than the fact that he or she has erroneous ideas, a mistaken lifestyle, and is moving in the wrong direction in life. Such a person is a discouraged individual, without common sense, and lacking in self-confidence. As I learned from Willard Beecher, my mentor and friend for a period of 15 years, a symptom is simply a person's unique way of falling apart.

A great many classification systems and typologies have been put forth by personality theorists and mental health professionals; however, when considered in its most basic form, just two broad ways of living exist, which go in opposite directions. One is living with reality on its terms in a well-adjusted manner. The other is living with maladjustment of one kind or another, with private logic that makes no sense to anyone but to oneself. One way makes for life, love, creation, and joy; the other way makes for death and destruction. One feels either adequate to life or not. One is either a giver and a maker or a taker and a breaker. A person is either a lover with good will toward others or a hater who displays hostility. Instead of live and let live, one's philosophy is kill or be killed.

Social Interest and Cooperation

Life is relationship. We are social organisms embedded in a social matrix. Our lives are filled with social activities of all kinds. Social interest in others and in all things that pertain to humankind, as well as the need for social cooperation, are necessary; in fact, they are absolutely indispensable. Social cooperation is essential for personal well-being and is also the key to the solution of the problems of humankind.

If the task is too great for a person and beyond his or her capabilities, then cooperation is the answer. What one cannot do alone can be done in concert and cooperation with others. As has been recognized and exclaimed, in unity is strength. Since social embeddedness is the reality of life, an important aspect is to be able to get close to people and to work with them for the common good and welfare. Social relationships without cooperation, friendship, and love will raise havoc.

Before one can cooperate with others, one must first be independent and self-sufficient. Self-reliance is a prerequisite for social cooperation (Beecher &

Beecher, 1966). A dependent person cannot cooperate. One has to be able to carry one's own weight and hold up one's end of the bargain before entering into a social situation where teamwork and cooperation are necessary.

The more of an ego one has, in the sense of wanting recognition and to make an impression, the less social interest the person has. Ego spurs on competition and makes cooperation difficult, if not impossible. Ego makes task centeredness difficult because the individual is more concerned about looking good, or at least not looking bad. The alternative to possessing an ego is to have self-esteem. This means liking yourself at all times with no contingencies or strings attached. Liking yourself is independent of winning or losing, succeeding or failing, or other people liking you (Beecher & Beecher, 1966). As Dreikurs pointed out, if you do not like yourself now the way you are, you probably never will like yourself (Terner & Pew, 1978).

Diagnosis and Treatment

The purpose of diagnosis is not simply classification on the basis of symptoms. A more basic purpose is the understanding of personal and social dynamics. When a clear and adequate understanding exists, a prescription for action is known. Seeing is the action, and knowing is the doing. This theme is very much a part of the teaching and writing of Jiddu Krishnamurti (1960, 1972, 1976, 1983). The ideas of Adler and Krishnamurti are very compatible.

The purposes of Adlerian psychotherapy include the following:

learning to live with reality on its terms rather than on one's own terms,
getting rid of mistaken certaintudes,
seeing reality as it is and coping with it as one finds it,
increasing self-reliance and lessening dependency,
gaining self-confidence,
increasing courage (the willingness to put oneself at risk and take a chance—
   not to be afraid to make a mistake or to fail),
getting rid of ego or the need to impress others,
having genuine self-esteem in that one likes oneself at all times no matter
   how things are going and what others think, and
increasing social interest and expanding the aptitude for social cooperation.

The interested reader can find much information about the theory and techniques of Adlerian therapy in other sources (Corsini, 1979; Dreikurs, 1973; Ford & Urban, 1963; Nikelly, 1971).

Adler once expressed the idea that the best we can hope to gain from therapy is to learn to make smaller mistakes. One should keep in mind the Chinese proverb that states that the start of a 10,000–mile journey is but a single step. The concern is with movement in the right direction and improvement, not perfection, and is with a strong sense of realism and optimism.

AN ADLERIAN INTERPRETATION
OF ANTISOCIAL PERSONALITY

Dreikurs (1973) distinguished among neurosis, psychosis, and psychopathy on the basis of a structural differentiation. This differentiation is based on the solution to the inner conflict between the spirit and the flesh. Adler spoke in terms of the conflict between *common sense* and *private sense*. Common sense refers to thinking that is general to the group, how one should act. However, note needs to be taken that common sense is not determined by the general consensus; it is dictated by the demands of reality. Usually the wise solution is generally known, but not always. Private sense conflicts with the general rules of common understanding and the needs of reality. Dreikurs expressed this well in the single sentence, "I know how one should act, but this is only true for others; I myself gain more if I act differently" (p. 124).

Dreikurs (1973) explained how the neurotic, the psychotic, and the psychopath solve their conflict between common and private sense differently.

The neurotic person

> . . . meets the conflict by hiding his private sense from his own
> consciousness, but not admitting his own tendencies when they
> conflict with his conscience, his common sense. He looks for alibis
> to excuse his social shortcomings. (Dreikurs, 1973, p. 124)

The psychotic resolves

> . . . his inner conflicts by changing, temporarily or indefinitely, his
> recognition of the common sense. Through delusions or hallucina-
> tions, he can impress himself with an assumed reality, which then
> conforms with his private sense. He lives in a world of his own;
> in which his personal goals find complete justification. He no longer
> adheres to the logic of life; he has his own logic shared by none.
> (Dreikurs, 1973, p. 125)

The psychopath

> . . . unlike the neurotic, has no inner conflict. He has failed to
> develop sufficient common sense. He denies the logic of others,
> never accepts their values and morals, and considers his own inter-
> ests as the only motivation which counts. Therefore, he needs no
> alibis and flaunts his own interests and tendencies. (Dreikurs, 1973,
> p. 125)

The neurotic is the only one of the three who is aware of the conflict between private sense and common sense. The psychotic avoids the realization by adjusting his or her common sense. The psychopath has never developed common sense.

Case of Tom

In the *DSM-III Casebook* (Spitzer, Skodol, Gibbon, & Williams, 1981), an historical case is presented. It is the case of Tom, extracted from the book *The Mask of Sanity* by Cleckley (1976). Tom is 21 years old. His manner and appearance are pleasing, and he creates a favorable impression. To reconcile his appearance and manner with what one knows about his extensive maladjustment and problems is hard to do. His family and legal authorities were in hope that if some psychiatric disorder could be discovered, he might escape a jail sentence for stealing. His maladjustment was evidenced in childhood. He never could be counted on to keep at any task and was frequently truant from school. Though he generally was provided for, he stole from home and from others. He lied, made excuses, and did not identify himself with others for long. At age 14 he became involved in stealing automobiles. At one point, as part of a therapeutic maneuver, a car was bought for him. Tom also was involved with forgery. He was sent to a federal institution and underwent a program of rehabilitation. He was impressive with his efforts to change his old ways and was released. Some time afterward, his deceitful and irresponsible behavior emerged and continued. He has been arrested and imprisoned approximately 50 times. On 150 other occasions, his family came to the rescue and made good his small thefts and damages, and paid fines for him. He never formed any substantial attachment for another person, including the other sex.

Cleckley's diagnosis of Tom was Psychopathic Personality. The DSM-III diagnosis was Antisocial Personality Disorder (301.70) on Axis II (Spitzer et al., 1981).

Discussion

The comments by Dreikurs about the psychopath are very apropos to the case of Tom. As an Adlerian psychologist, I would like to know about family constellation and birth-order dynamics and to elicit early recollections and memories if possible. These memories serve as an express route to the identification of lifestyle (Adler, 1958; Lombardi, 1975). Even with the limited information about the case, one easily can become aware of several important matters. Tom is impatient and impulsive with extremely low frustration tolerance, a central trait of Antisocial Personality and Personality Disorders generally. He has low social interest and is more concerned with his interests and needs. Likely he has a very pampered personality and does not wish to defer the gratification of his needs. Tom is a hedonistic individual who does not feel guilty about what he does. He is quick to have an explanation, alibi, or excuse for everything and projects blame to others so that he is always free from blame. No wonder he is so recidivistic in his behavior and cannot maintain good interpersonal relationships. He has a big ego in that he lacks genuine self-esteem and is selfish with no concern or regard for others. He has a consistency of irresponsible behavior from childhood through his adult years, which is an important diagnostic consideration for DSM-IV (American Psychiatric Association, 1994).

THE ADDICTIONS

At this point let us examine four addictions—alcoholism, drug addiction, pathological gambling, and obesity. In each situation, a case is presented to illustrate an Adlerian interpretation.

Alcoholism

Case of Bill.   Bill was in a hospital for detoxification and then in residence for a month in an alcohol rehabilitation program. As an oldest child, Bill had a lot of obligations and responsibility placed on him. He was a hard worker in and out of school, helpful, considerate, and a conforming and pleasing person. He assumed the mantle of parent as a teenager. Bill was a serious person for whom success and accomplishment were important. He is an achievement-oriented person. He is a perfectionist and likes to be in control and on top of things. He is idealistic in wanting things to be correct and done the right way. He has a strong fear of failure and, at times, he suffers from indecision. Bill has low self-esteem. He wishes he were very wealthy and is envious of others and their success. He does not like the unknown and the unfamiliar. At one point in his life, he was confused and lacked direction; he started drinking at that time.

When an individual has involvement with a number of different therapists and programs, as Bill did, it is likely that one could receive several different diagnoses at different times. A review of Bill's case history data reveals this to be the case. Diagnostic classifications are provided for Obsessive Compulsive Personality Disorder (301.40), Generalized Anxiety Disorder (300.02), and Alcohol Dependence in Remission (303.93) according to DSM-III (1980).

Discussion.   A person does not always fit into a mold or classification schema. From social psychology we know that a stereotype does not allow for the exception to the rule nor take into consideration the fine points and nuances. A particular theory or test may not capture the essence of the person. This is not surprising since each individual has a unique quality and aspect. Generalities are limited, and allowances have to be made for seeing the uniqueness and individuality of a given case. Understanding psychodynamics and group dynamics must be a part of any diagnostic effort and classification system. The understanding of individuality cannot be avoided.

As is widely known, alcohol is not a stimulant; it does not exhilarate. Instead it dulls the mind and critical faculty. The human cortex has the cognitive function of memory, learning, and judgment. The cortex remembers, compares, and classifies. Alcohol knocks out the cortex, also called the "fault finder." It makes one less critical, and much of human misery stems from comparison. Alcohol is a convenient painkiller. Pain can come from many sources, including the hurt from frustrated ego needs. One of the reasons people get drunk is to kill the irritation, envy, and humiliation that comes from being unable to cope with the reality of what is here and now. Alcohol is the poor man's self-medication to combat anxiety, depression, envy, and other kinds of hurt. The normal state of functioning requires alertness, consciousness, and activity. Alcohol reduces this state and brings calm. Increased consumption brings stupor and sleep. The final stage of this anesthetic process is death. If an alcoholic has to confront anything that is painful without this anesthetic, he or she relapses and experiences what is commonly called the dry jitters.

Drug Addiction

Case of Harry.   Harry grew up as the youngest child in a family of many achievers. The father was a highly successful professional person. The older siblings each had their claims to fame. The oldest child was a superstar whose picture was frequently in the newspapers. Harry was always in the shadow of stardom and felt insignificant, especially compared to the oldest child who was the family favorite. Growing up, Harry was pampered, spoiled, and babied by his mother. He got everything he wanted from his parents and older siblings. He felt no one ever really took him seriously. During childhood he was in a continuous parade of trouble and difficulties. Before the age of 15, he was classified as having a Conduct Disorder (American Psychiatric Association, 1987).

After the age of 15, his irresponsible and antisocial behavior increased in frequency, intensity, and seriousness. His mother felt he was weak and easily influenced by his peers. Harry had a charming personality, at least average intelligence, and was very popular with his friends. He was involved heavily with a criminal element. Compounding his difficulties was a serious drug problem. He used and experimented with many different kinds of drugs. His progression of drug use started with the weekend drinking of beer. He went onto cough medicine, onto pills and snorting, and onto skin popping and mainlining heroin (which was his favorite drug). He did not like to use marijuana or other psychedelic drugs. Several drug overdoses were a part of his drug history. Harry was in numerous drug rehabilitation programs and spent many years of his life in jail and behind bars. His reputation as a drug addict and criminal was well-known. Within the scenario of his family, if he could not be first best, he would be first worse. One of his outstanding traits was an extremely low frustration tolerance. Despite his horrible life experience and several broken marriages, Harry's case has a happy ending. He now is married happily, has a family, has a well-paying job, and is living a constructive life.

Discussion.   Szasz (1974) stated

> Powerful "addictions"—whether to smoking cigarettes or injecting heroin—are actually both very difficult and very easy to overcome. Some people struggle vainly against such a habit for decades; others "decide" to stop and are done with it; and sometimes those who have long struggled in vain manage suddenly to rid themselves of the habit. How can we account for this? Not only is the pharma-cology of the so-called addictive substance irrelevant to this riddle, but so is the personality of the so-called addict. What is relevant is whether "the addiction"—smoking, drinking, shooting heroin— is or is not a part of an internally significant dramatic production in which the "patient-victim" is the star. So long as it is (and if it is, the struggle to combat the addiction is only a part of the play), the person will find it difficult or impossible to give up his habit; whereas once he has decided to close down this play and leave

the stage, he will find the grip of the habit broken and will "cure"
himself of the "addiction" with surprising ease. (pp. 72–73)

From the point of view of a unitary concept of psychopathology, all abnormal
behavior, not only addiction, is a mistaken and erroneous way to achieve a
semblance of personal significance, save face, and avoid a painful clash with
reality (Lombardi, 1975). Some people do bizarre things to get attention. Some
people will do any number of things to be viewed and considered a star or a
hero, even at the high price of self-destructive behavior. Some of the facets of
drug addiction have been spelled out elsewhere (Gilbert & Lombardi, 1967;
Lombardi, 1969, 1971, 1973; Lombardi & Angers, 1967; Lombardi & DiPeri,
1965; Lombardi & Isele, 1967; Lombardi, O'Brien, & Isele, 1968).

Essentially, drug use and abuse are viewed as symptomatic of more basic
and underlying problems. The extent of drug use indicates the degree of the
underlying problem just as a thermometer indicates the degree of temperature in
the body. Addiction and drug use are merely a sideshow activity, a way of
avoiding the problems of everyday living (Beecher & Beecher, 1966). As I
learned from Willard Beecher, there are no addicting substances, only people.
Of course, some drugs like heroin produce physical dependence and tolerance,
but the more important concept is psychological dependence. The problem is not
a drug problem but a people problem. Drugs have no real power over people.
To deal with the physical problem of addiction is relatively easy, but to cope
with its psychological aspects is much more difficult. Also, like all other abnormal
behaviors, addiction is an achieved disability. Work and effort are necessary to
become what one is. Addiction is not without its purpose and gives the addict
a sense of comfort, an alibi, and a semblance of significance and security.

Obesity

Case of Joan.   Joan is hyper-obese, that is to say, more than 100 pounds
overweight. She is an only child and growing up she was pampered, indulged,
and spoiled. Nothing she ever wanted was denied her. Her birthday was celebrated
not yearly, but monthly. When she was single and living at home, her father
made sure that her car always was filled with gas and washed. In the winter, he
would start the car and let the engine and interior warm up before his daughter
drove it. This symbolizes the kind of care and child rearing she experienced.

Joan came into counseling because she was having personal and marital
problems. She would like to lose weight but is not ready to stop indulging herself
with the repetitive pleasure of eating. She is a very impatient person who cannot

tolerate irritation or annoyance. Her preference is to eat something that does not have to be prepared or cooked. She prefers a candy bar to a steak dinner, and candy, cake, bread, and ice cream are her nemeses. Pleasure is important to her, and she is a hedonistic person who relishes attention. She has an insatiable hunger for recognition and likes to have her way. Joan is very sensitive and quick to have her feelings hurt. She has practically no frustration tolerance and cannot stand delay or hassle of any kind. This is a hallmark trait of her personality. She often feels that she has been cheated or at least not given due consideration. She likes to be active, dominant, and ascendant. People are not always compatible with her needs and wishes. She operates on the basis of greed, not need. Eating lessens her deprivation, dulls her hurt, soothes her envy, and makes her feel happy and good.

Discussion.   With regard to the etiology of Joan's obesity, a major considera-tion is her wanting to be fussed over and catered to by others. The root cause of the problem is her belief that she has value and personal significance only when she is the focal point of attention and has whatever she wants or desires. Essential psychodynamics revolve around Joan's efforts to satisfy these needs. Whenever she feels frustrated and irritated, she looks for a quick fix to make things better.

Therapeutic goals that must be met in order to help Joan are as follows: increase patience and frustration tolerance, learn to place emphasis on we rather than me, become task-centered instead of self-centered, and learn to live as an equal rather than a privileged person. Understanding the psychodynamics provides a prescription for therapeutic action to be taken; however, these are difficult goals to achieve and one only can move gradually in the right direction. In Adlerian psychotherapy, the emphasis is on making smaller mistakes and striving for improvement, not perfection. Joan feels defeated and deprived and alienated from the world. With such frustrations, the desire is for instant rewards. And a fat person is an angry person because no one wants to be that fat. With a sensible approach in therapy, the prognosis is brightened with an element of optimism.

Pathological Gambling

Case of Frank.   Frank was the second oldest of seven children, but the oldest boy growing up. He took charge of the younger siblings and is an individual who tends to dominate and be in control. He was very intelligent, independent, and somewhat rebellious with a mind of his own. The family lived in a poverty-stricken area. The house in which he lived was small. Instead of friends coming to his house to visit, he would go to their homes. His house had little space and poor facilities. His father had a small business, but Frank thought that his father was afraid to take chances to increase business. As an adult, Frank was not at all conservative with either business or gambling. His preference is to gamble big or not at all. In the span of a few years, he has lost in excess of a million dollars.

He will not let anyone dominate or intimidate him. He wants to win and does not like to lose in anything he does or undertakes. He will put himself at risk, will take a chance, and is not afraid to lose. He is confident that he will make good. In the past this attitude has served him well, but as so often happens in life, what is an asset can turn out to be a liability. Frank has a supreme ego in that the odds pertain to other people but not to him. He knows he is intelligent and unafraid and thinks he has a special claim to fortune. He feels that he can do anything to which he puts his mind. For him money is important (he never had any when he was young); with money, he believes, one can do anything. Money is security, and gambling provides an opportunity to show how smart and clever he is. He feels that he is insignificant as a person and has nothing, but with money he has power.

Discussion.   In talking about the other addictions, the point was made that the basic problem is in the person, not in the substance used. If an obese person overeats food, this is not because food has some magical power or control over him or her. The problem is with the person, not the food. The same is true with all addictions, and this can be seem more easily with the problem of pathological gambling. The horseplayer does not get that way from eating horse meat.

Several additional points can be made about pathological gambling. A study by Graham cited in Carson and Butcher (1992) compared pathological gamblers, alcoholics, and heroin addicts on the MMPI. The results showed that they shared many similar characteristics. For example, they were self-centered, acting out and impulsive, and manipulative. This similarity in the three groups is very much in accord with the unitary concept of psychopathology.

A further study by Rosten cited in the same source (Carson & Butcher, 1992) found that pathological gamblers tended to love action and excitement, hated regulations, and felt that the odds did not apply to them. In other words, they believed they were special and above or exempt from the odds. Livingston (1974) in fact found that pathological gamblers had big egos. These findings are very much in accord with the interpretation of personality disorders and the addictions from the points of view of DSM-IV and Individual Psychology.

REFERENCES

Adler, A. (1958). *What life should mean to you*. New York: Capricorn Books. (Original work published 1930)

Allport, G.W. (1960). *Personality and social encounter*. Boston: Beacon Press.

American Psychiatric Association. (1952). *Diagnostic and statistical manual of mental disorders* (DSM-I). Washington, DC: Author.

American Psychiatric Association. (1968). *Diagnostic and statistical manual of mental disorders* (DSM-II) (2nd ed.). Washington, DC: Author

American Psychiatric Association. (1980). *Diagnostic and statistical manual of mental disorders* (DSM-III) (3rd ed.). Washington, DC: Author.

American Psychiatric Association. (1987). *Diagnostic and statistical manual of mental disorders* (DSM-III-R) (3rd ed., rev.). Washington, DC: Author.

American Psychiatric Association. (1994). *Diagnostic and statistical manual of mental disorders* (DSM-IV) (4th ed.). Washington, DC: Author.

Ansbacher, H.L., & Ansbacher, R.R. (1956). *The Individual Psychology of Alfred Adler*. New York: Harper & Row

Beecher, W., & Beecher, M. (1966). *Beyond success and failure*. New York: The Julian Press.

Carson, R.C., & Butcher, J.N. (1992). *Abnormal psychology and modern life* (9th ed.). New York: Harper Collins.

Carson, R.C., Butcher, J.N., & Coleman, J.C. (1988). *Abnormal psychology and modern life* (8th ed.). Glenville, IL: Scott, Foresman & Company.

Cleckley, H. (1976). *The mask of sanity* (5th ed.). St. Louis: C. V. Mosby.

Corsini, R.J. (Ed.). (1979). *Current psychotherapies*. Itasca, IL: F. E. Peacock.

Dreikurs, R. (1973). *Psychodynamics, psychotherapy and counseling*. Chicago: Alfred Adler Institute. (Original work published 1967)

Dreikurs, R., & Soltz, V. (1987). *Children: The challenge.* New York: E. P. Dutton. (Original work published 1964)

Ford, D.H., & Urban, H.B. (1963). *Systems of psychotherapy.* New York: John Wiley and Sons.

Gilbert, J. G., & Lombardi, D. N. (1967). Personality characteristics of young male narcotic addicts. *Journal of Consulting Psychology, 31*(5), 536–538.

Krishnamurti, J. (1960). *Commentaries of living* (3rd series). Wheaton, IL: The Theosophical Publishing House.

Krishnamurti, J. (1972). *You are the world.* New York: Harper & Row

Krishnamurti, J. (1976). *Krishnamurti's notebook.* New York: Harper & Row.

Krishnamurti, J. (1983). *The flame of attention.* San Francisco: Harper & Row.

Leman, K. (1985). *The birth order book.* New York: Dell Publishing.

Livingston, J. (1974, March). Compulsive gamblers: A culture of losers. *Psychology Today,* 51–55.

Lombardi, D.N. (1969). The special language of the addict. *Pastoral Psychology, 20*(195), 51–52.

Lombardi, D.N. (1971). Self-reliance and social cooperation. *Journal of Drug Education, 1*(3), 279–284.

Lombardi, D.N. (1973). The psychology of addiction. In H.H. Mosak (Ed.), *Alfred Adler, his influence on psychology today* (pp. 71–75). Park Ridge, NJ: Noyes Press.

Lombardi, D.N. (1975). *The search for significance.* Chicago: Nelson-Hall.

Lombardi, D.N., & Angers, W.P. (1967). First memories of drug addicts. *Individual Psychologist, 5*(1), 7–13.

Lombardi, D.N., & DiPeri, J.B. (1965). Heroin and God. *The Catholic Psychological Record, 3*(1), 35–38.

Lombardi, D.N., & Isele, F.W. (1967, February). The young drug addict. *NJEA Review,* 28–29.

Lombardi, D.N., O'Brien, B.J., & Isele, F.W. (1968). Differential responses of addicts and non-addicts on the MMPI. *Journal of Projective Techniques and Personality Assessment, 32*(5), 479–482.

Mays, H., Sperry, L., Pancner, R. J., & Shulman, L. (1988, May). *Psychotherapy and psychopharmacology: A challenge for Adlerian therapy and theory.* Symposium conducted at the annual meeting of the North American Society of Adlerian Psychology, Seattle, Washington.

McCord, W., & McCord, J. (1964). *The psychopath.* New York: Van Nostrand Company.

Mosak, H.H. (1968). The interrelatedness of the neuroses through central themes. *Journal of Individual Psychology, 24*(1), 67–70.

Nikelly, A. (Ed.). (1971). *Techniques for behavior change.* Springfield, IL: Charles C. Thomas.

Rosenhan, D.L., & Seligman, M.E.P. (1984). *Abnormal psychology.* New York: W. W. Norton.

Sperry, L. (1989a). DSM-III-R and Individual Psychology: A case summary. *NASAP Newsletter, 22*(2), 1–3.

Sperry, L. (1989b). Differential therapeutics and IP: The case of Mrs. A. revisited. *NASAP Newsletter, 22*(3), 3–6.

Spitzer, R.L., Skodol, A.E., Gibbon, M., & Williams, J.B.W. (1981). *DSM-III casebook* (1st ed.). Washington, DC: American Psychiatric Association.

Szasz, T. (1974). *The second sin.* Garden City, NY: Anchor Press/Doubleday.

Terner, J., & Pew, W.L. (1978). *Courage to be imperfect.* New York: Hawthorn Press.

Watkins, C.E. (1986). A research bibliography theory. *Journal of Individual Psychology, 42*(1), 123–132.

Zax, M., & Cowen, E.L. (1976). *Abnormal psychology* (2nd ed.). New York: Holt, Rinehart and Winston.

Chapter 15

SEXUAL DISORDERS FROM THE VIEWPOINT OF INDIVIDUAL PSYCHOLOGY

Dorothy E. Peven

Preface to the Second Edition

Since the publication of the first edition of this book, the most comprehensive survey on the sexual practices of American people has been published. It is the first publication of its kind since Kinsey's report in the 1940s, which, according to current research criteria, was seriously flawed. In a tour de force of scientific surveying, Robert Michael, John H. Gagnon, Edward Laumann, and Gina Kolata (1994) have collected information on a wide range of sexual behavior. It is a major contribution to the comprehension of sexual practices in America. Alas, there is no information about the sexual disorders.

There is a large body of research and an openness that is only recently in evidence concerning certain male sexual dysfunctions (e.g., impotence). In fact, the discussion of male sexual dysfunctions has become so popular that a recent weekly magazine has a cover with an advertisement for an antidepressant that promises to have a "minimal impact on sexual function" (i.e., impotence). Advertisements like this, in addition to the increase of eroticism in the media (X- and R-rated films, sensitive-issue talk shows, pornography), can lead to considerable confusion concerning personal sexual behavior. ("There must be something wrong with me; I don't do that.")

Figures 15.1 (men) and 15.2 (women) contain data about the selected sexual practices of the representative sample of Americans interviewed by Michael and his colleagues. You will notice that at least a two-thirds majority of those interviewed are "not at all" interested in sexual activities that, if used to the exclusion of all else, become the practices of paraphilias (e.g., voyeurism). In fact, the survey results run contrary to popular beliefs that everybody else is having erotic experiences often with many partners. The truth is, we are a nation of people who prefer monogamy, enjoy our partners, and do not practice kinky sex.

The following chapter, however, is not concerned with such issues—who is having sex with whom and how often. Here, we are interested in the Sexual and Gender Identity Disorders as listed in the DSM-IV (1994) from the viewpoint of Individual Psychology. The focus is on the *psychology* of sexual disorders.

INTRODUCTION

General observation leads us to the conclusion that much sexual behavior has motives that are not primarily sexual and often occurs for a great number of nonsexual reasons. Because the sexual act is a social function, it requires a significant amount of human cooperation. Furthermore,

> It is hedged around with taboos, and it makes a demand for a degree of intimacy uncomfortable to many . . . [thus] all the factors involved in human relationships can often be found in full regalia . . . [and] sex becomes an arena in which many desires and strivings interpose and influence the sexual behavior itself. (Shulman & Peven, 1971, p. 28)

For example, one may offer sexual opportunities to another in order to gain an advantage, or sexual intercourse can be forced on an unwilling partner for the purpose of establishing dominance. In both cases the principle is unmistakable: The motive behind the sexual behavior is not at all a sexual one.

For the Individual Psychologist, the use of sex for purposes other than intimacy and pleasure is considered "neurotic" (Ansbacher & Ansbacher, 1978, p. 187). Neurotic behavior is designed to create distance between people and life's challenges, and all sexual disorders are to be understood as distance-keeping

Selected Sexual Practices	Measure of Appeal Ages 18 through 44				Measure of Appeal Ages 45 through 59			
	Very	Somewhat	Not	Not at all	Very	Somewhat	Not	Not at all
Vaginal intercourse	83%	12%	1%	4%	85%	10%	1%	4%
Watching partner undress	50%	43%	3%	4%	40%	47%	7%	5%
Receiving oral sex	50%	33%	5%	12%	29%	32%	11%	28%
Giving oral sex	37%	39%	9%	15%	22%	33%	13%	32%
Group sex	14%	32%	20%	33%	10%	18%	22%	50%
Anus stimulated	6%	16%	24%	54%	4%	12%	23%	60%
Stimulate partner's anus	7%	19%	22%	52%	4%	16%	20%	60%
Using dildo/vibrator	5%	18%	27%	50%	3%	17%	24%	57%
Watching others	6%	34%	21%	39%	4%	25%	21%	50%
Same-gender partner	4%	2%	5%	89%	2%	1%	5%	92%
Sex with stranger	5%	29%	25%	42%	2%	52%	23%	52%
Anal intercourse/passive	3%	8%	15%	75%	2%	5%	10%	84%
Forcing sexual practices	0%	2%	14%	84%	1%	2%	12%	86%
Being forced	0%	3%	13%	84%	0%	2%	10%	89%
Anal intercourse/active	5%	9%	13%	73%	1%	7%	9%	83%

Figure 15.1. Selected sexual practices of the representative sample of American men. Based on Table 12 in Michael et al., *Sex in America*, Copyright 1994 by Little, Brown, p. 147.

Selected Sexual Practices	Measure of Appeal Ages 18 through 44				Measure of Appeal Ages 45 through 59			
	Very	Somewhat	Not	Not at all	Very	Somewhat	Not	Not at all
Vaginal intercourse	78%	18%	1%	3%	74%	19%	2%	6%
Watching partner undress	30%	51%	11%	9%	18%	49%	16%	17%
Receiving oral sex	33%	35%	11%	21%	16%	24%	14%	45%
Giving oral sex	19%	38%	15%	28%	11%	20%	17%	52%
Group sex	1%	8%	14%	78%	1%	4%	9%	87%
Anus stimulated	4%	14%	18%	65%	6%	12%	14%	60%
Stimulate partner's anus	2%	11%	16%	70%	4%	12%	12%	73%
Using dildo/vibrator	3%	13%	23%	61%	4%	14%	17%	65%
Watching others	2%	18%	15%	66%	2%	11%	13%	74%
Same-gender partner	3%	3%	9%	85%	2%	2%	6%	90%
Sex with stranger	1%	9%	11%	80%	1%	4%	6%	89%
Anal intercourse	1%	4%	9%	87%	1%	3%	8%	88%
Forcing sexual practices	0%	2%	7%	91%	0%	0%	5%	95%
Being forced	0%	2%	6%	92%	0%	1%	5%	95%

Figure 15.2. Selected sexual practices of the representative sample of American women. Based on Table 12 in Michael et al., *Sex in America*, Copyright 1994 by Little, Brown, p. 146.

behavior. Such behavior is used by those who are not prepared for cooperation and feel too uncertain about themselves to take risks. Neurotic people look for guarantees: they "hesitate," find detours, and create imaginary obstacles in order not to "expose" themselves. Such people look for sexual situations in which their fictional superiority, security, and status will be preserved. Often this leads to sexual behavior that appears incomprehensible to the observer because the behavior has so little to do with the sentiments of affection and closeness usually associated with sex.

Adler was one of the first to understand that many sexual behaviors did not have a primarily sexual purpose. He pointed out that certain sexual behaviors such as dominance and submission, or conquest and resistance, are "political" behaviors concerned with strivings for power and authority. Sexual conflicts, said Adler, were concerned with prestige and status, and he suggested that perhaps all sexual conflicts were really dominance conflicts. He observed that male dominance and female submission were socially determined and that the masculine protest was women's answer to the situation. He believed male-female relationships are a function of culture rather than a set of biologically determined behaviors. Not penis envy, but patriarchy and the superior position of the male in society, leads to the masculine protest. The masculine protest is the compensatory behavior demonstrated by both men and women in response to the cultural tendency to overvalue masculinity and depreciate femininity.

Freud, on the other hand, believed that all behavior was motivated by the libidinal energy of the id and that sexual disorders are the result of inadequately repressed libidinal urges expressed in ways repulsive to civilized societies.

In 1939, Kraft-Ebbing (1939) advanced the proposition that sexual disorders were "illnesses." Several decades went by before Masters and Johnson (1966) reintroduced the topic of sex to the medical field. Kinsey (1948) had made a significant contribution to the discussion of sexual practices, although he did not have a representative sample, verifying what many had long suspected—certain sexual behaviors that previously had been considered perversions, such as masturbation and adultery, were fairly common. The most recent survey of sex in America (Michael et al., 1994) discusses many sexual practices including oral and anal sex but, aside from forced sex, there is no discussion of the paraphilias.

ADLER'S VIEWPOINT

The decades of the 1980s and 1990s saw a great deal of research into the physiological, chemical, and even hydraulic understanding of some of the sexual dysfunctions. While the pendulum swings in the direction of biological physiological explanations for human behavior, here offered are the ideas of a philosopher-psychologist who understood all behavior, including the language of the body, in psychological terms—Alfred Adler.

Adler said, "While we do take the organic foundations of eroticism fully into account, we must assert that the individual attitude is decisive for the erotic direction and shortcomings" (Ansbacher & Ansbacher, 1978, p. 183). He took for granted the existence of the sexual drive, understood that it could be disturbed by organic factors, but also believed that the expression of sexuality is indistinguishable from the personality. The manner and mode in which people choose to express their sexual inclinations are to be considered reflections of lifestyle phenomena.

Adlerians, with their belief in the ultimate perfection of society, also look at sex from an ethical viewpoint and ask for what purpose is the sexual behavior used. The criterion by which the act is judged is the social purpose for which it is used (Shulman, 1967). Sex is not only something that happens to people, but it also is something that they *do*, and they use sex in ways related to their own personal opinions about sex and life.

When sexual behavior is used to promote pleasure and love, to increase feelings of belonging, and leads to conjunctive emotions, it is socially "useful." Such sexual behavior is prosocial and brings people closer together.

Sexual behavior that is antisocial leads people away from the group, produces social isolation, is exploitative, and produces dysjunctive emotions. Antisocial sexual behavior promotes suffering in others and is considered socially "useless" behavior. According to Individual Psychologists, all destructive and unethical sexual behavior is socially useless.

Human beings will reflect in their sexual behavior their own propensities. If they are competitive, they will be likewise in their sexual behavior. If they are antisocial in nature, the sexual behavior will be self-seeking and exploitative. Those who have intoxicated themselves with thoughts of power, control, and dominance over others will use sexual behavior to reflect such purposes. Those who are not ready for the cooperation and mutuality of sex often will use one of the sexual paraphilias as their mode of sexual expression.

SEXUAL AND GENDER IDENTITY DISORDERS

The *Diagnostic and Statistical Manual of Mental Disorders, Fourth Edition* (DSM-IV) (American Psychiatric Association, 1994) section on Sexual and Gender Identity Disorders includes criteria for four groups:

1. the Sexual Dysfunctions, which are typified by inhibitions in sexual desire or the psychophysiological changes that characterize the sexual response cycle;
2. the Paraphilias, which are conditions in which the sexual instinct is expressed in ways that are socially prohibited or unacceptable or ar biologically undesirable. Sexual arousal is in response to sexual objects or situations that are not part of normative arousal-activity patterns;
3. the Gender Identity Disorders, which are characterized by the individual's feelings of discomfort about his or her anatomic sex; and
4. A class of Other Psychosexual Disorders that shall not be discussed in this chapter.

Sexual Dysfunctions

Psychosexual dysfunctions are characterized by inhibition in the appetitive or psychophysiological changes that characterize the complete sexual response circle:

1. appetitive—the desire for sexual activity;
2. excitement—physiological changes;
3. orgasm—the release of sexual tension; and
4. resolution—the sense of general relaxation.

Usually disturbances are in both the subjective sense of desire and objective sense of performance. The dysfunction must be both recurrent and persistent to be given a designation, although some dysfunctions may be short-lived or episodic. What is not included is the whole sphere of "spectatoring" and "performance anxiety." More on this topic will be presented later. What is included in sexual dysfunctions are the following:

A   Sexual Desire Disorders
   a   Hypoactive Sexual Desire Disorder
   b   Sexual Aversion Disorder

B   Sexual Arousal Disorders
   a   Female Sexual Arousal Disorder
   b   Male Erectile Disorder

C   Orgasmic Disorder
   a   Female Orgasmic Disorder
   b   Male Orgasmic Disorder
   c   Premature Ejaculation

D   Sexual Pain Disorders
   a   Dyspareunia
   b   Vaginismus (not due to a general medical condition)

E   Sexual Dysfunction Due to a General Medical Condition

F   Substance-Induced Sexual Dysfunction

G   Sexual Dysfunction Not Otherwise Specified

Adler and Organ Jargon.   Adler said bodily symptoms often contained an organ dialect, a nonverbal statement that reflects an internal attitude. "Adler considered all kinds of sexual dysfunction . . . impotence, frigidity, premature ejaculation, etc., forms of 'organ dialect.' 'While the patient's words, his thoughts and desires express his longing, his body, his sexual organs, speak another language, expressing his cowardliness' " (Ansbacher & Ansbacher, 1978, p. 376).

Adler understood behavior as nonverbal language reflecting the apperceptive mode, the assumptive world—the lifestyle. For Adler, bodily functions are influenced by the style-of-life; the expression of the sexual urges are indistinguishable from the personality. "While we do take the organic foundations of eroticism fully into account, we must assert that the individual attitude is decisive for the erotic direction and shortcomings" (Ansbacher & Ansbacher, 1978, p. 183). There is considerable research demonstrating that about 50% of erectile dysfunctions are organic (Gregoire & Pryor, 1993; Jewelewicz, 1989), which leaves 50% due to psychological reasons.

Adler understood that there were biological forces at work but suggested that the sexual dysfunctions were psychological, and it is the meaning and the function of the disorder that is to be examined—what is being said in the language of the body by each particular dysfunction. Those who demonstrate failure, for example, may be saying "I can't do this correctly," or "I'm incompetent in this important area of life." Sexual dysfunctions are the unconscious expressions of deep feelings, beliefs, and values—the grammar of the genitals. Those who fail to function sexually are making statements about their sexuality. Their "failure" has a purpose. Adler said

> In sexual impotence the patient's faintheartedness is materialized
> in a main line of life. He evades the very aggression that he
> longingly desires. While his word, his thoughts, and his desires
> express his longing, his body, his sexual organ, speaks another
> language, expressing his cowardliness. (Ansbacher & Ansbacher,
> 1978, p. 189)

Those who suffer from sexual dysfunctions rarely understand what their body is telling the world. Men experiencing premature ejaculation feel as if they cannot restrain themselves, as if they have no control over their body functions. Yet one gentleman client explained his "quickie" by saying, "I was in a hurry," accompanied by a shy smile. Many others claim their inability to inhibit orgasm. "I tried but I couldn't control myself," or, as one unconsciously hostile client said when his wife complained during a marriage counseling session, "I didn't time it." These men characteristically ejaculate immediately prior to or immediately after penetration leading to frustration on the part of the woman, especially if all sexual activity ends with the ejaculation. The body language appears to be, "What do you expect from me?" Yet this is the most easily "treatable" of the sexual dysfunctions using training in sensate focus.

Adler believed that women with vaginismus (an involuntary spasm of the vagina that interferes with intercourse) showed ". . . tendencies toward isolation, aversion against the feminine role . . . and a fear of loss of one's own value, of depreciation and disappointment . . . a passive resistance" (Ansbacher & Ansbacher, 1978, p. 186). The body says "No!" even if the intentions are otherwise.

Psychologically, the hostility inherent in the dysfunctions is part of the hostility of all neurotics—the negativistic, pessimistic view of life, the fear of failure, the demand for service from others, and the desire to win without putting out effort. In the sexual dysfunctions, however, the body reveals the truth: They are not willing to perform under these circumstances no matter how much they protest their good intentions.

Sex requires cooperative endeavor, and the failure to understand this is at the core of the sexual dysfunctions. Those who suffer often are concerned with themselves and their performance to the exclusion of all else. Oblivious to the desires, feelings, and messages of the other, they concentrate on themselves. Welwood wrote

> We can maintain a hearty enjoyment of sex . . . only by immersing
> ourselves in the stream of its energy, letting go, and seeing where
> it takes us. If we want to keep lovemaking fresh, we need to put
> aside expectations and preconceptions, so we can be more sensitive

to the changing energies and feelings arising in each moment of
exchange with our partner. (Welwood, 1992, p. 34)

When people are self-absorbed, fearful of making a mistake, cower before
"normal" interpersonal activities, afraid that others will find out what they are
really like, is it any wonder that they falter before the sexual task? Sexual
gratification with a loving partner requires cooperation and self-revelation, a risk
of exposure to the eyes of another, for all imperfections are open to inspection.
Therefore, all sexual disorders are to be understood as distance-keeping behavior,
". . . a self-imposed distance from the other sex" (Ansbacher & Ansbacher,
1978, p. 380) in those who are generally neurotically disposed, who experience
discouragement about their sexual role or gender, and who have trained themselves in their disorders.

Special mention should be given to male impotence since there is considerable
discussion of this dysfunction in the popular magazines as well as the scientific
journals. Recent research suggests that as much as 50% of male erectile dysfunction is related to physiology. Among the physical causes are hardening of the
arteries, diabetes, high blood pressure, and the pills that are used to control high
blood pressure. Antihistamines, antidepressants, antibiotics, tranquilizers, and
medication for ulcers, heart disease, and hypertension also can be involved. While
treatment is still somewhat primitive and includes vacuum pumps or injections
of drugs, there are now clinics specializing in the treatment of male erectile
dysfunction since it has become such a popular subject.

Paraphilias

The essential feature of these disorders is that unusual or bizarre imagery
or acts are *necessary* for sexual arousal to occur. In the absence of paraphiliac
imagery, sexual excitement or orgasm is not attained. The acts are "involuntary,"
repetitive, and involve the following:

1. preference for the use of a nonhuman object for sexual arousal;
2. repetitive sexual activity with humans involving real or simulated suffer-
    ing or humiliation; and
3. repetitive sexual activity with nonconsenting partners, statistically male-
    related.

Because some of these disorders are associated with nonconsenting partners,
the paraphiliacs are often in conflict with society. The behavior not only has
legal significance, but there is an impairment in the individual's ability to become

involved in reciprocal affectionate relationships, and psychosexual dysfunctions are common.

The Individual Psychologist is not surprised to find paraphiliacs in conflict with society, for these are antisocial people who go through life on the useless side. Their behavior is destructive and exploitative. Virtually all reported cases of paraphilias are males (with the exception of sadism and masochism), and it is not difficult to understand behavior as often cultural in nature; that is, paraphiliac behavior is a manifestation of the Masculine Protest in the male. The onus of "performance" is usually on the male, and some men respond to this demand with behavior that means "I don't want to perform the prescribed male role. I don't want to service women. Leave me alone!" Some men take a detour away from "reciprocal affectionate sexual activity."

These are men who suffer from exaggerated feelings of inferiority. They see themselves as not capable of or not interested in "normal" sexual acts. Often, their self-image is "I'm weird," which enables them to claim a "disability grant": "Don't expect anything normal (like love and marriage) from me. I'm disqualified because I'm bizarre." Paraphiliacs demonstrate to the utmost degree the lack of preparation and willingness to join with others for mutually satisfying relationships.

Fetishism.   Fetishism is the use of nonliving objects (fetishes) as the preferred or exclusive method of achieving sexual excitement. Fetishes tend to be articles of clothing such as female undergarments, shoes, boots, or, more rarely, parts of the female anatomy such as breasts.

When a man, rather than make a date with a woman, steals her panties and masturbates into them, he is, in fact, disparaging and devaluing the female. Some unimportant detail like a shoe is given sexual rank and dignity. The female partner becomes object, not person; she is reduced to a slip or a breast rather than a living, breathing human being with interests and feelings of her own.

Adler said the fetishist is dependent on incidentals for he or she displaces sexual pleasure onto the fetish. These fetishists have freed themselves from dependency on a partner for they "fear and [have a] feeling of weakness toward the other sex" (Ansbacher & Ansbacher, 1978, p. 180).

Exhibitionism and Voyeurism.   The essential feature of exhibitionism is the repetitive act of exposing the genitals to an unsuspecting stranger for the purpose of achieving sexual excitement. No attempt is made at further sexual activity, only a desire to surprise and shock. While the voyeur gets sexually aroused by repeatedly looking at unsuspecting people who are naked, disrobing, or engaging in sexual activity, he or she also enjoys thinking about the observed people as being helpless and feeling humiliated if they knew they were being seen.

Adler suggested that both the exhibitionist and the voyeur are visual types who sexually do not get beyond showing and looking.

> . . . the cowardliness and low degree of activity of these persons can be readily observed also in their other life relationships. . . . Exhibitionism . . . always contains a battle against the norms of society. Furthermore, the urge to frighten and corrupt children through exposure of oneself, and to depreciate others by exposing them, places their deviation close to sadism. (Ansbacher & Ansbacher, 1978, p. 181)

Zoophilia, Necrophilia, and Pedophilia.   Zoophilia is the use of animals as the preferred or exclusive method of achieving sexual satisfaction. Necrophilia is intercourse with the dead. Pedophilia is achieving sexual satisfaction with prepubescent children.

According to Adler, people who commit sexual acts with animals are demonstrating an "extreme form of discouragement and despair regarding sexual possibilities" (Ansbacher & Ansbacher, 1978, p. 182). In these perversions, there is no human partner with whom to interact; the partner is devalued into the form of an animal. Necrophiliacs demonstrate a desire for the complete defenselessness of the partner and the "relief" from no obligations and consequences. In this paraphilia, there is a complete renunciation of the mutuality of sexual pleasure and an easily attained feeling of unrestrained domination over the partner. Like many paraphiliacs, the zoophilic, the necrophilic, and the pedophile get a great deal of sexual satisfaction from the utter defenselessness of their victims. The pedophile also exploits the innocence and innocence of children. Bentovim wrote

> [Adults abusing children represents] a view of women and children as appropriate victims of male sexual interest and therefore appropriate objects to meet sexual needs. . . . [t]he fact that most known sexual abusers are men seems to indicated that how boys and men are socialized is somehow connected with why they sexually abuse children.
>
> Among men who have poor self esteem and considerable anxieties about their identity and capacities, sexual activities with children may seem easier, with less resistance to overcome, and less chance of rejection and . . . humiliation. The child comes to be seen as an object rather than a person. (Bentovim, 1994, p. 144)

These people have failed completely at the challenge of relationships, have given up all hope of equality, and have rejected society and the social field entirely. They apparently have lost all hope of mutually satisfying cooperative sexual pleasure. Many detective/murder mysteries use prototypes of the sexual psychopaths as the antagonists in their stories, but the difference is that the psychopath has *never* been interested in cooperative endeavors. The stance is distance, the belief is they cannot make it like others do, and so they choose striving for dominance in "cheap" ways that are repulsive to society.

Sexual Sadism and Sexual Masochism. Sadists are people who become sexually aroused through inflicting physical or psychological suffering on another person. One of the following conditions must prevail if a diagnosis of sadism is to be made:

1. the sadist has inflicted suffering on a nonconsenting partner,
2. with a consenting partner, sexual excitement is achieved with humiliation or mildly injurious bodily suffering, and
3. body injury that is extensive, permanent, or possibly mortal is inflicted on a consenting partner for the purpose of sexual arousal.

Masochists are people whose preferred mode of producing sexual arousal is to be beaten, humiliated, bound, or made to suffer. Often the person has participated intentionally in an activity in which he or she was harmed physically or his or her life was threatened.

What is to be said of people who derive their sexual pleasure from torturing others and/or watching people suffer? Adler said biographical accounts of these people show

> a long history of erroneous training . . . [and that] the development
> of sadism and masochism always has an understandable history. . . .
> [T]he goal remains constant: the careful elimination and deprecia-
> tion of the normal . . . [and] the continuous attempt to harden
> oneself against initial inhibitions, and to learn to love abnormalities
> and horrors and to elaborate on them. (Ansbacher & Ansbacher,
> 1978, p. 174)

Adler believed that sexual perversions had nothing to do with any innate abnormality of drives or instincts, and that paraphiliacs moved easily from sadism to masochism and ". . . from homosexuality into masochism or sadism [because] in every person are traits of defiance and obedience, cravings for dominance and submission, that serve the striving for significance" (Ansbacher & Ansbacher, 1978, p. 174).

The Individual Psychologist will point to the "cowardliness" of the sexual deviate, especially the sadist and pedophile. In fear of defeat before the challenge of sexual relationships and egalitarian love, they choose children or defenseless people, for they see the least resistance as a threat to a very precarious self-esteem. Sadism is the quest for power in an easy way by people lacking the courage to meet the real problems of relationships. Sadists and pedophiles are people looking for ". . . the semblance of power, of a secret, often unconscious supermanliness in a situation of uncontested superiority" (Ansbacher & Ansbacher, 1978, p. 373).

The upward movement of all life in the direction perceived as superiority (significance) is seen by Adler even in the masochist. Adler said, "Even . . . in masochism, there is always a compensatory line upward, as when in flagellation the individual seeks a ridiculous justification in thoughts of penance." Adler thought that ". . . the partner falls under the dictates of the masochist . . . [and that] while the sadist is the triumphant vanquished, the masochist becomes the vanquished conqueror (Ansbacher & Ansbacher, 1978, p. 373).

While discussing nonsexual behavior Adler pointed out that obedience, submission, and humility were meant to "capture and conquer the other." He saw the "feeling of weakness" as a weapon which secured dominance over the environment" (Ansbacher & Ansbacher, 1978, p. 373). Haley, quoted by Ansbacher and Ansbacher, agreed and said that helpless behavior influences other people as much if not more than authoritarian behavior (Ansbacher & Ansbacher, 1978, p. 375) and gives the suffering victim control over what happens in a relationship. Dreikurs used to call this "the power of passivity" (R. Dreikurs, personal communication).

Shulman and Peven (1971) also believed that sadism is a perversion in which the desire to dominate is the most important issue.

> In DeSade's writings he [continually] deals with what is, to him, the main issue in sex or in life; namely, one person gaining complete control over another. Sex is merely one vehicle for achieving this goal. The sadist is excessively concerned with the issue of personal domination, but it also seems he must reduce his [victim] . . . to the status of an object so he can use the object without having to enter into a relationship between equals. (Shulman & Peven, 1971, p. 31)

The paradox is, who dominates whom?

> When a man pays a prostitute to whip him until he is aroused, who is dominant? When a girl can only achieve orgasm if her partner brutalizes her, which one is dominant? Many sadomasochistic relationships are really cooperative endeavors in which, often, the masochist is the one who calls the tune. (Shulman & Peven, 1971, p. 31)

Shulman and Peven (1971) also suggested that people who want to dominate others are people who want to establish authority over others because they do not trust or believe in democratic relationships. They make themselves bigger by trying to make others smaller and feel threatened if they cannot dominate.

Gender Identity Disorders

Gender Identity Disorder.   DSM-IV describes this disorder as

> A strong and persistent cross-gender identification. . . . [T]he disturbance is manifested by a stated desire to be the other sex . . . of the conviction that he or she has the . . . feelings and reaction of the other sex . . . [and] persistent discomfort with his or her sex or sense of inappropriateness in the gender role of that sex. (American Psychiatric Association, 1994, pp. 246–248)

DSM-IV also states that the disorder must cause "clinically significant distress or impairment" in the social or occupational areas of life. Clearly then, a great majority of those who profess themselves to be homosexual will not be included in this disorder. Adler, however, wrote a great deal about homosexuality, and it seems appropriate to describe his views in a paper that discusses the Individual Psychological viewpoint of sexual behavior even though homosexuality is no longer categorized as one of the paraphilias or even listed in DSM-IV as a dysfunction (except when it is ego-dystonic).

Homosexuality.   Adler believed homosexuality is psychological in origin and that the reason for a considerable public sentiment against homosexuals is not because homophobics have repressed their own homosexuality, but because ". . . the logic of man's living together, the urge to preserve the human race—in short, the inherent communal feeling in man—is what compels people toward the energetic rejection of homosexuality" (Ansbacher & Ansbacher, 1978, p. 150).

Adler said homosexuals are those who early on decide that they are inadequately equipped for "normal" sexual behavior and have not been prepared either because of improper education or faulty upbringing for the customary sexual role. Adler saw homosexuality as an "expression of great discouragement and hopeless pessimism, states in which one is satisfied with life in a small circle, far from the other sex" (Ansbacher & Ansbacher, 1978, p. 155). (Written many decades ago.)

Adler also made the observation that throughout history, whenever an increase has occurred in the emancipation of women (as in Greek culture), an increase also has occurred in homosexual trends. Adler believed that men, in an escape from feelings of insecurity, attempt to put distance between themselves and women; they take flight from females into exclusively male society.

ETIOLOGY

According to Adler, those suffering from psychosexual disorders are neurotic. Neurotic people are those who live their lives in a mistaken manner; they compete rather than cooperate as they strive for personal superiority over others. Neurotic people lack social interest, do not contribute to the community, lean on others, and take no responsibility for their behavior. When faced with situations calling for increased courage, they feel a threat to their self-esteem, to their fictitious goal of superiority. Many neurotic people develop disabling symptoms that serve as "excuses" for failures (real or imagined) and the general unwillingness to move forward into life.

The psychosexual disorders are understood as neurotic symptoms because they are part of an arrangement enabling retreat from the challenge of love. Those people who have trained themselves from childhood on to falter before a challenge develop psychosexual disorders.

Adler recognized the possible organic factors leading to sexual disorders and believed that "organ inferiority" is one possible factor in the developmental history of sufferers. Thus, some men may imagine their penis "too small" and develop feelings of inferiority vis-a-vis their genitalia. I once heard a gentleman tell Dr. Dreikurs there was something "wrong" with his penis preparatory to a lament about size. Dr. Dreikurs looked up and asked, "What's the matter? Is it too big?" Any exaggeration of normal inferiority feelings can lead to a neurotic lifeline and the avoidance of intimacy and love.

In the case of sadism and masochism, Adler observed that some children experience sexual excitement during situations that create anxiety. He thought that in some children, an organ inferiority of the nervous system leads to sexual arousal as well as ". . . excitation of the intestines, bladder, etc., [and that] this mind-body connection holds a strong temptation to get oneself into threatening, prohibited situations, and to provoke them in reality or fantasy" (Ansbacher & Ansbacher, 1978, p. 175).

Pampering and neglect are also important etiological factors in the developmental history of neurotic people and, therefore, in the history of those with psychosexual disorders. Pampered children are those who have managed to secure for themselves a position in which everything comes easily and people do for them. All wishes and desires are quickly granted. These pampered children often grow up to be discouraged adults for they have never learned to take care of themselves. When the time comes (as it must to everyone) to face up to responsibility, they respond with, "Who me? I've never had to do it before; why are you asking me now?" Never having developed their social interest, these children grow up to be ill-prepared and ill-equipped to deal with life-situation challenges.

Neglected children, on the other hand, may have never had the nourishing experience of the feeling of belonging and being cared for. Often no one has been available as a guide to the adult world to encourage these children to feel comfortable and at home in the world. Such children seldom develop feelings for others; they have never been loved themselves; and when the task of love appears, they do not understand how to behave. No guiding lines have been available.

Training and self-training play an important part in the development of the psychosexual disorders, for there could be ". . . no sexual deviation without training" (Ansbacher & Ansbacher, 1978, p. 393). The sexual disorders represent training from childhood on of people discouraged about their ability to function in a normal, gender-related role. The possibility of "exposure" is avoided by using devious modes of sexual expression.

Another factor in etiology is early sexual education. Adler believed that of the three life tasks, we are the least prepared for the task of love and marriage and suggested education in preparation for the task of marriage with a special emphasis on training for "equality" (equal worth between the genders).

The first five to six years of life will, according to Individual Psychologists, determine the lifestyle. Since sexual disorders are an expression of the lifestyle attitude about sex and intimacy, the Individual Psychologist will look there for indications of developmental disorders. Obviously, the more cooperation is modeled in the home, the more prepared the child will be for relationship tasks as they arise throughout life. If mother and father model a harmonious marriage, their children will be better equipped to meed the task of marriage. Other important early environmental factors include the relationship between siblings, family values, family atmosphere, and cultural norms. With the givens of heredity and environment, children will create their life plan, which includes all gender-related concepts as well as psychosexual role-related behaviors.

TREATMENT

The concept of accepting responsibility for the creation of our own lives carries with it the implication that, once aware of our fictitious goals, we can choose to make changes. The task of the Individual Psychologist is to convince clients to make these changes and discover for themselves that life can be different, better, and more comfortable. The therapist's job is to listen, understand, analyze, illuminate, and, most of all, encourage.

In a discussion of treatment of sexual disorders, Adler suggested that the outcome was highly dependent on the ability of the therapist to encourage, thus to rid the client of the always "erroneously created" psychological inhibitions. "The supreme remedy is change of the personality into a courageous, self-confident fellow man. Such a transformation should be carried out in a clear, deliberate manner (Ansbacher & Ansbacher, 1978, p. 191).

The treatment of paraphilias is difficult and there is virtually no literature is available on it. If therapy is going to succeed, according to Adler, an essential component is to destroy the tie between anxiety and sexual arousal. He suggested that paraphiliacs train themselves to increase the connection between anxiety arousal and sexual excitement and said paraphiliacs had to be encouraged to give up this "thrill" in order for therapy to be successful.

Based on the pioneering work of Masters and Johnson (1966, 1970), treatment of the psychosexual dysfunctions has evolved in the last few decades using a combination of behavior modification techniques as well as psychotherapy (and, or course, medication when indicated). A psychosexual history and anamnesis is taken, and on the basis of findings, a set of sexual techniques is prescribed usually starting with sensate focus. To describe each treatment developed for each sexual dysfunction is, however, beyond the scope of this chapter. Therefore, the reader is referred to Kaplan (1974) and Masters and Johnson (1970) for a full description of the treatment of psychosexual dysfunctions.

CONCLUSION

Adler believed that because humanity is divided into two sexes, there is an "eternal compulsion toward one another" (Ansbacher & Ansbacher, 1978, p. 321), and it is possible to recognize the amount of courage and the capacity to cooperate as revealed in sexual practices. Those who falter before the sexual challenge develop psychosexual disorders and are "neurotic." Psychosexual disorders are an attempt to run away from sexual obligations because neurotic people have developed limited social interest. From the Individual Psychological viewpoint, the sexual deviations are compensatory efforts created to alleviate a feeling of inferiority vis-a-vis sexuality and to exclude sexual commitment.

According to Adler, the sexual drive is the means by which men and women join together for the good of society. The interests of society in general are best served when the two sexes marry and fulfill their obligations to society. And, in an interesting update, the most recent research supports this view.

> We find . . . happiness with partnered sex is linked to happiness with life. . . . And happiness is clearly linked to having just one partner—which may not be too surprising since that is the situation that society smiles upon. Virtually all the people who were happy in general also said they were happy with their sex lives. And almost all of these happy people . . . were married and faithful to their spouse. . . . Those having the most partnered sex and enjoying it most are the married people. . . . In real life, the unheralded, seldom discussed world of married sex is actually the one that satisfies people the most. (Michael et al., 1994, pp. 130–131)

CASE EXAMPLE

Robert: A Case History

> "I desperately want to rid myself of my present feelings and be able to enjoy this life that God has given me. . . . I have tried to put my tragic feelings down on paper so you can help me. I find it difficult to put into words how terrible I feel. HELP! My home life is presently difficult because I can't find the right words with my wife, but I must talk to her or she'll think I'm dull. I agonize over the smallest things and force others to decide for me. I can't concentrate.

> Life doesn't seem like the gift it should be. I question its
> worth. My life doesn't have the happy atmosphere it used
> to have. I was able to be high on life and converse with lots
> of people. I want to be that happy person. My personality
> is almost nonexistent, and I am wasting my life. Mornings
> are the worst. I wake up in the morning and say I want to
> die. . . . I want to die."

A poignant letter from Robert, a 45-year-old man suffering from the down phase of his bipolar disorder. He had cycled up and down six times since he was 25 years old, but, like many bipolars, he refused to believe he suffered from a chronic disorder. With a great deal of urging, Robert agreed to a medication regime, including lithium, and as time rolled around he started to feel better. the major complaint that brought him into psychotherapy, however, continued— intermittent impotence.

Robert reported he was "successful" about every five or six attempts at intercourse but "failed" the rest of the time. There was little foreplay, and the sexual activity described was quite limited (e.g., intercourse was restricted to the missionary position).

Since Robert reported getting erections in the middle of the night and upon awakening in the morning, it was unlikely that the impotence was physiologically based. Still, I recommended a urologist who specialized in male sexual dysfunction, and Robert did go see him. After a number of tests proved negative, the urologist suggested that Robert's impotence was psychic. Robert and I then embarked on a psychological tour.

Robert was the youngest of two, the only boy, the very obvious favorite of his mother, pampered by her and kept somewhat distant from a very active, outgoing, friendly father. Older sister was like father, whereas Robert emulated mother—always looking for approval. Efforts to please included never confronting and always obliging. He remained forever the family favorite, the baby, who tried to go through life as Peter Pan. (Although I called him Robert, the rest of his world called him Bobby.) An early recollection from age 7 reads

> "I was in my front yard on my back on the ground. There
> was a fat guy sitting on my chest, and I was crying. I felt
> defeated."

This is the very picture of an unhappy, awkward little boy crushed by the big, fat responsibilities of life.

A Millon Clinical Inventory report of that time shows Robert as 100% on the dependent (submissive) scale as well as on the dysthymia scale. Other notable remarks include deficits in social attainments, self-deprecation, seeking reassurance from others, and vulnerability to rejection from supportive others. The Millon also says the test-taker's fear of loss of support makes him overtly compliant but so irritable he alienates others.

Thus, Robert had many fights with his wife whom he claimed avoided intercourse with him and was very demanding, bossy, and critical. Although his childhood history suggests that his dependent behavior was rewarded by mother, such behavior was rejected by his wife. In fact, Robert's wife experienced his dependency as a demand and responded to his passive resistance to growing up with hostility. According to Robert, his wife was a "prude" who resisted any effort on his part to talk about sex and, although she is an educated woman, was ashamed that Robert was seeing a psychotherapist and refused to come and see me. Robert's viewpoint was that, in the face of his wife's lack of support and demands, he was unable to get and maintain an erection, and he often ejaculated without erection. Every once in a while, the intercourse would succeed.

With great care, Robert and I went over every detail of sexual intercourse starting with the kiss. Robert was embarrassed by my frankness and often would respond with an uncontrollable giggle. Inexperienced men who have a childlike view of sex and women find it difficult to discuss sexual matters openly, and the giggle gives them away—it is the signal. If such a man is married to an inexperienced woman (both Robert and his wife were virgins before they met in college), the marriage bed becomes quite circumscribed and sex is stilted, enacted in the dark, confined to rote behavior. The partners are frightened of experimentation, and the man as well as the woman find it difficult to lead the partner into unexplored, experimental behavior. The partners are often clumsy and awkward and seem never able to discuss their frustration and what to do about it. There is a reluctance to expose themselves to the possibility of embarrassment and ridicule. Sex remains secretive, silent, dull, and boring.

I understood Robert's impotence as passive-aggressive behavior. In anger against his wife's demands for performance (in every aspect of life), Robert's response was to shout silently at her, "Don't expect anything of me. Don't you know I'm incompetent?" The loss of erection also seems to stand for the distaste he feels for his wife—she turns him off. Then how to explain the successes and the mid-night erections? Robert was 45, still young enough to have erections without volition—testimony to the resiliency of the human life force. Robert had erections literally in spite of himself.

Sexuality is an expression of the personality. Those who go through life suffering from performance anxiety naturally will suffer in the bedroom. The organ dialect of Robert's body distinctly says, "Expect nothing from me." I also understand Robert's impotence as a case of extreme self-interest.

Robert is so concerned with himself that he cannot relax enough to be able to concentrate on his partner. Self-absorption is the enemy of sexual performance. We get aroused because we see that we are arousing another. "I get off because I sense you're getting off on me, and that makes me turn on even higher (and so on and on)." It is the ability to tune in to another, to lose oneself in the "stream of energy" that enables us to let go, to become immersed in the sensations, and even, occasionally, to have an oceanic experience. We give to get is never more appropriate than in sexual behavior. Lastly, we cannot take ourselves too seriously—funny things do happen.

Robert's inability to forget himself and any possible inadequacies demonstrates a self-consciousness, an ego-centric view of the world that is incompatible with the concept of giving oneself to another. Only when he cycled high was Robert able to approach the marriage bed with any degree of confidence in himself and in his partner.

I wish I could report that Robert's sexual dysfunction is better after months of psychotherapy, but it is not. He has accepted the fact that he is cyclothymic; he takes his medications and comes to see me about once a month. Yet he continues to report intermittent failure to achieve satisfactory intercourse with his wife. He *has* grown up. He no longer plays the clown or the baby. His wife lost her lucrative job, and he has been supportive and encouraging. He is making decisions in his insurance business and, after the death of his father, he took over the obligation and responsibility for his sick mother. But Robert continues to obsess about this sexual performance and, as a result, approaches the marriage bed full of angst and dread, unable to just relax and enjoy himself. Too bad!

REFERENCES

American Psychiatric Association. (1987). *Diagnostic and statistical manual of mental disorders* (3rd ed., revised). Washington, DC: Author.

American Psychiatric Association. (1994). *Diagnostic and statistical manual of mental disorders* (4th ed.). Washington, DC: Author.

Ansbacher, H., & Ansbacher, R. (Eds.). (1978). *Alfred Adler: Cooperation between the sexes—Writings on women, love and marriage, sexuality and its disorders*. New York: Anchor Books, Doubleday & Co.

Bentovim, A. (1993). Why do adults sexually abuse children? *British Medical Journal, 307*, 144.

Gregoire, A., & Pryor, J. (1993). Impotence: An integrated approach to clinical practice. *The Lancet, 69*(3880), 1267.

Jewelewicz, R. (1989). The sexual dysfunctions. In *Sexual and reproductive health: The Columbia University College of Physicians & Surgeons complete home medical guide* (2nd ed.). New York: Columbia University Press.

Kaplan, H.S. (1974). *The new sex therapy: Active treatment of sexual dysfunctions*. New York: Brunner/Mazel.

Kinsey, A.C. (1948). *Sexual behavior in the human male*. Philadelphia: W.B. Saunders.

Kraft-Ebbing, R. von. (1939). *Psychopathia sexualis: A medical forensic study*. New York: Pioneer.

Masters, W.H., & Johnson, V.E. (1966). *Human sexual response*. Boston: Little, Brown.

Masters, W.H., & Johnson, V.E. (1970). *Human sexual inadequacy*. Boston: Little, Brown.

Michael, R.T., Gagnon, J.H., Laumann, E.O., & Kolata, G. (1994). *Sex in America: A definitive survey*. Boston: Little, Brown.

Shulman, B.H. (1967). The uses and abuses of sex. *Journal of Religion and Health, 6*(4).

Shulman, B.H., & Peven, D.E. (1971). Sex for domination. *Medical Aspects of Human Sexuality, 5*(10).

Welwood, J. (1992, November/December). Making love heart to heart: Exchanging spiritual energy during sexual intercourse. *East West Natural Health*, 34.

PART V
CHILDHOOD
AND
ADOLESCENT DISORDERS

OVERVIEW

Adler (1930a, 1930b, 1930/1963) was very concerned with the welfare of children and, unlike Freud, worked with children and families quite extensively throughout his professional career. He strongly stated that

> In the rearing of children there are some things which the parent or teacher must never allow to discourage him. He must never grow hopeless . . . he must not anticipate defeat . . . nor must he permit himself to be influenced by the superstition that there are gifted or ungifted children. Individual Psychology claims that the effort should be made with all children to stimulate their mental faculties by giving them more courage, more faith . . . by teaching them that difficulties are not . . . insurmountable obstacles, but a s problems to meet and conquer. (Adler, 1930a, p. 227)

Individual Psychologists have continued this effort and philosophy, working with children and families to provide education, guidance, and therapy in numerous formats across a wide variety of settings (Mosak & Maniacci, 1993). In the three chapters in this section are explored a variety of conditions.

Myers and Croake in Chapter 16 provide an extensive discussion of "Major Depressive Disorder During Childhood." They explore the relationship of childhood depression to adult depression and present guidelines for working with these issues as well as conduct disorders. They provide an excellent, in-depth review of the current literature and research.

Croake and Myers in Chapter 17 provide an extensive discussion of "Attention-Deficit/Hyperactivity Disorder and Specific Developmental Disorders." After an in-depth, broad review of the literature and current research in the field, they provide and Adlerian interpretation of the management and treatment strategies needed to deal effectively with such conditions. They highlight the interrelatedness of medication, family therapy, and psychological assessment in the treatment of these disorders.

Carlson in Chapter 18 presents the final chapter in this section, entitled "Eating Disorders." He reviews the various theoretical perspectives and integrates these with the Adlerian notions of purposiveness, sideshows, and the use of weakness in order to gain power.

REFERENCES

Adler, A. (1930a). *The education of children* (E. Jensen & F. Jensen, Trans.). South Bend, IN: Gateway Editions.

Adler, A. (1930b). *The pattern of life*. New York: Cosmopolitan Books.

Adler, A. (1963). *The problem child*. New York: Capricorn Books. (Original work published 1930)

Mosak, H.H., & Maniacci, M.P. (1993). Adlerian child psychotherapy. In R.J. Morris & T.R. Kratochwill (Eds.), *Handbook of psychotherapy with children and adolescents* (pp. 162–184). Boston: Allyn & Bacon.

Chapter 16

MAJOR DEPRESSIVE DISORDER DURING CHILDHOOD

Kathleen M. Myers
James W. Croake

The purpose of this chapter is to review the syndrome of Major Depressive Disorder (MDD) in children. The syndrome will be reviewed specifically according to diagnostic criteria of DSM-IV (American Psychiatric Association, 1994) and more generally with respect to phenomenology. MDD during childhood is an example of a disorder that usually is observed during adulthood but that may have an onset during earlier life as well. In this respect, Childhood-onset Major Depressive Disorder (COMDD) may be considered an example of a less common childhood disorder by DSM-IV criteria.

HISTORICAL

The diagnosis of MDD in children has aroused controversy. Early observations of young children separated from their mothers suggested that they developed a depressive disorder. Many institutionalized infants appeared devoid of interest in the outside world, apathetic, inconsolable, with poor developmental progression, sleep disturbances, and weight loss. They were termed "anaclitically depressed" (Spitz, 1946). Anaclitic depression in infants is a rare disorder, probably limited to infants who have been institutionalized early in life. A syndrome suggestive of a depressed state also was described in young children separated from their parents during wartime (Freud & Burlingham, 1974). Many of the children's features resembled a grieving process; however, the persistent and disabling course of their affective responses was similar to a depressed state. Other young children whose mothers were depressed also were observed to reciprocate their mothers' depressive affect (Freud, 1946). A developmental schema of separation, protest, and despair has been proposed to account for the depressive affects noted in these children (Bowlby, 1980). Initially, these young children protest separation from their parents with crying; later they despair that they will ever return and finally detach themselves from human bonding. This response is less likely to develop if the young child receives personal substitute parenting.

These infantile disorders associated with parental separation, however, never have been accepted as constituting the same depressive syndrome observed in later life. In the 1960s the argument was that children could not develop the full syndrome of depression despite their ability to sustain a depressed affect (Rie, 1966). The development of a full depressive disorder purportedly required psychological structures that were not developed until adolescence. Depressive affects were attributed to normal developmental processes. Piaget's studies lend credence to this theory, since "formal operations" in cognition do not become well developed until adolescence (Croake & Catlin, 1986).

By the 1970s the terms "masked depression" and "depressive equivalents" were used to conceptualize depression in children (Lefkowitz & Burton, 1978). Conduct problems, hyperactivity, and multiple other maladaptive behaviors were thought to represent behavioral manifestations of an underlying depression. According to this idea children could become depressed, but they displayed their depression through typical childhood misbehaviors. The affective components were obscured by the behavioral components. The phenomenology of childhood depression then would differ from adult depression. Under this schema, childhood depression also was overdiagnosed.

By 1980 several authors noted that depressive symptomatology could be distinguished from overlying "masking" behaviors when both occurred concurrently. They suggested applying to children the same criteria used to diagnose MDD in adults. The past decade has shown a growing consensus that children can experience an MDD syndrome that is consistent with adult diagnostic criteria and that is distinct from self-limited depressive symptoms (Carlson & Cantwell, 1980a, 1980b; Kovacs, Feinberg, & Crouse-Novak, 1984a; Mitchell, McCauley,

Burke, & Moss, 1988; Puig-Antich, 1980). Other disorders may occur with the depression and may appear to "mask" depressive symptomatology, but these disorders are diagnosed separately.

In DSM-IV (American Psychiatric Association, 1994) are delineated criteria for diagnosing Major Depressive Disorder (MDD) without reference to developmental period. If an infant, child, teen, or geriatric individual presents signs and symptoms that meet DSM-IV criteria for MDD, then the diagnosis may be made regardless of other coexisting diagnoses, symptoms, or behaviors. The application of DSM-IV criteria to childhood psychopathology has led to the recognition and general acceptance of Childhood-onset Major Depressive Disorder (COMDD).

Nevertheless, controversy persists. Specific questions include the following: Does COMDD represent a common nonspecific pathway during childhood to various adult Axis I or Axis II disorders? Alternatively, could it represent a self-limited syndrome phenomenologically similar to Adult-onset Major Depressive Disorder (AOMDD) that children will "outgrow"? Or does it represent an early-onset form of AOMDD syndrome? If the latter, does such early onset of MDD herald a more severe life course of the disorder? Current research is geared toward elucidating whether COMDD is the same disorder that at least 10% of men and 20% of women will experience at some time during their lives (Kaplan & Sadock, 1985), and how COMDD affects the holistic course of childhood development.

DSM-IV CRITERIA AND PHENOMENOLOGY OF COMDD

DSM-IV Diagnostic Criteria

The diagnostic criteria for Major Depressive Disorder (MDD) are listed in Table 16.1 (American Psychiatric Association, 1994, p. 327), Table 16.2 (pp. 377–378), and Table 16. 3 (p. 384). A pervasively depressed or anhedonic state must be present in addition to four other signs and symptoms.

Mood.   Most COMDD children will report a depressed mood; however, many may report a predominantly irritable mood without a depressed one. This is the only developmental concession made in DSM-IV to establish the diagnosis

TABLE 16.1
Criteria for Major Depressive Episode

A. Five (or more) of the following symptoms have been present during the same 2–week period and represent a change from previous functioning: at least one of the symptoms is either (1) depressed mood or (2) loss of interest or pleasure.

Note: Do not include symptoms that are clearly due to a general medical condition, or mood-incongruent delusions or hallucinations.

(1) depressed mood most of the day, early every day, as indicated by either subjective report (e.g., feels sad or empty) or observation made by others (e.g., appears tearful). **Note:** In children and adolescents, can be irritable mood.
(2) markedly diminished interest or pleasure in all, or almost all, activities most of the day, nearly every day (as indicated by either subjective account or observation made by others)
(3) significant weight loss when not dieting or weight gain (e.g., a change of more than 5% of body weight in a month), or decrease or increase in appetite nearly every day. **Note:** In children, consider failure to make expected weight gains.
(4) insomnia or hypersomnia nearly every day
(5) psychomotor agitation or retardation early every day (observable by others, not merely subjective feelings of restlessness or being slowed down)
(6) fatigue or loss of energy nearly every day
(7) feelings of worthlessness or excessive or inappropriate guilt (which may be delusional) nearly every day (not merely self-reproach or guilt about being sick)
(8) diminished ability to think or concentrate, or indecisiveness, nearly every day (either by subjective account or as observed by others)
(9) recurrent thoughts of death (not just fear of dying), recurrent suicidal ideation without a specific plan, or a suicide attempt or a specific plan for committing suicide

B. The symptoms do not meet criteria for a Mixed Episode (see p. 335).
C. The symptoms cause clinically significant distress or impairment in social, occupational, or other important areas of functioning.
D. The symptoms are not due to the direct physiological effects of a substance (e.g., a drug of abuse, a medication) or a general medical condition (e.g., hypothyroidism).
E. The symptoms are not better accounted for by Bereavement, i.e., after the loss of a loved one, the symptoms persist for longer than 2 months or are characterized by marked functional impairment, morbid preoccupation with worthlessness, suicidal ideation, psychotic symptoms, or psychomotor retardation.

From *Diagnostic and Statistical Manual of Mental Disorders, Fourth Edition* (DSM-IV). Copyright © 1994 by American Psychiatric Association. Reprinted with permission.

of MDD during the life span. The irritable mood may represent children's lesser ability to conceal the anger implicit during depressive episodes. Anger is even more commonly reported by MDD children than MDD adults (Mitchell et. al., 1988). It also may represent less discouragement. They have not withdrawn totally from others but continue to seek interpersonal contact, however negative.

TABLE 16.2
Criteria for Severity/Psychotic/Remission Specifiers for current (or most recent) Major Depressive Episode

Note: Code in fifth digit. Can be applied to the most recent Major Depressive Episode in Major Depressive Disorder and to a Major Depressive Episode in Bipolar I or II Disorder only if it is the most recent type of mood episode.

.x1—Mild: Few, if any symptoms in excess of those required to make the diagnosis and symptoms result in only minor impairment in occupational functioning or in usual social activities or relationships with others.

.x2—Moderate: Symptoms or functional impairment between "mild" and "severe."

.x3—Severe Without Psychotic Features: Several symptoms in excess of those required to make the diagnosis, **and** symptoms markedly interfere with occupational functioning or with usual social activities or relationships with others.

.x4—Severe with Psychotic Features: Delusions or hallucinations. If possible, specify whether the psychotic features are mood-congruent or mood-incongruent:

Mood-Congruent Psychotic Features: Delusions or hallucinations whose content is entirely consistent with the typical depressive themes of personal inadequacy, guilt, disease, death, nihilism, or deserved punishment.

Mood-Incongruent Psychotic Features: Delusions or hallucinations whose content does not involve typical depressive themes of personal inadequacy, guilt, disease, death, nihilism, or deserved punishment. Included are such symptoms as persecutory delusions (not directly related to depressive themes), thought insertion, thought broadcasting, and delusions of control.

.x5—In Partial Remission: Symptoms of a Major Depressive Episode are present but full criteria are not met, or there is a period without any significant symptoms of a Major Depressive Episode lasting less than 2 months following the end of the Major Depressive Episode. (If the Major Depressive Episode was superimposed on Dysthymic Disorder, the diagnosis of Dysthymic Disorder alone is given once the full criteria for a Major Depressive Episode are no longer met.)

.x6—In Full Remission: During the past 2 months, no significant signs or symptoms of the disturbance were present.

.x0—Unspecified.

From *Diagnostic and Statistical Manual of Mental Disorders, Fourth Edition* (DSM-IV). Copyright © 1994 by American Psychiatric Association. Reprinted with permission.

Children often do not recognize feeling depressed, especially if they have been depressed for a long time. Their current mood may be perceived as normal because they have lived with it for as long as they can remember. Hence, they cannot identify a premorbid state. Inquiry into related symptoms like sadness, gloominess, crankiness, or unhappiness may elicit unequivocal confirmation of a depressed or irritable mood. About one-half of the time, children cannot identify a reason for feeling so bad. It just seems to overcome them. They do not describe it as a reaction to life events. Other times they may offer a reason for their

TABLE 16.3
Criteria for Melancholic Features Specifier

Specify if:

With Melancholic Features (can be applied to the current or most recent Major Depressive Episode in Major Depressive Disorder and to a Major Depressive Episode in Bipolar I or Bipolar II Disorder only if it is the most recent type of mood episode)

A. Either of the following, occurring during the most severe period of the current episode:
     (1) loss of pleasure in all, or almost all, activities
     (2) lack of reactivity to usually pleasurable stimuli (does not feel much better, even temporarily, when something good happens)
B. Three (or more) of the following:
     (1) distinct quality of depressed mood (i.e., the depressed mood is experienced as distinctly different from the kind of feeling experienced after the death of a loved one)
     (2) depression regularly worse in the morning
     (3) early morning awakening (at least 2 hours before usual time of awakening)
     (4) marked psychomotor retardation or agitation
     (5) significant anorexia or weight loss
     (6) excessive or inappropriate guilt

From *Diagnostic and Statistical Manual of Mental Disorders, Fourth Edition* (DSM-IV). Copyright © 1994 by American Psychiatric Association. Reprinted with permission.

difficulties. Identifying a possible cause for the depression does not exclude the diagnosis. Many children who develop a depressed mood in response to a psychosocial stressor will not have a complete MDD syndrome but rather will meet DSM-IV criteria for an Adjustment Disorder with Depressed Mood. However, others will meet the full diagnostic criteria. Lack of an identifiable stressor is not part of the diagnostic criteria. Whether or not a stressor is identified, COMDD children usually report that their depressed or irritable mood lacks reactivity, i.e., their mood does not improve in response to positive external events (Mitchell et al., 1988). The disturbance seems pervasive to them. Parents, however, may note objective evidence of a favorable response to positive events.

Careful differentiation must be made of these mood states from the transitory unhappiness demonstrated by all children at stressful times during development. Such transitory unhappiness often reflects Goal I, attention getting, or Goal II, desire to dominate the adult misbehavior. Depression communicates greater discouragement and more frequently communicates Goal III misbehavior, in which the child feels hurt and wants to hurt back, or Goal IV misbehavior, in which the child wants to be left alone without the burden of expectations (Dreikurs, 1958).

Anhedonia.   Anhedonia does not appear to occur any more frequently in children than in adults, but it seems more striking (Mitchell et al., 1988). Adults are not accustomed to children lacking interest in any activities. Children often are better able to identify anhedonia than a depressed mood in themselves. They easily can understand feeling bored, not wanting to do anything, and that nothing is fun anymore. Sometimes they will state that they do have interests but do not feel like pursuing them. They may expect others to provide them with interesting activities. Parents often feel that they are supposed to entertain their depressed children. Some children do continue to participate in activities but with less fervor or pleasure. Others, especially eldest children, may continue with their perceived "obligations," especially if they hold positions of responsibility within their families. Their enjoyment of these activities must be determined. Care also must be taken not to confuse anhedonia with passivity or with Goal IV misbehavior (Dreikurs, 1973).

Other Diagnostic Symptoms.   Depressed or irritable mood and anhedonia are necessary but not sufficient criteria to diagnose the MDD syndrome. A total of five signs and symptoms of the nine listed in DSM-IV must be present. Compared to adults, children endorse significantly more guilt and have more suicide attempts, although the rate of suicidal ideation appears the same (Mitchell et al., 1988). Often these children will express their guilt as feeling responsible for things they did not do. Suicide attempts are typically of mild severity, but the children clearly identify wanting to die, not just wanting to hurt themselves. Some make serious attempts, as hanging; however, usually these attempts are made with an adult nearby. Frequently, these suicides are enacted impulsively. Reasons given typically include being reprimanded by a parent, feeling unloved, or feeling ridiculed by peers. Frequently, children state that they do not know why they made an attempt.

COMDD children endorse decreased appetite, weight loss, early morning awakening, and terminal insomnia, significantly less frequently than adults (Mitchell et al., 1988). Difficulty in getting to sleep, called initial insomnia, is common in MDD children and occurs at a rate comparable to MDD adults. Unlike AOMDD adults, children do not typically report their mood to be at its lowest ebb upon awakening and improving as the day progresses. Children generally do not describe any pattern of diurnal variability of their mood. Rather they describe a more consistently unhappy mood regardless of the time of day. Some children may state that their mood worsens during school hours. Careful inquiry must be made as to whether this is also true on weekends and whether their mood improves if they stay home from school. If the worsening of mood is related to school attendance, it is not considered a diurnal variation.

Psychotic Symptoms.   DSM-IV specifies that Major Depressive Episode With Psychotic Features is diagnosed if the individual experiences delusions or hallucinations during the depressive episode. Approximately 25% of AOMDD is of the psychotic subtype (Spitzer, Endicott, & Robins, 1978). The presence of such psychotic symptoms indicates greater severity of the depression and, therefore, greater self-absorbance and lower social interest. They do not feel that they have a place in society. The delusions are further categorized as congruent or incongruent with the depressive mood. Mood-congruent delusions are consistent with the depressive themes of personal inadequacy, guilt, death, and nihilism. Mood-incongruent delusions are those that emphasize thought control, paranoia, and other nondepressive themes. They more are commonly endorsed in schizophreniform psychoses.

Psychotic symptoms may occur during a COMDD episode (Chambers, Puig-Antich, & Tabrizi, 1982; Freeman, Poznanski, & Grossman, 1985; Mitchell et al., 1988); however, hallucinations are the only commonly reported psychotic symptom. These hallucinations are generally mild in severity, and frequently nondistressing, but may include self-destructive commands. COMDD children rarely report the mood-congruent delusions, mood-incongruent delusions, or other psychotic symptoms that characterize psychotically depressed adults.

Because psychotic disorders occur frequently in the parents of children who hallucinate, regardless of their diagnosis (Del Beccarro, Burke, & McCauley, 1988), COMDD children who hallucinate may be expressing a psychotic proclivity (Kemph, 1987). Hallucinations, however, are endorsed by children with various psychopathologies and even by normal children (Kotsopoulos, Kanigsberg, Cote, & Fiedorowicz, 1987). This nonspecificity of childhood hallucinations, their mild nature, and the lack of delusional thinking suggest that COMDD hallucinosis falls short of the psychotic depression syndrome observed in adults. However, according to DSM-IV, COMDD children who endorse hallucinations, and especially hallucinations with depressive themes such as self-destructive acts, should be considered to meet criteria for Major Depressive Episode With Psychotic Features.

Phenomenologically, hallucinations reported by COMDD children represent greater discouragement. Psychotically depressed children are demonstrating even greater reluctance to meet their life tasks than those COMDD children without psychotic features.

Sources of Information for Establishing a Diagnosis.   Information from both the child and parents is crucial to making the diagnosis. Children better describe subjective distress that their parents often underestimate, because parents just cannot imagine that their children feel as discouraged as they do. Parents, however, better describe objective behavioral signs that children underreport, because children are usually not aware of the distress their misbehaviors cause others (Herjanic, Herjanic, & Brown, 1975; Herjanic & Reich, 1982). When they are aware, they often feel guilty. This contrasts with childhood disturbances in which children do not seem to care how they affect others. Adjunctive information from auxiliary sources such as daycare, school, friends, or other family members is also helpful in establishing the diagnosis of MDD in children. In particular, teachers often have a better opportunity than parents to observe the MDD child's behavior around peers. Since depressed children feel alienated and withdraw from social activities even more than children with other psychiatric disorders, teachers can provide perspective on the extent to which the child is meeting responsibility to the life tasks of work, friendship, and community.

Related Signs and Symptoms

Cognitive Symptoms.   In addition to the DSM-IV (American Psychiatric Association, 1994) criteria, other symptoms typically characterize the depressed state in adults, contributing to MDD phenomenology. Depressed adults demonstrate a characteristic cognitive schemata in which they recurrently interpret themselves, their experiences, and the future in a negative manner (Kovacs & Beck, 1978). In Adlerian language, they lack courage, are overambitious and pessimistic.

Courage is the willingness to continue making efforts toward positive goals. *Overambition* is the opposite of self-confidence, characterized by the setting of unrealistic goals. *Pessimism* is the conviction that, whatever one attempts to accomplish, it will not come to a happy ending.

Depressed children may be similarly discouraged. They set unattainable goals, become increasingly self-absorbed, and give up on themselves and life. Like depressed adults, these children also may express negative views of themselves and exaggerate negative aspects of themselves, others, and the environment. Frequently, they see success as external to themselves and unpredictable. They do not feel in control of their fate. They harshly criticize themselves. As a result, depressed children feel hopeless, without self-control, and with little self-esteem compared to children with other psychiatric disorders (Haley, Fine, Marriage, Moretti, & Freeman, 1985; Kazdin, Unis, & French, 1983; McCauley, Mitchell, Burke, & Moss, 1988). The impaired self-esteem is profound and much more frequently endorsed by MDD children than MDD adults (Mitchell et al., 1988). This probably reflects children's lack of previously established cognitive mechanisms to mitigate the depressed state; however, lowered self-esteem is common to many childhood psychiatric disorders and may not be specific to the depressed state. Rather the pervasiveness of the impaired self-esteem may be that which characterizes depression. Maturation does not appear to make matters better. Depressed adolescents report even lower self-concept and greater depressive attributional style than depressed children (McCauley, Mitchell, Burke, & Moss, 1988).

According to Adler, these cognitive distortions, or negative self-talk, which result in mistakes relative to self and others, appear to resolve upon recovery from MDD, suggesting specificity to the depressed state. These cognitive distortions do not necessarily characterize the lifestyle. In this respect, the cognitive distortions resemble the Four Goals of Misbehavior. There are no such things as Goal I, Goal II, Goal III, or Goal IV children. Rather discouraged children demonstrate any of the Goals of Misbehavior to take unfair advantage of others at the moment. Similarly, negative self-talk is a *junctim*, a thought used to intensify an emotion, that guides children away from the life task that they are confronting at that instant (Adler, in Ansbacher & Ansbacher, 1956).

This ability to "catastrophize" (Ellis, 1973) is what many cognitively-oriented theorists view as a necessary prerequisite to the development of depression. The idea assumes that one can only take the depressive mental stance by going beyond the present moment and thinking to past apperceived negative situations and assuring oneself that the future will be even worse. The particular way in which one abstracts beyond the moment is in accord with one's lifestyle, one's characteristic pattern of movement.

Consistent with the Adlerian notion of holism, as the individual becomes discouraged, cognitive abilities are recruited into the movement toward depression. Children use their developing cognitive abilities to confirm their discouraged perception of life. Teens can emphasize their greater abstraction and conceptual ability to show further the ways in which they can be discouraged. All movement is toward an individual lifestyle goal, one's reason to be.

Somatic Symptoms.   One-quarter to one-third of AOMDD individuals present with somatic complaints and deny a depressed mood (Katon, Kleinman, & Rosen, 1982a; 1982b). These adults minimize the affective and cognitive components of their depression, while selectively emphasizing somatic symptoms (Katon, Kleinman, & Rosen, 1982a, 1982b). Somatic complaints are also frequently reported by COMDD children (McCauley, Carlson, & Calderon, 1991). Children are much more likely to endorse somatic complaints than are adults or children with other psychiatric disorders (Mitchell et al., 1988). They may deny depression stating that pain is the only thing distressing them (Hershberg, Carlson, Cantwell, & Strober, 1982; Hughes, 1984; Kashani, Lababidi, & Jones, 1982; Mitchell et al., 1988). Some may endorse both depression and physical symptoms. Hypochondriasis, however, is uncommon. The somatic complaints appear specific to the depressed state, since they resolve with remission of the MDD (Mitchell et al., 1988). This somatization may lead either to low-level discomfort that minimally interferes with life activities or to severe pain that interferes with most activities, especially with regular school attendance. The most common types of physical symptoms endorsed are abdominal pain, headaches, and chest pain.

The physical symptoms communicate these children's discouragement with their perceived inferiority. They are inadequately prepared for life's tasks. In their families of origin they have found that the reporting of physical symptoms allows them to escape responsibilities of school, friendship, and community involvement. When they do participate in these life tasks, they heroically surmount their feelings of inferiority by going on in spite of their claimed disability.

Concurrent Diagnoses

Phenomenologically, AOMDD frequently coexists with other DSM-IV diagnoses. The most common are Dysthymic Disorder (DD) and the Anxiety Disorders, specifically Panic Disorder (PD), Phobias, and Generalized Anxiety Disorder (GAD).

Overall, dual diagnoses are made in more than one-half of COMDD children (Kovacs, Feinberg, & Crouse-Novak, 1984a; Mitchell et al., 1988). As with AOMDD, the most common diagnoses concurrent with COMDD are DD, and Anxiety Disorders, especially Separation Anxiety Disorder (SAD). GAD occurs less commonly. Children with dual diagnoses do more poorly in meeting their life tasks than children with MDD alone (Mitchell et al., 1988).

Dysthymic Disorder.   DD affects about 38% of COMDD children (Kovacs et al., 1984a), which compares closely with the 26% reported in AOMDD patients (Keller & Shapiro, 1982). The DD may precede or follow an acute MDD episode, similar to the adult pattern. COMDD-DD children appear to have a poorer course than those with COMDD alone, consistent with the poor prognosis noted for adult "double depression" (Akiskal, 1983; Keller & Shapiro, 1982; Miller, Norman, & Dow, 1986). Their lives are experienced as constant disappointment with too many expectations that they believe they cannot meet (DD) and that only will get worse (MDD).

Anxiety Disorders.   Moderate to severe anxiety complicates the course of approximately half of AOMDD adults (Breier, Charney, & Heninger, 1985; Fawcett and Kravity, 1983; Leckman, Merikangas, & Pauls, 1983). DSM-IV is an improvement over previous diagnostic manuals, but one deficit is its lack of a mixed depression/anxiety diagnosis to describe this group of individuals.

Similarly, more than one-half of COMDD patients report anxiety symptoms (Hershberg et al., 1982; Puig-Antich & Rabinovich, 1986). SAD, the most common anxiety disorder in childhood, is diagnosed in approximately 40% of COMDD children (Kovacs et al., 1984a; Mitchell et al., 1988; Puig-Antich & Rabinovich, 1986). Other anxiety disorders occur much less frequently. It remains to be shown whether development may mediate the behavioral and experiential manifestations of anxiety. For example, Panic Disorder and Agoraphobia, which are frequently experienced by AOMDD adults but rarely by COMDD children, may be adult expressions of earlier SAD (Orvaschel & Weissman, 1986).

Separation anxiety is children's distress at being away from a nurturant adult figure. Their anxiety serves to control this significant other. They overcompensate feelings of inferiority by demonstrating how they can control another to their will. They demand the privilege of having their own mentor. They have learned that in their families the expression of such anxiety brings the special place of having no expectations placed on them (Goal IV misbehavior).

Conduct Disorders.   Many COMDD children, particularly COMDD boys, misbehave sufficiently to meet diagnostic criteria for Conduct Disorder (CD) (Kovacs et al., 1984a; Marriage, Fine, Moretti, & Haley, 1986; McGee & Williams, 1988; Mitchell et al., 1988; Puig-Antich, 1982). Because CD is a childhood diagnosis, a direct comparison of COMDD-CD children with AOMDD adults is not possible. CD is a precursor to Antisocial Personality Disorder (APD) in adulthood (Robins, 1978). Whether the co-occurrence of COMDD with CD also leads to adult APD or moderates the outcome is unknown.

Children who develop CD concurrently with MDD often will stop their CD misbehaviors upon recovery from depression (Puig-Antich, 1982), suggesting that CD may be an expression of MDD in some children. On the other hand, some COMDD children's depression develops secondary to a well-established CD (Anderson, Williams, McGee, & Silva, 1987). Other children appear to develop CD subsequent to an MDD episode (McGee & Williams, 1988). These sequences suggest that some COMDD-CD children may be evolving primary character disturbances (Axis II psychopathology) with secondary depression. In adults 40% of AOMDD occurs secondary to another psychiatric disorder (Spitzer et al., 1978; Weissman, Pottenger, & Kleber, 1977). Some COMDD children develop their depression secondary to Axis III medical illnesses as diabetes mellitus, or Axis I disorders as substance abuse or Attention-deficit Hyperactivity Disorder (Akiskal, Downs, & Jordan, 1985; Anderson et al., 1987; Biederman, Munir, & Knee, 1987), or Axis II Specific Developmental Disorders. COMDD secondary to an evolving Axis II character disorder is also possible. DSM-III (American Psychiatric Association, 1980) did not allow character disorders to be diagnosed in children, precluding consideration of such a diagnostic schema. A character disorder represents deficits in personality. But personality is not fully developed in children. DSM-III reasoned that a character disorder could not, therefore, be appropriately diagnosed in children. DSM-IV, however, has empirically removed this limitation, because many children and adolescents do demonstrate sufficiently dysfunctional personality structure to be considered characterologically impaired. Continuity between childhood and adulthood psychopathology, as observed between CD and APD, further supports the validity of diagnosing personality disorders at earlier developmental stages (Robins, 1978).

How the co-occurrence of MDD affects outcome of CD is unknown. It may attenuate Axis II Cluster B personality disorders away from APD toward other Cluster B disorders such as Borderline Personality Disorder (BPD). In adults, BPD is frequently associated with episodic MDD (Akiskal, 1981). Several studies have reported that COMDD-CD children meet criteria for BPD (Greenman, Gunderson, & Cane, 1986; McManus, Lerner, & Robbins, 1984).

COMDD-CD children believe that the world owes them. They are not constrained by the usual social mores. COMDD children with other concurrent diagnoses continue to make some movement toward meeting their life tasks, albeit within the constraints of their private logic. COMDD-CD children, however, make no movement toward meeting their life tasks. They do not feel part of the larger human community. They want the world to grant them special exemption.

Physiology and Organ Inferiority

Multiple studies have demonstrated physiological abnormalities in the neuroendocrine system of AOMDD adults during the depressed state. Three major areas of functioning are involved. First, sleep is disrupted, particularly the onset of rapid eye movement (REM) sleep. These abnormalities are well documented with sleep electroencephalography (S-EEG) (Gillin, Duncan, & Murphy, 1981). Second, neuroreceptors that control the output of hormones and other neuroendocrine substances are blunted or "downregulated" during the depressed state. A failure to appropriately regulate output of these body chemicals results (Willner, 1985). Affected hormones and other circulating substances include, among others, growth hormone, cortisol, epinephrine (Adrenalin), norepinephrine, serotonin, and beta-endorphin. Third, the hypothalamic-pituitary-adrenal axis (HPA) that controls basic bodily functions is overactive during MDD resulting in excessive production of selected hormones (Arans, Baldessarini, & Ornsteen, 1985). These abnormalities are not present in all AOMDD adults. They probably reflect in part the severity of the depression and more endogenous features. An adult who develops these abnormalities during a severe depression that has gone untreated for some time may not develop them during another depression that has been treated early in its course. These neuroendocrine abnormalities are present during the depressed state but not during recovery. Therefore, they reflect the acute depressed state rather than preexisting physiologic traits or organ inferiority.

The presence of an organ inferiority in MDD, however, is supported by inheritance studies. Methods for investigating possible genetic transmission of psychological disorders have included twin studies, family history studies, direct family pedigree studies, and adoption studies. Most of these studies have been conducted with adults in order to allow affected individuals sufficient time to develop the disorder. MDD has a lifetime risk, unlike many other DSM-IV disorders that have a limited age range for onset and usually are first demonstrated in young adulthood. Investigating children, teens, or young adults would not identify cases with later age-of-onset. All of these methodologies have supported a genetic component to the transmission of MDD (Nurnberger & Gershon, 1984; Wender, Kety, & Rosenthal, 1986). They support the Adlerian concept of an underlying organ inferiority leading to the expression of a psychiatric disorder. How this genetic proclivity, or organ inferiority, relates to the observed physiological changes is not yet known. No studies have yet attempted to correlate physiologic abnormalities in the acute state with inherited risk for MDD. At present, some individuals appear to have an inherited organ inferiority predisposing them to depression. Some of these individuals develop the disorder, and others do not. Of those who do become acutely depressed, some demonstrate physiologic changes in their neuroendocrine system. These changes resolve with recovery from the depression. Due to an underlying organ inferiority, they remain at-risk for recurrence of the disorder at another time during their lives.

The occurrence of physiological abnormalities in children with COMDD has not been as well investigated. Preliminary evidence supports some alteration in biological functions, but not with the same frequency or with the same pattern as noted in AOMDD. Sleep disturbances are common complaints of COMDD children. The S-EEG abnormalities noted for adults, however, have not been as strongly or consistently measured with children (Goetz, Puig-Antich, & Ryan, 1987; Lahmeyer, Poznanski, & Bellur, 1983; Puig-Antich, Goetz, & Hanlon, 1982, 1983; Young, Knowles, & MacLean, 1982). They are more frequently observed with depressed adolescents than depressed children, and especially with older rather than younger depressed adolescents.

On tests that measure neuroendocrine functioning and integrity of the HPA axis, children have shown some abnormalities, but again not with the same sensitivity as depressed adults (Doherty, Madansky, & Kraft, 1986; Freeman et al., 1985; Petty, Asarnow, & Carlson, 1985; Poznanski, Carroll, & Banegas, 1982; Weller, Weller, & Fristad, 1984, 1985). However, specificity of these abnormalities to the depressed state in children is high, similar to depression in adults.

Very few studies have investigated neuroreceptor control during COMDD. These few have reported that some children do show blunting or downregulation of neuroreceptors during COMDD, but less frequently than expected from adult studies (Cavallo, Holt, & Hejazi, 1987; Puig-Antich, Goetz, & Davies, 1984a, 1984b; Puig-Antich, Novacenko, & Davies, 1984a; 1984b; Puig-Antich, Novacenko, & Goetz, 1984). In particular, growth hormone and melatonin appear affected, but cortisol diurnal secretion does not.

Three conclusions relative to the phenomenology of COMDD have been proposed to account for these differences. First, children with COMDD may not develop physiological abnormalities during the depressed state as frequently as adults, because children may not become as severely depressed as adults. Second, children may not have the same disorder experienced by adults. In this case a different pattern of abnormalities would be expected. Third, children may experience the same disorder, but the receptors mediating physiological dysfunction during depression may not be fully developed and so the abnormalities cannot be as reliably measured (Davis, Davis, & Mathe, 1984; Gillin et al., 1981; Goetz et al., 1987). Receptor expression may accelerate with puberty, be completed with adulthood, and decline with senescence leading to a different pattern of physiological functioning at each developmental stage (Gillin et al., 1981). The development of neuroreceptor functioning in humans has not been well studied, and so this theory remains speculative.

Similar to adults, no studies have attempted to investigate these physiological abnormalities as a function of an underlying organ inferiority. Several studies, however, have shown that MDD in parents confers on their preadult children an increased risk of COMDD as well as an increased risk of other psychopathology and of impairments in overall functioning (Beardslee, Bemporad, & Keller, 1983; Keller, Beardslee, Dorer, Lavori, & Samuelson, 1986; Weissman, Gammon, & John, 1987; Weissman, Prusoff, & Gammon, 1984). Conversely, parents of mood-disordered children and adolescents show high occurrence of mood disorders but not higher than observed in the parents of children with other psychiatric disorders (Mitchell, McCauley, Burke, Calderon, & Schloredt, 1989; Puig-Antich, Goetz, Davies, 1989). Transmission of an organ inferiority is suggested by these studies, but it may not be specifically related to disturbances of mood. In this respect, children of mood-disordered parents may demonstrate problems related to temperament, behavior, mood, and intellectual performance in the absence of any signs of a depressive disorder. Whether these children are demonstrating effects of parenting and environmental stressors or an underlying organ inferiority that places them at-risk for development of MDD is unknown.

All COMDD is a holistic movement. The building blocks of heredity and environment are present with everyone (Adler, in Ansbacher & Ansbacher, 1956). The degree of influence from one or the other, from child to child is not known at this time. Further research is needed to determine whether this heterogeneous group of COMDD children with and without physiological abnormalities during the depressed state are differentiated by specific underlying organ inferiorities.

Demographic Phenomenology

Prevalence.   As many as one-third of normal school-aged children report depressive symptoms at some time during elementary school years (Kaslow, Tannenbaum, & Abramson, 1983; Seligman, Kaslow, & Alloy, 1984). Feeling depressed appears to be a common problem for children; however, the full COMDD syndrome occurs much less frequently. Approximately 1–2% of all preteen children have experienced an episode of MDD (Anderson et al., 1987; Kashani, McGee, Clarkson, Anderson, & Walton, 1983). Many children may never receive appropriate clinical evaluation. Those who do comprise from 13% to 34% of clinical samples (Carlson & Cantwell, 1980b; Hershberg et al., 1982).

COMDD probably is underdiagnosed in younger children. Children under 10 years of age have difficulty identifying their affect and labelling problems, and parents frequently underestimate the subjective distress experienced by their young children. Therefore, depression is likely to be underdiagnosed in this age group (Herjanic et al., 1975; Kazdin, French, & Unis, 1983). By 10 years of age children do reliably endorse their depression, and reported rates are more accurate (Herjanic & Reich, 1982; Reich, Herjanic, & Welner, 1982).

Age.   Many independent centers have reported MDD in children as young as 7 years of age (Carlson & Cantwell, 1980a; Chambers, Puig-Antich, & Hirsch, 1985; Kovacs et al., 1984a; Mitchell et al., 1988; Puig-Antich, Chambers, & Tabrizi, 1983); however, DSM-IV criteria allow the diagnosis to be made in any age range, including infants. MDD-like states have been identified in preschoolers (Kashani & Carlson, 1987; Kashani & Ray, 1987), but the occurrence in toddlers and infants is not well documented.

Age-of-onset may be a variable that integrates COMDD and AOMDD into a single depressive disorder across the life span. Epidemiologic studies with adults indicate that earlier age-at-onset for AOMDD correlates with more severe dysfunction and with a more familial type disorder; and older age-at-onset correlates with more sporadic type depression (Mendlewicz & Baron, 1981). AOMDD is unique among DSM-IV disorders in its cumulative risk throughout the life span. COMDD may represent the earliest end of a depression spectrum with increasing risk throughout the life span, and greater severity with younger age-at-onset.

Sex. The sex composition of AOMDD is complex. Higher rates of AOMDD for women frequently are reported (Myers, Weissman, & Tischler, 1984; Robins, Helzer, & Weissman, 1984). But marital status, presence of young children in the home, and differential patterns of help-seeking by sex may confound these reports (Radloff, 1975; Weissman & Klerman, 1977).

This issue is similarly complex with children. No sex differential has been established for COMDD (Carlson & Cantwell, 1980b; Kashani et al., 1983; Kovacs et al., 1984a; Mitchell et al., 1988); Puig-Antich, 1980). Girls, however, are overrepresented in clinical COMDD samples compared to other childhood DSM-IV disorders and, during adolescence, increasingly outnumber boys in rates of MDD (Rutter 1986). The role of sex in the expression of MDD in both adults and children remains unclear. Both sociocultural and biological factors are probably relevant to symptom expression. Females experience an inferior social status that they resent but are socially encouraged to maintain. Males enjoy the superior social standing that they are encouraged to exert. These social mores may contribute to the greater rate of depression observed in females and of sociopathy in males (Kaplan & Sadock, 1985). Biological factors probably contribute as well, because testosterone is associated with higher levels of aggressiveness and estrogen with passivity in primates. Both nature and nurture may be invoked by the individual's private logic to support a life stance.

Course of the Disorder

Recovery from an episode of Major Depression during childhood and the risk of relapse is important to understanding the phenomenology of this disorder for three reasons. First, if this is not a serious illness comparable to adult-onset

MDD, COMDD children might be expected to experience transient depressive states without significant morbidity. But if COMDD is comparable to AOMDD, then recovery and relapse patterns might be similar. This would portend a more serious life vulnerability to this disorder. Second, knowing the expected course would assist treatment planning for either a sporadic disability or a protracted impairment. Third, accurate determination of the onset and offset of the disorder is necessary to establish interepisode morbidity. For example, full recovery from an acute disorder is necessary in order to determine whether an underlying personality disorder is present, which may predispose to recurrence. Establishing remission of acute morbidity is the first step in beginning the evaluation for possible chronic morbidity.

Recovery.   AOMDD used to be described as an episodic disorder with full recovery between episodes. Research over the past two decades, however, reveals more variability in the course of the disorder. Approximately two-thirds of AOMDD patients experience only a single MDD episode, while others develop recurrent episodes, and approximately 15% suffer a chronic nonremitting disorder (Robins & Guze, 1972; Weissman & Klerman, 1977; Zis & Goodwin, 1979). Some individuals with a recurrent disorder do fully recover between episodes, but others do not. Minor depression or Dysthymic Disorder (DD) may be present between AOMDD episodes and may have preceded or followed the first AOMDD incident in natural history (Akiskal, 1983; Akiskal, King, & Rosenthal, 1981); however, the range is large, from four weeks to several years.

Rates of recovery from MDD during childhood are not well established; however, preliminary evidence indicates that COMDD is not a transient disorder (Kovacs et al., 1984a; McGee & Williams, 1988). The children are unlikely to recover within the first three months. Episodes average 32 weeks, with a range from 4 to 60 weeks (Kovacs et al., 1984a). A later age-of-onset appears to correlate with faster recovery, but with a shorter interim well-time to recurrence. As with adults, DD frequently precedes COMDD or develops subsequently (Kovacs et al., 1984a). More children seem to recover and do so more rapidly than adults. Only 50% of MDD adults reportedly recover by 12 months and 64% by 24 months (Akiskal et al., 1981; Keller, Shapiro, & Lavori, 1982a), compared to 92% of child subjects by 18 months (Kovacs et al., 1984a). Children may have an advantage toward recovery.

The presence of concurrent DD, however, negates this advantage. Adults with AOMDD superimposed on DD recover from the acute MDD episode more rapidly than adults with only AOMDD (Gonzales, Lewinsohn, & Clarke, 1985; Keller & Shapiro, 1982; Keller et al., 1982a), but children with and without DD do not appear to demonstrate such a recovery differential (Kovacs et al., 1984a).

To date, COMDD appears to run a moderately long course comparable to AOMDD, but children have a better prognosis for recovery from MDD episodes. Their course, however, may be complicated by continuing behavioral problems, including overt Conduct Disorders or other behavioral deviance (McGee & Williams, 1988). Developmental factors influencing outcome are not yet known.

Recurrence.   As indicated in Table 16.1, MDD may be either a single episode disorder or recurrent. Most, but not all, children initially presenting for help are usually experiencing their first episode, although it may be of long duration. Frequently parents think that their children are going through a difficult period or will outgrow whatever is distressing them. They will then delay treatment. Over time, many of these children will experience a course with several recurrences.

The rate of recurrence is high (Kovacs et al., 1984b; McCauley, Mitchell, Burke, Myers, Calderon, & Schloredt, 1988). The most current evidence ascertained from several independent studies suggests that 40% to 70% of COMDD children followed over three to five years will relapse at least once. Twenty-six percent may relapse within the first year of recovery (Kovacs et al., 1984b). This compares with a one-year relapse of 38% in adults (Keller, Shapiro, & Lavori, 1982b). At two years, 40% of COMDD children relapse. If COMDD children also have a Dysthymic Disorder (COMDD-DD), the risk for one-year recurrence increases from 9% (COMDD) to 43% (COMDD-DD) (Kovacs et al., 1984b). This large differential is not shown by AOMDD adults with DD (44%) and without DD (38%) (Keller & Shapiro, 1982); however, both MDD children and MDD adults with DD appear to have their greatest rate of relapse during the first four weeks following full recovery. Dysthymic Disorder is also one of the strongest predictors of later MDD for individuals who have not yet had an MDD episode. Fifty percent of DD children and 36% of DD adults will experience an MDD episode within three to four years.

Longitudinal information contributes to the phenomenology of COMDD by demonstrating a propensity for recurrence, especially in the first year, similar to that observed in AOMDD. The similar courses strengthen the use of DSM-IV criteria to diagnose the disorder in children. Unknown yet is whether the disability experienced by children with a recurrent disorder is comparable to that of adults. Recurrence suggests greater discouragement and increasing lack of social interest, a feeling that one is not a full member of society. However, knowing the disability incurred would reveal the direction of movement. Greater disability might suggest a perceived helplessness (Goal IV misbehavior) that justifies reneging on one's life responsibilities. Lesser disability might suggest heroism, of rising above it all, and putting oneself above others.

ADLERIAN DYNAMICS

Constitutional Factors

Adoption studies established a heredity component to MDD (Kaplan & Sadock, 1985). Regardless of the family in which an individual is reared, depression is highly correlated among first degree biological relatives. Among identical twins separated at birth and reared in different families, a 65% concordance rate has been found for mood disorders. Therefore, a constitutional predisposition exists toward depression that Adler (1927) termed an "organ inferiority." The specificity of that organ defect is not known at this time.

Early Training

Adlerr (1961) believed that these children, in addition to having an organ inferiority, are pampered, hated, or neglected. *Pampering* is doing for children that which they are capable of doing for themselves. This trains them to be overly dependent upon others and robs them of a normal, developmental self-confidence. Hating or neglecting children trains them to believe that others in the family are favored over them and the world is a hostile place.

This dependency upon others, most often mother (Kanoy & Miller, 1980; McDonald, 1980), becomes a generalized dependence upon others for support. These children rely on their parents' achievement rather than their own and believe that they are unable to attain the lofty recognition that they demand for themselves (Adler, 1969).

Lifestyle Themes

COMDD children are overambitious (Smith, 1981). The greater their depression, the greater their ambition. Mild depression shows itself in mild overambition. Severe depression is typified by extreme ambition (Adler, 1970). COMDD children want to give the impression that they are kind and noble. This exterior may appear to be humility, but it should never be taken as concern and consideration for others (Adler, 1961). Consideration is not extended toward others as can be seen by the self-pity that they demonstrate. Self-pity is not concern for others.

Anger

The absence of kindness and consideration for others is an expression of anger towards others. These children believe that they are not given the recognition that is due to them. They think that they have been unjustly cared for and have a right to be angry. They may recognize that they are treating others unkindly, but their private logic allows them to be unkind because others in the family have been favored in preference to them. Mosak (1971) repeats these children's private logic to them: "I may be wrong, but they are more wrong."

The hostility toward others is most often covert in the form of signs and symptoms of depression. Anyone who has lived with a depressed person knows how much everyone around the depressed person suffers. At times, the hostility will be more overt. Irritability is common. They may destroy property, including their own, and may verbally or physically attack others.

Pampering

Again, it is usually mother who is seen as the cause of their problems. Rather than allowing for normal successes and failures, the parents have protected them. The parents have pampered them in a misguided attempt to protect them. These children have not been allowed to assume increasing responsibilities with increasing age and ability. In an effort to be good parents, they have not allowed their children to do whatever they could for themselves, to experience the successes as well as the failures that follow in normal growth and development.

The parents' overindulgence is increasingly seen as being "not enough consideration for me" by COMDD children as they find themselves to be less capable than others. Upon inquiry they can readily point to a sister, brother, relative, school mate, and so forth, who is better treated. They reason that this favored treatment has enabled these "anointed beings" to achieve where the depressed children feel incapable. They know that their parents could have done much more to help them succeed in a hostile world.

Life Tasks

COMDD children are not preparing to meet the tasks of life: community, occupation, and love (Adler, in Ansbacher & Ansbacher, 1964). They demonstrate resentment toward others. They feel inferior to others and covertly desire to be above all others. They have not learned to cooperate with family members. They carry this lack of cooperation to peers, school, and the greater community as they age.

The pampering they receive does not allow them to master chores and develop a sense of competency that later would allow them to be willing and feel capable of making a contribution to self and others through useful work. They hesitate to involve themselves fully in school and in other work even when they are talented. They do not experience the satisfaction that commitment to work affords.

Lacking in Cooperation

The successes that they do have are selfishly guarded and are used to feel momentarily superior to others. They begrudge the accomplishments of peers and siblings and take another's achievement as a personal failure for themselves. They have not learned to cooperate.

This lack of cooperation is often first evident between children and parents. COMDD children may be demanding as infants, continue to wet the bed as they age, and even defecate on themselves. This self-soiling is a stealthy attack upon others who have to change the bedding, do extra washing, and put up with unpleasant odor and sanitation. It is a further example of their hostility. This hostility will carry over to dating and mating. They have not learned the value of cooperating as children but have learned to defeat others, to feel superior when others fail to succeed. They will use lovers for selfish gain. They do not know how to bond with others for the mutual good.

Recollections of punishment or unfairness are remembered and used as justification for not contributing, not trying, not treating others fairly, being angry, or harming another. Revenge is most often demonstrated through self-destruction (e.g., poor posture, sleep, and eating problems). These are sideshows (Adler, 1961).

Obfuscation

Sideshows are sign and symptom production for the purpose of avoiding the life tasks, for not cooperating. These children become consumed with their problems and have no time, energy, or ability to get on with life, to make a contribution to the common welfare. Their bid for nobility translates into "no-ability."

Using Others

COMDD is a demonstration of learning to elicit concern and help from others by showing weakness, sadness, and helplessness. The more help that is offered in the form of pampering and indulgence, the greater the number and intensity of signs and symptoms of depression. In this way they defeat those who offer to help them. If self-esteem is low enough, the principal feelings of superiority come from being unique in that no one can make life better for them.

Giving suggestions, assuming responsibility for these children only meets with further defeat. To fall into this trap is very tempting as COMDD children have mastered methods for gaining support from others. They seem so harmless and pitiful that others readily jump in and further the pampering. This behavior continues until others feel so defeated and inadequate in their efforts that they detach themselves from the child. The human compassion that leads people to reach out to COMDD children with common sense methods of helping is an opportunity to turn the helper into a servant. No amount of common sense help is quite enough.

Overambition

COMDD children set goals that are impossible to attain. They will not settle for normal step-by-step progress that carries no assurance of success. They want it all, and they want it now. The hostile world is an ever present opportunity to fail. This view leads to the idea that, "nothing ventured, nothing lost" (Mosak, 1971). Protecting their image of nobility and superiority becomes of paramount importance. They cannot risk the possibility of failure. Those involved with them misinterpret this behavior as a lack of ambition and will mistakenly attempt to motivate them through common sense methods. The predictable result is that those doing the motivating end up defeated. Again, the COMDD child has triumphed and attained a feeling of superiority at the expense of another victim.

Attitude to Fail

These children have lofty, high standards, but effort toward tasks means opening themselves to possible defeat and perceived scorn by others. The hostility that they have for others is turned into imagined contempt from others if they were to try but fail in their attempt to achieve. The result is a replacement of the attempts toward achieving tasks with an intense contemplation of all the many ways that they might try but fail. By focusing on the many ways in which they might fail, the calamitous results, they attain the proper corresponding affect that connotes to themselves and the world that if it were not for their problems, they would be successful. In this stance toward the world, they feel hopeless.

They demand a guarantee of perfect results before they will take on a task. The fear of failure leads to an investment in pride rather than effort. The greater the pride, the less one has about which to be proud.

Appearance

The hostility and attempts to elevate themselves by defeating others is rarely in their consciousness. They are mostly aware of how bad they feel. As they mature, they offer increasing feelings of guilt when they demonstrate their selfishness and hostility. Appearing noble rather than acting noble becomes more and more characteristic of their pattern of behavior. This is most evident in suicidal ideation: "I just don't wish to be a further burden to my family."

Family Dynamics

The mother may be lacking in cooperation to a degree that she fails to bond with the child (Adler, in Ansbacher & Ansbacher, 1956). Mother's self-absorption will not provide a secure attachment or a model for useful involvement with others.

Competition between the parents is most easily seen in increasingly different interests. With time and devotion to common tasks, the expectation is that a salubrious marriage will result in more similarity of interests. This marital competition also sets the stage for competition between the children and is the basis for differences in lifestyle (personality) characteristics between the siblings, especially the dissimilarities between the first and second children (Dreikurs, 1958).

The other children in the family may appear to be better adjusted at the expense of the depressed child. So long as signs and symptoms of depression are maintained, they elevate themselves at the expense of their depressed sibling. They can further this elevation by being "helpful" and "feeling sorry" for their depressed sibling. This results in the depressed child feeling even more incapable while furthering the belief that "I have been done wrong and deserve special consideration to make up for this unfairness."

First-born children are most likely to develop depression for many reasons, including family expectations for successfully carrying on the family's perceived image, fulfilling the parental and other family member's ambitions, inability of the parents to allow these first-borns to be their own persons, the desperate attempts of the oldest child to regain the focus of attention when the second child is born, feeling dethroned, believing achievement will result in regaining a favored position, and so forth.

More insidious is the tacit agreement of the parents to invest themselves in signs and symptoms of depression in their child as a method for avoiding looking at their dysfunctional marriage. The child's depression becomes a smoke screen for not moving forward with their love task. They too can appear to be nobly concerned, in this case "no-ability" to form a useful marital bond. The focus on their child provides them with an excuse for not attending to their marriage while elevating their "good parent" image. This parental behavior has the unfortunate result of modeling poor cooperation as well as making the child a scapegoat for their dysfunctional union.

Treatment Strategy

Therapy focuses on bringing to awareness the lofty ambition, the self-loathing, anger towards parents, and attempts to defeat others, particularly family members. The four goals of misbehavior (Dreikurs, 1958) are useful for detecting the immediate reason for maladaptive behavior and can guide one toward understanding the particular lifestyle that supports depression. The goals of misbehavior indicate the degree of discouragement and point to those adults who are the specific victims of these children.

Goals of Misbehavior

The children are asked in therapy several reasons for their behavior: if they possibly could be seeking attention (Goal I); or could they be attempting to demonstrate that they are more powerful than the adult in the situation (Goal II); or could it be that be that they are expressing their feelings of hurt by directly or furtively attacking the adult (Goal III); or could they be demonstrating their feelings of helplessness by demonstrating their inadequacy (Goal IV). With adolescents the questions are more pointed. "Everyone knows that depression is an expression of hostility and an effort to defeat people. Toward whom are you directing your anger?"

Self-pity

COMDD children believe that their situation is far worse than that of others, that too much is expected of them, that a constant demand to do for others is expected of them, and that too little is done for them. Asking them in counseling if it is possible that they are thinking these thoughts brings these attitudes to their and the family's awareness.

Fantasy

The reaction to revealing these private thoughts is often shock. The masquerade of nobility has been convincing to everyone. This can be further seen when a desire for fame has been revealed. The fame is characterized by fantasies of heroism. An extreme expression of this desire can be seen in suicidal ideation. These children may contemplate a TV program interruption bringing the late, breaking news of their death. This fantasy is followed by scenes of their family grieving.

A therapy question revealing this desire for heroism and notoriety is, "Would it be a fair statement to say that you want to be a hero (or that you desire to be famous)?" Adler (1927) termed this method of questioning as "spitting in the soup." These children and families have difficulty continuing to buy the apparent nobility and self-effacing image: They can continue to eat the soup, but it no longer is so appealing.

Family Therapy

The therapeutic setting of choice with children is with the entire family. This forum allows all members of the family to understand their roles in these dynamics. Adlerian family therapy is a systems approach with emphasis upon the family constellation. This approach considers the investment of the family in the depressive signs displayed by the identified child. Tactics such as focusing on potential problems of another family member who is seen as the best adjusted can be employed, as can other interventions familiar to family systems therapists.

Group treatment with peers, especially when adolescence has been attained, is also a good adjunctive therapy. The larger family is still an important involvement even when the focus is group therapy with peers. Parent education can also be an effective treatment method (Croake & Hinkle, 1983).

CASE VIGNETTE: JIMMY—
ACUTE-ONSET MDD FOLLOWING
RECENT SEVERE STRESSOR AND
PRODROMAL COMPULSIVE BEHAVIORS

History

Jimmy was an 11-year-old boy who presented to the clinic due to trash collecting. He had been collecting trash for seven months and now had a disarrayed room full of it. Jimmy's father's discovery of the malodorous trash motivated Jimmy's mother to seek treatment. Jimmy described feeling "sad" whenever he thought of throwing away any items. Multiple attempts by the family to dispose of the trash resulted in tearful, agitated tantrums. He always protested coming to therapy, although he always came. He would leave a session when we began to plan disposal of the trash. His mother insisted and Jimmy finally complied; however, he agreed to burn the trash, only if he could keep the ashes near the house. In four weeks all of the trash was burned. The family was advised to check back four weeks after school began. They did not return, "since things were going well and we did not want to rock the boat."

The family returned to the clinic four months later. Jimmy was asking to see the doctor due to growing distress. He described an increasing anger especially directed toward one boy whom he felt received special treatment at school and who was harassing him. He wanted to kill this boy. He did not want to attend school anymore.

Jimmy felt like crying all the time but did not endorse the sadness he previously had reported. His mother described him as constantly very irritable. He stated that he had great difficulty falling asleep, requiring one to three hours, but then slept well. He also reported wanting to eat all of the time and had gained 10 to 15 pounds. He had difficulty doing school work due to fatigue and decreased ability to concentrate. He tired very easily. Initially, he did not think of suicide; however, he did describe a desire to hurt himself or "to destroy something important to relieve the tension." He then began to scratch himself across the forehead with scissors, which "released the tension." Later he became suicidal. When he broke items, they were only his own possessions. This did not relieve the tension sufficiently, and he feared breaking more important things. He lost interest in most activities. Additionally, Jimmy was reluctant to go out of his home unless with a family member or with one friend who helped him by telling him what to do. He complained of several physical symptoms without detectable cause and often stayed home from school. He did not endorse any guilt or demonstrate any negative cognitive distortions. No endorsement of hallucinations or other psychotic symptoms was evident. He wanted to come to treatment as often as possible. Several unscheduled visits to the clinic were made.

Past Medical History.   Jimmy had mononucleosis eight months previously. During this illness, he experienced a respiratory arrest. He was intubated to assist breathing and spent four days in the intensive care unit (ICU). He knew that he had almost died but stated that no one had discussed this with him.

Social History.   Jimmy had always been an excellent student. He had an IQ in the superior range. His family was intact with no major family or marital problems endorsed. A 19-year-old sister lived at home while attending college. He had many friends but was "shy." His father held stable employment as an engineer and his mother as a special education teacher.

Family History.   There was no significant medical or psychiatric history in first degree relatives. A distant relative had Bipolar Disorder.

Mental Status Examination and Observations

Jimmy was seen alone and with his family. The most notable observations were a very rationalized and intellectualized psychological style in all family members. They also appeared very guarded even after knowing the treating therapist for many months and having enjoyed success with the initial treatment program. Jimmy's father and the sister kept particular distance and would not comply with recommended family treatment. Jimmy's mother was described by her daughter as overinvolved with her son. The father did not object to being left out or not being told about the trash collecting.

Jimmy seemed more agitated and irritable than depressed on each evaluation. Although endorsing "uncontrollable anger," he seemed worried, anxious, sad, with a very blunted affect. His mood was anxious and irritable. Jimmy demonstrated great concern in play and drawings with armor, self-defense, danger, and dying.

Jimmy offered the following Early Recollection at the first clinic visit. "I was at my fourth birthday party. I was walking through the dining room and looking at the toy helicopter in my hand. My uncle gave it to me as a birthday gift." When asked for the most important scene and his feeling, Jimmy responded "When I was looking at it. I felt excited."

When seen four months later, Jimmy gave the same Early Recollection. He also described the same "most important scene." However, when asked for his feeling he replied "I don't know; I can't tell what I feel."

Course of Treatment

Due to the previous episode of mononucleosis and his acute course, Jimmy received a comprehensive evaluation. A CT scan of his head, an electroencephalogram, neuropsychological testing, and projective testing revealed no indications of organicity or psychosis.

The father would not comply with regular family sessions, although he would attend sporadically. Due to the severity of Jimmy's depression with harm to himself and potential for harm to others, medication was started. The first medication chosen was ineffective and worsened his insomnia. Fluoxetine then was prescribed. This medication belongs to the alleged "serotonergic" medications, which have been efficacious for treating Obsessive-Compulsive Disorder (OCD), as well as depression. Although Jimmy had no more compulsive behaviors, he still described many obsessional features, such as overfocusing on his schoolmate, constant thoughts of harming himself, worry about leaving the house, and over-concern with self-defense. He still collected, although the items were age-appropriate toys.

Jimmy improved steadily during six weeks of medication and sporadic family sessions. Goal diagnosis in the family session indicated Goal III and IV to be the most common misbehaviors directed toward both parents. "Could it be" questions to Jimmy clearly indicated that hostility and attempts to defeat the mother were the purpose of many signs and symptoms.

Competition between the parents was addressed by having them agree to take one evening each week for an outing away from home where the two of them would have "fun." Obtaining mutual agreement for a strategy for dealing with Jimmy's signs of depression went a long way toward increasing marital cooperation. The older sister agreed to stop "mothering" Jimmy; albeit, she never did cease feeling sorry for him, but she would leave the house when those feelings came into her awareness.

Symptoms and signs persist, although significantly abated. In particular, he is no longer obsessed with the schoolmate, has no thoughts of hurting himself or of breaking things, and attends school regularly. He is playing baseball, his favorite sport; however, he joined the team only under the guidance of his trusted friend. His affect remains fairly blunted, although a sense of humor is returning. He remains concerned with self-defense and guns but tolerates less frequent therapy sessions, because he is "too busy."

Comment

Jimmy's case is rather atypical due to the initial presentation of obsessive-compulsive features; however, it is typical in other regards. Children may not demonstrate depression as the initial problem. A variety of symptoms may evolve over time to finally meet MDD criteria. Jimmy also demonstrated almost all of the criteria symptoms plus the adjunctive symptoms of somatic complaints. His acute stress, which is coded on Axis IV, had recently changed from none or mild to extreme due to the respiratory arrest with invasive procedures and intensive care hospitalization. Family dynamics may have contributed to Jimmy's depression; however, this was a better functioning family than many. Jimmy's chronic level of stress, or the enduring circumstances also coded on Axis IV, was mild. Jimmy's family was stable and basically, although not optimally, supportive and showed improvement with family therapy. Jimmy was a very intelligent child with many strengths and had an apparent successful life adjustment prior to onset of depression.

Jimmy's early recollection was the same at each presentation and indicated liking to get things or to be given to. He was a receiver; however, he changed his affect associated with receiving something from excited to confused. The positive affect reflected his concrete desire to collect and accumulate. With depression his goals were less clear to him; he felt confused because "getting" and "collecting" no longer contained his ambition and desire to have life his way.

DSM-IV Diagnoses

> Axis I: 296.23 Major Depressive Disorder, Single Episode
> Axis II: No disorder but compulsive personality traits
> Axis III: Status post mononucleosis and respiratory arrest
> Axis IV: Psychosocial Stressors:
> (a) respiratory arrest and ICU hospitalization
> Severity: 5—extreme (acute event)
> (b) chronic mild parental discord; overinvolvement of mother with son; underinvolvement of father
> Severity: 2—mild (enduring circumstances)
> Axis V: Current GAF: 35; Highest GAF Last Year: 92

CASE VIGNETTE: TIM—GRADUAL-ONSET MDD FOLLOWING CHRONIC STRESS AND DYSTHYMIA

History

Tim was a 10–year-old boy who came for treatment following his destruction of fence posts with an axe at camp. He said that he used the axe in response to teasing by his peers. He had demonstrated impulsive behaviors in the past but much more minor. He had broken small objects, walked out of class, and occasionally struck another student. Mostly Tim became very upset when teased. He would verbally berate his taunting peers and then run away crying. He had no friends. Despite these actions, Tim did not engage in antisocial activities, never bullied or teased others, and was generally well-behaved in class and elsewhere. He completed work in school and maintained average grades. His fraternal twin sister Taryn and older sister Kate (also a fraternal twin) described his teasing by others as due to his awkwardness with peers and his poor social presentation. Tim would often go to school in unkempt clothing, hair uncombed, and smelling of urine from not properly cleaning himself after nocturnal enuresis. He did not seem to know how to make small talk with peers. Mother and siblings described Tim as helpful but mostly keeping to himself. Free time was spent around other adults or with his "big brother," who was assigned to Tim four hours per week. He had locked up his belongings to keep them from his older bother Ken who would take Tim's belongings, break them, or tauntingly hide them. Although Tim frequently protested to Mother, she stated she had no control over Ken.

Neither Tim nor the family noted any recent change in Tim's behavior. He was also always irritable and quick to blow up but never showed any real tantrums. Between these sporadic episodes Tim was a calm and a "kind" boy. Detailed inquiry revealed a history of increased irritability with difficulty concentrating and difficulty getting up in the mornings. He always had insomnia, but this had increased recently. Both Tim and his mother attributed these problems to his change of schools the past September. Neither he nor his family endorsed depression. He had mentioned suicide a few times, but his mother thought that he was "discouraged from all the teasing."

Past Medical History.   Noncontributory except for enuresis.

Family History.   No known significant medical or psychological disorders.

Educational History.   Regular education with average grades.

Social History.   Tim's mother was married and delivered her first set of fraternal twins, Kate and Ken. Tim and Taryn were born 18 months after the first set of twins. When the youngest set of twins was 18 months old, the Father deserted the family leaving Mother with four preschool children. The family was on welfare for many years. Mother made several unsuccessful attempts to work after the children were all in school. She had successfully returned to work again eight months prior to Tim's referral to the clinic. She enjoyed her work but reported many conflicts with supervisory figures. She left this job for another position one year after hiring. During their rearing the children had to fend for themselves. Mother reared the children to be "independent." They were very good at "odd jobbing" to make spending money. In fact, the adult relationships Tim made through "odd jobbing" were his main positive social contacts. These adults felt sorry for him and tried to help him. Mother was a proud woman. She appeared overwhelmed but indicated that she had everything under good control. She had been very involved in organizing many social activities for the children who participated in multiple social organizations and activities. Mother often let the two boys work out their difficulties, but she intervened occasionally, which kept the conflict going between them. Ken escalated his harassment of Tim.

Mental Status Examination and Observations

Tim initially was seen with his family and then alone for evaluation. The family session was chaotic. All the children talked at once. They were evasive and seemed to play a game with the therapist. Mother sat back and just observed. She appeared overwhelmed, defensive, dysphoric, but not depressed. She seemed quite needy but unable or unwilling to express this. She also wanted to control the direction of the sessions and recommendations. She would not allow the interviewer to focus on her or the overall family. Kate, the older girl, had a motherly role in the family and was the most "responsible." She also stuck up for Tim. She felt sorry for him. His brother Ken was uncooperative and sarcastic; and his twin Taryn gave the appearance of being oblivious.

Tim presented as a socially awkward but outgoing boy. He was very desirous of attention. He liked to talk about himself, especially his perceived accomplishments. These accomplishments, however, were age-inappropriate simple acts, such as tracing a logo onto a piece of paper. He presented this as artistic talent. Other exaggerations of ability were common, and he sought confirmation of his capabilities. He had a fixed smile on his face. Tim always wanted to extend sessions. Many times he asked to take something from the office with him when he left. He was never daunted when refused the items and felt entitled to them. He seemed very vulnerable. Tim never spoke of his problems and tended to minimize them when addressed by the therapist, stating everything was going "fine." His scores on self-report questionnaires indicated severely impaired self-esteem, high level of anxiety, feelings of worthlessness, alienation from peers and family, negative distortions in his thinking, and suicidality. His scores were the worst the tester had seen in an outpatient setting. When carefully questioned, he did endorse feeling depressed and angry or irritable during part of every day. He felt guilty for what had happened to his mother in life. He also felt guilty about people starving in Ethiopia. He frequently thought about killing himself and occasionally about killing others. He took at least one hour to fall asleep at night, mostly because he felt worried. He had started to awaken during the night but did not have early morning awakening. Recent difficulty keeping his mind on school work was endorsed. He was not anhedonic nor anorectic. He clearly noted that his mood was worse in the morning, even on weekends when he did not have to attend school. Despite Tim's strong endorsement of feeling "depressed," his mother did not believe he felt that way.

Course of Treatment

Mother did not want to involve herself or the family in treatment. She wanted individual treatment for her son. She would not allow a second family session. Tim's situation was critical. Antidepressant medication was started, because Tim continued to have difficulty regulating his affect with resultant disciplinary action at school. Mother's refusal to allow family therapy greatly curtailed treatment possibilities. Tim was enrolled in social skills training and was seen with his older sister who attended his school and was "popular." Sessions focused on bringing to awareness his skill at involving school children and his older brother in taunting him, the power he exerted by stimulating them to pick on him. Asking Tim in the family session and with his sister if it were possible that he elicited this harassment met with denial; however, when asked if he knew of anyone who knew how to better entice Ken to harass, he gave a recognition reflex (Dreikurs, 1958) by smiling proudly. The therapist's spitting in his noble, victimized soup effectively ended these behaviors. Tim quickly stabilized; however, many issues persisted. Mother was again requested to involve the entire family in treatment. At this point, she changed health policies and transferred Tim's care to another facility.

Comment

Tim's presentation typifies MDD in many children. Onset is frequently chronic with exacerbation of preexisting symptoms rather than acute. The family and Tim did not perceive a change until a crisis developed. His symptoms included both depressed mood and irritability. Only the irritability was obvious, since it led to behaviors affecting others. He had grandiose ambitions for himself but depended upon the success and support of his motherly sister. He had increasing insomnia, feelings of excessive guilt and worthlessness, diminished ability to concentrate, and suicidal thoughts. Neither his appetite nor his weight changed. He was neither fatigued nor anhedonic. Some psychomotor agitation existed. He did not meet criteria for other diagnoses concurrent with the depression. Despite his misbehavior, he did not demonstrate a Conduct Disorder; however, his long-standing depressive and irritable feelings did meet criteria for a preexisting Dysthymic Disorder.

Several factors delayed diagnosis. The irritability impressed others. Tim's feelings of depression were not so impressive. Tim's mother was overwhelmed and felt that life had been unfair to her. She was relatively inattentive to her children's needs. When Tim's needs could no longer be ignored, she was still unwilling to act in her children's best interests if it meant puncturing her own pride. Tim's psychological style was to avoid his problems in favor of impressing others. Depressive symptoms were elicited only with self-report questionnaires and careful individual interviewing. Most of his symptoms were chronic and so the increased intensity was discounted. Finally, because he had recently changed schools, an event could be identified to which change of symptoms could be attributed. Indications of a serious disorder were minimized by attributing them to "stress."

DSM-IV Diagnoses

> Axis I: 296.22 Major Depressive Disorder, Single Episode
> 300.40 Dysthymia, Primary Type, Early-onset
> 307.60 Functional Enuresis, Primary, Nocturnal
> Axis II: No disorder; but personality traits of grandiosity, self-involve-ment, intrusiveness, praise-seeking, entitlement, no close friends
> Axis III: Deficits in personal hygiene
> Axis IV: Psychosocial Stressors:
> (a)   change of schools; mother takes job
> Severity: 2—mild (acute event)
> (b)   welfare, abandonment by father, chronic single parent home with multiple siblings, socioemotional neglect by mother, harass-ment by brother, chronic ridicule by peers
> Severity: 5—extreme (enduring circumstances)
> Axis V: Current GAF: 40; Highest GAF Past Year: 50

REFERENCES

Adler, A. (1927). *The practice and theory of Individual Psychology*. New York: Harcourt, Brace.

Adler, A. (1961). Depression in the light of Adlerian psychology. *Journal of Individual Psychology, 17*, 56–57.

Adler, A. (1969). *The science of living*. Garden City, NY: Anchor Books.

Adler, A. (1970). *Problems of neurosis: A book of case histories*. Chicago: Henry Regnery.

Akiskal, H.S. (1981). Subaffective disorders: Dysthymic, cyclothymic, and bipolar II disorders in the borderline realm. *Psychiatric Clinics of North America, 4*, 25–46.

Akiskal, H.S. (1983). Dysthymic disorder: Psychopathology of proposed chronic depressive subtypes. *American Journal of Psychiatry, 140*, 11–20.

Akiskal, H.S., Downs, J., & Jordan, P. (1985). Affective disorders in the referred children and younger siblings of manic-depressives: Mode of onset and prospective course. *Archives of General Psychiatry, 42*, 996–1003.

Akiskal, H.S., King, D., & Rosenthal, T.L. (1981). Chronic depressions, Part I: Clinical and familial characteristics in 137 probands. *Journal of Affective Disorders, 3*, 297–315.

American Psychiatric Association. (1980). *Diagnostic and statistical manual of mental disorders* (3rd ed.). Washington, DC: Author.

American Psychiatric Association. (1987). *Diagnostic and statistical manual of mental disorders* (3rd ed., rev.). Washington, DC: Author.

American Psychiatric Association. (1994). *Diagnostic and statistical manual of mental disorders* (4th ed.). Washington, DC: Author.

Anderson, J.C., Williams, S., McGee, R., & Silva, P.A. (1987). DSM-III disorders in preadolescent children. Prevalence in a large sample from the general population. *Archives of General Psychiatry, 44*, 69–76.

Ansbacher, H.H., & Ansbacher, R.R. (Eds.). (1956). *The Individual Psychology of Alfred Adler*. New York: Harper Torchbooks.

Ansbacher, H.L., & Ansbacher, R.R. (Eds.). (1964). *Superiority and social interest*. Evanston, IL: Northwestern University Press.

Arans, G.W., Baldessarini, M.D., & Ornsteen, M. (1985). The dexamethasone suppression test for diagnosis and prognosis in psychiatry. *Archives of General Psychiatry, 42*, 1193–1204.

Beardslee, W.R., Bemporad, J., & Keller, M.B. (1983). Children of parents with major affective disorder: A review. *American Journal of Psychiatry, 140*, 825–832.

Biederman, J., Munir, K., & Knee, D. (1987). High rates of affective disorders in probands with attention deficit disorder and in their relatives. *American Journal of Psychiatry, 144*, 330–333.

Bowlby, J. (1980). *Attachment and loss: III. Loss, sadness, and depression.* New York: Basic Books.

Breier, A., Charney, D.S., & Heninger, G.R. (1985). The diagnostic validity of anxiety disorders and their relationship to depressive illness. *American Journal of Psychiatry, 142*, 787–797.

Carlson, G.A., & Cantwell, D.P. (1980a). Unmasking masked depression in children and adolescents. *American Journal of Psychiatry, 137*, 445–449.

Carlson, G.A., & Cantwell, D.P. (1980b). A survey of depressive symptoms, syndrome and disorder in a child psychiatric population. *Journal of Child Psychology and Psychiatry, 21*, 19–25.

Cavallo, A., Holt, K.G., & Hejazi, M.S. (1987). Melatonin circadian rhythm in childhood depression. *Journal of American Academy of Child and Adolescent Psychiatry, 26*, 395–399.

Chambers, W.J., Puig-Antich, J., & Hirsch, M. (1985). The assessment of affective disorders in children and adolescents by semistructured interview: Test-retest reliability of the K-SADS-P. *Archives of General Psychiatry, 39*, 696–702.

Chambers, W.J., Puig-Antich J., & Tabrizi, M.A. (1982). Psychotic symptoms in prepubertal major depressive disorder. *Archives of General Psychiatry, 39*, 921–927.

Croake, J.W., & Catlin, N. (1986). *A teleoanalytic approach to adolescence.* Seattle, WA: Seattle Institute for Adlerian Studies.

Croake, J.W., & Hinkle, D.E. (1983). Adlerian family counseling education. *Journal of Individual Psychology, 39*, 247–258.

Davis, K.L., Davis, B.M., & Mathe, A.A. (1984). Age and the dexamethasone suppression test in depression. *American Journal of Psychiatry, 141*, 872–874.

Del Beccarro, M., Burke, P., & McCauley, E. (1988). Hallucinations in children: A follow-up study. *American Academy of Child and Adolescent Psychiatry, 27*, 462–465.

Doherty, M.B., Madansky, D., & Kraft, J. (1986). Cortisol dynamics and test performance of the dexamethasone suppression test in 97 psychiatrically hospitalized children aged 3–16 years. *American Academy of Child Psychiatry, 25*, 400–408.

Dreikurs, R. (1958). *The challenge of parenthood*. New York: Hawthorn Books.

Dreikurs, R. (1973). *Psychodynamics, psychotherapy, and counseling*. Chicago: Alfred Adler Institute.

Ellis, A. (1973). *Humanistic psychotherapy*. New York: McGraw-Hill.

Fawcett, J., & Kravity, H.M. (1983). Anxiety syndromes and their relationship to depressive illness. *Journal of Clinical Psychiatry, 44*, 8–11.

Freeman, L.N., Poznanski, E.O., & Grossman, J.A. (1985). Psychotic and depressed children: A new entity. *Journal of American Academy of Child Psychiatry, 24*, 95–102.

Freud, A. (1946). *The ego and the mechanisms of defense*. New York: International Universities Press.

Freud, A., & Burlingham, D. (1974). *Infants without families and reports on the Hamstead Nurseries 1939–1945*. London: Hogarth Press.

Gillin, J.C., Duncan, W.C., & Murphy, D.L. (1981). Age-related changes in sleep in depressed and normal subjects. *Psychiatry Research, 4*, 73–78.

Goetz, R.R., Puig-Antich, J., & Ryan, N. (1987). Electroencephalographic sleep of adolescents with major depression and normal controls. *Archives of General Psychiatry, 44*, 61–68.

Gonzales, L.R., Lewinsohn, P.M., & Clarke, G.N. (1985). Longitudinal follow-up on unipolar depressives: An investigation of predictors of relapse. *Journal of Consulting & Clinical Psychology, 53*, 461–469.

Greenman, D.A., Gunderson, J.G., & Cane, M. (1986). An examination of the borderline diagnosis in children. *American Journal of Psychiatry, 143*, 998–1003.

Haley, G.M.T., Fine, S., Marriage, K., Moretti, M.M., & Freeman, R.J. (1985). Brief reports: Cognitive bias and depression in psychiatrically disturbed children and adolescents. *Journal of Consulting & Clinical Psychology, 53*, 535–537.

Herjanic, B., Herjanic, M., & Brown, F. (1975). Are children reliable reporters? *Journal of Abnormal Child Psychology, 3*, 41–48.

Herjanic, B., & Reich, W. (1982). Development of a structured psychiatric interview for children: Agreement between child and parent on individual symptoms. *Journal of Abnormal Child Psychology, 10*, 307–324.

Hershberg, S.G., Carlson, G.A., Cantwell, D.P., & Strober, M. (1982). Anxiety and depressive disorders in psychiatrically disturbed children. *Journal of Clinical Psychiatry, 43*, 358–361.

Hughes, M.C. (1984). Recurrent abdominal pain and childhood depression: Clinical observations of 23 children and their families. *American Journal of Orthopsychiatry, 54*, 146–155.

Kanoy, K., & Miller, B. (1980). Children's impact on the parental decision to divorce. *Family Relations, 29*, 309–316.

Kaplan, H., & Sadock, B. (1985). *Synopsis of psychiatry*. Baltimore: Williams and Wilkins.

Kashani, J.H., & Carlson, G.A. (1987). Seriously depressed preschoolers. *American Journal of Psychiatry, 144*, 348–350.

Kashani, J., Lababidi, Z., & Jones, R. (1982). Depression in children and adolescence with cardiovascular symptomatology. *Journal of American Academy of Child Psychiatry, 21*, 187–189.

Kashani, J.H., McGee, R.O., Clarkson, S.G., Anderson, J.C., & Walton, L.E. (1983). Depression in a sample of 9–year-old children. *Archives of General Psychiatry, 40*, 1217–1223.

Kashani, J.H., & Ray, J.S. (1987). Major depression with delusional features in a preschool-age child. *American Academy of Child and Adolescent Psychiatry, 26*, 110–112.

Kaslow, N.J., Tannenbaum, R.L., & Abramson, L.Y. (1983). Problem-solving deficits and depressive symptoms among children. *Journal of Abnormal Child Psychology, 11*, 497–501.

Katon, W., Kleinman, A., & Rosen, G. (1982a). Depression and somatization: A review, Part I. *American Journal of Medicine, 72*, 127–136.

Katon, W., Kleinman, A., & Rosen, G. (1982b). Depression and somatization: A review, Part II. *American Journal of Medicine, 72*, 241–247.

Kazdin, A.E., French, N.H., & Unis, A.S. (1983). Child, mother, and father evaluations of depression in psychiatric inpatient children. *Journal of Abnormal Child Psychology, 11*, 167–180.

Kazdin, A.E., Unis, A.S., & French, N.H. (1983). Hopelessness, depression and suicidal intent among psychiatrically disturbed inpatient children. *Journal of Consulting & Clinical Psychology, 51*, 504–510.

Keller, M.B., Beardslee, W.R., Dorer, D.J., Lavori, P.W., & Samuelson, M.A. (1986). Impact of severity and chronicity of parental affective illness on adaptive functioning and psychopathology in children. *Archives of General Psychiatry, 43*, 930–937.

Keller, M.B., & Shapiro, R.W. (1982). "Double depression": Superimposition of acute depressive episodes on chronic depressive disorders. *American Journal of Psychiatry, 139*, 438–442.

Keller, M.B., Shapiro, R.W., & Lavori, P.W. (1982a). Recovery in major depressive disorder: Analysis with life table and regression models. *Archives of General Psychiatry, 39*, 905–910.

Keller, M.B., Shapiro, R.W., & Lavori, P.W. (1982b). Relapse in Major Depressive Disorder. *Archives of General Psychiatry, 39*, 911–915.

Kemph, J.P. (1987). Hallucination in psychotic children. *American Academy of Child and Adolescent Psychiatry, 26*, 556–559.

Kotsopoulos, S., Kanigsberg, J., Cote, A., & Fiedorowicz, C. (1987). Hallucinatory experiences in nonpsychotic children. *American Academy of Child and Adolescent Psychiatry, 26*, 375–380.

Kovacs, M., & Beck, A.T. (1978). Maladaptive cognitive structures in depression. *American Journal of Psychiatry, 135*, 525–533.

Kovacs, M., Feinberg, T.L., & Crouse-Novak, M.A. (1984a). Depressive disorders in childhood: A longitudinal prospective study of characteristics and recovery I. *Archives of General Psychiatry, 41*, 229–237.

Kovacs, M., Feinberg, T.L., & Crouse-Novak, M.A. (1984b). Depressive disorders in childhood: A longitudinal study of risk for subsequent major depression II. *Archives of General Psychiatry, 41*, 643–649.

Lahmeyer, H., Poznanski, E., & Bellur, S. (1983). EEG sleep in depressed adolescents. *American Journal of Psychiatry, 140*, 1150–1153.

Leckman, J.F., Merikangas, K.R., & Pauls, D.L. (1983). Anxiety disorders and depression: Contradictions between family study data and DSM-III conventions. *American Journal of Psychiatry, 140*, 880–882.

Lefkowitz, M.M., & Burton, N. (1978). Childhood depression: A critique of the concept. *Psychological Medicine, 85*, 716–726.

Marriage, K., Fine, S., Moretti, M., & Haley, G. (1986). Relationship between depression and conduct disorder in children and adolescents. *Journal of American Academy of Child Psychiatry, 25*, 687–691.

McCauley, E., Carlson, G.A., & Calderon, R. (1991). The role of somatic complaints in the diagnosis of depression in children and adolescents. *Journal of the American Academy of Child & Adolescent Psychiatry, 30*, 631–635.

McCauley, E., Mitchell, J., Burke, P., & Moss, S. (1988). Cognitive attributes of depression in children and adolescents. *Journal of Consulting & Clinical Psychology, 56*, 903–908.

McCauley, E., Mitchell, J., Burke, P., Myers, K., Calderon, R., & Schloredt, K. (1988). *Longitudinal assessment of depression in children and adolescents*. Paper presented at the annual meeting of the American Academy of Child & Adolescent Psychiatry, Seattle, WA.

McDonald, G. (1980). Parental power and adolescents' parental identification. *Journal of Marriage and the Family, 42*, 289–296.

McGee, R., & Williams, S. (1988). A longitudinal study of depression in nine-year- old children. *American Academy of Child and Adolescent Psychiatry, 27*, 342–348.

McManus, M., Lerner, H., & Robbins, D. (1984). Assessment of borderline symptomatology in hospitalized adolescents. *Journal of American Academy of Child Psychiatry, 23*, 685–694.

Mendlewicz, J., & Baron, M. (1981). Morbidity risks in subtypes of unipolar depressive illness: Differences between early and late onset forms. *British Journal of Psychiatry, 139*, 463–466.

Miller, I.W, Norman, W.H., & Dow, M.G. (1986). Psychosocial characteristics of "double depression." *American Journal of Psychiatry, 143*, 1042–1044.

Mitchell, J., McCauley, E., Burke, P., Calderon, R., & Schloredt, K. (1989). Psychopathology in parents of depressed children and adolescents. *American Academy of Child and Adolescent Psychiatry, 28*, 352–357.

Mitchell, J.R., McCauley, E., Burke, P.M., & Moss, S. (1988). Phenomenology of depression in children and adolescents. *American Academy of Child and Adolescent Psychiatry, 27*, 12–20.

Mosak, H.H. (1971). Lifestyle. In A. Nikelly (Ed.), *Techniques for behavioral change* (pp. 77–88). Springfield, IL: Charles C. Thomas.

Myers, J.K., Weissman, M.M., & Tischler, G.L. (1984). Six-months prevalence of psychiatric disorders in three communities: 1980–1982. *Archives of General Psychiatry, 41*, 959–967.

Nurnberger, J.I., & Gershon, E.S. (1984). Genetics of affective disorders. In R. Post & J. Ballenger (Eds.), *Neurobiology of mood disorders* (pp. 216–280). Baltimore: Williams & Wilkins.

Orvaschel, H., & Weissman, M.M. (1986). Epidemiology of anxiety disorders in children: A review. In R. Gittelman (Ed.), *Anxiety disorders of childhood* (pp. 58–71). New York: Guilford Press.

Petty, L.K., Asarnow, J.R., & Carlson, G.A. (1985). The dexamethasone suppression test—depressed, dysthymic, and nondepressed children. *American Journal of Psychiatry, 142*, 631–633.

Poznanski, E.O., Carroll, B.J., & Banegas, M.D. (1982). The dexamethasone suppression test in prepubertal depressed children. *American Journal of Psychiatry, 139*, 321–324.

Puig-Antich, J. (1980). Affective disorders in childhood: A review and perspective. *Psychiatric Clinics of North America, 3*, 403–424.

Puig-Antich, J. (1982). Major depression and conduct disorder in prepuberty. *American Academy of Child and Adolescent Psychiatry, 21*, 118–128.

Puig-Antich, J., Chambers, W., & Tabrizi, M. (1983). The clinical assessment of current depressive episodes in children and adolescents: Interview with parents and children. In D. Cantwell & G. Carlson (Eds.), *Affective disorders in children and adolescents: An update* (pp 157–180). New York: Spectrum Press.

Puig-Antich, J., Goetz, R., & Davies, M. (1984a). Growth hormone secretion in prepubertal children with major depression II: Sleep-related plasma concentrations during a depressive episode. *Archives of General Psychiatry, 41*, 463–466.

Puig-Antich, J., Goetz, R., & Davies, M. (1984b). Growth hormone secretion in prepubertal children with major depression IV: Sleep-related plasma concentrations in a drug-free, fully recovered clinical state. *Archives of General Psychiatry, 41*, 479–483.

Puig-Antich, J., Goetz, D., & Davies, M. (1989). A controlled family history study of prepubertal major depressive disorder. *Archives of General Psychiatry, 46*, 406–418.

Puig-Antich, J., Goetz, R., & Hanlon, C. (1982). Sleep architecture and REM sleep measures in prepubertal children with major depression. *Archives of General Psychiatry, 39*, 932–939.

Puig-Antich, J., Goetz, R., & Hanlon, C. (1983). Sleep architecture and REM sleep measures in prepubertal major depressives: Sleep during recovery from the depressive episode in a drug-free state. *Archives of General Psychiatry, 40*, 187–192.

Puig-Antich, J., Novacenko, H., & Davies, M. (1984a). Growth hormone secretion in prepubertal children with major depression I: Final report on response to insulin-induced hypoglycemia during a depressive episode. *Archives of General Psychiatry, 41*, 455–460.

Puig-Antich, J., Novacenko, H., & Davies, M. (1984b). Growth hormone secretion in prepubertal children with major depression III: Response to insulin-induced hypoglycemia after recovery from a depressive episode and in a drug-free state. *Archives of General Psychiatry, 41*, 471–475.

Puig-Antich, J., Novacenko, H., & Goetz, R. (1984). Cortisol and prolactin responses to insulin-induced hypoglycemia in prepubertal major depressives during episode and after recovery. *Journal of American Academy of Child Psychiatry, 23*, 49–57.

Puig-Antich, J., & Rabinovich, H. (1986). Relationship between affective and anxiety disorders in childhood. In R. Gittelman (Ed.), *Anxiety disorders of childhood* (pp. 136–156). New York: Guilford Press.

Radloff, L. (1975). Sex differences in depression: The effects of occupation and marital status. *Sex Roles, 1*, 249–269.

Reich, W., Herjanic, B., & Welner, Z. (1982). Development of a structured psychiatric interview for children: Agreement on diagnosis comparing child and parent interviews. *Journal of Abnormal Child Psychology, 10*, 325–336.

Rie, H.E. (1966). Depression in childhood: A survey of some pertinent contributions. *American Academy of Child and Adolescent Psychiatry, 5*, 653–686.

Robins, E., & Guze, S. (1972). Classification of affective disorders—the primary-secondary, the endogenous-reactive and the neurotic-psychotic dichotomies. In T.A. Williams, M.M. Katz, & J.A. Shield (Eds.), *Recent advances in psychobiology of the depressive illnesses* (pp. 212–250). Washington, DC: U.S. Printing Office.

Robins, L.N. (1978). Sturdy childhood predictors of adult antisocial behavior: Replications from longitudinal studies. *Psychological Medicine, 8*, 611–622.

Robins, L.N., Helzer, J.E., & Weissman, M.M. (1984). Lifetime prevalence of specific psychiatric disorders in three sites. *Archives of General Psychiatry, 41*, 949–958.

Rutter, M. (1986). The developmental psychopathology of depression: Issues and perspectives. In M. Rutter, C.E. Izard, & P.B. Read (Eds.), *Depression in young people: Developmental and clinical perspectives* (pp. 12–14). London: The Guilford Press.

Seligman, M.E.P., Kaslow, N.J., & Alloy, L.B. (1984). Attributional style and depressive symptoms among children. *Journal of Abnormal Psychology, 93*, 235–238.

Smith, E.T. (1981). Adolescent agreement with perceived maternal and paternal goals. *Journal of Marriage and the Family, 43*, 85–94.

Spitz, R. (1946). Anaclitic depression. *Psychoanalytic Study of the Child, 2*, 313–342.

Spitzer, R.L., Endicott, J., & Robins, E. (1978). Research diagnostic criteria: Rationale and reliability. *Archives of General Psychiatry, 35*, 773–782.

Weissman, M.M., Gammon, G.D., & John, K. (1987). Children of depressed parents: Increased psychopathology and early onset of major depression. *Archives of General Psychiatry, 44*, 847–853.

Weissman, M.M., & Klerman, G.L. (1977). Sex differences and the epidemiology of depression. *Archives of General Psychiatry, 34*, 98–111.

Weissman, M.M., Pottenger, M., & Kleber, H. (1977). Symptom patterns in primary and secondary depression: A comparison of primary depressives with depressed opiate addicts, alcoholics and schizophrenics. *Archives of General Psychiatry, 34*, 854–862.

Weissman, M.M., Prusoff, B.A., & Gammon, G.D. (1984). Psychopathology in the children (ages 6–18) of depressed and normal parents. *Journal of American Academy of Child Psychiatry, 23*, 78–84.

Weller, E.B., Weller, R.A., & Fristad, M.A. (1984). The dexamethasone suppression test in hospitalized prepubertal depressed children. *American Journal of Psychiatry, 141*, 290–291.

Weller, R.A., Weller, E.B., & Fristad, M.A. (1985). A comparison of the cortisol suppression index and the dexamethasone suppression test in prepubertal children. *American Journal of Psychiatry, 142*, 1370–1372.

Wender, P.H., Kety, S.S., & Rosenthal, D. (1986). Psychiatric disorders in the biological and adoptive families of adopted individuals with affective disorders. *Archives of General Psychiatry, 43*, 923–929.

Willner, P. (1985). *Depression: A psychobiological synthesis*. New York: John Wiley & Sons.

Young, W., Knowles, J., & MacLean, A. (1982). The sleep patterns of childhood depressives: Comparisons with age-matched controls. *Biological Psychiatry, 17*, 1163–1168.

Zis, A.P., & Goodwin, F.K. (1979). Major affective disorder as a recurrent illness: A critical review. *Archives of General Psychiatry, 36*, 835–839.

Chapter 17

ATTENTION-DEFICIT/ HYPERACTIVITY DISORDER AND SPECIFIC DEVELOPMENTAL DISORDERS

James W. Croake
Kathleen M. Myers

This chapter reviews the syndrome of Attention-Deficit/Hyperactivity Disorder (ADHD). The discussion will focus on two areas. First, ADHD is presented as an example of a very common childhood disorder with onset during the earliest childhood years. Second, it is presented as a disorder affecting overall biopsychosocial development and significantly overlapping with Axis II Specific Developmental Disorders.

HISTORICAL

The current DSM-IV description of the syndrome Attention-Deficit/Hyperactivity Disorder (ADHD) represents the most current conceptualization of a long-recognized disorder characterized by inattention, impulsivity, and excessive unfocused activity. The syndrome has been known by many different names over the past century. Still (1902) described a series of children with "defects in moral control." This term referred to his observation that these children had difficulty not only with attention, impulsivity, and hyperactivity, but frequently with socially appropriate behaviors as well.

Bradley (1937) reported a "paradoxical quieting effect" of amphetamines, which are stimulant medications, on children with these symptoms. He thought that they responded differently from normal children and that this paradoxical response was part of an underlying brain dysfunction.

From the 1940s to the 1960s this disorder was referred to as Minimal Cerebral Damage or Minimal Brain Damage. These terms connoted the then prevalent concept that these behaviors arose from underlying brain damage; however, no structural or anatomical abnormalities have ever been documented. This designation was slowly discarded in favor of the term Minimal Brain Dysfunction (MBD) (Clements & Peters, 1962; Knobloch & Pasamanick, 1959). This terminology still suggested an underlying etiology. Structural brain damage was replaced by abnormality in brain functioning.

Attempts to define a syndrome accelerated in the mid 1960s to the 1970s. In DSM-II this same constellation of signs and symptoms was referred to as the Hyperkinetic Reaction of Childhood (American Psychiatric Association, 1968; Bakwin & Bakwin, 1966; Bender, 1975; Laufer & Denhoff, 1957; Safer & Allen, 1976). This term carried no reference to brain abnormalities or other possible etiology. In it was also described the one symptom that most distresses parents and teachers—hyperactivity.

Later in the 1970s and 1980s the core problem was conceptualized as a disorder of faulty attention and inhibitory control (Dykman, Ackerman, Clements, & Peters, 1971). Therefore, in DSM-III the disorder was designated as "Attention-Deficit Disorder, with or without Hyperactivity" (American Psychiatric Association, 1980). This approach specified three constellations of diagnostic symptoms: inattentiveness, impulsivity, and overactivity or restlessness. This three-fold classification system impacted research and conceptualization of the disorder; however, it was short-lived.

In DSM-III-R this disorder was termed "Attention-Deficit Hyperactivity Disorder" (American Psychiatric Association, 1987). It reinstated hyperactivity in the diagnostic nomenclature and returned to an undifferentiated list of 14 diagnostic signs and symptoms without subtypes. Consistent with DSM-III-R's mandate to designate nomenclature descriptively and free from theoretical bias or potential etiology, no reference was made to etiology.

The nosology began with Still (1902), who described a series of children with "defects in moral control." This term referred to his observations that these children had difficulty not only with attention, impulsivity, and hyperactivity, but frequently with socially appropriate behaviors as well. DSM-IV has refined ADHD by removing theoretical influences, i.e., psychoanalysis or moral control defects. The description of the disorder is now divided into hyperactivity, inattention-impulsivity or a combination of hyperactivity and inattention-impulsivity. Specific behavioral categories are the desired direction for all of the disorders in DSM-IV. ADHD as a disorder is quite free of theoretical bias and moral interpretation in this latest nosological description.

DIAGNOSTIC CRITERIA AND PHENOMENOLOGY

Diagnostic Signs and Symptoms

DSM-IV diagnostic criteria for ADHD are listed in Table 17.1 (American Psychiatric Association, 1994, pp. 83–85). The classification is based upon ADHD subtyping: ADHD Combined Type, ADHD Predominantly Inattention Type, ADHD Predominantly Hyperactive-Impulsive Type. The Combined Type requires 6 (or more) signs from the Inattention list and 6 (or more) signs from the Hyperactivity-Impulsivity list. The predominantly Inattention Type requires 6 (or more) signs from the Inattention list. These signs must have persisted for at least 6 months and result in maladaptive behavior that is inappropriate to the developmental level of the individual. The ADHD Predominantly Hyperactive-Impulsive Type must meet the criteria listed in A2 of Table 17.1. Additionally, the individual must demonstrate the ADHD behavior in more than one setting (e.g., at home and at work).

Experienced clinicians can identify ADHD children with a high degree of reliability, even though the symptoms predominating in any one child vary greatly. A hallmark of this disorder is its variability from child to child. The current approach, therefore, addresses the heterogeneity of the ADHD syndrome, while preserving its easily identifiable essence.

Representative Behaviors

The behaviors noted in Table 17.1 represent developmentally inappropriate extremes in attention, hyperactivity, and impulsivity. Affected children generally

TABLE 17.1
Diagnostic criteria for Attention-Deficit/Hyperactivity Disorder

A. Either (1) or (2):
   (1) six (or more) of the following symptoms of **inattention** have persisted for at least
       6 months to a degree that is maladaptive and inconsistent with developmental level:
       Inattention
       (a) often fails to give close attention to details or makes careless mistakes in school-
           work, work, or other activities
       (b) often has difficulty sustaining attention in tasks or play activities
       (c) often does not seem to listen when spoken to directly
       (d) often does not follow through on instructions and fails to finish schoolwork,
           chores, or duties in the workplace (not due to oppositional behavior or failure to
           understand instructions)
       (e) often has difficulty organizing tasks and activities
       (f) often avoids, dislikes, or is reluctant to engage in tasks that require sustained
           mental effort (such as schoolwork or homework)
       (g) often loses things necessary for tasks or activities (e.g., toys, school assignments,
           pencils, books, or tools)
       (h) is often easily distracted by extraneous stimuli
       (i) is often forgetful in daily activities
   (2) six (or more) of the following symptoms of **hyperactivity-impulsivity** have persisted
       for at least 6 months to a degree that is maladaptive and inconsistent with develop-
       mental level:
       Hyperactivity
       (a) often fidgets with hands or feet or squirms in seat
       (b) often leaves seat in classroom or in other situations in which remaining seated
           is expected
       (c) often runs about or climbs excessively in situations in which it is inappropriate
           (in adolescents or adults, may be limited to subjective feelings of restlessness)
       (d) often has difficulty playing or engaging in leisure activities quietly
       (e) is often "on the go" or often acts as if "driven by a motor"
       (f) often talks excessively
       Impulsivity
       (g) often blurts out answers before questions have been completed
       (h) often has difficulty awaiting turn
       (i) often interrupts or intrudes on others (e.g., butts into conversations or games)
B. Some hyperactive-impulsive or inattentive symptoms that caused impairment were
   present before age 7 years.
C. Some impairment from the symptoms is present in two or more settings (e.g., at school
   [or work] and at home.)
D. There must be clear evidence of clinically significant impairment in social, academic,
   or occupational functioning.
E. The symptoms do not occur exclusively during the course of a Pervasive Developmental
   Disorder, Schizophrenia, or other Psychotic Disorder and are not better accounted for
   by another mental disorder (e.g., Mood Disorder, Anxiety Disorder, Dissociative Disorder, or a Personality Disorder.)

TABLE 17.1 (Continued)
Diagnostic criteria for Attention-Deficit/Hyperactivity Disorder

Code based on type:

> **314.01 Attention-Deficit/Hyperactivity Disorder, Combined Type:** if both Criteria A1 and A2 are met for the past 6 months
> **314.00 Attention-Deficit/Hyperactivity Disorder, Predominantly Inattentive Type:** if Criterion A1 is met but Criterion A2 is not met for the past 6 months
> **314.01 Attention-Deficit/Hyperactivity Disorder, Predominantly Hyperactive-Impulsive Type:** if Criterion A2 is met but Criterion A1 is not met for the past 6 months

From *Diagnostic and Statistical Manual of Mental Disorders, Fourth Edition* (DSM-IV). Copyright © 1994 by American Psychiatric Association. Reprinted with permission.

display deficits in all three behaviors, although to varying degrees. The behaviors are pervasive, manifesting in most areas of functioning. They are not intermittent but may wax and wane depending on environmental circumstances.

School Behaviors.   Teachers' descriptions of attentional deficits generally involve ADHD children's difficulty following directions, completing work, staying on task, or being easily distracted by classroom noise. Impulsivity is demonstrated by blurting out answers, starting an assignment before the directions have been completed, not waiting a turn, being easily angered, or not being able to work in groups. In the schoolyard they may be involved in frequent fights. Hyperactivity is noted in their frequent fidgeting, inability to remain in their seats, dropping items, or constant running at recess or in the halls. Uninformed teachers may describe ADHD children as daydreaming, lazy, unmotivated, or uncooperative. Poor school performance affects the eventual level of academic attainment. The presence of fighting is a very negative indicator for future social adjustment.

Home Behaviors.   At home, parents may describe difficulty getting ready for school in the morning, forgetfulness with chores or multiple commands, and inability to stick with tasks. They may break things accidentally by their rough play and impulsive acts. They are frequently accident prone. Fighting with siblings goes beyond simple sibling rivalry. Since they act impulsively, they may act before having understood what is requested of them. Apparently good intentions go awry. Their hyperactivity is described as being constantly on the go, as having "their motor running." They lack age-appropriate judgement.

Unlike many psychiatric disorders where symptoms are described by the individual or parent as beyond usual day-to-day experience, ADHD symptoms are typical of most children at some time during development. Parents will tolerate their young children's inability to sit still, shifting from one activity to another, not listening, interrupting others, impulsive acts, and even aggression; however, they will not tolerate these same behaviors by older children. Additionally, most parents will describe their ADHD children as displaying these behaviors to a much greater extent than other children their age, even when the children are very young. The signs of ADHD, therefore, appear to represent the extreme on a continuum of motoric and cognitive behaviors.

Peer Behaviors. Peers frequently will not play with ADHD children. They cite reasons such as their not following rules of games, not listening, and immaturity. Impulsivity is evident in other children's complaints that they are bossy, disrupt games, do not wait their turn, risk dangerous activity, and generally get their peers into trouble. Their activity level is high in quiet games or unstructured activities and they talk too much. In more exciting activities they may become frenetic and appear out of control.

Observations of these ADHD children with peers indicate that they very easily become stimulated by peer interactions and have difficulty disengaging or calming down. Other children quickly pick out the ADHD children and label them as undesirable, even when watching silent videotapes of ADHD children playing with peers (Whalen, Henker, Castro, & Granger, 1987). It does not take long for these new peers to assess ADHD children and rate them as negatively as their former peers had rated them (Henker & Whalen, 1989). They become unpopular.

Purposiveness of Behavior. Their social difficulties do not arise because of poor intellectual capacity. ADHD children generally have normal intellect and information processing skills (Henker & Whalen, 1989; Milich & Dodge, 1984). They are as socially aware as their peers (Whalen & Henker, 1985). Their main deficit appears to be in self-regulation (Dykman et al., 1971; Henker & Whalen, 1989; Laufer & Denhoff, 1957). Motivational factors play a central role, as indicated by their ability to attend and focus their activity when appropriately stimulated. ADHD may be described as an interpersonal disorder, that is, deficits in interfacing of the child with the social world (Henker & Whalen, 1989).

These behaviors may worsen in situations requiring self-application such as completing a task, or requiring sustained attention as listening to the teacher or sitting in church. Conversely, they may be minimized during novel activities, stimulating situations, individualized attention, strict control, or when receiving frequent reinforcement. Thus, adults will note that these children appear normal when they are examined at the clinician's office. Observations of their waiting room behavior provides a more diagnostic environment. They also do better when their desk is placed at the front of the room near the teacher's desk. Finally, they may do very well with computers and stimulating computer games.

Primary vs. Secondary Syndrome

ADHD most frequently occurs as a primary syndrome, diagnosed in children with no other overt disorder to explain the symptoms; however, it may exist concurrently with or secondary to other abnormalities (American Psychiatric Association, 1987). Children who experienced earlier damage to their central nervous system, such as brain infections, head injuries, birth complications, or premature birth, may later demonstrate signs consistent with ADHD. ADHD may be diagnosed in these children if the signs are excessive for the given condition. For example, if a mentally retarded child demonstrates symptoms of ADHD that are beyond the child's mental age, then ADHD is appropriately diagnosed. The frequent occurrence of ADHD in such cerebrally compromised children has contributed to etiologic theories of brain impairment.

Adjunctive Signs

The diagnostic criteria for ADHD reveal only a small part of the overall dysfunction experienced by these children and the impact they make on others. At this point in time, knowing whether impairments in the social, psychological, and physical domains are secondary to their inattention, impulsivity, and hyperactivity or whether all of these problems develop from a common developmental deficit is unclear. These adjunctive signs are the ones that are mostly distressing to parents and others who encounter ADHD children.

Social Development and Maladaptive Behavior

All four Goals of Misbehavior may be observed, and all within a very short time period. Dreikurs (1968) saw the purpose of children's misbehavior as falling into one of four categories: (a) attention getting, (b) power, (c) power with revenge, and (d) display of inadequacy. These are immediate goals of the situation aimed at the adults in the setting. With attention getting the children are attempting to keep adults busy with them. Power is a statement of, "I can do whatever I desire, and you can't stop me." Power with revenge is an indication that the child feels hurt and wants to hurt back. Display of inadequacy is a request to be left alone, to be free of expectations.

Power struggles of ADHD children with their parents are so common that even the smallest chores become major obstacles. They may be rigid, tolerating change poorly. They seem immature. Parents and teachers complain that the ADHD children do not learn from experience or from the consequences of their behavior. Praise and rewards are usually ineffective. They believe that punishment is the only recourse. They are convinced that they have to control their children. Peers exclude them. They may be enthusiastic and even charming so that they initially make friends, but they quickly antagonize these friends. Often they have no friends. They want their own way; they want what they want when they want it; they do not take no for an answer; they want to be the boss; and they play impulsively, often resulting in aggression. But they are not mean. Their violence often results from their impulsivity and other children's negative response to their domineering ways.

The preceding profile indicates why ADHD is classified in the DSM-IV with the Disruptive Behavior Disorders. The hallmark of ADHD and the other Disruptive Behavior Disorders is that the behaviors are usually more distressing to others than to the individual demonstrating them. For this reason, they have been termed "externalizing," as opposed to the "internalizing" symptoms seen with depression. ADHD children go through life apparently oblivious to the social codes and situational cues that guide others' behavior. They are often surprised to learn that others are very distressed by their behavior. Often they will blame their behavior and its consequences on others, taking no personal responsibility. The individual diagnostic signs and symptoms, therefore, do not convey the social disruption associated with this syndrome.

Emotional and Psychological Development

Three behavioral attributes seem to characterize the psychological profile of these children. Their moods are variable and unpredictable. They are fine one day, or even one minute, and impossible the next. Their moods may also be exaggerated. In pleasurable activities they may become overexcited so that they appear to lose control of themselves. They cannot "wind down." Secondly, they are generally irritable and easily frustrated. Their low frustration tolerance along with their impulsivity frequently leads to tantrums or temper outbursts. Thirdly, they seek stimulation. They may call attention to themselves, engage in novel activities, and even court danger. As part of their stimulus seeking, they are constantly unsatisfied and easily bored. Their impulsive behavior counters the boredom. They often have difficulty getting to sleep, perhaps reflecting their inability to "wind down" at the end of the day or their continued desire for stimulation. Many ADHD children do not appear affectionate, even as infants. Although attention-seeking, they are not affection-seeking.

Eventually, most ADHD children suffer impairments in their self-esteem. Usually this is evident by the second to fourth grade. They begin to recognize their social rejection; they feel different and may be very lonely. They may make statements about hurting themselves or wishing they were dead, and their impulsivity makes them a risk to incur some harm, either self-induced or by apparent accident. They are accident-prone. They may become depressed, and even if not depressed, they are often unhappy at a young age.

Physical and Neurological Development

Many, but not all, ADHD children demonstrate "soft neurological signs" (Werry, Minde, Guyman, Weiss, Dogan, & Hoy, 1972). These are observable neurological deficits of mild to moderate severity, which are not localized to a specific part of the brain, but which indicate diffuse motoric dysfunction. The most common soft neurological signs are deficits in fine motor skills. Approximately half of ADHD children demonstrate such incoordination. In school these children may color or write very poorly or be unable to cut with scissors. At home they may not be able to button their clothes, tie their shoes, or zipper their pants. They may have difficulty balancing themselves and therefore cannot learn to ride a bicycle. Others have poor hand-eye coordination, making them awkward at catching or throwing a ball, or at playing baseball or basketball. They tend to be clumsy and frequently break things accidentally. Some may not even respond to pain as robustly as other children. Gross motor skills are more frequently intact, so that even those children with fine motor deficits may still run and swim well, play soccer, or master martial arts. These gross motor activities can help them to focus some of their restlessness.

Related to incoordination is the inability to organize tasks appropriately. School papers appear disorganized, carelessly done. Test results show haphazard mistakes. They may miss easy questions and then correctly answer more difficult ones. They do not seem to plan their answers or problem solving. Chores at home are done poorly, if at all, without supervision. When they must work independently, they may not be able to organize the task to get started. They often do not have the skills that enable them to organize preparations for school in the morning. Continual parental supervision is typical.

CONCURRENT DISRUPTIVE BEHAVIOR DISORDERS

Approximately 50% of ADHD children also will meet criteria for other Disruptive Behavior Disorders, specifically Oppositional Defiant Disorder (ODD) or Conduct Disorder (CD) (Henker & Whalen, 1989; Sandberg, Wieselberg, & Shaffer, 1980). The high concurrence of these diagnoses with ADHD results in part because criteria for the three disorders overlap (American Psychiatric Association, 1987; Biederman, Munir, & Knee, 1987; Reeves, Werry, Elkind, & Zametkin, 1987; Sandberg et al., 1980; Shapiro & Garfinkel, 1986; Werry, Reeves, & Elkind, 1987).

Oppositional Defiant Disorder

Oppositionally Defiant ADHD children demonstrate greater difficulty regulating mood and behavior. Presenting signs shift to anger, instead of just irritability as with ADHD, and increased power struggles instead of just disorganization and distractibility. These children will not only have difficulty remembering or sticking with tasks, they will adamantly refuse to do them or put up a struggle before doing them. Everything they do seems to say "You can't make me." They seem to have a "chip on their shoulder." They seem provocative, resentful, and sometimes vindictive. They may treat others very poorly, being annoying and argumentative at the least to denigrating at worst. They disrespect parents especially, but authority figures in general. They are always showing that they are the boss. Other people are not as eager to reach out to help these children as the children with ADHD alone. Behavior is generally much worse at home, or around familiar people and situations; however, they do not generally break societal rules.

Conduct Disorder

Conduct Disordered ADHD children may have been diagnosed as having ODD when younger. CD supersedes ODD diagnostically, because the psychopathology is greater and ODD symptoms are generally present in CD youths. Basic age-appropriate societal rules are broken and the rights of others violated when ADHD children also demonstrate a CD. Such antisocial behaviors are not diagnostic of ADHD or ODD diagnoses without CD. Impairments of behavior are typically pervasive, occurring in most settings not just with authority figures, as is seen with ODD. Those ADHD children with better social skills are likely to develop the group type of CD, whereas those less skilled may develop the solitary aggressive type.

If a child does not present for therapeutic help until CD or ODD is present, parents will generally focus on these more disruptive and maladaptive behaviors. Careful assessment for underlying ADHD must then be undertaken and considered in treatment planning.

Mood Disorders

Some features of a Mood Disorder resemble symptoms of ADHD (Jensen, Burke, & Garfinkel, 1988). Both may demonstrate an irritable mood. The agitation of mood may resemble hyperactivity. Difficulty concentrating may be confused with inattention and distractibility. Both groups of children may display insomnia. Some of the mood lability seen in ADHD children suggests rapid cycling Bipolar Disorder. Therefore, Mood Disorders form part of the differential diagnosis of ADHD.

Additionally, ADHD children may develop a Mood Disorder subsequent to or concurrent with their ADHD. Major Depressive Disorder may develop. More commonly ADHD children will meet criteria for Dysthymia with either irritable or depressive mood (Anderson, Williams, McGee, & Silva, 1987; Jensen et al., 1988; McGee & Williams, 1988). The risk for a secondary Mood Disorder is increased by the increased rate of Mood Disorders in parents of ADHD children (Biederman et al., 1987; Lahey, Piacentini, McBurnett, Stone, Hartdagen, & Hynd, 1988). Some parents will have Mood Disorders undiagnosed prior to evaluation of their children's problems. Therefore, any symptomatic change of ADHD phenomenology must be reassessed with consideration of a Mood Disorder.

Specific Developmental Disorders

The Specific Developmental Disorders (SDDs) include academic skills disorders in arithmetic, expressive writing, and reading; language and speech disorders in articulation, expressive language, or receptive language; and motor skills disorders in coordination. Due to their large overlap with ADHD, a more comprehensive discussion is warranted.

Diagnosis.   In DSM-IV criteria for the various SDDs is the requirement that the individual's achievement in the particular developmental skill be "markedly below" what would be expected for the individual's age, schooling, and intellectual capacity. Additionally, the disturbance in the specific SDD must significantly interfere with academic achievement or activities of daily living related to that skill. Finally, the deficit in that SDD must not be due to any physical defect or other disorder. Also to be ruled out are psychosocial conditions that could lead to deprived educational opportunities. For example, children living in poverty or children from families where English is not the primary language need special consideration. The lack of appropriate motivation for learning also would preclude this diagnosis. In general, the SDD child is conceptualized as having average academic potential, but below-average academic performance, with academic difficulties resulting from a specific cognitive deficit, as language or perceptual-motor skills.

Diagnoses of the Academic Skills Disorders are made with tests that measure both the level of development of the impaired skill and the individual's intelligence. Additionally, the diagnosis of Developmental Expressive and Receptive Language Disorders requires that scores for these language skills be compared with scores for nonverbal intelligence. The Axis II Specific Developmental Disorders are unique among psychiatric disorders in that their diagnoses are dependent upon validating standardized tests; however, no comparable standardized tests are available to measure ADHD. ADHD children generally will demonstrate characteristic patterns on such testing that suggest inattention and impulsivity.

Detection.   These SDDs are usually diagnosed by 8 years of age. Some children escape detection until later ages. Criteria in the DSM-IV are vague. Multiple difficulties ensue when attempts are made to operationalize the definitions for SDDs, so that children may escape detection early in their schooling. Two major approaches have been used (Morris, 1988).

The first is an age-based definition that is used most commonly in educational settings. Schools require that children perform two years below their age or grade level in reading or other specific achievement area. This definition has many associated problems relating to the psychometric properties of scores, such as the use of age equivalents or grade equivalents (Reynolds, 1981).

The second approach has focused on the discrepancy between IQ and achievement measures, with a 1–standard-deviation difference being considered criterion to define a SDD child. The problem with such discrepancy-based classification relates to the use of standardized IQ tests, the choice of different achievement tests, and the definition of the skill being measured. Finally, the choice of the 1–standard-deviation discrepancy between IQ and performance is arbitrary. One of the most common uses of various discrepancy criteria is to control the number of children eligible for special services in relation to funding levels.

A final problem is the exclusionary criteria used in operationalizing definitions of SDD. Children with sensory-motor deficits, with psychiatric disorders, or from lower socioeconomic backgrounds would be excluded, although no operational criteria exist for identifying these problems that may contribute significantly to learning difficulties.

Current operationalized criteria group deficits in related skills as reading disorders, arithmetic disorders, or language disorders. Such grouping assumes homogeneous symptomatology and implies a known etiology, as underlying brain dysfunction; however, the most current research does not support these conclusions. Great variability occurs within the SDD population. This heterogeneity may reflect individual differences or the occurrence of variable subtypes that differ in etiology, task performance, and prognosis (Morris, 1988). This heterogeneity has been largely ignored in theories of SDD as well as in the development of services to treat SDD children. New approaches to classification are now being investigated (Morris, 1988).

As summarized previously, these operational criteria for identifying SDD children are variable and inconsistently applied. Definitions fail to acknowledge the multiple factors that influence academic development or the diversity of problems associated with academic handicaps (Taylor, 1988). As a result, many children who meet DSM-IV criteria will not meet the school criteria and will, therefore, not be eligible for remedial services. Children with milder SDDs and shy children are especially vulnerable to being overlooked. By contrast, SDD children with concurrent ADHD or other Disruptive Behavior Disorders will be less likely to escape detection.

Prevalence.   Individual SDDs affect approximately 2% to 11% of the general child population (American Psychiatric Association, 1987). Many children have more than one SDD. Among school-aged children, a prevalence rate of at least 10 to 15% is commonly reported for SDDs as a group (Heaton, 1988; Silver, 1989).

Different studies have variably reported that 20% to 40% of ADHD children have concurrent SDDs (Bashir, Wing, & Abrams, 1987; Denckla, 1978; Duane, 1985; Duffy, 1988; Forness, 1981; Halperin, Gittelman, Klein, & Rudel, 1984; Silver, 1981). This high overlap of the two disorders suggests a possible common etiology or predisposing factors. The inability to concentrate is a primary characteristic of perceptual dysfunction. A pupil who cannot focus and attend will have difficulty decoding sensory data efficiently. Achievement in all areas of learning will then be affected. ADHD children are prone to multiple developmental disorders. This makes them more easily identifiable but also makes academic achievement more difficult.

Maturation.   Previously, these disorders were designated as learning disabilities or developmental delays. These designations are misleading, implying that maturation brings improvement. Some developmentally disordered children do improve their abilities with age; however, most do not. Children with more severe forms of these disorders are especially unlikely to attain skills comparable to their adolescent or adult peers.

Disorders of inadequate development may be more diagnostically descriptive. SDDs and ADHD share this historic conceptualization that the dysfunction results from delays of maturation and represents normal functioning for earlier developmental stages. This terminology persists in part because accurate prediction is not possible during preschool and school years as to which children will "catch up" and which will not. Whether these children will "catch up" relates not only to their academic success but also to their success with life tasks.

Etiology.   In general, SDD children vary in their academic, cognitive, and social abilities. No individual child has all of the deficits that have been associated with specific academic learning problems. Attempts to establish causality are therefore difficult, and the etiology of SDDs remains unknown. The current consensus is that the etiology is heterogeneous. Complex cognitive operations and neural factors are associated with children's ability to learn any skill. Learning is influenced by multiple factors including intelligence, academic skills, stimulation, social interest, effort, and encouragement. Each of these factors is affected by a wide range of emotional and environmental considerations. If any of these factors for success is missing, the risk of learning disability increases.

Traditional concepts of SDD have rested on two presuppositions: first, that SDDs are due to deficits in basic psychological processes; and second, that these processing deficits are, in turn, a reflection of an organ inferiority in biological-genetic or constitutional factors (Taylor, 1988). These concepts are being rethought in the light of new research.

Support for a genetic organ inferiority has been best established for Developmental Reading Disorder or dyslexia (Pennington & Smith, 1988). Dyslexic children reportedly have a genetically influenced deficiency in single word recognition skills and the precursor to this deficit is in the domain of phonological processing skills (Pennington & Smith, 1988). Other SDDs have not been as well assessed for genetic influences. Indicators of organ inferiority, however, are supported by an association with biological markers such as positive family histories, electrophysiological abnormalities, and increased rates of prenatal and perinatal complications (Taylor, 1988).

In the DSM-IV no reference is made to any impairment of central nervous system organ inferiority or constitutional etiology. Such factors may be necessary, but they are not sufficient for the development of learning problems. The manifestations of these problems probably depend upon other factors, such as overcompensation, lack of encouragement, overambition, lack of social interest, as well as parental attitudes and educational approaches. "Encouragement" and "overambition" are technical terms in Adlerian theory. *Encouragement* is a willingness to go forth until the problem is solved. The opposite, *discouragement*, is characterized by not taking the sequential steps necessary for problem-solving. *Overambition* is the opposite of self-confidence. Overambition is a statement that "I am not enough. I am unable to do the job."

Interpersonal Disturbances. The SDDs are, by definition, associated with impairment in academic functioning and also have been associated with impairments in daily living. The latter impairments are the ones that generally bring SDD children to clinical awareness (Hunt & Cohen, 1984).

An original problem such as reading frequently will generalize to other school subjects that rely heavily on written material. They then are considered unintelligent, because they cannot master age-appropriate language skills. These skills are not limited to academic subjects. They include the time taken to understand material as well as to associate it with old knowledge. Therefore, skills requiring wit and humor or creativity and intuition may be beyond these children in daily social interactions. To other children these children appear to "not get it." They are then excluded. These additional failure experiences are perceived by SDD children as further indication of their inferiority. SDD children then become further stigmatized by their peers.

Adlerian theory is holistic: A deficit in one aspect of being will necessarily show itself in all areas of functioning to a lesser or greater degree. It can take the form of overcompensation as in the classic case of Demosthenes who used pebbles in his mouth to overcome a speech impediment. His overcompensation resulted in his fame for great oration. Adler (Ansbacher & Ansbacher, 1956) viewed all compensation as overcompensation. When one successfully strives to overcome a liability, the striving goes beyond a neutral position or average level of competence. Physical overcompensation is also seen. A broken bone heals stronger in the area of the wound than in the surrounding bone. Overcompensation requires courage, self-confidence, and optimism. Unsuccessful striving is characteristic of discouragement, a lack of self-confidence, and pessimism. These academic and functional impairments, interference with getting on with all aspects of life, are the bases for the inclusion of these disorders in psychiatric nomenclature. These children will go to extremes in their efforts to overcome their SDDs. They may fake a paragraph when it comes to their turn to read aloud. A "sour grapes" attitude can be a discouraged, unwillingness to try, response to confronting an academic task. Conduct Disorder commonly will be employed as a discouraged tactic in the avoidance of an academic challenge. A face-saving strategy obscures the fact that one cannot meet the academic requirements. All misbehaviors can be best viewed as an attempt to safeguard self-esteem. Overcompensation using misbehavior may bring admiration among some peers and give one a higher status position in certain circles. That method of attaining status will be an interference to achievement in academic areas where one might be successful. Coming to rely on misbehavior for finding one's place in the group can result in a life-long disability.

SDD children often will resist receiving special educational services because they are aware of the stigmatization that they will incur. Special education is an inferior station among peers. Special education encourages overcompensation in the direction of misbehavior because it sets these children in a socially inferior position. As Adler (Ansbacher & Ansbacher, 1956) made clear, all striving is from a position of felt inferiority to a position of felt superiority. The child who believes that academic success is not possible will overcompensate, and strive toward superiority, which is not useful. Placing children with ADHD and SDD apart from their peers in any form is best avoided. Their striving for superiority will likely move in a negative direction if they are seen as different by peers.

Since many ADHD children have concurrent SDDs, they face stigmatization by their peers even more than the those with only ADHD. ADHD children are easily picked out by their peers as undesirable because of their disruptive behaviors. As seen above, ADHD-SDD children may additionally be considered stupid, socially inept, moody, and different.

Discouragement.   Many studies have reported decreased self-esteem and social competence, poor social adjustment, emotional disturbances, conduct and family problems (Rourke, 1988). As discussed, SDD children must deal with interpersonal environments that differ markedly from their normally achieving peers whether they are merely handicapped or further stigmatized with special education. They are often perceived by parents, teachers, and peers as less pleasant and desirable and are the recipients of more negative communications and discouragement from these sources. They may be ignored and rejected by teachers, and treated in a more punitive and derogatory manner by parents.

Dreikurs (1958) clarified the problem. Teachers and parents do not know how to encourage these children. Hence, they resort to discouraging tactics typically in the form of punishment.

Classmates describe SDD children as less socially competent regardless of their attempts to overcompensate. SDD children may also have difficulty perceiving and interpreting the affective states of others. They lack social interest, that is, they do not feel part of the group, perceive the environment as unfriendly, and then respond with socially useless behavior (Dreikurs, 1958). It is likely that social awareness and responsiveness vary markedly for subtypes of SDD children depending upon the central processing abilities and deficits, the specific task demands (Ozols & Rourke, 1985), as well as the degree of personal courage, self-confidence, optimism, and development of social interest.

The association of socioemotional disturbances with SDDs does not necessarily imply that they are consequences of the learning deficits. A causal connection has been proposed between particular patterns of central processing abilities and deficits, on the one hand, and particular subtypes of learning disabilities and socioemotional functioning on the other (Rourke, 1988; Rourke & Fisk, 1981).

Idiographic. The Adlerian view is unwilling to compartmentalize brain functioning, behavioral manifestations, and interpersonal relationships. They are integral, an inseparable idiographic, and do not lend themselves to direction, specific stimulus-response predictability, or individual prognosis even if all of the objective variables could be determined.

Long-term Functioning. The long-term outcome for SDD children is of relevance for interpersonal, occupational, and emotional adjustment as well as for the school, economic, and judicial systems of society. Early studies painted a bleak picture of the adolescent and adult outcomes for SDD children who did not overcome their learning disabilities (Critchley, 1964). Increased risk for an antisocial behavior pattern was emphasized. Intervention did not appear to affect outcome. Only if the child came from upper socioeconomic status (Schonhaut & Satz, 1983) or had superior intelligence (Robinson & Smith, 1962) did the prospect for academic skill development appear hopeful.

The current consensus is that SDDs persist into adulthood to some degree. The severity of academic deficits in adulthood is associated with the severity of the disability as a child (Spreen, 1988a, 1988b). Once children have fallen behind academically, they are susceptible to further delays with increasing disability (Kistner & Torgesen, 1987; Stanovich, 1986).

How intervention affects adult achievement remains unclear. Some studies report good success with specific intervention models (Kline & Kline, 1975); others have demonstrated only modest success with general interventions (Bruck, 1985; Spreen, 1988b); and others have not demonstrated any effect of intervention on outcome (Frauenheim, 1978). Nomothetically, the single best predictor of overall adult outcome is general intelligence (Muehl & Forrell, 1973; Rawson, 1968; Spreen, 1988a, 1988b). Similarly, the absence of neurological impairment is highly predictive of better outcome (Jaklewicz, 1982; Spreen, 1988a, 1988b; Silver, 1977). Occupational achievement appears lower for SDD children (Finucci, Gottfredson, & Childs, 1985; Jaklewicz, 1982; Spreen, 1988a). The father's occupational and educational status appear to predict SDD children's later occupational outcome better than many other relevant factors except general intelligence and lack of neurological impairment (Buerger, 1968; O'Connor & Spreen, 1988).

Socioemotional disturbances appear to peak in late adolescence and decrease somewhat in the third decade of life. Women appear to be more affected than men (Spreen, 1988a). SDD children with socioemotional disturbances continue to demonstrate problems as adolescents and adults and may change the types of problems they have (Rourke, 1988); however, children without significant socioemotional disturbances are not likely to develop them later in life (Rourke, 1988).

ETIOLOGY OF ADHD

No structural or anatomical brain damage has been documented in ADHD. Many studies over the past three decades, however, have supported brain dysfunction in ADHD children, that is, an abnormality in how the brain functions rather than in tissue structure (Brown, Ebert, & Minichiello, 1985; Dykman et al., 1972; Ferguson & Pappas, 1979; Hastings & Barkley, 1978; Levy & Hobbs, 1988; Rapoport, Buchsbaum, Zahn, Weingartner, Ludlow, & Mikkelsen, 1978; Rapoport & Ferguson, 1981; Satterfield, 1973; Werry, Minde, Guyman, Weiss, Dogan, & Hoy, 1972; Wender, 1971; Zametkin & Rapoport, 1987). This dysfunction is detected by psychophysiological and neuropsychological testing, and neurochemical assays rather than by neurological examination or postmortem examinations of brain tissue. Recent developments in cerebral imaging techniques have revealed decreased blood perfusion of selected areas of brain tissue, which may be associated with these functional deficits (Loh, Hendrickson, & Bruhn, 1984). The "soft neurological signs," such as fine motor control (Werry et al., 1972), and the very frequent co-occurrence of SDDs with ADHD (Bashir et al., 1987; Denckla, 1978; Duane, 1985; Duffy, 1988; Forness, 1981; Halperin et al., 1984; Silver, 1981) also suggest underlying brain dysfunction.

Another line of thinking conceptualizes ADHD as a disorder of temperament with primary developmental deficits in self-control, interpersonal relatedness, and social transactions (Henker & Whalen, 1989; Wender, 1987). The high prevalence of personality disorders in adulthood and the enduring nature of ADHD deficits in those adults without personality disorders (Gittelman, Mannuzza, Shenker, & Bonagura, 1985; Hopkins, Perlman, Hechtman, & Weiss, 1979; Weiss & Hechtman, 1986; Weiss, Hechtman, & Perlman, 1978; Weiss, Hechtman, Perlman, Hopkins, & Wener, 1979) suggests an etiologic role for temperament.

DEMOGRAPHY

Prevalence

ADHD appears to affect approximately 3% to 5% of children in the United States (American Psychiatric Association, 1987; Lambert, Sandoval, & Sasone, 1981; Sandberg et al., 1980). It is the most common single disorder referred to child psychiatry (Safer & Allen, 1976). The onset of ADHD must be before 7 years old in order to meet DSM-IV diagnostic criteria. If clinical assessment does not occur until after this age, then the symptoms must still have been present before 7 years of age. Approximately half of ADHD children are diagnosed by age 4 years old (American Psychiatric Association, 1987). Most children are clinically identified by 10 years of age.

Masculine Protest

Males significantly outnumber females. In general population studies, the ratio approximates 3:1; but in clinical samples the ratio has been estimated between 6:1 and 10:1 (American Psychiatric Association, 1987; Lambert et al., 1981). The discrepancy probably reflects the differential misbehaviors demonstrated by boys and girls. Dreikurs (1968) suggested that this is a form of what Adler termed "the masculine protest." Striving from a position of felt inferiority toward superiority takes on the exaggerated caricature of masculinity. Misbehavior of an aggressive nature is supported by parents and culture as proof that one is a real man and reassures the boy that even if he is not as capable in academic areas at least he is powerful in the male arena. Parents and culture do not desire feminine males. Hence, the misbehavior may result in referral for treatment because it is disrupting, but it is better than being a "sissy."

DEVELOPMENTAL CHANGE OF SYMPTOMS

ADHD children generally demonstrate different signs at various developmental periods. This variability may represent a true maturational change. Alternatively, parents and teachers may differentially respond to signs with advancing age. If children are overly active as toddlers, they may well be called hyperactive. But if they are unable to stay in their seats and bother other pupils when placed in a large stimulating classroom, their disruptiveness becomes a major problem. Expectations of children's behavior depends largely on established age-appropriate normative behaviors. The exact reasons for the shifting behavior pattern is not clear. Due to their greater experience with these age-appropriate norms, teachers are often better reporters of whether ADHD children are demonstrating inappropriate behaviors.

Preschool

Many ADHD children show their first signs as infants. They are irritable, not easily consoled, colicky, and sleep poorly. Some parents describe them as not wanting to be held. Other parents, however, note a normal infancy. As toddlers, the main complaints almost always center on their gross motor activity. ADHD children seem to be motorically ahead of their peers from the very first crawl they take. They are quickly into and on top of everything and seem fearless. They may wander away if not carefully supervised, not seeming to mind separation from mother. They are constantly on the go and tantrums continue throughout the preschool period. They may also be especially violent with head banging or serious injury to other children. If enrolled in preschool, social misbehaviors start to dominate the picture. They want all of the attention, talk incessantly, do not share, try to dominate, tantrum, do not nap, and are generally annoying and uncooperative.

School-age

At the start of school many children are first diagnosed who had escaped detection previously. Children who are smart and charming may be well tolerated by adults who can give extra time. In the classroom such individualized attention is not practical. Teachers complain of hyperactivity or restlessness and of inattentiveness or distractibility. They may be aware of the social problems, even of the children's rejection by peers; but it is the inability to cooperate in class that is the most bothersome. Academic difficulties are usually noted in the first or second grade by an alert teacher but may be overshadowed by the social adjustment problems. Academic problems are seriously addressed around the fourth grade. By then ADHD children have sufficiently underachieved to warrant formal academic assessment. Specific developmental disorders may be first detected. Emphasis now centers on academic deficits. Aggression and antisocial behaviors may emerge around this time. Some children may be placed in special educational programs that further stigmatize them.

Adolescence

Adolescence often heralds a significant change (Lambert, 1988). Many ADHD children seem to grow out of the difficulties with inattention, hyperactivity, and impulsivity. This group has a relatively normal adolescence. Even specific developmental disorders may normalize. Another group no longer has hyperactivity but continues to display inattentiveness and impulsivity. Academics remain problematic. A third group shows antisocial and self-destructive behaviors, including serious drug and alcohol abuse. They are at-risk to drop out of school or to enter the juvenile justice system. Their social problems receive much more attention than their persistent academic problems. Not all ADHD children display gross maladaptive behaviors at all stages; the pattern is quite variable. Perhaps another hallmark of this disorder is the inconsistency across groups of children and within individual children.

OUTCOME

Long-term Functioning

Early studies concluded that ADHD resolved at puberty; however, those studies focused on the hyperactivity. When the entire syndrome is assessed longitudinally, another picture emerges. Approximately one-third to one-half of ADHD children at puberty seem either to have resolved this disorder or at least to have significantly mitigated it (Gittelman et al., 1985; Hechtman, Weiss, Perlman, & Tuck, 1981; Lambert, 1988; Mannuzza, Klein, Bonagura, Konig, & Shenker, 1988; Minde, Weiss, & Mendelson, 1972; Weiss & Hechtman, 1986).

They may have developed some problems with self-esteem but generally do well with the tasks of life.

Another third continues to experience chronic interpersonal disharmony, restlessness, and impulsivity that have been only partially contained (Weiss & Hechtman, 1986; Weiss et al., 1978; Weiss et al., 1979). These may persist into the third and fourth decades of adulthood. The three main tasks of life, occupation, marriage, and community relationships pose conflicts but do not totally preclude moderate interpersonal adjustment.

ADHD individuals in these first two groups who do attain some degree of social status, satisfying social ties, and stability may still have difficulty with social transactions and lack intimacy in their lives, as evidenced by lower participation in extracurricular and community activities (Mannuzza et al., 1988).

The last one-third of ADHD children as adults demonstrates serious problems throughout adolescence and adulthood (Wender, Reimherr, & Wood, 1981). These individuals experience significant failures in most domains of life. Multiple marriages and jobs fail. They frequently engage in antisocial activities and illicit substance usage. Incarceration is common. Their restlessness and impulsivity, chronic excitement-seeking, and rigidity indicate a lack of social interest and a serious failure with the tasks of life.

The decreased social interest of ADHD children in adulthood is further evidenced by an increased rate of personality disorders, particularly the DSM-IV Cluster B of Antisocial, Borderline, and Narcissistic Personality Disorders (Hechtman & Weiss, 1986). These individuals are more likely to have had concurrent diagnoses of ODD or CD as youths.

Predicting Outcome

Early identification of those ADHD children who will eventually succeed with life tasks and those who will fail defies prediction at present. Some indication is available that those who will fare poorest are those most severely afflicted during childhood. They demonstrate the most social and academic maladjustment and usually are diagnosed with other concurrent Disruptive Behavior Disorders (August & Holmes, 1984; August, Stewart, & Holmes, 1983; Gittelman et al., 1985; Loeber & Schmaling, 1985; Loney, 1987; Milich & Loney, 1979; Walker, Lahey, Hynd, & Frame, 1987; Weiss, Hechtman, Milroy, & Perlman, 1985).

Their fathers appear more frequently to be antisocial, to use illicit substances, or to abuse alcohol (Cantwell, 1972; Lahey et al., 1988; Stewart, DeBlois, &

Cummings, 1980). Overall parental psychopathology appears higher. Factors such as general intelligence, soft neurological signs, Specific Developmental Disorders, and treatment history have not been shown to definitively affect outcome.

The prediction of outcome for ADHD children, however, has been confounded by the heterogeneity of this disorder. Recent work has addressed the need to subtype ADHD children according to the concurrence of conduct problems and aggression (Loney, 1987; Loney, Langhorne, & Paternite, 1978; O'Leary & Steen, 1982). Children with only ADHD appear to meet the life tasks much more successfully than those ADHD children with other Disruptive Behavior Disorders.

Adlerian theory takes a different perspective. Outcome cannot be predicted because ADHD is not separable from the individual. It represents an idiographic. An ADHD individual's movement in life cannot be dissected into these discrete variables.

ADLERIAN DYNAMICS

Many dynamics addressed by Individual Psychology have been stated previously and will be further illustrated in the case vignettes. ADHD had not been a diagnostic entity when Adler was writing. Dreikurs, Adler's foremost student, was well familiar with the concept. Dreikurs (1968) believed that ADHD is a spurious diagnosis, as are most of the SDDs. The over-representation of males with these problems and the absence of hard diagnostic signs was evidence to him that these diagnoses are cultural artifacts. He agreed that intelligence is a strong influence with SDD. He further agreed that an optimal home and school environment will lessen the probability of any disorder developing; however, it is the masculine overemphasis discussed previously (masculine protest) that predominantly accounts for ADHD and the SDDs. Where no evidence of an organ inferiority is present, Dreikurs and Adler would have seen the cultural desire to be a real man as the largest culprit.

Organ Inferiority

As noted previously, the evidence is increasing that constitutional defects are present at birth in many children with ADHD and SDD diagnoses. Adler (Ansbacher & Ansbacher, 1956) believed that any organ inferiority poses the possibility of risk for maladjustment. Parents and other family members may pamper these children, or worse, feel sorry for them. Pampering, doing for them that which they can do for themselves, is discouraging. It robs children of the confidence that comes with increasing skill development. It deprives them of learning opportunities and retards their emotional and intellectual development.

Feeling sorry for children (Dreikurs, 1958) teaches them that they have been short-changed by life, and now life owes them. They then expect that others will treat them special because they have been short-changed. They claim special exemption due to their disability. They learn not to maximize their striving but to wait for life to come to them. Feeling sorry for these children provides them with evidence that they are inferior to others. Feelings of personal inferiority will result in a striving to be better than others. If that striving is not accomplished in culturally approved ways, for example, academics, it will take the form of misbehavior. Either way, striving for personal superiority is not social cooperation and can only be deleterious to the individual and others.

Competition

Parents who are unsure of their worth compete with each other for a place of significance. Their competition sets a model for the children to compete with them and with each other. If first-born children are well-behaved and academically successful, second children in these families are likely to misbehave and have academic problems. In other words, their ambition leads them to compete in areas not secured by the first born. If the "model child" position is occupied, a place for misbehavior and being the very best at failing is open and tempting to the second child. This competition can show in just the reverse. The first child can have the characteristics of the second child just described. Competition can also occur between any ordinal positions within the family (for example, between the first and third child). Competition is the key to diversity between siblings, whatever their ordinal position.

Lifestyle Theme

A representative lifestyle, pattern of behavior, might be as follows:

"I am less than others."
"I must be superior."
"Life is one big opportunity to fail."
"It is better not to try than to face the humiliation that comes with failure."

"If I don't put my neck out, no one will know that I can't succeed."

"My family expects too much of me."

"I have problems and they have to treat me differently."

"My siblings are favored and get all the breaks."

"My parents owe me and have to make up for what they should have done for me."

"I have been shorted by them and by life."

"Life is unfair."

"Too much is expected of me and too little has been given to me."

"If I can't be the best at that which is approved by my family, school, and community, I'll be the best at being the boss."

"I'll show others that they can't tell me what to do or make me do anything."

"I can't find a place among my peers in academics, but I can gain their admiration by my defiance of adults."

"I feel superior when I defeat adults."

"Besides they deserve it for what they have done to me."

TREATMENT STRATEGIES

Medication Treatment

Comments regarding the medication management of ADHD children are warranted. Stimulant medication is the most prevalent and effective therapy used for ADHD. It is also the most carefully studied therapy of all childhood therapies (Henker & Whalen, 1989). Three stimulant medications are routinely used according to physician preference and the child's tolerance: (a) methylphenidate (Ritalin), the most commonly prescribed stimulant; (b) dextroamphetamine (Dexedrine); and (c) Pemoline (Cylert). Medications other than stimulants are sometimes used. The most common is the tricyclic antidepressant imipramine or its metabolite desipramine (Pliszka, 1987). This medication is generally used if the child develops complications with the stimulants or has a concurrent Mood Disorder. Less frequently, antidepressants of the type termed monoamine oxidase inhibitors are chosen (Zametkin, Rapoport, Murphy, Linnoila, & Ismond, 1986; Zametkin, Rapoport, Murphy, Linnoila, Karoum, Potter, & Ismond, 1986).

Social Behaviors

Favorable stimulant-related changes are frequently immediate, dramatic, and multifaceted. They do not represent a placebo effect (Whalen, Henker, Swanson,

Granger, Kliewer, & Spencer, 1987). The noted changes affect everyday life activities and may be noted by parents, teachers, and other adults interacting with the ADHD child. Parents note decreases in demanding, oppositional, and disruptive behaviors. The children cooperate better with family responsibilities, because they are less impulsive and excitable. Transitions, such as bedtimes, getting ready for school in the morning, or family outings proceed more smoothly. They are better able to engage in peer activities, such as scouts or athletic events.

Teachers note that they are better able to stay on-task during classroom assignments, more frequently complete assignments, do not disrupt the class, and/or do not get into as much trouble on the schoolyard. Their fine motor control, as evidenced in their handwriting or artwork, may improve. Improvements in learning disabilities also may be noted (August & Holmes, 1984; Gittelman, Klein, & Feingold, 1983; Richardson, Kupietz, Winsberg, Richardson, Maitinsky, & Mendell, 1988).

Indirect benefits of the medication are observed in parents' and teachers' more positive and less controlling interactions with them (Barkley, 1985; Mash & Johnston, 1982; Whalen, Henker, & Dotemoto, 1980). They report that the child is more likeable and manageable. These improvements suggest that the negative family environment surrounding ADHD children may arise largely from the response of caretakers to these children's adverse behaviors. Containment of the children's symptoms may positively influence the family environment.

Less information has been obtained regarding peer relationships. Preliminary evidence is not encouraging. Some improvements in social standing may be realized, although still below that realized by their normal peers (Henker & Whalen, 1989). Their reputations and peer relationships do not seem to change, at least over the short-term (Cunningham, Siegel, & Offord, 1985; Pelham & Bender, 1982). Perhaps a longer time may be needed for these children to realize improved peer relationships. Alternatively, ADHD children taking stimulant medication may be better able to contain their adverse behaviors, but they may not replace these behaviors with more prosocial behaviors that build friendships. Achievement of social competence becomes the major focus of psychotherapeutic interventions (Henker & Whalen, 1989).

Cognitive Performance

Positive medication effects are also well-established on standardized neuropsychological measures (Campbell, Douglas, & Morgenstern, 1971; Sebrechts, Shaywitz, Shaywitz, Jatlow, Anderson, & Cohen, 1986), and classroom behavior

(Brown & Sleator, 1979; Rapport, Stoner, DuPaul, Birmingham, & Tucker, 1985; Rapport, Stoner, DuPaul, Kelly, Tucker, & Schoeler, 1988). The quantity, accuracy, and efficiency of completed classwork improves (Douglas, Barr, O'Neill, & Britton, 1986; Pelham, Bender, Caddell, Booth, & Moorer, 1986). Stimulant medication helps the children to focus, so that they make more effective use of their time and increase their speed and accuracy of response.

The larger question is whether stimulant medication facilitates these gains directly by improving information processing or whether the enhanced performance results from changes in attitude, motivation, and self-regulation, which allow ADHD children to cooperate and exert mental effort. The fact that stimulant treatment seems least effective in improving academic performance in children with learning disabilities, whether or not they also have ADHD, suggests that improved academic performance results from motivational and attitudinal change rather than from changes in the basic cognitive processes (Henker & Whalen, 1989).

Despite these significant short-term effects, long-term effects have not been consistently documented in major areas of functioning, including scholarship. Many methodological factors may contribute to the lack of measurable long-term gains. Stimulants, however, may improve ADHD children's ability to discern social cues and modulate their behavior appropriately but not provide the catch-up learning that many of these children may need. They also do not negate the effects of past experiences on ADHD children's motivation and self-perceived efficacy or the negative expectancies held by others for them (Henker & Whalen, 1989).

These long term studies indicate that these ADHD children need more than just medication therapy. They need individualized programs in education, social skills, development, and parent education.

Psychosocial Treatment

Treatment involves the school and the family. Structure, predictable schedules, and adult disengagement from the child's misbehavior are useful. Building on strengths at school and home gives more opportunities for success. Focusing on misbehaviors and inadequate skills only furthers everyone's discouragement.

An organized environment that provides novel and stimulating activities aids attention in ADHD. Teachers are asked not to involve the parents in schoolwork. Parents assure the teachers that they will support decisions between the school and their child. Teachers do not advise the parents, and parents do not give advice to the teachers.

Stimulant medication typically assists attention, contains impulsivity, and decreases restlessness, thereby allowing children to focus on more positive interactions. They become more educable. Hence, family therapy is facilitated as well as peer, school, and home behavior. Family therapy is a structure that assists the initiation of family council meetings. An ability to listen to one another is learned in family therapy.

Family therapy gives an understanding to everyone as to the intent of misbehaviors. The misbehaviors may lessen upon recognition (Dreikurs, 1958) and provide valuable information to the therapist for parental recommendations; for example, parents leave the house when the child misbehaves. Parents of children diagnosed with ADHD are more ready to admit defeat, and they will more likely follow advice. The advice is basic to child rearing principles (Dreikurs & Soltz, 1964) and teaches the family methods of encouragement, mutual respect, winning cooperation, and acting rather than speaking when it is time for discipline, refraining from pampering and overprotection, staying out of fights, stimulating independence, conducting family meetings for mutual problem solving, and emphasizing having fun together.

CASE EXAMPLES

Case of David: ADHD with Specific Developmental Disorder and Oppositional Defiant Disorder

Identified Patient.   David is a 7.5-year-old boy living with his biological parents and 11-year-old sister. He is in the second grade.

Chief Complaint.   "He just has a hard time coping."

History of Current Problem.   David had been receiving special education services for moderately severe Specific Developmental Disorder in Reading since starting school. He had made progress but had developed behavioral problems related to reading. He was not completing reading assignments in class and refused to do his reading homework. David had difficulty organizing work related to reading but not to writing. He could compose sentences that were grammatically correct and had appropriate understanding of the structure of language. He exhibited a low frustration tolerance during his reading homework and frequently ripped up his papers. He berated himself and his teacher during these episodes. He alternately requested and then rejected his parents help. Initially, his parents denied other problems. They were most concerned that he succeed in school.

A detailed history revealed other chronic problems, which his parents attributed to David's personality. He was a demanding child who would not take "no" for an answer even when he was very young. When refused a request, he would verbally demand what he wanted. He would then attempt to defy his parents. For example, David would demand food just after finishing dinner or prior to bedtime. His parents would calmly try to divert him. David would loudly threaten to take the food. His parents would cut him off at the kitchen. He would berate them and tell them "you can't stop me" (Goal II misbehavior). His parents would block the kitchen door. David would start to push them, and they would physically contain him. Both parents would sit their son in order to control his escalating tantrum. Strategies such as time-out had failed long ago. Inevitably they would escort him to his room and a physical confrontation would ensue. His parents felt confused. David had always been a difficult child requiring strict controls and did not seem to learn from his mistakes; however, he also could be charming and do well. He would then "become a terror" for no apparent reason. This would last for several days and then resolve. Parents could not predict the cycles.

Bedtimes were always difficult. He procrastinated and did not wash or brush his teeth (Goal IV was indicated). His mother would brush his teeth for him while he fought her. He took one to three hours to fall asleep. He wet his bed regularly (Goal IV was indicated upon questioning). He took a very long time to get ready for school. He was easily distracted with other activities. Additionally, he could not tie his shoes or button his shirts correctly, and so he fought about which clothing to wear. At mealtime he was up and down from the table and had difficulty controlling his knife and fork when eating. Chores were problematic. He dawdled and forgot what he was supposed to do (Goal IV was indicated upon questioning). Sometimes he refused adamantly to do them. He opposed his parents on most requests. He usually wanted his own way. He had not learned how to cooperate and had not experienced the satisfaction of contributing to the family welfare.

Problems at school were not as serious. He had difficulty staying on task with reading but not science or math. He was a "dreamer" but creative. He did fidget a lot, but so did some other first and second grade boys. He used to call out answers in class and not wait his turn. His handwriting was illegible. The greatest difficulty was on the schoolyard. He fought with other pupils who would set him up. He had few friends at school but was accepted on his sports teams.

In his special education reading class, he had more difficulty. He did not stick with the assignments. He did not receive as much attention due to the other students' similar needs. He would disrupt the class when he was not receiving the most attention. He intruded on other students and would annoy them willfully. He did comply with his teacher; however, he showed no tantruming behavior or physical violence.

David also had many strengths. He was athletic, excelling at swimming and soccer. Recently he started skateboarding and did well. He had some difficulty in baseball with both batting and throwing the ball but overall did average. He was the fastest runner on the team. He also excelled in science. He grasped science concepts quickly and received honors for his project at the school fair. He had encyclopedic knowledge about dinosaurs. He easily mastered computers. His regular teacher liked him, and he behaved well in her classroom where his desk was next to hers.

Two weeks after their initial evaluation, David's parents called with a new problem. Twice David had climbed out of the window onto the ledge and had threatened to jump off if his parents did not comply with his requests. His father had pulled him in. His parents were scared. They felt bankrupt.

Developmental History.   David suffered mild oxygen deprivation at birth due to a cervical umbilical cord. He did not like to be cuddled as an infant and slept poorly. Developmental milestones, however, were normal. In fact, he walked by 10 months. He was very active and into everything. He seemed very "curious," venturing where other preschoolers would not go, and getting lost. He did not seem to mind being away from his parents when young.

The oxygen deprivation may have resulted in an organ inferiority that contributed to his ADHD; however, the parents' handling of this early medical condition was helpful to David—they never considered it to be a problem.

Social History.   Parents endorsed no major problems, including no marital dysfunction. Father was an academic scientist and worked long hours. Mother wanted to return to work but was reluctant to do so due to her son's problems.

Family History.   No major medical or psychiatric problems were endorsed. David's sister also had difficulty organizing her work. She presented some minor behavioral problems.

Mental Status Examination and Observations.   During the initial three sessions, few unusual behaviors or family interactions were noted. In particular,

David was able to attend well, was interactive and charming, and displayed no behavioral problems. He appeared to have good receptive and expressive language skills. He and his sister argued but not inappropriately. David's father appeared anxious and bit his fingernails during the sessions. He generally deferred to his wife. David's mother was tearful on several occasions, as she expressed concern for her son's welfare, but was not depressed. She was reluctant to withdraw from her extensive role as social organizer and chauffeur for her son. She reasoned that he would not have positive outlets to counter his negative life experiences. She was also concerned that setting such limits would antagonize her son. In the sessions she did cue him frequently about his behavior.

The children were very verbal and outspoken. They chided their mother and mimicked her. Both complained that their mother wanted "perfection." She agreed that this might be so. The sister complained that the parents overprotected her. They described a series of activities in which their children could not engage. This included teen-like clothing and cosmetics for their daughter and toy weapons for David. They monitored their children's activities and interests closely.

As David became more familiar with the therapist and treatment format, he began to display his problematic behaviors. He never became violent; however, he demonstrated restlessness and inattentiveness with longer family sessions. He would impulsively provoke his sister by going to her chair and annoying her. Then he could not understand why he was in trouble. He talked excessively. He easily became excited while describing mundane events and then had difficulty calming down again. Oppositional and defiant behaviors were not displayed during treatment. He was not depressed. Parents were fully compliant with treatment and began to model their interactions with David according to the way the therapist related to him.

Evaluation.   Due to the history of birth hypoxia, David received neuropsychological testing to supplement the testing given by the school for the purpose of determining his reading disability. An electroencephalogram (EEG) was also obtained. His testing showed deficits in tasks requiring concentration, and he made impulsive mistakes on easy material. He also demonstrated perceptual deficits. His intellect was in the above-average range. Problem-solving skills were good. His EEG was normal and specifically did not reveal a static encephalopathy.

Medication Treatment.   Stimulant medication is useful in the treatment of ADHD when combined with school and family consultation. The stimulant improves attention, often reduces impulsiveness, and makes it easier for the child to attend to new learning opportunities whether in school, home, or therapy sessions. The child demonstrates better self-control. **Medication without therapy**

is not recommended, because it does not provide the family or child an opportunity to understand the purpose of the maladaptive behaviors and to develop greater social interest.

David was started on dextroamphetamine. The dosage was adjusted over 7 weeks to a therapeutic level and schedule. He did best using a long-acting preparation in the morning and at lunch time. He generally did not require any late afternoon dose; however, if he had to participate in an activity requiring sustained attention or interactions with peers, such as scouts or church activities, then he took an additional low dose.

Immediate benefits were noted and sustained over the first year of treatment. Specifically, David was able to complete work at school and at home. He was more patient at reading and no longer proclaimed that he "hated school." Fights were fewer. His handwriting improved dramatically. He mastered tying his shoes, buttoning his clothing, and controlling his fork at meals. He also was able to get to sleep in a much shorter time. He complied with his parents requests more frequently and less oppositionally. He was less volatile. Some provocative, impulsive, and violent behaviors persisted; however, his parents stated that the medication "took the edge off." They felt that they could usually handle him. Mother felt more hopeful. David noted only that his handwriting was better and that he might be getting teased less.

The medication was self-administered. The medication dosage was explained to David in his parents' presence. Because mother was most accessible, she kept the medication and it was up to David to request scheduled dosages from her. Neither she nor anyone else was to remind David when to take the medication. Frequently with ADHD, misbehaviors are attributed to "have you taken your medication." The goal of treatment was to put control in David's hands and remove the adults from potential power struggles.

School Intervention.   To address David's inability to stay on task in the classroom, his impulsive behaviors were addressed in consultation with his teacher. Closer attention was paid to keeping on schedule. Math would always begin at 9:00 a.m., writing at 9:45, and so forth. She ignored his out-of-turn responses. She addressed his desire for control by frequently asking his advice and letting him know that she believed that he could work out a particular problem, find the answers, join in activities, wait in line, wait his turn, and so forth.

Conflict on the playground was reinterpreted to him in therapy sessions to indicate that he was controlling several other boys by his "cooperating" behavior.

The other boys did not realize that he determined whether he would or would not provide them with a laugh. His playground interactions readily improved.

David's ability in sports was used as a strength upon which to build self-image and improved interactions. The suggestion was that he join the track club, attended by many of his peers at school, and participate in the relay team as well as short distance events. Peer recognition on the track team was immediate. He was given the nickname "rabbit" of which he was very proud. He was encouraged to participate in as many organized team sports as possible.

His science accomplishments were put in a perspective of greater social interest by suggesting that he represent his school, rather than himself, at the state fair. His class followed his project development closely. Also, his parents purchased a baseball statistics program for their home computer. Each week David entered statistics on the local minor league baseball team. He became a local expert on baseball in addition to his previous reputation as a dinosaur expert. David knew all the esoteric statistics on the team. He was able to channel his attention through use of the computer. He compiled tables of statistics, which the local paper published, bringing him community recognition.

Family Education and Therapy.   The parents' feeling of bankruptcy in dealing with their son's escalating behaviors was a fortuitous therapeutic moment. **"Bankruptcy," according to Dreikurs (1958), is the "teachable moment."** The parents are ready to listen to advice and change their behavior. In this case Goal II misbehavior was determined in David's climbing out the window and threatening to jump. The parents were instructed to call the fire department whenever David went out on the ledge. They were not to make any contact with him. The fire department had to make only one visit to the home.

David's tantrums were addressed by instructing the parents not to encourage their son's self-destructive behaviors. The parents were to walk away from their son and to leave the house whenever he started any of these Goal III misbehaviors. They were very reluctant to do this but complied. David quickly ceased tantruming.

The explanation to David of his control over peers who set him up seemed to have enlightened mother with respect to the ways in which her children set her up. She learned to go for a walk whenever she felt them baiting her. Disciplining the children was modeled in the therapy sessions. The parents had become fearful of "antagonizing" their son, because he might tantrum. They, therefore, tended to avoid addressing issues with him or exerting power over him. The therapist modeled discipline by "putting both children in the same boat" (Dreikurs, 1958). Both David and his sister were escorted to the waiting room by a coworker whenever David demonstrated misbehaviors with his sister. An arrangement was made prior to the second family session for another staff member to take both children to a waiting area if one of them misbehaved. Both children enjoyed the sessions: "I get treated as an adult," which helped to limit the times that they were removed. The therapist did not respond to David's request for explanations as to why he and his sister were removed.

Mother returned to work part-time and is requiring more cooperation from her husband and children in housework and schedules. She is no longer so involved with scheduling her son. They were all more encouraged. After these critical issues were addressed, family therapy focused on mother's demands for perfection from the family and more so from herself. Parental intrusiveness into their children's lives was also addressed in response to the sister's complaints of overprotectiveness. Focus was gradually shifted from David to his sister. The strategy of focusing on the "good" child helps to achieve a more salubrious balance in the family. The parents genuinely become concerned about the other child when attention is diverted from the identified patient. This speeds the therapy process of which Dreikurs and Stoltz (1964) noted: "I'll believe that the 'bad' one is getting better when the 'good' one gets worse." Dreikurs is pointing to the scapegoating function of the identified patient. This individual is the sign of a dysfunctional family interaction. Improvement can be seen when realignment is established within the family. This usually means strengthening the ties between the same generation, parent to parent and sibling to sibling, and weakening the ties between generations, parent to child. It has been shown that by focusing on parent education, improvement can be noted between the marital pair, even when the identified patient has a psychotic or mood disorder (Croake & Kelly, 1985; Croake & Kelly, manuscript in progress).

Diagnosis.

    Axis I: 314.01 Attention-Deficit/Hyperactivity Disorder, moderate
               313.81 Oppositional Defiant Disorder, moderate
               307.80 Functional Enuresis, primary type, nocturnal
    Axis II: 315.00 Developmental Reading Disorder
               315.40 Developmental Coordination Disorder
    Axis III: None
    Axis IV: Psychosocial Stressors:
               acute event: 2—mild (recent move back to home state with change
               of schools)
               enduring circumstance: 2—mild (placement in special education;
               chronic teasing by peers)
    Axis V: Current GAF: 55; Highest GAF past year: 60

Comment.   David's case is especially relevant in showing how such a pervasively impairing disorder can develop in a child for no obvious "reason." David was a typical child with ADHD. His Developmental Reading Disorder was established early in life before he showed serious behavioral problems. Therefore, the school system was attuned to possible other needs. Nevertheless, his ADHD was neglected until his behavioral problems escalated necessitating intervention. David had an intact, loving family. He had experienced no significant life stress. The family was readily amenable to therapeutic intervention.

Another asset of David's that helped him was his generally charming, attractive personality and good athletic skills. Others were, therefore, willing to extend themselves to him. He probably was more fortunate than many ADHD children in this respect. Most children would function well with these assets. The effects of ADHD are most impressive in a child with David's strengths.

Case of Cory: ADHD with Conduct Disorder

Identified Patient.   Cory is an 11-year-old boy living with his divorced mother. He is in the fifth grade in the public school system.

Chief Complaint.   "He needs a psychiatric evaluation before they will let him back into school."

History of Current Problem.   Cory had been suspended from school for the third time during the current year. He was recurrently violent on the school-yard, and this time had bloodied a child's nose. He also started fights in other unstructured settings, such as walking home from school or in the lunchroom. These fights frequently developed after he had intruded into other children's activities and they did not want to include him. Other problems at school included stealing from his classmates and at least once from a teacher, destroying other pupils' belongings, and frequent lying about these and other activities. Teachers and the school psychologist described Cory as "mean": He seemed to be vindictive and take pleasure from the harm he inflicted. He did not go around with a gang but rather was a loner. He was never truant from school; in fact, he liked school. His marks were good, although teachers said he was capable of much more if he would listen and settle down. They noted that he had difficulty concentrating on his work. He daydreamed and fidgeted constantly, which his teacher found annoying. He would impulsively respond to questions, wander about the class, and even leave the classroom. He generally blamed others for his misdeeds and took little responsibility for his behavior. He seemed to behave much better in structured settings where expectations were very clear and he could not act as impulsively. His teacher did not like him. The school had tried various programs, including denial of all unstructured activities, but to no avail. They had particular difficulty understanding Cory's behavior because he was quite bright and had no learning problems.

At home and outside of school, Cory also had problems. He had not tortured animals but was cruel to pets. He had run away from home three times but went to a friend's house. He argued regularly with his mother and had shoved her several times. He reports that these were after she had shoved him, which mother confirmed. He refused to do anything around the house. He had stolen from his mother twice. Multiple projects were started but never completed due to his apparent disorganization and boredom. He was not using drugs or alcohol.

Cory was excellent at skateboarding. He loved the excitement and skated alone for hours. He wanted to compete nationally. Although athletically endowed, he hated team sports and had been kicked off several teams for excessive violence and challenging the coaches. Anger was identified as a major problem wherever he went. Cory was aware of his problems and had expressed a desire to change.

Developmental History.   This was not known. Cory was adopted at age 4 years. He had achieved appropriate milestones and had continued normal development.

Family History.   This was not well known for the biological parents. His biological father had drug and alcohol problems and some legal infractions. His parents had never married.   No major medical or psychiatric problems in the adoptive family.

Social History.   Not much was known of Cory's early life except that he was physically abused by his mother and her boyfriend. Sexual abuse was suspected. His biological father was never involved with him. He had lived in a foster home for one year prior to adoption. Two years after his adoption, his new parents divorced. This was reportedly in part related to the mother's recurrent depressions and dependency. Initially the adoptive father maintained contact with Cory but had not seen him in the last two years. Mother worked steadily as an executive secretary. She had a few short-term relationships with men since the divorce but little other social life. An older biological daughter had moved away from home two years previously and had little contact with the family.

Mental Status Examination and Observations.   Cory was seen for initial evaluation with his mother twice and alone once. His mother appeared depressed. With his mother, Cory was obviously inattentive and misunderstood several issues being discussed. He jumped to conclusions. He fidgeted constantly and changed chairs several times. He alternately was angry, blamed his mother, made self-deprecating remarks, and expressed a desire to have friends. He also cried about his situation but then denied caring. Upon questioning, Goal III misbehavior was associated with his restlessness, anger, self-deprecation, and lack of friends. As the session progressed, he gradually moved his seat closer to the interviewer.

During his individual interview, Cory's presentation was similar but moderated. He was less agitated. He blamed the therapist for making him miss school and threatened to leave, but did not. Blaming the therapist felt like Goal II misbehavior. The therapist received confirmation from Cory in the form of a recognition reflex (Dreikurs, 1958). He smiled when asked, "Could it be that you want to show me that you are in charge here, that I cannot make you do anything?" Upon confirmation the therapist stated, "I cannot make you do anything and I will not try. You are too powerful." Cory seemed pleased with this confirmation. He calmed down and cried, stating that his life was miserable, that nobody cared. He wanted to take self-defense classes but asked that his mother not be told or "she would kill me." He asked if he could play a board game with the therapist, and he played appropriately. He was obviously impulsive in his play strategy.

Course of Treatment. Cory had multiple problems. The violence obscured the underlying ADHD. He had made himself so unlikable that others did not look further to understand his problems. To disentangle the effects of past environmental trauma, inadequate parenting by his mother, and his own possible organ inferiority is not possible. Clinic staffing of this family led to much controversy and an atmosphere of rejection.

Medication Treatment. A trial of a stimulant medication was initiated. At a moderate dosage of dextroamphetamine, he became depressed. The medication exacerbated the depressive feelings he had shown during previous sessions; however, he also had demonstrated markedly improved ability to concentrate and to control his restlessness and temper. A different stimulant, pemoline, was tried and he did well. After eight weeks of treatment his impulsivity and fighting also decreased. Problems still persisted with difficulty making friends, blaming others, and anger. No recurrence of depression occurred.

Family Education and Therapy. Psychotherapy was initiated with Cory and his mother to maintain and enhance the gains noted. The first issue addressed was having fun together. Having fun together is a Dreikursian technique (Dreikurs, 1958). This method is commonly used with any family. It is not anticipated. Family members expect an immediate focus on the negative ADHD signs. An agreement and plan for an afternoon of fun for the coming weekend was planned in the session. The two of them selected an outing to the community swimming pool. Thereafter, Sunday afternoons were reserved as fun times based on mutually agreed upon activities.

Next, Mother's depression, social isolation, overinvolvement with Cory, and tendency to self-defeating behaviors were addressed in relation to Cory's similar behaviors. Both were surprised at seeing the similarities. Mother seemed less overwhelmed at Cory's misbehavior when she could sympathize with her own discouragement. Recommended attendance at a parent study group (Dreikurs & Soltz, 1964) resulted in an improved relationship with Cory. Initiating a weekly family council meeting (Dreikurs & Soltz, 1964) relieved some of the pressure that mother felt about having to always be in charge. The family council meetings lasted about 15 minutes, consistent with Cory's attention span for such activities. These council meetings provided rules, regulations, and order for the two of them at home. Mutual decision-making resulted in much less desire by Cory to be the boss. Mother established two friendships with other women in the parenting group and was reserving one night each week for social activities with them.

Mother was unwilling to arrange martial arts classes for Cory. This training was recommended to teach discipline and self-regulation as well as a cooperative atmosphere for educating Cory in getting along with others. Therapy is ongoing with Cory and his Mother.

Diagnosis.

> Axis I: 314.01 Attention-Deficit/Hyperactivity Disorder, moderate
> 312.00 Conduct Disorder, Solitary aggressive
> Axis II: Depressive personality features
> Axis III: None
> Axis IV: Psychosocial Stressors:
> acute event: none
> enduring circumstance: 6—extreme (recurrent physical abuse as toddler, and possible sexual abuse; removal from biological parents; abandonment by adoptive father and sister; adoptive mother's depression
> Axis V: Current GAF: 40; Highest GAF Past Year: 55

Comment.   Cory presented diagnostic pitfalls common with ADHD children who also display behavioral problems. ADHD signs are integrated with behavior into holistic movement. They are reflective of a probable organ inferiority (biological disposition) and interpersonal conflict. Perhaps the attention deficit and hyperactivity are biologically inherited and the misbehavior is learned within the family context. The latter is a discouraged attempt to interact with the adult in the situation.

Cory's movement kept others at a distance and created an environment of rejection. Therefore, ADHD was not considered in his school assessment, and diagnosis was delayed. Additionally, Cory did not have any Specific Developmental Disorder. This further precluded him from any specialized services that many ADHD children receive.

Cory showed considerable depressive symptoms. They did not meet criteria for a Mood Disorder; however, both these depressive feelings and his early losses and abuse put him at-risk for a later depression. These depressive features may make him more amenable to treatment, since they may have related to his ability to establish a relationship with the therapist. Depression in an impulsive child, however, increases the risk of self-destructive behaviors.

For ADHD children treated with stimulants to develop an Organic Mood Disorder is not unusual. This disorder generally resolves with discontinuation of the stimulant. The occurrence of such a medication-induced Mood Disorder is not diagnostic of a proclivity for Mood Disorders.

Cory's vindictiveness and cruelty alienated others. His violence had resulted in punishment and rejection. Cory was so discouraged that he would not communicate his own dissatisfaction with his life. He had mostly given up on the idea of friendly relationships, was without skills for cooperation, and promoted alienation for himself. His adoptive family provided another model of discouragement. The parents had given up on their marriage, and Mother's depression indicated that she had lost heart. The tasks of life seemed overwhelming to her. She did not know how to parent. Her relationships with men were tenuous. She was not involved with her own family or the community. In Western culture, the emphasis is upon vocational attainment. Cooperation with the other sex is poorly achieved for most people. Community involvement is somewhat better. Cory's Mother fit the rule and enjoyed success at her job.

Cory's lack of social interest places him at-risk for ongoing problems. Rejection by peers continues despite less anger and fighting. A peer group counseling forum aimed at social skill improvement is planned for Cory to increase his social interest, his sense of belonging, and having a place in life.

REFERENCES

American Psychiatric Association. (1968). *Diagnostic and statistical manual of mental disorders* (2nd ed.). Washington, DC: Author.

American Psychiatric Association. (1980). *Diagnostic and statistical manual of mental disorders* (3rd ed.). Washington, DC: Author.

American Psychiatric Association. (1987). *Diagnostic and statistical manual of mental disorders* (3rd ed., rev.). Washington, DC: Author.

Anderson, J., Williams, S., McGee, R., & Silva, P.A. (1987). The prevalence of DSM-III disorders in a large sample of preadolescent children from the general population. *Archives of General Psychiatry, 44*, 69–81.

Ansbacher, H.L., & Ansbacher, R.R. (Eds.). (1956). *The Individual Psychology of Alfred Adler*. New York: Harper Torchbooks.

August, G.J., & Holmes, C.S. (1984). Behavior and academic achievement in hyperactive subgroups and learning disabled boys: A six year follow-up. *American Journal of Diseases of Childhood, 138*, 1025–1029.

August, G.J., Stewart, M.A., & Holmes, C.S. (1983). A four year follow-up of hyperactive boys with and without conduct disorder. *British Journal of Psychiatry, 143*, 192–198.

Bakwin, H., & Bakwin, R.M. (1966). *Clinical management of behavior disorders in children*. Philadelphia: Saunders.

Barkley, R.A. (1985). The parent-child interaction patterns of hyperactive children: Precursors to aggressive behaviors? In M. Wolraich & D. Routh (Eds.), *Advances in developmental and behavioral pediatrics* (Vol. 6) (pp. 117–150). Greenwich, CT: JAI Press.

Bashir, A.S., Wing, E.H., & Abrams, J.C. (1987). Language disorders in childhood and adolescence. *Pediatric Annals, 16*, 145–156.

Bender, L.S. (1975). Career in clinical research in child psychiatry. In E.J. Anthony (Ed.), *Exploration in child psychiatry* (pp. 10–68). New York: Plenum Press.

Biederman, J., Munir, K., & Knee, D. (1987). Conduct and oppositional disorder in clinically referred children with attention deficit disorder: A controlled family study. *American Academy of Child and Adolescent Psychiatry, 26*, 724–727.

Bradley, C. (1937). The behavior of children receiving Benzedrine. *American Journal of Psychiatry, 94*, 577–585.

Brown, G.L., Ebert, M.H., & Minichiello, M.D. (1985). Biochemical and pharmacological aspects of attention deficit disorder. In L.M. Bloomingdale (Ed.), *Attention deficit disorder: Identification, course, and rationale* (pp. 106–154). New York: Spectrum.

Brown, R.T., & Sleator, E.K. (1979). Methylphenidate in hyperkinetic children: Differences in dose effects on impulsive behavior. *Pediatrics, 64*, 408–411.

Bruck, M. (1985). The long-term prognosis of childhood learning disabilities. In P. Gerber & K. Garnett (Eds.), *Adults with learning disabilities: An international perspective* (pp. 165–178). New York: World Rehabilitation Fund.

Buerger, T.A. (1968). A follow-up of remedial reading instruction. *The Reading Teacher, 21*, 329–334.

Campbell, S.B., Douglas, V.I., & Morgenstern, G. (1971). Cognitive styles in hyperactive children and the effect of methylphenidate. *Journal of Child Psychology & Psychiatry, 12*, 55–67.

Cantwell, D.P. (1972). Psychiatric illness in the families of hyperactive children. *Archives of General Psychiatry, 27*, 414–417.

Clements, S.D., & Peters, J.E. (1962). Minimal Brain Dysfunction in the school age child. *Archives of General Psychiatry, 6*, 185–197.

Critchley, M. (1964). *Developmental dyslexia*. Springfield, IL: Charles C. Thomas.

Croake, J.W., & Kelly, D.F. (1985). Adlerian family therapy with depressed and schizophrenic patients. *Individual Psychology: The Journal of Adlerian Theory, Research, & Practice, 41*, 302–310.

Croake, J.W., & Kelly, D.F. (In progress). *Parent education for families in which the father has a diagnosis of psychosis.*

Cunningham, C.E., Siegel, L.S., & Offord, D.R. (1985). A developmental dose-response analysis of the effects of methylphenidate on the peer interactions of attention deficit disordered boys. *Journal of Child Psychology &Psychiatry, 26*, 955–971.

Denckla, M.D. (1978). Minimal brain dysfunction. In J.S. Chall & A.F. Mirsky (Eds.), *Education and the brain* (pp. 23–54). Chicago: University of Chicago Press.

Douglas, V.I., Barr, R.G., O'Neill, M.E., & Britton, B.G. (1986). Short-term effects of methylphenidate on the cognitive, learning and academic performance of children with attention deficit disorder in the laboratory and the classroom. *Journal of Child Psychology & Psychiatry, 27*, 191–211.

Dreikurs, R. (1958). *The challenge of parenthood*. New York: Hawthorn Books.

Dreikurs, R. (1968). *Psychology in the classroom*. New York: Harper & Row Publishers.

Dreikurs, R., & Soltz, V. (1964). *Children: The challenge*. New York: Hawthorn Books.

Duane, D.D. (1985). Neurodiagnostic tools in dyslexic syndromes in children: Pitfalls and proposed comparative study of computed tomography, nuclear magnetic resonance, and brain electrical activity mapping. In G. Pavlidis & D. Fisher (Eds.), *Dyslexia: Its neuropsychology and treatment* (pp. 159–237). New York: Wiley.

Duffy, F.H. (1988). Neurophysiological studies in dyslexia. In F. Plum (Ed.), *Language, communication and the brain* (pp. 34–42). New York: Raven Press.

Dykman, R.A., Ackerman, P.T., Clements, S.D., & Peters, J.E. (1971). Specific learning disabilities: An attention deficit syndrome. In H.R. Myklebust (Ed.), *Progress in learning disabilities* (Vol. 2) (pp. 174–233). New York: Grune and Stratton.

Ferguson, H.B., & Pappas, B.A. (1979). Evaluation of psychophysiological, neurochemical, and animal models of hyperactivity. In R.L. Trites (Ed.), *Hyperactivity in children* (pp. 48–61). Baltimore: University Park Press.

Finucci, J.M., Gottfredson, L.S., & Childs, B. (1985). A follow-up study of dyslexic boys. *Annals of Dyslexia, 35*, 117–136.

Forness, S.B. (1981). *Recent concepts in dyslexia: Implications for diagnosis and remediation*. Virginia: ERIC Exceptional Child Education Reports.

Frauenheim, J.G. (1978). Academic achievement characteristics of adult males who were diagnosed as dyslexic in childhood. *Journal of Learning Disabilities, 11*, 476–483.

Gittelman, R., Klein, D.F., & Feingold, I. (1983). Children with reading disorders II. Effects of methylphenidate in combination with reading remediation. *Journal of Child Psychology & Psychiatry, 24*, 193–212.

Gittelman, R., Mannuzza, S., Shenker, R., & Bonagura, N. (1985). Hyperactive boys almost grown up. *Archives of General Psychiatry, 42*, 937–947.

Halperin, J.M., Gittelman, R., Klein, D.F., & Rudel, R.G. (1984). Reading-disabled hyperactive children: A distinct subgroup of attention deficit disorder with hyperactivity. *Journal of Abnormal Child Psychology, 12*, 1–14.

Hastings, J.E., & Barkley, R.A. (1978). A review of psychophysiological research with hyperkinetic children. *Journal of Abnormal Child Psychology, 6*, 413–448.

Heaton, R.K. (1988). Introduction to the special series. *Journal of Consulting & Clinical Psychology, 56*, 787–788.

Hechtman, L., & Weiss, G. (1986). Controlled prospective 15–year follow-up of hyperactives as adults: nonmedical drug and alcohol use and antisocial behavior. *Canadian Journal of Psychiatry, 31*, 557–567.

Hechtman, L., Weiss, G., Perlman, T., & Tuck, D. (1981). Hyperactives as young adults: Various clinical outcomes. *Adolescent Psychiatry, 9*, 295–306.

Henker, B., & Whalen, C.K. (1989). Hyperactivity and attention deficits. *American Psychologist, 44*, 216–223.

Hopkins, J., Perlman, T., Hechtman, L., & Weiss, G. (1979). Cognitive style in adults originally diagnosed as hyperactives. *Journal of Child Psychology & Psychiatry, 20*, 209–216.

Hunt, R.D., & Cohen, D.J. (1984). Psychiatric aspects of learning difficulties. *Pediatric Clinics of North America, 31*, 471–497.

Jaklewicz, H. (1982). Dyslexia: Follow-up studies. *Thalamus (International Academy for Research in Learning Disabilities), 2*, 3–9.

Jensen, J.B., Burke, N., & Garfinkel, B.D. (1988). Depression and symptoms of attention deficit disorder with hyperactivity. *American Academy of Child and Adolescent Psychiatry, 27*, 742–747.

Kistner, J.A., & Torgesen, J.K. (1987). Motivational and cognitive aspects of learning disabilities. In B.B. Lahey & A.E. Kazdin (Eds.), *Advances in clinical child psychology* (Vol. 10) (pp. 289–333). New York: Plenum Press.

Kline, C., & Kline, C. (1975). Follow-up study of 211 dyslexic children. *Bulletin of the Orton Society, 25*, 127–144.

Knobloch, H., & Pasamanick, B. (1959). Syndrome of Minimal Cerebral Damage in infancy. *Journal of the American Medical Association, 170*, 1384–1387.

Lahey, B.B., Piacentini, J.C., McBurnett, K., Stone, P., Hartdagen, S., & Hynd, G. (1988). Psychopathology in the parents of children with conduct disorder and hyperactivity. *American Academy of Child and Adolescent Psychiatry, 27*, 163–170.

Lambert, M.N. (1988). Adolescent outcomes for hyperactive children: Perspectives on general and specific patterns of childhood risk for adolescent educational, social, and mental health problems. *American Psychologist, 43*, 786–799.

Lambert, M.N., Sandoval, J., & Sasone, D.M. (1981). Prevalence of hyperactivity and related treatments among elementary school children. In K.D. Gadow & J. Loney (Eds.), *Psychosocial aspects of drug treatment for hyperactivity* (pp. 10–15). Boulder, Colorado: Westview Press.

Laufer, M.W., & Denhoff, E. (1957). Hyperkinetic behavior syndrome in children. *Journal of Pediatrics, 50*, 463–474.

Levy, F., & Hobbs, G. (1988). The action of stimulant medication in attention deficit disorder with hyperactivity: Dopaminergic, noradrenergic, or both? *American Academy of Child and Adolescent Psychiatry, 27*, 802–805.

Loeber, R., & Schmaling, K.B. (1985). The utility of differentiating between mixed and pure forms of antisocial child behavior. *Journal of Abnormal Child Psychology, 13*, 315–336.

Loh, H.C., Hendrickson, L., & Bruhn, P. (1984). Focal cerebral hypoperfusion in children with dysphasia and/or attention deficit disorder. *Archives of Neurology, 41*, 825–829.

Loney, J. (1987). Hyperactivity and aggression in the diagnosis of attention deficit disorder. In B.B. Lahey & A.E. Kazdin (Eds.), *Advances in child psychology* (Vol. 10) (pp. 99–135). New York: Plenum.

Loney, J., Langhorne, J.E., & Paternite, C.E. (1978). An empirical basis for subgrouping the hyperkinetic/MBD syndrome. *Journal of Abnormal Child Psychology, 87*, 331–341.

Mannuzza, S., Klein, R.G., Bonagura, N., Konig, P.H., & Shenker, R. (1988). Hyperactive boys almost grown up II. Status of subjects without a mental disorder. *Archives of General Psychiatry, 45*, 13–18.

Mash, E.J., & Johnston, C. (1982). A comparison of the mother-child interactions of younger and older hyperactive and normal children. *Child Development, 53*, 1371–1381.

McGee, R., & Williams, S. (1988). A longitudinal study of depression in nine-year-old children. *American Academy of Child and Adolescent Psychiatry, 27*, 342–348.

Milich, R.S., & Dodge, K.A. (1984). Social information processing in child psychiatric populations. *Journal of Abnormal Child Psychology, 12*, 471–489.

Milich, R.S., & Loney, J. (1979). The role of hyperactive and aggressive symptomatology in predicting adolescent outcome among hyperactive children. *Journal of Pediatric Psychology, 4*, 93–108.

Minde, K., Weiss, G., & Mendelson, N. (1972). A five-year follow-up study of 91 hyperactive school children. *Journal of American Academy of Child Psychiatry, 11*, 595–619.

Morris, R.D. (1988). Classification of learning disabilities: Old problems and new approaches. *Journal of Consulting & Clinical Psychology, 56*, 789–794.

Muehl, S., & Forrell, E.R. (1973). A follow-up study of disabled readers: Variables related to high school reading performance. *Reading Research Quarterly, 9*, 110–123.

O'Connor, S.C., & Spreen, O. (1988). The relationship between parents' socioeconomic status and education level and adult occupational and educational achievement of children with learning disability. *Journal of Learning Disabilities, 21*, 148–153.

O'Leary, S.G., & Steen, P.L. (1982). Subcategorizing hyperactivity: The Stony Brook Scale. *Journal of Consulting & Clinical Psychology, 50*, 426–432.

Ozols, E.J., & Rourke, B.P. (1985). Dimensions of social sensitivity in two types of learning-disabled children. In B.P. Rourke (Ed.), *Neuropsychology of learning disabilities: Essentials of subtype analysis* (pp. 281–301). New York: Guilford Press.

Pelham, W.E., & Bender, M.E. (1982). Peer relationships in hyperactive children: Description and treatment. In K.D. Gadow & I. Bialer (Eds.), *Advances in learning and behavioral disabilities: A research annual* (Vol. 1) (pp. 365–436). Greenwich, CT: JAI Press.

Pelham, W.E., Bender, M.E., Caddell,. J., Booth, S.B., & Moorer, S.J. (1986). Methylphenidate and children with attention deficit disorder. *Archives of General Psychiatry, 42*, 948–952.

Pennington, B.F., & Smith, S.D. (1988). Genetic influences on learning disabilities: An update. *Journal of Consulting & Clinical Psychology, 56*, 817–823.

Pliszka, S.R. (1987). Tricyclic antidepressants in the treatment of children with attention deficit disorder. *American Academy of Child and Adolescent Psychiatry, 26*, 127–132.

Rapoport, J.L., Buchsbaum, M.S., Zahn, T.P., Weingartner, H., Ludlow, C., & Mikkelsen, E.J. (1978). Dextroamphetamine: Cognitive and behavioral effects in normal prepubertal boys. *Science, 199*, 560–563.

Rapoport, J.L., & Ferguson, H.B. (1981). Biological validation of the hyperkinetic syndrome. *Developmental Medicine in Child Neurology, 23*, 667–682.

Rapport, M.D., Stoner, G., DuPaul, G.J., Birmingham, B.K., & Tucker, S. (1985). Methylphenidate in hyperactive children: Differential effects of dose on academic, learning, and social behavior. *Journal of Abnormal Child Psychology, 13*, 227–244.

Rapport, M.D., Stoner, G., DuPaul, G., Kelly, K.L., Tucker, S.B., & Schoeler,

T. (1988). Attention deficit disorder and methylphenidate: A mutilevel analysis of dose-response effects on children's impulsivity across settings. *American Academy of Child and Adolescent Psychiatry, 27*, 60–69.

Rawson, M. (1968). *Developmental language disability: Adult accomplishment of dyslexic boys*. Baltimore, MD: Johns Hopkins University Press.

Reeves, J.C., Werry, J.S., Elkind, G.S., & Zametkin, A. (1987). Attention deficit disorder, conduct, oppositional, and anxiety disorders in children: II. Clinical characteristics. *American Academy of Child and Adolescent Psychiatry, 26*, 144–155.

Reynolds, C.R. (1981). The fallacy of "two years below grade level for age" as a diagnostic criterion for reading disorders. *Journal of School Psychology, 19*, 350–358.

Richardson, E., Kupietz, S.S., Winsberg, B.G., Richardson, E., Maitinsky, S., & Mendell, N. (1988). Effects of methylphenidate dosage in hyperactive reading-disabled children II. Reading achievement. *American Academy of Child and Adolescent Psychiatry, 27*, 78–87.

Robinson, H.M., & Smith, H.K. (1962). Reading clinic clients—Ten years after. *Elementary School Journal, 63*, 22–27.

Rourke, B.P. (1988). Socioemotional disturbances of learning disabled children. *Journal of Consulting & Clinical Psychology, 56*, 801–810.

Rourke, B.P., & Fisk, J.L. (1981). Socio-emotional disturbances of learning disabled children: The role of central processing deficits. *Bulletin of the Orton Society, 31*, 77–78.

Safer, D.J., & Allen, R.P. (1976). *Hyperactive children: Diagnosis and management*. Baltimore: University Park Press.

Sandberg, S.T., Wieselberg, M., & Shaffer, D. (1980). Hyperkinetic and conduct problems in a primary school population: Some epidemiological considerations. *Journal of Child Psychology & Psychiatry, 21*, 293–311.

Satterfield, J.H. (1973). EEG issues in children with Minimal Brain Dysfunction. *Seminars in Psychiatry, 5*, 35–46.

Schonhaut, S., & Satz, P. (1983). Prognosis for children with learning disabilities:

A review of follow-up studies. In M. Rutter (Ed.), *Developmental neuropsychiatry* (pp. 542–574). New York: Guilford Press.

Sebrechts, M.M., Shaywitz, S.E., Shaywitz, B.A., Jatlow, P., Anderson, G.M., & Cohen, D.J. (1986). Components of attention, methylphenidate dosage, and blood levels in children with attention deficit disorder. *Pediatrics, 77*, 222–228.

Shapiro, S.K., & Garfinkel, B.D. (1986). The occurrence of behavior disorders in children: The interdependence of attention deficit disorder and conduct disorder. *American Academy of Child and Adolescent Psychiatry, 25*, 809–819.

Silver, A.A. (1977). Prevention. In A.L. Benton & D. Pearl (Eds.), *Dyslexia, an appraisal of current knowledge* (pp. 351–376). New York: Oxford University Press.

Silver, L.B. (1981). The relationship between learning disabilities, hyperactivity, distractibility, and behavioral problems. *Journal of American Academy of Child Psychiatry, 20*, 385–397.

Silver, L.B. (1989). Learning disabilities: Introduction. *American Academy of Child and Adolescent Psychiatry, 28*, 309–313.

Spreen, O. (1988a). Prognosis of learning disability. *Journal of Consulting & Clinical Psychology, 56*, 836–842.

Spreen, O. (1988b). *Learning disabled children growing up*. New York: Oxford University Press.

Stanovich, K. (1986). Cognitive processes and the reading problems of learning disabled children: Evaluating the assumption of specificity. In J. Torgesen & B. Wong (Eds.), *Psychological and educational perspectives on learning disabilities* (pp. 87–131). Orlando, FL: Academic Press.

Stewart, M.A., DeBlois, C.S., & Cummings, C. (1980). Psychiatric disorder in the parents of hyperactive boys and those with conduct disorder. *Journal of Child Psychology & Psychiatry, 21*, 283–329.

Still, G.F. (1902). The Coulstonian lectures on some abnormal physical conditions in children. *Lancet, 1*, 1008–1012, 1077–1082, 1163–1168.

Taylor, H.G. (1988). Neuropsychological testing: Relevance for assessing children's learning disabilities. *Journal of Consulting & Clinical Psychology, 56,* 795–800.

Walker, J.L., Lahey, B.B., Hynd, G.W., & Frame, C.L. (1987). Comparison of specific patterns of antisocial behavior in children with conduct disorder with or without coexisting hyperactivity. *Journal of Consulting & Clinical Psychology, 55,* 910–913.

Weiss, G., & Hechtman, L. (1986). *Hyperactive children grown up.* New York: Guilford Press.

Weiss, G., Hechtman, L., Milroy, T., & Perlman, T. (1985). Psychiatric status of hyperactive adults: A controlled prospective 15–year follow-up of 63 hyperactive children. *Journal of American Academy of Child Psychiatry, 24,* 211–220.

Weiss, G., Hechtman, L., & Perlman, T. (1978). Hyperactives as young adults: School, employer, and self-rating scales obtained during ten year follow-up evaluation. *American Journal of Orthopsychiatry, 48,* 438–445.

Weiss, G., Hechtman, L., Perlman, T., Hopkins, J., & Wener, A. (1979). Hyperactives as young adults: A controlled prospective ten-year follow-up of 75 children. *Archives of General Psychiatry, 36,* 675–681.

Wender, P.H. (1971). *Minimal brain dysfunction in children.* New York: Wiley-Interscience.

Wender, P.H. (1987). *The hyperactive child, adolescent, and adult: Attention deficit disorder through the lifespan.* New York: Oxford University Press.

Wender, P.H., Reimherr, F.W., & Wood, D.R. (1981). Attention deficit disorder ("Minimal Brain Dysfunction") in adults. *Archives of General Psychiatry, 38,* 449–456.

Werry, J.S., Minde, K., Guyman, A., Weiss, G., Dogan, K., & Hoy, E. (1972). Studies on the hyperactive child VII. Neurological status compared with neurotic and normal children. *American Journal of Orthopsychiatry, 42,* 441–451.

Werry, J.S., Reeves, J.C., & Elkind, G.S. (1987). Attention deficit, conduct, oppositional, and anxiety disorders in children: I. A review of research on differentiating characteristics. *American Academy of Child and Adolescent Psychiatry, 26,* 133–143.

Whalen, C.K., & Henker, B. (1985). The social worlds of hyperactive children. *Clinical Psychology Review, 5,* 1–32.

Whalen, C.K., Henker, B., Castro, J., & Granger, D. (1987). Peer perceptions of hyperactivity and medication effects. *Child Development, 58,* 816–828.

Whalen, C.K., Henker, B., & Dotemoto, S. (1980). Methylphenidate and hyperactivity: Effects on teacher behaviors. *Science, 208,* 1280–1282.

Whalen, C.K., Henker, B., Swanson, J.M., Granger, D., Kliewer, W., & Spencer, J. (1987). Natural social behaviors in hyperactive children: Dose effects of methylphenidate. *Journal of Consulting & Clinical Psychology, 55,* 187–193.

Zametkin, A.J., & Rapoport, J.L. (1986). The pathophysiology of attention deficit disorder with hyperactivity: A review. In B.B. Lahey & A.E. Kazdin (Eds.), *Advances in clinical child psychology, 9* (pp. 177–216). New York: Plenum.

Zametkin, A.J., & Rapoport, J.L. (1987). Neurobiology of attention deficit disorder with hyperactivity: Where have we come in 50 years? *American Academy of Child and Adolescent Psychiatry, 26,* 676–686.

Zametkin, A.J., Rapoport, J.L., Murphy, D.L., Linnoila, M., & Ismond, D. (1986). Treatment of hyperactive children with monoamine oxidase inhibitors I. Clinical efficacy. *Archives of General Psychiatry, 42,* 962–968.

Zametkin, A.J., Rapoport, J.L., Murphy, D.L., Linnoila, M., Karoum, F., Potter, W.Z., & Ismond, D. (1986). Treatment of hyperactive children with monoamine oxidase inhibitors II. Plasma and urinary monoamine findings after treatment. *Archives of General Psychiatry, 42,* 969–973.

Chapter **18**

EATING DISORDERS

Jon Carlson

Vast parts of the world's population are faced with problems of malnutrition and starvation; however, people in more developed nations face a different type of problem concerning eating—eating disorders. Eating disorders are characterized by a preoccupation with food. The shift in societal preference toward a thin physique has led to an increasing prevalence of dieting such that normal eating for North American women is now characterized by dieting. Anorexia Nervosa and Bulimia Nervosa are conditions involving disturbed eating behavior and distorted body image. They involve refusal to eat, overeating, impulse eating, and purging. Eating disorders are often a more passive form of rebellion combined with an exaggerated acceptance of society's idealized "perfect" image and are much more common in females than in males (Wadden & Stunkard, 1987; Ruderman, 1986); however, disorders seem to be increasing in males (Andersen, 1990). In the DSM-III-R were listed five Axis I eating disorders.

07.10 Anorexia Nervosa
307.51 Bulimia Nervosa
307.52 Pica
307.53 Rumination Disorder of Infancy
307.50 Eating Disorder NOS

Of the five, pica and rumination usually occur during infancy and early childhood, whereas the others are predominantly an adolescent or early adulthood phenomenon. Therefore, in DSM-IV a new category, "Feeding and Eating Disorders of Infancy or Early Childhood," has been added. Pica and rumination disorders are placed in this section as well as new category Feeding Disorder of Infancy and Early Childhood. Anorexia Nervosa, Bulimia Nervosa, and Eating Disorder NOS remain in the Axis I Eating Disorder section. Simple obesity is a physical disorder and, although included in the International Classification of Diseases (ICD) as a general medical condition, it is not included in DSM-IV, the reason being it generally is not associated with any distinctly psychological or behavioral syndrome. When evidence is available that psychological factors are important in the course of a particular case of obesity, however, it is often noted under the category of Psychological Factors Affecting Medical Condition.

Pica, which is the persistent consumption of non-nutritive substances such as dirt, plaster, hair, bugs, and pebbles, usually has an onset of between 12 to 24 months of age with remission in childhood. Pica rarely persists into adolescence or adulthood. *Rumination Disorder of Infancy* is a well-defined syndrome. Although it has been described in adult patients, it is much more common in children. The essential feature is a repeated regurgitation of partially digested food that then is chewed, spit out, or swallowed without nausea, retching, or other signs of gastrointestinal distress. The condition is potentially fatal because of weight loss or no weight gain and subsequent malnutrition. *Feeding Disorder of Infancy or Early Childhood* involves the persistent failure to eat adequately as reflected by the failure to gain weight or significant weight loss over at least one month. This disorder must be before age six and not accounted for by a medical condition, mental disorder, or lack of available food. The purpose of this chapter is to concentrate on the two major categories, *Anorexia Nervosa* and *Bulimia Nervosa.*

Anorexia Nervosa and Bulimia Nervosa may affect as many as 5% to 10% of young women. Morbidity and mortality rates associated with eating disorders are among the highest for any psychiatric disorder. The diagnostic criteria in DSM-IV for Anorexia Nervosa (American Psychiatric Association, 1994, pp. 544–545) are as follows:

A. Refusal to maintain body weight at or above a minimally normal weight for age and height (e.g., weight loss leading to maintenance of body weight less than 85% of that expected; or failure to make expected weight gain during period of growth, leading to body weight less than 85% of that expected).

B. Intense fear of gaining weight or becoming fat, even though underweight.

C. Disturbance in the way in which one's body weight or shape is experienced, undue influence of body weight or shape on self-evaluation, or denial of the seriousness of the current low body weight.

D. In postmenarcheal females, amenorrhea, i.e., the absence of at least three consecutive menstrual cycles. (A woman is considered to have amenorrhea if her periods occur only following hormone, e.g., estrogen, administration.)

The diagnostic criteria in DSM-IV for Bulimia Nervosa (American Psychiatric Association, 1994, pp. 549–550) are as follows:

A. Recurrent episodes of binge eating. An episode of binge eating is characterized by both of the following:

   (1) eating, in a discrete period of time (e.g., within any 2–hour period), an amount of food that is definitely larger than most people would eat during a similar period of time and under similar circumstances
   (2) a sense of lack of control over eating during the episode (e.g., a feeling that one cannot stop eating or control what or how much one is eating)

B. Recurrent inappropriate compensatory behavior in order to prevent weight gain, such as self-induced vomiting; misuse of laxatives, diuretics, enemas, or other medications; fasting; or excessive exercise.

C. The binge eating and inappropriate compensatory behaviors both occur, on average, at least twice a week for 3 months.

D. Self-evaluation is unduly influenced by body shape and weight.

E. The disturbance does not occur exclusively during episodes of Anorexia Nervosa.

Anorectics are fearful of becoming overweight and perceive themselves as being fat, despite being emaciated. They describe themselves as having felt moderately overweight as teenagers and therefore began to diet in early to mid-teens, which led to weight becoming an obsession. Seldom do anorectics come to treatment on their own but usually are coerced by families, friends, employers, or physicians. ***Denial is the hallmark of an anorectic***.

Anorectics may present for treatment with a variety of moods, from being full of energy and cheerful to being depressed and lethargic. At some point during the course of the illness, however, over one-half of these clients meet the criteria for major depression. This problem may begin quickly or gradually and its course can be chronic, self-limited, or cyclical.

As previously mentioned, bulimics binge on huge quantities of food, usually in private, followed by purging in order to produce weight loss or weight maintenance. Purging is accomplished through such methods as self-induced vomiting, laxative abuse, Ipecac abuse, diuretics, or restriction. Bulimics often will present for treatment feeling ashamed or distressed about their symptoms and are much more open about their problems than anorectics. The bulimics, in contrast to the anorectics, may look much better than they feel. They can appear strong, sociable, and assertive but frequently are tormented by low self-esteem, fear of intimacy, and aggression. Physical signs of Bulimia Nervosa include a swelling of the parotid glands, which produces a chipmunk-like appearance, scars on the back of the hand from vomiting, chronic hoarseness or throat problems, and a dryness of the mouth. Physiological reactions to the disorder include dental cavities and enamel loss, electrolyte imbalance, cardiac and renal problems, and esophageal tears (Agras, 1987).

Clients with Anorexia Nervosa often come from families where food has an important role (Gutwill, 1994). They are characterized as having been very well-behaved children and have a major role in holding the family together. Many have been parentified children in enmeshed families and have been overprotected and overregulated. Clients with Anorexia Nervosa often are described as dependent, introverted, compulsive, stubborn, perfectionistic, asexual, and shy (Gutsch, 1988). These clients have low self-esteem and often use their eating disorder as a form of rebellion or a way to get attention from their families and therefore avoid having to be mature and responsible. Their disorder is generally classified as egosyntonic and they feel little hunger or discomfort with their symptoms.

Bulimic clients, however, tend to be anxious and depressed, self-critical, socially inhibited, secretive, and ashamed of their Bulimia. According to Gutsch (1988) and Bloom and Kogel (1994), they have conflicted feelings about relationships and sex, feel angry and powerless, and have difficulty handling pain, loss, and conflict. Bulimics are characterized by their feeling out of control, and they often have a high incidence of other impulse control problems such as alcohol abuse, self-mutilation, and overexercising. Families of bulimics are often low in cohesiveness with high levels of conflict. Unlike anorectics, bulimics tend to be egodystonic and experience considerable hunger and disappointment with their need to binge and purge. Bulimic binging episodes are often later in the day and tend to relate to mood change, stress, or unstructured time. According to Brotman and Herzog (1990), impaired psychological development may play a role in eating disorders. Impaired mother-child relationships have been described by psychoanalysts as central to the development of eating disorders. Self psychologists and proponents of feminist psychological theory have proposed that a history of sexual abuse is common in clients with eating disorders, and therefore, exploration of this subject during the initial evaluation would seem important. Many writers have tried to find a neurochemical explanation for both Anorexia Nervosa and Bulimia Nervosa. Researchers have often been frustrated by this, as neurochemical imbalances are often the result of the disorder and it is often hard to determine their etiology.

Although both bulimics and anorectics tend to have friends and have fairly successful lifestyles, they also have a tendency towards isolation and social difficulties. It is likely that this was developed in their troubled and chaotic families. Additionally some researchers (Atwood & Chester, 1987) have noticed that they have a tendency to have mothers who doubt themselves and are unresponsive to their daughters and distant fathers who have high expectations for their daughters. Agras (1987) has also noticed that they have siblings and parents who have a high incidence of eating disorders and major depression.

TREATMENT FORMULATION

The anorectic personality is often described as submissive (although often stubbornly so), timid, duty-bound, rigidly disciplined, and achievement-oriented. Individuals also are quite moralistic and have underlying doubts and anxious hesitancy about social skills. In contrast to the typically shy anorectics, bulimics are more likely to be outgoing and friendly perfectionists who attempt to control the people around them by more direct means (Agras, 1987; Bruch, 1982). Bulimics generally show one of two patterns—either obsessive-compulsive or addictive features.

Several personality factors increase the tendency in adolescents to develop a bulimic pattern:

1. acceptance of a traditional feminine role,
2. middle- to upper-class social status,
3. attendance away at college or boarding school,
4. early physical maturation,
5. a lower metabolic rate,
6. higher stress,
7. tendency toward depression,
8. a high belief in the ability to control one's world,
9. a prolonged history of dieting attempts, and

10.   a family that promotes psychological isolation from other people (Casper, Eckert, Halmi, Goldberg, & Davis, 1980; Striegel-Moore, Silberstein, & Rodin, 1986; Yager, Landsverk, & Edelstein, 1987).

The typical bulimic patient is Caucasian, female, single, in her mid-teens to mid-20s, well-educated, and close to her ideal weight. A binge episode usually is done in secret and commonly follows a sequence of stages including the following:

1.   anticipation and planning,
2.   anxiety,
3.   urgency to begin,
4.   rapid uncontrollable consumption of food,
5.   relief, usually by purging and relaxation,
6.   disappointment, and
7.   shame or disgust.

Many theories have been offered in an attempt to account for eating disorders. Psychodynamic theories tend to see anorectics as having a core conflict. Initially their core conflict was felt to be a fear of oral impregnation, while later analysts blamed domineering mothers for preventing the anorectic from completing the two chief psychosocial tasks of adolescence—individuating and separating. The theories are accurate in the fact that anorectics do fear sex and they also demand independence while clinging to their mothers.

Family therapists often have noted that anorectics' fathers are ineffective, mothers overbearing, and both parents intrusive. The family system generally seems to be dysfunctional with the parents acting in inappropriate ways. (However, if one's daughter is starving to death, it is unlikely that any family would stay intact.)

Social theorists feel that society places an inordinate value on thinness, beauty, proper behavior, diets, nutrition, exercise, health clubs, etc. This provides adolescents a way to rebel.

The biological research has been inconclusive; however, affective disorders seem to be closely correlated with eating disorders.

Adlerians tend to formulate eating disorders in a similar fashion to that of depression. Eating disorders are conceptualized as a result of overcontrolled behavior. Eating disorders are viewed as an expression of a combination of perfectionism and pessimism. Young girls are used by their parents in a way to live out unfulfilled ambitions. They are overprotected, overindulged, overcontrolled, with at least one parent having unrealistic hopes on her with the expectation of a perfect individual. The other parent and siblings indulge or compete in this arrangement but never directly challenge it. The young girl then becomes discouraged about her own abilities, wants, and worth, and eventually develops a compliant attitude that says "I must be like my parents to be approved" or a complaining attitude that says "If I do what you want, I'm entitled to your approval." She is therefore trapped and finds her place in the family by being obedient.

As she gets older, her high degree of perfectionism without any of her own goals often leads toward disaster. The young woman is discouraged and both unwilling and perhaps unable to make an effort for herself. She is often a pessimist and believes that her efforts will not turn out well. She is overambitious and believes that she must be perfect—and yet perfect by other people's standards.

Many theorists are puzzled why eating disorders affect primarily girls and surface as more of a behavioral rather than a mood disorder. Probably this relates to a young girl's close connection to a family, and this disorder can be a socially acceptable way to rebel against improper socialization. Also to have a physical problem is more socially acceptable than to have a mental illness or mood disorder.

In a controlled, strongly physically, vocationally, or socially competitive family, depression is effectively ruled out as a behavior that the family will tolerate. The family emphasis on eating or appearance, however, can be selected as a vulnerable point by the child, or the refusal to eat or look good is a behavior reinforced in the family by their efforts to discourage it. Depression is not reinforced; it is not responded to (Slavik, 1990).

An adolescent girl seeking a more egalitarian place in this family, while still complying with family rules (and not face a father who speaks for most of them), must develop the whole repertoire of acceptable rebellious behaviors. A man in a similar family might develop a compulsive overwork schedule. The woman, however, has her body and her relationships. Her strategy might include stubbornness; a tendency to engage in power struggles; denial of body sensations and functions, hunger, and feelings; an apparent inability to perceive how she appears to others; and obsessions, anxieties, and preoccupation with useless activities such as exercise. The anorectic woman has found the ultimate strategy to comply with all the family rules and still be most visible: a preoccupation with food yet refusing to eat. When these behaviors, obsessive plans, and vigilance begin to wear her down, then she may slip into depression. In an eating disorder, the woman chooses rebellion against the rules of appropriate performance. In depression, one rebels against the rules of appropriate affect. Both follow the family rules, and an eating disorder can thus easily be concurrent with depression (Slavik, 1990).

Adlerians, therefore, target therapy at how children are used for their parents' ambitions, children's profound discouragement, and their lack of skills and values. Often early recollections are a useful tool in order to enter into this process.

CLINICAL COURSE AND COMPLICATIONS

Anorexia Nervosa

Anorexia Nervosa often persists for years with active and inactive periods. Some clients, however, have stopped within 12 months and have not had recurrences. Physiologically, patients recover in two to three years from the nutritional deficits; however, many will continue to have menstrual problems, sexual and social maladjustment, weight fluctuations, disturbed appetite, and continued body and weight image problems. According to Hsu (1990), in terms of their overall prognosis, 40% are completely recovered, 30% are considerably improved, 20% are unimproved or severely impaired, and 5 to 10% prematurely die, usually by starvation, electrolyte imbalance (from vomiting or purging), or suicide.

How Anorexia Nervosa begins has little bearing on its course or outcome. Instead, predictors of a favorable outcome include a good premorbid level of functioning, more education, early age of onset, less weight loss, less denial of illness, overactivity, a greater psychosexual maturity, and feeling hunger when hospitalized. Indicators of a poor prognosis are the opposite of the above plus perinatal complications; binging, self-induced vomiting, and purging; longer duration of illness; longer delay in initially obtaining treatment; severe dysthymia; and obsessions and greater exaggeration of body width (Maxmen, 1986).

Bulimia Nervosa

Bulimia Nervosa occurs during the teenage or early 20s and rarely after the age of 30. It is a chronic disorder with fluctuating intensity and alternating periods of normal eating and binging. Sometimes normal eating does not occur, and the patient cycles between periods of binging and fasting. Bulimics generally improve and completely recover and seldom die. Connors, Johnson, and Stuckey (1984) found that 80% of the bulimic clients stopped their dysfunctional behavior in 10 weeks of treatment, 93% in 14 weeks. A positive prognosis is associated with good premorbid functioning, high educational level, early age of onset, feelings of hunger and low weight loss, short duration of disorder, acceptance of illness, overactivity, and psychosexual maturity (Seligman, 1990). Relapses are common and are often related to stressful life events. Therefore treatment should be extended through follow-up or support groups to prevent setbacks. Follow-up treatment also should be helpful in reducing the family, social, and occupational difficulties that often persist after the eating disorder has been eliminated. In addition to direct therapeutic follow-up, eating disorder assistance programs are available (Kapoor, 1988; Sandbek, 1986; Siegel, Brisman, & Weinshel, 1988).

THERAPIST CHARACTERISTICS

Clients presenting with eating disorders need considerable support and approval to make the difficult behavioral changes required. Engaging the client and developing strong rapport is an integral part of treatment. The individuality of these clients often has been denied in their families, and that should not happen in therapy (Bruch, 1982). They need to be heard, encouraged, and helped to develop a separate identity. Treatment needs to be similar to that for clients with dependent personality features, with the therapist needing to encourage self-control and independence. Additionally, therapists will need to be firm and set limits in order to protect the client. Sometimes hospitalization will be necessary. Many writers also feel that women with eating disorders are uncomfortable with men and will prefer a female therapist or a male-female therapy team (Seligman, 1990).

According to Brouwers (1990), before counselors can ethically work on body image issues with their clients, they need to examine their own beliefs about weight and appearance. The worst thing to do with a bulimic client is to endorse the view that she must lose weight. The counselor's attitude is not only unhelpful but also actually colludes with the client in maintaining appearance-oriented attitudes that contribute to the bulimia. In the event that the client actually does need to lose weight for health reasons, the counselor must state clearly that bulimia is much worse for health than being overweight. Regardless of her appearance, the client must *accept herself as he or she is.*

"Fatism" is alive and well in our culture. Counselors owe it to themselves and to their clients to combat this form of prejudice. A counselor who believes the cultural indoctrinations that women must be thin to be happy, and that overweight people are lazy, lack willpower, or are less intelligent must seriously look at the effect that these beliefs are having on his or her own life and work. Counselors would do well to examine their own conscious and unconscious attitudes about appearance and work toward acceptance of their own bodies. Until a counselor works toward his or her own freedom from cultural slavery regarding appearance, he or she cannot effectively work with clients struggling with body image issues (Brouwers, 1990, p. 147).

TREATMENT

The client's initial evaluation should include a physical examination with a blood screen and a nutritional history in addition to a normal clinical intake (Garner & Davis, 1986). Because of these requirements, a treatment team consisting of a physician, therapist, nutritionist, and, in some cases, family therapist is often required (Bauer & Anderson, 1989a, 1989b; Bauer, Anderson, & Hyatt, 1986). Initially it is also necessary to have an initial treatment period where the client has behavioral treatment to help control the binging and purging and to closely monitor the weight. Fremouw, Wiener, and Seime (1987) have developed a useful set of forms for self-monitoring eating behavior. When the weight loss is severe or the client's medical condition is serious, hospitalization that includes a supervised eating program to prevent vomiting and laxative use and promote weight gain may be needed. An interesting point to note, however, is that although hospitalization can stabilize a patient, most have eating problems after discharge (Agras, 1987). If the client does not seem to be in immediate danger, outpatient treatment is adequate as long as steps are taken to normalize weight and to stop self-damaging behaviors.

The treatment of eating disorders is often difficult because the clients and families tend to deny the illness. Premature termination of therapy frequently occurs. Power and control issues often inhibit the progress of therapy. Clients are resistant to changing behaviors that have served as coping mechanisms, even feeling as if they are giving up a part of themselves. The therapist needs to take control, yet to avoid triggering control issues or engaging in power struggles. This can be done in several ways (Sallas, 1985; Schwartz, 1986).

1. Therapists should allow clients to know that no one can make them change. The choice is one they can make. This reinforces that the client is in control and provides a sense of security so they can explore new behaviors.
2. Therapists should acknowledge that the evident goal (for the clients to

be in control of their lives) is appropriate, but the methods for achieving the goal are inappropriate.

3. Therapists should presently suggest (occasionally through hypnosis) though not demand that the patient exercise some up-front and appropriate control over symptom behaviors.
4. Therapists should encourage the establishment of a support system for the patient by incorporating group therapy into the treatment plan.
5. Therapists should acknowledge that the symptom behaviors are important to the client and have functioned as part of their identity for a long time. This allows the client to be less defensive and more willing to seek alternative behaviors. The recognition of the interplay between physiology and psychology in the eating disordered client is imperative for successful treatment (Garner & Isaacs, 1986).

According to Seligman (1990), most treatment programs for clients with eating disorders tend to be relatively brief, 8 to 20 sessions, but sometimes include extended follow-up treatment. Therapy for clients with eating disorders, as for most clients with behavioral disorders, typically has several components. Behavioral therapy to promote healthy eating and to eliminate purging is the core of the treatment. Procedures usually include gathering baseline data on client's weight and related dysfunctional behaviors such as laxative use, establishment of goals, contingency contracting, monitoring of progress via diary or scale in the office if necessary, reinforcement and rewards for positive change, and relaxation strategies to reduce anxiety and to improve self-image and sense of control. Other behavioral techniques, such as assertiveness, communication, and social skills training can enhance treatment, as can the development of leisure activities and improved relationships to provide alternatives to the dysfunctional eating (p. 192).

In order to help clients gain insight into the dynamics of the disorder, both cognitive and insight-oriented approaches have been useful. These approaches tend to improve self-esteem, provide a sense of control, and contribute to the development of better eating. Therapists additionally need to deal with the conflicts that include the client's concurrent desire for autonomy and dependence and the need to be in complete control of a body that refuses to cease having appetites. During the course of treatment, attitudes and assumptions are identified, defined, and evaluated within a context of a firm yet supportive therapeutic relationship.

Many treatment programs are available in the literature that would be compatible with Adlerian thinking. These programs combine cognitive and behavioral interventions with some attention to affect in the structured format that could be used with either individuals or with groups. The psychoeducational aspects of treatment and the group dynamics are important. The programs basically shape diet, provide education, explore antecedents of the disorder, prevent vomiting, examine cognitions, teach problem-solving and coping mechanisms, provide group support, and prevent relapse. Boskind-White and White (1983) found that group therapy with a male-female leadership team can be particularly helpful for bulimic women. Their approach to treating Bulimia has the following elements:

1. exploring affect, for example, shame, hostility, isolation, self-esteem, designed to clarify connection between emotions and eating;
2. understanding relationships and the connection between intimacy and responsibility—improvement of social skills;
3. awareness of eating patterns and cues to dysfunctional eating and purging;
4. role-playing to develop assertiveness, communication, and other skills; and
5. developing coping strategies—techniques such as the writing of autobiographies, feedback, values clarification, and self-disclosure also are used to help clients establish and work toward goals.

The eating-disordered client also may need counseling regarding diet facts and simple control of eating behaviors, counseling of the type used with the more common problem of obesity and persistent eating disorders (Ruderman, 1986) such as the following:

1. a biological drive exists toward high fat and very sweet foods, so control should be directed toward "what" as much as "when" and "how much";
2. weight loss is not hard to attain—keeping it off is;
3. more difficulty is experienced in losing weight during the second diet than the first;
4. most diets are broken in the late afternoon;
5. if the activity level remains the same and a cessation of smoking occurs, a weight gain also will occur; and
6. changing exercise amounts and patterns are usually more effective in generating weight loss than changing diet amounts and patterns.

Many creative therapeutic approaches are used in treating eating disorders. O'Connor (1984) suggested a paradoxical intervention for bulimic clients. In this approach, clients are instructed to think obsessively about food for 30 minutes daily, to develop a mutually exclusive behavior such as shopping that they can engage in whenever they feel the urge to purge, and to binge on a schedule. This approach might be effective with clients who are highly resistant to straightforward treatment of their symptoms.

Bloom, Kogel, and Zaphiropoulous (1994) believed that all clients must be taught about hunger, satiety, and food choice. Although they use a didactic model, it incorporates psychoanalytic tasks in order to work through conflicts and defenses.

Madanes (1990) suggested a family intervention strategy where mass quantities of food that a bulimic would ordinarily eat are mixed on a table all together by the client with the family watching and then carried by hand and thrown into the toilet bowl all at one time, and then having the father clean it out so that the toilet would work again. By exaggerating and bringing out into the open this behavior, Madanes has found that this often provides a quick stop to this problem.

In order to treat the negative thinking related to distorted body image, the counselor and client must first discover the self-defeating thoughts that the client holds about her body. Thoughts are examined in terms of associated feelings, rationality, and their connection with the eating behavior. The counselor then asks the client to generate alternative thoughts that encourage flexibility and self-acceptance (Ellis & Bernard, 1985). The client is encouraged to practice these alternative thoughts outside of the counseling office. Practice can involve writing them, saying them out loud to herself, or reminding herself quietly. In Figure 18.1 are listed examples of self-defeating thoughts, associated feelings, and alternative thoughts related to body image dissatisfaction (Brouwers, 1990).

Bauer and Anderson (1989a, 1989b) have discovered that individuals who suffer from Bulimia Nervosa share a characteristic pattern of thinking that needs to be understood if effective treatment is to take place. The following are the constructs and their corresponding beliefs.

A   Being or becoming overweight is the worst thing that can happen to me.
   a   Fat is disgusting and repulsive.
   b   To be fat is to be a failure.

B   Certain foods are good foods; other foods are bad foods.
   a   Good foods are "diet" foods; bad foods are fattening.
   b   Eating bad foods makes me a bad person; eating good foods makes me a good person.
   c   Bad food is turned directly into body fat.

C   I must have control over all of my actions to feel safe.
   a   Self-control is a sign of strength and discipline.

Self-defeating Thoughts	Associated Feelings	Alternative Thoughts
1. I am so fat and ugly.	1. Inadequate, judged, depressed.	1. My body is healthy and functional.
2. My thighs are disgusting.	2. Inadequate, trapped, judged.	2. This is the way my thighs are, and I accept them.
3. Fat people are gross and disgusting.	3. Fearful, loathsome	3. Overweight people are people with strengths and weaknesses. Their appearance has nothing to do with their value as human beings.
4. I should be able to control my appearance.	4. Anxious, guilty inadequate.	4. My appearance is largely genetic, and I accept the way I look.
5. My boyfriend (husband, mother) wants me to be thin.	5. Angry, fearful, resentful.	5. I will not live to please others.
6. No one will like me if I'm fat.	6. Fearful, inadequate, anxious.	6. Appearance has nothing to do with being likable.

Figure 18.1. Examples of thoughts and feelings associated with body image dissatisfaction. Adapted from M. Brouwers (1990), Treatment of Body Image Dissatisfaction among Women with Bulimia Nervosa. *Journal of Counseling and Development, 69,* 144–147.

  b Minor dietary indiscretions are indicative of a complete loss of self-control.

  c Trying harder is the answer to my food problems.

D I must do everything perfectly or what I do is worthless.

  a I hold myself to standards that I would never apply to another individual.

  b I feel bad regardless of performance. I could have done even better if I had tried harder.

  c I negate accomplishments and dwell on failures.

E   Everyone is aware of and interested in what I'm doing.
   a   If I hear people laughing, I know it is about me.
   b   Other people watch and are critical of what I eat and know if I have gained weight.

F   Everyone must love me and approve of what I do.
   a   I must keep others happy regardless of the cost to me.
   b   I feel so unworthy of love that I attempt to buy it.
   c   I perceive rejection whether it is intended or not.
   d   I'm basically a bad person.

G   External validation is everything.
   a   Numbers are very important: calories, weight, grade point average, score on any type of competition.
   b   I take opinion polls every time I need to make a decision to be sure I am making the right choice.

H   As soon as I _____, I will be able to give up bulimia.

I   To be successful, a woman must combine the traditional values of women with the aggressive career orientation of men.
   a   I must be dependent and subservient like my mother.
   b   I must be aggressive and competitive like my father.
   c   I must be attractive and feminine but never sexual.

Some researchers (Bauer & Anderson, 1989a, 1989b) have found bizarre assignments designed to counter the perfectionism so integral to the personality of a bulimic to be highly effective. They suggest doing activities like balancing half a checkbook, leaving one corner of a bed unmade, or starting a letter and stopping in the middle of a sentence.

Andreas and Andreas (1989) believed that an important procedure is to help clients learn to think and respond the way naturally slender people do, rather than wage a constant battle with food. These authors believed that to teach the following naturally slender eating method is important. This procedure helps people to learn and think how healthy people eat.

1. First, something makes me think of food. This might be seeing that it's time for lunch, hearing someone mention lunch, feeling hunger, or seeing food.
2. I check how my stomach feels now.
3. I ask myself "what would feel good in my stomach?"
4. I visualize a possible portion of food: a sandwich, a bowl of soup, a dinner salad, etc.

5. I imagine eating this food. I think of the taste of this food and then feel the food slipping into my mouth and get a feeling of how this amount of this food will feel in my stomach over time if I eat it now.
6. If I like this feeling better than how I will feel if I eat no food at all, I keep this food item as one possibility. It not, I discard it.
7. Next I visualize another food I might eat.
8. I imagine tasting this second item and feel how it feels as it goes into my stomach and stays in my system for some hours to come.
9. I notice how I like this feeling. Do I like it more than my first choice so far? I keep in mind the food item that makes me feel best to compare to my next choice.
10. Now I repeat steps 7, 8, and 9 as often as I want to, always keeping in mind the kind of food that I imagine would make me feel the best over time if I eat it. I compare each new possibility to that.
11. When I'm satisfied that I have considered enough options, I eat the food that I imagine would make me feel best over time so that I'll get to feel that good.

Other researchers (Humphrey, 1992; Root, Fallon, & Friedrich, 1986; Russell, Dare, Eisler, & LeGrange, 1992; Schwartz, 1987) have found family therapy to be very effective in the treatment of eating disorders, as well as an important adjunct to treatment. The classic study by Minuchin, Rosman, and Baker (1978) reported an 86% success rate with anorexics.

Many professionals are experimenting with the use of medications and eating disorders (Walsh, 1992). It seems that at best medications will have a limited role in the current treatment of Anorexia Nervosa (Gitlin, 1990). The reasons for this are as follows.

> First, anorexic patients, especially in the early stages of treatment when their weight is very low, are at a high risk to have a variety of metabolic and other biological disturbances from the self-induced starvation. Because of this, an increased danger exists in using any medication. Second, patients with Anorexia Nervosa are exceedingly sensitive to and intolerant of nondangerous medication side effects, both from the starvation effects and from their own sensitivity to unwanted feelings or changes in their bodies. Third, these patients often equate taking medication with losing control, further increasing the resistance to taking them. (Gitlin, 1990, p. 141)

The most promising drug for Anorexia Nervosa is cyproheptadina (Periactin), which blocks the effect of serotonin. Because serotonin increases feelings of satiety (being full) through an effect in the hypothalamus, cyproheptadina stimulates appetite. Unfortunately, its major side effect is sedation.

In contrast to Anorexia Nervosa, medications, specifically antidepressants, have documented efficacy in decreasing the binge-purge cycle of Bulimia Nervosa (Walsh, 1987). The guidelines that a therapist should use before considering referral of a bulimic patient for possible antidepressant treatment are as follows.

1. It is important to acknowledge that medications are far from being the only well-documented treatment for Bulimia. A variety of psychological approaches utilizing cognitive, behavioral, educational, psychodynamic, and supportive techniques in both individual and group formats have shown clear evidence of efficacy (Yager, 1988).
2. Studies comparing antidepressants to educational/cognitive/behavioral approaches are rare.
3. Medications are sometimes difficult to use in bulimic patients: side effects are often problematic, affecting compliance. Vomiting can cause erratic medication blood levels, making pharmacotherapy inconsistent, and the necessary dietary restrictions with the MAO inhibitors make these particular medications acceptable for only a subset of those with Bulimia.
4. No established predictors are known for antidepressant responses with bulimic patients. Since the issues of control are so central to Bulimia Nervosa, patients often are frightened of being addicted to medications and are concerned that taking medication is an indication of lack of self-control. Bulimics also fear that the medications will make them fat (Edelstein, 1989).

CASE EXAMPLE

Case of Judy

Judy is a single 17-year-old who lives with her parents, who insisted that she be seen by the counselor because of binge eating and vomiting. She achieved her greatest weight of 180 pounds at 16 years of age; her lowest weight since she reached her present height of 5'9" has been 150 pounds, and her present weight is about 160 pounds. Judy's parents are both professionals with advanced college degrees. Judy is the middle of three daughters.

Judy stated that she has been dieting since the age of 12 and said that she has always been tall and chubby. At age 14 she started to binge eat and vomit.

She was a serious competitive swimmer at that time and she felt it was necessary for her to keep her weight down in order to be the state champion that her father desired. She would deprive herself of food for a few days and then get an urge to eat. She could not control the urge and would raid the refrigerator and cupboards for desserts, potato chips, and whatever else caught her fancy. She would often do this in the evening when no one was looking and would eat everything in one sitting. While binging she knew that her eating was out of control but would only stop when she felt physical discomfort. She would then feel depressed and afraid of gaining weight and would self-induce vomiting by sticking a finger down her throat.

Judy has always been concerned about the effect this behavior was having on her weight and constantly has feared being overweight. Sometimes she would resort to laxatives to help her lose weight. When she was 15 she was having eating binges and vomiting four days per week. She has obtained very good grades in junior high school and high school and tends to be a student who works very hard.

Recently Judy has been drinking wine and beer on weekends. She drinks mostly with girlfriends. She dates infrequently, never getting very close to any boys, but Judy states that she wants to date. She feels ashamed of the way she looks and does not put herself in the right places at the right times. Four months ago she was hospitalized for two weeks in order to control her eating binges. During the time in the hospital she became very depressed, talked about suicide, and attempted to cut her wrist.

Judy is very well-dressed, well-oriented, and is able to answer questions with great psychological insight. During the interview, she indicates that she has a serious problem but feels hopeless about getting the behavior under control.

Diagnosis.

>Axis I: 307.51 Bulimia Nervosa
>   Rule out: Psychoactive substance abuse
>Axis II: 301.83 Borderline personality disorder
>Axis III: None
>Axis IV: 3; eating disorder
>Axis V: Current GAF: 65; Highest GAF Past 12 Months: 65

Initial Intake.   Judy described herself as being "born fat" and always being a chubby kid, not really fat but somewhat overweight. She reports not liking this and having her mom and dad caring about the way she looked and always on her case about her weight. Her dad was always trying to get her to diet in order to be a better swimmer. Her parents often commented on everything she put on her mouth, making mealtime an awful experience. Her two sisters did not get it as bad as Judy. Actually, her sisters would even tell on her if they saw her eating stuff she was not supposed to.

Food issues are often the stated topic of power struggles between parents, though the subtext was typically a fight over who is in charge of the daughter's life. Therefore, one can easily see how a youngster such as Judy who was in the process of individuation is having a difficult time. Though Judy wants to please her parents and appear perfect on the outside, down inside she needs to rebel in order to establish her own identity.

Summary of the Family Constellation Information.   Judy is the middle of three girls in a family with extremely high standards. These standards have led each girl to seek the goal of perfection. Judy's older sister has out-achieved Judy by being perfectly good and capable, and her younger sister acted out her perfect goals by being perfectly lousy. Judy supposed that her father wanted a boy and tried to be a reasonable facsimile, and although she did gain some of her father's favor, doing so did not give her a place with the power person in the family—her mom. By following an overachieving sister, she felt as though she had no ability, so she tried to win approval by trying to please her parents. Her academics and success in swimming were plays to accomplish this; however, as she approached adolescence and individuation, she began a war with herself.

Summary of Early Recollections.

"Life is a fight and dangerous."
"Everyone will give you a hard time unless you can remain perfect."
"People don't treat me the way that I should be treated."

Basic Mistakes.

1.   She cannot conceive of the possibility of good relationships.
2.   She can do nothing to solve the situation except to look up to the upper dogs and down to the underdogs.
3.   She sees life as a jungle and is so busy defending herself that she often provokes the battles.
4.   She feels like Cinderella—a deprived princess in disguise.

Treatment.   In order to help Judy with her problem, the therapist first received the medical records verifying that her medical condition was stable.

Next, the therapist began individual therapy with a cognitive focus to look at many of the beliefs that Judy had that were getting in her way, particularly the beliefs of perfectionism and pessimism. The therapist helped to build up her self-esteem and to empower her. Instruction was provided in healthy eating, and a consultation with a dietitian was arranged. A further suggestion was that Judy attend a local Overeaters Anonymous group and that her family contract to attend five sessions of family therapy focused on changing some of the family expectations.

CONCLUSION

Eating disorders are among the most challenging problems facing counselors and psychologists today. Their successful treatment involves a multimodal approach that seems to be well-suited to Adlerian orientation.

RESOURCES FOR EATING DISORDERS

Organizations

American Anorexia/Bulimia Association, Inc.
425 East 61st Street, Sixth Floor
New York, NY 10021
(212) 891–8686

FEED—Foundation for Education about Eating Disorders
5238 Duvall Drive
Bethesda, MD 20816
(Send a self-addressed, stamped envelope.)

Information Resources and Inquiries Branch
National Institute of Mental Health
5600 Fishers Lane, Room 7C-02
Rockville, MD 20857

National Association of Anorexia Nervosa and Associated Disorders
P.O. Box 7
Highland Park, IL 60035
(708) 831–3438

National Eating Disorders Organization
445 East Granville Road
Worthington, OH 43085
(614) 436–1112

Overeaters Anonymous - National Office
4025 Spencer Street, Suite 203
Torrance, CA 90504
(213) 542–8363

O-Anon
(Check local listings .)

Publications

Eating Disorders Review
P.O. Box 2468
Van Nuys, CA 91404–9983
(A bi-monthly publication providing current information to professionals treating eating disorders.)

Hazledon Educational Materials
Pleasant Valley Road
P.O. Box 176
Center City, MN 55012–0176
(Publisher of many useful books and pamphlets in the 12-Step Tradition for compulsive overeaters. Catalog available upon request.)

Carle Medical Communication
611 West Park
Urbana, IL 61801
(Publisher of media on eating disorders for professionals and clients. Catalog available upon request.)

Gurze Books
P.O. Box 2238
Carlsbad, CA 92018
(800) 756–7533
(The leading distributor of books and tapes on Bulimia Nervosa, Anorexia Nervosa, and compulsive eating. Catalog available upon request.)

REFERENCES

Agras, W.S. (1987). *Eating disorders*. Elmsford, NY: Pergamon Press.

American Psychiatric Association. (1994). *Diagnostic and statistical manual of mental disorders* (4th ed.). Washington, DC: Author.

Andersen, A.E. (1990). *Males with eating disorders*. New York: Brunner/Mazel.

Andreas, C., & Andreas, S. (1989). *Heart of the mind*. Moab, UT: Real Person Press.

Atwood, J.D., & Chester, R. (1987). *Treatment techniques for common mental disorders*. New York: Jason Aronson.

Bauer, B.G., & Anderson, W.P. (1989a). Bulimic beliefs: Food for thought. *Journal of Counseling and Development, 67,* 416–419.

Bauer, B., & Anderson, A. (1989b, September). Turning around Bulimia with therapy. *Psychology Today,* p. 14.

Bauer, B., Anderson, A., & Hyatt, R. (1986). *Bulimia: Book for therapist and client*. Muncie, IN: Accelerated Development.

Bloom, C., & Kogel, L. (1994). Symbolic meaning of food and body. In C. Bloom, A. Getter, S. Gutwill, L. Kogel, & C. Zaphiropoulous (Eds.), *Eating problems: A feminist psychoanalytic treatment model* (pp. 57–66). New York: Harper Collins.

Bloom, C., Kogel, L., & Zaphiropoulous, C. (1994). Learning to feed oneself: A psychodynamic model. In C. Bloom, A. Getter, S. Gutwill, L. Kogel, & C. Zaphiropoulous (Eds.), *Eating problems: A feminist psychoanalytic treatment model* (pp. 83–115). New York: Harper Collins.

Boskind-White, M., & White, W.C., Jr. (1983). *Bulimarexia: The binge-purge cycle*. New York: Norton.

Brotman, A.W., & Herzog, D.B. (1990). Eating disorders. In S.E. Hyman & M.A. Jenike (Eds.), *Manual of clinical problems in psychiatry with annotated key references* (pp. 214–220). Boston: Little, Brown & Company.

Brouwers, M. (1990). Treatment of body image dissatisfaction among women with Bulimia Nervosa. *Journal of Counseling and Development, 69,* 144–147.

Bruch, H. (1982). Anorexia Nervosa: Therapy and theory. *American Journal of Psychiatry, 139,* 1531–1538.

Casper, R.C., Eckert, E.D., Halmi, K.A., Goldberg, S.C., & Davis, J.M. (1980). Bulimia. *Archives of General Psychiatry, 37,* 1030–1035.

Connors, M.E., Johnson, C.L., & Stuckey, M.K. (1984). Treatment of Bulimia with brief psychoeducational group therapy. *American Journal of Psychiatry, 141,* 1512–1516.

Edelstein, C. (1989). *Mood disorders and eating disorders.* Presented at the 142nd American Psychiatric Association annual meeting, San Francisco, CA.

Ellis, A., & Bernard, M.E. (Eds.). (1985). *Clinical applications of rational emotive therapy.* New York: Plenum.

Fremouw, W.J., Wiener, A.L., & Seime, R.J. (1987). Self-monitoring forms for Bulimia. In P.A. Keller & S.A. Heymen (Eds.), *Innovations in Clinical Practice and Sourcebook, 6,* 325–332. Sarasota, FL: Professional Resource Exchange.

Garner, D.M., & Davis, R. (1986). The clinical assessment of Anorexia Nervosa and Bulimia Nervosa. In P.A. Keller & L.G. Ritt (Eds.), *Innovations in Clinical Practice and Sourcebook, 5,* 5–28. Sarasota, FL: Professional Resource Exchange.

Garner, D.M., & Isaacs, P. (1986). The fundamentals of psychotherapy for Anorexia Nervosa and Bulimia Nervosa. In P.A. Keller & L.G. Ritt (Eds.), *Innovations in Clinical Practice and Sourcebook, 5,* 29–44. Sarasota, FL: Professional Resource Exchange.

Gitlin, M.J. (1990). *The psychotherapist's guide to psychopharmacology.* New York: The Free Press.

Gutsch, K.U. (1988). *Psychotherapeutic approaches to specific DSM-III-R categories.* Springfield, IL: C. C. Thomas.

Gutwill, S. (1994). Women's eating problems: Social context and the internalization of culture. In C. Bloom, A. Getter, S. Gutwill, L. Kogel, & C. Zaphiropoulos (Eds.), *Eating problems: A feminist psychoanalytic treatment model* (pp. 1–27). New York: Harper Collins.

Hsu, L.K.G. (1990). *Eating disorders*. New York: The Guilford Press.

Humphrey, L.L. (1992). Family relationships. In K.A. Halmi (Ed.), *Psychobiology and treatment of Anorexia Nervosa and Bulimia Nervosa* (pp. 263–285). Washington, DC: American Psychiatric Press.

Kapoor, S. (1988). *Bulimia: A program for friends and family members*. Springfield, IL: C. C. Thomas.

Madanes, C. (1990). *Metaphors and paradoxes*. San Francisco: Jossey-Bass.

Maxmen, J.S. (1986). *Essential psychopathology*. New York: W. W. Norton.

Minuchin, S., Rosman, B.L., & Baker, L. (1978). *Psychosomatic families: Anorexia Nervosa in context*. Cambridge, MA: Harvard University Press.

O'Connor, J. (1984). Strategic individual psychotherapy with bulimic women. *Psychotherapy: Theory, research, and practice, 21*, 491–499.

Root, M.P., Fallon, P., & Friedrich, W.N. (1986). *Bulimia: A systems approach to treatment*. New York: W.W. Norton.

Ruderman, A. (1986). Dietary restraint: A theoretical and empirical review. *Psychological Bulletin, 99*, 247–262.

Russell, G.F.M., Dare, C., Eisler, I., & LeGrange, P.D.F. (1992). Controlled trials of family treatments in Anorexia Nervosa. In K.A. Halmi (Ed.), *Psychobiology and treatment of Anorexia Nervosa and Bulimia Nervosa* (pp. 237–262). Washington, DC: American Psychiatric Press.

Sallas, R. (1985). Winning the war against eating disorders without doing battle. *The Journal of Psychiatric Research, 19*, 445–448.

Sandbek, T.J. (1986). *The deadly diet: Recovering from Anorexia and Bulimia*. Oakland, CA: New Harbinger Publications.

Schwartz, R. (1986). Eating disorders. *New England Journal of Medicine, 313*, 295–303.

Schwartz, R.C. (1987). Working with internal and external families in the treatment of Bulimia. *Family Relations, 36*, 242–245.

Seligman, L. (1990). *Selecting effective treatments*. San Francisco: Jossey-Bass.

Siegel, M., Brisman, J., & Weinshel, M. (1988). *Surviving an eating disorder: New perspectives and strategies for family and friends*. New York: Harper & Row.

Slavik, S. (1990). *Speculations on eating disorders in Adlerian framework*. Mimeographed form, 4391 Torrington Place, Victoria, B.C. Canada V8N 4T3.

Striegel-Moore, R., Silberstein, L., & Rodin, J. (1986). Toward an understanding of risk factors for Bulimia. *American Psychologist, 43*, 246–263.

Wadden, T., & Stunkard, A. (1987). Psychopathology and obesity. In R. Wurtman & J. Wurtman (Eds.), *Human obesity*. New York: New York Academy of Sciences.

Walsh, B.T. (1992). Pharmacological treatment. In K.A. Halmi (Ed.), *Psychobiology and treatment of Anorexia Nervosa and Bulimia Nervosa* (pp. 329–340). Washington, DC: American Psychiatric Press.

Walsh, B.T. (1987). Psychopharmacology of Bulimia. In H.Y. Meltzer (Ed.), *Psychopharmacology: The third generation of progress*. New York: Rabin Press.

Yager, J. (1988). The treatment of eating disorders. *Journal of Clinical Psychiatry, 49*(9), 18–25.

Yager, J., Landsverk, J., Edelstein, C.K. (1987). A twenty-month follow-up study of 628 women with eating disorders. I: Course and severity. *American Journal of Psychiatry, 144*, 1172–1177.

APPENDIX
DSM-IV Classification:
Axis I and II Categories
and Codes*

*Extracted from American Psychiatric Association. (1994). *Diagnostic and statistical manual of mental disorders* (4th ed.), pp. 13–24. Washington, DC: Author.

**DISORDERS USUALLY FIRST
DIAGNOSED IN INFANCY,
CHILDHOOD, OR ADOLESCENCE**

Mental retardation
Note: These are coded on Axis II.
317   Mild mental retardation
318.0   Moderate mental retardation
318.1   Severe mental retardation
318.2   Profound mental retardation
319   Mental retardation, severity unspecified

Learning disorders
315.00 Reading disorder
315.1   Mathematics disorder
315.2   Disorder of written expression
315.9   Learning disorder NOS

Motor skills disorder
315.4   Developmental coordination disorder

Communication disorders
315.31 Expressive language disorder
315.31 Mixed receptive/expressive language
        disorder
315.39 Phonological disorder
307.0   Stuttering
307.9   Communication disorder NOS

Pervasive developmental disorders
299.00 Autistic disorder
299.80 Rett's disorder
299.10 Childhood disintegrative disorder
299.80 Asperger's disorder
299.80 Pervasive developmental disorder NOS

**Attention-deficit and disruptive behavior
disorders**
314.xx Attention-deficit/hyperactivity disorder
    .01   combined type
    .00   predominantly inattentive type
    .01   predominantly hyperactive-impulsive
            type
314.9   Attention-deficit/hyperactivity disorder
        NOS
313.81 Oppositional defiant disorder
312.8   Conduct disorder
312.9   Disruptive behavior disorder NOS

**Feeding and eating disorders of infancy or
early childhood**
307.52 Pica
307.53 Rumination disorder
307.59 Feeding disorder of infancy or early
        childhood

Tic disorders
307.23 Tourette's disorder
307.22 Chronic motor or vocal tic disorder
307.21 Transient tic disorder
307.20 Tic disorder NOS

Elimination disorders
787.6   Encopresis with constipation and over-
        flow incontinence
307.7   Encopresis without constipation and
        overflow incontinence
307.6   Enuresis (not due to a general medical
        condition)

**Other disorders of infancy, childhood, or
adolescence**
309.21 Separation anxiety disorder
313.23 Selective mutism
313.89 Reactive attachment disorder of in-
        fancy or early childhood
307.3   Stereotypic movement disorder
313.9   Disorder of infancy, childhood, or ado-
        lescence NOS

**DELIRIUM, DEMENTIA, AMNESTIC
AND OTHER COGNITIVE DISORDERS**

Delirium
293.0   Delirium due to *[indicate the general
        medical condition]*
___.__ Substance-intoxication delirium *(refer
        to substance-related disorders for sub-
        stance-specific codes)*
___.__ Substance withdrawal delirium *(refer
        to substance-related disorders for sub-
        stance-specific codes)*
___.__ Delirium due to multiple etiologies
        (code each of the specific etiologies)
780.89 Delirium NOS

Dementia
290.xx Dementia of the Alzheimer's type
With early onset: at age 65 or before
    .10   uncomplicated
    .11   with delirium
    .12   with delusions
    .13   with depressed mood
With late onset: after age 65
    .00   uncomplicated
    .30   with delirium
    .20   with delusions
    .21   with depressed mood
Vascular dementia
    .40   uncomplicated
    .41   with delirium

.42 with delusions
.43 with depressed mood

Dementia due to other general medical conditions
294.9 Dementia due to HIV disease *(also code 043.1 on Axis III)*
294.1 Dementia due to head trauma *(also code 854.00 on Axis III)*
294.1 Dementia due to Parkinson's disease *(also code 332.0 on Axis III)*
294.1 Dementia due to Huntington's disease *(also code 333.4 on Axis III)*
290.10 Dementia due to Creutzfeldt-Jakob disease *(also code 046.1 on Axis III)*
294.1 Dementia due to *[indicate the general medical condition not listed above]*
___.__ Substance-induced persisting dementia *(refer to substance-related disorder for substance-specific codes)*
___.__ Dementia due to multiple etiologies *(code each of the specific etiologies)*
294.8 Dementia NOS

Amnestic disorders
294.0 Amnestic disorder due to *[indicate the general medical condition]*
___.__ Substance-induced persisting amnestic disorder *(refer to substance-related disorders for specific substance-specific codes)*
294.8 Amnestic disorder NOS

Other cognitive disorders
294.9 Cognitive disorder NOS

MENTAL DISORDERS DUE TO A GENERAL MEDICAL CONDITION NOT ELSEWHERE CLASSIFIED

293.89 Catatonic disorder due to *[indicate the general medical condition]*
310.1 Personality change due to *[indicate the general medical condition]*
293.9 Mental disorder NOS due to *[indicate general medical condition]*

SUBSTANCE-RELATED DISORDERS

Alcohol use disorders
303.90 Alcohol dependence
305.00 Alcohol abuse

Alcohol-induced disorders
303.00 Alcohol intoxication
291.8 Alcohol withdrawal

291.0 Alcohol intoxication delirium
291.0 Alcohol withdrawal delirium
291.2 Alcohol-induced persisting dementia
291.1 Alcohol-induced persisting amnestic disorder
291.x Alcohol-induced psychotic disorder
.5 with delusions
.3 with hallucinations
291.8 Alcohol-induced mood disorder
291.8 Alcohol-induced anxiety disorder
291.8 Alcohol-induced sexual dysfunction
291.8 Alcohol-induced sleep disorder
291.9 Alcohol-related disorder NOS

Amphetamine use disorders
304.40 Amphetamine dependence
305.70 Amphetamine abuse

Amphetamine-induced disorders
292.89 Amphetamine intoxication
292.0 Amphetamine withdrawal
292.81 Amphetamine intoxication delirium
292.xx Amphetamine-induced psychotic disorder
.11 with delusions
.12 with hallucinations
292.84 Amphetamine-induced mood disorder
292.89 Amphetamine-induced anxiety disorder
292.89 Amphetamine-induced sexual dysfunction
292.89 Amphetamine-induced sleep disorder
292.9 Amphetamine-related disorder NOS

Caffeine-induced disorders
305.90 Caffeine intoxication
292.89 Caffeine-induced anxiety disorder
292.89 Caffeine-induced sleep disorder
292.9 Caffeine-related disorder NOS

Cannabis use disorders
304.30 Cannabis dependence
305.20 Cannabis abuse

Cannabis-induced disorders
292.89 Cannabis intoxication
292.81 Cannabis intoxication delirium
292.xx Cannabis-induced psychotic disorder
.11 with delusions
.12 with hallucinations
292.89 Cannabis-induced anxiety disorder
292.9 Cannabis-related disorder NOS

Cocaine use disorders
304.20 Cocaine dependence
305.60 Cocaine abuse

Cocaine-induced disorders
292.89 Cocaine intoxication
292.0   Cocaine withdrawal
292.81 Cocaine intoxication delirium
292.xx Cocaine-induced psychotic disorder
   .11   with delusions
   .12   with hallucinations
292.84 Cocaine-induced mood disorder
292.89 Cocaine-induced anxiety disorder
292.89 Cocaine-induced sexual dysfunction
292.89 Cocaine-induced sleep disorder
292.9   Cocaine-related disorder NOS

Hallucinogen use disorders
304.50 Hallucinogen dependence
305.30 Hallucinogen abuse

Hallucinogen-induced disorders
292.89 Hallucinogen intoxication
292.89 Hallucinogen persisting perception disorder (flashbacks)
292.81 Hallucinogen intoxication delirium
292.xx Hallucinogen-induced psychotic disorder
   .11   with delusions
   .12   with hallucinations
292.84 Hallucinogen-induced mood disorder
292.89 Hallucinogen-induced anxiety disorder
292.9   Hallucinogen-related disorder NOS

Inhalant use disorders
304.60 Inhalant dependence
305.90 Inhalant abuse

Inhalant-induced disorders
292.89 Inhalant intoxication
292.81 Inhalant intoxication delirium
292.82 Inhalant-induced persisting dementia
292.xx Inhalant-induced psychotic disorder
   .11   with delusions
   .12   with hallucinations
292.84 Inhalant-induced mood disorder
292.89 Inhalant-induced anxiety disorder
292.9   Inhalant-related disorder NOS

Nicotine use disorders
305.10 Nicotine dependence

Nicotine-induced disorders
292.0   Nicotine withdrawal
292.9   Nicotine-related disorder NOS

Opioid use disorders
304.00 Opioid dependence
305.50 Opioid abuse

Opioid-induced disorders
292.89 Opioid intoxication
292.0   Opioid withdrawal
292.81 Opioid intoxication delirium
292.xx Opioid-induced psychotic disorder
   .11   with delusions
   .12   with hallucinations
292.84 Opioid-induced mood disorder
292.89 Opioid-induced sexual dysfunction
292.89 Opioid-induced sleep disorder
292.9   Opioid-related disorder NOS

Phencyclidine use disorders
304.90 Phencyclidine dependence
305.90 Phencyclidine abuse

Phencyclidine-induced disorders
292.89 Phencyclidine intoxication
292.81 Phencyclidine intoxication delirium
292.xx Phencyclidine-induced psychotic disorder
   .11   with delusions
   .12   with hallucinations
292.84 Phencyclidine-induced mood disorder
292.89 Phencyclidine-induced anxiety disorder
292.9   Phencyclidine-related use disorder NOS

Sedative, hypnotic, or anxiolytic use disorders
304.10 Sedative, hypnotic, or anxiolytic dependence
305.40 Sedative, hypnotic, or anxiolytic abuse

Sedative-, hypnotic-, or anxiolytic-induced disorders
292.89 Sedative, hypnotic, or anxiolytic intoxication
292.0   Sedative, hypnotic, or anxiolytic withdrawal
292.81 Sedative, hypnotic, or anxiolytic intoxication delirium
292.81 Sedative, hypnotic, or anxiolytic withdrawal delirium
292.82 Sedative-, hypnotic-, or anxiolytic-induced persisting dementia
292.93 Sedative-, hypnotic-, or anxiolytic-induced persisting amnestic disorder
292.xx Sedative-, hypnotic-, or anxiolytic-induced psychotic disorder
   .11   with delusions
   .12   with hallucinations
292.84 Sedative-, hypnotic-, or anxiolytic-induced mood disorder
292.89 Sedative-, hypnotic-, or anxiolytic-induced anxiety disorder

292.89 Sedative-, hypnotic-, or anxiolytic-induced sexual dysfunction

292.89 Sedative-, hypnotic-, or anxiolytic-induced sleep disorder

292.9 Sedative-, hypnotic-, or anxiolytic-related use disorder NOS

Polysubstance-related disorder

304.80 Polysubstance dependence

Other (or unknown) substance use disorders

304.90 Other (or unknown) substance dependence

305.90 Other (or unknown) substance abuse

Other (or unknown substance-induced disorders

292.89 Other (or unknown) substance intoxication

292.0 Other (or unknown) substance withdrawal

292.81 Other (or unknown) substance-induced delirium

292.82 Other (or unknown) substance-induced persisting dementia

292.93 Other (or unknown) substance-induced persisting amnestic disorder

292.xx Other (or unknown) substance-induced psychotic disorder

  .11   with delusions

  .12   with hallucinations

292.84 Other (or unknown) substance-induced mood disorder

292.89 Other (or unknown) substance-induced anxiety disorder

292.89 Other (or unknown) substance-induced sexual dysfunction

292.89 Other (or unknown) substance-induced sleep disorder

292.9 Other (or unknown) substance-related use disorder NOS

SCHIZOPHRENIA AND OTHER PSYCHOTIC DISORDERS

295.xx Schizophrenia

  .30   paranoid type

  .10   disorganized type

  .20   catatonic type

  .90   undifferentiated type

  .60   residual type

295.40 Schizophreniform disorder

295.70 Schizoaffective disorder

297.1 Delusional disorder

298.8 Brief psychotic disorder

297.3 Shared psychotic disorder

293.xx Psychotic disorder due to *[indicate the general medical condition]*

  .81   with delusions

  .82   with hallucinations

___._ Substance-induced psychotic disorder *(refer to substance-related disorders for substance-specific codes)*

298.9 Psychotic disorder NOS

MOOD DISORDERS

Code current state of major depressive disorder or bipolar I disorder in fifth digit:

1 = mild

2 = moderate

3 = severe, without psychotic features

4 = severe, with psychotic features

5 = in partial remission

6 = in full remission

0 = unspecified

Depressive disorders

296.xx Major depressive disorder

  .2x   single episode

  .3x   recurrent

300.4 Dysthymic disorder

311 Depressive disorder NOS

Bipolar disorders

296.xx Bipolar I disorder

  .0x   single manic episode

  .40   most recent episode hypomanic

  .4x   most recent episode manic

  .6x   most recent episode mixed

  .5x   most recent episode depressed

  .7   most recent episode unspecified

296.89 Bipolar II disorder

301.13 Cyclothymic disorder

296.80 Bipolar disorder NOS

293.83 Mood disorder due to *[indicate the general medical condition]*

___._ Substance-induced mood disorder *(refer to substance-related disorders for substance-specific codes)*

296.90 Mood disorder NOS

ANXIETY DISORDERS

300.01 Panic disorder without agoraphobia

300.21 Panic disorder with agoraphobia

300.22 Agoraphobia without history of panic disorder

300.29 Specific phobia

300.23 Social phobia

300.3 Obsessive-compulsive disorder

309.81 Posttraumatic stress disorder
308.3   Acute stress disorder
300.02 Generalized anxiety disorder
293.89 Anxiety disorder due to *[indicate the general medical condition]*
___.__ Substance-induced anxiety disorder *(refer to substance-related disorders for substance-specific codes)*
300.00 Anxiety disorder NOS

SOMATOFORM DISORDERS

300.81 Somatization disorder
300.81 Undifferentiated somatization disorder
300.11 Conversion disorder
307.xx Pain disorder
   .80   associated with psychological factors
   .89   associated with both psychological factors and a general medical condition
300.7   Hypochondriasis
300.7   Body dysmorphic disorder
300.81 Somatoform disorder NOS

FACTITIOUS DISORDERS

300.xx Factitious disorder
   .16   with predominantly psychological signs and symptoms
   .19   with predominantly physical signs and symptoms
   .19   with combined psychological and physical signs and symptoms
300.19 Factitious disorder NOS

DISSOCIATIVE DISORDERS

300.12 Dissociative amnesia
300.13 Dissociative fugue
300.14 Dissociative identity disorder
300.6   Depersonalization disorder
300.15 Dissociative disorder NOS

SEXUAL AND GENDER IDENTITY DISORDERS

Sexual desire disorders
302.71 Hypoactive sexual desire disorder
302.79 Sexual aversion disorder

Sexual arousal disorders
302.72 Female sexual arousal disorder
302.72 Male erectile disorder

Orgasm disorders
302.73 Female orgasmic disorder
302.74 Male orgasmic disorder
302.75 Premature ejaculation

Sexual pain disorders
302.76 Dyspareunia (not due to a general medical condition)
306.51 Vaginismus (not due to a general medical condition)

Sexual dysfunction due to a general medical condition
625.8   Female hypoactive sexual desire disorder due to *[indicate the general medical condition]*
608.89 Male hypoactive sexual desire disorder due to *[indicate the general medical condition]*
607.84 Male erectile disorder due to *[indicate the general medical condition]*
625.0   Female dyspareunia due to *[indicate the general medical condition]*
608.89 Male dyspareunia due to *[indicate the general medical condition]*
625.8   Other female sexual dysfunction due to *[indicate the general medical condition]*
608.89 Other male sexual dysfunction due to *[indicate the general medical condition]*
___.__ Substance-related sexual dysfunction *(refer to substance-related disorders for substance-specific codes)*
302.70 Sexual dysfunction NOS

Paraphilias
302.4   Exhibitionism
302.81 Fetishism
302.89 Frotteurism
302.2   Pedophilia
302.83 Sexual masochism
302.84 Sexual sadism
302.3   Transvestic fetishism
302.82 Voyeurism
302.9   Paraphilia NOS

Gender identity disorders
302.xx Gender identity disorder
   .6   in children
   .85   in adolescents and adults
302.6   Gender identity disorder NOS
302.9   Sexual disorder NOS

EATING DISORDERS

307.1 Anorexia nervosa
307.51 Bulimia nervosa
307.50 Eating disorder NOS

SLEEP DISORDERS

Dyssomnias
307.42 Primary insomnia
307.44 Primary hypersomnia
347   Narcolepsy
780.59 Breathing-related sleep disorder
307.45 Circadian rhythm sleep disorder
307.47 Dyssomnia NOS

Parasomnias
307.47 Nightmare disorder
307.46 Sleep terror disorder
307.46 Sleepwalking disorder
307.47 Parasomnia NOS

Sleep disorders related to another mental disorder
307.42 Insomnia related to *[indicate the Axis I or Axis II disorder]*
307.44 Hypersomnia related to *[indicate the Axis I or Axis II disorder]*

Other sleep disorders
780.xx Sleep disorder due to *[indicate the general medical condition]*
   .52 insomnia type
   .54 hypersomnia type
   .59 parasomnia type
   .59 mixed type
___.__ Substance-induced sleep disorder *(refer to substance-related disorders for substance-specific codes)*

IMPULSE-CONTROL DISORDERS NOT ELSEWHERE CLASSIFIED

312.34 Intermittent explosive disorder
312.32 Kleptomania
312.33 Pyromania
312.31 Pathological gambling
312.39 Trichotillomania
312.30 Impulse-control disorder NOS

ADJUSTMENT DISORDERS

309.xx Adjustment disorder
   .0   with depressed mood
   .24 with anxiety
   .28 with mixed anxiety and depressed mood
   .3   with disturbance of conduct
   .4   with mixed disturbance of emotions and conduct
   .9   unspecified

PERSONALITY DISORDERS

Note: These are coded on Axis II.
301.0 Paranoid personality disorder
301.20 Schizoid personality disorder
301.22 Schizotypal personality disorder
301.7 Antisocial personality disorder
301.83 Borderline personality disorder
301.50 Histrionic personality disorder
301.81 Narcissistic personality disorder
301.82 Avoidant personality disorder
301.6 Dependent personality disorder
301.4 Obsessive-compulsive personality disorder
301.9 Personality disorder NOS

OTHER CONDITIONS THAT MAY BE A FOCUS OF CLINICAL ATTENTION

Psychological factors affecting medical condition
316 . . . *[specified psychological factors]* affecting *[indicate the general medical condition]* . . .
   Choose name based on nature of factors:
   Mental disorder affecting medical condition
   Psychological symptoms affecting medical condition
   Personality traits or coping style affecting medical condition
   Maladaptive health behaviors affecting medical condition
   Stress-related physiological response affecting medical condition
   Other or unspecified psychological factors affecting medical condition

Medication-induced movement disorders
332.1 Neuroleptic-induced Parkinsonism
333.92 Neuroleptic malignant syndrome
333.7 Neuroleptic-induced acute dystonia
333.99 Neuroleptic-induced acute akathisia
333.82 Neuroleptic-induced tardive dyskinesia
333.1 Medication-induced postural tremor
333.90 Medication-induced movement disorder NOS

Other medication-induced disorder
995.2   Adverse effects of medication NOS

Relational problems
V61.9   Relational problem related to a mental disorder or general medical condition
V61.20 Parent-child relational problem
V61.1   Partner relational problem
V61.8   Sibling relational problem
V62.81 Relational problem NOS

Problems related to abuse or neglect
V61.21 Physical abuse of child
V61.21 Sexual abuse of child
V61.21 Neglect of child
V61.1   Physical abuse of adult
V61.1   Sexual abuse of adult

Additional conditions that may be a focus of clinical attention
V15.81 Noncompliance with treatment
V65.2   Malingering

V71.01 Adult antisocial behavior
V71.02 Childhood or adolescent antisocial behavior
V62.89 Borderline intellectual functioning
        Note: This is coded on Axis II.
780.9   Age-related cognitive decline
V62.82 Bereavement
V62.3   Academic problem
V62.2   Occupational problem
313.82 Identity problem
V62.89 Religious or spiritual problem
V62.4   Acculturation problem
V62.89 Phase of life problem

ADDITIONAL CODES

300.9   Unspecified mental disorder (non psychotic)
V71.09 No diagnosis or condition on Axis I
799.9   Diagnosis or condition deferred on Axis I
V71.09 No diagnosis on Axis II
799.9   Diagnosis deferred on Axis II

INDEX

BIOGRAPHIES

Heinz L. Ansbacher, Ph.D., Emeritus Professor of Psychology, University of Vermont, and past president of the North American Society of Adlerian Psychology, is an Honorary President of the International Association of Individual Psychology. He and his wife, Rowena, have edited three volumes of Alfred Adler's writings: *The Individual Psychology of Alfred Adler* (1956), *Superiority and Social Interest* (1964), and *Cooperation between the Sexes* (1978). They also have edited 17 volumes of the *Journal of Individual Psychology* (1957–1973). Dr. Ansbacher has written numerous chapters and journal articles on various topics of Adlerian psychology; he currently is engaged in synthesizing some of these.

James W. Croake, Ph.D., is Professor of Psychiatry, Professor of Psychology, and Professor of Neurology, University of South Alabama College of Medicine in Mobile. He is also Clinical Professor of Psychiatry and Behavioral Sciences, University of Washington in Seattle, and Adjunct Professor at the Adler School of Professional Psychology in Chicago. He has written numerous articles and books in Adlerian psychology. His most recent texts are *Dreikursian Theory Part I and II* with Dick Fowler and *Toward an Adlerian Theory of Learning.* The former is the unpublished writings of Rudolf Dreikurs obtained from the Library of Congress.

Elizabeth Hooker, Ph.D., served as a primary therapist and Clinical Coordinator of an inpatient behavioral health unit specializing in anxiety disorders and trauma/PTSD for 16 months. For over 11 years she has studied various forms and the residual effects of abuse. On the practical side, working as a therapist in private practice, Dr. Hooker has specialized in treating victim behavior, and as a seminar/lecture presenter and trainer for mental health professionals, she has shared this knowledge with others. Dr. Hooker has written one book on the assessment and treatment of victim behavior and has just completed a second one that moves beyond identifying the abuse into the healing/change process.

Carl W. Jylland, Psy.D., is a licensed clinical psychologist in private practice in Fort Wayne, Indiana. Dr. Jylland is a graduate of the Alfred Adler Institute of Chicago. Dr. Jylland is a board member of the Alfred Adler Institute of Fort Wayne as well as a faculty member of that institute. Dr. Jylland works with families, children, and adolescents with an emphasis on adopting families, foster families, and the impact of gender issues on families.

Judith Lewis, Ph.D., is a professor in the College of Health Professions at Governors State University, where she currently teaches in a graduate program focused on alcoholism and drug abuse. She is a licensed psychologist in Illinois. Dr. Lewis does extensive publishing, training, and consulting in the fields of substance abuse and counseling. Among her recent publications are *Addictions: Concepts and Strategies in Treatment* (Aspen), and *Health Counseling* (Brooks/Cole). She is associate editor of *The Family Journal* and *The Family Psychology and Counseling Series.*

Donald N. Lombardi, Ph.D., is a Professor of Psychology, Seton Hall University, and licensed practicing psychologist in New Jersey. He was attracted to Individual Psychology after reading *The Individual Psychology of Alfred Adler.* Dr. Lombardi learned much about Adlerian psychology in his 15–year association with Willard and Marguerite Beecher. He has authored numerous articles and a book, *Search for Significance,* in 1975.

Michael P. Maniacci, Psy.D., is a licensed clinical psychologist and a graduate of the State University of New York at Stony Brook and the Alfred Adler Institute of Chicago. Currently, he is core faculty and clinical supervisor at the Adler School of Professional Psychology and in private practice in Chicago, Illinois. He is a member of the North American Society of Adlerian Psychology, the American Psychological Association, and the Society for the Exploration of Psychotherapy Integration. Dr. Maniacci has contributed numerous articles and book chapters on psychopathology and psychotherapy with diverse populations.

Mark Mays, Ph.D., J.D., is a psychologist in private practice in Spokane, Washington. Dr. Mays serves on the faculty of the University of Washington Medical School, Department of Psychiatry, and is also an adjunct faculty member of the Gonzaga School of Law. He has served as president of the Washington State Psychological Association, as chair of the Committee of Professional Practice for

APA, and on the Council of Representatives for the American Psychological Association. He is a consulting editor of *Individual Psychology.*

Harold H. Mosak, Ph.D., is a Distinguished Service Professor at the Adler School of Professional Psychology in Chicago where he has taught for the last 40 years. He is also currently Chairman of the Board of Trustees. Among his publications are *On Purpose; Alfred Adler: His Influence on Psychology Today; Manual for Life Style Assessment* (with B.H. Shulman); and *Ha, Ha, and Aha: The Role of Humor in Psychotherapy.*

Kathleen M. Myers, M.D., M.P.H., M.S., is Associate Professor and Director of Outpatient Child and Adolescent Psychiatry Clinic at the Oregon Health Sciences University in Portland. Dr. Myers has published research regarding developmental psychopathology and mood disorders. She and James Croake, Ph.D., together have written and taught about the application of Adlerian methods to child development, therapy, and parenting. They have contributed several articles to *Individual Psychology.*

Walter "Buzz" O'Connell, Ph.D., is active in private practice and senior center groups in his retirement in the Lost Pines of Bastrop, Texas. Buzz was both research and clinical psychologist at Veterans Administration Medical Centers in Texas for over 30 years. At the same time, he taught at Baylor University (Waco), University of St. Thomas, University of Houston, and Baylor College of Medicine. Dr. O'Connell is a Fellow of the American Psychological Association, the Academy of Clinical Psychology, and the International Academy of Eclectic Psychotherapists. Buzz is considered to be an expert in psychodrama, the sense of humor, and death and transformation. Most of his 400 publications are concerned with those topics.

Ronald J. Pancner, M.D., is in the private practice of psychiatry in Fort Wayne, Indiana, and is the Medical Director of Charter Beacon Behavioral Health System. He is a core professor of the Adler School of Professional Psychology in Chicago and the Alfred Adler Institute of Fort Wayne, and is also a clinical Assistant Professor of Psychiatry at the Indiana University School of Medicine at Fort Wayne. He is a past president of the North American Society of Adlerian Psychology and is on the council of the International Association of Individual Psychology and served as Assistant Secretary General. He and his wife have authored several articles in *Individual Psychology.* He has given numerous presentations at professional conventions and institutes on psychiatry and Individual Psychology.

Dorothy E. Peven, M.S.W., is a Licensed Clinical Social Worker in private practice in the Chicago metropolitan area and a professor at the Adler School of Professional Psychology, Chicago. She has served as Vice President of the North American Society of Adlerian Psychology and has consulted and lectured to the Alfred Adler Institutes in the United States, Canada, the Netherlands, and Japan. She is a Diplomate in Clinical Social Work and a clinical member of the American Association of Marriage and Family Therapy. Ms. Peven has published several articles on Adlerian theory and practice and in the field of social psychology.

Bernard H. Shulman, M.D., is a past president of the North American Society of Adlerian Psychology and of the International Association of Individual Psychology. He is a Life Fellow of the American Psychiatric Association and formerly was a Clinical Professor of Psychiatry at both Northwestern Medical School and Loyola Medical School. He has made many contributions to the literature of Adlerian psychology, including *Essays on Schizophrenia*.

ABOUT THE EDITORS

Len Sperry, M.D., Ph.D., is Professor of Psychiatry and Behavioral Medicine and Professor also of Preventive Medicine at the Medical College of Wisconsin. He is Codirector of its Foley Center for Aging and Development. Board certified in both psychiatry and clinical psychology, he has published over 200 professional articles and books and is associate editor of *Individual Psychology* and *The Family Journal*. He is also on the editorial board of the *American Journal of Family Therapy* and *Depression and Stress*.

Jon Carlson, Psy.D., Ed.D., is a Professor of Psychology and Counseling at Governors State University, University Park, Illinois, and a psychologist in Lake Geneva, Wisconsin. Dr. Carlson is a Fellow of the American Psychological Association, a Diplomate in Family Psychology of the American Board of Professional Psychology, and holds a certificate in psychotherapy from the Alfred Adler Institute in Chicago. Dr. Carlson has authored 17 books, 110 professional articles, and is the editor of two journals: *Individual Psychology: The Journal of Adlerian Theory, Research, and Practice,* and *The Family Journal: Counseling and Therapy for Couples and Families.*